Contents: 1 Book   1 CD-ROM

Distance Learning and Copyright

A GUIDE TO LEGAL ISSUES

STEVEN A. ARMATAS

D1417701

ABA
Defending Liberty
Pursuing Justice

THE ABA SECTION OF
Intellectual Property Law

Cover design by ABA Publishing.

The materials contained herein represent the opinions and views of the authors and/or the editors, and should not be construed to be the views or opinions of the law firms or companies with whom such persons are in partnership with, associated with, or employed by, nor of the American Bar Association or the Intellectual Property Law Section, unless adopted pursuant to the bylaws of the Association.

Nothing contained in this book is to be considered as the rendering of legal advice, either generally or in connection with any specific issue or case; nor do these materials purport to explain or interpret any specific bond or policy, or any provisions thereof, issued by any particular franchise company, or to render franchise or other professional advice. Readers are responsible for obtaining advice from their own lawyers or other professionals. This book and any forms and agreements herein are intended for educational and informational purposes only.

Library of Congress Cataloging-in-Publication Data
Armatas, Steven A.
  Distance learning and copyright: a guide to legal issues / Steven A. Armatas.—1st ed.
    p. cm.
  ISBN 978-1-60442-101-9
  1. Fair use (Copyright)—United States. 2. Copyright—United States. 3. Distance education—United States. 4. Telecommunication in higher education—United States. 5. Internet in education—United States. I. Title.

  KF3030.1.A947 2008
  346.7304'82—dc22

                                                    2008025606

Discounts are available for books ordered in bulk. Special consideration is given to state bars, CLE programs, and other bar-related organizations. Inquire at Book Publishing, ABA Publishing, American Bar Association, 321 North Clark Street, Chicago, Illinois 60654-7598.

www.ababooks.org

For my Suzanne

About the ABA Section of Intellectual Property Law

From its strength within the American Bar Association, the ABA Section of Intellectual Property Law (ABA-IPL) advances the development and improvement of intellectual property laws and their fair and just administration. The Section furthers the goals of its members by sharing knowledge and balanced insight on the full spectrum of intellectual property law and practice, including patents, trademarks, copyright, industrial design, literary and artistic works, scientific works, and innovation. Providing a forum for rich perspectives and reasoned commentary, ABA-IPL serves as the ABA voice of intellectual property law within the profession, before policy makers, and with the public.

Contents

Preface

My first experience with copyright law came nearly twenty-five years ago when I selected it as an elective course in my second year of law school. I ashamedly now admit that I signed up for it because it yielded two desperately needed credits and met only once a week on Tuesdays, thus permitting me to have a lighter schedule for the next term (and a three-day weekend for the current one). It turned out to be a wonderful decision for reasons far apart from credits or scheduling and consequently influenced my career in ways I could not then foresee. The class was taught by Professor Benjamin Kaplan, a soft-spoken gentleman of immense standing in the Harvard Law School community and a renowned expert in both federal civil procedure and copyright law. His brilliance, wit, and ability to combine theory with real-world examples would help shed a beam of light onto a maze of mysterious new terms and concepts.

I recall being initially intrigued by one of the major premises of copyright—that certain mental exercises such as expression of thoughts could be "owned" while others, like ideas, could not. Also compelling to me were the competing (and somewhat contradictory) objectives that the Copyright Act was always attempting to balance—promoting the creation of *new* works while compensating authors for *old* ones, and encouraging the public to experience and build on someone's creations while simultaneously limiting their use. These tensions and inherent conflicts in the law were the subject of many spirited discussions among Professor Kaplan and my classmates. These same types of issues continue to be debated today over innovations such as the Internet, DVDs, and iPods—things none of us could even imagine back in the early 1980s.

Professor Kaplan's course was also my initial encounter with what was then the relatively new field of "intellectual property," a discipline attempting to apply long-held ownership concepts for static tangibles (e.g., land, tools, buildings) to technological innovations and advances that were in a continuous state of evolution. Theory would give way to practicality only a few years later when I began my legal career. One day I was asked by a senior partner at my firm to assist a university client who wanted to establish a fiber-optic link to a local high school. The purpose of the connection was to permit high school seniors to participate via a live audio and video feed in a freshman English class being offered at the college. My initial task of negotiating and drafting an agreement with the local public utility providing the cable link soon grew more complex and became my first foray into something called "distance learning."

Soon after the contract between the university and utility company was signed, a dean from the college called me to pose what appeared a rather simple question. It seemed the professor teaching the new distance learning course always liked to show a movie version of *Macbeth* to his lecture hall students when covering the works of Shakespeare. The instructor wanted to know whether there was any copyright problem in doing the same for his remote-site students since he was now "broadcasting" the film. In other words, would transmitting the lesson electronically alter the wide latitude teachers were normally afforded in performing and displaying copyrighted works as part of their lessons? My initial (but unexpressed) reaction was no, how could it? What rationale would there be for imposing one set of rules for traditional classroom lectures and another for students sitting in front of a monitor only a few miles away? The professor himself would be doing nothing different. The only change would be the use of a television camera to carry his words and image to a separate, yet equally interested and deserving audience.

While I was still relatively new to the practice of law, I had already learned the cardinal rule of never expressing an opinion on a subject one knows little, if anything, about. I told the dean I would get back to him with an answer shortly, hung up the telephone, and began making some inquiries around the office. This initial strategy proved rather fruitless, however, as none of my colleagues knew anything about this very narrow field of copyright law. As one of them courteously advised, I now had to make myself the expert in the area in order to effectively service our college and university clients. I managed to locate my old lecture notes from Professor Kaplan's course and discovered that indeed there were separate provisions in the Copyright Act covering face-to-face versus "transmitted" classes. Thus began my new and primarily self-taught education concerning the interrelationship between distance learning and copyright.

As I began delving into the statutes, regulations, and court cases involving federal copyright law, I discovered, much to my surprise, that often what was permissible in face-to-face teaching constituted copyright infringement when used in a distance learning setting. Specifically, I found that while the English professor at the local college could show the movie *Macbeth* to his lecture hall class, transmitting it to the local high school constituted a violation of the then existing Copyright Act. I promptly informed the dean regarding the results of my research (but not about my initial assumption being dead wrong). The key reason for this separate (and arguably unfair) treatment for distance students was congressional concern that transmitted broadcasts containing copyrighted material (even in a nonprofit educational setting) could be intercepted and viewed by interlopers. As such, these individuals could then forgo purchasing an original of the copyrighted work and thus deprive its creator of revenue, something Congress strongly wanted to discourage.

These concerns ultimately led to unequal treatment for distance learning students finding its way into the 1976 amendments to the Copyright Act, which at the time constituted the most significant revamping of the federal statute in close to seventy years. Concern was also fomented because the most prevalent form of distance education at that time was over-the-air television and radio broadcasts. These media were by their nature particularly vulnerable to unwanted interception as universities lacked the technology currently available to either scramble or "close-circuit" their transmissions. Differences in the type and format of performances and displays of copyrighted material that distance rather than traditional students may receive continues to this day, although the gaps were somewhat narrowed by enactment of the TEACH Act in late 2002. (But more on that in Chapter Six.)

Regardless of the policy considerations behind the 1976 Act amendments, the result led to one set of rules for face-to-face instructors using copyrighted works and another (much more restrictive) one for distance educators. Not surprisingly, the existence of this dichotomy was, and is still, not well known or understood among educators. For these reasons, about ten years ago I started offering seminars to teachers and administrators affiliated with local colleges and school systems with the goal of alerting them to the pitfalls of potential copyright infringement when offering a distance learning course. In August 2000, I was asked to conduct a half-day workshop on this topic at the 16th Annual Distance Teaching & Learning Conference sponsored by the University of Wisconsin at Madison.

While I expected a dozen people, at most, to attend a three-hour presentation on as esoteric a topic as "Distance Learning and Copyright," I was presently surprised to have over sixty educators sign up for my class. This experience proved informative and enlightening in many ways. To begin with, I discovered what I perceived to be a dearth of knowledge of basic copyright principles among teachers at all levels. While I realized that my audience did not have the benefit of a law degree, I had assumed most educational institutions would attempt to give their faculty and staff at least a grounding in copyright basics. Since almost every instructor has to reference and use the works of others in his or her teaching, I envisioned many schools would offer such training for no other reason than to avoid unnecessary and unwanted infringement liability. In discussing this topic with several participants at the Madison conference, I discovered my assumption to be incorrect. While I found that some universities, particularly larger ones, either conducted copyright compliance courses for their faculty or distributed written materials to them outlining copyright law, most did neither. Training at the K–12 level was even more wanting.

Indeed, many of the comments I received in response to my seminar regarded the need to go into more detail on the basics of copyright law as well as its application to the burgeoning field of distance education. Many respondents suggested a full-day course as a more appropriate method to present the material. Based on those suggestions, I subsequently developed a six-hour workshop on the topic, which I began offering in 2001. The seminar was given in several major cities over the next few years and continues to be offered nationally today. Each program was well attended, and the questions I fielded both during and after the sessions further elucidated for me the many common misperceptions about copyright law held by members of the educational community.

One major area of confusion concerned the doctrine of "fair use" and its applicability to nonprofit, educational settings. Many seminar participants labored under the false notion that any use of a copyrighted work in a school environment constituted fair use. Nothing, of course, could be further from the truth. Others misunderstood the concept of "public domain" and assumed that anything placed on the Internet, because it was made available to the public, lost copyright protection. Again, a faulty and quite dangerous assumption. Several attendees believed that as long as the author or creator of a work was clearly identified, any use of his or her work was permitted for scholarly purposes. As I always liked to say in answer to that question, "Congratulations; you may not be a plagiarizer, but you are still a copyright infringer."

Attendees often inquired about the various copyright "guidelines" their institutions occasionally distributed to them. Many were confused about what guidelines actually emanated from the Copyright Act and which of them served as mere suggestions. Others wanted to know more about the operation of the Digital Millennium Copyright Act and its applicability to colleges and local school systems. Several participants sought information about the most efficient way of determining whether a work was still protected by copyright. A large number expressed frustration over dealing with copyright owners and/or their agents in obtaining permission or licenses to use their works. School administrators often asked whether their institutions could be held liable for the acts of their faculty and students, and wanted to know what policies, if any, could be implemented to prevent such exposure.

It was in response to these and many other questions posed in my workshops that I first decided to write this book. I also perceived a need for educators and attorneys who represent colleges and school systems to have essential copyright information available to them in one convenient resource rather than having to search for answers in a plethora of government and commercial publications. A great deal of information about copyright law is available from the U.S. Copyright Office and other agencies of the federal government. In fact, several portions of this book were prepared by using this material (which is not protected by copyright) as a base and then editing, supplementing, updating, and refining it to conform to the remainder of the text. As such, I express my gratitude to a host of unknown (and underappreciated) federal employees who provided a valuable starting point for several sections contained herein.

The Copyright Act and international treaties concerning it are also available on the Internet or can be ordered from the United States Government Printing office. However, as in the case of the Digital Millennium Copyright Act, only portions of many lengthy and detailed statutes have applicability to educational institutions. An explanation of which provisions are germane to educators and how these laws relate to one another is much more difficult, if not impossible, to locate online or by more traditional means. Many "copyright guidelines" for instructors are also available on the World Wide Web if one knows where to search. What is not generally available, however, is any cogent discussion of who created these guidelines, what authority they had to do so, how the guidelines work together, and what weight, if any, they are accorded legally.

Giving this complex and enormously important area greater coherence for educators and lawyers practicing in the field was thus another major aim of this work. The book is divided into six chapters. Chapter One defines distance education and presents an overview of how it is offered and who is using it in today's world. Chapter Two is essentially a primer on copyright law and covers the basics every educator (and most lawyers) should know. Chapter Three discusses the fair use doctrine by exploring its role in both the commercial and nonprofit sector and analyzing fair use guidelines for various educational activities (e.g., classroom photocopying, music, library reserves, multimedia presentations, etc.).

Chapter Four focuses on effective ways of locating copyright owners, with particular emphasis on understanding and negotiating licensing agreements with them. Chapter Five concerns the growing interrelationship between the Internet and distance learning with a section dedicated to clarifying how the Digital Millennium Copyright Act affects schools, their faculty, and students. Chapter Six explores the evolving rules governing the performances and displays of copyrighted works in traditional and distance classrooms. Much of the chapter is devoted to an analysis of the history, scope, and operation of the recently enacted TEACH Act.

As mentioned above, this book was designed for both educators involved with and lawyers needing more information about distance learning and copyright. Writing for such a diverse audience presented a difficult challenge in itself. While this text is intended to be a practical guide to copyright law for those with little to no training in the area, I also wanted it to serve as a resource for those seeking a greater understanding of the discipline's legal nuances. In striking this balance, I attempted to draft the main body of material with as little "legalease" as possible, instead placing the bulk of applicable case law and legislative history in the accompanying footnotes. As such, readers can get a generous "layman's" explanation of the topics by reading the principal text alone. Those conducting research or seeking specific legal authority should be aided by the footnote material. How successful I was in accomplishing this dual objective, I leave to the readers to decide.

A few notes about the organization of this book. First, all footnotes are listed at the bottom of the page, are numbered consecutively for each chapter (not the entire book), and conform to the Harvard *Bluebook* citation format. Second, books, printed government publications, printed journal and newspaper articles, and titles of materials found on the Internet are cited using the *Bluebook* "Bluepages" style (used for materials that are neither law reviews nor journal articles). For Internet materials, a URL is also given for the site where the work was posted and located during my research, although its current availability cannot be guaranteed. Third, I have attempted to be consistently gender neutral in the use of pronouns (e.g., "his or her" course), but at times use only the masculine or feminine case where style or word economy considerations come into play.

Lastly, like most authors, I envisioned my book would be read from beginning to end. However, I recognize that many people may choose to use this work as a reference or spend time on only those chapters of most relevance to them or their field of study. In that regard, it was necessary at times to repeat certain concepts or citations in order to give a section more cogency and provide the reader with the needed framework to better comprehend the material. These repetitions are minimal, however, and should not hinder or unduly delay anyone reading the text in its entirety.

After practicing law for over twenty years now, I can honestly say my greatest satisfaction still remains in taking a complex set of facts and legal doctrine and communicating it in a precise, yet highly understandable, fashion to nonlawyers (as most of my clients remain). Perhaps it is a buried or latent teaching instinct in me attempting to surface. Regardless, it was with that goal primarily in mind that I undertook to write this book. I can only hope that its audience derives even a portion of the same intellectual satisfaction and learning experience in reading its pages that I gained from writing them.

S.A.A.

About the Author

Steven A. Armatas currently resides and practices law in the State of Ohio. He is a graduate of Harvard College (A.B. 1981) and Harvard Law School (J.D. 1984). Mr. Armatas has over 20 years of experience in the field of copyright law and its implications for educational institutions.

Mr. Armatas has served as legal counsel to both colleges and local school systems, advising them on a variety of contractual and intellectual property issues associated with distance learning. This representation has included negotiating and preparing software and hardware acquisition agreements, joint venture arrangements between schools and commercial enterprises, intellectual property licenses, publishing contracts, assignments of copyrights and trademarks, instructor employment and consulting agreements, student and faculty manuals on copyright compliance, and institutional policies relating to online piracy, Internet acceptable use, and ownership of distance learning courseware.

Mr. Armatas is also a frequent lecturer on the topic of copyright law for schools, and has spoken on the subject to educators across the country, including presenting to faculty members on campus, attendees at various national and regional distance education conferences, and participants in his day-long "Distance Learning and Copyright" seminar sponsored by various syndicators of educational programming.

CHAPTER 1

Overview of Distance Learning

This chapter provides an overview of the burgeoning field of distance education. Section 1.1 defines some key terms and explores the levels of classes, technologies, and related school resources associated with providing distance education. It also examines the characteristics of those persons and organizations who, respectively, take and provide distance learning courses. Section 1.2 discusses distance education's future, while Section 1.3 explains how the concepts underlying the relationship between distance learning and copyright will be analyzed in this work.

1.1 THE NATURE OF DISTANCE EDUCATION TODAY

[1] What Is Distance Education?

In 1998, as part of its directive from Congress under Section 403 of the Digital Millennium Copyright Act,[1] the United States Copyright Office sought comment from interested persons on what constituted "distance education" in America at that time. The Office began with these basic questions:

> How may distance education be defined? In what sense does it differ from traditional face-to-face education? To what extent does it utilize digital technologies? In what sense does it differ from the general use of electronic communications in educational settings?[2]

A consensus emerged on the most fundamental definition: distance education is a form of learning in which students are separated from their instructors by time and/or space. This characteristic is central to all variants of the field.

---

1. Pub. L. No. 105–304, 112 Stat. 2860 (1998) (hereinafter the DMCA). For a more detailed discussion of the DMCA, *see infra* Chapter Five, Section 5.4.

2. *See* 63 Fed. Reg. 71,167 (1998).

Various terminology is used in discussing distance education, most notably the corresponding terms "distance learning," "distributed learning," and "distributed education." Some use these terms interchangeably, while others employ them to refer to different activities. Despite the lack of standard definitions, "distance education" generally involves the delivery of instruction with a teacher active in determining pace and content, but normally removed from his or her students by time, space, or both. As such, it is differentiated from unstructured learning using resource materials.

Distance learning is not necessarily separate and distinct from on-campus education, however. An individual course may contain both classroom and distance components. Some online courses require brief periods of on-campus instruction; conversely, classroom courses often use digital technology for directed research or to deliver resource materials. In other instances, a student in a regular classroom may periodically receive live or delayed instruction from a teacher in another part of the country or even the world. All of these examples constitute distance learning.

The distance education courses available today are many and varied. They are geared toward all levels of students, from kindergartners through retirees, and take advantage of a wide range of technologies to enrich and expand the educational experience. Distance programs have become integrated into most educational institutions. In connection with their distance learning activities, these schools are also drawing upon their library resources, employing new technology, promulgating copyright compliance policies, and participating in the accreditation process. These activities are discussed below.

[2] Levels of Courses

Distance learning is now utilized at every stage of the educational spectrum. It takes various forms at different levels, however. Currently, its most extensive use as a substitute for the classroom experience occurs in higher education, but distance education has applicability to the K–12 environment as well. Elementary and secondary school students are using computers in increasing numbers. According to the United States Department of Education (DOE), 91% of students in grades K through 12 had used computers, and 59% had "surfed" the Internet. Such use begins quite early; 80% of children in kindergarten had used computers, while almost one-third (32%) had experience with the Internet.[3] Computer use at the elementary level, however, does not generally involve remote course deliv-

---

3. National Center for Education Statistics, U.S. Dept. of Education, *Issue Brief: Rates of Computer and Internet Use by Children in Nursery School and K–12: 2003* (June 2005).

ery. Rather, education here tends to focus on software and Internet visits used to supplement classroom instruction.[4]

At the secondary level, distance education activities are more extensive. Distance learning programs across the country provide high school students with the opportunity to take classes not otherwise available to them, such as advanced placement or college equivalency courses. A third of public school divisions nationwide had students enrolled in distance learning during the 2002–2003 school year, the most recent year for which data is available, according to a report from the National Center for Education Statistics.[5] Currently, about half the states allow for online charter schools, while fourteen have state-sanctioned cyber-schools, including Florida, which has more than 10,000 students enrolled in its Florida Virtual School.[6] As of September 2006, thirty-eight states had either state-led online learning programs and/or significant policies regulating the field.[7] A recent study indicates that 40 percent of K–12 distance learning programs saw their enrollments increase by at least 25 percent in 2006.[8]

Postsecondary distance education is the fastest-growing field of all.[9] Courses are available at most colleges and universities, at both the undergraduate and postgraduate level, and for post-professional development and training. Community colleges, with their history of serving local and continuing education needs, have been particularly active in the field.[10] In a recent survey, it was reported that online enrollments at community colleges had increased by 15 percent on average in 2006, while total enrollment at such institutions was only up 2 percent for the same period.[11]

---

4. *See* Program for Copyright Office Demonstrations of Distance Education Programs Using Digital Technologies, *available as* Appendix D to U.S. Copyright Office, *Report on Copyright and Digital Distance Education* (1999) (hereinafter *DDE Report*).

5. L. Williams, *Distance Learning: Making a Connection,* dailypress.com (Mar. 28, 2005), http://www.chicagotribune.com/topic/dp-local-distance-learning,1,4608518.story.

6. Mendoza, *Arizona to Add 10 Online Schools,* Arizona Rep., June 8, 2003.

7. P. Deubel, *Should States Mandate Online Learning?* TheJournal.com (Nov. 2004), http://www.thejournal.com/articles/20003.

8. L. Devaney, *Reports Reveal Online Learning's Successes, Needs,* eSchool news (Nov. 21, 2007), http://www.eschoolnews.com/news/top-news/?i=50614;_hbguid=6c7e3d93-fda9-41e4-941c-c83e6b4c7793.

9. *See Growth in Distance Education Programs and Implications for Federal Policy: Hearings Before the Senate Committee on Health, Education, Labor, and Pensions,* 107th Cong. 2nd Sess. 4 (2002) (statement of Cornelia M. Ashby, Director, Education, Workforce, and Income Security Issues), reprinted in GAO-02-1125T.

10. N. Easterday, *Distance Learning and 2-Year Colleges,* Community C.J. of Research and Prac., 1997, at 21(1), 23–36.

11. *See* S. Jaschik, *Surge in Distance Ed at Community Colleges,* insidehighered.com (April 16, 2007), http://insidehighered.com/news/2007/04/16/aacc.

[3] Technologies

Today's distance education courses use digital technology extensively for multiple purposes. Adding these technologies has produced new models of learning, resulting in a richer and more interactive classroom environment.

[a] Evolution

Radio was the favored medium for distance education in the first part of the twentieth century, with television supplanting it in the 1950s.[12] Telecourses produced by educators and distributed by the Public Broadcasting System (PBS), for example, garnered large audiences for decades. Such programs are still widely used, and they are expanding their services in both the analog and digital environment.[13]

The 1990s saw the advent of computer networks and multimedia technologies as powerful new tools for distance education.[14] According to a DOE study conducted in 1995, over 70 percent of higher education institutions were planning to start or increase offering courses using online or other computer-based technologies.[15] This growth has continued unabated

---

12. S. Cassidy et al., Learning Technologies Division, U.S. Dep't of Education, *Developing a Vision for Distance Education in the 21st Century* 2–3; Western Cooperative for Educational Telecommunications, The Distance Learner's Guide 5 (G. C. Connick, ed.) (1999).

13. Many states have active distance education telecourse programs, often distributed through state educational networks. Examples include the Education Network in Maine, BadgerNet in Wisconsin, and the Utah Education Network. *See* National Center for Education Statistics, *Distance Education in Higher Education Institutions* 1 (1997). The role of the Public Broadcasting System (PBS) in this area has diminished significantly, however. On February 10, 2005, PBS announced plans to cease operations of its Adult Learning Service effective September 30, 2005. *See* PBS Announcement at http://www.pbs.org/als/transition .html. In 1996, there were 400,000 students enrolled in PBS courses, as compared to only 180,000 in 2004 and 153,000 in 2005. *See* S. Behrens, *PBS Drops its Middleman Role in College Courses,* current.org (April 25, 2005), http://www.current.org/education/ed0507adult .shtml.

14. Students and educators fueled the vigorous growth of distance education in the 1990s by capitalizing on these opportunities. Educational computer use increased rapidly in traditional classroom courses as well as in distance education. According to the 1998 Campus Computing Project, which surveyed 571 technology officials at two- and four-year colleges nationwide, 44% of on-campus courses used e-mail in some way, growing from 32.8% in 1997 and only 8% in 1994. The project further reported that 16% of courses used computers for simulations of exercises and 15% to launch CD-ROMs. As of 1996, more than 7 million college students and faculty were routinely using the Internet and the World Wide Web as part of their daily and weekly activities. *See* Mendels, *Survey Shows a Sharp Rise in Net-Savvy Academics,* N.Y. Times, Nov. 4, 1998.

15. *See* National Center for Education Statistics, *Issue Brief: Distance Education in Higher Education Institutions: Incidence, Audiences, and Plans to Expand* (Feb. 1998).

over the last decade. American colleges and universities spent over $5.2 billion on information technology in 2003, reflecting a 5 percent increase over the prior year.[16]

Currently, distance programs use combinations of technologies in varied ways. These involve e-mail among teachers and students, class chat rooms, links to resources on the World Wide Web, incorporation of preexisting content into reading materials, mediated instruction from a distance, and the delivery of supplemental materials in electronic form. The use of older technologies, like videoconferencing, is also prevalent, particularly in rural schools. Even in courses delivered entirely through digital media, however, students continue to use textbooks.[17]

Determining the appropriate technology to use in a distance course is generally based on the availability and cost thereof and on satisfying the intended audience. Older working adults, for example, may require fewer multimedia "bells and whistles" than the average college student. Unfortunately, such choices may not be available for rural or foreign students, who generally have less access to sophisticated equipment and software.

[b] New Characteristics

One significant manner in which distance education has evolved is a shift from one-way to interactive communication. The original model for distance learning was one-way transmission of instruction from teacher to remote students, with communication among them often limited to telephone lines or correspondence. The advent of digital technologies has enabled more teacher-to-student and student-to-student interaction. E-mail and chat rooms, for example, allow continuous discourse among participants separated by distance. As a result of these advances, distance programs may now offer experiences more closely paralleling face-to-face teaching.[18]

---

16. The Chron. of Higher Educ., Mar. 26, 2003.

17. *See, e.g.,* I. Hinds, *Marketplace for Licensing in Digital Distance Education* 8–9 (1998), *available as* Appendix E to *DDE Report.*

18. Cassidy et al., *supra* note 12, at 12: "During most of this century, distance learning has provided important educational opportunities, which bridged differences in location or time, with interactivity limited to the particular form of communications being used. With the advent of electronic technologies and their use in distance education, the emergence of school reform efforts and the support of the Federal government, new models of distance and distributed education have emerged to allow us to envision more highly interactive, global, distance-distributed models for learning in the 21st century."

New technologies have also made distance courses more convenient and better suited to student needs. Historically, distance learning has been divided into synchronous and asynchronous programs. Synchronous programs are usually delivered by broadcast and closed-circuit technologies, set in real time, allowing the student to participate from afar but imposing scheduling constraints. Asynchronous programs are exemplified by correspondence, videotape, and computer network courses, and allow for a time lapse between the delivery of material and its reception by a student.

With the advent of interoperable digital media, distance education has increasingly incorporated both synchronous and asynchronous tools into the same course. Asynchronous technologies, such as e-mail, threaded discussion, "stored" lessons, and self-paced testing, are often used in conjunction with synchronous elements such as chat rooms and streaming video. The same material may be delivered by both methods. For example, a lecture may be given in real time by streaming audio or video and then archived on a server to be made available to students for later viewing or review.

[4] Library Resources

In the course of providing distance programs, educational institutions draw on their library resources in several ways. Often, they rely on librarians for negotiating and obtaining licenses, since many times these professionals have the requisite experience. Libraries also provide facilities and support staff for developing online courses, preparing digital materials, and advising on copyright law. Frequently, distance educators provide their classes with selected library resources in digital form. These materials are designated as electronic reserves, or "e-reserves," and are similar to textual works set aside on campus by an instructor for outside reading. These and other electronic resources are often made available to both on-campus and remote-site students pursuant to institutional licenses obtained through the library's efforts.

[5] Copyright Policies

Many educational institutions are now making efforts to adopt and implement appropriate policies on copyright issues involved with distance learning. These endeavors include promulgating written policies, conducting training for faculty and staff, and educating students about copyright law. Copyright policies usually take one of two forms. The first involves allocating ownership rights between the institution and its faculty for works created as part of the educational experience.

A second type of document educates faculty, staff, and students about the principles of copyright law and is often called a "copyright compliance manual."[19] While the preparation of such policies and the training of faculty, staff, and students has always been sound policy, such acts are now required by both the Digital Millennium Copyright Act (DMCA) and the Technology, Education, and Copyright Harmonization Act of 2002, more commonly known as the "TEACH Act."[20]

[6] Accreditation

As distance education becomes increasingly incorporated into mainstream curricula, more focus has been paid to the issue of accreditation. For distance education to gain true public acceptance, it must be viewed as comparable in quality to classroom instruction. This is an important issue both for students, who must choose among available programs, and for educators who must assess the knowledge imparted by those classes. Formal accreditation has traditionally provided that assurance of quality.

The Higher Education Act,[21] among other items, focuses on accreditation, a task undertaken by outside bodies, as the main tool for ensuring quality in postsecondary education.[22] Under the act, accreditation may only be granted by one of 62 agencies specifically "recognized" by the DOE.[23] Some agencies, such as the Middle States Association of Colleges and Schools, accredit entire institutions falling under their geographic or other purview. Others, such as the American Bar Association, Council of

---

19. In a recent survey conducted by the Recording Industry Association of America, of the top fifty-five doctoral institutions as ranked by *U.S. News and World Report,* it was discovered that less than three-quarters of the institutions had online-accessible institutional policies containing more than a cursory treatment of copyright law, and only one-fourth had policies treating the issue in depth. *See* Education Task Force of the Joint Committee of the Higher Education and Entertainment Communities, *University Policies and Practices Addressing Improper Peer-to-Peer File Sharing* (April 2004), http://www.acenet.edu.

20. Pub. L. No. 107–273, 116 Stat. 1758 (2002). *See infra* Chapter Six, Section 6.4, for extensive discussion of the TEACH Act.

21. Pub. L. No. 89–329, 79 Stat. 319 (1965).

22. In general, there are two main types of accrediting agencies—regional and national. Regional accrediting agencies review institutions in a region of the United States that includes at least three states that are reasonably close to one another. National accrediting agencies review programs or specialized institutions, such as acupuncture or business schools, on a national basis.

23. U.S. General Accounting Office, *Distance Education: Improved Data on Program Costs and Guidelines on Quality Assessments Needed to Inform Federal Policy,* GA0-04-279 (Feb. 2004) (hereinafter *GAO Report*).

the Section of Legal Education, and Admissions to the Bar, accredit specific programs or departments. Collectively, accrediting agencies cover public and private two- and four-year colleges, for-profit vocational schools, and nondegree training programs. Thirty-nine agencies are permitted to accredit schools for participation in federal student aid programs. DOE is required to recognize or re-recognize these agencies every five years.

To achieve DOE recognition, accrediting agencies must, in addition to meeting basic criteria, establish standards addressing ten broad areas of institutional quality, including student support services, facilities and equipment, and success with respect to student achievement.[24] While these standards must be consistently applied to an institution's programs of study, including distance education courses,[25] the law grants agencies flexibility in determining the requirements under each area. This flexibility includes whether and how to assess distance education as part of the review process. Ongoing accreditation is being carried out against a backdrop of holding schools more accountable for student learning results. For example, concerns have been expressed about the following:

- Program completion—the percentage of full-time students who graduate with a 4-year post-secondary degree within six years of initial enrollment was about 52 percent in 2000.[26]
- Unprepared workforce—business leaders and educators have expressed concern over gaps between many students' problem-solving, communications, and analytical thinking skills and what the workplace actually requires.[27]

To address these issues, an increased interest has developed in using "outcomes" to ensure quality in distance and campus-based education. The Council for Higher Education Accreditation, a national association representing accreditors, has issued guidelines on distance education and on-campus programs that, among other things, call for greater attention to student learning outcomes.[28] Additionally, in May 2003, the U.S. Gen-

---

24. 20 U.S.C. § 1099b(a)(5).

25. 20 U.S.C. § 1099b(a)(4).

26. U.S. Department of Education, *Fiscal Year 2004 Annual Plan* (Mar. 2003).

27. Business–Higher Education Forum, *Building a Nation of Learners: The Need for Changes in Teaching and Learning to Meet Global Challenges* (June 2003).

28. *See* Council for Higher Education Accreditation, *Statement of Mutual Responsibilities for Student Learning Outcomes: Accreditation, Institutions, and Programs* (Sept. 2003). Also, in May 2003, the Council identified six areas for accreditation and accountability reform, including expanding the use of student learning outcomes in accreditation reviews, offering more information to the public on the findings of these reviews, and reviewing any distance learning providers or offerings that may become eligible for federal student aid programs.

eral Accounting Office (GAO) reported eighteen states were promoting accountability by publishing the performance measures of their colleges and universities, including retention and graduation rates.[29] At the national level, DOE announced in its 2004 Annual Plan that it would propose to hold institutions more accountable for results, such as ensuring that a higher percentage of students complete their programs on schedule.[30]

The congressionally appointed Web-based Education Commission[31] has also called for greater attention to student outcomes. The commission has reported that "quality assurance has too often measured educational inputs (e.g., number of books in the library, etc.) rather than student outcomes."[32] Finally, the Business Higher Education Forum, an organization representing business executives and leaders in postsecondary education, has reported improvements are needed in adapting objectives to specific outcomes and certifiable job skills.[33]

In this same vein, GAO recently examined how accrediting agencies evaluate distance education programs. The office focused on the policies of seven such agencies collectively responsible for more than two-thirds of all distance education programs.[34] It specifically evaluated the extent to which these bodies assess student learning outcomes using criteria GAO

---

29. *See* U.S. General Accounting Office, *College Completion: Additional Efforts Could Help Education with Its Completion Goals*, GAO-03-568 (May 23, 2003).

30. *GAO Report* at 10.

31. Congress established the Web-based Education Commission to prepare a report to the President and Congress containing recommendations for legislation and administrative actions, including those pertaining to the appropriate federal rule in determining the quality of educational software products. Members of the Commission included senators, representatives, and leaders from postsecondary institutions.

32. *See* Web-Based Education Commission, *The Power of the Internet for Learning: Moving from Promise to Practice* (Dec. 2000).

33. *See supra* note 27.

34. The seven agencies are (1) Middle States Association of Colleges and Schools, (2) Western Association of Schools and Colleges–Accrediting Commission for Community and Junior Colleges, (3) New England Association of Schools and Colleges, (4) North Central Association of Colleges and Schools, (5) Northwest Association of Schools and Colleges, (6) Southern Association of Colleges and Schools, and (7) the Accrediting Council for Independent Colleges and Schools. In December 2004, the United States Distance Learning Association (USDLA) announced the formation of the Distance Learning Association Board (DLAB). The DLAB was formed to review and accredit distance learning institutions and distance education components of degree-granting institutions in the United States and abroad. DLAB accreditation will be based on the institution's successful completion of a detailed self-study and on-site visit by a peer-review team. A complete version of the USDLA Release is available at http://www.usdla.org/html/resources/accreditation.htm.

had developed in past work.[35] GAO conducted its work between October 2002 and February 2004 in accordance with generally accepted government auditing standards.[36]

The agencies reviewed by GAO all had standards for evaluating distance education programs.[37] The Higher Education Act does not specify how these programs should be reviewed, but instead directs agencies to cover key subject areas, such as student achievement, curricula, and faculty. The act also does not specify what the appropriate standards are. Interestingly, all seven agencies used the same standards to assess a school's distance education program as they did to evaluate its campus-based curricula.[38] The six regional accrediting agencies within the group have all adopted supplemental guidelines[39] to help schools assess their own distance education programs.[40]

In reviewing these standards, however, GAO found significant variations among the agencies. Five of the seven agencies required schools to demonstrate comparability between distance education programs and campus-based ones. For example, one agency required each school to evaluate "the educational effectiveness of its distance education programs (including assessments of student learning outcomes, student retention, and student satisfaction) to ensure comparability to campus-based programs."[41] Another agency required the successful completion of distance programs to be similar to campus-based courses. The remaining two agencies did not require schools to demonstrate comparability in any tangible way.[42]

A second area of variation was the threshold for deciding when to review a distance education program. While accrediting agencies generally review schools on a multiyear cycle, federal regulations provide that they

---

35. *See* U.S. General Accounting Office, *Executive Guide: Effectively Implementing the Government Performance and Results Act,* GAO/GGD-96-118 (June 1996).

36. *GAO Report* at 5.

37. *Id.* at 18.

38. *Id.* at 19.

39. The "Best Practices for Electronically Offered Degree and Certificate Programs" was drafted by the Western Cooperative for Educational Telecommunications in Colorado. The executive directors of the eight regional accrediting agencies (including six covered in GAO's review) requested the study on best practices to assist institutions in planning distance education activities and to provide a self-assessment framework for those already involved. According to the "best practices," overall program effectiveness is determined by such measures as student retention rates and student competence in fundamental skills such as communication, comprehension, and analysis.

40. Four of six regional accrediting agencies GAO reviewed also had additional standards or policies that applied to schools with a distance education program.

41. *GAO Report* at 19.

42. *Id.*

must also approve any "substantive changes" to an institution's educational mission or program.[43] The regulations prescribe seven types of events an agency must include in this definition. For example, beginning a distance education program might be considered a substantive change. However, the seven agencies vary in their definition of "substantive." Three of the seven choose to review distance education programs only when at least half of all courses in a program are offered in such manner.[44] A fourth agency reviews only when 25 percent or more of a degree or certificate program is offered through distance learning. The remaining three have still other polices in place.[45]

These differences likely result from the statutory latitude provided agencies in carrying out their roles. While such variations do not necessarily lead to significant gradations in educational quality, they potentially increase the odds of some schools being held to higher standards than others.[46] A growing awareness has arisen in the postsecondary education community that additional steps may be needed to evaluate and ensure the quality of distance education. As such, several agencies have taken significant steps toward applying an outcome-based, results-oriented approach to their accreditation process for distance learning.[47]

[7] Who Is Taking the Courses?

[a] In General

Distance education helps individuals overcome such barriers as full-time work, geographic inaccessibility, obtaining timely child or elder care, and physical disabilities. It further provides the advantages of convenience and flexibility. With digital technologies allowing courses to reach and appeal to wider audiences, interest in distance education has grown exponentially.[48] While almost all segments of the population may now access distance education, the college audience is increasing at the highest rate. Surveys predicted the number of college students enrolled in distance courses would reach 2.2 million by 2003, up from 710,000 in 1998.[49] Distance

---

43. 34 C.F.R. §§ 602.22(a)(2)(i)–(vii).

44. *GAO Report* at 20.

45. *Id.*

46. *Id.*

47. *GAO Report* at 25.

48. Press Release of International Data Corp., *Distance Learning Takes Off, Fueled by Growth in Internet Access* (Feb. 2, 1999), http://www.idc.com/Data/Consumer/content/CSB020999PR.htm.

49. *Id.* By the fall of 2006, close to 3.5 million college students were enrolled in at least one online course. *See* M. Cawvey, *Community Colleges Lead Online Demand,* Washingtontimes.com (April 15, 2008).

education owes much of its explosive growth to being able to respond to the needs of older, nontraditional students. The average distance student is thirty-four, employed full-time and with previous college experience.[50] More than half are female.[51]

Many persons drawn to distance education are professionals with jobs preventing them from attending on-campus classes. Even prestigious private universities such as Harvard, Stanford, and Duke, known for their traditional degree programs, are developing distance courses for working adults.[52] Retirees often take advantage of distance education opportunities too. More disposable income and/or greater leisure leads older students to enroll in courses for life-enhancing reasons, rather than academic or professional advancement. Senior citizens often take courses online due to restricted mobility or a desire to study privately.

[b] Current Trends

More and more students are being exposed to distance learning in their local school systems. About 36 percent of public school districts offered online courses in 2002–2003, enrolling more than 328,000 students.[53] Slightly over 19 percent of the 1.1 million students being homeschooled in 2003 also took an online course according to a 2006 report by the National Center for Education Statistics.[54] In the year 2000, about 1 in every 13 postsecondary students enrolled in at least one distance education course. By the fall of 2006, that number had risen to one in five.[55]

Students taking primarily distance learning courses in college differ from their postsecondary counterparts in several respects. First, they tend to be older and are more likely to be employed full-time. They also have higher incomes and are more likely to be married. Most students take distance classes at public institutions, with more matriculating at two-year

---

50. Peterson's, *Who Is Learning at a Distance?* http://www.petersons.com/dlearn/who .html.

51. *Id.*

52. Mendels, *Universities Embrace Distance Learning for Busy Professionals,* N.Y. Times, July 29, 1998.

53. R. Borja, *States Urged to Adopt Rules to Keep Pace with Growth in Online-Learning Options* 2 (Nov. 8, 2006), http://www.edweek.org/ew/Articles/2006/11/08/11online.h26 .html.

54. *Id.*

55. I. Elaine Allen & Jeff Seaman, *Online Nation: Five Years of Growth in Online Learning,* Babson Survey Research Group (Oct. 2007), http://www.sloan-c.org/publications/survey/ index.asp.

rather than four-year schools. The Internet is the most common mode of delivery for them in receiving distance education.[56]

[8] Who Is Providing Distance Education?

The expansion of distance education has led to significant changes among its providers. Although many distance programs are offered by established public and private colleges, the traditional model of nonprofit, K–12, and postsecondary education is no longer as predominant. Distance courses are now offered by both nonprofit and for-profit entities and through various partnerships involving educational institutions, government bodies, and private corporations.

[a] Providers in General

Distance education providers cover a broad spectrum and exist at the K–12 level, among community colleges, at public and private universities, in continuing education, and through educational publishers. Some providers are engaged exclusively in the offering of distance courses and are called "virtual" universities. With greater technological capabilities available and increasing technical sophistication among teachers, the number of institutions offering digital distance education has correspondingly increased. It was predicted that by 2002, 85% of two-year colleges would be offering these courses, up from 58% in 1998; and 84% of four-year institutions would be doing so, up from 62% in 1998.[57] Some large traditional schools, such as Stanford and the University of Illinois, are already offering entire degree programs online.[58]

Numerous consortia have also been formed to pool resources and offer classes from multiple institutions. For example, Colorado Community College Online offers 35 courses from 12 different accredited institutions.[59]

---

56. This data comes from the National Postsecondary Student Aid Study (NPSAS), a DOE database covering more than 19 million postsecondary students. The NPSAS is conducted approximately every three to four years by the National Center for Education Statistics in the Department of Education. It is a nationwide survey designed to collect demographic information on postsecondary students, as well as information on how such students fund their education. The most recent NPSAS covers students attending over 6,000 Title IV eligible institutions during the 1999–2000 school year. NPSAS defines distance education as courses delivered off-campus using live, interactive television or audio; prerecorded television or video; CD-ROM; or a computer-based system such as the Internet, e-mail, or chat rooms. NPSAS does not cover correspondence students.

57. International Data Corp., *supra* note 48, at 2.

58. Mendels, *Online University Set to Open Its (Virtual) Doors,* N.Y. Times, Mar. 4, 1998; Koeppel, *A Sample of Cyberschools,* N.Y. Times, April 4, 1999.

59. *See* Colorado Community College Online website, http://www.ccconline.org.

The Southern Regional Electronic Campus offers approximately 1,500 credit courses and 60 degree programs from 175 different colleges.[60] Western Governors University (WGU), an online "virtual university," was the brainchild of then governor Michael Leavitt of the State of Utah and began offering courses in 1998 with the support of 19 Western state governors and several corporations.[61] WGU offers courses from over 30 institutions and has over 1,200 enrolled students.[62]

[b] Postsecondary Statistics

Many postsecondary schools have added or expanded electronically based programs, so that distance education is now relatively common at this level.[63] In addition to the demographics of distance students, the National Postsecondary Student Aid Study (or NPSAS) also provides information on the modes of distance education delivery and the types of schools offering such courses.[64]

[i] Public Institutions Enrolled the Most Distance Education Students

For undergraduates, public institutions enrolled more distance students than either private or proprietary schools.[65] Of undergraduates taking at least one distance education class, 85%[66] did so at a public institution (79% of all undergraduates attend public institutions), 12% did so at private nonprofit institutions (16% of all undergraduates attend private nonprofit institutions), and 3% did so at proprietary schools (5% of all undergraduates attend proprietary schools). For graduate students, public institutions

---

60. *See* Southern Regional Electronic Campus website, http://www.electroniccampus.org (85 percent of these courses are web-based, about 10 percent are live and satellite-delivered, and the remainder are CD-ROM and videotape).

61. *Leavitt Says Western Governors University on Brink of Accreditation,* Casper Star & Tribune, Feb. 26, 2003. Mr. Leavitt is currently United States Secretary for Health and Human Services.

62. *See* Western Governors University website, http://www.wgu.edu/.

63. *See* Ashby Statement, *supra* note 9, at 4.

64. *See supra* note 56. The design for NPSAS involves selecting a nationally representative sample of postsecondary education institutions and students within those institutions. NPSAS information comes from multiple sources and includes data on institutional characteristics. This information is useful in developing some limited insights on institutions offering distance education programs.

65. Proprietary schools are for-profit, postsecondary institutions. They can include traditional two- and four-year colleges and universities as well as trade and technical schools.

66. Of the 85% of undergraduate students who took at least one distance education course at a public institution, 55% did so at two-year or less institutions and 30% did so at four-year institutions.

also enrolled more—63.5%—distance students than did private nonprofit or proprietary schools (32% and 4.5%, respectively). Approximately 58%, 40%, and 2% of all graduate students attended public institutions, private nonprofit institutions, and proprietary schools, respectively.

[ii] Institutions Predominantly Use the Internet to Deliver Distance Education

Postsecondary institutions used the Internet more than any other mode of communication to deliver distance education. At the three main types of institutions, over half the undergraduates taking at least one distance course did so over the Internet. Fifty-eight percent of undergraduate distance students at public institutions used the Internet; over 70% did so at both private nonprofit and proprietary schools. Institutions offering graduate programs also used the Internet as the primary means of delivery. For graduate students taking at least one distance education class, 65% of those at public colleges used the Internet, compared with 69% at private nonprofit schools and 94% at proprietary institutions.

[iii] Institutions Enrolled the Most Distance Education Students in Subjects Related to Business, Humanities, and Education

For undergraduates, 21% of those taking their entire program through distance education studied business, while 13% enrolled in humanities. Traditional students show similar patterns with 18% studying business and 15% humanities. For graduate students, 24% of those taking their entire program through distance education enrolled in education courses, while 19% majored in business. Again, this pattern is similar to that for traditional classroom graduate students, of whom 23% studied education while 17% pursued a business degree.

[c] Nonprofit versus For-Profit Education

In the United States, academic and professional education became a business earning $100 billion per year plus in the 1990s.[67] The increasing public appetite for distance learning has significantly affected the role played by providers. Once a primarily nonprofit activity, distance education has proven a lucrative commercial venture for some. While nonprofit schools continue to offer the vast majority of distance courses, new for-profit educational institutions have also entered the field. In addition, some nonprofit institutions have begun to engage in for-profit distance learning activities.

---

67. R. Vigilante, "Semesters in Cyberspace, New York University Virtual College" 1 (Sept. 1996) (pamphlet).

The predominant distance learning model remains a nonprofit one as schools at all levels continue to produce distance offerings. The tuition paid for distance courses at these institutions is typically the same as charged for on-campus classes, with supplemental fees occasionally added to cover technology costs. However, for-profit entities are now playing a larger role; the University of Phoenix (UOP) became the best known example. As the largest for-profit university in the country, the UOP online campus has granted over 171,000 degrees since 1976.[68] UOP has increased its enrollment dramatically since its inception and primarily serves older, adult learners.[69]

A hybrid category of provider consists of nonprofit educational institutions launching for-profit divisions. New York University (NYU), for example, created a wholly owned, for-profit subsidiary in 1998 to offer online courses separate from those given by its traditional college. These courses were marketed to corporations, other colleges and universities, and individual students. The subsidiary was intended to enable NYU to raise money through an eventual stock offering or sale of partnership interests.[70]

NYU's program, "NYUOnline," was closed in 2002, however, because of financial difficulties. The venture lost nearly $25 million of its parent's money before ceasing operations.[71] A similar for-profit venture, initiated in 2001 by Columbia University and called "Fathom," was dissolved in January 2003 after posting significant losses. Strikingly, Columbia contributed nearly $15 million to Fathom only to see a mere $700,000 in revenue.[72] Temple University's "Virtual Temple" program also closed its doors in 2001 after failing to meet expectations.[73] More recently, the University of Illinois announced its for-profit "Global Campus" initiative would be replaced with a nonprofit model under academic control of the faculty.[74]

Several for-profit subsidiaries of nonprofit schools continue to demonstrate viability, however, including the University of Maryland's "UMUC-

---

68. Figures provided by the University of Phoenix website, http://www.uopxonline.com/aboutus.asp.

69. Hobson, *Translation Troubles,* U.S. News & World Rep., Oct. 25, 2001, at 58.

70. Arenson, *N.Y.U. Sees Profits in Virtual Classes,* N.Y. Times, Oct. 7, 1998; Arenson, *More Colleges Plunging into Uncharted Waters of Online Courses,* N.Y. Times, Nov. 2, 1998.

71. Gordon, *College Online Learning Programs Falter,* The Daily Pennsylvanian, Jan. 31, 2003.

72. Carlson, *After Losing Millions, Columbia U. Will Close its Online-Learning Venture,* The Chron. of Higher Educ., Jan. 7, 2003.

73. See Gordon, *supra* note 71.

74. S. Jaschik, *Defeat for For-Profit Model,* insidehighered.com (Jan. 12, 2007), http://insidehighered.com/news/2007/01/12/illinois.

Online," Pennsylvania State University's "World Campus," and the University of Massachusetts's "UMassOnline."[75] The latter recently announced that online program education revenues grew 32% for the 2005–2006 academic year, while enrollment increased 23% for the same period.[76] This compares to an increase of 39% for revenues in fiscal 2004 and an enrollment surge in such programs of 32% for that period.[77]

[d] Partnerships

Several distinct varieties of partnership have emerged from the growth of distance education, including collaborations between nonprofit and commercial entities, otherwise unaffiliated educational institutions, and even foreign governments. Recognizing the value of the educational market, and the need for classes tailored to accommodate busy corporate schedules, companies have partnered with universities to design, produce, and transmit distance courses. The synergies associated with these arrangements are obvious. Educational institutions can shift the costs of expensive distance education technologies to the private sector, while their corporate partners "acquire an invaluable 'laboratory' for application of their technology in educational environments, and often gain access to the latest research of leading academics. . . ."[78]

AT&T, for example, designed a Learning Network Virtual Academy, in partnership with several colleges, that offers a range of professional development options for educators.[79] In August 2001, Thomson Corp. announced it would invest $25 million in "Universitas 21 Global," an online university targeting Latin America and Asia for English-language training. The venture will involve 16 colleges, including the University of Virginia and NYU.[80] Private corporations are internally involved in distance learning as well. On January 19, 2005, *Distance-Educator.com*, a daily Internet publication, reported that Canon had recently announced its intention to make e-learning courses in information technology and professional skills available to over 11,000 of its employees in Europe.[81]

---

75. Wilson, *Is There a Future for Online Ed?* Univ. Bus., Mar. 31, 2003.

76. "UMass Online Growing," UMassOnline.net (Sept. 7, 2006).

77. "UMass Online Revenue Grows," Distance-Educator.com (Mar. 31, 2004).

78. A. Chute & K. Gulliver, *Distance Education and Partnerships: Tools for the Future* (1996), http://www.lucent.com/cedl/distedpart.html.

79. U.S. Dep't of Education, *Star Schools Makes a Difference* (pamphlet; 1998–1999).

80. *See* Hobson, *supra* note 69, at 58.

81. The copyright laws applicable to private companies, as opposed to educational institutions, are a separate topic and will not be directly dealt with in this book.

Educational institutions, recognizing the potential of sharing resources and expertise in this expanding field, are joining forces to create programs that span state borders. Colleges have a long history of collaborative association, and distance education has provided new incentives to develop partnerships.[82] Foreign governments are also involved in similar distance education efforts. In November 2003, the Government of Japan and the World Bank announced the establishment of the "Japan/World Bank Distance Learning Partnership." The project's aim is to assist East Asia and the Pacific region's Global Development Learning Network to become a more effective teaching tool.[83] In March 2004, Gilat Satellite Networks Ltd. announced an agreement to supply Russia's Modern Institute for the Humanities, one of the world's largest universities with over 145,000 students enrolled, with a satellite-based network to provide Internet access, distance learning, and videoconferencing to the university's branches located throughout the Russian Federation.[84]

1.2 THE FUTURE OF DISTANCE EDUCATION

While the growth of distance education in the United States has been dramatic, it has experienced its share of setbacks. As Michael Lambert, executive director of the Distance Education and Training Council, has stated: "You will see a lot of mistakes committed and a lot of money spent with little results."[85]

One recent victim was MindEdge.com, a website originally designed as a search engine allowing students to look for, compare, and enroll in online courses while the company earned commissions for these referrals. Unfortunately for the venture, students found it easier to proceed directly to a particular college's website to register for courses.[86] The ill-fated California Virtual University, described by its own CEO, Stanley Chodorow, as "a flawed idea,"[87] ceased most of its operations in late 1999. According to

---

82. Distance-Educator.com (Mar. 26, 2003), at 1.

83. *Press Release of Foreign Policy Association Job Board* (Nov. 24, 2003), http://www.fpa .org/jobs_contact2423.

84. *Gilat Signs Agreement with Russia's Largest Open University,* Distance-Educator.com (Mar. 25, 2004).

85. Quoted in C. Thomas, *The Future of Distance Learning* 2 (2003), http://www .distance-learning-programs.info/the-future-of-distance-learning.html.

86. *See* E. Horowitz, *Charting the Future of Distance Education,* Faculty Forum, The Newsletter of the U.S.C. Academic Senate (Vol. 2, No. 3/4, 2000–2001), http://www.usc.edu/ academe/acsen/resources/newsletter/0001v2n34/0001vol2num34article02.shtml.

87. The Chron. of Higher Educ., May 19, 2000. *See also* Section 1.1, subsection [8]c *supra* for other examples of distance education ventures that have failed recently.

Mr. Chodorow: "There was an absence of an adequate financial structure. Member institutions never contributed much money to it, and private companies were not enthusiastic either."[88]

Despite such publicized failures, distance learning has continued to become an accepted form of education. The DOE's 2004 National Education Technology Plan included a specific recommendation that states and school districts "provide every student access to e-learning."[89] The real question now is not whether distance learning has a role in education, but what form that role will ultimately take. Commenting on a recent poll by the National Education Association (NEA), NEA President Robert Chase noted: "For those who continue to divide higher education into 'for' and 'against' distance learning camps . . . this poll will be a surprise . . . [because] from the faculty perspective [it is] clear that distance learning can be quality learning."[90] The NEA poll revealed that 75 percent of the 400 instructors surveyed conveyed positive feelings about distance education, while only 14 percent were critical of the trend.[91]

A more recent study found that nearly 70 percent of academic leaders believe student demand for online learning is still growing, while 83 percent of those institutions with online offerings expect their distance education enrollments to increase in the near term.[92] The growth of distance education in the United States will not necessarily lead to a decline in on-campus learning, however. Frank Mayadas, program director at the Alfred P. Sloan Foundation's Asynchronous Learning Networks, speculates that: "[o]ver a period of many years . . . the differences between campus-based and distance learning will be minimal."[93] Mary Beth Almeda, Director of the Center for Media and Independent Learning at the University of California, concurs by saying: "Technology won't replace or supercede the classroom. There's room for everything."[94] Michael Lambert best sums up

---

88. *Id.*

89. U.S. Department of Education, National Education Technology Plan, *Toward a New Golden Age in American Education: How the Internet, the Law and Today's Students are Revolutionizing Expectation* (2004), http://www.ed.gov/about/offices/list/os/technology/plan/2004/site/edlite-default.html.

90. News Release of the National Education Association, *Confronting the Future of Distance Learning—Placing Quality in Reach* (June 14, 2000), http://www.nea.org/nr/nr000614.html.

91. *Id. See also* Jaschik, *supra* note 11, at 2 ("A few years back, those organizing distance programs at community colleges would complain that faculty skepticism was a big obstacle, but . . . the survey found that is no longer the case.").

92. Babson Survey, *supra* note 55, at 2.

93. Quoted in Thomas, *supra* note 85, at 2.

94. *Id.*

the situation by noting distance learning "will not replace traditional education but will enhance it."[95] Mr. Lambert points out that approximately 85 percent of "distance education" students are taught on-campus and use distance learning to supplement the classroom environment.[96]

A recent survey of distance education programs in higher education found that their revenues grew by a mean of 15.52 percent in 2006 and that more than two-thirds of the colleges in the sample viewed their distance programs "as a financial resource . . . expected to produce a surplus for the college."[97] As such, the future debate over distance education will not involve its viability, which is a given, but its impact on faculty, institutional, and student relationships. One leading educator has expressed concern that distance learning will contribute to the commercialization of academia by forcing universities to be more interested in profits rather than educational standing.[98] Other thought-provoking questions raised by faculty across the country concern whether:

- the creation of for-profit subsidiaries will reduce the number of tenured professorial positions
- universities will become more consumer oriented rather than student oriented
- the financial rewards associated with online courses will distract faculty from their traditional roles
- professors will maintain control over the material they produce
- faculty will have the same oversight regarding electronic courses as they do face-to-face ones
- professors ultimately will be replaced by the very materials they created[99]

These challenges and concerns will no doubt be the subject of much discussion over the coming years.

1.3 THE CLASH OF LAW AND TECHNOLOGY

While new technology has been a driving force behind distance education, there is little doubt that, at least until recently, copyright law has been viewed as a significant hindrance to its development. As will be explored

---

95. *Id.*

96. *Id.*

97. Primary Research Group, Inc., *Press Release* (Sept. 20, 2007), http://www.prweb.com/releases/2007/9/prweb544787.html.

98. D. Noble, *Digital Diploma Mills: The Coming Battle Over Online Instruction* (Mar. 1998), http://www.communication.ucsd.edu/dl/ddm2.html.

99. *See* Horowitz, *supra* note 86, at 3. Several of these questions are considered and discussed in more detail in Chapter Five.

later, the law (which often evolves slowly) has struggled to maintain pace with technology in many areas. Distance learning is only one example of this phenomenon.

For years, educators have grappled with applying the murky doctrine of "fair use" to their lesson plans in order to avoid copyright infringement liability. The advent of digital distance learning has only made such application more difficult. Chapters Two and Three of this book deal with the basics of copyright law and the fair use doctrine in detail to assist distance educators in making better-informed decisions when teaching.

Digital technology has also made it easier to duplicate and distribute copyrighted works. As such, copyright owners have been reticent to license their works to colleges and universities for fear of the havoc students may cause by facilitating the worldwide, unauthorized dissemination of their materials. Advances in technology and a better understanding of licensing procedures have alleviated this problem to some extent. These topics and other licensing issues are covered in more detail in Chapter Four.

Using the Internet as the primary medium of distance education also carries with it legal risk. For years, Internet service providers, including colleges and universities, faced the prospect of being held vicariously or contributorily liable for the copyright piracy and associated legal misconduct of their subscribers or students. Recent federal legislation has lessened such exposure to providers in exchange for mandating cooperation with copyright owners and/or their agents who wish to identify and prosecute infringers. This and other related topics are discussed in Chapter Five.

Finally, for almost twenty-five years, copyright law placed severe constraints on the types of works that educators could perform or display in their electronic courses, and on where such courses could be transmitted. New federal statutes have eased such restrictions but in turn have imposed greater legal and technological burdens on educational institutions and their faculty. This is the principal topic of Chapter Six.

A word about the importance of these laws for educators is merited. In conducting seminars across the country, this author has often been asked whether teachers "really" need to have an understanding of copyright law. This skeptical inquiry arises, I believe, from a false sense of security propagated within the walls of academia. Many faculty simply dismiss the notion of ever being sued for infringement for reasons such as "content owners will never figure out what I'm doing in my classroom"; "lawsuits are too expensive"; "I'm not charging anybody"; and "there's too much bad publicity in suing a school."

While these rationalizations seem somewhat compelling, the reality is that while the prospect of legal action against educators for copyright infringement is currently remote, the threat is real and growing. Those teachers who do not consider themselves potential targets may wish to reconsider in light of the thousands of college students now being sued by the music industry for illegally downloading songs from the Internet.[100] One can assume most of those individuals also viewed themselves as too small to ever appear on anyone's radar screen. However, new evidence suggests "investigators are now shifting their focus from companies profiting from the reproduction of copyrighted academic materials to individuals acquiring and exchanging those materials online for educational purposes, most often professors and students."[101] Participants at a recent national workshop on how copyright law affects educational policy expressed awareness of recent litigation threats publishers have made against several colleges and their faculty.[102]

The *Google* case, discussed in more detail in Chapter Three, demonstrates the proclivity of copyright owners to pursue what they perceive as threats to their financial revenue stream. While the principal defendant in *Google* is an Internet search engine, that company is scanning and indexing books made available to it by a number of universities. In time, those institutions may well be added as defendants.[103] They are already involved in having to defend and justify their actions publicly.[104]

Lastly, educational institutions must weigh the odds of being sued against the potential costs of such an event. Under the law, instead of proving actual damages (which are often negligible), copyright owners may elect to recover "statutory" damages for each act of infringement.[105] These amounts range from $750 to $30,000, and may reach as high as $150,000 if the plaintiff can demonstrate the infringement was "willful."[106] As such,

---

100. As of late 2004, the Recording Industry of America had filed over 6,200 such suits. *See* A. Ramasastry, *Privacy, Piracy and Due Process in Peer-to-Peer File Swapping Suits* (Nov. 10, 2004), http://writ.findlaw.com/ramasastry/20041110.html.

101. C. Toth, *E-violations of Copyright a Problem for Faculty, Students,* dailyvanguard .com (May 23, 2006), http://www.media.dailyvanguard.com/media/storage/paper941/news/ 2006/05/23/News/Eviolations.Of.Copyright.A.Problem.For.Faculty.Students-2607072.shtml.

102. W. Fisher & W. McGeveran, *Obstacles to Educational Uses of Copyrighted Material in the Digital Age* 54 (August 10, 2006), Berkman Center Research Publication No. 2006–09, http://ssrn.com/abstract=923465.

103. *UC Libraries Join Google's Book-Scanning Project Despite Lawsuits,* siliconvalley.com (Aug. 9, 2006) ("Although the lawsuits aren't directly targeting the university libraries, [the University of California's] alliance with Google [has] irritated the publishing community.").

104. *Id.* at 2, *quoting* Jennifer Colvin, a spokesperson for the University of California's library system: "There are so many benefits to this. We respect copyrights, but also want to give full access to our public domain material."

105. 17 U.S.C. §§ 504(a) and (b).

106. 17 U.S.C. §§ 504(c)(1) and (2).

illegally duplicating only a few works (even unintentionally) may expose the university or its faculty to significant liability. Even if these persons are successful in raising fair use or other educational exemptions to justify their conduct, the expense of litigating such suits is exorbitant. Current studies estimate the costs of defending a major copyright infringement action at close to $1,000,000.[107]

As such, the growing risk of litigation coupled with the prospect of paying out disproportionate damages and incurring substantial legal fees should be a warning bell to every educational institution or school system that copyright law education and compliance should be an important component of its agenda. At present, however, such copyright awareness on campus seems to be lacking. The publishing community has estimated that professors illegally posting long excerpts of works on the Internet have cost that industry over $20 million per year.[108] The issue has also raised national concern. In May of 2006, the United States Senate unanimously passed a nonbinding resolution that "institutions of higher learning should adopt policies and educational programs on their campuses to help deter and eliminate illicit copyright infringement."[109] Two months earlier, the U.S. House reauthorized the Higher Education Act and included language therein to use federal funds to combat copyright piracy on campus.[110]

However these issues are resolved, distance learning will remain a significant component of education at all levels for many years to come. How copyright law affects and interacts with distance education is the subject of the remainder of this book.

---

107. Fisher, *supra* note 102, at 57.

108. J. O'Neill, *Professors Get "F" in Copyright Protection Knowledge* (Nov. 20, 2006), http://Seattlepi.nwsource.com/business/292898-copyright20.html.

109. S. Res. 488, 109th Cong., 2d Sess. (May 22, 2006). *See* Chapter Three, Section 3.2, subsection [5] for a discussion of steps schools are taking to deal with this issue.

110. House Committee on Education and the Workforce, Press Release (Sept. 26, 2006).

CHAPTER **2**

Basics of Copyright Law

Since a general understanding of copyright law is necessary for every instructor incorporating another's works into his or her course, Section 2.1 of this chapter first provides some historical perspective and then addresses United States copyright laws focusing on such questions as:

- What is copyright?
- How long does copyright protection last?
- What works are eligible for protection?
- How does one register a new work for protection?
- What constitutes "fair use" of a copyrighted work?
- What are the penalties for infringing use?

This first part also covers the assignment and licensing of copyrights and discusses recent case law involving use of the sovereign immunity defense by state universities against intellectual property infringement claims. Section 2.2 deals with international treaties and issues regarding foreign copyright protection.

2.1 UNITED STATES COPYRIGHT LAW

[1] Purpose of Copyright Law

The Constitution of the United States provides that Congress has the power to "promote the Progress of Science and useful Arts, by securing for limited Times to Authors and Inventors the exclusive Right to their respective Writings and Discoveries."[1] Ironically, the Framers did not discuss this

---

1. *See* U.S. Const. art. I, § 8, cl. 8.

clause at length either before or after its adoption.[2] The purpose of the clause was described in the Federalist Papers by James Madison:

> The utility of this power will scarcely be questioned. The copyright of authors has been solemnly adjudged, in Great Britain, to be a right of common law. The right to useful inventions seems with equal reason to belong to the inventors. The public good fully coincides in both cases with the claims of individuals.[3]

The Constitution, therefore, outlines both the *goal* Congress is attempting to achieve (promoting the progress of science and useful arts) and the *means* to accomplish that goal (securing for limited times to authors and inventors the exclusive right to their respective writings and discoveries).[4] Over history, the United States Supreme Court has described the various objectives of copyright in terms of supplying the economic incentive to create and disseminate ideas;[5] serving the public good;[6] encouraging others to build freely upon the ideas and information conveyed by a work;[7] advancing the public welfare;[8] allowing the public access to the products of creators' genius;[9] assuring contributors to the store of knowledge;[10] and inducing release of creative works.[11]

---

2. On August 18, 1787, James Madison submitted to the delegates at the Constitutional Convention a list of powers to be granted Congress, which included the power "[t]o secure to literary authors their copyrights for a limited time" and "[t]o encourage, by premiums and provisions, the advancement of useful knowledge and discoveries." At the same time, Charles Pinckney submitted a list that included the power "[t]o grant patents for useful inventions" and "[t]o secure to authors exclusive rights for a certain time." On September 5, 1787, the clause "[t]o promote the progress of science and the useful arts, by securing for limited times, to authors and inventors, the exclusive right to their respective writings and discoveries" was agreed to unanimously. On September 17, 1787, the draft was signed by the delegates to the convention with no substantive changes. *See Debates on the Adoption of the Federal Constitution* as reported by James Madison. The clause was finally ratified in its present form in 1788. George Washington signed the first copyright law on May 31, 1790.

3. *The Federalist* No. 43 (J. Madison).

4. *Goldstein v. California*, 412 U.S. 546, 555 (1973).

5. *Harper & Row, Publishers, Inc. v. Nation Enterprises*, 471 U.S. 539, 558 (1985). *See also id.* at 546 ("monopoly created by copyright thus rewards the individual author in order to benefit the public").

6. *Fogerty v. Fantasy, Inc.*, 114 S. Ct. 1023, 1029 (1994).

7. *Feist Publication, Inc. v. Rural Telephone Service Co.*, 499 U.S. 340, 349–50 (1991).

8. *Mazer v. Stein*, 347 U.S. 201, 219 (1954).

9. *Sony Corp. v. Universal City Studios, Inc.*, 464 U.S. 417, 429 (1984).

10. *Harper & Row, supra* note 5, at 545–46 (citing *Twentieth Century Music Corp. v. Aiken*, 422 U.S. 151, 156 (1975)).

11. *United States v. Paramount Pictures, Inc.*, 334 U.S. 131, 158 (1948).

Copyright is thus "intended definitely to grant valuable, enforceable rights to authors . . . 'to afford greater encouragement to the production of literary works of lasting benefit to the world.'"[12] The purpose is to reward the author, but the law does so to achieve its ultimate purpose—inducing him or her to release the products of their genius.[13] The "immediate effect" of copyright law is that authors receive a "fair return for [their] creative labor," however, the "ultimate aim is, by this incentive, to stimulate artistic creativity for the general public good."[14] Congress also interpreted this constitutional clause when it enacted the Copyright Act of 1909:

> The enactment of copyright legislation by Congress under the terms of the Constitution is not based upon any natural right that the author has in his writings, . . . but upon the ground that the welfare of the public will be served and progress of science and useful arts will be promoted by securing to authors for limited periods the exclusive rights to their writings . . . .[15]

By being granted exclusive rights, authors receive economic rewards and the public obtains literature, music, and other creative works that might not have been created or disseminated otherwise. The public also benefits from the limited scope and duration of the rights granted.[16] The free flow of thoughts is promoted by the denial of protection for facts and ideas.[17] The granting of exclusive rights to the author "does not preclude others from using the ideas or information revealed by the author's work."[18]

While copyright law "ultimately serves the purpose of enriching the general public through access to creative works,"[19] it imposes no obligation upon copyright owners to make their works available. While it is hoped that the potential economic benefits to doing so will induce them, such owners do not have to provide access to their works, either during the term of protection or after. Hence, unpublished works never distributed to the public are granted as much (if not more) protection than published

---

12. *Washingtonian Publishing Co. v. Pearson*, 306 U.S. 30, 36 (1939).

13. *Paramount, supra* note 11, at 158.

14. *Twentieth Century Music Corp. v. Aiken*, 422 U.S. 151, 156 (1975).

15. H.R. Rep. No. 2222, 60th Cong., 2d Sess. 7 (1909) (report accompanying the Copyright Act of 1909, the first comprehensive revision of the copyright laws).

16. *See* discussion of term of protection, fair use, and other limitations on an author's exclusive rights in subsections [4] through [7] of Section 2.1 of this chapter.

17. *See* discussion of unprotected subject matter, *infra* Section 2.1[2][c].

18. *See* H.R. Rep. No. 1476, 94th Cong., 2d Sess. 47 (1976) (hereinafter *House Report*), at 56.

19. *Fogerty, supra* note 6, at 1030.

ones. However, once an author publishes a work, copies thereof must be deposited with the Library of Congress for the public's benefit.

[2] Subject Matter and Scope of Protection

[a] Eligibility for Protection

The subject matter eligible for protection under the Copyright Act is set forth in Section 102(a):

> Copyright protection subsists . . . in original works of authorship fixed in any tangible medium of expression, now known or later developed, from which they can be perceived, reproduced, or otherwise communicated, either directly or with the aid of a machine or device.[20]

From this provision, the courts have derived three basic requirements for copyright protection—originality, creativity, and fixation.[21]

The requirements of originality and creativity are derived from the statutory qualification that copyright protection extends only to "original works of authorship."[22] To be original, a work merely must be one of independent creation, that is, not copied from another. There is no requirement the work be novel (as in patent law), unique, or ingenious. To be creative, there must only be a modicum of creativity. The level required is

---

20. 17 U.S.C. § 102(a). The Copyright Act specifically excludes from protectible subject matter any "idea, procedure, process, system, method of operation, concept, principle or discovery" even if it meets the criteria for protection. *See* 17 U.S.C. § 102(b). The Copyright Act also preempts any grant of equivalent rights for works of authorship within the specified subject matter. Section 301 provides:

> On and after January 1, 1978, all legal or equitable rights that are equivalent to any of the exclusive rights within the general scope of copyright as specified by section 106 in works of authorship that are fixed in a tangible medium of expression and come within the subject matter of copyright as specified by sections 102 and 103, whether created before or after that date and whether published or unpublished, are governed exclusively by this title. Thereafter, no person is entitled to any such right or equivalent right in any such work under the common law or statutes of any State.

17 U.S.C. § 301(a). *See infra* Section 2.1[3][c], for a more detailed discussion of the doctrine of preemption.

21. Many courts consider creativity to be an element of originality. For purposes of this discussion, we examine originality and creativity as separate requirements.

22. *See* 17 U.S.C. § 102(a). The statutory qualification is derived from the limited constitutional authority of Congress to grant copyright protection to "authors" for their "writings." *See* U.S. Const. art. I, § 8, cl. 8.

exceedingly low; "even a slight amount will suffice."[23] The third and final requirement for copyright protection is fixation in a tangible medium of expression. Protection attaches *automatically* to an eligible work the moment it is fixed.[24] A work is fixed "when its embodiment in a copy or phonorecord . . . is sufficiently permanent or stable to permit it to be perceived, reproduced, or otherwise communicated for a period of more than transitory duration."[25]

Congress left considerable room for technological advances in the area of fixation by providing that the method thereof may be "now known or later developed."[26] The Copyright Act divides the possible media for fixation into only two categories—"copies" and "phonorecords":

> "Copies" are material objects, other than phonorecords, in which a work is fixed by any method now known or later developed, and from which the work can be perceived, reproduced, or otherwise communicated, either directly or with the aid of a machine or device.[27]
>
> "Phonorecords" are material objects in which sounds, other than those accompanying a motion picture or other audiovisual work, are fixed by any method now known or later developed, and from which the sounds can be perceived, reproduced, or otherwise communicated, either directly or with the aid of a machine or device.[28]

According to the House Report accompanying the Copyright Act of 1976, Congress intended the terms "copies" and "phonorecords" to "comprise all of the material objects in which copyrightable works are capable of being fixed."[29] The form of fixation and the manner, method, or medium used are virtually unlimited. A work may be fixed in "words, numbers, notes, sounds, pictures, or any other graphic or symbolic indicia"; may be embodied in a physical object in "written, printed, photographic, sculptural, punched, magnetic, or

---

23. *Feist, supra* note 7, at 345 ("vast majority of works make the grade quite easily, as they possess some creative spark").

24. Copyright protection literally begins when, for instance, the ink dries on the paper or someone's voice is recorded on a dictating machine. There are no longer any prerequisites, such as registration or affixation of a copyright notice, for obtaining or enjoying copyright protection.

25. 17 U.S.C. § 101 (definition of "fixed").

26. *See* 17 U.S.C. § 102(a) .

27. 17 U.S.C. § 101 (definition of "copies").

28. 17 U.S.C. § 101 (definition of "phonorecords").

29. *House Report* at 53. This work generally uses the term "copy" or "copies" to refer to copies *and* phonorecords except in those instances where the distinction is relevant.

any other stable form"; and may be capable of perception either "directly or by means of any machine or device 'now known or later developed.'"[30]

In digital form, a work is generally recorded (and thus fixed) as a sequence of binary digits (zeros and ones) using media-specific encoding. This fits within the House Report's list of permissible manners of fixation.[31] Virtually all works may be fixed in acceptable material objects, that is, copies or phonorecords. For instance, floppy disks, compact discs (CDs), CD-ROMs, optical disks, compact discs-interactive (CD-Is), digital tape, DVDs, and other digital storage devices are all stable forms in which works may be fixed and from which they may be perceived, reproduced, or communicated by means of a machine or device.[32] The question of whether interactive works (e.g., video games) are sufficiently fixed to qualify for protection (given the user's ability to constantly alter the sequence of the "action") has been resolved by courts in the affirmative.[33]

A transmission, in and of itself, however, is not a fixation. While a transmission may result in a fixation, a work is not fixed by virtue of the transmission alone. Therefore, "live" broadcasts fail to meet the fixation requirement and are not protected by the Copyright Act. An exception exists if the work is being fixed or recorded while being transmitted.[34] The Copyright Act provides that a work "consisting of sounds, images, or both, that are being transmitted" meets the fixation requirement "if a fixation of the work is being made simultaneously with its transmission."[35]

A simultaneous (or any other) fixation meets the requirements if its embodiment in a copy is "sufficiently permanent or stable to permit it to be perceived, reproduced, or otherwise communicated for a period of more than transitory duration."[36] Works are not sufficiently fixed if they

---

30. *House Report* at 52.

31. *Id.*

32. *See, e.g., Stern Electronics, Inc. v. Kaufman*, 669 F.2d 852, 855 (2d Cir. 1982) (putting work in "memory devices" of a computer "satisf[ies] the statutory requirement of a 'copy' in which the work is 'fixed'").

33. *See, e.g., Atari Games Corp. v. Oman*, 888 F.2d 878 (D.C. Cir. 1989).

34. Unfixed broadcasts are not within the subject matter of federal copyright law. Therefore, protection of such works is not preempted and may be provided by state statutory or common law. *See* 17 U.S.C. § 301.

35. *See* 17 U.S.C. § 101 (definition of "fixed"); *see also Baltimore Orioles, Inc. v. Major League Baseball Players Assoc.*, 805 F.2d 663, 668 (7th Cir. 1986) (telecasts that are video-taped at the same time that they are broadcast are fixed in tangible form), *cert. denied*, 480 U.S. 941 (1987); *National Football League v. McBee & Bruno's, Inc.*, 792 F.2d 726, 731–32 (8th Cir. 1986) ("the legislative history [of the Copyright Act] demonstrates a clear intent on the part of Congress to resolve, through the definition of 'fixation' . . . the status of live broadcasts, using—coincidentally but not insignificantly—the example of a live football game"). It is understood that the "fixation" must be made or authorized by the author.

36. 17 U.S.C. § 101 (definition of "fixed").

are "purely evanescent or transient" in nature, "such as those projected briefly on a screen, [or] shown electronically on a television or cathode ray tube. . . ."[37] On the other hand, electronic network transmissions from one computer to another, such as e-mail, even though they may only reside on each computer in RAM (random access memory), have still been found by courts to constitute sufficient fixation.[38]

For example, a professor having his lecture broadcast live by a cable feed to students at a regional campus of his university in another part of the state is not creating a "copyrightable" work, unless the lecture is being simultaneously videotaped. Ironically, if the same lecture were being "webcast" over the Internet to these same students (even without videotaping), it would be deemed a copyrightable work because of the transmission into the RAM of the student's computer. As will be discussed later, however, this does little good as the professor does not have a "replayable" version to file with the Copyright Office to register his work. Without registration, he may not pursue an infringer in federal court. Regardless, the professor would not lose his copyright to a student secretly videotaping the class, because that fixation was not authorized by the instructor.

[b] Published and Unpublished Works

Historically, the concept of publication has been a major underpinning of copyright law. Under the dual system of protection that existed until the 1976 Copyright Act took effect, unpublished works were generally protected under state law. Published works, on the other hand, were subject to federal copyright protection.[39] On the effective date of the 1976 act, January 1, 1978, federal copyright protection became available for both unpublished and published works.[40] The concept of publication thus lost its "all-embracing

---

37. *House Report* at 53.

38. *See Advanced Computer Services of Michigan Inc. v. MAI Systems Corp.*, 845 F. Supp. 356, 363 (E.D. Va. 1994) (conclusion that program stored only in RAM is sufficiently fixed is confirmed, not refuted, by argument that it "disappears from RAM the instant the computer is turned off"; if power remains on (and the work remains in RAM) for only seconds or fractions of a second, "the resulting RAM representation of the program arguably would be too ephemeral to be considered 'fixed'"); *Triad Systems Corp. v. Southeastern Express Co.*, 1994 U.S. Dist. LEXIS 5390, at *15–19 (N.D. Cal. 1994) ("[C]opyright law is not so much concerned with the temporal 'duration' of a copy as it is with what that copy does, and what it is capable of doing, while it exists. 'Transitory duration' is a relative term that must be interpreted and applied in context.").

39. *See Wheaton v. Peters*, 33 U.S. (1 Peters) 591, 662–63 (1834).

40. *See* 17 U.S.C. § 104. Prior to 1978, certain unpublished works, particularly dramatic works and musical compositions, could obtain federal copyright protection through registration with the Copyright Office. Since 1978, all otherwise eligible unpublished works are protected under federal law. *See* 17 U.S.C. § 104(a).

importance" as the threshold to federal statutory protection.[41] However, while the importance of publication has been reduced through amendment to the law (e.g., granting federal protection to unpublished works and removing the notice requirement for published ones), the status of a work as either published or unpublished still retains some significance. For example:

- only works that are published in the United States are subject to mandatory deposit in the Library of Congress;[42]
- deposit requirements for registration with the Copyright Office differ depending on whether a work is published or unpublished;[43]
- the scope of the fair use defense is generally narrower for unpublished works;[44]
- unpublished works are eligible for protection without regard to the nationality or domicile of the author;[45]
- published works must bear a copyright notice if published before March 1, 1989;[46] and

---

41. *House Report* at 129.

42. 17 U.S.C. § 407. "[T]he owner of copyright or of the exclusive right of publication in a work published in the United States shall deposit, within three months after the date of publication—(1) two complete copies of the best edition; or (2) if the work is a sound recording, two complete phonorecords of the best edition, together with any printed or other visually perceptible material published with such phonorecords." 17 U.S.C. § 407(a). The deposit requirements are not conditions of copyright protection, but failure to deposit copies of a published work may subject the copyright owner to significant fines. *See* 17 U.S.C. §§ 407(a), (d).

43. *See* 17 U.S.C. § 408(b) ("the material deposited for registration shall include—(1) in the case of an unpublished work, one complete copy or phonorecord; (2) in the case of a published work, two complete copies or phonorecords of the best edition; (3) in the case of a work first published outside the United States, one complete copy or phonorecord as so published; (4) in the case of a contribution to a collective work, one complete copy or phonorecord of the best edition of the collective work").

44. The first factor of the fair use analysis—the nature of the copyrighted work—generally weighs against a finding of fair use if the work is unpublished. *See Harper & Row, supra* note 5. In 1992, Congress was prompted to amend Section 107 by the near determinative weight courts were giving to the unpublished nature of a work. *See* Act of October 24, 1992, Pub. L. No. 102–492, 106 Stat. 3145 (1992) (adding to the fair use provisions, "The fact that a work is unpublished shall not itself bar a finding of fair use if such finding is made upon consideration of all the above factors.").

45. 17 U.S.C. § 104(a); *House Report* at 58 (Section 104(a) "imposes no qualification of nationality and domicile with respect to unpublished works"); *see also* 17 U.S.C. § 104(b) (national origin requirements for published works).

46. 17 U.S.C. § 405. For such works, failure to include a copyright notice risks total loss of copyright protection. *See id.* Works published after March 1, 1989 (the effective date of the Berne Implementation Act) may (but are not required to) bear a copyright notice identifying the year of publication and the name of the copyright owner. *See* 17 U.S.C. § 401.

- certain limitations on the exclusive rights of a copyright owner are applicable only to published works.[47]

The Copyright Act provides a definition of "publication" to distinguish between published and unpublished works:

> "Publication" is the distribution of copies or phonorecords of a work to the public by sale or other transfer of ownership, or by rental, lease, or lending. The offering to distribute copies or phonorecords to a group of persons for purposes of further distribution, public performance, or public display, constitutes publication. A public performance or display of a work does not of itself constitute publication.[48]

The definition uses the language of Section 106 describing the exclusive right of distribution and was intended to make clear that "any form of dissemination in which a material object does not change hands—performances or displays on television, for example—is not a publication no matter how many people are exposed to the work."[49] It also underscores that the distribution must be "to the public."[50] In general, the definition continues principles that had evolved through prior case law,[51] including the doctrine of limited publication.[52]

The latter doctrine was developed by courts to save works from losing copyright protection when copies thereof were distributed to only a limited

---

47. *See generally* 17 U.S.C. §§ 107—120. *See, e.g.,* 17 U.S.C. § 118 (compulsory license is available for the use of certain published works in connection with noncommercial broadcasting).

48. 17 U.S.C. § 101 (definition of "publication").

49. *See House Report* at 138.

50. *See, e.g., Salinger v. Random House, Inc.,* 811 F.2d 90 (2d Cir.), *supplemented, reh'g denied,* 818 F.2d 252, *cert. denied,* 484 U.S. 890 (1987) (copyrighted letters did not lose unpublished status by placement in library); *WPOW, Inc. v. MRLJ Enterprises,* 584 F. Supp. 132 (D.D.C. 1984) (filing of work with federal agency did not constitute publication).

51. *See* 1 M. Nimmer & D. Nimmer, *Nimmer on Copyright* § 4.04 (1994) (hereinafter *Nimmer on Copyright*). In a couple of aspects, the concept of publication was broadened to include the authorization of offers to distribute copies in a commercial setting and the distribution to certain middlemen, such as retailers, motion picture exhibitors, and television stations. *See Paramount Pictures Corp. v. Rubinowitz,* 217 U.S.P.Q. 48, 50 (E.D.N.Y. 1981) (discussing evolution of definition of publication); *National Broadcasting Co., Inc. v. Sonneborn,* 630 F. Supp. 524, 532–33 (D. Conn. 1985).

52. *See* 1 *Nimmer on Copyright* § 4.13[B]; *Kunycia v. Melville Realty Co. Inc.,* 755 F. Supp. 566, 574 (S.D.N.Y. 1990).

number of people for a restricted purpose without a copyright notice.[53] Those works would not be considered distributed to the public (i.e., published) and, therefore, not subject to the notice requirement. Although the notice requirement has been eliminated, the few cases dealing with publication since 1989 suggest courts continue to apply the "limited publication" doctrine.[54]

[c] Works Not Eligible for Protection

Certain works and subject matter are expressly excluded from protection under the Copyright Act, regardless of their originality, creativity, and fixation. Titles, names, short phrases, and slogans generally do not enjoy copyright protection.[55] Other material ineligible for protection includes the utilitarian elements of industrial designs;[56] familiar symbols; simple

---

53. *See White v. Kimmell,* 193 F.2d 744, 746–47 (9th Cir. 1952). Before the notice requirement was eliminated, the Copyright Act generally provided for the invalidation of copyright in a work if copies thereof were distributed to the public, under the authority of the copyright owner, without a copyright notice. In virtually all instances where limited publication was applied, the distribution was noncommercial in nature.

54. *See Academy of Motion Picture Arts and Sciences v. Creative House Promotions, Inc.,* 944 F.2d 1446, 1451–54 (9th Cir. 1991) (distribution of personalized Oscar statuettes to select group of distinguished artists constituted limited publication); *Lish v. Harper's Magazine Found.,* 807 F. Supp. 1090, 1102 (S.D.N.Y. 1992) (letter distributed to members of class remained unpublished).

55. *See* 37 C.F.R. § 202.1(a); *see also, e.g., Takeall v. PepsiCo Inc.,* 29 U.S.P.Q.2d 1913, 1918 (4th Cir. 1993) (unpublished) (holding phrase "You Got the Right One, Uh-Huh" is not copyrightable and, thus, was not infringed by commercial using phrase "You Got the Right One Baby, Uh-Huh"). While short phrases may not be copyrightable standing alone, they may be protected as part of a larger, copyrighted work. *See, e.g., Dawn Assocs. v. Links,* 203 U.S.P.Q. 831, 835 (N.D. Ill. 1978) (holding phrase "When there is no room in hell . . . the dead will walk the earth" to be an integral part of a copyrighted advertisement, and defendant's unauthorized use of it demonstrated likelihood of success on the merits of infringement suit); *Grand Upright Music Ltd. v. Warner Bros. Records, Inc.,* 780 F. Supp. 182, 183–85 (S.D.N.Y. 1991) (finding lyric "alone again" to be protected as part of a copyrighted work and infringed by defendant rap artist's "sampling"). Short phrases may also be eligible for trademark protection if used to identify goods or services.

56. In *Mazer v. Stein,* the Supreme Court held that works of art that are incorporated into the design of useful articles, but that can stand by themselves as artworks separate from the useful articles, are copyrightable. *See supra* note 8, at 214–17. *See also* 17 U.S.C. § 101 (defining "useful article" as "an article having an intrinsic utilitarian function that is not merely to portray the appearance of the article or to convey information"); 17 U.S.C. § 101 (in the definition of "pictorial, graphic, and sculptural works" noting that "the design of a useful article . . . shall be considered a pictorial, graphic, or sculptural work only if, and only to the extent that, such design incorporates pictorial, graphic, or sculptural features that can be identified separately from, and are capable of existing independently of, the utilitarian aspects of the article"). The *House Report* indicates the required separability may be physical or conceptual. *See House Report* at 55; *see also Kieselstein-Cord v. Accessories By Pearl, Inc.,* 632 F.2d 989, 993 (2d Cir. 1980).

geometrical shapes; mere variations of typographic ornamentation, lettering, or coloring; and common works considered public property, such as standard calendars, height and weight charts, tape measures, and rulers.

Copyright protection also does not extend to any "idea, procedure, process, system, method of operation, concept, principle, or discovery, regardless of the form in which it is described, explained, illustrated, or embodied" in such work.[57] Thus, although a magazine article on how to tune a car engine is protected by copyright, that protection extends only to the *expression* of the ideas, facts, and procedures in the article—not the principles themselves, no matter how creative or original they may be. Anyone may "use" these ideas, facts, and procedures to tune an engine or write another article on the same subject. What may not be taken is the expression used by the original author to describe or explain those concepts.[58]

> Copyright does not prevent subsequent users from copying from a prior author's work those constituent elements that are not original—for example . . . facts or materials in the public domain—as long as such use does not unfairly appropriate the author's original contributions.[59]

This idea–expression dichotomy "assures authors the right to their original expression, but encourages others to build freely upon the ideas and information conveyed by a work."[60] Although it "may seem unfair that

---

57. 17 U.S.C. § 102(b); *see Feist, supra* note 7, at 359 ("facts contained in existing works may be freely copied"); *Harper & Row, supra* note 5, at 547 ("no author may copyright facts or ideas").

58. The ideas are not protected; the expression is. *Baker v. Seldon*, 101 U.S. 99, 103 (1879); *Beal v. Paramount Pictures Corp.*, 20 F.3d 454, 458–59 (11th Cir.), *cert. denied*, 115 S. Ct. 675 (1994); *see also Harper & Row, supra* note 5, at 547–48 ("copyright is limited to those aspects of the work—termed 'expression'—that display the stamp of the author's originality"). The line between idea and expression is not easy to draw. The distinction is not that one is fixed and the other is not—they are both fixed in the copyrighted work of authorship. At some point, the idea becomes detailed enough to constitute expression. Judge Learned Hand explained:

> Upon any work . . . a great number of patterns of increasing generality will fit equally well, as more and more of the incident is left out. The last may perhaps be no more than the most general statement of what the [work] is about, and at times might consist only of its title; but there is a point in this series of abstractions where they are no longer protected, since otherwise the [author] could prevent the use of his "ideas," to which, apart from their expression, his property is never extended.

Nichols v. Universal Pictures Corp., 45 F.2d 119, 121 (2d Cir. 1930).

59. *Harper & Row, supra* note 5, at 548.

60. *Feist, supra* note 7, at 349–50 (citing *Harper & Row, supra* note 5, at 556–57).

much of the fruit of the [author's] labor may be used by others without compensation," it is "a constitutional requirement—the 'means by which copyright advances the progress of science and art.'"[61]

As a matter of law, copyright protection is also not extended to works of the U.S. government.[62] Therefore, nearly all federally created works may be reproduced, distributed, adapted, or publicly performed and displayed without infringement liability in the United States.[63] While the Copyright Act leaves most works created by the federal government unprotected under domestic laws, Congress did not intend for the section to have any effect on the protection of these works abroad.[64]

[d] Categories of Protectable Works

The Copyright Act enumerates eight broad categories of protectable subject matter:

  (1) literary works;
  (2) musical works, including any accompanying words;
  (3) dramatic works, including any accompanying music;
  (4) pantomimes and choreographic works;
  (5) pictorial, graphic and sculptural works;
  (6) motion pictures and other audiovisual works;
  (7) sound recordings; and
  (8) architectural works.[65]

[i] Literary Works

"Literary works" are works, other than audiovisual works, expressed in words, numbers, or other verbal or numerical symbols or indicia, regard-

---

61. *Feist, supra* note 7, at 349–50.

62. 17 U.S.C. § 105. There are limited exceptions to this non-copyrightability provision. For instance, the Secretary of Commerce is authorized to secure copyright on behalf of the United States "in all or any part of any standard reference data which he prepares or makes available" under the Standard Reference Data Program. *See* 15 U.S.C. § 290(e). Works of the U.S. Postal Service, such as designs on postage stamps, are also copyrightable by the Postal Service. *See House Report* at 60 ("the Postal Service could . . . use the copyright law to prevent the reproduction of postage stamp designs for private or commercial non-postal services"). Copyright interests transferred to the U.S. Government by assignment, bequest, or otherwise may be held and enforced by it. *See* 17 U.S.C. § 105.

63. A work of the U.S. Government is a work "prepared by an officer or employee of the United States Government as part of that person's official duties." 17 U.S.C. § 101 (definition of "work of the United States Government"). Although the wording of this definition is not identical to that of a "work made for hire," the concepts "are intended to be construed in the same way." *House Report* at 58.

64. *See House Report* at 59.

65. 17 U.S.C. § 102(a).

less of the nature of the material objects—such as books, periodicals, manuscripts, phonorecords, films, tapes, disks, or cards—in which they are embodied.[66] Literary works include newspapers, magazines, computer programs,[67] articles, novels, essays, catalogs, poetry, dictionaries, encyclopedias, and other reference materials.[68]

[ii] Musical Works

A musical work consists of the notes and lyrics (if any) in a musical composition.[69] A musical work may be fixed in any form, such as a piece of sheet music or a compact disc.[70] Musical works may be "dramatic," that is, written as part of a musical or play, or "nondramatic," that is, an individual, free-standing composition.

[iii] Dramatic Works

Generally, a dramatic work is one in which a series of events is presented to the audience by characters through dialogue and action as the events happen, such as in a play.[71]

[iv] Pantomimes and Choreographic Works

This category was first added to the list of protectable subject matter in 1976.[72] While pantomimes and choreographic works, such as dances, can be fixed in a series of drawings or notations, they are usually placed on film or videotape.

---

66. 17 U.S.C. § 101 (definition of "literary works").

67. Following the recommendation of the National Commission on New Technological Uses of Copyrighted Works (CONTU), Congress amended the Copyright Act in 1980 to recognize that computer programs are protected works. *See* Act of December 12, 1980, Pub. L. No. 96–517, 94 Stat. 3015, 3028 (1980). "Computer programs" are defined as a "set of statements or instructions to be used directly or indirectly in a computer in order to bring about a certain result." *See* 17 U.S.C. § 101.

68. *See House Report* at 54.

69. Congress did not define the term "musical work" in the statute based on the assumption that it had a "fairly settled" meaning. *See House Report* at 53.

70. A phonorecord generally embodies two works—a musical work (or, in the case of spoken word recordings, a literary work) and a sound recording. Musical works available through services on the Internet may also be the subject of musical instrument digital interface (MIDI) recordings. A MIDI is a data stream between a musical unit in a computer and a music-producing instrument. The data stream instructs the instrument, such as a synthesizer, on what notes to play.

71. *See* H. Abrams, *The Law of Copyright* § 204[C][3][b][iv] (1993). The term "dramatic works" is not defined in the Copyright Act. *See House Report* at 53.

72. Congress also declined to define the terms "pantomimes" and "choreographic works," again relying on "fairly settled meanings." *See House Report* at 53.

[v] Pictorial, Graphic, and Sculptural Works

This category includes two-dimensional and three-dimensional works of fine, graphic, and applied art, photographs, prints and art reproductions, maps, globes, charts, diagrams, models, and technical drawings, including architectural plans.[73] A work of art that is incorporated into the design of a useful article, but that can stand by itself as artwork separate therefrom, is copyrightable; but the design of the useful article is not.[74]

[vi] Motion Pictures and Other Audiovisual Works

The Copyright Act provides definitions of "audiovisual works" and the subcategory "motion pictures." "Audiovisual works" consist of a series of related images that are intrinsically intended to be shown by the use of machines, or devices such as projectors, viewers, or electronic equipment, together with accompanying sounds, if any, regardless of the nature of the material objects, such as films or tapes, in which the works are embodied.[75]

"Motion pictures" are audiovisual works consisting of a series of related images that, when shown in succession, impart an impression of motion, together with accompanying sounds, if any.[76] The House Report notes that the key to the subcategory "motion pictures" is the conveyance of the impression of movement. Such impression alone is not required to qualify as an audiovisual work.[77]

[vii] Sound Recordings

A "sound recording" is the work resulting from the fixation of sounds, including musical or spoken ones.[78] When those sounds are included in an audiovisual work, such as a music video, they are considered part of the audiovisual work rather than a sound recording.[79]

[viii] Architectural Works

An "architectural work" is "the design of a building as embodied in any tangible medium of expression, including a building, architectural plans,

---

73. 17 U.S.C. § 101 (definition of "pictorial, graphic, and sculptural works").

74. *Mazer v. Stein, supra* note 8, at 214–17.

75. 17 U.S.C. § 101 (definition of "audiovisual works").

76. 17 U.S.C. § 101 (definition of "motion pictures").

77. *See House Report* at 56.

78. *See* 17 U.S.C. § 101 (definition of "sound recordings").

79. The sounds accompanying an audiovisual work are specifically excluded from the definition of sound recordings. *See id.*

or drawings."[80] It includes the overall form as well as the "arrangement and composition of spaces and elements" in the design of the building.[81]

[ix] Compilations and Derivative Works

A compilation is "a work formed by the collection and assembling of pre-existing materials or of data that are selected, coordinated, or arranged in such a way that the resulting work as a whole constitutes an original work of authorship."[82] Magazines and anthologies are types of compilations. A derivative work is "based upon" one or more preexisting works[83] and created when one or more of them is "recast, transformed, or adapted" into a new work, such as when a novel is used as the basis of a movie or a drawing is transformed into a sculpture.[84] Translations, musical arrangements, and abridgments are also examples of derivative works.

The Copyright Act makes clear that the subject matter specified in Section 102 (literary works, musical works, sound recordings, etc.) includes compilations and derivative works thereof.[85] The copyright in a derivative work or compilation, however, extends only to the contribution of the author thereto (the compiler) and does not affect the copyright protection granted the preexisting material.[86] Protection for an individual musical work, for instance, is not reduced, enlarged, shortened, or extended if the work is included in a collection, such as a medley of songs.

Moreover, copyright in a compilation or derivative work does not imply any exclusive right in the preexisting material incorporated in such new work.[87] The copyright in a compilation, for example, is limited to the original selection or arrangement of the facts or other elements compiled. Protection in no way extends to the facts or elements themselves.[88] Copyright protection is also not granted simply for the hard work that may be

---

80. 17 U.S.C. § 101 (definition of "architectural work"). The category of architectural works was added in 1990 by the Architectural Works Copyright Protection Act, Pub. L. No. 101–650, 104 Stat. 5089, 5133 (1990).

81. *Id.*

82. 17 U.S.C. § 101 (definition of "compilation"). A "collective work," which is one kind of "compilation," is "a work, such as a periodical issue, anthology, or encyclopedia, in which a number of contributions, constituting separate and independent works in themselves, are assembled into a collective whole." 17 U.S.C. § 101 (definition of "collective work").

83. 17 U.S.C. § 101 (definition of "derivative work").

84. *Id.*

85. *See* 17 U.S.C. § 103(a).

86. 17 U.S.C. § 103(b).

87. *Id.*

88. *See Feist, supra* note 7, at 350–51 (alphabetical "arrangement" of comprehensive list of telephone subscribers not sufficiently "original" and therefore non-copyrightable).

involved in compiling those facts. In 1991, the U.S. Supreme Court struck down a doctrine that had protected such efforts, known as the "sweat of the brow" or "industrial collection" theory.[89]

[x] Multimedia Works

Increasingly, works from different categories are fixed in a single tangible medium of expression.[90] Theses works are often labeled "multimedia" or "mixed media" products. A prefatory note may be warranted because of the manner in which these terms are used in the context of copyright law. The terms "multimedia" and "mixed media" are, in fact, misnomers. In these situations, it is the categories of *works* that are "multiple" or "mixed," not the types of *media*.

The very premise of a so-called multimedia work is that it combines several different types of works (e.g., text (literary works), sound (sound recordings), still images (pictorial works), and moving images (audiovisual works) into a *single medium* (e.g., a CD-ROM), not multiple media.[91] Multimedia works are not categorized separately under the Copyright Act; nor are they explicitly included in any of the eight enumerated categories. While most current multimedia works would be considered compilations,[92] that classification does not resolve the issue of subject matter categorization.[93]

While the Copyright Act enumerates only eight categories of works, those works not falling clearly within the categories may, nevertheless, be protected because the list of protectable works in Section 102 is illustrative

---

89. *See Feist, supra* note 7, at 354 ("to accord copyright protection on this basis alone distorts basic copyright principles in that it creates a monopoly in public domain materials without the necessary justification of protecting and encouraging the creation of 'writings' by 'authors'").

90. The embodiment of two or more different types of works in one medium is not a new concept. For instance, a book may contain both literary and pictorial works. A compact disc may contain a musical work and a sound recording.

91. A true "multimedia" work would be one in which several material objects, such as a book, a videocassette, and an audiocassette, are bundled into one product.

92. *See* discussion of compilations, *supra* Section 2.1[2][d][ix].

93. While expressly protected under the Copyright Act, the category of "compilations" is not a particularly useful subject matter category. Works in any of the eight enumerated categories of protectible subject matter outlined above may take the form of a compilation, and a protectible compilation must fit into one or more of the subject matter categories. "A compilation or derivative work is copyrightable if it represents an 'original work of authorship' *and* falls within one or more of the categories listed in section 102." *House Report* at 57 (emphasis added).

rather than exclusive.[94] The House Report explains that such categories "do not necessarily exhaust the scope of 'original works of authorship' that the [Copyright Act] is intended to protect."[95] However, absent the addition of a new category, a work not fitting into one of the enumerated categories is, in a sense, in a copyright no-man's land.[96] Under current law, the categorization of a work still holds a great deal of significance. For instance, two of the exclusive rights granted in Section 106 apply only to certain categories.[97] In addition, many of the limitations on rights in Sections 108 through 120 are not applicable to all types of works.[98]

Generally, multimedia works include two or more of the following preexisting elements: text (literary works), computer programs (literary

---

94. The list "sets out the general area of copyrightable subject matter, but with sufficient flexibility to free the courts from rigid or outmoded concepts of the scope of particular categories." *House Report* at 53.

95. *House Report* at 53. Indeed, Congress amended the Copyright Act in 1990 to add "architectural works" as a category of protectible works. *See supra* note 80.

96. It should be noted that the Copyright Office classifies works into four broad categories for purposes of registration: nondramatic literary works, works of performing arts, works of visual arts, and sound recordings. *See* 37 C.F.R. § 202.3(b)(i)–(iv). The Copyright Office notes that in cases "where a work contains elements of authorship in which copyright is claimed which fall into two or more classes, the application should be submitted in the class most appropriate to the type of authorship that predominates in the work as a whole." *See* 37 C.F.R. § 202.3(b)(2). However, the Copyright Act makes clear the Copyright Office classification of works for purposes of registration "has no significance with respect to the subject matter of copyright or the exclusive rights provided." *See* 17 U.S.C. § 408(c)(1); *see also House Report* at 153 ("[i]t is important that the statutory provisions setting forth the subject matter of copyright be kept entirely separate from any classification of copyrightable works for practical administrative purposes").

97. *See* 17 U.S.C. § 106(4), (5). The public performance right is limited to literary, musical, dramatic, and choreographic works, pantomimes, and motion pictures and other audiovisual works. The public display right is limited to literary, musical, dramatic, and choreographic works; pantomimes; and pictorial, graphic, or sculptural works, including the individual images of a motion picture or other audiovisual work. *Id.*

98. *See, e.g.,* 17 U.S.C. § 108(h) (limitation not applicable to musical works; pictorial, graphic, or sculptural works; or motion pictures or other audiovisual works other than audiovisual works dealing with news); 17 U.S.C. § 109(b) (certain limitations not applicable to sound recordings and musical works embodied in sound recordings or to computer programs); 17 U.S.C. § 110(4) (limitation applicable only to nondramatic literary or musical works); 17 U.S.C § 110(8) (limitation applicable only to nondramatic literary works); 17 U.S.C. § 110(9) (limitation applicable only to dramatic literary works); 17 U.S.C. § 112(a) (limitation not applicable to motion pictures or other audiovisual works); 17 U.S.C. § 113 (limitation applicable only to pictorial, graphic, or sculptural works); 17 U.S.C. § 114 (limitation applicable only to sound recordings); 17 U.S.C. § 115 (limitation applicable only to nondramatic musical works); and 17 U.S.C. § 120 (limitation applicable only to architectural works).

works), music (musical works and sound recordings), still images (pictorial and graphic works), and moving images (audiovisual works). The definition of "literary works" begins with the phrase "works, *other than audiovisual works* . . . ."[99] Therefore, a reasonable interpretation may be that text and computer programs otherwise categorized as literary works could be considered part of an audiovisual work if included therein.

Such is also the case with sound recordings. A music video is not categorized as both a sound recording and an audiovisual work; it is viewed only as the latter.[100] Audiovisual works also include still images, at least related ones.[101] Therefore, in many instances, a multimedia work may be considered, as a whole, an audiovisual work. The legislative history makes clear that a work in one category may contain works from other headings.[102]

[3] Copyright Ownership

Copyright ownership in a work initially vests in the author thereof.[103] If the work is a "joint work" (a work with two or more authors), such authors are co-owners of the copyright therein and each one "automatically acquires an individual ownership in the entire work," including any portion thereof.[104]

Under certain circumstances, the copyright in a work is not granted to its actual preparer. In the case of "works made for hire," the employer of the preparer or the person for whom the work was prepared, in some instances, is considered the "author" under the Copyright Act.[105] There are two types of works made for hire—those prepared by an employee and

---

99. *See* 17 U.S.C. § 101 (definition of "literary works") (emphasis added).

100. The definition of "sound recordings" explicitly excludes from the category thereof musical, spoken, or other sounds "accompanying a motion picture or other audiovisual work . . . ." *See* 17 U.S.C. § 101 (definition of "sound recordings"). The definition of "audiovisual works" also expressly includes any "accompanying sounds." *See* 17 U.S.C. § 101 (definition of "audiovisual works").

101. Audiovisual works are "works that consist of a series of related images which are intrinsically intended to be shown by the use of machines or devices such as projectors, viewers, or electronic equipment . . . ." 17 U.S.C. § 101 (definition of "audiovisual works").

102. Categories are "overlapping in the sense that a work falling within one class may encompass works coming within some or all of the other categories." *House Report* at 53.

103. 17 U.S.C. § 201(a).

104. *Id.* A "joint work" is "a work prepared by two or more authors with the intention that their contributions be merged into inseparable or interdependent parts of a unitary whole." 17 U.S.C. § 101 (definition of "joint work"). *See also* 1 *Nimmer on Copyright* § 6.03, at 6–6. *See also* discussion of joint works in Chapter 5, Section 5.2.

105. *See* 17 U.S.C. § 201(b). This legal conclusion may be altered only by the parties in a written instrument signed by them expressly agreeing otherwise. *Id.*

those created by an independent contractor by special order or commission. The copyright in a work prepared by an employee within the scope of his or her employment vests in the employer, and the employer is considered the author thereof.[106] The copyright in a work specially ordered or commissioned vests in the person for whom the work was prepared *if* the work falls into one of nine specified categories *and* the parties expressly agree in writing beforehand that it will be considered a work made for hire.[107]

Copyright ownership entitles the copyright owner to:

- exercise the exclusive rights granted under Section 106 of the Copyright Act;
- authorize others to exercise any of those exclusive rights; and
- prevent others from exercising any of those exclusive rights.

An important distinction to comprehend is the difference between ownership of a *copyright* in a work and ownership of a *copy* thereof. Ownership of a copy, the material object in which a work is embodied (e.g., a book, CD, or videocassette), carries with it no interest in the copyright.[108]

---

106. The Copyright Act does not define "employee." In 1989, the Supreme Court held that an employment relationship determination for copyright purposes should be made by reference to the "general common law of agency." *See Community for Creative Non-Violence v. Reid*, 490 U.S. 730, 740–41 (1989). The central question in an agency law inquiry is whether the hiring party has the "right to control the manner and means by which the product is accomplished." *Id.* at 751. The factors to be considered include the skill required, the source of the instrumentalities and tools used in the work, where the work was created, the duration of the relationship between the parties, whether the hiring party has the right to assign additional projects to the hired party, the method of payment, the extent of the hired party's discretion over when and how long to work, the hired party's role in hiring and paying assistants, whether the hiring party is in business, whether the work is part of the regular business of the hiring party, the provision of employee benefits, and the tax treatment of the hired party. *Id.* at 751–52. The Court did not specify any factors that should be weighed more heavily than others, but made clear that an "employee" under the Copyright Act is not limited to a formal, salaried employee. *See infra* Chapter Five, Section 5.3, for a more detailed discussion of this issue in the educational context.

107. To qualify as a work made for hire under the first prong, the work must be specially ordered or commissioned for use as (1) a contribution to a collective work, (2) part of an audiovisual work, (3) a translation, (4) a supplementary work, (5) a compilation, (6) an instructional text, (7) a test, (8) answer material for a test, or (9) an atlas. 17 U.S.C. § 101 (definition of "work made for hire"). "Sound recordings" were added as an eligible category in 1999, but Congress repealed such addition in 2000. *See* 1 *Nimmer on Copyright* § 5.03[B][2][a][ii].

108. *See* 17 U.S.C. § 202.

Ownership of a copyright, or any of the exclusive rights under a copyright, is distinct from ownership of any material object in which the work is embodied. Transfer of ownership of any material object, including the copy or phonorecord in which the work is first fixed, does not of itself convey any rights in the copyrighted work embodied in the object; nor, in the absence of an agreement, does transfer of ownership of a copyright or of any exclusive rights under a copyright convey property rights in any material object.[109]

Similarly, ownership, possession, or any other attachment to or relationship with a copy of a copyrighted work (including obtaining access to it through a computer network or other service) does not entitle one to exercise any of the exclusive rights of the copyright owner (e.g., to reproduce it or to perform it publicly).

[a] *Transfer of Ownership*

Copyright ownership, or ownership of any one or more of the exclusive rights in a work, may be transferred to one or more persons.[110] A transfer of rights must be in writing and signed by the transferor.[111] A transfer may occur through an assignment, exclusive license, mortgage, "or any other conveyance, alienation, or hypothecation" of a copyright or any of the exclusive rights thereof.[112] A transfer of copyright ownership may be limited in time or place, but must be an exclusive transfer of whatever right or rights are involved (i.e., nonexclusive licenses are not considered transfers of ownership).[113] Any of the exclusive rights in the work[114] may

---

109. *Id.*

110. *See* 17 U.S.C. § 201(d)(1) ("ownership of a copyright may be transferred in whole or in part by any means of conveyance or by operation of law, and may be bequeathed by will or pass as personal property by the applicable laws of intestate succession").

111. 17 U.S.C. § 204(a). An exclusive license is considered a transfer of copyright and, therefore, must be in writing. Although an exclusive license may be limited in time, place, or scope, it nevertheless extends the benefits of copyright ownership with respect to the rights granted to the licensee for the duration of the license. The rights of a copyright owner may also be licensed on a nonexclusive basis to one or more licensees. The Copyright Act does not require nonexclusive licenses to be in writing. For a more detailed discussion of licensing in the educational context, *see* Chapter Four.

112. 17 U.S.C. § 101 (definition of "transfer of copyright ownership"). With the exception of transfers by operation of law, all transfers of copyright ownership must be in writing. 17 U.S.C. § 204(a) ("transfer of copyright ownership, other than by operation of law, is not valid unless an instrument of conveyance, or a note or memorandum of the transfer, is in writing and signed by the owner of the rights conveyed or such owner's duly authorized agent").

113. *See* 17 U.S.C. § 204(a).

114. *See* discussion of the exclusive rights of a copyright owner, *infra* Section 2.1[6].

be separately transferred and owned, and the owner of a particular right is considered the "copyright owner" with respect thereto.[115]

In the case of any copyrighted work other than a "work made for hire," all transfers of ownership (as well as all nonexclusive licenses) executed by the author of the work may be terminated by him or her 35 years after such transfer.[116] This right to terminate, intended to protect authors, cannot be waived by contract or other agreement.[117] However, termination is not automatic; an author (or his or her heirs) must assert such termination rights and comply with certain statutory requirements to regain copyright ownership.[118]

[b] Licensing

The rights of a copyright owner may be licensed on an exclusive (i.e., copyright ownership is transferred in its entirety by the owner) or nonexclusive basis (i.e., the owner retains ownership of the copyright and may grant similar licenses to others). A nonexclusive licensee is not considered a copyright owner and thus does not have standing to sue for any infringement in the work by others.[119] Unlike exclusive licenses, nonexclusive licenses need not be in writing.[120]

Limitations on exclusive rights, such as the first sale doctrine, fair use, or the library exemptions, may, under certain limited circumstances, be overridden by a license or other form of contract.[121] However, such contract

---

115. *See* 17 U.S.C. § 201(d)(2); 17 U.S.C. § 101 (definition of "copyright owner").

116. *See* 17 U.S.C. § 203(a) *see also* 17 U.S.C. § 304(c).

117. 17 U.S.C. § 203(a)(5) ("[t]ermination of the grant may be effected notwithstanding any agreement to the contrary, including an agreement to make a will or to make any future grant").

118. *See* 17 U.S.C. § 203(a).

119. *See* 17 U.S.C. § 501(b) ("legal or beneficial owner of an exclusive right under a copyright is entitled . . . to institute an action for any infringement of that particular right committed while he or she is the owner of it"). In certain circumstances, television broadcast stations and others are treated as legal or beneficial owners and may bring actions for infringement by cable systems and satellite carriers. *See* 17 U.S.C. §§ 501(c), (d), and (e).

120. However, like exclusive licenses, nonexclusive licenses may be terminated 35 years after the effective date of the license. *See* 17 U.S.C. §§ 203(a), 304(c).

121. To avoid these issues, a user could decide to participate in a licensing program covering all copies made, for a nominal fee per copy, rather than to indulge in the record keeping necessary to determine which copies are subject to a licensing fee and which are fair use. Copyright owners may not be allowed, however, to seek to increase the term of protection without implicating the doctrine of copyright misuse. *Compare Saturday Evening Post Co. v. Rumbleseat Press, Inc.*, 816 F.2d 1191, 1200 (7th Cir. 1987) (claims of misuse must be judged by antitrust standards); *Lasercomb America, Inc. v. Reynolds*, 911 F.2d 970, 979 (4th Cir. 1990) (contract purporting to license copyright for 99 years rendered copyright owner guilty of copyright misuse). The doctrine of copyright misuse may be implicated in other situations where the scope of protection is significantly expanded.

terms can be enforced only under state law. For instance, the fair use of a work (outside the scope of the license) by a licensee who is precluded from using the work other than as specified by the license, would not be an infringement of copyright, but could be a breach of the agreement. Licenses and other contracts cannot transform noninfringing uses (such as fair uses) into infringements; they can, however, depending on a variety of factors, make such uses violations of the terms and conditions of specific agreements.

> A library that has acquired ownership of a copy is entitled [under the Copyright Act] to lend it under any conditions it chooses to impose. This does not mean that conditions on future disposition of copies or phonorecords, imposed by a contract between their buyer and seller, would be unenforceable between the parties as a breach of contract, but it does mean that they could not be enforced by an action for infringement of copyright.[122]

A major exception to this analysis arises, however, when state law interferes with a clear federal policy and falls within what is termed the "federal preemption" doctrine. This doctrine is the subject of the next section.

[c] Preemption of State Law Claims

Section 301 of the Copyright Act governs preemption of state law claims that conflict with the federal policies embedded in the Copyright Act.[123] Preemption comes into play only if two conditions are satisfied: (1) the work in which the state law right is asserted comes within the "subject matter" of copyright, as specified in Sections 102 or 103 of the Copyright Act; and (2) the state law right asserted is equivalent to any of the rights specified in Section 106 of the Act.[124] A more careful examination of both of these conditions is warranted.

[i] Subject Matter of Copyright

In general, courts have found the "subject matter of copyright" includes all works that fall within the scope of Sections 102 and 103 of the Copyright Act, whether or not the works themselves qualify for actual protection.[125] This topic was discussed in *Baltimore Orioles v. Major League Baseball Players*, where the issue was whether major league baseball clubs

---

122. *House Report* at 79.
123. 17 U.S.C. § 301.
124. *Baltimore Orioles, supra* note 35, at 674.
125. *Id.*

owned exclusive rights to the televised performances of the players during games.[126] The players argued they had a state law right of publicity in their performances, while the clubs contended federal copyright law preempted this right.

The court rejected the players' argument that because their performances lacked sufficient creativity and were not copyrightable, they fell outside the subject matter of copyright law. In its ruling, the court relied on a House of Representatives report stating: "As long as a work fits within one of the general subject matter categories of sections 102 and 103. . . [section 301(a)] prevents the States from protecting it even if it fails to achieve Federal copyright because it is too minimal or lacking in originality to qualify."[127]

The Court of Appeals for the Seventh Circuit touched on this same issue in *United States Trotting Ass'n v. Chicago Downs Ass'n, Inc.*[128] The court held that a misappropriation claim was not preempted, because it did not fall within the realm of federal copyright law.[129] Although this same court did not mention *United States Trotting Ass'n* in *Baltimore Orioles*, its decision in the latter case seems to overrule any suggestion in the first that non-copyrightable material cannot fall within the subject matter of copyright law.[130]

[ii] Equivalency of Asserted Rights to Rights Specified in Section 106

A right is equivalent to one of the rights set forth in Section 106 if it "is infringed by the mere act of reproduction, performance, distribution or

---

126. *Id.* at 665.

127. *Id.* at 676 (*citing House Report* at 51). Other courts have ruled similarly. *See Harper & Row, Publishers, Inc. v. Nation Enterprises,* 723 F.2d 195, 201 (2d Cir. 1983), *rev'd on other grounds,* 471 U.S. 539 (1985) (accepting opposite position would allow states to "expand the perimeters of copyright protection to their own liking" and would "run directly afoul of one of the Copyright Act's central purposes, to 'avoid the development of any vague borderline areas between State and Federal protection.'" (*citing House Report* at 50); *Ehat v. Tanner,* 780 F.2d 876, 877 (10th Cir. 1985), *cert. denied,* 479 U.S. 820 (1986) (Congress stated expressly that § 301 is intended to prevent "the States from protecting . . . [a work] even if it fails to achieve Federal statutory copyright because it is too minimal or lacking in originality to qualify") (*citing House Report* at 51). *See also Nash v. CBS, Inc.,* 704 F. Supp. 823, 832 (N.D. Ill. 1989) (state law claims do not avoid preemption simply because they are based upon improper use of uncopyrightable material contained in works properly subject to copyright).

128. 665 F.2d 781 (7th Cir. 1981).

129. *Id.* at 786 n.6.

130. *Baltimore Orioles, supra* note 35, at 676.

display."[131] Thus to avoid federal preemption, a cause of action defined by state law must incorporate an "extra element" beyond those necessary to prove copyright infringement.[132] The "extra element" test, in essence, requires an element making the state law claim qualitatively different from the underlying copyright claim.[133] Several federal courts have held breach of contract claims not to be preempted by Section 301 of the Copyright Act on this basis.[134]

For example, in *National Car Rental Sys., Inc. v. Computer Assoc. Int'l. Inc.*,[135] plaintiff licensed the defendant to use its software for internal operations and for the processing of the defendant's data. When defendant used the software to process the data of a third party, the plaintiff sued, contending defendant used the software in a manner outside the bounds of the contract. The court found the agreement created a right that did not exist under copyright law, an "extra element" that made the breach of contract claim qualitatively different from an infringement action.[136] The plaintiff did not argue that defendant had improperly reproduced, distributed, or displayed the software—all claims that would need to have been brought under federal copyright law.

Other federal cases contain reasoning similar to *National Car Rental*. In *Taquino v. Teledyne Monarch Rubber*,[137] the court held the provisions in a covenant not to compete were valid and the rights plaintiff sought to protect were sufficiently distinct from reproduction and distribution as not to be preempted by the Copyright Act. In *Trenton v. Infinity Broadcasting Corp.*, the court found a breach of contract claim was not federally preempted because "the contract-based causes of action . . . allege[d] more than the unauthorized use of a copyrighted work. They also claim[ed] that there ha[d] been a breach of an underlying contract."[138]

---

131. *Baltimore Orioles, supra* note 35, at 677 (*citing* 1 *Nimmer on Copyright* § 1.01[B][1]).

132. *Trandes Corp. v. Guy F. Atkinson Co.*, 996 F.2d 655, 659 (4th Cir.), *cert. denied*, 114 S. Ct. 443 (1993).

133. *See Data General Corp. v. Grumman Sys. Support Corp.*, 36 F.3d 1147, 1164 (1st Cir. 1994) ("Not every 'extra element' of a state claim will establish a qualitative variance between the rights protected by federal copyright law and those protected by state law"); *Harper & Row, Publishers, supra* note 127, at 201 (additional elements did not establish a fundamental nonequivalence between state and federal rights implicated).

134. *See, e.g., Acorn Structures, Inc. v. Swantz*, 846 F.2d 923, 926 (4th Cir. 1988).

135. 991 F.2d 426 (8th Cir. 1993), *cert. denied*, 114 S. Ct. 176 (1993).

136. *Id.* at 433.

137. 893 F.2d 1488 (5th Cir. 1990).

138. 865 F. Supp. 1416, 1429 (C.D. Cal. 1994).

However, courts have also ruled that where a plaintiff's action is not qualitatively different from charging copyright infringement, plaintiff's claims become equivalent to federal rights and are thus preempted by the Copyright Act.[139] In such cases, plaintiff's non-copyright claims are usually dismissed and the issues resolved under federal copyright law. Unfortunately, the doctrine of federal preemption remains less than clear and will continue to evolve. Ultimately, due to the seeming inconsistency of federal court rulings, the issue may need to be decided by the United States Supreme Court.

[4] Term of Protection

The Copyright Act of 1976 (sometimes hereinafter, the "1976 Act") made significant changes to the term of protection for copyrighted works. Since the effective date of the 1976 Act was January 1, 1978, many of those changes use that date as a line of demarcation.

[a] Works Not Protected Before January 1, 1978

For works not protected before January 1, 1978, the Copyright Act establishes a single copyright term and different methods for computing the duration thereof. Works of this sort fall into two categories:

[i] Works Created On or After January 1, 1978

For works created after the effective date of the Copyright Act of 1976, U.S. copyright law adopts the basic "life-plus-seventy" system already in effect in most countries. A work created (fixed in tangible form for the first time) on or after January 1, 1978, is automatically protected from the moment of its creation and given a term lasting for the author's life plus 70 years.[140] In the case of joint works, copyright protection is granted until

---

139. *See Videotronics, Inc. v. Bend Elecs.*, 564 F. Supp. 1471 (D. Nev. 1983) (applying state law of misappropriation to protect intellectual property would create on unacceptable conflict with federal policy). *See also* 1 *Nimmer on Copyright* § 1.01[B][1][a] ("although the vast majority of contract claims will presumably survive scrutiny . . . nonetheless pre-emption claims should continue to strike down claims that, though denominated 'contract,' nonetheless complain directly about the reproduction of expressive materials."). Contra *Pro CD, Inc. v. Zeidenberg*, 86 F.3d 1447, 1454 (7th Cir. 1996) ("Contracts . . . generally affect only their parties; strangers may do as they please, so contracts do not create 'exclusive rights'"). However, the court in *Pro CD* went on to write: "[w]e think it prudent to refrain from adopting a rule that anything with the label 'contract' is necessarily outside the preemption clause." *Id.* at 1455.

140. *See* 17 U.S.C. § 302(a). The terms of protection for works created before January 1, 1978, are set forth in Sections 303 and 304 of the Copyright Act. *See* 17 U.S.C. §§ 303, 304.

the death of the last surviving author plus another 70 years.[141] Works made for hire, as well as anonymous and pseudonymous works, are protected for a term of either 95 years from first publication or 120 years from creation, whichever is shorter.[142] When the term of protection for a copyrighted work expires, the work falls into the "public domain."[143]

[ii] Works in Existence but Not Published or Copyrighted by January 1, 1978

Works created before the current law came into effect, but that had neither been published nor registered for copyright before January 1, 1978, were automatically given copyright protection by the 1976 Act. The duration of copyright in these works will generally be computed in the same way as for new works—life-plus-70 years or the 95-/120-year term for entity-created works. However, all works in this category were guaranteed at least 25 years of statutory protection. For instance, in no case would copyright in a work of this sort have expired before December 31, 2002, regardless of when its author died. If the work was published before that date, the term would extend another 45 years, through the end of 2047.

[b] Works Already under Statutory Protection before January 1, 1978

For works that had already secured statutory copyright protection before January 1, 1978, the 1976 law retained the old system for computing the duration of protection, but with some changes.

[i] Duration under the Prior Law

Under the statute in effect before 1978, copyright was secured either on the date a work was published or registered with the Copyright Office, if registered in unpublished form. In either case, the copyright lasted for a term of 28 years and was eligible for renewal during the last (28th) year. If renewed, it was extended for an additional 28 years.[144] If not renewed, the copyright expired at the end of the first term. The term of copyright for

---

141. 17 U.S.C. § 302(b).

142. 17 U.S.C. § 302(c). The term for anonymous or pseudonymous works differs if the identity of one or more of the authors is revealed before the end of the term of protection. *See id.*

143. The "public domain" is the legal status of works whose term of copyright protection has ended or that are not protected for other reasons, such as the non-copyrightability of the subject matter. The term has nothing to do with either publication of the work or disseminating it to the public. For a description of all works in the public domain by January 1, 2007, see the chart compiled by Peter B. Hirtle of Cornell University, http://www.copyright.cornell.edu/public_domain/.

144. For a number of copyrights, the second term was extended beyond 28 years by special legislation.

works published with a year in the notice that was earlier than the actual date of publication was computed from the year contained in the notice.

[ii] Effect of the Present Law on Length of Subsisting Copyrights

The old system of computing the duration of protection was carried over into the 1976 Act with one major change—the length of the second term was increased to 67 years.[145] Thus, the maximum total term of copyright protection for works protected by federal statute prior to 1978 was increased from 56 years (a first term of 28 years plus a renewal term of 28 years) to 95 years (a first term of 28 years plus a renewal term of 67 years). The specific situation for works copyrighted before 1978 depends on whether the copyright had already been renewed or was still in its first term on December 31, 1977.

- **Works originally copyrighted before 1950 and renewed before 1978:** These works were automatically given a longer copyright term. Copyrights that had already been renewed and were in their second term at any time between December 31, 1976, and December 31, 1977, inclusive, did not need to be renewed again. They were automatically extended to last for a total term of 95 years (a first term of 28 years plus a renewal term of 67 years) from the end of the year in which they were originally secured. This extension applied not only to copyrights less than 56 years old but also to older copyrights that had previously been extended in duration under a series of congressional enactments beginning in 1962. As in the case of all other copyrights subsisting in their second term between December 31, 1976, and December 31, 1977, inclusive, these copyrights expire at the end of the calendar year in which the 95th anniversary of the original date of copyright occurs.

- **Works originally copyrighted between January 1, 1950 and December 31, 1963:** Copyrights in their first 28-year term on January 1, 1978, still had to be renewed in order to be protected for the second term. If a valid renewal was made, the second term now lasts for 67 years. However, if a proper renewal was not made within the statutory time limits, a copyright originally secured between 1950 and 1963 expired on December 31st of its 28th year, and protection was permanently lost.

---

145. Prior to 1998, this second term was 47 years. The Sonny Bono Copyright Term Extension Act, Pub. L. No. 105–298, 112 Stat. 2827, 2830, enacted October 27, 1998, extended the second 47-year term an additional 20 years.

- **Works originally copyrighted between January 1, 1964 and December 31, 1977:** An amendment enacted on June 26, 1992,[146] makes renewal registration optional for these works. The copyright is still divided between a 28-year original term and a 67-year renewal term, but a renewal registration is not required to secure the additional term. The renewal vests on behalf of the appropriate claimant upon registration or, if there is no renewal registration, on December 31 of the 28th year.

[5] Notice, Deposit, and Registration

In 1989, the United States became a party to the principal international copyright treaty, commonly known as the Berne Convention. Prior to U.S. accession thereto and the concomitant amendments to the Copyright Act, a copyright notice was required on all publicly distributed works. Omission of the notice usually resulted in loss of copyright protection for the work. However, in 1989, the use of a copyright notice became permissive rather than required.[147] Section 401(a) of the Copyright Act provides:

> Whenever a work protected under this title is published in the United States or elsewhere by authority of the copyright owner, a notice of copyright . . . *may be* placed on publicly distributed copies from which the work can be visually perceived, either directly or with the aid of a machine or device.[148]

If a copyright notice is used, it generally must consist of three elements:

- the letter "C" in a circle (©), the word "Copyright" or the abbreviation "Copr." (in the case of sound recordings embodied in phonorecords, the letter "P" in a circle);
- the year of first publication of the work; and
- the name of the copyright owner.[149]

As a general rule, two copies of a published work must be deposited in the Copyright Office within three months of publication for the benefit of

---

146. Copyright Renewal Act of 1992, Pub. L. No. 102–307, 106 Stat. 264 (1992).

147. *See* Berne Convention Implementation Act of 1988, Pub. L. No. 100–568, 102 Stat. 2853, 2857, enacted October 31, 1988. Copyright notice is still required on copies and phonorecords of works publicly distributed prior to March 1, 1989, the effective date of the act. For more information on the Berne Convention, *see* Section 2.2 of this chapter.

148. 17 U.S.C. § 401(a) (emphasis added). The copyright owner of a sound recording may also place a notice of copyright on publicly distributed phonorecords of the sound recording. 17 U.S.C. § 402(b).

149. *See* 17 U.S.C. §§ 401(b), 402(b).

the Library of Congress.[150] The Register of Copyrights may exempt certain works from this deposit requirement. The Register may also require only one copy of the work or allow alternative forms of deposit.[151] Although required by the Copyright Act, the deposit of copies is not a prerequisite to or condition of copyright protection. Failure to deposit copies after receipt of a written demand by the Register of Copyrights may, however, result in the imposition of a fine.[152]

Since registration with the Copyright Office is permissive, rather than mandatory, it is not a prerequisite to the grant of exclusive rights.[153] It is, however, generally a prerequisite to the enforcement of those rights in court.[154] The owner of a work (or the owner of any exclusive rights therein) may register a copyright by filing with the Copyright Office a completed application form, registration fee and sufficient copies of the work.[155] The Library of Congress deposit requirement under the act may be fulfilled through the registration process.[156]

The Family Entertainment and Copyright Act of 2005[157] amended U.S. copyright law by adding a new section establishing preregistration. Preregistration, as distinct from registration, is available only for certain types of unpublished works that the Register of Copyrights finds to have a history of infringement prior to commercial distribution. On October 27, 2005, the Copyright Office issued an interim regulation in which it identified motion pictures, sound recordings, musical compositions, literary works

---

150. *See* 17 U.S.C. § 407.

151. *See* 17 U.S.C. § 407(c); *see also* 37 C.F.R. § 202.19(e).

152. *See* 17 U.S.C. § 407(d).

153. 17 U.S.C. § 408(a).

154. 17 U.S.C. § 411(a). Registration is required before a suit for infringement may be brought for works of U.S. origin and for foreign works from countries that are not members of the Berne Convention. While most jurisdictions require the plaintiff to hold a certificate of registration prior to commencing suit, one federal circuit has held that "[i]n order to bring suit for copyright infringement, it is not necessary to prove possession of a registration certificate. One need only prove payment of the required fee, deposit of the work in question, and receipt by the Copyright Office of a registration application." *See Apple Barrel Products, Inc. v. R.D. Beard*, 730 F.2d 384 (5th Cir. 1984).

155. *See* 17 U.S.C. §§ 408 (a), (b). Only one copy of the work is required for certain types of works, including unpublished works. The basic registration fee was raised to $45.00 per work, effective July 1, 2006. *See Annual Report of the Copyright Office for Fiscal 2006* (hereinafter 2006 *Annual Report*), at 20.

156. 17 U.S.C. § 408(b). The value of these mandatory deposits was estimated at $17.6 million to fiscal 2006. *See* 2006 *Annual Report* at 13. The Copyright Office may request the Department of Justice to bring suit under 17 U.S.C. § 407 to compel the deposit of copies of a work published in the U.S. *Id.* at 32.

157. Pub. L. No. 109–9, 119 Stat. 218 (2005).

being prepared for publication in book form, computer programs, and advertising or marketing photographs as the six classes of works eligible for preregistration.[158]

Unlike registration, preregistration requires only an application with a brief description of the work, some other basic information, and a fee. Preregistration is not a substitute for registration because after publication, a follow-up filing is required. The Copyright Office implemented preregistration and the first use of the electronic Copyright Office, or eCO, the Office's new information technology system to process regular work, on November 15, 2005.[159]

It is anticipated that eCO will enable the Copyright Office to provide its services to the public online and manage its internal processes through a centralized case management system. Besides enabling copyright owners or their agents to submit electronic applications for registration, eCO will allow users of Copyright Office services to check the status of their requests, supply additional information, and resolve discrepancies. The new service was expected to be instituted as a pilot program by the end of 2007.[160]

Although not required, registration is still advisable. A certificate of copyright registration constitutes prima facie evidence of the validity of the copyright and the facts stated therein, if registration is made within five years of first publication.[161] In addition, the remedies of obtaining statutory damages and recovering attorney's fees are available only in infringement suits regarding unpublished works if registration is made prior to the date of the infringement. For published works, those remedies are available only if the copyright owner registered his work within three months of publication, regardless of when the infringement occurred, or at any time before the date of infringement if the three-month deadline was missed.[162]

Under current law, the Register of Copyrights may determine that the material deposited for copyright registration does not constitute copyrightable subject matter or that the claim is invalid for other reasons. In such cases, the Register refuses registration and notifies the applicant in writing of its reason(s) therefor. Applicants whose claims for registration are rejected can seek reconsideration of such decisions in a two-stage process. The claimant first requests reconsideration by the Examining Division. If the division upholds the refusal, the claimant may make a second

---

158. 2006 *Annual Report* at 19.

159. *Id* at 8.

160. *Id.*

161. 17 U.S.C. § 410(c); *Bibbero Systems, Inc. v. Colwell Systems, Inc.*, 893 F.2d 1104, 1106 (9th Cir. 1990). The weight to be accorded a certificate when registration has been made more than five years from the date of first publication is within the discretion of the court.

162. 17 U.S.C. §§ 412(1), (2).

request to the Copyright Office Review Board, composed of the Register of Copyrights, the Office's General Counsel, and a third member designated by the Register.[163]

The lack of notice and registration requirements obviously make it more difficult in today's world to differentiate between protected and unprotected works, including those in the public domain or for which the author does not assert copyright. It also complicates the task of identifying the copyright owner. This has led some to suggest, at least with respect to works disseminated via computer networks, that one should be free to copy any work that does not contain a copyright notice[164] or that registration should be required again.

While these arguments may have some merit, the balance of interests has not changed since these issues were considered by Congress and the notice and registration requirements eliminated. Conditioning copyright protection on the affixation of copyright notices and/or registration would be inconsistent with the obligations of the United States under the Berne Convention.[165] Further, the benefits of utilizing copyright management information (more fully discussed in Chapter Five) should encourage owners to affix the same items historically included in copyright notices, as well as additional information for consumers, such as terms and conditions of use.

[6] Exclusive Rights

The Copyright Act grants owners of works certain exclusive rights that, together, comprise the bundle of rights known as "copyright." Limitations on exclusive rights and infringement of those rights are discussed in subsequent sections. The fact that a particular use of a work is said to "implicate" one or more of these rights, therefore, does not necessarily mean that such use is an infringement or unlawful.

The exclusive rights of a copyright owner include the right:

1. to *reproduce* the work in copies or phonorecords;
2. to prepare *derivative* works based thereon;
3. to *distribute* copies or phonorecords to the public by sale or other transfer of ownership, or by rental, lease, or lending;
4. in the case of literary, musical, dramatic, and choreographic works, pantomimes, and motion pictures and other audiovisual works, to *perform* the work publicly; and

---

163. 2006 *Annual Report* at 9.

164. *See, e.g.,* University of Toledo Investigation Panel, "Final Report on Allegations of Misconduct in Research," at 14 (Jan. 30, 2001) (unpublished report).

165. *See* Article 5 of the Berne Convention, which prohibits member states from conditioning copyright protection for works of Berne nationals on compliance with formalities.

5. in the case of literary, musical, dramatic, and choreographic works, pantomimes, and pictorial, graphic, or sculptural works, including the individual images of a motion picture or other audiovisual work, to *display* the work publicly.[166]

These rights, in most instances, have been elaborated upon by Congress and the courts in both "conventional" and digital contexts. A more detailed discussion of such rights is contained below.

[a] The Right to Reproduce the Work

The fundamental right to reproduce copyrighted works is implicated in innumerable transactions. Indeed, due to the nature of computer-to-computer communications, it is implicated in most electronic transmissions. For example, when someone accesses a document resident on another computer, the image on the user's screen exists, under contemporary technology, only by virtue of the copy being *reproduced* in the user's computer memory. Under federal copyright law, the placement of material into a computer's memory (whether it be the hard drive or RAM) constitutes a reproduction of that material (because the work in memory then may be, in the law's terms, "perceived, reproduced, or . . . communicated . . . with the aid of a machine or device").[167]

The Copyright Act, its legislative history, and repeated holdings by courts make it clear that in each instance below (most of which are associated with distance learning), one or more copies are made.[168]

- When a work is placed into a computer, whether on a disk, diskette, ROM, or other storage device, or in RAM for more than a very brief period[169]
- When a printed work is scanned into a digital file
- When other works, including photographs, motion pictures, or sound recordings, are digitized

---

166. 17 U.S.C. § 106. Section 106(A) grants additional rights for certain works of visual art in single copies or limited editions. *See* 17 U.S.C. § 106(A).

167. *See MAI Systems Corp. v. Peak Computer, Inc.*, 991 F.2d 511, 519 (9th Cir. 1993), *cert. denied*, 114 S. Ct. 671 (1994); *Vault Corp. v. Quaid Software Ltd.*, 847 F.2d 255, 260 (5th Cir. 1988); *Advanced Computer Services, supra* note 38; *Triad Systems Corp., supra* note 38; *2 Nimmer on Copyright* § 8.08[A].

168. That copying has occurred does not necessarily mean that infringement has occurred. When copying is (1) authorized by the copyright owner, (2) exempt from liability as a fair use, (3) otherwise exempt under the provisions of Sections 108–119 of the Copyright Act, or (4) of such a small amount as to be de minimis, then there is no infringement liability.

169. *See, e.g., MAI Systems Corp. v. Peak Computer, Inc., supra* note 167, at 519.

- Whenever a digitized file is "uploaded" from a user's computer to a bulletin board system (bbs) or other server
- Whenever a digitized file is "downloaded" from a bbs or other server
- When a file is transferred from one computer network user to another[170]

[b] The Right to Prepare Derivative Works

Copyright law grants copyright owners the right to control the abridgment, adaptation, translation, revision, or other "transformation" of their works.[171] Anyone who modifies, by annotating, editing, translating, or otherwise significantly changing the contents of a downloaded file, creates a derivative work. Derivative works may also be created by transforming a work, such as an audiovisual work, into an interactive one.

[c] The Right to Distribute Copies

Before addressing issues raised by the distribution right, it is necessary to understand its application and limitations with respect to conventional modes of exploitation and infringement. The right to distribute legitimate copies of works is substantially circumscribed by the "first sale" doctrine:

> Notwithstanding the provisions of section 106(3), the owner of a particular copy or phonorecord lawfully made under this title, or any person authorized by such owner, is entitled, without the authority of the copyright owner, to sell or otherwise dispose of the possession of that copy or phonorecord.[172]

---

170. For example, if an author transfers a file (such as a manuscript) to a publisher with an Internet account, copies will typically, at a minimum, be made (a) in the author's Internet server, (b) in the publisher's Internet server, (c) in the publisher's local area network server, and (d) in the editor's microcomputer. It has been suggested that such "copying" of files in intermediate servers is only of transitory duration and consequently not covered by the reproduction right. However, it is clear that if the "copy" exists for more than a period of transitory duration, the reproduction right is implicated. Whether such reproduction is an infringement would be a separate determination. Such analysis has great significance for distance learning technology, as well. *See* Chapter Six for a more detailed discussion of this issue.

171. *See* 17 U.S.C. § 106(2). "A 'derivative work' is a work based upon one or more pre-existing works, such as a translation, musical arrangement, dramatization, fictionalization, motion picture version, sound recording, art reproduction, abridgment, condensation, or any other form in which a work may be recast, transformed, or adapted. A work consisting of editorial revisions, annotations, elaborations, or other modifications which, as a whole, represent an original work of authorship, is a 'derivative work.'" 17 U.S.C. § 101 (definition of "derivative work").

172. 17 U.S.C. § 109(a).

This means that the copyright owner generally processes only the right to authorize or prohibit the *initial* distribution of a particular *lawful* copy of a copyrighted work. It is important to understand, however, that the distribution of an *unlawfully* made (i.e., infringing) copy will subject any distributor to liability for infringement.[173]

One court decision has construed the downloading of digitized photographic images (whose reproduction was unauthorized) by bbs subscribers as "implicating" the distribution right.[174] The discussion in *Playboy Enterprises Inc. v. Frena*[175] reflects the reach of this right:

> Public distribution of a copyrighted work is a right reserved to the copyright owner, and usurpation of that right constitutes infringement . . . . [Playboy Enterprise's] right under 17 U.S.C. § 106 to distribute copies to the public has been implicated by Defendant Frena [the bbs operator]. Section 106(3) grants the copyright owner "the exclusive right to sell, give away, rent or lend any material embodiment of his work." There is no dispute that Defendant Frena supplied a product containing unauthorized copies of a copyrighted work. It does not matter that Defendant Frena claims it did not make the copies itself.[176]

The court may not have focused on the reproduction right, apparently because of its uncertainty whether the operator of the bulletin board system could itself be held to have reproduced a work that was uploaded by one subscriber and downloaded by another. (As discussed below, the bbs operator publicly displayed the works by the same conduct, and was found liable by the court for infringing the owner's display right as well.)

Whether the litigants in *Playboy* put the issue properly in dispute or not, the right to distribute copies of a work has traditionally covered the ability to convey a possessory interest in a *tangible* copy.[177] Indeed, the first

---

173. Furthermore, with respect to international distributions, Section 602 of the Copyright Act makes unauthorized importations a violation of the distribution right.

174. The court elsewhere in its opinion, in a small but perhaps significant deviation from conventional usage, appears to use "implicate" to mean "infringe" rather than "involve."

175. 839 F. Supp. 1552 (M.D. Fla. 1993).

176. *Id.* at 1556.

177. *See Perfect 10 v. Amazon.com*, 508 F.3d 1146, 1162 (9th Cir. 2007) ("distribution requires an 'actual dissemination' of a copy"); *Agee v. Paramount Comm., Inc.*, 59 F.3d 317, 325 (2d Cir. 1995) ("[i]t is clear that merely transmitting a sound recording to the public does not constitute a 'distribution' . . . "); W. F. Patry, 4 *Patry on Copyright* § 13.9 (2007) ("[W]ithout actual distribution of copies . . ., there is no violation of the distribution right.").

sale doctrine implements the common law's abhorrence of restraints on alienation of property by providing the distribution right does *not* generally prevent owners of lawfully obtained copies from alienating them in a manner of their own choosing.[178] It is certain that a Frena subscriber, at the end of a transaction, possessed a copy of a *Playboy* photograph; but it is less clear whether, under the current law, Frena "distributed" that photograph, or if he or the subscriber "reproduced" it (and, if the latter, whether current law clearly would have made Frena contributorily liable for the unauthorized reproduction).[179]

In a related case, *Sega Enterprises Ltd. v. MAPHIA*,[180] a court, on a motion for a preliminary injunction, made findings of fact regarding (a) the use of a bulletin board system to "make and distribute" copies of video games, (b) the "unauthorized copying and distribution" of such games on the bulletin board, and (c) the profits made by the defendant from this "distribution." The court held the owner's reproduction right was infringed, but apparently did not reach a similar conclusion with respect to distribution.

[d] The Right to Perform the Work Publicly

The public performance right is available to all types of "performable" works—literary, musical, dramatic, and choreographic works, pantomimes, motion pictures, and other audiovisual works, with the exception of nondigital sound recordings.[181] It is therefore important to understand:

---

178. Owners of copyrights in computer programs and sound recordings have the right to control post-first-sale rentals of copies of their works; owners of copyrights in other works do not. *See* 17 U.S.C. § 109.

179. Adding to the confusion is that Section 106(3) encompasses the distribution of "copies or phonorecords" that are limited to "material objects" by 17 U.S.C. § 101, thus arguably excluding all electronic transmissions from the scope of the distribution right. *See also* discussion of contributory infringement and vicarious liability, *infra* Section 2.1[8][c].

180. 857 F. Supp. 679 (N.D. Cal. 1994). *Compare A&M Records v. Napster, Inc.*, 284 F.3d 1091 (9th Cir. 2002), in which a panel for the Ninth Circuit ruled that plaintiff record companies had presented a prima facie case of direct copyright infringement against users of a "peer-to-peer" file-sharing network, but not the defendant network facilitator itself. The court did find, however, that the defendant was contributorily liable for such infringement.

181. *See* 17 U.S.C. § 106(4). Current law now provides an exclusive right to perform sound recordings publicly by means of a digital audio transmission, subject to a number of limitations. *See* Digital Performance Rights in Sound Recordings Act of 1995, Pub. L No. 104–39, 109 Stat. 336 (1995).

- the definition of "perform" in copyright law,[182]
- that only "public" performances are covered thereby,[183] and
- the limitations set forth in the statute rendering the performance right inapplicable in a variety of circumstances (mostly of a non-profit nature).[184]

A distinction must be made between transmissions of *copies* of works and transmitting *performances* or *displays* thereof.[185] When a copy of a work is sent over wires, fiber optics, satellite signals, or other modes in digital form so that it may be captured in a user's computer, without the capability of simultaneous "rendering" or "showing," it has rather clearly not been performed. Thus, for example, a file comprising the digitized version of a motion picture might be transferred from a copyright owner to an end user via the Internet without the public performance right being implicated. When, however, the motion picture is "rendered," by showing its images in sequence, so that users with the requisite hardware and software might watch it *with or without copying the performance*, then, under current law, a "performance" has occurred.

The "public" nature of a performance, which brings it within the scope of copyright, is sufficiently broadly defined to apply to multiple individual viewers watching a work in a variety of locations at several different times. Courts have repeatedly imposed public performance infringement liability upon entities that, for example, develop novel modes of deliver-

---

182. "To 'perform' a work means to recite, render, play, dance, or act it, either directly or by means of any device or process or, in the case of a motion picture or other audiovisual work, to show its images in any sequence or to make the sounds accompanying it audible." 17 U.S.C. § 101 (definition of "perform").

183. To perform or display a work "publicly" means—

   (1) to perform or display it at a place open to the public or at any place where a substantial number of persons outside of a normal circle of a family and its social acquaintances is gathered; or

   (2) to transmit or otherwise communicate a performance or display of the work to a place specified by clause (1) or to the public, by means of any device or process, whether the members of the public capable of receiving the performance or display receive it in the same place or in separate places and at the same time or at different times.

   17 U.S.C. § 101 (definition of "publicly").

184. *See* 17 U.S.C. § 110.

185. The current law addresses only transmissions of "performances" and "displays."

ing motion picture performances to customers.[186] Therefore, the fact that performances and displays may take these less traditional forms will not exempt them from the exclusive rights of the creator.

[e] The Right to Display the Work Publicly

To display a work means to "show a copy of it, either directly or by means of a . . . television image, or any other device or process . . . ."[187] Complex analyses to determine whether a particular transmission amounts to a "distribution" or "performance" are rarely necessary in this context. The definition of "display" clearly encompasses, for instance, the actions of the defendant bbs operator in the *Playboy* case.[188]

Thus, when any user visually "browses" through copies of works in any medium (but not through a list of titles or other "menus" that are not copies of the works),[189] a public display has occurred. A display is "public" on the same terms as a performance is. Therefore, many Internet uses would fall within the law's current comprehension of public display.[190] Whether such acts necessarily constitute infringement is determined by separate analyses.

---

186. *See, e.g., Columbia Pictures Indus. v. Redd Horne, Inc.*, 749 F.2d 154 (3d Cir. 1984) (video store operator liable for public performance violation where he rented tapes of motion pictures to customers and provided semiprivate screening rooms where the tapes could be viewed); *Columbia Pictures Indus. v. Aveco, Inc.*, 800 F.2d 59 (3d Cir. 1986) (same result where customers also rented rooms for viewing); *On Command Video Corp. v. Columbia Pictures Indus.*, 777 F. Supp. 787 (N.D. Cal. 1991) (infringement found where hotel guests in rooms selected tapes to be played on remotely controlled console in hotel basement with signal then sent to rooms); *Red Baron-Franklin Park, Inc. v. Taito Corp.*, 883 F.2d 275 (4th Cir. 1989), *cert. denied*, 493 U.S. 1058 (1990) (arcade owner's use of circuit boards in coin-operated video machines constituted public performance); *But cf. Allen v. Academic Games League of America*, 89 F.3d 614 (9th Cir. 1996) (playing of copyrighted academic games in tournament sponsored by nonprofit corporation not deemed "performance").

187. 17 U.S.C. § 101 (definition of "display").

188. *See* discussion of *Playboy* case, *supra* Section 2.1[6][c].

189. Of course, to the extent that such lists or menus are protectible under the Copyright Act, the authors of such lists would have the exclusive right to publicly display them.

190. The copyright law's legislative history, describing the introduction of the display right, distinguishes displays "on a screen or tube" from reproductions. This language, written before the advent of the personal computer, applies easily to displays with which Congress was familiar in 1976 (those rendered by broadcast television receivers), but is inapplicable to digital "browsing" where the law itself clearly, without resort to explanatory congressional language, defines such acts as implicating the display *and* reproduction rights.

[7] Limitations on Exclusive Rights

The Copyright Act provides a number of exceptions to the "exclusive" rights of copyright owners by specifying that certain uses of works are outside the control of their owner.[191] While many regard these exceptions as "rights" of users, they are, as a technical matter, outright exemptions from liability or affirmative defenses to what would otherwise be acts of infringement.

[a] Fair Use

The most significant and, perhaps, murkiest of the limitations on a copyright owner's exclusive rights is the doctrine of fair use.[192] Fair use is an affirmative defense to an action for copyright infringement.[193] It is potentially available for all manners of unauthorized use of any type of work. When it exists, the user is not required to seek permission from the copyright owner or pay a license fee. The doctrine is rooted in some 200 years of judicial decisions.

The most common example is when someone incorporates a portion of a preexisting work into a new work of authorship,[194] such as a quotation from a book or play by a reviewer. In *Campbell v. Acuff-Rose Music, Inc.*, the U.S. Supreme Court expressly accepted the proposition that "transformative" uses are more favored than those amounting to little more than verbatim copying.[195] As one moves away from transformative uses into acts that, for practical purposes, compete with the copyright owner's dominion, the use is less likely to be deemed fair.

Before examining the doctrine as developed by the courts, it is useful to read the statutory language concerning fair use. Section 107 of the Copyright Act provides:

---

191. It has been argued that the Copyright Act would be unconstitutional if such limitations did not exist, as they reduce First Amendment and other concerns. *See, e.g., Saenz v. Roe*, 526 U.S. 489 (1999) (legislation promulgated pursuant to the Copyright Clause must still comport with other express limitations of the Constitution); *Eldred v. Ashcroft*, 537 U.S. 186, 221 (2003) (an act of Congress would be subject to First Amendment review if it "altered the traditional contours of copyright protection").

192. *See* 17 U.S.C. § 107. The judicially created doctrine, although now codified in the Copyright Act, has been described as "so flexible as virtually to defy definition." *See Time Inc. v. Bernard Geis Assoc.*, 293 F. Supp. 130, 144 (S.D.N.Y. 1968).

193. *Campbell v. Acuff-Rose Music, Inc.*, 114 S. Ct. 1164, 1177 (1994). As an affirmative defense, the burdens of persuasion and coming forward with evidence both must be carried by defendants to avoid liability (i.e., a copyright owner need not prove an accused use not fair; rather, the defendant must prove its fairness).

194. *Id.*

195. *Id.* at 1171.

Notwithstanding the provisions of sections 106 and 106A, the fair use of a copyrighted work, including such use by reproduction in copies or phonorecords or by any other means specified by that section [*sic*], for purposes such as criticism, comment, news reporting, teaching (including multiple copies for classroom use), scholarship, or research, is not an infringement of copyright. In determining whether the use made of a work in any particular case is a fair use the factors to be considered shall include—

(1) the purpose and character of the use, including whether such use is of a commercial nature or is for nonprofit educational purposes;
(2) the nature of the copyrighted work;
(3) the amount and substantiality of the portion used in relation to the copyrighted work as a whole; and
(4) the effect of the use upon the potential market for or value of the copyrighted work.

The fact a work is unpublished shall not itself bar a finding of fair use if such holding is made upon consideration of all the above factors.[196]

The language may usefully be divided into two parts—the first sentence, which is largely tautological ("fair use . . . is not an infringement of copyright"), and the analysis required by the second sentence. The recitation of assorted uses in the middle of the first sentence has been held neither to prevent a fair use analysis from being applied to other "unlisted" uses nor to create the suggestion that the listed uses are always fair.[197] It does, however, provide some guidance on what may be considered fair use. The core of Section 107 is the second sentence, which elaborates a test similar to one articulated by Justice Story more than 160 years ago.[198] It is clear courts must evaluate all four factors in determining whether a particular use is fair, but may also take into account unenumerated "extra" factors, when appropriate. The four factors are examined in more detail below.

[i] The Purpose and Character of the Use

Although the fourth factor has repeatedly been held as the most important, the first one often plays a major role in determining the result of a

---

196. 17 U.S.C. § 107.

197. *Harper & Row, supra* note 5, at 561.

198. Justice Story stated that courts should "look to the nature and the objects of the selections made, the quantity and value of the material used, and the degree in which the use may prejudice the sale, or diminish the profits, or supersede the objects, of the original work." *Folsom v. Marsh*, 9 F. Cas. 342, 348 (C.C.D. Mass. 1841) (No. 4,901).

fair use defense. This factor contrasts "commercial" uses with "nonprofit educational" ones. There is, of course, a continuum between these two opposites, with most uses not falling neatly into either category. The weight of the factor may be inferred from the Supreme Court's very limited fair use jurisprudence. In the four fair use cases it has decided, one noncommercial, noneducational use was held fair,[199] two commercial uses were held unfair,[200] and one commercial use was held potentially fair.[201] In the famous *Sony* case involving videocassette recording for home use, the Court announced a "presumption" that all commercial uses were deemed unfair,[202] thus placing a substantial burden on any profit-seeking defendant.

For the most part, "mere reproduction" has fared rather badly in court under the Copyright Act, even in actual and ostensible educational contexts.[203] Courts have denied fair use,[204] for example, to a teacher's reproduction, in text materials, of the copyrighted material of another

---

199. *See Sony, supra* note 9, at 456 (videotaping by individuals at home of off-the-air television broadcast programming for purpose of "time shifting"—as distinguished from "librarying"—held fair use). A current debate, not completely resolved, suggests "space shifting," which permits one to transfer a work from one medium to another, is also fair use. *See RIAA v. Diamond MultiMedia Systems, Inc.,* 180 F.3d 1072, 1079 (9th Cir. 1999).

200. *See Stewart v. Abend,* 495 U.S. 207, 216 (1990) (theatrical and television distribution of motion picture over objection of owner of renewal copyright in underlying short story held infringing); *Harper & Row, supra* note 5, at 569 (*Nation* magazine's scoop of *Time* magazine's first serial rights in President Ford's memoirs held infringing, notwithstanding newsworthiness of the account of the Nixon pardon set out therein).

201. *See Campbell, supra* note 193, at 1177–79 (parodic lyrics of popular song not per se unfair by virtue of commercial purpose of parody; case remanded for further factual determination).

202. *See Sony, supra* note 9, at 451. The subsequent *Campbell* decision indicates that the presumption is strongest in cases of "mere duplication" and weakest when a second commercial comer makes a transformative use and creates a derivative work. *See Campbell, supra* note 193, at 1177.

203. Congress has expressly declined to enact a specific exemption from copyright liability for educational uses. *See House Report* at 66–67. Cases holding reproduction of an entire work as fair use are few. In *Haberman v. Hustler Magazine, Inc.,* 626 F. Supp. 201, 212 (D. Mass. 1986), a magazine's reproduction of an artist's postcards was found to be fair use because there was no market harm.

204. The consequences of denying a fair use defense in certain legitimate educational contexts are far smaller than in the commercial context. Under the provisions of Section 504(c)(2), statutory damages (damages that may be imposed without proof of the quantum of actual harm to the copyright owner) may not be imposed against a nonprofit educational institution, its employees or agents, when acting within the scope of their employment, in respect of copying performed with reasonably based grounds for believing such copying was fair use. 17 U.S.C. § 504(c)(2).

teacher;[205] a school system's practice of taping educational broadcasts for later use in classrooms;[206] and off-campus copy shops' manufacture, per teachers' specifications, and distribution of photocopies of anthologies containing portions of textbooks and periodicals.[207]

[ii] The Nature of the Copyrighted Work

This second factor tends to play a less significant role than the first in fair use litigation. Courts have held this factor weighs in the copyright owner's favor when fictional[208] and unpublished works[209] are involved, and in the defendant's favor when factual[210] and published works[211] are used. In the electronic context, it is possible a court may take into consideration whether a digital work should be treated differently from one in conventional print or other analog form because of the ease with which it could be copied and distributed.

[ii] The Amount and Substantiality of the Portion Used

This is probably the least important factor, given that even taking a small amount, if considered the "heart" of the work, can lead to a finding of infringement.[212] Indeed, the most frequently cited copyright treatise devotes only four sentences to its discussion:

> The third factor listed in § 107 is "the amount and substantiality of the portion used in relation to the copyrighted work as a whole." This raises an issue discussed in a preceding section [concerning the quantum of copying that constitutes infringement], and may be regarded as relating to the question of substantial similarity rather than whether the use is "fair." This includes a

---

205. *Marcus v. Rowley*, 695 F.2d 1171 (9th Cir. 1983).

206. *Encyclopedia Britannica Educ. Corp. v. Crooks*, 558 F. Supp. 1247 (W.D.N.Y. 1983).

207. *Basic Books, Inc. v. Kinko's Graphics Corp.*, 758 F. Supp. 1522 (S.D.N.Y. 1991).

208. *See Twin Peaks Prods., Inc. v. Publications Int'l, Ltd.*, 996 F.2d 1366, 1376 (2d Cir. 1993).

209. *See New Era Publications Int'l, ApS v. Henry Holt & Co.*, 873 F.2d 576 (2d Cir. 1989), *cert. denied*, 493 U.S. 1094 (1990).

210. *See National Rifle Ass'n v. Handgun Control Fed'n*, 15 F.3d 559, 562 (6th Cir. 1994).

211. *See New Era Publications Int'l, ApS v. Carol Publishing Group*, 904 F.2d 152, 157 (2d Cir. 1990).

212. *See Harper & Row, supra* note 5, at 569 (taking of some 300 words held infringing). *But cf. SunTrust v. Houghton Mifflin*, 252 F.3d 1165, 1172 (11th Cir. 2001) (novel that was largely "an encapsulation of [*Gone With the Wind*] [that exploits] its copyrighted characters, story lines, and settings as the palette for the new story" was entitled to fair use defense because it served as "specific criticism of and rejoinder to depiction of slavery and relationships between blacks and whites in *Gone With the Wind*.").

determination of not just quantitative, but also qualitative substantiality. In any event, whatever the use, generally it may not
constitute a fair use if the entire work is reproduced.[213]

[iv] The Economic Effect of the Use

Courts have repeatedly identified this as the most significant of the four
factors.[214] It weighs against a defendant not only when a *current*, but also
a *potential*, market exists for a work that could be exploited by a copyright owner. Harm in either market will, in most instances, render a use
unfair.[215] Several Supreme Court decisions demonstrate the significant
weight given this factor:

- In *Sony*, the absence of any market for home taping licenses, combined with the testimony of some copyright owners that they were
  indifferent to home copying, led the Court to conclude there was
  no cognizable harm.[216]
- In *Harper & Row*, the Court accepted the argument that defendant's "scooping" of *Time* magazine's right to make the first serial
  publication of President Ford's memoirs, which caused cancellation
  of the magazine's contract with *Harper & Row*, resulted in harm to
  the copyright owner.[217]
- In *Stewart v. Abend*, performances of a movie palpably harmed the
  economic interests of the copyright owner in the underlying short
  story.[218]
- In *Campbell*, the Court, because the parody was "transformative,"
  rejected the court of appeals' determination that the commercial

---

213. 3 *Nimmer on Copyright* § 13.05[A] (footnotes omitted).

214. *See Stewart v. Abend, supra* note 200, at 238.

215. *American Geophysical Union v. Texaco, Inc.*, 37 F.3d 881, 895 (2d Cir. 1994) ("analysis under the fourth factor must focus on the effect of [defendant's] photocopying upon the
potential market for or value of these individual articles"); *Salinger v. Random House, Inc.*,
811 F.2d 90, 99 (2d Cir.), *cert. denied*, 484 U.S. 890 (1987) (protecting potential market for
author's letters notwithstanding author's profound disinclination ever to publish them); *But
compare Bill Graham Archives v. Dorling Kindersley*, 448 F.3d 605, 614 (2d Cir. 2006) (suggesting the impact on potential revenues should be analyzed only for "traditional, reasonable, or likely to be developed markets").

216. *See Sony, supra* note 9, at 443–47 (plaintiffs "failed to carry their burden with
regard to [the harm of] time-shifting . . . . Harm from time-shifting is speculative and, at
best, minimal").

217. *See Harper & Row, supra* note 5, at 562.

218. *See Stewart v. Abend, supra* note 200, at 238.

purpose of the parody required the parodist to overcome *Sony's* presumption of market harm.[219]

Commercial uses involving no "transformation" by users and that harm actual or potential markets will likely always be infringing, while nonprofit educational, transformative uses will likely often be fair. Between these extremes, courts must engage in the same type of fact-intensive analysis typifying fair use litigation and frustrating those who seek "bright lines" between the lawful and unlawful.[220]

Courts in two cases concerning the unauthorized "uploading" and "downloading" of copyrighted materials to and from bulletin board services (bbs) have held such activity did not constitute fair use.[221] In the *Playboy* case discussed earlier, the court characterized the issue as whether "unrestricted and widespread conduct of the sort engaged in by the defendant bulletin board system operator (whether in fact engaged in by the defendant or others) would result in a substantially adverse impact on the potential market for or value of [Playboy's copyrighted photographs],"[222] and determined it would.

In the *MAPHIA* case,[223] the court found that Sega had established a prima facie case of direct and contributory infringement in the operation of defendant's bulletin board system where Sega's copyrighted video game programs were uploaded and downloaded. In issuing a preliminary injunction, the court held each of the four factors weighed against a finding of fair use but found the fourth factor, in particular, weighed "heavily" against such conclusion:

> Based on Defendants' own statement that 45,000 bulletin boards like MAPHIA operate in this country, it is obvious that should the unauthorized copying of Sega's video games by Defendants and others become widespread, there would be a substantial and

---

219. *See Campbell, supra* note 193, at 1173.

220. The inability of our common-law system to provide guidance covering every possible permutation of behavior is not necessarily a weakness. By permitting courts to reach decisions on a case-by-case basis, our system permits both necessary gap-filling and jurisprudential evolution without requiring repeated pleas to Congress for additional elaboration. For more on the fair use doctrine as it applies to education, *see* Chapter Three.

221. *See supra* notes 174–180 and accompanying text (discussing *Playboy* and *MAPHIA* decisions).

222. *Playboy, supra* note 175, at 1558.

223. *MAPHIA, supra* note 180.

immeasurable adverse effect on the market for Sega's copyrighted video game programs.[224]

[b] Library Exemptions

Section 108 of the Copyright Act provides that under certain conditions it is not infringement for a library or archives, or its employees acting within the scope of their employment,[225] to reproduce or distribute one copy of a work (and in some instances, three copies)[226] in situations that would typically go beyond fair use. The general conditions of this exemption are (1) the reproduction or distribution must be made without any purpose of direct or indirect commercial advantage; (2) the collections of the library must be open to the public or available not only to researchers affiliated with the library but also to other persons doing research in a specialized field; (3) the reproduction or distribution must include a notice of copyright or a legend stating the work may be protected by copyright if no notice is found thereon;[227] and (4) a specific exemption in subsections (b) through (g) of Section 108 applies.

The exemptions granted under Section 108 extend only to isolated and unrelated reproduction of a copy of the same material on separate occasions,[228] and do not apply to (1) musical works; (2) pictorial, graphic, or sculptural works; or (3) motion pictures or other audiovisual works, except news programs.[229] The circumstances under which a library may reproduce or distribute a copyrighted work without infringement liability include the following.

[i] Archival Copies

Three copies of an unpublished work may be reproduced in facsimile form if the sole purpose is preservation and security or for deposit for research use in another library, provided the copy reproduced is currently in the

---

224. *MAPHIA, supra* note 180, at 688.

225. Hereinafter, the term "library" will be used to refer to a library or archives, or any of its employees acting within the scope of their employment. For a more detailed discussion of Section 108, *see* Chapter Three, Section 3.3[2].

226. *See* 17 U.S.C. § 108(a). Section 108 limitations are *additional* exemptions provided specifically for certain libraries. Libraries, of course, may also take advantage of fair use privileges or any other exemptions contained in Copyright Act (*see* 17 U.S.C. § 108(f)(4)), but the exemptions in Section 108 generally exceed fair use. *See generally Copyright Office Report of the Register of Copyrights on Library Reproduction of Copyrighted Works* (1983).

227. 17 U.S.C. § 108(a).

228. 17 U.S.C. § 108(g).

229. 17 U.S.C. § 108(i).

library's collection.[230] The House Report notes this right "would extend to any type of work, including photographs, motion pictures and sound recordings."[231] Any such copy may be reproduced in digital format provided it is not otherwise distributed in that way or made available to the public outside the library premises.[232]

[ii] Replacement Copies

Up to three copies of a published work may be reproduced solely for the purpose of replacing a copy that is damaged, deteriorated, lost, or stolen—if the library has, after reasonable efforts, determined an unused replacement cannot be obtained at a fair price, and any such copy reproduced digitally is not made available to the public outside the library.[233]

[iii] Articles and Short Excerpts for Users

A copy of one article or other contribution to a collection or periodical issue, or a copy of a small part of any other copyrighted work, may be made at the request of a user, subject to two conditions.[234] First, the copy must become the property of the user, and the library has no notice such copy will be used for any purpose other than private study, scholarship, or research. Second, the library must prominently display a warning of copyright at the place where orders are accepted and on its standard request form.[235]

[iv] Out-of-Print Works for Scholarly Purposes

A copy of an entire work may be made if the library has determined a copy thereof cannot be obtained at a fair price,[236] subject to the same two additional conditions applicable to articles and short excerpts—property transfer and proper copyright warning display.[237]

[v] News Programs

A library may reproduce and distribute by lending a limited number of copies of an audiovisual news program.[238]

---

230. 17 U.S.C. § 108(b).
231. *House Report* at 75.
232. 17 U.S.C. § 108(b)(2).
233. 17 U.S.C. § 108(c); *see House Report* at 75.
234. 17 U.S.C. § 108(d).
235. *Id. See* Appendix 3-B for examples of such warnings.
236. 17 U.S.C. § 108(e).
237. *Id.*
238. 17 U.S.C. § 108(f)(3).

[vi] Educational Uses

During the last twenty years of the copyright term of a *published* work, a library, including a nonprofit educational institution that functions as such, may reproduce, distribute, display, or perform in facsimile or digital form a copy of such work, or portions thereof, for purposes of preservation, scholarship, or research, if such library has first determined, based on a reasonable investigation, that (1) the work is not subject to normal commercial exploitation; (2) a copy of the work cannot be obtained at a reasonable price; and (3) the copyright owner or its agent has not provided notice pursuant to regulations promulgated by the Register of Copyrights that either of the conditions set forth above applies.[239]

[vii] Interlibrary Loans

The Copyright Act allows a library to make single copies of works and enter into interlibrary arrangements, but prohibits copying "in such aggregate quantities as to substitute for a subscription to or purchase of [a copyrighted] work."[240] In the mid-1970s, the National Commission on New Technological Uses of Copyrighted Works (CONTU) offered its services to interested parties, including copyright owners, educators, and libraries, to develop guidelines to interpret the quoted phrase. The parties were successful in establishing how much copying for interlibrary "borrowing" was appropriate. These so-called CONTU Guidelines were later included in the Conference Report on the Copyright Act of 1976.[241] The guidelines permit a library to "borrow" not more than five copies per year of articles from the most recent five years of any journal title.[242]

[c] First Sale Doctrine

Another major limitation on the exclusive rights of a copyright holder is the "first sale doctrine," which prevents such an owner from controlling subsequent transfers of his or her work. Once the copyright holder transfers ownership of a particular copy (a material object), his exclusive right of distribution is "extinguished" with respect thereto.[243] Section 109(a) of the Copyright Act provides:

---

239. 17 U.S.C. § 108(h).

240. 17 U.S.C. § 108(g)(2).

241. *See* H.R. Rep. No. 1733, 94th Cong., 2d Sess. 72–73 (1976).

242. *Id.* at 72. For a more detailed analysis of the CONTU Guidelines, *see* Chapter Three, Section 3.3[5].

243. *See T.B. Harms Co. v. Jem Records, Inc.*, 655 F. Supp. 1575, 1582 (D.N.J. 1987); *Columbia Pictures Indus., Inc. v. Aveco, Inc.*, 612 F. Supp. 315, 319–20 (M.D. Pa. 1985), *aff'd*, 800 F.2d 59 (3d Cir. 1986).

> Notwithstanding the provisions of section 106(3) [which grants copyright owners the exclusive right to distribute copies or pho-norecords of a work], the owner of a particular copy or phono-record lawfully made under this title, or any person authorized by such owner, is entitled, without the authority of the copyright owner, to sell or otherwise dispose of the possession of that copy or phono-record.[244]

This limitation allows wholesalers to, for example, distribute books to retailers, and retailers to sell them to consumers, and consumers to give them to friends, and friends to sell them in garage sales and so on, all without permission of (or payment to) the copyright owner.

The first sale doctrine thus allows someone holding a tangible copy of a work to dispose of it in any way (e.g., by selling, leasing, loaning, or giving it away). However, an exception exists for computer programs and sound recordings. The owner of a particular copy of those two items may not rent, lease, or lend such copy for the purpose of direct or indirect commercial advantage.[245] These exceptions were enacted because of the ease with which a person could reproduce these works at low cost and with minimum degradation in quality.[246] Additional items could be added to this exception in the future as more products are digitized and the "nexus" of rental and reproduction of those works "may directly and adversely affect the ability of copyright holders to exercise their reproduction and distribution rights under the Copyright Act."[247]

While the first sale doctrine limits the copyright owner's distribution right, it does not affect the reproduction right. Thus, the doctrine does not allow the electronic transmission of a work (through a computer network,

---

244. 17 U.S.C. § 109(a).

245. *See* 17 U.S.C. § 109(b)(1)(A). The prohibition with respect to record rental does not apply to nonprofit libraries or nonprofit educational institutions for nonprofit purposes. *Id.* In addition, a nonprofit educational institution may transfer possession of a lawfully made copy of a computer program to another nonprofit educational institution or to faculty, staff, and students. *Id.* Nonprofit libraries may also lend a computer program for nonprofit purposes if each copy has a copyright warning affixed to the package. 17 U.S.C. § 109(b)(2)(A). The prohibition does not apply to a computer program "which is embodied in a machine or product and which cannot be copied during the ordinary operation or use of the machine or product" or "a computer program embodied in or used in conjunction with a limited purpose computer that is designed for playing video games and may be designed for other purposes." 17 U.S.C. § 109(b)(1)(B).

246. Corsello, *The Computer Software Rental Amendments Act of 1990: Another Bend in the First Sale Doctrine*, 41 Cath. U. L. Rev. 177, 192 (1991).

247. *See* H.R. Rep. No. 987, 98th Cong., 2d Sess. 2 (1984) (justifying the Record Rental Amendment of 1984).

for instance) because, under current technology, the transmitter retains the original copy while the recipient obtains a reproduction thereof (i.e., a *new* copy). The Copyright Act, its legislative history, and relevant case law make clear the doctrine is applicable only to situations where the owner of a particular copy physically disposes of that same copy.[248]

Simply stated, the owner of a tangible copy of a copyrighted work may distribute but not reproduce it.[249] Therefore, any electronic transmission would constitute infringement.[250] If the reproduction is not authorized, further distribution thereof would also be illegal because the copy distributed was not "lawfully made." This "lawfully made" proviso does not limit the first sale doctrine's application to only copies made or authorized by the copyright owner.[251] For example, a "lawfully made" copy may also exist under the fair use doctrine.

Some have suggested the first sale doctrine should also apply to electronic transmissions, as long as the transmitter deletes the original copy from his or her computer. Proponents of this view note that at the completion of such activity, only one copy exists between the original owner and recipient, the same number as at the beginning. However, this zero-sum game analysis misses the point. The question is not whether the same number of copies exist at the completion of the transaction. Instead, it is whether the transaction violates one or more of the copyright owner's exclusive rights.

In this case, without any doubt, a reproduction of the work takes place in the receiving computer. To apply the first sale doctrine to this example would vitiate the reproduction right. To reinforce this point, the Register of Copyrights recently declined to endorse recommendations by some public commentators to create a "digital first sale doctrine," thus permit-

---

248. *See* 17 U.S.C. § 109(a) ("the owner of a particular copy or phonorecord . . . is entitled . . . to sell or otherwise dispose of the possession of that copy or phonorecord"); *House Report* at 79 (under the first sale doctrine in Section 109, "the copyright owner's exclusive right of public distribution would have no effect upon anyone who owns a particular copy or phonorecord lawfully made under this title and who wishes to transfer it to someone else . . .") *See also, e.g., Columbia Pictures Indus. v. Redd Horne, Inc., supra* note 186, at 159 ("first sale doctrine prevents the copyright owner from controlling the future transfer of a particular copy once its material ownership has been transferred").

249. *House Report* at 79 (under the first sale doctrine, "the owner of the physical copy or phonorecord cannot reproduce or perform the copyrighted work publicly without the copyright owner's consent").

250. If the reproduction is lawful under another provision of the Copyright Act, the transmission would likely not be an infringement.

251. *See House Report* at 79.

ting the owner of a digital work to transmit it to another person, provided the transferor subsequently deleted his copy.[252]

A copyright owner's exclusive right to publicly display copies of her work is also limited by Section 109 of the Copyright Act:

> Notwithstanding the provisions of section 106(5) [which grants copyright owners the exclusive right to display publicly copies of a work], the owner of a particular copy lawfully made under this title, or any person authorized by such owner, is entitled, without the authority of the copyright owner, to display that copy publicly, either directly or by the projection of no more than one image at a time, to viewers present at the place where the copy is located.[253]

Thus, an art gallery purchasing a print may publicly display it without liability. Similarly, the owner of a particular copy of an electronic audiovisual game intended for use in coin-operated equipment may also publicly perform or display that game in such equipment without fear of suit.[254]

This exemption does not, however, apply to the public display of a work on a bulletin board system or other computer, because more than one image is displayed at a time (to different viewers) and viewers are not present at the place where the copy is located. As such, our friend Mr. Frena from the *Playboy* case could not escape liability by purchasing a copy of *Playboy Magazine*, fixing a live camera on its pictorials, and streaming it out over the Internet to his subscribers. This same section also precludes someone from renting a video and showing it to a large gathering outside of his normal circle of acquaintances because it would involve the projection of "more than one image at a time."

[d] Educational Use Exemptions

Section 110(1) of the Copyright Act exempts from infringement liability the performance or display of a copyrighted work in the course of face-to-face

---

252. U.S. Copyright Office, *Digital Millennium Copyright Act Section 104 Report* (August 2001).

253. 17 U.S.C. § 109(c).

254. Section 109(e) reversed the decision in *Red Baron-Franklin Park, Inc. v. Taito Corp., supra* note 186, which held that video games could not be operated in an arcade without the permission of the copyright owner because such operation entailed violation of the copyright owner's exclusive rights to perform and display the work publicly. Section 109(e); however, does not allow the public display or performance of any other work of authorship embodied in the audiovisual game if the copyright owner of the game is not also the copyright owner of the other work. *See* 17 U.S.C. § 109(e).

teaching activities by a nonprofit educational institution in a classroom or similar setting.[255]

Prior to adoption of the Technology, Education, and Copyright Harmonization Act (the "TEACH Act") in the fall of 2002,[256] Section 110(2) of the Copyright Act exempted from liability the transmission of a performance or display of certain, limited copyrighted works if (1) such performance or display was a regular part of the systematic instructional activities of the nonprofit educational institution; (2) the performance or display was directly related and of material assistance to the teaching content of the transmission; and (3) the transmission was made primarily for reception in classrooms or similar places devoted to instruction or to persons with disabilities located elsewhere.[257]

As noted above, on November 2, 2002, President George W. Bush signed the TEACH Act into law. This particular legislation updated the distance education provisions of the Copyright Act and affected all colleges, universities, and K–12 school systems utilizing distance learning technologies. The TEACH Act essentially changed the terms and conditions under which eligible educational institutions could incorporate copyrighted works into their electronically transmitted courses.

Specifically, the new act amended Sections 110(2) and 112 of the Copyright Act to facilitate the growth and development of digital distance education. In doing so, it enlarged the number and types of copyrighted works an instructor could use without the need to obtain permission, pay licensing fees, or rely on items already in the public domain. Among its benefits, the TEACH Act expanded the categories of works the "distance learning" exemption applied to, allowed content to be transmitted to students at any location rather than just classrooms (as used to be the law), and permitted institutions to digitize certain works.[258]

To secure these benefits, however, the TEACH Act imposed a host of new legal and technical requirements on those schools seeking to take advantage of its measures. Among those are the need to employ technology to prevent unauthorized access to and downstream copying of educational broadcasts. The school must also assure all copyrighted works are used in conjunction with "mediated instructional activities." Of par-

---

255. See 17 U.S.C. § 110(1).

256. Pub. L. No. 107–273, 116 Stat. 1911 (2002). See Chapter Six for an extensive and detailed discussion of this legislation.

257. See 17 U.S.C. § 110(2) (1988).

258. See Gasaway, Balancing Copyright Concerns: The TEACH Act of 2001, EDUCAUSE Rev., Nov./Dec. 2001, at 2.

ticular significance, the TEACH Act now *requires* educational institutions to establish policies regarding copyright and to provide information to faculty, students, and staff members accurately describing and promoting compliance with copyright law.[259] The TEACH Act complements and coexists with the fair use doctrine and library exemptions already available to educational institutions.[260]

[e] Other Limitations

[i] Reproduction of Computer Programs

The rights of a copyright owner in a computer program are limited such that a software purchaser may make a copy or adaptation thereof as an "essential step" in using the program in a computer or for archival purposes.[261] This limitation applies only to "owners" of copies of programs— not licensees, borrowers, or mere possessors. The provision was added to the Copyright Act to essentially permit software purchasers to load and "boot up" computer programs and make "backup" copies thereof without facing infringement liability.

[ii] Certain Performances and Displays

Certain performances and displays in addition to the educational use exemptions described in Sections 110(1) and 110(2) are permitted under the Copyright Act, including

---

259. *Id.*

260. *See* Chapter Three, Section 3.3, for a detailed discussion of educational fair use exemptions.

261. Section 117 of the Copyright Act provides:

Notwithstanding the provisions of section 106, it is not an infringement for the owner of a copy of a computer program to make or authorize the making of another copy or adaptation of that computer program provided:

(1) that such a new copy or adaptation is created as an essential step in the utilization of the computer program in conjunction with a machine and that it is used in no other manner, or

(2) that such new copy or adaptation is for archival purposes only and that all archival copies are destroyed in the event that continued possession of the computer program should cease to be rightful.

17 U.S.C. § 117. Any identical copies made in accordance with Section 117 "may be leased, sold, or otherwise transferred, along with the copy from which such copies were prepared, only as part of the lease, sale, or other transfer of all rights in the program." Adaptations made may be transferred only with the authorization of the owner of the copyright in the original program. *Id.*

- the performance or display of certain works in the course of religious services;[262]
- the performance of certain works by governmental or nonprofit agricultural or horticultural organizations;[263]
- the performance of certain musical works in retail outlets for the sole purpose of promoting retail sales;[264]
- the transmission of performances of certain works to disabled persons;[265] and
- the performance of certain works at nonprofit veterans' or fraternal organizations for charitable purposes.[266]

The "communication of a transmission embodying a performance or display of a work by the public reception of the transmission on a single receiving apparatus of a kind commonly used in private homes" is also exempted if there is no direct charge to see or hear the transmission and it is not further transmitted to the public.[267] This exemption allows proprietors to play radios or televisions in public establishments such as restaurants, beauty shops, and bars.[268] The applicability of this exemption is extremely fact specific. Also, what qualifies as a type of receiving apparatus "commonly used in private homes" will certainly change as home equipment expands (e.g., satellite TV) or merges and becomes more sophisticated (e.g., combined radio/television /computer units).

[iii] Ephemeral Recordings

Section 112 provides it is not copyright infringement for a "transmitting organization" having the right to transmit to the public a performance or display of a work "to make no more than one copy or phonorecord of a

---

262. *See* 17 U.S.C. § 110(3).

263. *See* 17 U.S.C. § 110(6).

264. *See* 17 U.S.C. § 110(7).

265. *See* 17 U.S.C. §§ 110(8), (9).

266. *See* 17 U.S.C. § 110(10).

267. *See* 17 U.S.C. § 110(5).

268. *See, e.g.,* the decision in *Twentieth Century Music Corp. v. Aiken*, 422 U.S. 151 (1975), which was essentially codified in Section 110(5) (owner of a small food establishment exempt from infringement liability for the performance of copyrighted works via a radio and four small ceiling speakers). *See also Sailor Music v. The Gap Stores, Inc.*, 516 F. Supp. 923 (S.D.N.Y.), *aff'd*, 668 F.2d 84 (2d Cir. 1981), *cert. denied*, 456 U.S. 945 (1982); *Rodgers v. Eighty Four Lumber Co.*, 617 F. Supp. 1021 (W.D. Pa. 1985); *Springsteen v. Plaza Roller Dome, Inc.*, 602 F. Supp. 1113 (M.D.N.C. 1985).

particular transmission program embodying the performance or display" under certain conditions.[269]

[iv] Compulsory Licenses

Sections 111 and 119 are compulsory licensing provisions allowing cable systems and satellite operators to retransmit copyrighted programming without infringement liability by paying a statutory licensing fee (which is then distributed among the copyright owners of such programming).[270] A compulsory license under Section 111 is available only to a "cable system," which is defined as "a facility . . . that in whole or in part receives signals transmitted or programs broadcast by one or more television broadcast stations . . . ." This license generally would not be available for Internet or e-mail transmissions, because a "cable system" does not encompass facilities such as computer networks.[271] Similarly, a compulsory license under

---

269. *See* 17 U.S.C. § 112(a). This limitation of the copyright owner's reproduction right is applicable only if:

> (1) the copy or phonorecord is retained and used solely by the transmitting organization that made it, and no further copies or phonorecords are reproduced from it; and
>
> (2) the copy or phonorecord is used solely for the transmitting organization's own transmissions within its local service area, or for purposes of archival preservation or security; and
>
> (3) unless preserved exclusively for archival purposes, the copy or phonorecord is destroyed within six months from the date the transmission program was first transmitted to the public.

> *Id.*

270. *See* 17 U.S.C. §§ 111, 119. These provisions are referred to as "compulsory licenses" because copyright owners are compelled to grant them. No license agreements are actually signed, and the terms thereof are set forth in the statute. The copyright owner cannot object to the use of the work and must be satisfied with the license fees collected under the statute, which are distributed among all of the affected owners by arbitrators impaneled by the Librarian of Congress.

271. The Copyright Office issued a regulation in 1992 stating a cable system is a facility that both receives and transmits signals from within the same state. *See* 37 C.F.R. § 201.17(k). This ruling makes clear that Section 111 would not be applicable to entities other than community-based cable systems. Moreover, in *Satellite Broadcast Networks, Inc. v. Oman*, 17 F.3d 344 (11th Cir.), *cert. denied*, 115 S. Ct. 88 (1994), the Eleventh Circuit upheld the regulation, finding it valid, enforceable, and to be used by courts when determining whether a facility qualifies as a cable system. Since facilities used to transmit works through the Internet will generally be inherently capable of receiving and transmitting outside any particular state, these facilities will not qualify for the cable compulsory license.

Section 119 would not be available unless the transmitting entity qualified as a "satellite carrier" and met other statutory criteria.[272]

Compulsory licenses are also available for the public performance of nondramatic musical works by means of jukeboxes,[273] for the use of certain works in connection with noncommercial broadcasting,[274] and for the reproduction and distribution of nondramatic musical works in the course of making and distributing phonorecords of such works.[275]

[8] Copyright Infringement

[a] General

Anyone who, without the authorization of the copyright owner, exercises any of such owner's exclusive rights, as granted and limited by the Copyright Act, is an infringer of copyright.[276] Thus, any activity falling within the scope of such exclusive rights is an infringement; and the infringer is liable for damages, unless authorized by the owner or excused by a defense (such as fair use) or a specific exemption.[277] For purposes of the discussion in this section, the lack of such authorization, defense, or exemption is presumed.

---

272. A "satellite carrier" is defined as "an entity that uses facilities of a satellite service licensed by the Federal Communications Commission to establish and operate a channel of communications for point-to-multipoint distribution of television station signals . . . ." *See* 17 U.S.C. § 119(d)(6). Unless the Internet transmission occurs through a satellite service licensed by the FCC for the statutorily prescribed purposes, the compulsory license provisions are not applicable.

273. *See* 17 U.S.C. § 116. This compulsory license may be invoked only if private negotiations fail to produce a consensual license.

274. *See* 17 U.S.C. § 118.

275. *See* 17 U.S.C. § 115.

276. *See* 17 U.S.C. § 501(a). Anyone who "trespasses into [the copyright owner's] exclusive domain by using or authorizing the use of the copyrighted work in one of the five ways set forth in the statute" is an infringer of the copyright. *Sony, supra* note 9, at 433.

277. *See* discussion of the scope of the exclusive rights, *supra* Sections 2.1[6] and [7]. For instance, activities such as loading a work into a computer, scanning a printed work into a digital file, uploading or downloading a work between a user's computer and a bbs or other server, and transmitting a work from one computer to another may be infringements (in those cases, of the reproduction right). *See, e.g., MAI Systems Corp., supra* note 38 (the turning on of the computer, thereby causing the operating system to be copied into RAM, constituted an infringing reproduction of the copyrighted software); *Advanced Computer Services, supra* note 38 (loading software into computer's random access memory constituted infringing reproduction); *see also* 2 *Nimmer on Copyright* § 8.08 ("input of a work into a computer results in the making of a copy, and hence . . . such unauthorized input infringes the copyright owner's reproduction right").

Copyright infringement is determined *without* regard to the intent or state of mind of the infringer; "innocent" infringement is infringement nonetheless.[278] Moreover, although the exclusive rights refer to "copies" (plural) of the work,[279] there is no question the Copyright Act views the making of even a single unauthorized copy as infringement.[280] Courts generally use the term "copying" as shorthand for violating any of the copyright owner's exclusive rights (not just the reproduction right), and usually require a complainant to prove both ownership of his or her work and "copying" by the defendant to prevail in an infringement action.

Since there is seldom direct evidence of copying (witnesses who actually saw the defendant reproduce the work, for instance), an owner may prove copying through circumstantial evidence establishing the defendant had access to the original work and that the two works are substantially similar. Other indications of copying, such as the existence of common errors, have also been accepted as evidence of infringement.[281] The copying of the work must include the taking of protected expression and not just its ideas.[282] Likewise, the similarity between the two works must be similarity of protected elements (the expression), not unprotected elements (the facts, ideas, etc.). The portion taken must also be more than de minimis.

---

278. The innocence or willfulness of the infringing activity may be relevant with regard to the award of statutory damages. *See* 17 U.S.C. § 504(c); *see also* discussion of remedies, *infra* Section 2.1[8][d].

279. *See* 17 U.S.C. § 106.

280. *See House Report* at 61 ("references to 'copies or phonorecords' are intended [in Section 106(1)–(3)] and throughout the bill to include the singular"; "the right 'to reproduce the copyright work in copies or phonorecords' means the right to produce *a* material object in which the work is duplicated, transcribed, imitated, or simulated . . ."). Further evidence of the intent of Congress to make even a single act of unauthorized reproduction an infringement is found in specific exemptions created for certain single-copy uses. *See, e.g.,* 17 U.S.C. §§ 108(a), 108(f)(2), 112(a).

281. *See, e.g., Rockford Map Publishers, Inc. v. Directory Serv. Co.,* 224 U.S.P.Q. 851 (C.D. Ill. 1984), *aff'd,* 768 F.2d 145 (7th Cir. 1985), *cert. denied,* 474 U.S. 1061 (1986); *Sub-Contractors Register, Inc. v. McGovern's Contractors & Builders Manual, Inc.,* 69 F. Supp. 507, 509 (S.D.N.Y. 1946). It is common for publishers of directories and other compilations to deliberately insert mistakes into the work (such as periodically adding a fictitious name, address, and phone number in a telephone directory) to detect and help establish copying. *See* 2 H. Abrams, *The Law of Copyright* § 14.02[B][3][c] at 14–19 to 20 (1993).

282. Ideas and facts, of course, are not copyrightable. In the case of compilations, such as databases, if enough facts are copied, the copyrighted expression (the selection, arrangement, or coordination of the facts) may be copied and infringement found. *See Key Publications, Inc. v. Chinatown Today Publishing Enters., Inc.,* 945 F.2d 509, 515–16 (2d Cir. 1991); *Mid America Title Co. v. Kirk,* No. 86-C-2853, 1991 U.S. Dist. LEXIS 11168 at *8–*9 (N.D. Ill. 1991) (denying summary judgment on grounds that plaintiff's "use of judgment in determining which land title facts should be included" was question of fact.)

The similarity between the two works need not be literal (i.e., phrases, sentences, or paragraphs need not be copied verbatim); substantial similarity may be found even if none of the words, brush strokes, or musical notes are identical.[283] Various tests have been developed to determine whether there has been sufficient nonliteral copying to constitute substantial similarity between the copyrighted and allegedly infringing work.[284] Judge Learned Hand articulated the well-known "abstractions test," where the expression and idea are, in essence, treated as ends of a continuum, with infringement found if the "second" work crosses the line delineating the two.[285] Such a line, as Judge Hand recognized, is not fixed in stone; indeed, as he put it, its location must "inevitably be *ad hoc* . . . ."[286] The "pattern" test has also been suggested where the "pattern" of the work is taken (in a play, for instance, the "sequence of events, and the development of the interplay of characters").[287]

The "subtractive" test, which dissects the original work, disregards the non-copyrightable portions, and compares the copyrightable elements with the second work, has been the traditional method for determining substantial similarity.[288] Following the 1970 decision in *Roth Greeting Cards*

---

283. *See Donald v. Zack Meyer's T.V. Sales & Service*, 426 F.2d 1027, 1030 (5th Cir. 1970) ("paraphrasing is equivalent to outright copying"), *cert. denied*, 400 U.S. 992 (1971); *Davis v. E.I. DuPont de Nemours & Co.*, 240 F. Supp. 612, 621 (S.D.N.Y. 1965) ("paraphrasing is tantamount to copying in copyright law"); *see generally* 3 *Nimmer on Copyright* § 13.03[A] at 13-28 to 13-58. Nimmer identifies two bases upon which courts impose liability for less than 100 percent verbatim copying: (1) "fragmented literal similarity" (where words, lines, or paragraphs are copied virtually word for word, although not necessarily verbatim) and (2) "comprehensive nonliteral similarity" (where the "fundamental essence or structure" of a work is copied); *see also* P. Goldstein, *Copyright* § 7.2.1 at 13–17 (1989). Goldstein identifies three types of similarity: (1) where the infringing work "tracks" the original work "in every detail," (2) "striking similarity" (where a brief portion of both works is "so idiosyncratic in its treatment as to preclude coincidence") and (3) similarities that "lie beneath the surface" of the works ("[i]ncident and characterization in literature, composition and form in art, and rhythm, harmony and musical phrases in musical composition"). *Id.* at 13 (citations omitted).

284. For analyses of the various tests used, *see* 3 *Nimmer on Copyright* § 13.03[A]; M. Leaffer, *Understanding Copyright Law* §§ 9.5–9.7 at 268–76 (1989).

285. *See Nichols v. Universal Pictures, Corp.*, 45 F.2d 119, 121 (2d Cir. 1930).

286. *See Peter Pan Fabrics Inc. v. Martin Weiner Corp.*, 274 F.2d 487 (2d Cir. 1960).

287. *See* Chaffee, *Reflections on the Law of Copyright: I*, 45 COLUM. L. REV. 503, 513 (1945).

288. *See Universal Athletic Sales Co. v. Salkeld*, 511 F.2d 904, 908–09 (3d Cir.), *cert. denied*, 423 U.S. 863 (1975) (subtracting all but the "stick figures" from chart as unprotectable subject matter); *Alexander v. Haley*, 460 F. Supp 40, 46 (S.D.N.Y. 1978) (finding "alleged infringements display no similarity at all in terms of expression or language, but show at most some similarity of theme or setting. These items, the skeleton of creative work rather than the flesh, are not protected by the copyright laws.").

v. United Card Co.,[289] the "totality" test also became popular. This test compares works using a "total concept and feel" approach, and although chiefly used by the Ninth Circuit in the 1970s and 1980s,[290] has also been adopted by other federal circuits.[291]

The Ninth Circuit further defined an "extrinsic/intrinsic" test in proof of substantial similarity in *Sid & Marty Krofft Television Productions, Inc. v. McDonald's Corp.*[292] The intrinsic portion of the test measures whether an observer "would find the total concept and feel of the works" to be substantially similar.[293] The extrinsic portion, meanwhile, is an objective analysis of similarity based on "specific criteria that can be listed and analyzed."[294] Thus, this test requires substantial similarity "not only of the general ideas but of the expressions of those ideas as well."[295]

Both the Ninth and Second Circuits have moved away from the totality test with respect to computer applications, however. In *Data East USA, Inc. v. Epyx, Inc.,*[296] the Ninth Circuit rediscovered "analytic dissection of similarities" in the substantial similarity determination of video games.[297] Similarly, the Second Circuit, in *Computer Associates International, Inc. v. Altai, Inc.,*[298] fashioned an "abstraction-filtration-comparison test" for computer programs that combined Judge Learned Hand's "abstraction" test (to separate ideas from expression) and "filtration" reminiscent of traditional "subtraction" analysis in distinguishing protectable from unprotectable material.[299]

---

289. 429 F.2d 1106 (9th Cir. 1970).

290. *See, e.g., Sid & Marty Krofft Television Prods., Inc. v. McDonald's Corp.*, 562 F.2d 1157 (9th Cir. 1977); *McCulloch v. Albert E. Price, Inc.*, 823 F.2d 316 (9th Cir. 1987).

291. *See, e.g., Reyher v. Children's Television Workshop*, 533 F.2d 87 (2d Cir. 1976); *Atari, Inc. v. North American Philips Consumer Electronics Corp.*, 672 F.2d 607 (7th Cir.), *cert. denied*, 459 U.S. 880 (1982); *Atari Games, supra* note 33; *Whelan Assocs., Inc. v. Jaslow Dental Lab., Inc.*, 797 F.2d 1222 (3d Cir. 1986), *cert. denied*, 479 U.S. 877 (1987).

292. *See supra* note 290.

293. *See Pasillas v. McDonald's Corp.*, 927 F.2d 440, 442 (9th Cir. 1991).

294. *See Brown Bag Software v. Symantec Corp.*, 960 F.2d 1465, 1475 (9th Cir. 1992).

295. *Krofft, supra* note 290, at 1164.

296. 862 F.2d 204 (9th Cir. 1988).

297. *See also Apple Computer, Inc. v. Microsoft Corp.*, 35 F.3d 1435, 1445 (9th Cir. 1994) (approving of district court's use of analytical dissection and agreeing with other courts' use of the "same analysis although articulated differently").

298. 982 F.2d 693 (2d Cir. 1992). *See also Autoskill Inc. v. National Educational Support Systems, Inc.*, 994 F.2d 1476, 1490–91 (10th Cir. 1993).

299. Other circuits have applied this test. *See Engineering Dynamics, Inc. v. Structural Software, Inc.*, 26 F.3d 1335, 1343 (5th Cir. 1994); *Gates Rubber Co. v. Bando Chemical Indus., Ltd.*, 9 F.3d 823, 834 (10th Cir. 1993).

Aside from determining the proper test to use, there is also disagreement among the federal circuits as to the appropriate "audience" to employ for determining substantial similarity. The "ordinary observer test," alluded to in *Arnstein v. Porter*[300] and followed in a number of Second Circuit decisions,[301] considers the question from the viewpoint of the "average lay observer."[302] The Fourth Circuit, however, set forth a modified test in *Dawson v. Hinshaw Music Inc.*,[303] requiring the ordinary observer to be the "intended" audience for a particular work. Relying on decisions by both the Ninth and Seventh Circuits,[304] the court in *Dawson* wrote:

> [i]f the lay public fairly represents the intended audience, the court should apply the lay observer formulation of the ordinary observer test. However, if the intended audience is more narrow in that it possesses specialized expertise, . . . the court's inquiry should focus on whether a member of the intended audience would find the two works to be substantially similar.[305]

The challenge of this standard, especially in more advanced technologies, is determining when, if ever, a work is not directed to an audience possessing specialized expertise, and at what point a work once intended for a specialized audience becomes accepted by the general public.

The ability to manipulate works in digital form raises an issue with respect to infringement of the reproduction and derivative right. A photograph, for instance, can be manipulated in the user's computer in such a way that the resulting work is not substantially similar to the copyrighted work (in fact, it may bear little or no resemblance to the original). The initial input of the copyrighted work into the user's computer may be an

---

300. 154 F.2d 464 (2d Cir. 1946).

301. *See, e.g., Peter Pan Fabrics, Inc. v. Martin Weiner Corp.*, 274 F.2d 487 (2d Cir. 1960); *Ideal Toy Corp. v. Fab-Lu Ltd.*, 360 F.2d 1021 (2d Cir. 1966); *Eden Toys, Inc. v. Marshall Field & Co.*, 675 F.2d 498 (2d Cir. 1982).

302. *Ideal Toy Corp. supra* note 301, at 1023 n.2.

303. 905 F.2d 731 (4th Cir. 1990).

304. *See Aliotti v. R. Dakin & Co.*, 831 F.2d 898, 902 (9th Cir. 1987) (holding that perceptions of children must be considered in substantial similarity analysis because they are the intended market for product); *Atari, Inc. v. North American Philips Consumer Electronics Corp., supra* note 291, at 619 (holding that "[v]ideo games, unlike an artist's painting, . . . appeal to an audience that is fairly undiscriminating insofar as their concern about more subtle differences in artistic expression").

305. *Dawson, supra* note 303, at 736.

infringement of the reproduction right, but the infringing (or noninfring-ing) nature of the resulting work is less clear.

Although courts traditionally rely on a "substantial similarity" test to determine liability, including with regard to derivative works, neither the meaning of "derivative work" nor the statutory standard for infringement appears to require an infringing derivative work to be substantially simi-lar.[306] This dichotomy remains unresolved by the courts and unaddressed by Congress.

[b] Infringing Importation

The exclusive right to distribute includes the ability to limit importing a work into the country without authority of the copyright owner.[307] Such unauthorized importation, whether it be of pirated items (i.e., "copies or phonorecords made without any authorization of the copyright owner")[308] or "gray market" products (i.e., copies legally produced overseas for for-eign distribution, but not authorized for the U.S. market),[309] is an infringe-ment of the distribution right.[310] Several exceptions exist to this importa-tion right, including permitting one copy of a work at a time to be brought

---

306. An infringer is anyone who violates "any of the exclusive rights" of the copyright owner. 17 U.S.C. § 501(a). One of the exclusive rights is "to prepare derivative works based upon the copyrighted work." 17 U.S.C. § 106(2). A "derivative work" is a work "based upon one or more preexisting works, such as a ... condensation, or any other form in which a work may be recast, transformed, or adapted." 17 U.S.C. § 101 (definition of "derivative work"). The Ninth Circuit has suggested that "a work is not derivative unless it has been substantially *copied* from the prior work." *See Litchfield v. Spielberg,* 736 F.2d 1352, 1357 (9th Cir. 1984) (emphasis added). It is unclear; however, whether the court is suggesting a deriv-ative work must be substantially *similar* to the prior work or that it simply must incorpo-rate in some form a portion of the prior work, as noted in the legislative history. *See House Report* at 62. The court noted that there is "little available authority" on infringement of the derivative works right. *See Litchfield* at 1357.

307. 17 U.S.C. § 602(a).

308. *House Report* at 169–70.

309. *Id.* (Section 602 of the Copyright Act covers "unauthorized importation of copies or phonorecords that were lawfully made").

310. *See T.B. Harms Co., supra* note 243; *Parfums Givenchy, Inc. v. C&C Beauty Sales, Inc.,* 832 F. Supp. 1378 (C.D. Cal. 1993). Courts are divided as to whether the first sale doc-trine limits the ability of copyright owners to enforce the importation rights (as it does with respect to the domestic distribution right). *Compare BMG Music v. Perez,* 952 F.2d 318, 319 (9th Cir. 1991) (first sale doctrine does not circumscribe importation rights under Section 602) with *Sebastian Int'l, Inc. v. Consumer Contacts (PTY) Ltd.,* 847 F.2d 1093, 1097 (3d Cir. 1988) (*contra*).

in for the private use of an importer or articles contained in the personal baggage of travelers entering the United States.[311]

The applicability of these importation provisions to works transmitted into the United States via the Internet is subject to dispute. For instance, the importation right is an outgrowth of the distribution right, both of which refer to "copies or phonorecords."[312] A data stream can contain a work in the form of electronic impulses, but those impulses do not fall within the definition of "copies" or "phonorecords." Therefore, it may be argued that transmitting a copyrighted work into the United States via international communication links fails to constitute an "importation" under current law.

[c] Contributory and Vicarious Liability

Direct participation in infringing activity is not a prerequisite for liability under copyright law. The Copyright Act grants owners the exclusive right "to authorize" the exercise of their rights. This right was "intended to avoid any questions as to the liability of contributory infringers"; that is, those who do not directly exercise the copyright owner's rights, but "authorize" others to do so.[313] Other than this reference to authorization, the Copyright Act does not mention or define "contributory infringement" or "vicarious liability," the standards for which have developed through case law.[314]

---

311. *See* 17 U.S.C. § 602(a) (subsection does not apply to "(1) importation of copies or phonorecords under the authority or for the use of the Government of the United States or of any State or political subdivision of a State, but not including copies or phonorecords for use in schools, or copies of any audiovisual work imported for purposes other than archival use; (2) importation, for the private use of the importer and not for distribution, by any person with respect to no more than one copy or phonorecord of any one work at any one time, or by any person arriving from outside the United States with respect to copies or phonorecords forming part of such person's personal baggage; or (3) importation by or for an organization operated for scholarly, educational, or religious purposes and not for private gain, with respect to no more than one copy of an audiovisual work solely for its archival purposes, and no more than five copies or phonorecords of any other work for its library lending or archival purposes, unless the importation of such copies or phonorecords is part of an activity consisting of systematic reproduction or distribution, engaged in by such organization in violation of the provisions of section 108(g)(2)"); *House Report* at 170.

312. *See* discussion of transmissions and the distribution right, *supra* Section 2.1[6][c].

313. *See House Report* at 61. There must be a direct infringement upon which contributory infringement or vicarious liability is based.

314. The concepts of contributory and vicarious liability are well established in tort law. Contributory infringement of intellectual property rights was first codified in patent law. *See* 35 U.S.C. § 271(c).

If someone has the "right and ability" to supervise the infringing action of another, and such right and ability "coalesce with an obvious and direct financial interest in the exploitation of copyrighted materials, even in the absence of actual knowledge" of the infringement, such "supervisor" may be held vicariously liable.[315] Vicarious liability is based, therefore, on a connection to the direct infringer and not necessarily the infringing activity. The best-known examples involving this liability are the so-called dance hall cases. There, dance hall owners who permitted the unauthorized public performance of musical works by bands they hired were deemed culpable, even though the owners themselves had no knowledge of the infringements. In one case, a proprietor had even expressly warned the bands not to perform copyrighted music without the proper license.[316]

"Contributory infringement" may be found when "one who, with knowledge of the infringing activity, induces, causes or materially contributes to the infringing conduct of another."[317] Contributory infringement is also based on a connection to the illegal activity (not necessarily the actual wrongdoer). A person may thus be deemed liable merely based on providing services or equipment related to the direct infringement.[318] These two scenarios are explored next.

---

315. *Shapiro, Bernstein & Co. v. H.L. Green Co.*, 316 F.2d 304, 307 (2d Cir. 1963) (holding company leasing floor space to phonograph record department liable for record department's sales of "bootleg" records despite absence of actual knowledge of infringement, because of company's beneficial relationship to sales).

316. *See, e.g., Dreamland Ball Room, Inc. v. Shapiro, Bernstein & Co.*, 36 F.2d 354 (7th Cir. 1929); *Famous Music Corp. v. Bay State Harness Horse Racing & Breeding Ass'n, Inc.*, 554 F.2d 1213 (1st Cir. 1977); *KECA Music, Inc. v. Dingus McGee's Co.*, 432 F. Supp. 72 (W.D. Mo. 1977). Indeed, the "cases are legion which hold the dance hall proprietor liable for the infringement of copyright resulting from the performance of a musical composition by a band or orchestra whose activities provide the proprietor with a source of customers and enhanced income. He is liable whether the bandleader is considered, as a technical matter, an employee or an independent contractor, and whether or not the proprietor has knowledge of the compositions to be played or any control over their selection." *See Shapiro, Bernstein & Co. v. H.L. Green Co., supra* note 315, at 307 (citing some ten cases).

317. *Gershwin Publishing Corp. v. Columbia Artists Management, Inc.*, 443 F.2d 1159, 1162 (2d Cir. 1971) (holding management firm's authorization of clients' performances of copyrighted compositions to be contributory infringement).

318. A library is exempted from liability for the unsupervised use of reproducing equipment located on its premises provided that the equipment displays a copyright law notice. 17 U.S.C. § 108(f)(1). This exemption does not apply to the user of such equipment, and no other provider of equipment enjoys any statutory immunity. *See* 17 U.S.C. § 108(f)(2).

[i] Services

Contributory infringement liability may arise from providing services related to the infringement. Courts have found persons guilty, for instance, when they chose the material to be used in the direct infringer's work,[319] and vicarious liability when a defendant was responsible for the day-to-day activities where the infringement took place.[320]

In *A&M Records v. Napster, Inc.*,[321] the Ninth Circuit concluded that the defendant, a designer and operator of a system permitting computer users to transmit and retain digital music recordings, could be guilty of contributory infringement to the extent that it knew of specific infringing files, knew or should have known that such files were available on its system, and failed to act to prevent the distribution thereof. The court found the defendant could also be vicariously liable because it failed to patrol its system and preclude access to the files listed in its search index.

[ii] Equipment

Contributory infringement liability may also be based on supplying the equipment, instrumentalities, or other goods used in or related to the infringement. However, the U.S. Supreme Court in *Sony Corp. v. Universal City Studios, Inc.*[322] held manufacturers of videocassette recorders were not contributory infringers for providing the equipment used in the unauthorized reproduction of copyrighted works. Borrowing a patent law principle, the Court reasoned that manufacturers of staple articles of commerce also capable of substantial noninfringing uses should not be deemed infringers.[323] The Court wrote:

> [T]he sale of copying equipment, like the sale of other articles of commerce, does not constitute contributory infringement if the product is widely used for legitimate, unobjectionable purposes.

---

319. *See Universal Pictures Co. v. Harold Lloyd Corp.*, 162 F.2d 354, 366 (9th Cir. 1947) (rejecting defendant's argument that as an employee, he was not responsible for his employer's decision to use infringing material, in light of defendant's personal selection and appropriation of the protected material).

320. *See Boz Scaggs Music v. KND Corp.*, 491 F. Supp. 908, 913 (D. Conn. 1980) (finding defendant liable based on own admission of responsibility and control over radio performances of protected works).

321. *See supra* note 180.

322. *See supra* note 9.

323. *Id.* at 440.

Indeed, it need merely be capable of substantial non-infringing uses.[324]

The Court saw the key question as whether videocassette recorders were "capable of commercially significant non-infringing uses."[325] The Court held that in such an action, "the copyright holder may not prevail unless the relief that he seeks affects only his programs, or unless he speaks for virtually all copyright holders with an interest in the outcome."[326]

---

324. *Id.* at 442. The Court cited two principles of patent law, but used only one as the appropriate analogy for copyright:

> The Copyright Act does not expressly render anyone liable for infringement committed by another. In contrast, the Patent Act expressly brands anyone who "actively induces infringement of a patent" as an infringer, 35 U.S.C. § 271(b), and further imposes liability on certain individuals labeled "contributory" infringers, § 271(c).

Id. at 434–35. Section 271(b) of the Patent Act provides: "Whoever actively induces infringement of a patent shall be liable as an infringer." 35 U.S.C. § 271(b). Section 271(c) provides: "Whoever sells a component of a patented machine, manufacture, combination or composition, or a material or apparatus for use in practicing a patented process, constituting a material part of the invention, knowing the same to be especially made or especially adapted for use in an infringement of such patent, and not a staple article or commodity of commerce suitable for substantial non-infringing use, shall be liable as a contributory infringer." 35 U.S.C. § 271(c).

325. *Sony, supra* note 9, at 442. "In order to resolve that question, we need not explore *all* the different potential uses of the machine and determine whether or not they would constitute infringement. Rather, we need only consider whether on the basis of the facts as found by the District Court a significant number of them would be non-infringing." *Id.* The Court declined to "give precise content" to the issue of how much use is needed to rise to the level of "commercially significant." *See id.*

The four dissenting justices did not agree that the patent "staple article of commerce" doctrine of contributory infringement was applicable to copyright law. *See Sony, supra* note 9, at 490–91 n.41 (Blackmun, J., dissenting) ("[t]he doctrine of contributory patent infringement has been the subject of attention by the courts and by Congress . . . and has been codified since 1952, . . . but was never mentioned during the copyright law revision process as having any relevance to contributory *copyright* infringement"); *see also id.* at 491 (disagreeing that "this technical judge-made doctrine of patent law, based in part on considerations irrelevant to the field of copyright . . . should be imported wholesale into copyright law. Despite their common constitutional source, . . . patent and copyright protections have not developed in a parallel fashion, and this Court in copyright cases in the past has borrowed patent concepts only sparingly.") Recognizing the "concerns underlying the 'staple article of commerce' doctrine," the dissent concluded that "if a *significant* portion of the product's use is *non-infringing*, the manufacturers and sellers cannot be held contributorily liable for the product's infringing uses." *See id.* at 491 (Blackmun, J., dissenting).

326. *Id.* at 446.

Other actions against producers or providers of the instrumentalities of infringement since *Sony* generally have been more successful, however.[327] In the most recent case, the U.S. Supreme Court ruled that the distributors of two popular file-sharing programs (often used on the Internet to swap copyrighted music and songs) could be liable for copyright infringement because they distributed their product "with the object of promoting its use to infringe copyright, as shown by clear expression or other affirmative steps taken to foster infringement."[328] Similarly, the court in *Sega Enterprises Ltd. v. MAPHIA* issued a preliminary injunction against a bbs operator who sold special copiers, the "only substantial use" of which was to copy Sega's video games.[329] The court found Sega had established a *prima facie* case of contributory infringement based on the bbs operator's "advertising, sale and distribution" of these products.[330]

[d] Civil Remedies

Various remedies are available to copyright holders in infringement actions. Such owners may seek a preliminary or permanent injunction to prevent or restrain infringement.[331] Courts generally grant permanent injunctions where liability is established and the threat of wrongdoing continues.[332] Courts may also order all copies impounded any time an action is pending.[333] As part of a final judgment, the court may also direct the destruction (or any other "reasonable disposition") of these infringing items.[334]

---

327. *See, e.g., Vault Corp. v. Quaid Software Ltd., supra* note 167 (seller of computer programs that defeat anti-copying protection is not liable as contributory infringer because programs can be used to enable user to make legal archival copies of copyrighted computer programs under Section 117, which the court found to be a substantial noninfringing use). *But see RCA Records v. All-Fast Systems, Inc.*, 594 F. Supp. 335 (S.D.N.Y. 1984) (operator is liable for contributory infringement based on its provision of sound recording facilities where public could make unauthorized phonorecords).

328. *Metro-Goldwyn-Mayer Studios, Inc., et al. v. Grokster, Ltd., et al.*, 545 U.S. 913, 914 (2005). The Court distinguished *Sony* on the basis that nothing therein "requires courts to ignore evidence of intent to promote infringement if such evidence exists." *Sony, supra* note 9, at 439. *See* Chapter Three, Section 3.3[6][e], for a more detailed discussion of the popularity of these "peer-to-peer" systems on college campuses and recent legislative and administrative attempts to halt the use thereof.

329. *Sega, supra* note 180, at 685.

330. *See id.* at 687. The court found there was "no need to make archival copies of [Sega's] ROM game cartridges" because the "ROM cartridge format is not susceptible to breakdown" and Sega would replace defective cartridges. *Id.* at 685. The court also found it was unlikely customers would buy the copiers, at a cost of $350, for the purpose of backing up Sega's video game programs, which sold for $30 to $70 each. *Id.* at 685.

331. *See* 17 U.S.C. § 502.

332. *Superhype Publishing, Inc. v. Vasiliou*, 838 F. Supp. 1220, 1226 (S.D. Ohio 1993).

333. *See* 17 U.S.C. § 503(a).

334. *See* 17 U.S.C. § 503(b).

Before a final judgment is rendered, a copyright owner may elect to recover actual damages and profits of the infringer or be awarded statutory damages.[335] Actual damages include the owner's losses plus any profits made by the infringer (excluding those factored into calculating losses).[336] Conversely, statutory damages range between $750 to $30,000 per work infringed.[337] If an infringer can show he or she was not aware and had no reason to believe the activity was illegal, the court may find "innocent infringement."[338] Such a finding is a factual determination and does not absolve the defendant of guilt.[339] It does, however, give the court discretion to significantly reduce the damage award.[340]

If a copyright owner can demonstrate the defendant's infringement was willful, the court may increase statutory damages up to a maximum of $150,000.[341] "Willful" infringement means the defendant had knowledge

---

335. 17 U.S.C. § 504. For unpublished works, statutory damages are available only if the infringement occurred after the effective date of registration of the work. *See* 17 U.S.C. § 412(1). For published works, statutory damages are available if the work was registered within three months of its publication or any time before the date of infringement. *See* 17 U.S.C. § 412(2). This right is somewhat circumscribed by the fact that in 1998, the U.S. Supreme Court held there is a constitutional right to a jury trial on the question of statutory damages awarded in a copyright case. *See Feltner v. Columbia Pictures Television, Inc.,* 523 U.S. 340 (1998).

336. *See* 17 U.S.C. § 504(b).

337. *See* 17 U.S.C. § 504(c)(1).

338. 17 U.S.C. § 504(c)(2).

339. *D.C. Comics Inc. v. Mini Gift Shop*, 912 F.2d 29, 35 (2d Cir. 1990); *Innovative Networks, Inc. v. Satellite Airlines Ticketing, Inc.*, 871 F. Supp. 709, 721 (S.D.N.Y. 1995). However, the court is required to remit statutory damages if (1) the infringer "believed and had reasonable grounds for believing" that the use was a fair use, and (2) the infringer was a nonprofit educational institution, library, or archives (or its employee or agent) and infringed the reproduction right or a public broadcasting entity (or a person who "as a regular part of the nonprofit activities" of a public broadcasting entity) that infringed by performing a published nondramatic literary work or reproducing a transmission program embodying a performance of such work. *See* 17 U.S.C. § 504(c)(2).

340. *See* 17 U.S.C. § 504(c)(2) ("where the infringer sustains the burden of proving, and the court finds, that such infringer was not aware and had no reason to believe that his or her acts constituted an infringement of copyright, the court . . . may reduce the award of statutory damages to a sum of not less than $200"); *D.C. Comics Inc., supra* note 339, at 35 (defendant's lack of business sophistication and absence of copyright notice on copies were basis for a finding of innocent infringement and statutory damages of only $200). A person who is misled and innocently infringes by relying on the lack of a copyright notice on a copy of a work that was lawfully publicly distributed before March 1, 1989, is not liable for any damages (actual or statutory) for infringements committed before actual notice of registration of the work is received. 17 U.S.C. § 405(b). The court may allow, however, the recovery of any of the infringer's profits attributable to the infringement. *Id.*

341. *See* 17 U.S.C. § 504(c)(2).

his activity was illegal or recklessly disregarded the possibility thereof.[342] In copyright cases, judges have discretion to allow the recovery of court costs by or against any party other than the United States or its officers.[343] Courts may also award reasonable attorney's fees to the prevailing party under certain circumstances.[344]

[e] Criminal Offenses

Criminal sanctions may be levied against infringers if their actions were willful and taken for commercial advantage or private financial gain.[345] Any criminal proceedings must commence within three years after the wrongful act took place. If the defendant is convicted, the court must order the forfeiture and destruction (or other disposition) of all infringing copies and "all implements, devices, or equipment" used in the manufacture thereof.[346] The law leaves a loophole for certain nonmonetary violations, however. In *United States v. LaMacchia*,[347] a university student provided clandestine bbs locations on the Internet for the receipt and distribution of copyrighted software. Since no profit was derived from his actions, he could not be charged criminally and the court dismissed his indictment.[348]

---

342. *Twin Peaks Prods., Inc. v. Publications Int'l, Ltd., supra* note 208, at 1382; *Video Views, Inc. v. Studio 21, Ltd.*, 925 F.2d 1010, 1020 (7th Cir.), *cert. denied*, 502 U.S. 861 (1991).

343. 17 U.S.C. § 505.

344. *Id.; see also Roth v. Pritikin*, 787 F.2d 54, 57 (2d Cir. 1986) (attorney's fees generally awarded to prevailing plaintiffs because Copyright Act is intended to encourage suits to redress infringement); *Chi-boy Music v. Charlie Club, Inc.*, 930 F.2d 1224, 1230 (7th Cir. 1991) (attorney's fees and costs serve to deter infringement, dissuade defendant's disdain for copyright law, and encourage plaintiffs to bring colorable claims against infringers). No attorney's fees may be awarded for infringement of an unpublished work occurring before its registration. 17 U.S.C. § 412(1). In the case of published works, attorney's fees may be awarded if the infringement occurred after registration or at any time if registration was made within three months of first publication. 17 U.S.C. § 412(2).

345. *See* 17 U.S.C. § 506(a).

346. 17 U.S.C. § 506(b).

347. 871 F. Supp. 535 (D. Mass. 1994).

348. The indictment alleged that the resultant loss of revenue to the copyright owners was in excess of $1,000,000 over a period of approximately six weeks. The defendant would appear, nevertheless, to have committed many civil infringements. In 1997, Congress partially closed this loophole by enacting the No Electronic Theft Act (NET Act) (Pub. L. No. 105–147, 111 Stat. 2673 (1997)) permitting criminal prosecution of those who commit acts detrimental to copyright owners without necessarily personally benefiting therefrom. The NET Act imposes liability on persons who willfully infringe copyrights by the "reproduction or distribution, including by electronic means, during any 180-day period, or 1 or more copies or phonorecords of 1 or more copyrighted works, which have a total retail value of more than $1,000." 17 U.S.C. § 506(a)(2).

The Copyright Act also makes certain noninfringements criminal acts, including

- the placement on any article, with fraudulent intent, of a copyright notice a person knows to be false;[349]
- the public distribution or importation for public distribution, with fraudulent intent, of any article containing a copyright notice the distributor or importer knows to be false;[350]
- the removal or alteration, with fraudulent intent, of any notice of copyright on a copyrighted work;[351] and
- intentional false representation of a material fact in an application for copyright registration or in any written statement filed in connection therewith.[352]

[f] Defenses

The United States Supreme Court has written that "[a] successful defense of a copyright infringement action may further the policies of the Copyright Act every bit as much as a successful prosecution of an infringement claim by the holder of the copyright."[353] A number of legal and equitable defenses are available for infringement actions, of which fair use is the most common.[354] Others include misuse of copyright by the owner thereof,[355] abandonment of copyright,[356] estoppel, collateral estoppel, laches, res judicata, acquiescence, and unclean hands.

Generally, a claim of innocent infringement is not a defense against a finding of wrongdoing. An innocent infringer remains liable for his or her conduct, but a court may reduce or, in some instances, remit altogether the

---

349. 17 U.S.C. § 506(c). The penalties in Section 506(c) apply with regard to copyright notices or "words of the same purport." *Id.*

350. *Id.*

351. 17 U.S.C. § 506(d).

352. 17 U.S.C. § 506(e).

353. *See Fogerty, supra* note 6, at 1029.

354. *See* discussion of the fair use defense, *supra* Section 2.1[7][a].

355. *See F.E.L. Publications, Ltd. v. Catholic Bishop of Chicago*, 754 F.2d 216, 220–22 (7th Cir. 1985); *but see Redd Horne, Inc., supra* note 186, at 161–62.

356. *See Pacific & Southern Co., Inc. v. Duncan*, 572 F. Supp. 1186 (N.D. Ga. 1983), *aff'd*, 744 F.2d 1490 (11th Cir. 1984).

amount of damages.[357] However, under certain, specified circumstances, a good faith reliance on a presumption that the term of protection for a work had expired is a complete defense to an infringement claim.[358]

As noted earlier, certain incidental uses of a work fall short of constituting infringement, such as the reproduction of a de minimis portion thereof. In those cases, the plaintiff will not be able to sustain its burden of proof and no defense will be necessary.[359] In other cases, a defendant may successfully assert that the activity is noninfringing due to the existence of a license, whether statutory, negotiated, or implied.[360] Finally, one defense of long-standing existence, but of newfound potency, is that of sovereign immunity. The next section explores this doctrine in greater detail.

---

357. *See* 17 U.S.C. § 504(c)(2). If a proper copyright notice was affixed to the published copy to which the infringer had access, the court may not give any weight to a claim of innocent infringement in mitigation of damages, except in limited circumstances involving certain infringers (including nonprofit educational institutions and libraries) who violated certain exclusive rights and who believed, and had reasonable grounds for believing, that the use was a fair use. *See* §§ 401(d), 504(c)(2); *see also* 17 U.S.C. § 405(b) (effect on innocent infringers of omission of copyright notice on copies publicly distributed before March 1, 1989).

358. *See* 17 U.S.C. § 302(e) (after a period of 95 years from first publication of a work, or 120 years from its creation, whichever is shorter, a person who obtains from the Copyright Office a certified report that the records relating to the deaths of authors disclose nothing to indicate the author is living, or died less than 70 years before, may presume the author has been dead for at least 70 years, and good faith reliance on such presumption is a complete defense).

359. The de minimis doctrine is not found in the actual text of the Copyright Act, but is instead rooted in case law. Essentially, it provides that where unauthorized copying is sufficiently trivial, "the law will not impose legal consequences." *Ringgold v. Black Entertainment Television*, 126 F.3d 70, 74 (2d Cir. 1997). *See also Knickerbocker Toy Co. v. Azrak-Hamway Int'l, Inc.*, 668 F.2d 699, 703 (2d Cir. 1982) (denying relief under de minimis doctrine where defendant had made a copy of plaintiff's work, but copy was never used); *American Geophysical Union v. Texaco, Inc.*, *supra* note 215, at 916 (suggesting that if photocopying for individual use in research is de minimis, it would not constitute an infringement); Pierre N. Leval, *Nimmer Lecture: Fair Use Rescued*, 44 UCLA L. Rev. 1449, 1457–58 (1997).

360. A nonexclusive license may be implied from conduct. *See Effects Assocs., Inc. v. Cohen*, 908 F.2d 555, 558 (9th Cir. 1990), *cert. denied*, 498 U.S. 1103 (1991); *MacLean Assocs., Inc. v. Wm. M. Mercer-Meidinger-Hansen, Inc.*, 952 F.2d 769, 779 (3d Cir. 1991); *see also* 3 *Nimmer on Copyright* § 10.03[A]. Implied licenses, like oral licenses, are always nonexclusive in nature and may be limited in scope. *See Oddo v. Ries*, 743 F.2d 630, 634 (9th Cir. 1984); *Gilliam v. American Broadcasting Cos.*, 538 F.2d 14, 19–21 (2d Cir. 1976). For instance, delivery of a work by the copyright owner to the moderator of a newsgroup may imply a license to reproduce and distribute copies of that work to the newsgroup's subscribers, but may not be evidence of an implied license to reproduce and distribute copies to other newsgroups.

[9] Sovereign Immunity

[a] General

The doctrine of sovereign immunity is grounded in the Eleventh Amendment to the United States Constitution. For over 200 years, however, it was generally assumed that states and their instrumentalities and agencies, such as state colleges and universities, were subject, like any other private party, to legal claims alleging patent, trademark, and copyright infringement. In 1999, the United States Supreme Court altered those assumptions by expanding the scope of the sovereign immunity doctrine and correspondingly narrowing the powers of the federal government.

[b] Background of the Litigation³⁶¹

[i] Parties and Claims

In two companion cases known, respectively, as *College Savings Bank v. Florida Prepaid Postsecondary Education Expense Board*,³⁶² and *Florida Prepaid Postsecondary Education Expense Board v. College Savings Bank*,³⁶³ the U.S. Supreme Court held that states are immune from lawsuits for patent and trademark infringement brought in federal court by virtue of the Eleventh Amendment. The cases involved College Savings Bank, a New Jersey financial institution ("College Savings"), that offered and sold certificates of deposit designed to finance the costs of a college education for the purchaser's children.

College Savings held a patent on the methodology of administering these certificates and brought suit against Florida Prepaid Postsecondary Education Expense Board, an agency of the State of Florida ("Florida Prepaid"), for allegedly infringing this patent by operating a similar tuition prepayment program. College Savings also alleged Florida Prepaid had violated Section 43(a) of the Trademark Act of 1946 (the "Lanham Act")³⁶⁴ by making misstatements about the former's tuition savings plan in agency brochures and annual reports.

[ii] Arguments

In court, Florida Prepaid moved to dismiss the claims against it on grounds they were barred by the Eleventh Amendment and the protection of sovereign immunity granted to the states. The two cases, originally

---

361. Portions of this section are excerpted from S. Armatas, *State Educational Institutions Granted Immunity for Patent and Trademark Infringement*, ITPE J., Sept. 14, 1999, at 6.

362. 119 S. Ct. 790 (1999) (hereinafter *College Savings*).

363. 119 S. Ct. 2199 (1999) (hereinafter *Florida Prepaid*).

364. 15 U.S.C. § 1125(a).

filed in federal court, wound their way to the U.S. Supreme Court, where College Savings argued Congress had validly abrogated Florida's sovereign immunity in 1992 when it passed the Patent and Plant Variety Protection Remedy Clarification Act ("Patent Remedy Act").[365]

Prior to that, the U.S. Supreme Court had ruled congressional abrogation of state sovereign immunity would be recognized only if the relevant federal statue was "unmistakably clear" that states were to be included in the defendant class.[366] Congress had enacted the Patent Remedy Act to do just that—specify that states, instrumentalities of states, and officers and employees thereof, acting in their official capacity, could be subject to suit in federal court by any person claiming patent infringement.

College Savings also alleged standing under the Trademark Remedy Clarification Act ("TRCA"),[367] also enacted by Congress in 1992, which subjected states and their instrumentalities to suits brought under Section 43(a) of the Lanham Act for false and misleading advertising. Both statutes were passed in response to earlier lower federal court rulings[368] that had limited plaintiffs' rights in suing state entities.[369] Florida Prepaid responded that its sovereign immunity was not validly abrogated under either statute, because Congress had overstepped its authority when relying upon Section 5 of the Fourteenth Amendment as the basis for enacting such legislation.

Section 1 of the Fourteenth Amendment, more commonly known as the "Due Process Clause," provides no state shall "deprive any person of life, liberty, or property, without due process of law." Section 5 of the amendment reads: "Congress shall have power to enforce, by appropriate legislation, the provisions of this article." In *Seminole Tribe of Florida v. Florida*,[370] the Supreme Court found the enforcement power of Section 5 to be the sole source of constitutional authority from which Congress could abrogate state sovereign immunity. In short, Congress viewed patent and trademark rights granted under federal law as legitimate "property" interests eligible for protection under the Fourteenth Amendment

---

365. 35 U.S.C. §§ 271(h), 296(a).

366. *See Seminole Tribe of Florida v. Florida,* 517 U.S. 44 (1996).

367. 106 Stat. 3567.

368. *See, e.g., Chew v. California,* 893 F.2d 331 (1989).

369. Pub. L. No. 102-560, preamble, 106 Stat. 4230 (1992); *see also* H.R. Rep. No. 101-960, pt. 1, pp. 7, 33 (1990); S. Rep. No. 102-280, pp. 1, 5–6 (1992). Section 271(h) now states: "As used in this section, the term 'whoever' includes any State, any instrumentality of a State, and any officer or employee of a State or instrumentality of a State acting in his official capacity."

370. *See supra* note 366.

against any person who infringed upon same, including states and their instrumentalities.

[c] The Supreme Court's Analysis

[i] Property Interests and Conduct

While acknowledging patents were legitimate property interests entitled to constitutional protection, the Supreme Court held that in order for Congress to invoke its Section 5 power, it had to *first*, specifically identify conduct transgressing the Fourteenth Amendment and *second*, tailor its legislative scheme proportionately to remedy or prevent such conduct.[371] In enacting the Patent Remedy Act, the Supreme Court found, however, that Congress had not met this burden because it had failed to delineate any pattern of preexisting patent infringement by the states.[372]

[ii] State Remedies

In addition, the Court ruled Congress had not taken into account the existence or adequacy of state remedies prior to enacting the legislation.[373] As such, the Court essentially found there was no deprivation of property

---

371. *See Florida Prepaid, supra* note 363, at 2206.

372. *Id.* at 2207.

373. The court acknowledged Congress did hear a limited amount of testimony to the effect that remedies available in some states were uncertain. *See, e.g., Patent Remedy Clarification Act: Hearing On H.R. 3886 before the Subcommittee on Courts, Intellectual Property and the Administration of Justice of the House Committee on the Judiciary,* 101st Cong., 2d Sess. 56 (1990) (hereinafter *PRCA House Hearing*) at 33 (statement of Robert Merges) ("Thus a patentee . . . would apparently have to draft her cause of action as a general tort claim—or perhaps one for restitution—to come within the statute. This might be impossible, or at least difficult under California law"); *Id.* at 43 ("It is true that you may have State remedies, alternative State remedies . . . . You could bring a deceit suit. You could try just a general unfair competition suit. A restitution is one that has occurred to me as a possible basis of recovery."); *Id.* at 34 ("Another problem with this approach is that it assumes that such state law remedies will be available in every state in which the patentee's product is sold. This may or may not be true."); *Id.* at 47 (statement of William Thompson) ("In this case there is no balance, since there are no—or at least there are not very effective patent remedies at the State level."); *Id.* at 57 ("The court in *Lane* [*v. First Nat. Bank of Boston,* 687 F. Supp. 11 (Mass. 1988),] pointed out that the appellant may be able to obtain money damages by recourse to the Massachusetts tort claims act or sue the state for deceit, conversion, or unfair competition under Massachusetts law. The court also noted a Massachusetts statute which provides that damages may be recovered from the state when private property is confiscated for a public purpose. While many states may have similar statutes, the courts' surmise that intellectual property infringement cases may be pursued in some state courts offer us little comfort."); *Id.* at 60 ("It sounds to me like it is a very difficult area to predict what would happen. There is a rich variety of potential causes of action, as the prior speaker [Merges] pointed out.").

"without due process" as claimants could have availed themselves of state law remedies in seeking redress against infringers.[374] The Court even more firmly dismissed College Savings' TRCA claims holding that neither the right to be "free from a business competitor's false advertising about its product" nor "secure in one's business interests" qualified as legitimate property interests under the Constitution.[375]

[iii] Intentional Acts

The Supreme Court also wrote that "a state actor's negligent act that causes unintended injury to a person's property does not 'deprive' that person of property within the meaning of the Due Process Clause."[376] In other words, the Court deemed intent to be an inherent prerequisite before a "deprivation" of property could be established. Because a claim for patent infringement does not require a showing of intent, the Court held the law's potential application was unduly broad.[377]

[iv] Waiver by Conduct

Lastly, the Court considered College Savings' assertion that Florida Prepaid's sovereign immunity was voluntarily waived by its willing participation in interstate commerce.[378] According to this theory, Florida Prepaid had constructively waived its immunity from suit by engaging in the voluntary and nonessential activity of selling and advertising a for-profit investment vehicle in interstate commerce. The Court rejected this argument by holding there was no recognized doctrine of constructive waiver and that sovereign immunity could be waived only through express statutory language.[379]

---

374. The State of Florida, for example, provides remedies to patent owners for alleged infringement on the part of the State. Aggrieved parties may pursue a legislative remedy through a claims bill for payment in full, Fla. Stat. § 11.065 (1997), or a judicial remedy through a takings or conversion claim, *see Jacobs Wind Electric Co. v. Florida Dept. of Transp.*, 626 So. 2d 1333 (Fla. 1993).

375. *College Savings Bank, supra* note 362, at 791.

376. *Florida Prepaid, supra* note 363, at 2209.

377. *See Daniels v. Williams*, 474 U.S. 327, 328 (1986). Actions predicated on direct patent infringement do not require any showing of intent to infringe; instead, knowledge and intent are considered only with respect to damages. *See* 35 U.S.C. § 271(a); 5 D. Chisum, *Patents* § 16.02[2] at 16–31 (1998) ("It is, of course, elementary, that an infringement may be entirely inadvertent and unintentional and without knowledge of the patent").

378. This theory arose out of the holding of the U.S. Supreme Court in *Parden v. Terminal Ry. of Ala. State Docks Dep't*, 377 U.S. 184 (1964).

379. *College Savings, supra* note 362, at 792. In essence, *College Savings* expressly overruled *Parden* and its implied waiver theory. As such, that theory is no longer available to support an Article I abrogation of Eleventh Amendment immunity.

[d] Impact

[i] Private Partnering

While seemingly a windfall for state colleges and universities, the *College Savings* and *Florida Prepaid* decisions may carry with them several unintended and negative consequences for these institutions, particularly those fostering distance learning programs. One result may be that private companies partnering with state universities in joint research projects or for delivering distance learning will be much more aggressive in seeking indemnification from their college partners for potential intellectual property infringement. The Supreme Court decision grants absolutely no protection to these private actors, and in fact may well leave them as the only exposed party in a successfully prosecuted intellectual property suit. If state universities are unable or unwilling to provide such indemnification or similar protection, these arrangements may become less prevalent.

[ii] State Impediments

Even those state colleges and universities willing to grant contractual protections to private parties may be precluded from doing so under local law. Some states already bar their agencies and instrumentalities from indemnifying private individuals and entities.[380] Even if permitted to enter into these arrangements, such contracts provide little comfort if the state defaults on its obligation and cannot be sued thereon. For instance, a number of states still have not abrogated their sovereign immunity from legal claims, and among those that have, the contours of this waiver vary widely.[381]

Again, without these protections, private companies stand as the only viable defendants in patent and trademark cases. While plaintiffs remain free to assert state law remedies in most jurisdictions, these causes of action are typically more difficult to sustain and document and often limit

---

380. *See, e.g., CSX Transp., Inc. v. City of Garden City*, No. 02-12261, slip op. at 4 (11th Cir. Mar. 27, 2003).

381. *See, e.g.*, Ala. Code § 41-9-60 (1991) (claims may only be brought administratively); W. Va. Const., art. VI § 35 ("The State of West Virginia shall never be made a defendant in any court of law or equity . . ."); Colo. Rev. Stat. § 24-10-106 (1998) (waiving immunity in tort claims only for injuries resulting from operation of a motor vehicle, operation of a public hospital or a correctional facility, the dangerous condition of public building, the dangerous condition of a public highway or road, a dangerous condition caused by snow or ice, or from the operation of any public utility facility); Minn. Stat. Ann. § 3.736 (Supp. 1998–1999) (waiver of immunity invalid when loss arises from state employee who exercises due care or performance or failure to perform discretionary duty); Md. Cts. & Jud. Proc. Code Ann. § 5–522(a)(5) (1998) (immunity not waived if a claim from a single occurrence exceeds $100,000).

the type and amount of recovery.[382] Since *College Savings* and *Florida Prepaid* effectively bar plaintiffs from bringing patent and trademark claims in federal court, the inability to proceed in a state forum leaves aggrieved owners with absolutely no remedy or recourse against state-affiliated infringers.

[iii] Copyright Matters

While the *College Savings* and *Florida Prepaid* decisions do not specifically address copyright infringement, their reasoning may be easily applied to such cases. In fact, in *Chavez v. Arte Publico Press*,[383] the Fifth Circuit Court of Appeals used the Supreme Court's analysis from *College Savings* and *Florida Prepaid* in dismissing a suit by an author claiming infringement of her book by the University of Houston, a state institution. In *Chavez*, the lower court considered whether Congress had authority to abrogate state sovereign immunity by enacting the Copyright Remedy Clarification Act (CRCA),[384] which explicitly required states to submit to suit in federal court for copyright violations.

Much as the U.S. Supreme Court had concluded in *Florida Prepaid* that "Congress identified no pattern of patent infringement by the States, let alone a pattern of constitutional violations,"[385] the *Chavez* court found the CRCA's legislative history exhibited similar deficiencies. For example, the court cited testimony before a House subcommittee in favor of the bill acknowledging that "the States are not going to get involved in wholesale violation of the copyright laws."[386] The court further noted that per a congressional request, the Copyright Office had previously reported on the nexus between states' copyright liability and the Eleventh Amendment. In that report, only seven incidents of state copyright infringement enabled by the Eleventh Amendment were documented.[387]

---

382. *See Chew v. California, supra* note 368, at 336 and *PRCA House Hearings* at 33 (statement of Robert Merges) ("In short, these [state] remedies are simply no substitute for patent infringement actions.").

383. 204 F.3d 601 (5th Cir. 2000).

384. Copyright Remedy Clarification Act, Pub. L. No. 101–553, 104 Stat. 2749 (1990) (codified at 17 U.S.C. §§ 501(a), 511).

385. *Florida Prepaid, supra* note 363, at 2207.

386. *Copyright Remedy Clarification Act and Copyright Office Report on Copyright Liability of States: Hearings Before the Subcomm. on Courts, Intellectual Property, and the Administration of Justice of the House Comm. on the Judiciary*, 101st Cong., 1st Sess. 53 (1989) (hereinafter *CRCA House Hearings*) (statement of Ralph Oman, Register of Copyrights, Library of Congress). In addition, the bill's sponsor stated that "thus far there have not been any significant number of wholesale takings of copyright rights by States or State entities." *Id.* at 48 (statement of Rep. Kastenmeier).

387. *Register of Copyrights, Copyright Liability of States and the Eleventh Amendment* 5–9 (1988).

As in *Florida Prepaid*, the *Chavez* court next considered whether Congress had adequately explored the existence and adequacy of state law remedies for aggrieved copyright owners.[388] It found the legislative histories of the PRCA and CRCA were again parallel. In each case, the court concluded Congress had barely reviewed the availability of state causes of action for infringement and noted only two references to state remedies in the act's legislative history.[389] Therefore, when enacting the CRCA, the Fifth Circuit found Congress had done nothing "to confine the reach of the Act by limiting the remedy to certain types of infringement . . . or providing for suits only against States with questionable remedies or a high incidence of infringement."[390]

Lastly, just as the U.S. Supreme Court had ruled in *Florida Prepaid*, the *Chavez* court held that for there to be a deprivation of property under the Due Process Clause of the Fourteenth Amendment, the act causing deprivation had to be intentional; a negligent act was not sufficient. The Fifth Circuit noted copyright actions, like those for patent infringement, ordinarily require no showing of intent. Instead, knowledge and purpose are relevant in regard only to damages.[391] As such, the *Chavez* court found that since the CRCA's coverage was not limited solely to constitutional violations, it represented an improper exercise of congressional power.

The *Chavez* decision may well have a chilling effect on a school's ability to obtain copyrighted material. Educational institutions often seek to license such works for use in regular classroom and distance learning settings. The remarkable growth of digital technology and the ensuing ability to quickly, accurately, and widely reproduce the texts and images of others has already caused many creators and authors to be reticent in forging such dealings. The prospect that these owners could find themselves without a remedy when a state college or university, either willfully or unintentionally,

---

388. *Florida Prepaid, supra* note 363, at 2208.

389. *See CRCA House Hearings* at 51 (statement of James Healy, Vice President of Enterprise Media).

390. *Citing Florida Prepaid, supra* note 363, at 2210.

391. *See* 1 N. Boorstyn, *Boorstyn on Copyright* § 12.15 (1999) ("Although defendant's innocent intent is no defense to an infringement action, it may affect recoverable damages."); *Compare Florida Prepaid, supra* note 363, at 2209 ("Actions predicated on direct patent infringement . . . do not require any showing of intent to infringe; instead, knowledge and intent are considered only with respect to damages."). In addition, Mr. Oman, the Register of Copyrights, acknowledged most copyright infringement by states is unintentional, stating: "[the States] would want [immunity] only as a shield for the State treasury from the occasional error or misunderstanding or innocent infringement." *CRCA House Hearings* at 8.

infringes on their copyright may further dissuade them from entering into these types of arrangements.[392]

2.2 INTERNATIONAL IMPLICATIONS OF COPYRIGHT LAW

[1] International Framework

The advent and growth of the Internet and digital technology have made the world a much smaller place. This phenomenon has also created the need to evaluate the applicability of copyright in view of the complexities of international commerce in information and educational products.

In examining the field, one must first understand there is no such thing as an international copyright, but instead an international system establishing norms for protection to be implemented in each country. Several international treaties link the major trading nations and establish both minimum standards for protecting, under their own laws, each others' copyrighted works, and the basis upon which such protection is extended (e.g., national treatment). The situation is further complicated by the existence of two major legal traditions that apply to the protection of copyrighted works. To begin to comprehend the underpinnings of the international copyright system and multinational treaties, it is necessary to have a basic appreciation of these two major legal regimes.[393]

The United States and other countries following the Anglo-American or "common law" tradition have "copyright" systems aimed to promote the creation of new works for the public benefit by protecting the author's economic rights. This is seen as part of the basic "social contract" between the state and its citizens and is reflected in the patent and copyright clause of the U.S. Constitution. The premise is that providing such protection induces the creation of more works, which will "promote the progress of

---

392. Senator Patrick Leahy of Vermont has on several occasions introduced a bill in Congress, entitled the "Intellectual Property Protection Restoration Act," to restore federal remedies for violations of intellectual property rights by the states. *See, e.g.,* S. 1611, 107th Cong., 1st Sess. (2001). Senator Leahy describes his legislation as providing a damages remedy to redress constitutional violations and ensure the availability of the full range of prospective equitable relief. *See* 145 Cong. Rec. S13552-04, S13558 (daily ed. Oct. 29, 1999) (statement of Sen. Leahy).

393. *See generally* S. Stewart, *International Copyright and Neighbouring Rights* (1989). Stewart presents a summary of international copyright principles and synopses of the copyright laws of several countries. Stewart also identifies socialist copyright laws as a category. However, since the demise of the USSR, many of the former socialist countries have moved to enact modern copyright legislation. The copyright laws of the People's Republic of China and Russia follow the civil-law model.

science" and redound to the public benefit. "So deeply did the Framers, in their founding document, embrace the concept of 'progress' advanced through devotion to intellectual labor, that they mention it 24 separate times in the *Federalist Papers*."[394]

Countries following the civil law tradition, however, regard authors' rights as natural human rights, or part of one's right of personality. As part of this tradition, the author's "economic" and "moral" rights are both protected.[395] Moral rights, as reflected in Article 6*bis* of the Berne Convention (discussed later), include a creator's right to be recognized as the author of a work and to object to those uses thereof that bring dishonor or discredit on him or her. Often moral rights reflect a part of the author's personality and are neither transferable nor waivable. Economic rights, in some instances, may be subordinated to moral rights. Under these systems, only original works, because they reflect the personality of the author, are entitled to authors' rights protection. Productions not meeting this originality requirement, but still meriting some protection, are protected under a system of "neighboring rights."

Needless to say, with such divergent theoretical bases, the copyright and authors' rights systems are sometimes in conflict. One area of dispute is the nature and level of protections for owners of neighboring rights. Neighboring rights are similar to the rights protected by copyright or authors' rights and are primarily used to protect performers, broadcasters, and producers of phonograms. Under the American system, many privileges covered under neighboring rights are protected the same as copyright. For example, under U.S. law, recording producers and performers are regarded as joint authors of sound recordings. Under *droit d'auteur* (or authors' rights) systems, such producers and performers are protected by neighboring rights that are entirely separate and distinct from the higher-level rights granted authors.

---

394. E. Meese, III, "Copyright is Copyright is Copyright," The Heritage Foundation Newsletter (Jan. 10, 2005), http://www.heritage.org/Press/commentary/ed010305b.cfm.

395. Stewart, *supra* note 393, at 6. In some common law countries, moral rights are protected by a combination of statutory provisions and common law. In the United States, for instance, this protection is found in federal legislation, such as the Lanham Act and the Copyright Act, various state legislative provisions, and the common law of privacy and defamation. *See Final Report of the Ad Hoc Working Group on U.S. Adherence to the Berne Convention*, 10 Colum. VLA J.L. & Arts 513, 548–57 (1986); 2 *Nimmer on Copyright* § 8D.02[A].

[2] International Treaties and Agreements

[a] The World Intellectual Property Organization (WIPO)

The WIPO is responsible for administering and revising the international intellectual property treaties.[396] The principal WIPO copyright and neighboring rights treaties include the Berne Convention for the Protection of Literary and Artistic Works ("Berne Convention"),[397] the International Convention for the Protection of Performers, Producers of Phonograms and Broadcasting Organizations ("Rome Convention"),[398] and the Geneva Convention for the Protection of Producers of Phonograms Against the Unauthorized Reproduction of their Phonograms ("Geneva Phonograms Convention").[399]

The United Nations Educational, Scientific and Cultural Organization (UNESCO) and the WIPO jointly administer the Universal Copyright Convention,[400] which is a lower-level treaty negotiated following World War II largely to bring the United States into the world of international copyright. Virtually all members of the Universal Copyright Convention

---

396. There were 184 members of the Convention Establishing the World Intellectual Property Organization (WIPO) as of November 1, 2007. Done at Stockholm on July 14, 1967; entered into force for the United States on August 25, 1970. 21 UST 1749; TIAS 6932; 828 UNTS 3. A copy of this convention is available at http://www.wipo.int/treaties/en/convention/trtdocs_wo029.html. WIPO also administers the Paris Convention for the Protection of Industrial Property (Stockholm 1967), which is not discussed herein.

397. Berne Convention (with Appendix) for the Protection of Literary and Artistic Works of September 9, 1886; completed at Paris on May 4, 1896; revised at Berlin on November 13, 1908; completed at Berne on March 20, 1914; revised at Rome on June 2, 1928; at Brussels on June 26, 1948; at Stockholm on July 14, 1967; and at Paris on July 24, 1971; amended at Paris on July 24, 1979. Done at Paris on July 24, 1971; entered into force for the United States on March 1, 1989. A copy of the Berne Convention is available at http://www.law.cornell.edu/treaties/berne/overview.html.

398. There were 86 members of the Rome Convention as of November 1, 2007, of which the United States is not one. The Rome Convention is jointly administered by WIPO, the International Labor Organization (ILO), and the United Nations Educational, Scientific and Cultural Organization (UNESCO). A copy of the Rome Convention is available at http://portal.unesco.org/culture/en/ev.php-URL ID=14207&URL_DO=DO_TOPIC&URL_SECTION=201.html.

399. Done at Geneva on October 29, 1971; entered into force on April 18, 1973; for the United States on March 10, 1974. 25 UST 309; TIAS 7808; 888 UNTS 67. There were 76 members of the Geneva Phonograms Convention as of November 1, 2007. A copy of the Geneva Phonograms Convention is available at http://www.wipo.org/treaties/ip/geneva/geneva.html.

400. Universal Copyright Convention, as revised, with two protocols annexed thereto. Done at Paris on July 24, 1971; entered into force on July 10, 1974. 25 UST 1341; TIAS 7868. As of November 1, 2007, there were 164 members of the Universal Copyright Convention. A copy of this convention is available at http://www.cni.org/docs/infopols/US.universal.copyright.conv.html.

are also parties to the Berne Convention, and by the terms thereof, the Berne Convention governs relations between members of both.

The Berne Convention is the principal international copyright treaty and was joined by the United States in 1989.[401] While generally viewed as providing adequate international standards of protection, it has yet to be updated to account for advances in electronic communications and information technology. Its members come from the world's two major legal traditions—the Anglo-American common law copyright system and the European civil law *droit d'auteur* approach. However, despite its level of detail and because it must accommodate differing legal systems, its standards may be insufficient to deal with today's reality regarding the digital dissemination of copyrighted works.

The primary treaty for the protection of neighboring rights, the Rome Convention, was adopted in 1961. It protects producers of phonograms against unauthorized reproduction of their works, and artists from certain reproductions and fixations of their performances. It also provides limited rights for broadcasting organizations. The Rome Convention requires these rights last for twenty years and protects against certain "secondary uses" of phonograms, such as broadcasting. The United States is not a signatory thereto. The Geneva Phonograms Convention, to which the United States does belong, protects phonograms against unauthorized reproduction and distribution for a minimum of twenty years.

Since many of these treaties have not been revised in decades, their provisions may not always be easily adaptable to today's digital technology. To address these concerns, the WIPO has convened a Committee of Experts on a Possible Protocol to the Berne Convention to account for developments since 1971 and a Committee of Experts on a Possible New Instrument for the Protection of Performers and Producers of Phonograms to consider providing enhanced rights for such persons.[402]

[b] The World Trade Organization

In addition to the WIPO, other international fora now play significant roles in intellectual property policy formulation. The TRIPs Agreement[403]

---

401. As of November 1, 2007, there were 163 signatories to the Berne Convention.

402. WIPO, Press Release PR/98/127 (June 12, 1998), http://www.wipo.int/pressroom/en/releases/1998/p.127htm.

403. The full name is the Agreement on Trade-Related Aspects of Intellectual Property Rights. The TRIPs Agreement forms part of the WTO Agreement, which was concluded at the end of the GATT Uruguay Round in 1994. The TRIPs Agreement was entered into force on January 1, 1995. A copy is available at http://www.wto.org/english/tratop_e/trips_e/t_agm0_e.htm.

is administered by the World Trade Organization (WTO) and sets significant standards for the protection of copyright and related rights. Perhaps most importantly, it contains provisions ensuring member countries fully implement its obligations. Similar to the U.S. Copyright Act, the TRIPs Agreement reiterates a basic principle in the international arena that copyright protection extends only to expression and not ideas, methods of operation, or mathematical concepts.[404]

Article 10 of the TRIPs Agreement confirms computer programs are "literary works" under the Berne Convention and requires each WTO country to protect them as such. It also requires copyright protection for compilations of data or other material deemed original by reason of its selection or arrangement. Article 11 requires member countries to provide exclusive rights for authors to allow or prohibit commercial rental to the public of copies of their computer programs and cinematographic works. The obligation as to the latter need not be implemented unless rental has led to widespread copying having a material effect on the author's exclusive right of reproduction.

Article 12 of the TRIPs Agreement provides minimum terms of protection for copyrighted works. The term for most works is the life of the author plus fifty years. Whenever a term is not linked to the life of a person, it must be a minimum of fifty years, except for works of applied art or photographs. Article 9(2) of the Berne Convention bars imposition of limitations on, or exceptions to, the reproduction right except when not in conflict with normal exploitation of the work. Article 13 widens the scope of this provision to all exclusive rights in copyright, thus narrowly circumscribing the limitations and exceptions that WTO member countries may impose.[405]

Article 14 of the TRIPs Agreement goes beyond the obligations of the Rome Convention and the Geneva Phonograms Convention and requires member countries to provide sound recording producers a fifty-year term of protection and the rights to authorize or prohibit the direct or indirect reproduction and commercial rental of their sound recordings. However, a WTO member country that on April 15, 1994, had an equitable remuneration payment system to compensate for rental of recordings is permitted to retain that system.[406]

The TRIPS Agreement requires WTO countries to make it possible for performers to prevent unauthorized sound recording or reproduction of

---

404. This fundamental principle is set forth Section 1, Article 9(2) of the TRIPs Agreement and in Section 102(b) of the Copyright Act.

405. This approach is consistent with Section 107 of the U.S. Copyright Act (relating to fair use of copyrighted works).

406. Only Japan and Switzerland qualify under this exception.

their live performances. Broadcasting organizations are accorded similar rights, although member countries have the option of providing protection consistent with the Rome Convention or giving owners of works broadcast the right to prevent the same acts. The agreement also makes Article 18 of the Berne Convention regarding copyright protection of existing works applicable to sound recordings.

[3] Copyright Compared to Author's Rights

Countries with common law copyright systems, such as the United States, and those with authors' rights systems, such as most nations in Europe, have sometimes defined the rights of certain categories of owners differently. For instance, European performers, both in audiovisual works and sound recordings, enjoy certain statutory rights that American performers do not. In the United States, these performers' rights are guaranteed under contractual or collective bargaining agreements between the audiovisual producers and performers' unions. Broadcasters have been concerned that harmonization of protection along European lines may lead to the establishment of performance rights in all sound recordings. A consequence of this divergence is that American performers and producers have been denied the ability to share in remuneration for the use of their products and performances in some countries.

[4] National Treatment

The principle of national treatment is the cornerstone of the great international intellectual property treaties—Berne and Paris. It is also the foundation of international trade treaties, such as the General Agreement on Tariffs and Trade and the recently established WTO. As a general matter, this principle means that under a nation's laws, a foreigner enjoys no lesser rights and benefits than a citizen of that country receives, subject to the specific terms of the relevant international conventions. In copyright terms, for example, a German work for which copyright enforcement is sought in the United States would be treated under U.S. law exactly as if it were a domestic work.

This is somewhat different from the concept of reciprocity, which means the United States would grant a foreigner a specific right only if his or her country granted U.S. citizens the same right. Under this scenario, the work of a German citizen would be protected under U.S. law only to the extent German law provided the same, or at least equivalent, protection to works of an American citizen.

[a] The Berne Convention

Articles 5(1) and 5(2) of the Berne Convention establish the principle of national treatment for works protected by copyright.[407] Under Article 5(1), member countries must grant citizens of member states national treatment for those rights specifically covered by the convention. While this principle clearly applies to the minimum rights set forth in the convention,[408]

---

407. Article 5 provides:

> (1) Authors shall enjoy, in respect of works for which they are protected under this Convention, in countries of the Union other than the country of origin, the rights which their respective laws do now or may hereafter grant to their nationals, as well as the rights specially granted by this Convention.

> (2) The enjoyment and the exercise of these rights shall not be subject to any formality; such enjoyment and such exercise shall be independent of the existence of protection in the country of origin of the work. Consequently, apart from the provisions of this Convention, the extent of protection, as well as the means of redress afforded to the author to protect his rights, shall be governed exclusively by the laws of the country where protection is claimed.

> (3) Protection in the country of origin is governed by domestic law. However, when the author is not a national of the country of origin of the work for which he is protected under this Convention, he shall enjoy in that country the same rights as national authors.

> (4) The country of origin shall be considered to be:

>> (a) in the case of works first published in a country of the Union, that country; in the case of works published simultaneously in several countries of the Union which grant different terms of protection, the country whose legislation grants the shortest term of protection;

>> (b) in the case of works published simultaneously in a country outside the Union and in a country of the Union, the latter country;

>> (c) in the case of unpublished works or of works first published in a country outside the Union, without simultaneous publication in a country of the Union, the country of the Union of which the author is a national, provided that:

>>> (i) when these are cinematographic works the maker of which has his headquarters or his habitual residence in a country of the Union, the country of origin shall be that country, and

>>> (ii) when these are works of architecture erected in a country of the Union or other artistic works incorporated in a building or other structure located in a country of the Union, the country of origin shall be that country.

408. *See* World Intellectual Property Organization, BCP/CE/III/3, *Report of the Committee of Experts on a Possible Protocol to the Berne Convention, Third Session,* June 21 to 25, 1993, at 20–21 (1993).

there is some question whether the obligation would apply to any future or expanded rights promulgated by a member state.[409]

[b] The Rome Convention

A fundamental problem with the Rome Convention is that, while it generally imposes national treatment, it also permits several important reservations and exceptions thereto. Article 3.1 of the TRIPs Agreement provides that "[i]n respect of performers, producers of phonograms and broadcasting organizations, this obligation [national treatment] only applies in respect of the rights provided under this Agreement."[410] It also provides a member may avail itself of the "possibilities provided in . . . paragraph 1(b) of Article 16 of the Rome Convention . . ." relating to reciprocity for the broadcasting right in respect of phonograms.[411]

[c] The TRIPs Agreement

The TRIPs Agreement also includes a national treatment obligation.[412] For copyright, the TRIPs provision incorporates the standards of the Berne

---

409. *Id.* at 21.

410. *See* Office of the U.S. Trade Representative, *Trade-Related Aspects of Intellectual Property, Final Act Embodying the Results of the Uruguay Round of the Multilateral Trade Negotiations* (1993).

411. *Id.*

412. Article 3 (National Treatment) provides:

> 1. Each Member shall accord to the nationals of other Members treatment no less favorable than that it accords to its own nationals with regard to the protection of intellectual property, subject to the exceptions already provided in, respectively, the Paris Convention (1967), the Berne Convention (1971), the Rome Convention and the Treaty on Intellectual Property in Respect of Integrated Circuits. In respect of performers, producers of phonograms and broadcasting organizations, this obligation only applies in respect of the rights provided under this Agreement. Any Member availing itself of the possibilities provided in Article 6 of the Berne Convention and paragraph 1(b) of Article 16 of the Rome Convention shall make a notification as foreseen in those provisions to the Council for Trade-Related Aspects of Intellectual Property Rights.
>
> 2. Members may avail themselves of the exceptions permitted under paragraph 1 above in relation to judicial and administrative procedures, including the designation of an address for service or the appointment of an agent within the jurisdiction of a Member, only where such exceptions are necessary to secure compliance with laws and regulations which are not inconsistent with the provisions of this Agreement and where such practices are not applied in a manner which would constitute a disguised restriction on trade.

Convention; but for neighboring rights, it allows members to impose those exceptions to national treatment permitted by the Rome Convention.[413]

[d] NAFTA

The North American Free Trade Agreement (NAFTA) also includes a very broad national treatment provision. It does not, however, permit the broad exceptions provided for under the TRIPs Agreement.[414]

[5] Private Copying Royalty Systems

The manner in which audio and video private copying royalties collected in some European countries are distributed to claimants may serve as an impediment to a more uniform international system of copyright. To illustrate, France's Law of July 3, 1985 ("1985 Law") establishes a platform of neighboring rights protection for performers, audiovisual communication enterprises, and producers of phonograms and videograms. The 1985 Law grants specified categories of rights holders an entitlement to equitable remuneration for private copying of their works. Some of the 1985 Law's provisions are based on reciprocity and thus discriminate against, for example, foreign motion picture interests. Consequently, those provisions

---

413. Article 4 of TRIPs (Most-Favoured-Nation Treatment) provides:

> With regard to the protection of intellectual property, any advantage, favour, privilege or immunity granted by a Member to the nationals of any other country shall be accorded immediately and unconditionally to the nationals of all other Members. Exempted from this obligation are any advantage, favour, privilege or immunity accorded by a Member:
>
> (a) deriving from international agreements on judicial assistance and law enforcement of a general nature and not particularly confined to the protection of intellectual property;
>
> (b) granted in accordance with the provisions of the Berne Convention (1971) or the Rome Convention authorizing that the treatment accorded be a function not of national treatment but of the treatment accorded in another country;
>
> (c) in respect of the rights of performers, producers of phonograms and broadcasting organizations not provided under this Agreement;
>
> (d) deriving from international agreements related to the protection of intellectual property which entered into force prior to the entry into force of the WTO Agreement, provided that such agreements are notified to the Council for TRIPs and do not constitute an arbitrary or unjustifiable discrimination against nationals of other Members.

414. See NAFTA, H.R. Doc. No. 159, 103d Cong., 1st Sess. (1993); 32 I.L.M. 289–456, 605–799 (1993). NAFTA is binding among the United States, Mexico, and Canada.

may be inconsistent with France's obligations under the Berne and Universal Copyright Conventions.

[6] Moral Rights

Article 6*bis* of the Berne Convention grants a creator the right to be named as the author of a work (the "right of paternity") and to object to uses thereof that bring dishonor or discredit upon him (the "right of integrity").[415] The controversy over "moral rights" kept the United States out of the Berne Convention for over a century. However, during that time, America's legal regime evolved significantly. When the United States finally joined Berne, Congress determined no changes to U.S. law were necessary to comply with this provision because the existing panoply of remedies available under common law and the various state and federal statutes provided sufficient protection.[416] When Congress became convinced that enhanced protection for moral rights was necessary, supplemental legislation was passed.[417]

For the United States, the scope of moral rights remains an important issue. Constitutional concerns exist about any new copyright legislation because it must be seen as promoting the progress of science and useful arts. In other words, moral rights still have to be viewed as part of the constitutional quid pro quo of providing protection in order to promote creativity. Even among Berne Convention members, the nature and scope of moral rights varies considerably. This fact may create difficulties for the

---

415. Article 6*bis* provides:

    (1) Independently of the author's economic rights, and even after the transfer of the said rights, the author shall have the right to claim authorship of the work and to object to any distortion, mutilation or other modification of, or other derogatory action in relation to, the said work, which would be prejudicial to his honor or reputation.

    (2) The rights granted to the author in accordance with the preceding paragraph shall, after his death, be maintained, at least until the expiry of the economic rights, and shall be exercisable by the persons or institutions authorized by the legislation of the country where protection is claimed. However, those countries whose legislation, at the moment of their ratification of or accession to this Act, does not provide for the protection after the death of the author of all the rights set out in the preceding paragraph may provide that some of these rights may, after his death, cease to be maintained.

    (3) The means of redress for safeguarding the rights granted by this Article shall be governed by the legislation of the country where protection is claimed.

416. *See* Berne Convention Implementation Act, *supra* note 147.

417. *See* Visual Artists Rights Act of 1990, Pub. L. No. 101–650, 104 Stat. 5128 (1990).

commercialization of works in the global environment. A recent report suggests there may be a need either to permit the specific waiver of the right of integrity or to limit its application in the digital world.[418]

[7] Conflict of Laws

Issues regarding conflict of laws often arise in cross-border infringement actions. Resolution of these matters determines what country's law applies to the action. If the infringer and infringement are in the United States, clearly the Copyright Act would govern. However, different situations raise more complex problems. For instance, users in country A, where certain actions are not considered copyright infringement, may use works located on servers in country B, where such actions are.

Which country's law then controls the resolution of a dispute? Is it the country from which a copyrighted work is uploaded? What about the law governing the jurisdiction where the work is downloaded or the host server is located? In the case of direct transmissions, which country's law applies? Is it the country where the transmission originates, or where it is received? It may be that rights of copyright owners are exercised in each country. These questions are complicated, and their answers currently unclear. Regardless, they are beyond the scope of this work.

---

418. *See Exposure '94: A Proposal for the New Rule of Intellectual Property for Multimedia*, Inst. of Intell. Prop., Feb. 1994, at 18.

CHAPTER **3**

Fair Use Guidelines

In ascertaining how to use the works of others in their research, writings, courses, and libraries, without committing copyright infringement, educators have traditionally had three sources to consult: (1) the provisions of the Copyright Act; (2) the doctrine of "fair use," the elements of which are incorporated within the Copyright Act; and (3) the various official and unofficial "guidelines" emanating out of the fair use doctrine. The language of the Copyright Act itself addresses relatively few educational situations. Those that it does deal with are found in Section 108, which governs copying by libraries; Section 110(1), which sets forth rules for performances and displays of copyrighted works in face-to-face teaching; and Section 110(2), which covers incorporating the works of others into distance learning situations.

Since these specific provisions govern relatively limited circumstances in which teachers use copyrighted works, educators must often rely on the principle of fair use to determine whether incorporating a copyrighted work into an instructional setting constitutes infringement. The doctrine of fair use has been recognized by courts for over 200 years. The most common example is when a person takes a small portion of a preexisting work to use as part of a new work. For example, when a reviewer quotes from a book or play or a scholar excerpts passages from other authors to analyze or comment on, this usually constitutes fair use.

Although hundreds of cases have dealt with the issue, no precise definition of fair use has ever emerged. Indeed, since the doctrine is inherently flexible, no exact definition is possible. Each case raising this defense must be decided on its own facts and circumstances. To aid in fostering compliance, courts have promulgated a set of criteria that provide some gauge for balancing various considerations. Thus, Section 3.1 of this chapter examines the current state of fair use in the commercial and business sector.

Section 3.2 is devoted to an extensive analysis of the doctrine as applied to education.

Recognizing the amorphousness of fair use in general and the need for educators to have clearer parameters to work with, Congress and various presidential administrations have, over the years, invited and urged representatives of libraries, universities, copyright owners, and others to meet and develop "fair use guidelines." The most successful of these efforts came in the mid-1970s as part of the legislative debate culminating in the revised Copyright Act of 1976.

Pursuant to that process, various contending groups formed, met, discussed, and ultimately agreed upon guidelines covering the copying of (1) printed material by and for teachers in classrooms, (2) music for educational purposes, (3) current journal articles by one library for another, and (4) certain programs broadcast on free television. These guidelines were eventually read into the *Congressional Record* and made part of the legislative history of the Copyright Act. As such, while they do not have the force of law, a number of courts have cited these guidelines in evaluating fair use claims and ruled in accordance with their principles.[1]

To determine whether educational fair use guidelines could be promulgated in the context of the Internet and distance learning, the Clinton administration convened a conference of more than 60 interested parties in September 1994. This group was charged with developing rules with greater relevance to the electronic and digital age. Participants in this Conference on Fair Use, or "CONFU" for short, considered guidelines on such topics as multimedia, library preservation, browsing, and distance learning. Unfortunately, with the exception of educational multimedia, no overall consensus was reached by the participants for any specific field.

Despite the inability to achieve formal agreement, several sets of guidelines (including one on distance learning) were published and publicly disseminated by CONFU. To further confuse matters, guidelines for other educational uses, such as the establishment of traditional and electronic library reserves, have been unilaterally developed and published by several organizations outside the CONFU process. In short, educators have been presented over the last three decades with a plethora of "fair use guidelines," some of which are part of the Copyright Act (and, therefore, actually not "guidelines" per se, but statutory law), others of which have been drafted by ad hoc committees of educators and copyright owners and "blessed" by

---

1. *See, e.g., Basic Books, Inc. v. Kinko's Graphics Corp.*, 758 F. Supp. 1522 (S.D.N.Y. 1991) (for-profit copy center held liable for photocopying book excerpts for sale to students as "coursepacks" for university courses).

Congress, and the remainder of which been developed by smaller groups and disseminated widely, but whose legal status is uncertain.

As such, Section 3.3 of this chapter is devoted to the most important and often referred to of these fair use guidelines.

3.1 FAIR USE IN THE COMMERCIAL SECTOR

[1] Introduction

Before examining fair use in the context of education, it is helpful to see how the principle has recently fared in the private, commercial sector where the bulk of cases interpreting it are found. As noted earlier, the fair use doctrine, codified in Section 107 of the Copyright Act, provides an affirmative defense to claims of copyright infringement. The doctrine recognizes circumstances exist in which the Copyright Act's objectives of encouraging creative and original works are better served by allowing, rather than prohibiting, the use of a work.[2]

The consent of the author of a work is implied as to reasonable uses thereof "since a prohibition of such use would inhibit subsequent writers from attempting to improve upon prior works and thus . . . frustrate the very ends sought to be attained" by copyright laws.[3] In essence, therefore, the fair use inquiry is whether a reasonable author would consent to such use.[4] The alleged infringer carries the burden of proof to show his use is fair.[5]

The four factors courts weigh in deciding these issues are the same in both the commercial and nonprofit sector. Only the presumption afforded to those factors is altered. Those factors are (1) the purpose and character of the use, (2) the nature of the copyrighted work, (3) the amount and substantiality of the portion used in relation to the copyrighted work as a whole, and (4) the effect of the use on the potential market for, or value of, the copyrighted work.[6] The doctrine is an equitable rule of reason, and each case must be decided on its own facts.[7]

[a] The Purpose and Character of the Use

The first factor in any fair use analysis examines "the purpose and character of the use, including whether such use is of a commercial nature

---

2. *Arica Institute, Inc. v. Palmer,* 970 F.2d 1067, 1077 (2d Cir. 1992).

3. *Harper & Row, Publishers, Inc. v. Nation Enterprises,* 471 U.S. 539, 549 (1985).

4. *Id.* at 550.

5. *See American Geophysical Union v. Texaco, Inc.,* 37 F.3d 881, 886 (2d Cir. 1994), *modified by* No. 92-9341 (2d Cir. Dec. 23, 1994).

6. *See* 17 U.S.C. § 107; *Arica, supra* note 2, at 1077.

7. *See Harper & Row, supra* note 3, at 560.

or is for nonprofit educational purposes."[8] This factor "asks whether the original was copied in good faith to benefit the public or primarily for the commercial interests of the infringer."[9] Uses of copyrighted works for purposes such as "criticism, comment, news reporting, teaching . . ., scholarship, or research" are given more latitude than commercial uses.[10] Indeed, these so-called presumptions aptly illustrate the importance of the distinction between the enumerated favored uses and commercial ones. If a use fits within the former, it is considered presumptively fair;[11] if, on the other hand, the use is commercial, the presumption is that it is unfair.[12]

Despite these "presumptions," the first factor is not decided in an all-or-nothing fashion based merely on how one labels the use. The case law has recognized that the character and nature of a use are often mixed. For instance, a use may fit within a favored category, but still be for commercial purposes to a significant or substantial degree.[13] Indeed, because nearly all authors hope to make a profit or gain recognition from their work, courts are wary of overemphasizing the commercial nature in a fair use determination.[14]

Recent cases, however, have made it clear that any first-factor analysis must also involve some qualitative measure of the value generated by the secondary use of the copyrighted material and the manner in which it is used.[15] As the Supreme Court has written:

> The central purpose of this investigation is to see . . . whether the new work merely "supersede[s] the objects" of the original creation . . . or instead adds something new, with a further purpose or different character, altering the first with new expression, meaning or message; it asks, in other words, whether and to what

---

8. 17 U.S.C. § 107(1).

9. *Rogers v. Koons*, 960 F.2d 301, 309 (2d Cir.), *cert. denied*, 113 S. Ct. 365 (1992).

10. 17 U.S.C. § 107; *see Twin Peaks Productions v. Publications International, Ltd.*, 996 F.2d 1366, 1375 (2d Cir. 1993).

11. *See Wright v. Warner Books, Inc.*, 953 F.2d 731, 736 (2d Cir. 1991).

12. *Rogers, supra* note 9, at 309 (citing *Sony Corp. of America v. Universal City Studios, Inc.*, 464 U.S. 417 (1984)).

13. *See, e.g., American Geophysical Union v. Texaco*, No. 93-9341, slip op. at 7951(c) (2d Cir. Dec. 23, 1994) (noting the Supreme Court has abandoned "presumption" language in favor of a more subtle approach), *modifying* 37 F.3d 881 (2d Cir. 1994); *Twin Peaks, supra* note 10, at 1374 (favored uses matter of degree); *Maxtone-Graham v. Burtchaell*, 803 F.2d 1253, 1262 (2d Cir. 1986), *cert. denied*, 481 U.S. 1059 (1987) (commercial use matter of degree).

14. *See Texaco, supra* note 5, at 889; *Twin Peaks Productions, supra* note 10, at 1374.

15. *See Texaco, supra* note 5, at 891.

extent the new work is "transformative . . . ." The more transformative the new work, the less will be the significance of other factors, like commercialism, that may weigh against a finding of fair use.[16]

When the secondary use involves an untransformed duplication, it adds nothing to the value already present in the original work.[17] As the Second Circuit has opined: "[R]ather than making some contribution of new intellectual value and thereby fostering the advancement of the arts and sciences, an untransformed copy is likely to be used simply for the same purpose as the original, thereby providing limited justification for a finding of fair use."[18]

Two other first-factor issues also militate against a finding of fair use. First, the propriety of the alleged infringer's conduct is relevant to a determination of the character of the subsequent use.[19] Someone who fails to quote, cite to, or even acknowledge the original places that person far closer to the scissors-wielding, cut-and-paste plagiarist than to the scholar building on others' efforts. Second, confusion between the original and infringing work may also be considered.[20] For instance, a situation in which a reader would have absolutely no knowledge that a significant amount of words used in one work were actually penned by another would weigh heavily against a fair use determination.

[b] Nature of the Copyrighted Work

The second factor analysis provides additional protection to works that are unpublished and/or creative or fictional.[21] The case law is clear that subsequent authors may rely more heavily on works of fact,[22] and, particularly, historical fact.[23] No biographer, for example, holds a monopoly

---

16. *Campbell v. Acuff-Rose Music, Inc.*, 114 S. Ct. 1164, 1171 (1994) (citations omitted).

17. *See Texaco, supra* note 5, at 891.

18. *Id.*

19. *See Harper & Row, supra* note 3, at 562.

20. *See Maxtone-Graham, supra* note 13, at 1260 (fact that objective reader would not confuse two works favored finding of fair use).

21. *See Harper & Row, supra* note 3, at 563 (law recognizes greater need to disseminate factual works than fiction; unpublished nature of work is critical to factor two analysis); *Texaco, supra* note 5, at 893 (scope of fair use greater for factual works); *Arica, supra* note 2, at 1078 (scope of fair use less for unpublished works).

22. *See Maxtone-Graham, supra* note 13, at 1263.

23. *See Wright, supra* note 11, at 735 ("As a threshold matter, section 102 of the Copyright Act does not extend copyright protection to ideas or facts.").

on the story of the subject's life.[24] Moreover, because the retelling of history necessarily proceeds in chronological order, an author cannot hold a copyright in the sequence of a story's elements.[25] An author's expression of historical facts, on the other hand, is protected by the Copyright Act. As the Second Circuit has opined:

> What is protected is the manner of expression, the author's analysis or interpretation of events, the way he structures his material and marshals facts, his choice of words, and the emphasis he gives to particular developments. Thus, the essence of infringement lies not in taking a general theme or in coverage of the reports as events, but in appropriating the "particular expression through similarities of treatment, details, scenes, events and characterization."[26]

This fact–expression dichotomy[27] also applies to cases involving biographies or historical nonfiction.[28] Indeed, a case involving famed author J. D. Salinger's private letters outlines the rights of a subsequent biographer to use facts contained in a copyrighted work without appropriating the protected expression of his source:

> When dealing with copyrighted expression, a biographer (or any other copier) may frequently have to content himself with reporting only the fact of what his subject did, even if he thereby pens a "pedestrian" sentence. The copier is not at liberty to avoid "pedestrian" reportage by appropriating his subject's literary devices.[29]

---

24. *See Hoehling v. Universal City Studios, Inc.*, 618 F.2d 972, 978 n.5 (citing cases), *cert. denied*, 449 U.S. 841 (1980).

25. *See Arica, supra* note 2, at 1075 (chronological narration of events not protected); *Hoehling, supra* note 24, at 978 ("There cannot be any such thing as copyright in the order of presentation of the facts, nor, indeed, in their selection." (*quoting Myers v. Mail & Express Co.*, 36 C.O. Bull. 478, 479 (S.D.N.Y. 1919)) (Hand, J.)).

26. *Wainwright Securities, Inc. v. Wall Street Transcript Corp.*, 558 F.2d 91, 95–96 (2d Cir. 1977) (*quoting Reyher v. Children's Television Workshop*, 533 F.2d 87, 91 (2d Cir.), *cert. denied*, 429 U.S. 980 (1976)), *cert. denied*, 434 U.S. 1014 (1978).

27. When the expression of an idea is inseparable from the idea itself; however, the expression will not be protected. *See CCC Information Services, Inc. v. Maclean Hunter Market Reports, Inc.*, Nos. 1312, 93-7687, 1994 WL 685689, at *6 (2d Cir. December 5, 1994) (*citing Kregos v. Associated Press*, 937 F.2d 700, 705 (2d Cir. 1991) and *Herbert Rosenthal Jewelry Corp. v. Kalpakian*, 446 F.2d 738, 742 (9th Cir. 1971)).

28. *See Salinger v. Random House, Inc.*, 811 F.2d 90, 96–97 (2d Cir.), *cert. denied*, 484 U.S. 890 (1987); *Craft v. Kobler*, 667 F. Supp. 120, 123 (S.D.N.Y. 1987).

29. *Salinger, supra* note 28, at 96–97.

[c] Amount and Substantiality of the Portion Used

The third factor in the fair use analysis is "the amount and substantiality of the portion used in relation to the copyrighted work as a whole."[30] This factor involves both a quantitative and qualitative review of how much of the original work was used.[31] The amount of permissible copying hereunder will vary depending on the nature of the use.[32] Although no given percentage of taking is per se unreasonable, even a small amount may constitute infringement.[33] Although the third factor looks only at the amount of the copyrighted work taken, "the fact that a substantial portion of the infringing work was copied verbatim is evidence of the qualitative value of the copied material, both to the originator and to the plagiarist . . . ."[34]

[d] Effect on the Market for the Original Work

The fourth factor, which examines the effect the infringing work has on the market for the original work, is the most important factor in a fair use analysis.[35] This inquiry requires courts to consider not only the extent of market harm caused by the actions of the alleged infringer, but also "whether unrestricted and wide-spread conduct of the sort engaged in by the defendant . . . would result in a substantially adverse impact on the potential market for the original."[36] Harm to both the original work and any derivative thereof must be taken into account.[37]

When a secondary work is substantially a non-transformative duplication made for commercial purposes, there is a strong inference of market harm to the original. As the Supreme Court explained in *Campbell v. Acuff-Rose Music, Inc.*, a non-transformative duplication merely serves as a marketplace substitute for the original work.[38] In addition, the fact that a work is out of print or not available is not dispositive—the statute focuses

---

30. 17 U.S.C. § 107(3).

31. *See Campbell, supra* note 16, at 1175; *Harper & Row, supra* note 2, at 565.

32. *See Campbell, supra* note 16, at 1175; *Texaco, supra* note 5, at 894.

33. *Harper & Row, supra* note 3, at 2233 (taking of 13% found to be unfair); *Salinger, supra* note 28, at 98 (taking of 10% found to be unfair); *Craft, supra* note 28, at 129 (taking of 3% found to be unfair); *But compare, e.g., Arica, supra* note 2, at 1078 (taking of only three passages found to be fair); *Wright, supra* note 11, at 738 (taking of 1% found to be fair); *Maxtone-Graham, supra* note 13, at 1263 (taking of 4.3% found to be fair).

34. *Harper & Row, supra* note 3, at 565.

35. *Id.* at 566. However, the Second Circuit has opined that the Supreme Court has moved away from an approach that favors one factor over another. *See American Geophysical Union, supra* note 13, slip op. at 7951(c).

36. *Campbell, supra* note 16, at 1177 (citations omitted).

37. *See Harper & Row, supra* note 3, at 568.

38. *See Campbell, supra* note 16, at 1177.

on the *potential* market for the original work.[39] As enunciated by the Second Circuit, "in the cases where . . . the fourth factor . . . favor[s] the defendant, the defendant's work filled a market niche that the plaintiff simply had no interest in occupying."[40] As such, the fair use doctrine attempts to "distinguish between a true scholar and a chiseler who infringes a work for personal profit."[41]

[e] Summary Judgment Standard

Under the rules of the federal judiciary and most state courts, a party may ask the presiding judge to dispense with a trial and render a ruling on the law that governs the case if no material facts are in dispute. While a useful tool, this standard is often difficult to apply when considering a fair use defense. Under Federal Rule of Civil Procedure 56(c), summary judgment:

> shall be rendered forthwith if the pleadings, depositions, answers to interrogatories, and admissions on file, together with the affidavits, if any, show that there is no genuine issue as to any material fact and that the moving party is entitled to a judgment as a matter of law.[42]

The moving party has the initial burden of "informing the district court of the basis for its motion" and identifying the matter "it believes demonstrate[s] the absence of a genuine issue of material fact."[43] The substantive law determines which facts are material to the outcome of a particular litigation.[44] In determining whether summary judgment is appropriate, a court must resolve all ambiguities, and draw all reasonable inferences, against the moving party.[45]

If the moving party meets its burden, the onus shifts to the nonmoving party to come forward with "specific facts showing that there is a genuine issue for trial."[46] The nonmoving party must "do more than simply

---

39. *See Craft, supra* note 28, at 129.

40. *Twin Peaks Productions, supra* note 10, at 1377.

41. *Wainwright Securities Inc., supra* note 26, at 94 (internal quotation omitted).

42. Fed. R. Civ. P. § 56(c); see *Anderson v. Liberty Lobby*, 477 U.S. 242 (1986).

43. *Celotex Corp. v. Catrett*, 477 U.S. 317, 323 (1986).

44. *See Anderson, supra* note 42, at 250; *Heyman v. Commerce & Indus. Ins. Co.*, 524 F.2d 1317, 1320 (2d Cir. 1975).

45. *See Matsushita Electrical Industrial Co. v. Zenith Radio Corp.*, 475 U.S. 574, 586 (1986) (citing *U.S. v. Diebold, Inc.*, 369 U.S. 654, 655 (1962)).

46. Fed. R. Civ. P. 56(e).

show that there is some metaphysical doubt as to the material facts."[47] Only when it is apparent, however, that no rational finder of fact "could find in favor of the non-moving party because the evidence to support its case is so slight" would a summary judgment motion be granted.[48] In light of the factual nature of many aspects of copyright litigation, federal courts are especially wary of granting summary judgment in cases alleging infringement.[49] In cases involving the fair use doctrine, "because the . . . question is so highly dependent on the particular facts of each case, courts . . . have usually found it appropriate to allow the issue to proceed to trial."[50]

Summary judgment may still be appropriate under some circumstances, however. Several cases have upheld summary judgment in favor of the defendant when no copyrightable material was taken or a finding of fair use was made as a matter of law.[51] Other cases have found in favor of plaintiffs and against the fair use defense at the summary judgment stage. Specifically, the Second Circuit has ruled that summary judgment was proper when the direct evidence was undisputed, or when it was such that no reasonable jury could differ.[52]

[2] Medium of Expression

Is the doctrine of fair use rendered more or less applicable depending upon the medium in which a particular work is replicated? Recent cases from the commercial sector indicate strongly that it does not. A list of various media and some fair use cases associated therewith are summarized below.

[a] Unpublished Works

When a biographer of Richard Wright, the famed African American novelist, quoted from six of his unpublished letters and ten unpublished journal entries, a court held that since less than 1 percent of Mr. Wright's

---

47. *Matsushita, supra* note 45, at 586.

48. *Gallo v. Prudential Residential Services, Ltd. Partnership*, 22 F.3d 1219, 1223 (2d Cir. 1994).

49. *See Hoehling, supra* note 24, at 977 (summary judgment traditionally frowned upon in copyright litigation).

50. *Maxtone-Graham, supra* note 13, at 1258.

51. *See, e.g., Wright, supra* note 11 (use of copyrighted material not unfair as a matter of law); *Maxtone-Graham, supra* note 50, at 1253 (same); *Hoehling, supra* note 24, at 972 (summary judgment appropriate when no copyrighted material taken).

52. *Rogers, supra* note 9, at 307; *see also United Feature Syndicate, Inc. v. Koons*, 817 F. Supp. 370 (S.D.N.Y. 1993) (granting summary judgment in favor of plaintiff after rejecting fair use defense).

works were copied, and the purpose was informational, it was fair use.[53] Conversely, an author who copied more than one-half of an unpublished manuscript describing events related to the overthrow of the Iranian government was deemed not to be a fair user.[54] Likewise, when a biographer paraphrased portions of unpublished letters written by J. D. Salinger, even though the letters were available at university libraries, the court ruled the reproduction and paraphrasing thereof was not fair use.[55]

[b] Published Books

When author Alice Randall used significant portions of virtually identical scenes, settings, and characters from Margaret Mitchell's classic *Gone With the Wind* for her satirical work, *The Wind Done Gone*, a court held the book's social commentary qualified it for fair use protection.[56] However, when *Welcome to Twin Peaks: A Complete Guide to Who's Who and What's What* was published, the guide contained direct quotes as well as paraphrases from the television series *Twin Peaks*. It also gave a detailed description of the plot, characters, and setting from the program.

The court concluded that since the guide could harm the market for authorized books about the show, it was not a fair use.[57] Similarly, when a commercial copy shop reproduced substantial segments of copyrighted works of scholarship, bound the copies into "course packs," and sold them to students to fulfill college reading assignments, the court determined such activity was not fair use.[58]

[c] Newspapers and Magazines

When Larry Flynt, publisher of *Hustler Magazine*, made disparaging statements in his publication about the Reverend Jerry Falwell, Reverend Falwell made several thousand copies of such statements to distribute as part of his own fundraising effort. A court held the photocopying to be fair use since it did not diminish sales of the magazine or adversely affect its marketability.[59] However, when the magazine *The Nation* published excerpts from former president Gerald R. Ford's unpublished memoirs several weeks before the book was to be serialized in *Time*, the U.S.

---

53. *Wright, supra* note 11.
54. *Love v. Kwitny*, 772 F. Supp 1367 (S.D.N.Y. 1989).
55. *Salinger, supra* note 28.
56. *SunTrust Bank v. Houghton Mifflin Co.*, 268 F.3d 1257 (11th Cir. 2001).
57. *Twin Peaks Productions, supra* note 10.
58. *Princeton University Press v. Michigan Document Services, Inc.*, 74 F.3d 1512 (6th Cir. 1994).
59. *Hustler Magazine, Inc. v. Moral Majority, Inc.*, 606 F. Supp. 1526 (C.D. Cal. 1985).

Supreme Court ruled that since the unauthorized publication potentially harmed sales, it was not fair use.[60]

[d] Film

When a film biography of Muhammad Ali used 41 seconds from a copyrighted boxing match clip, the court held fair use applied since only a small portion was taken and the purpose was informational.[61] Conversely, when a television news show copied a 1-minute, 15-second excerpt from a 72-minute Charlie Chaplin film to report on Chaplin's death, a court held that since the portions taken constituted the "heart" of the original film, it was not fair use.[62] Similarly, a television news broadcast that used 30 seconds from a 4-minute copyrighted videotape of the 1992 Los Angeles beating of truck driver Reginald Denny was also deemed not to be fair use.[63]

[e] Internet

A search engine's practice of creating low-quality thumbnails of pictures and placing them on its website was deemed fair use because it did not impact the sale or licensing of those images by their creator.[64] Likewise, when the *Washington Post* used three quotations from a Church of Scientology website, a court held that since only a small portion was used and the purpose was for news commentary, the use was fair.[65] However, when entire publications of the Church of Scientology were posted on the Internet by several persons without the church's permission, such copying was deemed unfair use.[66]

[f] Music

When *Saturday Night Live* parodied the song "I Love New York" with "I Love Sodom" using only the words "I Love" in four musical notes taken from the original, it was determined to be fair use.[67] Similarly, when an office seeker used fifteen seconds of his opponent's campaign song in his

---

60. *Harper & Row, supra* note 3.

61. *Monster Communications, Inc. v. Turner Broadcasting Systems, Inc.*, 935 F. Supp. 490 (S.D.N.Y. 1996).

62. *Roy Export Co. Establishment of Vaduz v. Columbia Broadcasting System, Inc.*, 672 F.2d 1095, 1100 (2nd Cir. 1982).

63. *Los Angeles News Service v. KCAL-TV Channel 9*, 108 F.3d 1119 (9th Cir. 1997).

64. *Kelly v. Ariba Soft Corporation*, 280 F.3d 934 (9th Cir. 2002).

65. *Religious Technology Center v. Pagliarina*, 908 F. Supp. 1353 (E.D. Va. 1995).

66. *Religious Technology Center v. Lerma*, 40 U.S.P.Q. 2d 1569 (E.D. Va. 1996).

67. *Elsmere Music, Inc. v. National Broadcasting Co.*, 482 F. Supp. 741 (S.D.N.Y.), *aff'd*, 632 F.2d 252 (2nd Cir. 1980).

own political ad, the court found it fair use because only a small portion was used and the purpose was for political debate.[68] However, using certain copyrighted music as background to a BBC story on Irish terrorists was deemed unfair.[69]

[g] Photographs

While the reproduction of a "screen shot" from Sony's copyrighted game to show the superior resolution of defendant's hardware was deemed fair use,[70] the use of plaintiff's photo as a starting point to produce a digitally altered scene of the Las Vegas strip was not.[71] And again, while the use of a Laurel and Hardy photograph showing the duo at the edge of a skyscraper to publicize a "Special Effects and Stunts" section in a magazine was ruled unfair,[72] another court found it acceptable for a Hollywood studio to use fleeting and obscured versions of copyrighted photographs in their film sequence.[73]

[3] The Fair Use Factors: Just a Means to an End?

The doctrine of fair use has been described as "so flexible as to virtually defy definition."[74] This flexibility and amorphousness have greatly frustrated authors, judges, juries, lawyers, legal commentators, and educators over the years. The U.S. Supreme Court itself is not immune to strong disagreements regarding the doctrine. In *Harper & Row, Publishers, Inc. v. Nation Enterprises*,[75] six justices analyzed each of the four factors as disfavoring fair use, while the three dissenters reached the opposite conclusion on *each* factor.[76]

As discussed above, cases with very similar fact patterns are often decided differently. Some cases may find fair use when large amounts of materials are taken, while others see no fair use where only miniscule portions are involved. One reason for this apparent inconsistency is the U.S.

---

68. *Keep Thomson Governor Comm. v. Citizens for Gallen Comm.*, 457 F. Supp. 957 (D.N.H. 1978).

69. *Byrne v. British Broadcasting Corporation*, 132 F. Supp. 2d 229 (S.D.N.Y. 2001).

70. *Sony Computer Entertainment of America, Inc. v. Bleem, LLC*, 214 F.3d 1022 (9th Cir. 2000).

71. *Tiffany Design, Inc. v. Reno-Tahoe Specialty, Inc.*, 55 F. Supp. 2d 1113 (D. Nev. 1999).

72. *Richard Feiner & Co. v. H.R.I. Indus.*, 10 F. Supp. 2d 310 (S.D.N.Y. 1998).

73. *Sandoval v. New Line Cinema*, 973 F. Supp. 409 (S.D.N.Y. 1997).

74. *Time, Inc. v. Bernard Geis Associates*, 293 F. Supp. 130, 144 (S.D.N.Y. 1968).

75. *See supra* note 3.

76. *See* 4 M. Nimmer & D. Nimmer, *Nimmer on Copyright* at § 13.05[A][5] (1994) (hereinafter *Nimmer on Copyright*).

Supreme Court's reluctance to establish clearer parameters regarding the doctrine. In this vein, the Court has written:

> A task is not to be simplified with bright line rules, for the statute, like the doctrine it recognizes, calls for case-by-case analysis . . . . Nor may the four statutory factors be treated in isolation, one from another. All are to be explored, and the results weighed together, in light of the purposes of copyright.[77]

To further complicate matters, a party need not prevail on all four factors to win a fair use case.[78] In fact, winning three out of four does not assure victory. In a most enlightening article on this topic, David Nimmer, noted scholar and Visiting Professor at the UCLA School of Law, studied and summarized sixty recent copyright cases that turned on an evaluation of the fair use doctrine.[79] For each, Nimmer looked at the four factors and analyzed whether a reasonable interpretation thereof would result in a "fair" or "unfair" determination.[80]

Those results were then compared to the court's judgment on whether the defendant's activity constituted fair or unfair use.[81] In a startling revelation, Nimmer found that in 23 of the 60 cases, while at least three of the factors could reasonably weigh in favor of one determination, the court chose the other.[82] In other words, Nimmer found cases where three out of the four factors could lead to a finding of fair use, but the court found the use unfair and vice versa.

Even more surprising, Nimmer identified five cases where all four factors could reasonably have led to one result, while the court ruled the opposite way.[83] These so-called shutouts[84] were found for both scenarios— where the factors leaned toward fair use while the court found infringement; and conversely, where the factors sided with the copyright owner but the court ruled for the defendant. Such results led Nimmer to conclude that "[c]ourts tend to first make a judgment that the ultimate disposition is fair use or unfair use, and then align the four factors to fit the result as best they can. At best, therefore, the four factors fail to drive the

---

77. *Campbell v. Acuff-Rose Music, Inc.*, 510 U.S. 569, 577–78 (1994).

78. *See Wright, supra* note 11, at 740.

79. Nimmer, *"Fairest of Them All" and Other Fairy Tales of Fair Use*, 66 Law & Contemp. Probs. 263 (2003), http://law.duke.edu./journals/66LCPnimmer.

80. *Id.* at 268.

81. *Id.* at 278.

82. *Id.* at 269–77.

83. *Id.*

84. *Id.* at 282.

analysis, but rather serve as convenient pegs on which to hang antecedent conclusions."[85] Professor Nimmer was quick to note, however, that judges seldom, if ever, expose their true methodology.[86]

One of the most prominent examples of the four fair use factors reasonably pointing to one conclusion, while the court finds another, occurred in *SunTrust v. Houghton Mifflin Company*.[87] Here, the issue before the court was whether publication of the book *The Wind Done Gone* (TWDG), a fictional work admittedly based on Margaret Mitchell's *Gone With the Wind* (sometimes hereinafter, the "Mitchell Book"), should have been enjoined from publication based on alleged copyright violations. The plaintiff was trustee of the Mitchell Trust, owner of the copyright in the Mitchell Book. The Mitchell Trust actively managed the copyright and authorized derivative works in a variety of commercial items.

Alice Randall, the author of TWDG, claimed her novel was a critique of *Gone With the Wind*'s depiction of slavery and the Civil War era American South. To that end, she appropriated the characters, plot, and major scenes from the Mitchell Book into the first half of her novel. SunTrust sought to bar publication of TWDG because it "(1) explicitly refer[red] to [the Mitchell Book] in its forward; (2) copied core characters, character traits, and relationships from [the Mitchell Book]; (3) copied and summarized famous scenes and other elements of the plot from [the Mitchell Book]; and (4) copied verbatim dialogs and descriptions from [the Mitchell Book]."[88] The defendant publisher contended the doctrine of fair use protected TWDG because it was primarily a parody of *Gone With the Wind*.

In examining the four fair use factors, it is quite logical that the court could have ruled in favor of the plaintiff, or against a finding of fair use, on all four. For factor one, the purpose and character of the work, it was undisputed that TWDG served primarily a commercial rather than a nonprofit educational purpose.[89] This factor could thus easily have gone in plaintiff's column. Regarding factor number two, the nature of the copyrighted work, since original, creative works are afforded greater protection than factual compilations, the Mitchell Book was undoubtedly entitled to a larger shield as a work of fiction. As such, this factor also leaned toward a finding of unfair use.

---

85. *Id.* at 281.

86. *Id.* at 280.

87. *See supra* note 56.

88. *SunTrust Bank v. Houghton Mifflin Co.*, 136 F. Supp. 2d 1357, 1364 (N.D. Ga. 2001), *vacated* 252 F.3d 1165 (11th Cir. 2001).

89. *SunTrust, supra* note 56, at 9.

Factor number three, the amount and substantiality of the portion used, also could have been found for plaintiff. The Eleventh Circuit, in its opinion, stated that "TWDG appropriated a substantial portion of the protected elements of *Gone With the Wind.*"[90] The last factor, the effect on the potential market, also seems to fall on plaintiff's side. SunTrust proffered substantial evidence of the value of its copyright and that several derivative works it had authorized, including the movie with Clark Gable and Vivien Leigh, had garnered millions of dollars for the Mitchell Trust.

Despite this evidence, the court found that "under the present state of the record, it appears that a viable fair use defense is available."[91] In short, the court believed Ms. Randall's work was entitled to fair use protection because it served as a "specific criticism of and rejoinder to the depiction of slavery and relationships between blacks and whites"[92] and a rebuttal to "the classic novel's particular perspective on the Civil War and slavery."[93] By finding the work to be a parody, TWDG was able to enjoy "significant value as free speech under the First Amendment."[94]

3.2 THE DOCTRINE OF FAIR USE AND EDUCATION

Chapter Two dealt in some detail with the doctrine of fair use and its elements, progeny and evolution. This section concerns the application of fair use in the educational arena with emphasis on distance learning. One common misconception about the doctrine is that any nonprofit educational use of a copyrighted work always qualifies as fair use. This erroneous perception likely arises from the wording of Section 107 of the Copyright Act, which incorporates fair use into the federal statute. The Section reads as follows:

> Notwithstanding the provisions of sections 106 and 106A, the fair use of a copyrighted work, including such use by reproduction in copies or phonorecords or by any other means specified by that section [*sic*], for purposes such as criticism, comment, news reporting, *teaching (including multiple copies for classroom use), scholarship, or research*, is not an infringement of copyright.

---

90. *Id.* at 11.

91. *Id.* at 14.

92. *Id.* at 8.

93. *Id.* at 15.

94. *Id.* at 15, *quoting Dr. Seuss Enterprises, LP v. Penguin Books U.S.A., Inc.*, 109 F.3d 1394, 1400 (9th Cir. 1997).

In determining whether the use made of a work in any particular case is a fair use the factors to be considered shall include—

(1) the purpose and character of the use, including whether such use is of a commercial nature or is for *nonprofit educational purposes*;

(2) the nature of the copyrighted work;

(3) the amount and substantiality of the portion used in relation to the copyrighted work as a whole; and

(4) the effect of the use upon the potential market for or value of the copyrighted work. (emphasis added)

One who stops reading after the first sentence of the preamble may indeed leave with the impression that any educational use is inherently fair use.[95] The second sentence of the provision makes clear, however, that any analysis must consider all four factors. Suffice it to say that the educator should normally prevail on factor number (1).[96] Winning one factor is seldom sufficient to carry the day, however. While courts do not require a fair use claimant to prevail on all four factors, normally a presumption on at least half, if not a majority, is needed. Of course, further complicating matters is that some factors are accorded more weight than others.

The U.S. Supreme Court has made clear that fair use carries no bright line test. It must, instead, be adjudicated on a case-by-case basis.[97] The fact-based nature of the inquiry often makes it difficult to predict outcomes, as does the fact that "virtually no decisions apply the fair use test directly to educational defendants who made educational uses of content."[98] Most of the so-called educational fair use cases have actually dealt with private businesses serving colleges.[99] Regardless, a court's analysis will depend on

---

95. This is a faulty assumption, however, as "[c]ourts rarely rely on the preamble of Section 107 as the basis for decisions on fair use." *See* W. Fisher and W. McGeveran, *Obstacles to Educational Uses of Copyrighted Material in the Digital Age*, 54 (Aug. 10, 2006), Berkman Center Research Publication No. 2006–09, http://ssrn.com/abstract=923465 (hereinafter *Fisher Report*).

96. This assumes, however, that there is no commercial component to the educational use, such as teaching business executives as part of the curriculum of a for-profit subsidiary of the school.

97. *Acuff-Rose, supra* note 77, at 577.

98. *Fisher Report* at 52. *See also* J. Band, "Educational Fair Use Today," Paper Prepared for the Association of Research Libraries 2, http://www.arl.org (referencing the "remarkable paucity of judicial decisions considering fair use by educational institutions").

99. *See, e.g., Marcus v. Rowley*, 695 F.2d 1171, 1174–79 (9th Cir. 1983) (distribution of multiple copies of copyrighted works to public school students held not fair use); *Wihtol v. Crow*, 309 F.2d 777, 780–81 (8th Cir. 1962) (same); *Encyclopedia Britannica Educational Corp. v. Crooks*, 542 F. Supp. 1156 (W.D.N.Y. 1982) (consortium of public school districts held liable for recording educational motion pictures and videos broadcast on public television stations, and providing copies of the tapes to member schools).

elements such as the subject matter of the course, the nature of the educational institution, the ways in which instructors use the materials, the mode of delivery, the kinds and amounts of materials used, and, of course, a consideration of the four fair use factors.

The first statutory factor, the purpose and character of the use, encompasses several variables. As noted above, Section 107 cites teaching, scholarship, and research as examples of "nonprofit educational purposes," that are more likely to be held fair. In addition, "transformative" uses, as opposed to merely reproductive or "consumptive" ones, are favored.[100] A transformative use is one that employs a copyrighted work as raw material to produce insight or understanding, usually expressed in the form of a new creative work.[101] Education often involves such transformative measures. Whether the educational use takes place in a distance learning or traditional classroom setting makes little difference here.

While outside of the traditional education context, one of the most controversial current "transformative" uses involves the efforts of the search engine Google to scan all the books contained in several major university libraries and create a searchable database of their content. Users will then be able to browse this resource and retrieve either entire texts of works that are in the public domain or a few sentences of those that are not.[102] While some publishers oppose this project and have filed lawsuits to stop it,[103] Google has defended its actions on the basis of fair use and contends the project is in the public interest as it "helps users discover new books and publishers discover new readers."[104] The matter and its ultimate disposition will probably remain in the courts for years.[105]

The second factor in a fair use analysis is the nature of the copyrighted work. In analyzing this factor, courts generally examine whether the work

---

100. *Acuff-Rose, supra* note 77, at 577; *Sony Corp. v. Universal City Studios, Inc.*, 464 U.S. 417, 450 n.33 (1984).

101. *Acuff-Rose, supra* note 77, at 577; Leval, *Toward a Fair Use Standard*, 103 Harv. L. Rev. 1105, 1111 (1990) (use is transformative when "quoted matter is used as raw material, transformed in the creation of new information, new aesthetics, new insights and understandings").

102. *See Fisher Report* at 10.

103. *See, e.g.,* Plaintiffs' Complaint, *The McGraw-Hill Companies, Inc., et al. v. Google, Inc.*, No. 05-CV-881 (S.D.N.Y. Oct. 19, 2005), http://publishers.org/main/PressCenter/ Archicves/2005_Oct/attachments/40_McGraw-Hill_v._Google.pdf.

104. *See* Google Library Project website at http://books.google.com/googlebooks/ library.html.

105. For an excellent discussion of how the doctrine of fair use might apply to the matter, *see* J. Band, *The Google Print Library Project: A Copyright Analysis*, http://www.policy bandwidth.com/doc/googleprint.pdf.

is creative or factual, and unpublished or published.[106] Creative works are considered "closer to the core of intended copyright protection" than factual ones are, and they are therefore less subject to a fair use defense.[107] Whether a work used in a classroom is factual or creative will vary with the subject matter. For example, a history course is likely to rely on factual material, while an expository writing class is more apt to use creative works. Unpublished works are less subject to fair use than published ones because of the author's right to control the "first public appearance of his undisseminated expression."[108] While educators are more likely to rely on published, available works to teach their classes, certain courses, such as political science seminars, may incorporate the unpublished letters or diaries of public figures.

Several additional elements are relevant in evaluating the second fair use factor. In teaching, a court may look at the intended audience for the copyrighted work. If the work is prepared primarily for school markets, such as a textbook, "the defense of fair use would be far less appropriate than if the work were material prepared for the general public."[109] Similarly, it is unlikely a digital course produced primarily for the distance education market could ever be excerpted under fair use. The work's commercial availability may also be considered.[110] An educator may be more justified in using a work without permission if it is unavailable for purchase through normal channels,[111] such as where students are asked to review older, out-of-print material.

The third fair use factor is the amount and substantiality of the work used. The portion used in teaching will vary according to the style of the instructor and the subject matter of the course. In some instances only brief excerpts will be used, such as in a survey course of English literature. In other cases the nature of the content being studied, such as short poems, paintings, or statues, will make it likely the entire work will be copied or

---

106. *Acuff-Rose, supra* note 77, at 580; *Stewart v. Abend,* 495 U.S. 207, 237–38 (1990); *Harper & Row, supra* note 3, at 563–64.

107. *Acuff-Rose, supra* note 77, at 580 (collecting cases); *see also American Geophysical Union v. Texaco, Inc.,* 60 F.3d 913, 924–25 (2d Cir. 1994), *cert. dismissed,* 516 U.S. 1005 (1995).

108. *Harper & Row, supra* note 3. Although fair use of unpublished works is narrow, "[t]he fact that a work is unpublished shall not itself bar a finding of fair use if such finding is made upon consideration of all the . . . factors." 17 U.S.C. § 107 (*as amended by* Act of October 24, 1992, Pub. L. No. 102–492, 106 Stat. 3145 (1992)).

109. *Triangle Pubs., Inc. v. Knight-Ridder Newspapers, Inc.,* 626 F.2d 1171, 1176 n.14 (5th Cir. 1980); *see also* S. Rep. No. 473, 94th Cong., 1st Sess. 60 (1975) (hereinafter *Senate Report*).

110. H.R. Rep. No. 1476, 94th Cong., 2d Sess. 47, 67 (1976) (hereinafter *House Report*).

111. *Senate Report* at 64.

displayed. Because "the extent of permissible copying varies with the purpose and character of the use," the evaluation of the amount taken will relate to the first factor as well.[112] Again, whether the extracted portion is used in a traditional or distance learning setting bears little weight.

The fourth factor, the effect of the use upon the potential market for or value of the work, considers the actual and/or potential market harm caused by the user's conduct.[113] The market considered includes both opportunities for sale and licensing of the work and its derivatives.[114] Certain works are more susceptible to harm than others, such as movies or plays intended for wide public distribution. On the other hand, to the extent a class is shown only a short excerpt thereof, the impact on the market is likely to be reduced or nonexistent. In addition, the availability of licenses may come into play. For instance, having a convenient mechanism for securing a license at a reasonable cost, such as the Copyright Clearance Center, has been taken into account by the courts.[115] As a corollary, the unavailability of an effective licensing mechanism could weigh in favor of a finding of fair use.[116]

In distance education, characteristics specific to digital technologies are likely to be relevant. Even though the fair use doctrine is technologically neutral, its application to particular circumstances may be influenced by the technology used. In particular, the ability in the digital environment to easily make and distribute vast numbers of perfect copies could alter a court's evaluation.[117] Although this aspect of the technology increases the

---

112. *Acuff-Rose, supra* note 77, at 586–87.

113. While this factor has been described as the most important, *Harper, supra* note 3, at 566, the Supreme Court has made clear that "all [four factors] are to be explored, and the results weighed together, in light of the purposes of copyright." *Acuff-Rose, supra* note 77, at 578; *see Leibovitz v. Paramount Pictures Corp.*, 137 F.3d 109, 113 (2d Cir. 1998); *Ringgold v. Black Entertainment Television, Inc.*, 126 F.3d 70, 77 n.8 (2d Cir. 1977); *American Geophysical, supra* note 101, at 926.

114. *American Geophysical Union, supra* note 107; *Acuff-Rose, supra* note 77, at 593.

115. *See American Geophysical Union v. Texaco, Inc.*, 802 F. Supp. 1 (S.D.N.Y. 1992) (availability of CCC and other licensing systems for "prompt[ ] and inexpensive[ ]" access to articles weighed against fair use); *aff'd* 60 F.3d 913, 929–31 (1994) (including potential licensing revenues under fourth factor of fair use test).

116. *Cf. Senate Report* at 64 (if work is "unavailable for purchase through normal channels the user may have more justification for reproducing it"); *see also Texaco, supra* note 115, at 24 (distinguishing *Williams & Wilkins v. National Institute of Health*, 487 F.2d 1345 (1973), *aff'd by an equally divided Court*, 420 U.S. 376 (1975), on grounds that licensing options available to defendant did not exist when *Williams & Wilkins* was decided).

117. *Cf. House Report* at 72 (in the cases of copies of works made in educational broadcasts, "the number of copies reproduced and the extent of their reuse or exchange" should be weighed in applying the criteria of fair use).

risk to copyright owners, countervailing elements exist as well. For example, the deployment of technological measures to control access to works, or inhibit their downstream dissemination, may also be considered by the courts.

In short, an educational institution, or its faculty, staff, or students, like any other defendant, will be subjected to a complete four-factor analysis of their actions before a court determines whether their use of a copyrighted work was "fair" or not. Congress, for its part, has pressed its thumb on the scales of justice on the side of the nonprofit, educational user. As evidence, the legislative history of the Copyright Act includes explicit references to educational settings. As one congressional document reported: "Assuming the applicable criteria are met, fair use can extend to the reproduction of copyrighted material for purposes of classroom teaching."[118] A later House report listed, among other examples of fair use, the "reproduction by a teacher or student of a small part of a work to illustrate a lesson . . . ."[119]

The courts, on the other hand, have not always been as supportive of teachers in their rulings. As noted above, a nonprofit, educational purpose does not automatically compel a finding of fair use. As early as 1914, a Massachusetts federal district court was presented with the issue.[120] In that case, plaintiff, an economics instructor at Harvard, had written a textbook entitled *Principles of Economics*. The defendant had acted as a private tutor and assembled a typewritten outline of lessons mirroring the organization of plaintiff's textbook and containing quotations therefrom.

Interestingly, no outlines were ever sold, and defendant claimed the fee charged for tutoring sessions was the same regardless of whether an outline was prepared. The court ultimately found plaintiff's copyright had been infringed due to "an appropriation [by the defendant] of the author's ideas and language more extensive than the copyright law permits."[121] With respect to the tutor's defense that educational use permitted the copying, the judge wrote:

> If the above conclusions are right, I am unable to believe that the defendant's use of the outlines is any the less infringement of the copyright because he is a teacher, because he uses them in teaching the contents of the book, because he might lecture upon the con-

---

118. H.R. Rep. No. 83, 90th Cong., 1st Sess. 33 (1967) (hereinafter 1967 *House Report*).

119. *House Report* at 65.

120. *MacMillan v. King*, 223 F. 862 (D. Mass. 1914).

121. *Id.* at 866.

tents of the book without infringing, or because his pupils might have taken their own notes of his lectures without infringing.[122]

The court's analysis was somewhat cursory in this case and did not specifically address the four fair use elements because these tests were not fully developed yet. Regardless, it may be helpful, at this point, to examine a hypothetical infringement situation (one based on a true case) and analyze how a court might apply the fair use factors in today's educational environment.

Let's assume the following facts: From 1990 to 1994, our plaintiff, Miss Author (hereinafter "Miss Author" or "Plaintiff") was employed by defendant, Acme Unified School District (hereinafter, the "District") as a teacher of home economics. Plaintiff left the District's employ in 1994 and taught adult education classes intermittently from 1995 to 2000. Shortly after leaving her position, Miss Author created a booklet entitled "Cake Decorating Made Easy." After completing her work, Miss Author promptly registered it with the Copyright Office in Washington, D.C. Plaintiff subsequently printed and sold 125 copies of her booklet for $2.00 each to students in her adult education cake decorating classes. Her profit was $1.00 on each sale of the work. The booklet was never sold by a bookstore or other outlet. In addition, Miss Author never authorized anyone else to copy or sell her work.

Defendant, Shirley Infringer (hereinafter "Miss Infringer" or "Defendant") taught food service career classes as a full-time teacher for the District. In the spring of 1995, she enrolled in one of Plaintiff's classes and purchased a copy of the booklet. The following summer, Miss Infringer prepared a short work entitled "Cake Decorating Learning Activity Package" (LAP) for use in her food service career classes. The LAP consisted of twenty-four pages. Miss Infringer ultimately admitted retyping eleven of those pages from Plaintiff's booklet and acknowledged she never cited Plaintiff as the creator thereof. Defendant made fifteen copies of the LAP available to her students. Neither Miss Infringer nor the District ever derived any profit from selling the LAP.

Miss Author learned of the LAP in the summer of 1997 and promptly filed a suit against Miss Infringer and the District for copyright infringement. The Defendants moved for dismissal on the grounds that Miss Infringer's copying of Plaintiff's material for nonprofit educational purposes constituted fair use.

---

122. *Id.* at 867.

How should a court decide the case? As with all fair use defenses, we start with a consideration of the four factors delineated in Section 107 of the Copyright Act.

[1] The Purpose and Character of the Use

As noted above, the first factor is the purpose and character of the use, with special emphasis on whether the use is for commercial or nonprofit purposes. Defendant clearly used the LAP for nonprofit, educational objectives; and her work was distributed to students at no charge. These facts necessarily weigh in Miss Infringer's favor. However, using the material for the same intrinsic purpose as the copyright owner intended often contradicts fair use.[123] Specifically, "textbooks and other material prepared primarily for the school market would be less susceptible to reproduction for classroom use than material prepared for general public distribution,"[124] if the fair use defense was properly interpreted.

In our example, both Plaintiff's and Defendant's booklets were prepared to help teach cake decorating. In other words, there was no "transformation" of the material, an element that often aids in a fair use defense.[125] Also, because fair use presupposes a defendant has acted fairly and in good faith, the propriety of such defendant's conduct must also be considered.[126] Here, no attempt was made by Defendant to secure Plaintiff's permission or credit her for the material, even though Defendant's copying was almost

---

123. *Jartech, Inc. v. Clancy*, 666 F.2d 403 (9th Cir. 1982); *Universal City Studios, Inc. v. Sony Corp.*, 659 F.2d 963, 969 (9th Cir. 1981). *See also Iowa State University v. American Broadcasting Cos.*, 621 F.2d 57 (2d Cir. 1980) (the scope of fair use is constricted when the original and the copy serve the same function).

124. *1967 House Report* at 34.

125. *Acuff-Rose, supra* note 77, at 577.

126. In *Schroeder v. William Morrow & Co.*, 566 F.2d 3 (7th Cir. 1977), the compilers of the allegedly infringing garden catalogue had copied names and addresses of florists and gardeners from plaintiff's similar compilation. Although the copied information was easily accessible from the telephone book, defendants did not check or verify plaintiff's list. The court found that defendants' shortcut saved them a lot of time and enabled them to meet a deadline. Although the court was not addressing the fair use issue at this point, it stated the "appropriation of the fruits of another's labor and skill in order to publish a rival work without the expenditure of the time and effort required for independently arrived at results is copyright infringement." *Id.* at 6. Later, the court explicitly rejected the fair use defense. *See also Baker v. Selden*, 101 U.S. 99 (1879) (the use of the same words or illustrations in a book teaching an art is undoubtedly infringement) and *Runge v. Lee*, 441 F.2d 579 (9th Cir. 1971), *cert. denied*, 404 U.S. 887 (1971).

verbatim.[127] Miss Infringer's conduct in this respect clearly weighs *against* a finding of fair use.

[2] The Nature of the Copyrighted Work

The second factor is the nature of the copyrighted work. Courts often begin their analysis here by considering whether the work is "informational" or "creative."[128] As a general proposition, "the scope of fair use is greater when informational type works, as opposed to more creative products, are involved."[129] Here, Plaintiff's booklet involved both informational and creative aspects. Some pages undoubtedly contained information available in other recipe books, while others featured Plaintiff's own expression of her experiences and ideas. Also, the manner in which Miss Author organized her book represented a creative expression. Thus, on balance, it appears this factor weighs slightly *against* a finding of fair use. Courts also give greater protection to unpublished material. Since Plaintiff's booklet was registered, but never published, this too weighs *against* a finding of fair use.

[3] The Amount and Substantiality of the Portion Used

The third factor is the amount and substantiality of the portion used in relation to the copyrighted work as a whole. This factor requires an analysis of both the quantity and quality of the alleged infringement.[130] Courts have long maintained that wholesale reproduction of material precludes application of the fair use doctrine.[131] Two cases have specifically addressed the issue with regard to copying in a nonprofit or educational setting.

The first involved alleged infringement by a church choir director of a hymn entitled "My God and I."[132] There, the defendant, Mr. Crow, incorporated plaintiff's original piano composition into an arrangement for his choir. He then made forty-eight copies of the piece and performed it on two occasions, neither time for money. The music was identified as

---

127. Attribution is, of course, but one factor. Moreover, acknowledgment of a source does not excuse infringement when the other factors listed in Section 107 are present. *See, e.g., Toksvig v. Bruce Publishing Co.,* 181 F.2d 664 (7th Cir. 1950).

128. *Universal City Studios, Inc., supra* note 123.

129. *Id.* at 972.

130. *Nimmer on Copyright* at § 13.05[A][3].

131. *Benny v. Loew's, Inc.,* 239 F.2d 532 (9th Cir. 1956), *aff'd by an equally divided Court sub nom. Columbia Broadcasting System v. Loew's, Inc.,* 356 U.S. 43 (1958). *See also Walt Disney Productions v. Air Pirates,* 581 F.2d 751, 758 (9th Cir. 1978) and *Universal City Studios, Inc., supra* note 123, at 973.

132. *Wihtol v. Crow, supra* note 99.

"arranged Nelson E. Crow," with no reference to the plaintiff. In addressing the issue, the court held that "whatever may be the breadth of the doctrine of 'fair use', it is not conceivable to us that the copying of all, or substantially all, of a copyrighted song can be held to be a 'fair use' merely because the infringer had no intent to infringe."[133]

In a second nonprofit-related case, three producers of educational motion picture films sued the Board of Cooperative Educational Services of Erie County (BOCES) in New York for videotaping several of their copyrighted films without permission.[134] BOCES later distributed the films to schools for delayed student viewing. In considering the matter, the Court found that although BOCES was involved in noncommercial copying to promote science and education, the taping of entire copyrighted films was too excessive for the fair use defense to apply.[135]

In our hypothetical scenario, almost half of Defendant's LAP was a verbatim copy of Plaintiff's booklet and could have been a photocopy thereof but for the fact that Defendant retyped the material. This factor presents a clear example of both substantial quantitative and qualitative copying and weighs *against* a finding of fair use.

[4] The Effect of the Use on the Potential Market for or Value of the Copyrighted Work

The final factor considered is the effect of the use on the potential market for or value of the copyrighted work. While often viewed as the most important criterion of fair use, it "must almost always be judged in conjunction with the other three criteria."[136] One legislative report suggests that "a use which supplants any part of the normal market for a copyrighted work would ordinarily be considered an infringement."[137]

Recall from our example, however, that neither Miss Infringer nor the District made any money from the LAP. In addition, Miss Author's profits amounted to a mere $125 and no evidence was presented that the LAP had diminished Plaintiff's sales. Most courts would find these facts irrelevant, however. The fourth factor's wording makes clear that *actual* eco-

---

133. *Id.* at 780.

134. *Encyclopedia Britannica, supra* note 99.

135. *Id.* at 251. *See also Quinto v. Legal Times of Washington, Inc.*, 506 F. Supp. 554, 560 (D.D.C. 1981). *Compare Williams & Wilkins Co. v. United States*, 487 F.2d 1345, 1352–54 (Ct. Cl. 1973), *aff'd*, 420 U.S. 376 (1975) (the existence of verbatim copying was not dispositive when the conduct encouraged scientific progress and did not cause plaintiff substantial monetary harm).

136. 1967 *House Report* at 35.

137. *Id.*

nomic harm need not be shown, only an effect on the "potential market" for the work. Therefore, absence of measurable pecuniary damage does not necessarily lead to a finding of fair use.[138] As such, the factor weighs *against* the Defendant's conduct.

Since fair use must be determined by considering all the evidence in a case,[139] it is probable Miss Author would prevail on her copyright infringement claim. What does our Plaintiff receive for winning, though? Since Miss Infringer did not sell her LAP, and Miss Author lost no revenues, what are the damages here? Was Plaintiff's lawsuit only a moral win? Even worse, was it a Pyrrhic victory since she now has to pay court costs and her lawyer? The answer, fortunately for her, is "no."

Recall from the fact pattern that Miss Author had the prescience to register her work with the Copyright Office prior to its printing. As such, she may elect to receive statutory rather than actual damages, which range from $750 to $30,000 per work infringed.[140] Courts may also award reasonable attorneys' fees to the prevailing party under certain circumstances.[141] Thus, despite no actual economic harm, Miss Author may still receive up to $30,000 in damages and have her legal fees paid by the Defendant. Even in a case involving educational uses and a small amount of money, the lesson is clear: *Let the infringer beware!*

Bear in the mind that the above hypothetical represents only one of an infinite number of situations involving education and fair use. Other cases could be decided differently. Even an identical fact pattern could result in a contrary holding, depending on the weight given each factor by a judge. The dearth of case law in the education arena makes it particularly challenging for instructors and academic administrators to draw clear boundaries around the concept of fair use.[142] What accounts for the few reported cases in this important area? A number of factors.

---

138. *Universal City Studios, Inc., supra* note 123, at 974.

139. *Mathews Conveyer Co. v. Palmer-Bee Co.,* 135 F.2d 73, 85 (6th Cir. 1943).

140. 17 U.S.C. § 504(c)(1). *See* Chapter Two, Section 2.1[8][d], for a more detailed discussion of actual versus statutory damages.

141. *Chi-boy Music v. Charlie Club, Inc.,* 930 F.2d 1224, 1230 (7th Cir. 1991).

142. M. Heins & T. Beckles, *Will Fair Use Survive? Free Expression in the Age of Copyright Control,* 26 (2005), Brennan Center for Justice, http://www.fepproject.org/policy reports/WillFairUseSurvive.pdf. A recent study conducted by Temple University interviewed 63 educational professionals and "found that nearly all were confused about 'fair use' and their rights as educators to use media materials." *See* Meris Stansbury, *Fair Use Confusion Threatens Media Literacy,* eSchool News (Oct. 9, 2007), http://www.eschoolnews.com/news/showStoryRSS.cfm?ArticleID=7430.

First, educational use infringements are difficult to detect. Copyright owners do not have the resources to police every classroom to ascertain whether teachers and students are using their works appropriately. Absent infringing material being posted on the Internet, such activity is virtually impossible to uncover. Second, even when an infringement is unmasked, the matter seldom reaches a court of law. Despite valid claims, copyright owners may choose not to sue educational institutions in order to avoid unpleasant publicity.[143] Many schools and their students are, of course, major purchasers of copyrighted works and therefore valued customers. These owners may be willing to overlook minor infringements if textbook sales are good.

Even when substantial economic harm is involved, a copyright holder or publisher generally opts to first notify the alleged infringer of its claim and request that it stop engaging in the disputed activity. Such notice usually arrives in the form of a "cease and desist" letter from a lawyer. These letters normally identify the copyrighted work and the alleged infringement thereof. They further request that the recipient either immediately discontinue its infringing practice or obtain a license for continued use. The letters generally conclude with a threat of a lawsuit being filed if the author's demands are not met.

Some schools that receive such a letter do not cease and desist, as requested, because they feel their actions are protected by fair use. In these cases, institutions are best advised to have legal counsel respond with a detailed defense of their position. Ignoring the letter or doing nothing merely invites disaster. In many instances, an institution with a defensible legal position still chooses to acquiesce to the publisher's demand in order to avoid a costly legal battle.[144]

If a school's conduct does not constitute fair use, the best course of action is to promptly notify the owner's lawyer that the school will adhere to her request. Apologies or explanations for the misbehavior are unnecessary and often counterproductive. Discontinuing infringing activity after being asked to do so makes one no less culpable than the bank robber who agrees to give back the money after being detained by the police in the park-

---

143. *Fisher Report* at 29. ("Film studios appear unwilling to take the potentially unpopular step of suing professors for stealing their work.").

144. Tricia Beckles & Marjorie Heins, *A Preliminary Report on the Chilling Effects of Cease and Desist Letters*, 5 (Oct. 26, 2004), http://www.feproject.org/commentaries/ceaseanddesist.html.

ing lot. There is also nothing preventing the school's "apology" from being introduced as evidence at trial should matters proceed to that stage.[145]

Lastly, there are few reported cases in this field because the financial incentive to initiate litigation against schools is generally low. Recall that the Copyright Act nullifies statutory damages against nonprofit educational institutions, or their agents or employees, who reasonably believed their conduct constituted fair use.[146] Regardless, given the paucity of case law in the area and the murky nature of the fair use doctrine in general, colleges and school systems need to be extremely cautious when employing fair use and should seek the advice of counsel when necessary. Compliance with the various "fair use guidelines" can also be an aid, if not always a complete source of comfort, as seen in Section 3.3 below.

3.3 FAIR USE GUIDELINES FOR EDUCATORS

As noted above, providing greater certainty for both educational users and copyright owners under Section 107 has long been sought.[147] One method for achieving this objective is to craft "guidelines" explaining how fair use applies to various educational situations. Guidelines are detailed standards describing permissible uses that represent a negotiated consensus among groups of interested parties. They do not, however, have the force of law; nor do they control or alter statutory language. Their primary purpose is to establish a "safe harbor" of conduct—a minimum standard that those endorsing the guidelines would agree qualifies as fair use.[148]

Guidelines typically provide direction as to how much of a work may be reproduced, how many copies can be made, and over what time periods they may be used. Operating within such guidelines substantially reduces

---

145. Only in the event that such a letter was deemed part of settlement discussions between the parties could it be legally excluded from evidence. *See generally* Fed. R. Evid. 503.

146. 17 U.S.C. § 504(c)(2). In addition, the doctrine of sovereign immunity makes it difficult for an owner to seek redress from a state college or university. *See* Chapter Two, Section 2.1[9], for a more detailed discussion of this doctrine.

147. *Fisher Report* at 51, 106. *See also* C. Toth, *E-violations of Copyright a Problem for Faculty, Students,* dailyvangard.com (May 23, 2006) ("Most faculty are accidentally breaking the law.").

148. *See Uniform Preamble for All Fair Use Guidelines, Conference on Fair Use, Final Report to the Commissioner on the Conclusion of the Conference on Fair Use* 31 (1998): "While only the courts can authoritatively determine whether a particular use is fair use, these guidelines represent the endorsers' consensus of conditions under which fair use should generally apply and examples of when permission is required. Uses that exceed these guidelines may or may not be fair use. The endorsers also agree that the more one exceeds these guidelines, the greater the risk that fair use does not apply."

the risk of infringement liability. Accordingly, guidelines should aid educators in planning their lessons and courses. It is important to stress, however, that these guidelines are designed as a floor and not a ceiling. Conduct falling outside their scope may still qualify as fair use.[149] Despite the lack of legal force, courts have considered several of these guidelines in evaluating fair use claims and have ruled in accordance with their principles.[150]

The most important of these guidelines are summarized and discussed below. In certain instances, their full text can be found in the appendices to this chapter. While some commentators have questioned both the neutrality and wisdom of such guidelines,[151] their place in education is well established as over 80 percent of American colleges have adopted various versions thereof as internal policies.[152]

[1] Classroom Photocopying

In a joint letter to the Chairman of the House Judiciary Subcommittee on Courts, Civil Liberties and the Administration of Justice (dated March 19, 1976), representatives of the Ad Hoc Committee of Educational Institutions and Organizations on Copyright Law Revision, the Authors League of America, Inc., and the Association of American Publishers, Inc., submitted to Congress their "Agreement on Guidelines for Classroom Copying in Not-for-Profit Educational Institutions with Respect to Books and Periodicals" (hereinafter, the "Photocopying Guidelines"). In preparing the Photocopying Guidelines, these organizations[153] agreed that:

- the purpose of the guidelines was to state the minimum and not the maximum standards of educational fair use under Section 107 of the Copyright Act;

---

149. *House Report* at 70 ("The purpose of the following guidelines is to state the minimum and not the maximum standards of educational fair use under Section 107.").

150. *See Princeton Univ. Press v. Michigan Doc. Svcs., Inc.*, 99 F.3d 1381, 1390–91 (6th Cir. 1996) (en banc) (discussing legal effect of guidelines), *cert. denied*, 520 U.S. 1156 (1997); *Kinko's, supra* note 1, at 1527 (citing and discussing classroom photocopying guidelines); 3 *Nimmer on Copyright* at § 13.05[E][3][a].

151. *See* K. Crews, *The Law of Fair Use and the Illusion of Fair Use Guidelines*, 62 Ohio St. L.J. 599, 694 (2001) (suggesting the guidelines "bear little relationship . . . to the law of fair use" and "have had contrary and destructive effects").

152. B. Zidar, *Fair Use and the Code of the Schoolyard: Can Copyshops Compile Coursepacks Consistent with Copyright?* 46 Emory L.J. 1363, 1386 (1997).

153. It should be noted that the American Association of University Professors and other educational groups have not approved these guidelines. *See Fisher Report* at 86.

- the conditions determining the extent of permissible copying for educational purposes may change in the future;
- certain types of copying permitted under the guidelines may not be permissible in the future;
- in the future, other types of copying not permitted under these guidelines may be permissible under revised guidelines; and
- there may be instances in which copying does not fall within the guidelines, but may nonetheless be permitted under the criteria of fair use.

The Photocopying Guidelines were included in H.R. Rep. No. 94–1476 and made part of the legislative history of the 1976 Copyright Act. They are reproduced in their entirety in Appendix 3-A. Pertinent provisions are paraphrased below:

I. *Single Copying for Teachers*

For scholarly research or use in teaching or preparing to teach a class, an instructor may make, or have made at his or her individual request, a single copy of:

A. a chapter from a book;

B. an article from a periodical or newspaper;

C. a short story, essay, or short poem, whether or not from a collective work; or

D. a chart, graph, diagram, drawing, cartoon, or picture from a book, periodical, or newspaper.

II. *Multiple Copies for Classroom Use*

Multiple copies may be made by or for the teacher giving the course for classroom use or discussion, if he or she:

A. makes no more than one copy for each pupil in a course;

B. includes a notice of copyright on each copy;

C. does not charge the student beyond the actual cost of the photocopying; and

D. meets the "brevity," "spontaneity," and "cumulative effect" tests outlined below:

a. "*Brevity.*" Copying of the following types of works in the amount prescribed is permitted:

(i) *Poetry:* a complete poem if less than 250 words and printed on not more than two pages, or an excerpt from a longer poem not to exceed 250 words.

(ii) *Prose:* a complete article, story or essay of less than 2500 words, or an excerpt from any prose work of not more than 1000 words or 10% of the work, whichever is less, but in any event a minimum of 500 words.

[The limits of (i) and (ii) above may be expanded to permit the completion of an unfinished line of a poem or prose paragraph.]

(iii) *Illustration:* one chart, graph, diagram, drawing, cartoon or picture per book or periodical issue.

(iv) *"Special" works* (poetry and/or prose which often combine language with illustrations and that is sometimes intended for children, but less than 2500 words): may not be reproduced in its entirety, however, excerpts may be up to two pages, but not more than 10% of the work.

b. *"Spontaneity."*

  (i) The copying is at the instance and inspiration of the individual teacher; and

  (ii) The inspiration and decision to use the work and the moment of its use for maximum teaching effectiveness are so close in time that it would be unreasonable to expect a timely reply to a request for permission.[154]

c. *"Cumulative" Effect.*

  (i) The material copied is for only one course in the school in which the copies are made;

  (ii) Not more than one short poem, article, story or essay or two excerpts may be copied from the same author, and not more than three from the same collective work or periodical volume during one class term (except for current news periodicals and newspapers and current news sections of other periodicals); and

  (iii) No more than nine instances of such multiple copying for one course during one class term (except for current news periodicals and newspapers and current news sections of other periodicals).

III. *Prohibitions as to I and II Above*

The Photocopying Guidelines specifically prohibit copying:

  (A) used to create, replace, or substitute for anthologies, compilations or collective works. (Such replacement or substitution may

---

154. *See Fisher Report* at 86 (criticizing the spontaneity requirement by characterizing it as "essentially imposing a general presumption that teachers seek licenses in all but the most extraordinary instances").

still occur even if copies of various works or excerpts therefrom are accumulated or reproduced and used separately.)

(B) of or from works intended to be "consumable" in the course of studying or teaching. (These include workbooks, exercises, standardized tests, test booklets, answer sheets, and similar educational material.)

(C) as a substitute for the purchase of books, magazines, or reprints.

(D) to be directed by an authority higher than the individual instructor.

(E) to be repeated with respect to the same item by the same teacher from term to term.

[2] General Library Exceptions

Section 108 of the Copyright Act sets forth the general conditions for libraries and archives[155] to avoid infringement liability when attempting to service patrons and preserve items within their collections. For convenience, a summary of the statute is included as Appendix 3-B at the end of this chapter. A more detailed explanation is contained below. As part of the Copyright Act, Section 108 is established law and therefore afforded greater judicial weight than the other guidelines addressed herein. It is dealt with here for ease of reference and because one of its subsections, 108(g)(2) regarding interlibrary loans, is the subject of negotiated guidelines, as discussed in subsection [5].

Paragraph (a) of Section 108 has been a source of some confusion, appearing to grant an independent exception allowing single copies. However, the legislative history of the 1976 Act clarifies that this paragraph

---

155. For convenience, the term "libraries" as used herein will refer to both "libraries and archives." While Section 108 does not define these terms, the 1976 *House Report* states that "a purely commercial enterprise could not establish a collection of copyrighted works, call itself a library or archive, and engage in for-profit reproduction and distribution of photocopies." *House Report* at 74. In addition, a subsequent Senate report notes that "just as when section 108 of the Copyright Act was first enacted, the term 'libraries' and 'archives' as used and described in this provision still refer to such institutions only in the conventional sense of entities that are established as, and conduct their operations through, physical premises in which collections of information may be used by researchers and other members of the public." S. Rep. No. 105–190, at 62 (1998) (hereinafter 1998 *Senate Report*). *See also Pacific & Southern Co. v. Duncan*, 744 F.2d 1490, 1494 n.6 (11th Cir. 1984) (noting that a commercial organization that videotapes television news programs and sells the tapes is not an "archive" within the meaning of Section 108); *United States v. Moran*, 757 F. Supp. 1046, 1051 (D. Neb. 1991) (indicating that a commercial video rental store does not operate as a library or archives, and thus cannot make unauthorized "replacement" copies of copyrighted works under Section 108).

serves as a qualifier for the specific exceptions set forth in subsequent clauses.[156] Essentially, 108 (a) lays out the general conditions that must be met in order to take advantage of the law. These conditions are as follows:

- Only one copy of a work can be made, unless otherwise specified.
- Library copies cannot be made for direct or indirect commercial advantage. Libraries in for-profit organizations (such as law firms or industrial research centers) may rely on the law because it bars commercial advantage only from attaching to the act of reproduction, not the overall goal of the institution where the copying takes place.[157] However, such libraries may be excluded from Section 108 privileges by virtue of the next condition.
- Collections must be open to the public or unaffiliated researchers in a specialized field. Thus, unless a company opens its library to nonaffiliated persons (including potential competitors), it cannot claim a Section 108 privilege.[158] Opening a collection to the public solely through interlibrary loans also fails to meet the test.[159]
- Prior to 1998, all works reproduced or distributed by a library had to contain a "notice of copyright." This created a problem if the original work bore no such notice. The situation was clarified by the Digital Millennium Copyright Act[160] (hereinafter, "DMCA") which modified 108(a) to provide that all library items had to bear a copyright notice identical to that on the original work. If the item did not have one, the library copy had to include a legend stating the work may be protected under copyright.[161]

Section 108(i) also sets forth another general qualifier. The reproduction and distribution of a musical, pictorial, graphic, or sculptural work, or a motion picture or other audiovisual work (other than one dealing with news), are allowed only for preservation and replacement purposes. However, duplicating pictorial and graphic works published as parts of nonex-

---

156. *House Report* at 75.

157. *Id.* Note, however, that the earlier Senate report states that Section 108(a)(1) "is intended to preclude a library or archives in a profit-making organization from providing photocopies of copyrighted materials to employees engaged in furtherance of the organization's commercial enterprise." *Senate Report* at 67. These conflicting stances have never been reconciled by subsequent laws or judicial opinions.

158. *The Register of Copyrights, Library Reproduction of Copyrighted Works* (17 U.S.C. §108) 78–79 (1983) (hereinafter 1983 *Register's Report*).

159. *Id.* at 78.

160. Pub. L. No. 105–304, 112 Stat. 2680 (1998).

161. 1998 *Senate Report* at 60.

cluded items is permitted. Basically, these provisions limit research-related copying to traditional print materials.

[a] Exceptions for Preservation and Replacement

Sections 108(b) and (c) of the Copyright Act permit libraries to reproduce works for preservation, deposit or replacement purposes, under certain circumstances. Specifically, Section 108(b) allows a library to reproduce and distribute up to *three* copies of an *unpublished* work solely for purposes of preservation, security, or deposit for research in another library. This provision applies to "an archival collection of original manuscripts, papers, and the like, most of which are unpublished, and for which a rigorous preservation regime serves the needs of archives and scholars."[162] Libraries may not loan unpublished preservation copies to their patrons, however, as this could infringe the copyright owner's right of first publication.[163] The limit was raised from one to three copies as part of the DMCA amendments in 1998.[164]

Fixing the number of preservation copies at three, as opposed to a "reasonable number," arose from the 1995 National Information Infrastructure Task Force Report, a foundational document for the DMCA drafters,[165] which recommended permitting "three copies of works in digital form," "to accommodate the reality of the computerized library."[166] However, the three-copy rule more closely tracks the analog (e.g., microform) preservation standard consisting of an "iron mountain," master, and a use copy,[167] than it does the realities of today's digital preservation standards.[168]

Triplicate reproduction and distribution of *unpublished* works are subject to two additional conditions:

- The work must already reside in the library making the copy, but need *not* be part of the library collection where it is deposited for research.[169]

---

162. 1983 *Register's Report* at 105.

163. *Id.* at 105–106.

164. 1998 *Senate Report* at 61.

165. *See, e.g., id.* at 2–3.

166. *Working Group on Intellectual Property Rights, Intellectual Property and the National Information Infrastructure* 227 (1995).

167. C. Henderson, *American Library Ass'n, Library Preservation: Changes Incorporated in H.R. 2281 The Digital Millennium Copyright Act of 1998* (Pub. L. No. 105–304 (1998)), http://www.ala.org/ala/washoff/WOissues/copyrightb/dmca/preservation.pdf.

168. Anyone owning a computer knows to save important items on backup media as digital copies are highly unstable and cannot be simply made once and for all and stored away.

169. *House Report* at 75.

- The library's distribution right is confined to its physical premises for digitally reproduced works.[170]

Section 108(c) allows a library to reproduce up to *three* copies of an entire *published* work, provided it is doing so to replace a work that is damaged, deteriorating, lost, stolen, or in an obsolete format. Two additional conditions must be met:

- No copies may be made until the library first consults the copyright owner and standard trade sources[171] to determine that an *unused* copy cannot be purchased at a fair price.
- The copy cannot be made available to the public outside the library's premises if reproduced in a digital format.

This provision (initially applicable to only a single copy) ensures that items are preserved in usable form despite factors—like time, accidents, and technology—that are beyond the library's reasonable control.[172] Unlike Section 108(b), which pertains to unpublished works, Section 108(c) does not expressly grant distribution rights to libraries.[173] However, the right to distribute the copy the same as the original under the first sale doctrine is implied, since providing continued access to a work is the provision's principal objective.[174] A library's ability to make a replacement copy for another institution is also implied where the second library's only copy is lost, stolen, or so badly damaged as to make it unusable.[175] Lastly, the DMCA permits duplication to replace an obsolete version of a work.[176]

[b] Exceptions for Patron Research

Sections 108(d) and (e) of the Copyright Act permit reproduction and distribution of potential works at the request of library patrons under cer-

---

170. 1998 *Senate Report* at 61–62. This limitation is designed to reduce the risk of digital copies entering into widespread circulation and thus harming the owner's potential market.

171. *House Report* at 75–76.

172. 1998 *Senate Report* at 62.

173. Note that a federal district court has ruled that "a library distributes a published work, within the meaning of the Copyright Act . . . when it places an unauthorized copy of the work in its collection, includes the copy in its catalog or index system, and makes the copy available to the public." *Hotaling v. Church of Jesus Christ of Latter-Day Saints*, 118 F.3d 199, 201 (4th Cir. 1997). The meaning of this rule for libraries that make replacement copies under Section 108 is unclear, as the *Hotaling* court declined to address the defendant's 108(c) arguments. *See id.* at 204.

174. 1998 *Senate Report* at 62.

175. 1983 *Register's Report* at 114.

176. A format is considered obsolete if the machine or device necessary to render a work stored in that format perceptible is no longer manufactured or reasonably available in the commercial marketplace. *See* 1998 *Senate Report* at 62.

tain limited circumstances. These rights vary depending on whether the request involves (1) one article or other contribution to a collection or periodical issue, (2) a small part of any work; or (3) an entire work or substantial part thereof.

Pursuant to Section 108(d), a library may make *one* copy of a single article from a collection or a small part of a larger work for a patron or another library, under the following four conditions:

1. The work is housed in the library where the patron makes the request, or another library.
2. The copy becomes the property of the requesting patron, and is not added to the library's collection.
3. The library has no notice that the copy will be used for anything other than research purposes.
4. The library displays a copyright warning where copy orders are made, and attaches that same warning to copy order forms.

Libraries are also permitted to make *single* copies of *entire* works, or substantial parts thereof, pursuant to patron requests, under the four conditions listed above if they also first consult with the copyright owner and standard trade sources[177] to determine whether a used or unused copy can be purchased at a fair price.

[c] Further Limitations on Reproductions for Patrons

While isolated and unrelated reproductions of similar items can be made on separate occasions, a library must refrain from such copying if it knows or has substantial reason to believe that it is engaged in the related or concerted reproduction or distribution of multiple reproductions of the same material.[178] Such "systematic" reproduction involves any copying done via a common plan, regular interaction, or an organized or established procedure.[179] The 1975 U.S. Senate Report, while failing to specifically define such practices, provided three examples:

(a) A library informs other libraries that it will maintain and build its own collection of frequently used biology journals and make copies of articles therefrom available to them and their patrons on request. Accordingly, the other libraries discontinue or refrain from purchasing similar subscriptions.

---

177. *House Report* at 75–76.
178. 17 U.S.C. § 108(g).
179. 1983 *Register's Report* at 139.

(b) A research center employing scientists and technicians subscribes to several relevant periodicals. By reproducing photocopies of articles contained therein, the center is able to make this material available to its staff and avoid multiple subscriptions.

(c) Several branches of a library system agree that each location will subscribe to specified journals only and provide copies of articles contained therein to the other branches.[180]

The "systematic copying" restriction does not prevent libraries from participating in interlibrary arrangements, provided the aggregate quantities of material received do not serve as a substitute for subscriptions to or purchases of the subject works. In crafting this proviso, Congress intended the meaning of "aggregate quantities" and "substitute for a subscription to or purchase of" to be clarified by private guidelines. These guidelines are discussed in Section 3.3[5].

[d] Exceptions for Newscasts

Section 108(f)(3) of the Copyright Act permits libraries to tape and distribute (by lending)[181] a limited number of copies and excerpts of audiovisual news programs provided the general conditions of Section 108(a) are met. These programs are defined as "daily newscasts of the national television networks, which report the major events of the day."[182] It is unclear whether cable news network broadcasts are covered by the statute because the law predates the advent of such programming.

[e] Exceptions for Orphan Works in Last Twenty Years of Their Term

Section 108(h) was added pursuant to the Sonny Bono Copyright Term Extension Act,[183] which added twenty years to the "life" of a copyright.[184] Congress enacted paragraph (h) over concerns older works would remain outside the public domain even though they were no longer available for

---

180. *Senate Report* at 70. In addition, the U.S. Court of Appeals for the Second Circuit has analyzed the meaning of "systematic" copying in the context of actions by a library in a for-profit corporation. This analysis, however, was within the fair use context, and did not directly address Section 108(g). *See American Geophysical Union, supra* note 107, at 916, 919–20, and 924–25.

181. *House Report* at 77 (distribution of such copies is limited to lending in order to prevent performance or sale by the recipients).

182. *Id.*

183. Pub. L. No. 105–298, 112 Stat. 2827 (1998).

184. H.R. Rep. No. 105–452, at 2 (1998).

purchase.[185] In essence, the law provides that once a *published* work reaches the last twenty years of its copyright term, a library or archives, including a nonprofit educational institution, may reproduce, distribute, display, or perform it, provided such organization has determined after a reasonable investigation that:

- The work is *not* currently subject to normal commercial exploitation;
- A *new or used* copy thereof is *not* available at a reasonable price; and
- The rights holder has not notified the Copyright Office that one or both of the above two assumptions is inaccurate.

Section 108(h) was originally modified by paragraph (i) so as to exclude those categories of works (e.g., pictorial, graphical, and sculptural) listed therein. This exclusion, however, was the result of a legislative oversight, and Congress corrected the lacuna shortly thereafter.[186] Interestingly, 108(h) applies only to the library itself and not its patrons or other downstream users. Also, the exception is not limited to analog reproduction, nor does it require that the subject work already be in the library's collection. The general Section 108(a) conditions continue to apply, however.

[f] Liability

Section 108(f)(1) of the Copyright Act immunizes libraries and their employees from infringement liability for the unsupervised use of their photocopying equipment, provided such equipment bears a notice stating the user is subject to copyright law. Correspondingly, Section 108(f)(2) makes clear that library patrons who engage in unsupervised copying or exceed the boundaries of fair use with such copies are subject to infringement penalties.

---

185. *See, e.g.,* A. P. Lutzker, *American Library Ass'n, Primer on the Digital Millennium Copyright Act*, 24 (1999), http://www.ala.org/ala/washoff/WOissues/copyrightb/dmca/dmca primer.pdf.

186. Preservation and Restoration of Orphan Works for Use in Scholarship and Education (PRO-USE) Act of 2005, H.R. 24, 109th Cong. 1st Sess. (2005). According to Register of Copyrights Marybeth Peters, the failure to carve out subsection (h) from subsection (i) was an oversight. *Oversight Hearing on the "Operations of the Copyright Office" Before the Subcomm. on Courts, the Internet, and Intellectual Property of the Comm. on the Judiciary, United States House of Representatives*, 108th Cong. at 28 (2004) (statement of Marybeth Peters, Register of Copyrights, U.S. Copyright Office), http://judiciary.house.gov/oversight .aspx?ID=49; Marybeth Peters, *Copyright Enters the Public Domain*, 51 J. Copyright Soc'y U.S. 701, 713 (2004).

[g] Fair Use and Contracts

Finally, Section 108(f)(4) confirms the statute does not in any way nullify or affect a library's fair use rights or contractual obligations. As a matter of practice, libraries continue to rely heavily on the fair use doctrine, particularly with respect to digital works for which little legislative guidance currently exists. The clarification regarding contracts ensures libraries honor agreements with donors who often gift or bequeath works to institutions with the understanding that these items will never be copied or loaned to the general public.[187]

[h] Section 108 Study Group

The Section 108 Study Group (hereinafter, the "Study Group") was convened in April 2005, under the auspices of the Library of Congress National Digital Information Infrastructure and Preservation Program (NDIIPP).[188] The Study Group is charged with examining how Section 108 may need to be amended in light of the impact of digital technologies on traditional analog works. The nineteen-member Study Group is composed of copyright experts from various companies, libraries, archives, and museums and intends to submit its findings and recommendations to the Librarian of Congress by late 2008.[189]

To date, the Study Group has primarily focused on the following issues: (1) making additional institutions eligible for Section 108 treatment; (2) amending the preservation and replacement exceptions in subsections (b) and (c) by: (i) raising the three-copy limit, (ii) adding other "triggers" to 108(c), (iii) no longer differentiating between published and unpublished works, and (iv) easing off-site access restrictions for digital works; (3) creating a preservation-only copy exception for certain works; (4) allowing the "capture" of websites and other online content; and (5) permitting libraries to circumvent "copyright-protected" works for Section 108 purposes. The Study Group has sought input, through both written and oral comments, on whether any of these areas merit a legislative solution and, if so, what changes might effectively address those problems while balancing the interests of libraries and copyright holders.[190]

---

187. *House Report* at 77.

188. The Miscellaneous Appropriations Act of 2001, Pub. L. No. 106–554, 114 Stat. 2763 (2000), appropriated $100,000,000 to plan and execute the NDIIPP legislation pursuant to which the Library of Congress, in cooperation with the U.S. Copyright Office, is charged with overseeing the effort to create a national digital collection and preservation strategy. *See* http://www.digitalpreservation.gov for more information regarding the NDIIPP.

189. Additional information regarding the Section 108 Study Group can be found at http://www.loc.gov/section108.

190. *Section 108 Study Group, Information for the March 2006 Public Roundtables and Request for Written Comments* (Feb. 10, 2006).

Some background on each of these five areas and why they are of current concern is included below.

[i] Institutions Eligible for Section 108

As noted above, the provisions of Section 108 apply only to "libraries" and "archives." Neither word is defined in the statute. Over the years, these terms have increasingly been used in a generic sense to embrace collections of information outside of local public or school libraries. In contemplating revisions to Section 108, the Study Group has discussed what types of institutions should now be covered by it.

For instance, the group has considered whether only nonprofit or government bodies providing materials and services for public, and not private, benefit should be eligible.[191] The Study Group has also examined whether "virtual" libraries and archives (i.e., institutions that provide access only electronically) should be included under the exemption as well. The U.S. Senate report on the DMCA indicated that Section 108 applied only to "brick and mortar" institutions.[192] Increasingly, however, libraries are building digital collections and making their works available on electronic networks.

Questions have also been raised regarding museums and outsourcing. Museums, for instance, increasingly provide services that overlap with libraries and often deal with digital and other materials that raise copyright issues. As for outsourcing, nothing in the current law covers such activities, but many libraries and archives engage contractors to digitize analog materials and perform other traditional library functions.

[ii] Amendments to Current Sections 108(b) and (c), Including (1) the Three-Copy Limit, (2) New Triggers Under 108(c), (3) Published versus Unpublished Works, and (4) Off-Premises Access to Digital Copies

Several revisions to Sections 108(b) and (c) have been considered, including proposals to (1) replace the three-copy limit in both (b) and (c) with language allowing a "reasonable/limited" number of copies; (2) add additional "triggers" under 108(c) to permit duplication where the original library copy is inherently unstable or at risk of loss; (3) no longer differentiate between unpublished and published works; and (4) permit limited

---

191. The 1975 *Senate Report* views 108(a)(1) as "intended to preclude a library or archives in a profit-making organization from providing photocopies of copyrighted materials to employees engaged in furtherance of the organization's commercial enterprise." *Senate Report* at 67.

192. 1998 *Senate Report* at 62 ("Although online interactive digital networks have since given birth to online digital 'libraries' and 'archives' that exist only in the virtual (rather than physical) sense on websites, bulletin boards and homepages across the Internet, it is not the Committee's intent that section 108 as revised apply to such collections of information.").

off-site use of digital copies. Each of these four issues is examined briefly below.

1) The Three-Copy Limit   Using digital technologies to preserve analog versions of works helps find shelf space and deal with chemical deterioration, but it also presents its own set of challenges. Among these are the need to make multiple backup copies, create preservation-ready formats, and combine those formats with new display technologies. Moreover, digital works are often distributed and accessed electronically among library staff for purposes of cataloging and storage. Each of these steps involves making either a permanent or temporary copy of the work and thereby implicates the owner's copyright therein.

In light of these technical realities, it is virtually impossible to preserve digital versions without making more than three copies of a work over the term of its copyright. The Study Group has thus considered replacing the fixed "three copy" rule with more flexible language (e.g., "a limited number of copies as reasonably necessary for the permitted purpose").

2) Additional Triggers under 108(c)   Digital works often require replacement "in anticipation of" future damage or loss, since such media tend to lose their integrity more quickly than analog materials. At the same time, the deterioration of digital objects, unlike like that of physical works, is not always apparent. For example, when a book becomes brittle, the decay is visible to the naked eye, but its text is often still legible. A digital work, on the other hand, may lose data before anyone notices. Moreover, once bits are lost, they are difficult if not impossible to restore.[193]

The Study Group has thus considered whether the "triggers" to replace copies under 108(c) should be expanded to include adjectives such as "unstable" or "fragile" and/or permit the unconditional replacement of digital materials. More precise definitions for these terms may be required to limit their scope. However, eligible institutions would still be required to first make a reasonable effort to find an unused copy at a fair price.

3) Published versus Unpublished Works   Section 108(b) makes it easier for libraries to reproduce and distribute unpublished works for preservation than 108(c) does for published ones. For instance, up to three copies of

---

193. For background on the problems surrounding digital preservation, *see, e.g.,* Jeff Rothenberg, *Counsel on Library and Info. Res., Avoiding Technological Quicksand: Finding a Viable Foundation for Digital Preservation* (1999), http://www.clir.org/pubs/abstract/pub77 .html.

unpublished materials can be made "for preservation and security or for deposit for research use in another library or archives." Unlike published works, the original need not be damaged, deteriorating, lost, stolen, or in obsolete format, and no effort need be made to find an unused copy.

The principal reason for this distinction is that unpublished items collected by libraries are frequently unique and rare. Moreover, there is less likelihood of economic harm or displacing demand for a work since these materials are not generally available. Conversely, some unpublished works are intended to be published or may nevertheless have a potential future market. In light of this, the Study Group has considered amending Section 108 to no longer distinguish between the two categories.

4) Access to Digital Copies Made under 108(b) and (c)　Currently, Section 108 requires libraries making digital copies for preservation or replacement purposes to permit access thereto only on their "premises." This applies to both tangible digital media (e.g., CDs and DVDs) and purely electronic materials (e.g., e-journals). "Premises" are understood to mean the actual buildings housing the library, and not the wider campus or community of which they are a part. Increasingly, though, libraries need to make digital copies available online or otherwise off-site for various preservation, access, or storage reasons. Expanding unlicensed electronic access to digital works, however, raises concerns for publishers and authors, given the ease of copying and retransmitting these materials.[194] Moreover, given the growing demand for digital products, copyright owners fear that permitting libraries to place more of their works online could usurp potential markets and decrease revenues.

On the other hand, libraries sense an increasing public appetite for electronic services. For example, patrons are often geographically dispersed and hampered by having to travel long distances to obtain materials and conduct research. Being able to retrieve information electronically would diminish this burden. However, the Study Group believes a balance needs to be struck between the current "physical premises" restriction, which appears anachronistic given existing technologies, and the prospect of unauthorized distribution of digital materials.

As such, the group has considered several ways to achieve this balance, including

- limiting the number of simultaneous users of a work to one per each legally acquired copy thereof,

---

194. It is for this very reason that the on-premises restriction for digital copies was included in the DMCA revisions to Section 108. *See* 1998 *Senate Report* at 61–62.

- restricting off-site access to the library's community of users, where a sufficiently well-defined community exists, and
- requiring technological measures and user agreements to enforce the above limits and prevent downloading or further transmission by the user.

[iii] New Preservation—Only Exception

As mentioned above, the inherently unstable nature of digital materials presents unique preservation problems. The loss of integrity, deterioration of bits, and obsolescence of hardware and software can often occur without notice. As such, measures need to be taken early in the "life" of such materials to safeguard them. However, the current parameters of the law make this difficult, as libraries must first wait for a work to become damaged, lost, stolen, or obsolete, or to deteriorate (as currently required by Section 108(c)) before initiating action.

The Study Group has proposed that certain institutions be allowed to make copies of "at risk" works, thus permitting a select group of qualifying libraries to duplicate all works in their collections solely for preservation purposes. Such a plan would still protect copyright owners' exclusive rights, while permitting recognized bodies to create up-front digital copies as insurance against future loss.

[iv] New Website Preservation Exception

The Study Group has also discussed allowing libraries to capture and memorialize certain publicly available Internet sites without permission of or license with their owner. The group believes websites present unique preservation problems that merit special attention. For instance, online content is particularly ephemeral in nature, and most noncommercial sites are not archived. However, these sites often contain a rich record of our social and political history that should be "captured." Currently, no legal mechanism exists for libraries to obtain a copy or duplicate the contents of a site on a particular date.

A new Section 108 exception would afford libraries this option. Since Internet sites arguably carry implicit permission to download their content,[195] it is anticipated that rights holders will have few, if any, objections to such a proposal. In addition, precedent currently exists for this type of exception. In 1976, Congress determined that, given the importance of national television news broadcasts, libraries should be able to copy them

---

195. *See* Chapter Four, note 16.

off the air for preservation and lending purposes.[196] That same reasoning could be applied to today's online content.

[v] Circumvention of TPMs

Finally, the Study Group has observed that many new works are encrypted or "copyright-protected" by their publishers. If a library is not permitted to circumvent such technological protection measures (TPMs), it cannot take advantage of any Section 108 exceptions. Given the increasing use of TPMs, the inability to circumvent them could eventually nullify any broadening of the statute, or render it altogether moot. One suggestion from the Study Group is to craft an exception similar to current Section 112(e)(8) of the Copyright Act, that would, for example, require owners to either provide the means to make a permitted copy or allow the library to circumvent the TPM for that work. Currently, the DMCA permits the circumvention of TPMs for only a few classes of works by selected users thereof.[197]

The prospects of the Study Group achieving consensus and ultimately recommending that Congress make specific amendments to the Copyright Act are currently uncertain.

[3] Traditional Library Reserves at Educational Institutions

No provision of the Copyright Act directly relates to copying educational materials for placement on reserve at a college or university library. The American Library Association published a set of guidelines as part of its Model Policy Concerning College and University Photocopying for Class-room, Research and Library Reserve Use in March, 1982 (the "ALA Guide-lines") to provide educational institutions some direction in this area. The ALA Guidelines were never formally adopted by any committee of educa-tors or copyright owners, nor made part of the *Congressional Record*, as were the Photocopying Guidelines. As such, their standing and impact are subject to uncertainty. The ALA Guidelines may be found in their entirety at http://www.cni.org/docs/infopols/ALA.html.

The ALA Guidelines permit librarians to photocopy materials to place on reserve, at the request of a professor, to assist students in preparing class assignments and for advanced independent study and research. This copying must be done in accordance with certain rules, however. For instance, the amount of material and copies thereof should be reasonable

---

196. 17 U.S.C. § 108(f)(3); *See Senate Report* at 69. Section 108(f)(3) legitimized the Vanderbilt University library program of capturing television news programs off-air and allowed it to build its Television News Archive into a resource of national importance.

197. *See* Chapter Five, Section 5.4[1][b], for a more detailed discussion of permitted TPM circumvention.

considering the total amount of material assigned for a class and the number of students enrolled therein. The material must also contain a copyright notice, and the photocopying may not significantly impact the market for the work. Copies may be used only in the same semester they were placed on reserve.

[4] Electronic Reserves at Educational Institutions

Making educational materials accessible through electronic reserve systems raises significant copyright issues.[198] Electronic reserve operations include digitizing text, displaying and distributing scanned works at computer terminals, and downloading and printing copies thereof. No specific provision of the Copyright Act addresses electronic reserves. The Fair Use Guidelines for Electronic Reserve Systems (the "ERS Guidelines"), which are paraphrased below, were developed by the Conference on Fair Use but did not gain universal support among participants. As such, their standing and impact are subject to much uncertainty. The ERS Guidelines are reproduced in their entirety in Appendix 3-C.

A. **Introduction**

Many college, university, and school system libraries have established reserve operations for readings and other materials that support the instructional requirements of specific courses. Some educational institutions now provide systems allowing storage of electronic versions of materials that students may retrieve on a computer screen and possibly print out for their personal study. When relying on fair use, electronic reserve systems should constitute an ad hoc or supplemental source of information for students, beyond a textbook or other materials. If included by permission of the copyright owner, however, the scope and range of materials is potentially unlimited. Although fair use is determined on a case-by-case basis, the following guidelines identify an understanding thereof for the reproduction, distribution, display, and performance of materials in the context of creating and using an electronic reserve system.

B. **Scope of Material**

1. In accordance with the fair use doctrine, electronic reserve systems may include copyrighted materials at the request of an individual instructor.

---

198. One way colleges are attempting to circumvent this issue is to have their professors provide links to the articles they wish their students to read instead of duplicating the material. *See* Toth, *supra* note 147, at 2. *See also* Chapter Four *infra*, note 29 (linking does not constitute copying).

2. Electronic reserve systems may include short items (such as an article from a journal, a chapter from a book or conference proceedings, or a poem from a collective work) or excerpts from longer items. "Longer items" include articles, chapters, poems, and other works that are of such length as to constitute a substantial portion of a book, journal, or other work. "Short items" include articles, chapters, poems, and other works of a customary length and structure as to be a small part of a book, journal, or other work, even if that work may be marketed individually.

3. Electronic reserve systems should not include any material unless the instructor, the library, or another unit of the educational institution possesses a lawfully obtained copy.

4. The total amount of material included in electronic reserve systems for a specific course should be small in proportion to the total assigned reading for such course.

C. **Notices and Attributions**

1. On a preliminary or introductory screen, electronic reserve systems should display a notice described in Section 108(f)(1) of the Copyright Act. The notice should include language cautioning against further electronic distribution of a work.

2. If a copyright notice appears on the copy of a work included in an electronic reserve system, the following statement should be positioned where users will likely see it in connection with accessing the work:

> "The work from which this copy is made includes this notice: [restate the elements of the statutory copyright notice: e.g., Copyright 2000, XXX Corp.]"

3. Materials included in electronic reserve systems should include appropriate citations or attributions to their sources.

D. **Access and Use**

1. Electronic reserve systems should be designed to permit access only to those students registered for the course in which the reserve items will be studied, and to instructors and staff responsible for the course or electronic system.

2. Appropriate methods for limiting access will depend on available technology, but may include one or more of the following:
   a. individual password controls or verification of a student's registration status;
   b. password system for each class;
   c. retrieval of works by course number or instructor name, but not by author or title thereof; or

    d. access limited to workstations ordinarily used by, or accessible to, enrolled students or appropriate staff.

  3. Students should not be charged specifically or directly for access to electronic reserve systems.

E. Storage and Reuse

  1. Permission from the copyright holder is required if the item is to be reused in a subsequent academic term for the same course offered by the same instructor, or constitutes standard assigned or optional reading for an individual course taught in multiple sections by many instructors.

  2. Material may be retained in electronic form while permission is being sought or until the next academic term in which the material might be used, but in no event for more than three calendar years, including the year in which the materials are last used.

  3. Short-term access to materials included on electronic reserve systems in previous academic terms may be provided to students who have not completed the course.

Prominent library and higher education associations did not endorse the ERS Guidelines, because they were deemed highly proscriptive and not sufficiently flexible.[199] In response to ongoing uncertainty regarding electronic reserves, in November 2003, the Association of College and Research Libraries, American Library Association, Association of Research Libraries, Association of American Law Libraries, Medical Library Association, and the Special Libraries Association endorsed and distributed a document entitled "Applying Fair Use in the Development of Electronic Reserve Systems."[200]

Instead of drafting new guidelines, though, the relevant parties sought to develop a framework within which libraries could assess risk when applying the doctrine of fair use to electronic reserve systems.[201] Unfortunately, the two-page document is little more than a recitation of the four fair use factors and provides little practical guidance to librarians or others.

[5] Interlibrary Loans

As noted in subsection [2], Section 108(g)(2) of the Copyright Act deals with, among other things, limits on interlibrary consortiums for copying. It prohibits systematic photocopying of material but permits interlibrary

---

199. American Library Association, Washington Office Newsline, Vol. 12, No. 98 (Nov. 19, 2003).

200. The complete document is available at http://www.nacua.org/documents/FairUse ElectronicReserves.doc.

201. See D. Webster, *Electronic Reserves and Fair Use*, Memorandum to ARL Directors (Nov. 5, 2003), http://fairuse.stanford.edu/library_resources/arl.html.

arrangements "that do not have, as their purpose or effect, that the library or archives receiving such copies or phonorecords for distribution does so in such aggregate quantities as to substitute for a subscription to or purchase of such work." The National Commission on New Technological Uses of Copyrighted Works (CONTU) assisted Congress in 1976 to forge a consensus among organizations representing libraries, publishers, and authors to define "such aggregate quantities."[202]

This definition was incorporated into a document called the "CONTU Guidelines" which was subsequently included in the final legislative report on the 1976 Copyright Act.[203] As such, while these guidelines do not have the actual force of law, they were endorsed by the conference committee as "a reasonable interpretation of the proviso of section 108(g)(2) in the most common situations to which they apply today."[204] The CONTU Guidelines are included in their entirety in Appendix 3-D. Pertinent excerpts therefrom are paraphrased below:

I. Requesting Libraries
Within any calendar year, a library may request (the "Requesting Library") no more than five copies of articles published within the last five years in a periodical volume (as opposed to any given issue of a periodical). The Guidelines leave the status of older articles to future determination.

II. Supplying Libraries
Within any calendar year, a supplying library (the "Supplying Library") may fulfill requests for no more than five small excerpts from any other copyrighted work regardless of its publication date.

III. Exception
The above limitations do not apply if the Requesting Library has an existing or ordered subscription to the periodical, or owns or has ordered a copy of the copyrighted work, but such material is not reasonably available for use (i.e., the material is lost, stolen, destroyed, or has not yet arrived).

IV. Representative
Any request must be accompanied by a representation of the Requesting Library that it is made in conformity with these guidelines.

---

202. CONTU was established under separate legislation in 1974 to study the use and reproduction of copyrighted works by computers and other machines. *See* S. Rep. No. 94–92, at 15–16 (1975).

203. Conf. Rep. No. 94–1733, at 72–74 (1976).

204. *Id.* at 71–72.

V. Records

The Requesting Library must maintain records of requested and fulfilled orders for three years after the end of the calendar year in which the request was made.

VI. Section 108 Compliance

A Requesting Library may request a copy from a Supplying Library only under those circumstances where the Requesting Library would have been able, under Section 108 of the Copyright Act, to supply such copy from materials in its own collection. Therefore, the following rules also apply:

A. In the case of an entire work or journal issue, the Requesting Library must determine, on the basis of a reasonable investigation, that a copy cannot be obtained at a fair price.

B. The copy must become the property of the Requesting Library.

C. The Supplying Library must not have received notice that the copy is to be used for any purpose other than private study, scholarship, or research.

D. The Supplying Library should permanently display where orders are taken and on its order form the "Warning of Copyright." (See Appendix 3-B.)

E. The Supplying Library must not be aware or have substantial reason to believe it is engaging in related or concerted reproduction or distribution of multiple copies of the same material.

F. In the case of articles and small parts of a work, the Requesting Library must keep records for a period of at least three full years following the year in which the request was made.

[6] Copyrighted Music

Representatives of the Music Publishers' Association of the United States, Inc., the National Music Publishers' Association, Inc., the Music Teachers National Association, the Music Educators National Conference, the National Association of Schools of Music and the Ad Hoc Committee on Copyright Law Revision submitted draft guidelines to Congress on April 30, 1976, setting forth proposed minimum standards of educational fair use for copyrighted music (the "Music Guidelines").

The organizations involved in drafting these guidelines agreed that conditions could change in the future to permit less or more expansive copying of music. The Music Guidelines are not intended to limit copying otherwise permitted under the standards of fair use. As such, copying not within the guidelines may nonetheless be permitted under the fair use doctrine. The Music Guidelines summarized below were made part of the legislative history of the Copyright Act of 1976. Therefore, while they do not have the force of law, they may be safely relied on by music educators. The guidelines are reproduced in their entirety in Appendix 3-E.

For purposes of interpreting the Music Guidelines, it is important to note that music involves two types of works: (1) the "musical work" (the "arrangement of notes" or "sheet music") and (2) the recorded version of such music, generally referred to in the Copyright Act as a "sound recording."

[a] Copying Sheet Music

Copying of sheet music is permitted under the following circumstances:

1. emergency copying to replace purchased copies which for any reason are not available for an imminent performance, provided purchased replacement copies are substituted in due course; or
2. for academic purposes other than performance, single or multiple copies of excerpts of works may be made, provided the excerpts do not constitute a performable unit, such as a section, movement or aria, but in no case more than 10 percent of the work, and never more than one copy per student; or
3. for academic purposes other than performance, a single copy of an entire performable unit that is (a) confirmed by the copyright owner to be out of print, or (b) unavailable except in a larger work; if made by or for a teacher for (i) the teacher's scholarly research, or (ii) preparation for teaching a class; and
4. a notice of copyright appears on the printed copy; and
5. the copying is never intended to:
   a. create, replace, or substitute for anthologies, compilations, or collective works;
   b. serve as a substitute for "consumables" such as educational workbooks, exercises, standardized tools, answer sheets, or similar material;
   c. substitute for the purchase of music (except as specifically permitted above); or
   d. be used for performances (except as specifically permitted above).

[b] Creating Derivative Works

Section 106(2) of the Copyright Act grants copyright owners the exclusive right to control the abridgement, adaptation, translation, revision or other "transformation" of their works (the so-called derivative right). Two exceptions exist for this right as it relates to musical works.

1. Printed copies that have been purchased may be edited or simplified, provided the fundamental character of the work is not distorted or the lyrics, if any, are not altered or, if no lyrics exist, that none are added.
2. Section 115(2) of the Copyright Act permits making a musical arrangement of a nondramatic musical work for which a compulsory license is sought to the extent necessary to conform it to the style or manner of interpretation of the performance involved, provided the arrangement does not change the basic melody or fundamental character of the work.

[c] Recording Music

Section 101 of the Copyright Act defines "sound recordings" as works resulting from the fixation of musical or spoken sounds, and grants a copyright holder the exclusive right to reproduce his or her sound recordings into a "phonorecord." Anyone else who does so without permission is a copyright infringer except under the following limited circumstances:

- "A single copy of recordings of performances by students may be made for evaluation or rehearsal purposes and retained by the educational institution or individual teacher."
- "A single copy of a sound recording of copyrighted music may be made from sound recordings owned by an educational institution or an individual teacher for the purpose of constructing aural exercises or examinations and retained by the educational institution or individual teacher. (This pertains only to the copyrights of the music itself and not to any copyright which may exist in the sound recording)."
- Once phonorecords of a nondramatic musical work have been distributed to the public in the United States under authority of the copyright owner, any person may obtain a compulsory license to make or distribute phonorecords of the work by complying with certain procedures and paying royalties as provided in Section 115 of the Copyright Act.

[d] Performing Music

A copyright owner generally has the exclusive right to control the public performance of his or her musical work or digital sound recording. However, the Copyright Act exempts certain performances from infringement liability when related to nonprofit activities, such as performances of:

1. a musical work or sound recording by instructors or pupils in the course of face-to-face teaching activities of a nonprofit educational institution in a classroom or similar place devoted to instruction (Section 110(1));
2. an entire nondramatic musical work by electronic transmission if the other requirements of Section 110(2) of the Copyright Act are met (See subsection [9]);
3. "reasonable and limited" portions of dramatic musical works and sound recordings via electronic transmission if the other requirements of Section 110(2) of the Copyright Act are met (See subsection [9]);
4. a nondramatic musical work, with no transmission to the public, without any purpose of direct or indirect commercial advantage, and no fee or other compensation for the performance paid to the performers, promoters, or organizers, if there is no direct or indirect admission charge; or if there is an admission charge, the proceeds, after deducting the reasonable costs of producing the performance, are used exclusively for educational or charitable purposes; except where the copyright owner, or his duly authorized agent, objects in writing at least seven days prior to the performance, which writing is
   a. signed,
   b. states the reasons for his objection,
   c. is served on the person responsible for the performance, and
   d. complies with any other requirements the Copyright Office prescribes (Section 110(4)); or
5. nondramatic musical works or dramatico-musical works of a religious nature in the course of services at a place of worship or other religious assembly (Section 110(3)).

[e] Downloading Music

Few copyright issues have garnered more attention on campus recently than peer-to-peer (P2P) file swapping. P2P file-sharing programs enable direct communication between users, allowing them to access each other's files and share digital music, software, images, and videos. By permitting fast, inexpensive, and easy production of identical copies, file-sharing applications have facilitated both the legitimate sale of copyrighted materials by their owners and the illegal piracy and distribution thereof by unauthorized users.

P2P file sharing has grown dramatically in recent years. According to one estimate, an average of 8 million users were online and sharing

10 million gigabytes of data on those networks at any given time during June 2004.[205] In addition, KaZaa, a file-sharing application, has become the world's most downloaded software program.[206] It is estimated that over 3 million people shared more than half a billion music files in 2003 alone, and that over 60 million Americans have downloaded music at one time or another.[207]

According to the music industry, an increasing number of students are using fast Internet connections offered by college computer networks to illegally download and share massive volumes of copyrighted songs, movies, and video games on P2P networks.[208] The U.S. film industry estimates that 44 percent of its domestic losses due to piracy (over $500 million annually) are attributable to college students.[209] In light of this, the Recording Industry Association of America (RIAA) has filed lawsuits against music swappers with a renewed focus on university students. RIAA announced in March 2004 that it had initiated suit against 532 anonymous individuals, including 89 people at 21 separate universities.[210] Thus far, these suits have targeted students only and not the universities they attend. If identified and prosecuted, these individuals probably have little chance of prevailing based on existing copyright infringement defenses.

A successful fair use defense is unlikely because, normally, an entire work is copied and distributed during file swapping with no transformative use occurring. Recent court cases have also held file sharing inherently damages the market for copyrighted works.[211] Thus, the key fair use factors all lean toward a finding of infringement. Some commentators have suggested that the Audio Home Recording Act of 1992 (AHRA)[212] and cases interpreting it may provide a fair use defense to music downloaders, much

---

205. J. Borland, *Survey: Movie-Swapping Up; KaZaa Down*, CNETNews.com (July 13, 2004), http://news.cnet.com/survey-movie-swapping-up-kazaa-down/2100-1025_3-5267992 .html.

206. *Consumer Privacy and Government Technology Mandates in the Digital Media Marketplace; Hearings on S. 253 Before Senate Committee on Commerce, Science and Transportation* (Sept. 17, 2003) (testimony of Cary Sherman, President, Recording Industry Association of America), http://commerce.senate.gov/hearings /testimony.cfm?id=919&wit_id=2584.

207. F. Oberholzer & K. Strumpf, *The Effect of File Sharing on Record Sales: An Empirical Analysis* (Mar. 2004), http://www.unc.edu/~cigar/papers/FileSharing_March2004.pdf.

208. *U.S. General Accounting Office, File Sharing*, GAO-04-503 (May 2004) (hereinafter *GAO P2P Report*), at 1.

209. *House Committee on Education and the Workforce, Press Release* (Sept. 26, 2006).

210. J. Borland, *New RIAA File-Swapping Suits Filed*, CNETNews.com (Mar. 23, 2004), http://news.com.com/2100-1027_3-5177933.html.

211. *See, e.g., A&M Records, Inc. v. Napster*, 239 F.3d 1004 (9th Cir. 2001).

212. Pub. L. No. 102–563, 106 Stat. 4237 (1992).

as the *Sony* case did for VCR users. AHRA was an attempt to balance the rights of copyright owners and consumers.

Prompted by the emergence of digital equipment capable of making flawless reproductions of musical recordings, AHRA prohibited the manufacture or import of "digital audio recording devices" unless such equipment incorporated a mandated technology (or its equivalent) to prevent serial copying. It also imposed a levy on the sale of such equipment and on the digital recording media, such as digital audiotapes, associated with it. In exchange, AHRA explicitly granted consumers an exemption from copyright infringement for their use of either an approved digital audio recording device or analog equipment to make personal copies of musical recordings.

Some observers cite the decision in *Recording Industry Association of America, Inc. v. Diamond Multimedia Systems, Inc.*[213] to support their view that using a computer to make personal copies of digital music files constitutes fair use. In that case, the U.S. Court of Appeals for the Ninth Circuit considered allegations that the defendant had violated AHRA in its manufacture of portable (Diamond Rio) MP3 players, which make copies of digital audio files from a computer hard drive and store them for replay. The Court found that, since the MP3 player in question could reproduce digital music files only through an attached computer, and a computer did not qualify as a "digital audio recording device" under AHRA; therefore, the manufacturer was not required to incorporate technology to prevent serial copying or pay royalties.

However, the Court addressed only whether the MP3 player was covered by AHRA; it did not explicitly address whether copying from computers for personal use constitutes a general limitation—as an element of fair use—on the exclusive rights of copyright owners. Hence, *Diamond* did not establish a general precedent for personal copying, but rather interpreted a specific clause of the Copyright Act in the context of a particular type of digital copying.[214]

Some have suggested the "first sale" doctrine provides a defense to unauthorized music downloading. Under the first-sale doctrine, once an owner sells physical copies of his or her copyrighted work, he or she may

---

213. 180 F.3d 1072 (9th Cir. 1999).

214. However, the ruling did point out that "the Rio's operation is entirely consistent with the [AHRA's] main purpose—the facilitation of personal use," and cited the Senate report accompanying the AHRA, which stated that "[t]he purpose of [the Act] is to ensure the right of consumers to make analog or digital audio recordings of copyrighted music for their private, noncommercial use." *See* S. Rep. No. 294, 102d Cong., 2d Sess. 52–53 (1992).

no longer control the distribution thereof.[215] This doctrine thus permits lawfully purchased CDs to be resold, loaned, or given to someone else. Does file swapping simply mirror this activity in an electronic environment? The answer has to be no, because in a digital context files are also *copied* through the downloading and uploading process, thus negating the analogy.[216]

Copyright owners have attempted to avoid the first-sale doctrine altogether by licensing rather than selling physical products containing digital works. Although a legally effective license can avoid creation of rights under the first-sale doctrine, mass market licenses—for example, those on widely distributed software products—are not traditional "offer-and-acceptance" licensing agreements. The courts have not yet ruled on the viability of mass market licensing practices intended to avoid the first-sale doctrine.[217]

Having thus far failed to establish either valid fair use or first-sale doctrine defenses, P2P users who are students may try to employ educational use exemptions from the Copyright Act. To date, the statutory exemptions for classroom teaching activities,[218] distance learning,[219] or compulsory licenses have not been deemed applicable to P2P file sharing in any reported case.

Colleges and universities themselves have thus far avoided exposure for the P2P activities of their students because existing theories of copyright leave them outside the scope of infringement liability. Under current law, infringement may be found if a person's activities are directly involved with, contributory to, or vicariously associated with the illegal act. Direct infringement occurs when anyone "violates any of the exclusive rights of the copyright owner as provided by Sections 106 through 122 . . ."[220] of the Copyright Act. Since, in most cases of music piracy, the infringing materi-

---

215. 17 U.S.C. § 109(a).

216. M. J. Remington, Esq., Paper Prepared for the Education Task Force of the Joint Committee of the Higher Education and Entertainment Communities, *Potential Liability for Students Engaged in P2P File Sharing* (Aug. 8, 2003), http://www.acenet.edu/am/template .cfm?section=Home&TEMPLATE=/cm/ContentDisplay.cfm&CONTENTID=11008.

217. A notable example is a software manufacturer's attempts to prevent the unbundling of components of a software suite at resale. In that case, the U.S. District Court for the Central District of California held that the restrictive licensing practices of the defendant software maker were unenforceable, but it did so on a very narrow basis. See *Softman Products Co., LLC v. Adobe Systems, Inc.*, 171 F. Supp. 2d 1075 (C.D. Cal. 2001).

218. 17 U.S.C. § 110(1).

219. 17 U.S.C. § 110(2).

220. 17 U.S.C. § 501(a).

als are copied and stored on the student's computer, and not the facilities of the university, the college itself is not deemed a direct infringer.[221]

Similarly, contributory infringement may be asserted against "one who, with knowledge of the infringing activity, induces, causes or materially contributes to the infringing conduct of another . . ."[222] "Contributory infringement [thus] stems from the notion that a person who directly contributes to another's infringement should be held accountable."[223] Again, however, it is unlikely a university would be held culpable unless it had *actual* knowledge of the specific file-sharing activity and "knowingly provided software or a network that materially contributed to infringements by its students."[224] However, courts have recently refined the parameters of contributory liability in the context of cyberspace[225] to determine when such liability can be imposed on a provider of Internet access or services, such as a university.

For instance, in *A & M Records, Inc. v. Napster Inc.*,[226] the Ninth Circuit Court of Appeals considered claims that Napster, an electronic file-sharing system operator, was contributorily liable for assisting individuals in trading copyrighted music files stored on their home computers.[227] The court wrote that "if a computer system operator learns of specific infringing material available on his system and fails to purge such material from the system, the operator knows of and contributes to direct infringement."[228] Because Napster knew of the availability of infringing music files, assisted users in accessing them, and failed to block access to such files, the court concluded the company materially contributed to the infringement.[229]

Accordingly, it was recently held in another case that a computer system operator could be contributorily liable if it had actual knowledge that specific infringing material was available using its system, and failed to take

---

221. *Perfect 10 v. Google, Inc.*, 416 F. Supp. 2d 828, 843–45 (C.D. Cal. 2006) (the owner of a computer that does not store and serve the electronic information for a user is not deemed to be "displaying" that information).

222. *Gershwin Publishing Corp. v. Columbia Artist Management, Inc.*, 443 F.3d 1159, 1162 (2nd Cir. 1971). *See also* Chapter Two, Section 2.1[8][c].

223. Remington, *supra* note 216, at 5.

224. *Id.*

225. "Cyberspace is a popular term for the world of electronic communications over computer networks." *Religious Tech. Ctr. v. NetCom On-Line Communications Services, Inc.*, 907 F. Supp. 1361, 1365 n.1 (N.D. Cal. 1995).

226. *Supra* note 211.

227. *Id.* at 1011–13, 1019–22.

228. *Id.* at 1021.

229. *Id.* at 1022.

simple measures to prevent further dissemination thereof.[230] Applying this test, a college or university could theoretically be held contributorily liable if it had knowledge that infringing images or songs were available using its computer network and subsequently failed to take appropriate measures to prevent such activity. To date, this issue has not come before the courts in an educational context.[231]

The scope of vicarious liability in the context of copyright has also recently been expanded by the U.S. Supreme Court. In *Metro-Goldwyn-Mayer Studios, Inc. v. Grokster, Ltd.*, the Court held that in order to succeed in imposing vicarious liability, a plaintiff must establish that the defendant exercised the requisite control over the direct infringer and that he derived a direct financial benefit from the infringing activity.[232] *Grokster* further describes the "control" element as the defendant's "right and ability to supervise the direct infringer"[233] or its legal "right to stop or limit"[234] the infringing conduct, as well as the practical ability to do so.

Because most universities have a closed computer system requiring user registration, and could terminate their users' accounts and/or block access thereto, schools seemingly have the right and ability to prevent (or at least inhibit) their students from engaging in the illegal downloading of copyrighted music and video files from the Internet. As for deriving a financial benefit from such activity (the second prong of the vicarious liability test), while schools do receive tuition payments from most students, their connection to the actual wrongdoing seems sufficiently attenuated as to negate the "direct financial interest"[235] needed to ascribe liability.[236]

Apart from simply avoiding legal liability, colleges and universities may wish to discourage their students from engaging in P2P file sharing for other important reasons, such as minimizing network disruptions and not

---

230. *Perfect 10 v. Amazon.com*, 487 F.3d 701 (9th Cir. 2007).

231. If it did, a defendant university would still be able to avail itself of those defenses provided by the Digital Millennium Copyright Act (DMCA), Pub. L. No. 105–304, 112 Stat. 2860 (1998) and codified at 17 U.S.C. §512. *See* Chapter Five, Section 5.4, for a more detailed discussion of the DMCA.

232. 545 U.S. 913, 930 (2005).

233. *Id.* at 930.

234. *Id.* at 930 n.9.

235. *Fonovisa, Inc. v. Cherry Auction, Inc.*, 76 F.3d 259, 262 (9th Cir. 1996).

236. *Grokster* may also be distinguished by virtue of the Court's emphasis on the company's business model, which showed "a clear intention to promote piracy as a way of increasing ad revenue." *See* Timothy B. Lee, *Circumventing Competition: The Perverse Consequences of the Digital Millennium Copyright Act* 5 (March 21, 2006).

impeding other legitimate educational activities.[237] According to a recent General Accounting Office (GAO) study, most university officials interviewed indicated they had experienced some network performance or security problems resulting from P2P file-sharing applications. The most common incidents reported were the introduction of viruses or malicious code and the temporary loss of network resources.[238]

Schools addressing unauthorized P2P file swapping have chosen several methods to deal with the problem. These include educating students, using blocking or limiting technology, adopting network acceptable use policies, disciplining violators, and developing legal alternatives for file sharing.[239] These options are discussed in more detail below.

- *Education.* According to the GAO, those university officials interviewed estimate 30 percent or more of their students used file-sharing applications to download or share music during the 2003–2004 academic year, with one school placing the number at closer to 90 percent.[240] Education of network users thus becomes an important early step and often takes the form of making students sign acknowledgements before using computer resources, or delivering information to them via poster campaigns, advertisements, e-mail messages, or brochures.[241] Some institutions train "not only students, but also those responsible for oversight . . . such as deans, IT staff, faculty, resident and graduate assistants, and other administrators."[242]

- *Network Management Technologies.* Schools routinely use technological tools to manage their computer networks. Some universities are now taking preemptive steps to block P2P file sharing by students. According to the GAO study, most school officials interviewed indicated they had the right tools and knowledge to deal with the problem and considered their approaches either somewhat or very successful.[243] For instance, Emory University in Atlanta recently adjusted its firewall to prevent students from creating web pages and stop persons outside the network from downloading

---

237. Paper prepared by the Education Task Force of the Joint Committee of the Higher Education and Entertainment Communities, *University Policies and Practices Addressing Improper Peer-to-Peer File Sharing* (April 2004), http://net.educause.edu/ir/library/pdf/CSD3092.pdf.

238. *GAO P2P Report* at 10.

239. Education Task Force, *supra* note 237, at 3.

240. *GAO P2P Report* at 9.

241. Education Task Force, *supra* note 237, at 3.

242. *Id.*

243. *GAO P2P Report* at 8.

files.[244] At the University of Florida, a software management tool called ICARUS detects any P2P use and promptly disconnects the user from the network for increased periods of time based on the number of prior offenses.[245] The university has reported over a 90 percent decrease in P2P use since ICARUS's implementation.[246]

- *Policies.* Universities typically have policies in place to cover the use of their computer networks, technological resources, and copyrights. Most policies are fairly straightforward, noting copyright infringement is illegal, and describing the potential penalties for violators. Many now describe how the institution's monitoring of bandwidth can be used to identify and potentially prosecute infringers.[247] According to the GAO, most of the universities studied routinely monitor their networks for P2P file-sharing applications.[248]

- *Disciplinary Action.* Interestingly, the GAO reported that all schools in its study had received notices from representatives of copyright holders alleging file-sharing violations by students. Over half had received more than 100 notifications. In most cases, university officials were able to trace the infringement notification to an individual student.[249] Once an infringer is identified, penalties imposed on him or her vary widely. One school's policy lists potential punishment as "fines, restitution of funds, termination of computer and network access, probation, suspension, separation, or exclusion from the university."[250] Other institutions are less specific and simply state the matter will be "referred to the appropriate officials for review and disciplinary action as warranted."[251]

- *Legal File Sharing.* Another approach to addressing unauthorized P2P file sharing on campus is to provide students with an alternative legitimate, commercial online music provider service. A pilot project at Pennsylvania State University currently supplies pupils

---

244. Education Task Force, *supra* note 237, at 4.

245. *Id.*

246. *Id.*

247. *Id.* The College Opportunity and Affordability Act, currently before Congress, would make such disclosures mandatory for all colleges and require "universities to publicly disclose their policies and procedures [regarding] copyright enforcement." *See* Tom Corelis, *New Bill Threatens University Funding If Schools Don't Play Ball with RIAA*, Daily-Tech.com (Nov. 12, 2007), http://www.dailytech.com/article.aspx?newsid=9629.

248. *GAO P2P Report* at 9.

249. *Id.*

250. Education Task Force, *supra* note 237, at 5.

251. *Id.*

with downloadable, online music already paid for by a portion of the existing student technology fee. Trinity University in San Antonio, Texas, recently reached an agreement with digital music provider Cdigix to allow the school's 2,700 students to legally download music and movies. The Colorado-based private company currently has similar arrangements with eighteen colleges.[252]

Measures taken by educational institutions seem to have been insufficient, however, to placate the RIAA and other copyright owners. As such, Congress has recently considered several pieces of legislation to increase penalties for P2P piracy and augment federal enforcement mechanisms. For instance, on March 31, 2004, the House Judiciary Intellectual Property Subcommittee voted out the Piracy Deterrence and Education Act (PDEA).[253]

The PDEA directs the FBI to (1) develop a program (including suitable warnings) deterring members of the public from making or offering unauthorized copies of works on the Internet; and (2) facilitate the sharing among law enforcement agencies, Internet service providers, and copyright owners of information concerning such activities. The proposed legislation subjects an Internet user who makes available $1,000 or more in copyrighted material to a prison term of up to three years and a fine of up to $250,000.[254]

A different bill sponsored by Senators Orrin Hatch and Patrick Leahy, labeled the "Protecting Intellectual Property Rights Against Theft and Expropriation Act of 2004" (or the "Pirate Act"), was introduced in the U.S. Senate on March 26, 2004. That legislation proposed that anyone sharing 2,500 or more pieces of content, such as songs or movies, face significant fines or imprisonment. In addition, persons distributing content not yet widely released (such as an upcoming movie) would also face criminal penalties.[255] Congressional efforts have focused not only on actual infringers, such as members of the public who illegally download music, but also on the companies and industries facilitating such behavior.

---

252. *Id.* at 6. *See also Trinity University Signs Digital Musical Agreement with Cdigix*, San Antonio Bus. J. (Feb. 2, 2005), http://sanantonio.bizjournals.com/sanantonio/stories/2005/01/31/daily24.html.

253. H.R. 2517, 108th Cong., 1st Sess. (2003). *See also* D. McCullagh, *House Panel Approves Copyright Bill*, CNETNews.com (Mar. 31, 2004), http://news.com.com/2100-1028_3-5182898.html.

254. McCullagh, *supra* note 253, at 1.

255. X. Jardin, *Congress Moves to Criminalize P2P*, Wired News (Mar. 26, 2004), http://wired.com/entertainment/music/news/2004/03/62830.

For example, on June 22, 2004, Senators Hatch and Leahy also introduced in the Senate the Inducing Infringement of Copyrights Act of 2004 (the "Induce Act" or "S. 2560"), which would hold individuals or corporations liable for infringing acts that they "intentionally induce."[256] "Intentional" was defined as "conscious and deliberate affirmative acts which a reasonable person would expect to result in widespread violations."[257] Opponents of the Induce Act contended it would undermine the U.S. Supreme Court decision in *Sony Corp. v. Universal City Studios, Inc.*[258] that held the manufacturer of a product could not be held liable for infringing uses facilitated thereby so long as it was also capable of "substantial non-infringing uses." [259] In other words, "technology, in and of itself, could rarely be considered unlawful in the copyright context."[260] The act's proponents believed it did not overrule or limit *Sony* because S. 2560 addressed only cases of intentional inducement that were not covered by *Sony*.[261]

The act's advocates also suggested it would not affect most Internet service providers because of certain "safe harbors" granted them in the Digital Millennium Copyright Act.[262] They further pointed out that S. 2560 permits civil enforcement only against persons whose acts already trigger criminal liability because intentional inducement of infringement is currently a felony.[263] The act was also technology-neutral, proponents suggested, in aiming to target behavior rather than any particular type of technology.[264] Finally, S. 2560 supporters argued, the bill did not affect anyone's ability to make "fair use" of copyrighted works.[265]

---

256. S. 2560, 108th Cong., 2d Sess. (2004).

257. R. Mark, *New Induce Act Prompts Old Complaints*, internetnews.com (Sept. 28, 2004), http://www.internetnews.com/infra/article.php/3414241.

258. 464 U.S. 417 (1984).

259. *Id.* at 435.

260. American Electronics Association, et al., *Letter sent to Senator Orrin Hatch regarding S. 2560, the "Inducing Infringement of Copyrights Act of 2004"* (July 6, 2004), http://news.clmusic.com/article/13109.

261. *Sony, supra* note 258, at 439, n.19. "Sony certainly does not 'intentionally induce' its customers to make infringing uses of respondent's copyrights, nor does it supply its products to identified individuals known by it to be engaging in continuing infringement of respondents' copyrights."

262. For a more detailed discussion of this act, *see* Chapter Five, Section 5.4.

263. News Release from the Office of U.S. Senator Orrin Hatch, *Hatch Introduces a Bill to Stop Inducement of Children to Commit Crimes* (June 22, 2004), http://www.lessig.org/blog/archives/floor.pdf.

264. *Id.*

265. *Id.*

Opponents suggested the bill would chill innovation and drive techno-logical investment abroad.[266] They believed S. 2560 "would have the unin-tended consequence of punishing individuals and companies that create and distribute consumer, business, and professional products that might be used by others for unlawful purposes."[267] These critics argued that the future development of many consumer products, such as personal com-puters, scanners, CD burners, modems, instant messaging products, and the software that enables them to operate, would be threatened by the leg-islation.[268] In the end, neither the PDEA, the Pirate Act, nor the Induce Act passed the 108th Congress.

The 109th Congress that convened in January 2005 had greater success in reaching accord on some of these issues, however. On April 27, 2005, President Bush signed into law the Family Entertainment and Copyright Act (FECA).[269] The new law authorizes the use of technologies that can delete offensive content from a film.[270] It also, for the first time nationally, criminalizes the unauthorized, knowing use of a video camera or similar device to transmit or make a copy of a motion picture in a movie the-ater.[271] It sets forth significant penalties for such a violation, including a prison term of up to three years for a first-time offender. The legislation further requires the forfeiture and destruction of all copies of motion pic-tures or audiovisual works made and any equipment used in connection with the crime.

More importantly, FECA establishes criminal penalties for willful copy-right infringement committed (1) for purposes of commercial advantage or private financial gain, (2) by the reproduction or distribution during any six-month period of one or more copies of copyrighted work(s) with a total retail value exceeding $1,000, or (3) by the distribution of a computer program, musical work, motion picture or other audiovisual work, or sound recording not yet commercially distributed by making it available on a computer network accessible to members of the public, if the person knew or should have known that the work was intended for commercial

---

266. American Electronics Association, et. al. *Letter, supra* note 260, at 2.

267. *Id.*

268. *Id.*

269. Pub. L. No. 109–9, 119 Stat. 218 (2005).

270. D. McCullagh, *US Cracks Down on Peer-to-Peer Pirates*, CNET News.com (April 28, 2005), http://networks.silicon.com/webwatch/0,39024667,39129955,00.htm.

271. T. Mennecke, *New Copyright Amendments Target P2P Users*, Slyck.com (April 28, 2005), http://www.slyck.com/news.php?story=766.

distribution.[272] The second category seems to cover any copyrighted work illegally in one's possession, while the third grouping applies only to items pirated before they are made commercially available. In the case of motion pictures, a "release" of the work does not commence upon distribution of the film to movie theaters, but at the time of its sale or lease on DVDs or videocassettes.

FECA does contain an exemption for certain nonprofit activities. For instance, the legislation provides that the limitation on rights of reproduction and distribution of copyrighted works does not apply to the authority of libraries or archives, during the last twenty years of any copyright term of a published work, to reproduce, distribute, display, or perform in facsimile or digital form a copy of such work for purposes of preservation, scholarship, or research when certain conditions apply.[273]

By virtue of the criminalization of copyright infringement with statutes like FECA, the involvement of law enforcement personnel is becoming more prevalent in these matters. On March 31, 2004, the Justice Department announced the creation of a task force to evaluate copyright prosecutions and recommend improvements. "The task force will determine how to meet the evolving challenges that law enforcement faces in the intellectual property arena," said David Israelite, deputy chief of staff to former Attorney General John Ashcroft and the task force chairman.[274]

Enforcement abroad is also becoming increasingly important for U.S. copyright owners. For example, the Motion Picture Association of America claims that global piracy of DVDs cost its members $3.5 billion in revenue during 2003.[275] Consequently, the protection of intellectual property has become prominent in both multilateral and bilateral trade negotiations between the United States and other nations.[276]

Federal law enforcement officials have already taken major steps to investigate and prosecute cross-border organizations involved in copyright infringement, such as the "warez groups"—loosely affiliated networks

---

272. FECA at § 103(a)(1)(A)–(C). A bill introduced in the 110th Congress, H.R. 4279, 110th Cong., 2d Sess. (2007), "would allow a copyright owner to collect statutory damages for each [stolen] copyrighted work" and create a "permanent intellectual property division within the Department of Justice." *See* Chloe Albanesius, *DOJ Blasts New 'Copyright Czar' Bill,* PCMag.com (Dec. 13, 2007), http://www.pcmag.com/article2/0,2704,2234098,00.asp.

273. *Id.* at § 402.

274. D. McCullagh, *Ashcroft Creates Task Force for Copyright Violation,* CNETNews .com (Mar. 31, 2004), http://news.cnet.com/2110-1023-5182781.html.

275. Fowler, *Hollywood's Burning Issue Is Piracy of DVDs and CDs,* Wall St. J., Sept. 18, 2003.

276. Landler, *U.S. Is Only the Tip of Pirated Music Iceberg,* N.Y. Times, Sept. 26, 2003.

that specialize in "cracking" the copyright protection on software, movies, games, and music files. According to the U.S. Department of Justice (DOJ), these outfits use a wide range of technologies, including file sharing over peer-to-peer networks, to illegally distribute copyrighted materials.[277] The DOJ's Operation Fastlink and the U.S. Customs Service's Operation Buccaneer are two recent examples of federal law enforcement efforts focusing on international piracy groups.

Fastlink is the largest international enforcement effort ever undertaken against online piracy. As part of its plan, on April 21, 2004, U.S. and foreign law enforcement officials executed more than 120 simultaneous searches across multiple time zones. In addition to the United States, action was taken in Belgium, Denmark, France, Germany, Hungary, Israel, the Netherlands, Singapore, Sweden, Great Britain, and Northern Ireland. As a result, more than 100 individuals believed to be engaged in online piracy were identified and arrested.[278]

Operation Buccaneer was an international investigation and prosecution led by the U.S. Customs Service. The endeavor resulted in the seizure of pirated copies of software, music, and computer games worth millions of dollars and led to thirty convictions worldwide. As part of the effort, on December 11, 2001, the U.S. Customs Service and law enforcement officials from Australia, Finland, Norway, Sweden, and the United Kingdom simultaneously executed over seventy search warrants.[279] Approximately 40 of those were executed in 27 cities across the United States, including several at universities. As a result, law enforcement seized ten computer "archive sites" containing tens of thousands of pirated copies of software, movies, music, and computer games.[280]

It is difficult to assess whether the recent RIAA lawsuits and other enforcement actions have had much impact on illegal file sharing. In a February 2004 survey, the Pew Internet & American Life Project and comScore Media Metrix reported 18 percent of Internet users said they downloaded music files online—well below the 29 percent who admitted doing so in the spring of 2003.[281] Because music downloading activity reported for February 2004 included both licensed and unauthorized downloads, the decline may actually have been sharper. During the same 2003–2004 period, the number of users of the most popular file-sharing networks also fell sharply.

---

277. *GAO P2P Report* at 15.

278. *Id.*

279. *Id.* at 16.

280. *Id.*

281. Pew Internet & American Life Project, *The State of Music Downloading and File-Sharing Online* (April 2004), http://www.pewinternet.org/pdfs/PIP_Filesharing_April_04.pdf.

The Pew Internet Project's survey also found that 14 percent of Internet users, or over 17 million people, reported they had stopped downloading music files and that the RIAA's decision to sue individuals who engaged in such conduct played some role therein. Survey respondents who had never engaged in music downloading also acknowledged the RIAA's lawsuits would deter them from undertaking such activity in the future.

In contrast, firms specializing in tracking Internet activity claim there has not been a substantial decline in the use of file-sharing networks. While conceding the RIAA's legal campaign has had some impact on illegal downloads, those firms contend the Pew Internet Project's survey results were not entirely representative of file-sharing activities. For instance, the Pew results were based on telephone interviews with individuals 18 years and older. Relative to adolescents, who are considered very active file sharers, such respondents would be more likely either to have curtailed or, in the context of a telephone interview, denied their file-sharing activity.[282]

Similarly, comScore Media Metrix data on file-sharing networks was obtained from consensual monitoring of individuals' computers, which could also lead to an understatement of illicit activity. Internet tracking firms suggest their measures, based on anonymous monitoring, show a 19 percent increase in the number of file-sharing network users in one year, from 6.8 million in June 2003 to 8.3 million in June 2004. Further, file-sharing as a proportion of total Internet traffic in the United States declined only slightly, from 70 to 65 percent during 2003.[283]

Surveys of *attitudes* toward file sharing also bring into question the effectiveness of the RIAA's legal strategy. According to one survey, the number of respondents in the United States who consider unauthorized file sharing illegal rose from 37 percent, before the RIAA announced its lawsuits in June 2003, to 64 percent by December 2003.[284] In contrast, a Harris Interactive poll conducted in September 2003 found that between two-thirds and three-quarters of respondents consider downloading or sharing music files for personal use to be "all right" or "legal."[285] Similarly,

---

282. McGuire, *Report: Kids Pirate Music Freely*, Wash. Post, May 18, 2004.

283. Graham, *Online File Swapping Endures*, USA Today, July 11, 2004; and W. Knight, *Net Traffic Shows File-Sharing Undented*, NewScientist.com (May 26, 2004), http://www.newscientist.com/article/dn5045-net-traffic-shows-filesharing-undented.html.

284. *IFPI Online Music Report 2004*, http://www.ifpi.org/content/library/digital-music-report-2004.pdf.

285. R. Leitman, *Americans Think Downloading Music for Personal Use Is an Innocent Act*, Harris Poll, no. 5 (Jan. 28, 2004), http://www.harrisinteractive.com/harris_poll/index.asp?PID=434.

the Pew Internet Project's February 2004 survey found 58 percent of those who downloaded music files said they did not care about copyright.[286]

These conflicting results may reflect individuals' unfamiliarity with copyright law. In a study conducted for the Pew Internet Project in November–December 2003, only 43 percent of respondents claimed they were "very familiar" or "somewhat familiar" with copyright law and regulations. Asked about "fair use" in particular, 81 percent said they were either "not too familiar" or "not familiar at all" with the concept.[287]

Ironically, these educational and law enforcement initiatives coincide with a new study questioning whether P2P file sharing actually affects record sales. In "The Effect of File Sharing on Record Sales," Felix Oberholzer of the Harvard Business School and Coleman Strumpf of UNC Chapel Hill have concluded that "file sharing has no statistical significant effect on purchases of the average album."[288] At most, these researchers conclude, file sharing explains only a small fraction of recent declines in CD sales. Indeed, even music industry executives have recently begun to acknowledge that file sharing may not be the entire cause of declining sales.[289]

Considered to have had a larger impact are "poor economic conditions, a reduction in the number of album releases, growing competition from other forms of entertainment such as video games and DVDs, . . . the rise of independent promoter fees to gain airplay, and possibly a consumer backlash against record industry tactics."[290] The authors of the Oberholzer study point out that similar drops in sales occurred in the late 1970s and early 1980s, and that "record sales in the 1990s may have been abnormally high as individuals replaced older formats with CDs."[291]

Others have suggested the music industry is also garnering far too much attention compared to other creators of copyrightable works. The gross revenues of the core copyright industries totaled $441.4 billion in 2002. Nearly a third of that total ($143.4 billion) came from the newspaper, periodical,

---

286. Pew Internet & American Life Project, *The State of Music Downloading and File-Sharing Online* (Feb. 2004).

287. Pew Internet & American Life Project, *November 2003 Tracking Survey.*

288. Oberholzer, *supra* note 207, at 24. For a contrary view, *see* Stephen E. Siwek, *The True Cost of Copyright Industry Piracy to the U.S. Economy,* IPI Policy Report No. 189 (Oct. 3, 2007). Siwek suggests that copyright piracy not only costs the entertainment industries billions of dollars annually but also has deleterious effects on the U.S. economy as a whole.

289. Strauss, *Executives Can See Problems Beyond File-Sharing,* N.Y. Times, Sept. 9, 2003. For links to recent academic research on Internet file sharing, *see* http://www.utdallas.edu/~liebowit/intprop/main.htm.

290. Oberholzer, *supra* note 207, at 24.

291. *Id.*

and book publishing industries. The music industry, which generated $13.9 billion in revenues in 2002, was the smallest segment.[292]

[7] Off-Air Recording of Television Broadcasts

Audiovisual works, such as television programs, constitute a specific category of work protected by federal copyright law.[293] Therefore, videotaping TV broadcasts without the copyright owner's permission may be deemed infringement unless the copier can avail himself of a specific defense. In the famous case of *Sony Corporation of America, et al. v. Universal City Studios, Inc., et al.*,[294] the United States Supreme Court held that videotaping television programs on VCRs in order to view them at a later time was fair use.

The Court, in rendering its decision, took note of substantial evidence that significant amounts of television programming had already been time-shifted without objection from copyright owners. Also, no proof was submitted that the practice impaired the commercial value of copyrights or created any likelihood of future harm. In other words, viewers were not taping the programs to resell them, only to watch them at a more convenient time.

Since *Sony* applied only to home viewing, it had no impact on educational institutions. Hence, most schools must still rely on licensing agreements with educational video producers and/or television stations to replicate broadcasts for their students. In the absence of a formal license, however, educational institutions may rely on the Guidelines for the Off-the-Air Recording of Broadcast Programming for Educational Purposes (the "Broadcast Guidelines"). Created in 1979, these guidelines reflect a consensus of interested parties as to the application of "fair use" to the recording, retention, and use of television broadcast programs for educational purposes. They specify periods of retention and conditions for use of such off-air recordings in classrooms and similar places devoted to instruction.

The Broadcast Guidelines apply only to nonprofit, educational institutions and television programs transmitted to the general public without

---

292. U.S. Census Bureau, *2002 Service Annual Survey.* The film industry also seems to have exaggerated the impact that on-campus piracy has on its industry. In 2005, it commissioned a study concluding that college students accounted for 44 percent of movie industry losses due to piracy. In 2008, the Motion Picture Association of America acknowledged an error in that study and revised its figures to suggest that college students were responsible for only 15 percent of such losses. *See* Wendy Davis, *MPAA Admits Stats Inflated as Congress Considers Copyright Protection Bill*, MediaPost.com (Jan. 24, 2008), http://publications .mediapost.com/index.cfm?fuseaction=Articles.showArticleHomePage&Art-aid74968.

293. 17 U.S.C. § 102(a)(6).

294. *See supra* note 258.

charge. In other words, only those TV shows one could normally receive with the use of a standard UHF-VHF antenna are covered. "Pay Programming," such as networks capable of reception only via cable or satellite are not included. The fact that an otherwise "over-the-air" channel is received via a cable or satellite provider in the home does not negate the Guidelines' coverage, however. The Broadcast Guidelines impose the following additional limitations:

1. The taped program
   - may not be kept for more than 45 calendar days following its recording;
   - must be erased at the end of such 45-day period;
   - may be shown to students only once within the first 10 school days of the 45-day period;
   - may be repeated once for instructional reinforcement;
   - may be viewed after the 10-day period only by instructors for evaluation purposes;
   - must be made at the request of an individual instructor;
   - may not be physically or electronically altered;
   - may not be combined with other programs to form anthologies or collections;
   - need not be shown in its entirety; and
   - must include the copyright notice from the original program.
2. Students viewing the taped program must be in
   - classrooms or similar places devoted to instruction within a single building, cluster or campus; or
   - their homes.
3. Educational institutions relying on the Broadcast Guidelines must
   - ensure that no broadcast program be recorded off-air more than once at the request of the same teacher; and
   - establish appropriate controls to maintain the integrity of the Broadcast Guidelines.

A complete version of the Broadcast Guidelines appears in Appendix 3-F and H.R. Rep. 97–495. By being incorporated into a congressional report, the Guidelines do not carry the force of law, but they may be safely relied on by educators.

[8] CONFU Fair Use Guidelines for Distance Learning

As mentioned in the introduction, CONFU, which was convened in September 1994 by the Clinton Administration's Working Group on Intellectual Property Rights, established committees for different topics, including one on distance learning.[295] The distance learning group sought to develop fair use guidelines for educational uses of copyrighted works employing digital technology. The CONFU Working Group on Distance Learning (the "Working Group"), composed of interested parties from the educational, library, and copyright owner communities, debated the relevant issues for several years. The Working Group[296] eventually prepared and distributed guidelines dealing with the performance and display of copyrighted works in distance learning classes (hereinafter, the "CONFU Distance Learning Guidelines").

Unfortunately, though, the entire process became controversial, both because of conflicting views regarding the value and function of fair use guidelines and the anticipation of congressional action in the field. As a result, the CONFU Distance Learning Guidelines were never formally adopted by the conference. However, several organizations have officially endorsed them or unofficially rely on them for guidance.

As drafted, the CONFU Distance Learning Guidelines apply only to the *performance* and *display* of lawfully acquired copyrighted works and not to the copying or distribution thereof. They address both live interactive distance learning classes (i.e., a teacher in a real-time class with all or some of the students at remote locations), and faculty instruction recorded without students present for later transmission. The guidelines apply only to nonprofit educational institutions and specify that any use thereunder must be noncommercial. Therefore, classes for private business executives or transmissions of a for-profit educational subsidiary are not covered. All students viewing the transmission must be officially enrolled in the course, thereby excluding auditors and visitors from participating. The guidelines apply to delivery via satellite, closed-circuit television, or computer network and require any such transmission to be made over a secure network with technological limitations placed on access to the class or program.

---

295. *Notice of First Meeting of Conference on Fair Use and the National Information Infrastructure*, 59 Fed. Reg. 46, 823 (1994).

296. Organizations participating in developing but not necessarily endorsing or supporting these guidelines: American Association of Community Colleges; American Association of Law Libraries; American Council of Learned Societies; Association of American Publishers; Association of American Universities; Association of College and Research Libraries; Association of Research Libraries; Broadcast Music, Inc.; City University of New York; Coalition of College and University Media Centers; Creative Incentive Coalition; Houghton Mifflin; Indiana Partnership; John Wiley & Sons, Inc.; Kent State University; National Association of State Universities and Land Grant Colleges; National Geographic; National School Board Association; Special Libraries Association; State University of New York; U.S. Copyright Office; University of Texas System; Viacom.

Additional restrictions are placed on the class session itself. First, the works performed must be integrated into the course, be part of systematic instruction, and be directly related and of material assistance to the teaching content of the transmission. In other words, the performance must be for pure instructional and not entertainment purposes. Second, technological measures must be implemented to prevent unauthorized access or copying. Third, the transmission must be received in a classroom or other location where the reception can be controlled by the institution. Reception in dormitory rooms and/or private homes is therefore outside the scope of the guidelines. Finally, while any amount of a work may be used, if an entire work or large portion thereof is performed, it may be transmitted only once without the owner's permission.

Although the Working Group considered many facets of distance learning, the guidelines focused solely on synchronous or "real-time" delivery. Some participants believed the time was not ripe for consideration of asynchronous delivery over a computer network. Other members, primarily those from the academic community, considered not covering delayed delivery as a serious failure. Given this lack of consensus and the limited time available, the Working Group chose *not* to incorporate asynchronous delivery into its final report.

The CONFU Distance Learning Guidelines did address some incidental asynchronous uses, however. Under the guidelines, an eligible institution may record classes, including the performance of an entire copyrighted work or a large portion thereof, and retain the recording for up to fifteen consecutive class days (i.e., days in which the institution is open for regular instruction) for viewing by students enrolled in the course. Permission from the copyright owner is required, however, for further dissemination of recorded courses.

The CONFU Distance Learning Guidelines were endorsed by some entities, including library and educational associations.[297] Several institutions continue to use them as a reference or link to them on their websites. The entire text of the guidelines is included in Appendix 3-G. Following the enactment of the Technology, Education, and Copyright Harmonization Act in November 2002 (the "TEACH Act"),[298] which amended the rules governing performance and display of copyrighted works in distance learning, the guidelines possess significantly less importance to the educational community. However, since the legislative history of the TEACH

---

297. Those organizations endorsing the guidelines were not specifically identified in CONFU's final report, however.

298. Pub. L. No. 107–273, 116 Stat. 1511 (2002).

Act states its provisions are still subject to the doctrine of fair use, the guidelines may still have some limited applicability.[299]

[9] Performance and Display of Works while Teaching

Section 110(1) of the Copyright Act grants instructors wide latitude in incorporating the performance and display of copyrighted works into their traditional classroom courses to enhance the educational experience. However, often what is permissible in face-to-face teaching constitutes copyright infringement when employed in distance learning. This occurs because a completely different provision of the Copyright Act, namely Section 110(2), covers distance education. As federal statutes, these two sections carry far more authority than do advisory guidelines. Educators are therefore best advised to adhere strictly to the requirements of these laws when using the works of others in their traditional or electronic classrooms. The salient features of these two provisions are outlined below.

[a] Face-to-Face Teaching

Section 110(1) of the Copyright Act permits the *performance* or *display* (but not the reproduction or distribution) of

- any copyrighted work;
- by instructors or pupils;
- in the course of face-to-face teaching activity;
- of a nonprofit educational institution;
- in a classroom or similar place devoted to instruction;
- unless, in the case of a motion picture or other audiovisual work, the performance or the display of individual images is given by means of a copy that was not lawfully made, and the person responsible for the performance knew or had reason to know of such illegality.

[b] Distance Learning

Section 110(2) of the Copyright Act, which was updated and amended in 2002 by the TEACH Act (included herein as Appendix 6-A), permits the performance and display plus the transient or temporary storage of material carried out through the automatic technical process of a digital transmission under the following circumstances:

I. The educator may
   A. *display* any work in an amount comparable to what is displayed in a live classroom;

---

299. *See* Chapter Six, Section 6.4[2][j], for a more detailed discussion of the remaining role of fair use in the TEACH Act.

B. *perform* entire portions of nondramatic literary or musical works;

C. *perform* only reasonable and limited portions of any other work, except for works produced or marketed as part of mediated instructional activities transmitted by digital networks, and

D. *convert* print or analog works into digital form only if: (1) no digital work is available; *or* (2) the available digital work is subject to technological protective measures; *and* (3) the amount digitized is limited to the portion authorized to be performed or displayed.

II. Such performance or display must be

A. by, at the direction of, or under the actual supervision of an instructor;

B. a regular part of systematic mediated instructional activities;

C. directly related and of material assistance to the teaching content of the transmission; and

D. an integral part of the class session offered.

III. The transmitting institution must

A. be an "accredited" nonprofit educational institution;

1. for K–12 school systems, the accreditation is determined by applicable state certification or licensing procedures;

2. for postsecondary institutions, such accreditation is determined by a regional or national accrediting agency recognized by the Council on Higher Education Accreditation or the United States Department of Education.

B. in the case of digital transmissions, not interfere with technological copyright protective measures;

C. institute written policies regarding copyright;

D. provide information to faculty, students, and staff that accurately describe and promote compliance with copyright law;

E. provide notice to students that material used in the course may be subject to copyright protection; and

F. in the case of digital transmissions, apply technological measures reasonably preventing

1. retention of the work by a recipient for longer than the class session, and

2. further dissemination thereof.

IV. The student–recipient

A. may receive the transmission at any location; and

B. must be officially enrolled in the course.

V. The transmission must be made solely for and the reception thereof limited to anticipated recipients.

VI. The performance or display must be made by means of lawfully made or acquired copy.

[10] Educational Multimedia Guidelines

After two years of negotiation, a working group coordinated by the Consortium of College and University Media Centers issued a set of guidelines on educational multimedia in September 1996 (the "Multimedia Guidelines"), and proceeded with its own process for review and endorsement. The Multimedia Guidelines were subsequently published in a non-legislative report of the House of Representatives Subcommittee on Courts and Intellectual Property[300] and endorsed by numerous associations representing educational institutions, licensing organizations, and content providers.[301] Thus, while lacking the force of law, these guidelines have been effectively "endorsed" by Congress and therefore afforded greater weight than the unilateral guidelines discussed earlier.[302]

The Multimedia Guidelines provide educators with parameters for the "fair use of portions of lawfully acquired copyrighted works in educational multimedia projects which are created by educators or students as part of a systematic learning activity at educational institutions." "Educational multimedia projects" are defined as copyrighted media formats, including

---

300. This report may be reviewed in its entirety at http://eric.ed.gov/ERICDocs/data/ericdocs2sql/Content_storage_01/0000019b/80/14/cd/54.pdf.

301. (1) Organizations endorsing these guidelines: Agency for Instructional Technology (AIT); American Association of Community Colleges (AACC); American Society of Journalists and Authors (ASJA); American Society of Media Photographers, Inc. (ASMP); American Society of Composers, Authors and Publishers (ASCAP); Association for Educational Communications and Technology (AECT); Association for Information Media and Equipment (AIME); Association of American Publishers (AAP); Association of American Colleges and Universities (AAC&U); Association of American University Presses, Inc. (AAUP); Broadcast Music, Inc. (BMI); Consortium of College and University Media Centers (CCUMC); Creative Incentive Coalition (CIC); Iowa Association for Communications Technology (IACT); Information Industry Association (IIA); Instructional Telecommunications Council (ITC); Maricopa Community Colleges/Phoenix; Motion Picture Association of America (MPAA); Music Publishers' Association of the United States (MPA); National Association of Regional Media Centers (NARMC); Recording Industry Association of America (RIAA); Software Publishers Association (SPA). (2) U.S. government agencies supporting these guidelines: U.S. National Endowment for the Arts (NEA); U.S. Copyright Office; U.S. Patent and Trademark Office. (3) Individual companies and institutions endorsing these guidelines: Houghton-Mifflin; John Wiley & Sons, Inc; McGraw-Hill; Time Warner, Inc.

302. Despite widespread approval, the multimedia guidelines were "soundly rejected by national library associations and a K–12 coalition led by the National School Boards Association." See Meris Stansbury, Fair Use Confusion Threatens Media Literacy, eSchool News (Oct. 9, 2007), http://eschoolnews.com/news/top-news/index.cfm?i=49095&cFIO=304099&CFTOKEN=35953654.

but not limited to motion media, music, text material, graphics, illustrations, photographs, and digital software that are combined into an integrated presentation. "Educational institutions" are defined as nonprofit organizations whose primary focus is supporting research and the instructional activities of educators and students for noncommercial purposes. The Multimedia Guidelines are reproduced in their entirety in Appendix 3-H. Pertinent provisions are paraphrased below:

I. Preparation of Projects
   A. *Students* may incorporate copyrighted works of others when producing their own projects for a specific course.
   B. *Educators* may incorporate copyrighted works of others when producing programs for their own teaching tools in support of curriculum-based instructional activities.
II. Permitted Uses of Programs
   A. *Students* may perform and display projects in the course for which they were created and use them later as examples of their academic work for job and graduate school interviews.
   B. *Educators* may perform and display their own projects for curriculum-based instruction to students in the following situations:
   1. face-to-face instruction;
   2. assignment to students for directed self-study; or
   3. remote instruction to students enrolled in curriculum-based courses and located at remote sites provided over the educational institution's secure electronic network in real time, or for after class review or directed self-study, provided:
      a) technological limitations are placed on access to the network and project (such as a password or PIN), and
      b) the technology used by the institution prevents the reproduction of copyrighted material by any recipient.

         If the educational institution's network or technology used to access the project cannot prevent duplication of copyrighted material, students or educators may only use the project over an otherwise secure network for a period of:
         (1) 15 days after its initial real-time remote use in the course of instruction; or
         (2) 15 days following its assignment for directed self-study.

            After that period, one of the two use copies of the project may be placed on reserve in a learning resource center, library or similar facility for on-site use by students enrolled in the course. Students must be advised not to make their own copies of the multimedia project.

C. *Educators* may also perform or display their own multimedia projects in presentations to peers at workshops and conferences. They are permitted to retain projects in their portfolios for later personal uses such as tenure review or job interviews.

III. **Time Limitations**

A. The Multimedia Guidelines do not specify how long a student may keep his or her project.

B. Educators may retain their projects for teaching courses for two years after the first instructional use. After that, they must obtain permission from the owner for each copyrighted portion incorporated into their production.

IV. **Portion Limitations**

Only those portions of the type of media specified below may be used in a project:

A. *Motion Media:* Up to 10% or 3 minutes, whichever is less.

B. *Text Material:* Up to 10% or 1000 words, whichever is less. An entire poem of less than 250 words may be used, but no more than three poems by one poet, or five poems by different poets from any anthology. For poems of greater length, 250 words may be used, but no more than three excerpts by a poet, or five excerpts by different poets from a single anthology.

C. *Music, Lyrics, and Music Video:* Up to 10%, but in no event more than 30 seconds, of the music and lyrics from an individual musical work (or in the aggregate of extracts from an individual work), whether it is embodied in copies or audio or audiovisual works. Any alterations to a musical work may not change its basic melody or fundamental character.

D. *Illustrations and Photographs:* A photograph or illustration may be used in its entirety, but no more than 5 images by an artist or photographer. When using photographs and illustrations from a published collective work, not more than 10% or 15 images, whichever is less.

E. *Numerical Data Sets:* Up to 10% or 2500 fields or cell entries, whichever is less, from a database or data table. A field entry is defined as a specific item of information, such as a name or Social Security number, in a record of a database file. A cell entry is defined as the intersection where a row and a column meet on a spreadsheet.

V. **Copying Limitations**

    A. No more than two use copies of the project may be made, only one of which may be placed on reserve as described above for distance learning purposes.

    B. One additional copy may be made for preservation purposes, but only to replace a use copy that has been lost, stolen, or damaged.

VI. **Miscellaneous**

    The Multimedia Guidelines also:

    A. recommend that students be instructed about the reasons for copyright protection and the need to follow the guidelines;

    B. remind both educators and students to provide attribution and acknowledgments for works they are incorporating; and

    C. require users to include a notice of use restriction on the opening screen of their program and any accompanying print material.

[11] ACRL Guidelines for Distance Learning Library Services

The Association of College and Research Libraries (ACRL) has promulgated its own set of guidelines regarding the role of educational libraries in promoting distance learning (the "ACRL Guidelines").[303] These guidelines recognize the importance of a higher education library to meet the needs of its faculty, students, and academic support staff, wherever these individuals are located. Unlike Section 108 of the Copyright Act and the guidelines for traditional and electronic reserves, the ACRL Guidelines do *not* attempt to quantify the amount of reference material that may be reproduced or distributed by a library without the owner's permission. Instead, these guidelines serve more as a philosophical backdrop to the role that libraries should play in their communities in developing and promoting distance learning.

As such, the ACRL Guidelines are of limited use in assisting educators to avoid copyright infringement and, therefore, are not really "fair use guidelines" at all. Regardless, they are worth reading as a collective response of the library community to the "increased concern and demand for equitable services for all students in higher education, no matter where the 'classroom' may be."[304]

---

303. *Guidelines for Distance Learning Library Services*, American Library Association (June 29, 2004), http://www.ala.org/ala/acrl/acrlstandards/guidelinesdistancelearning.cfm.

304. *Id.* at 1.

[12] Interrelationship of the Fair Use Guidelines

Anyone relying on the "fair use guidelines" described above should be aware that each set of guidelines, in essence, stands on its own. Guideline requirements must be fulfilled in their entirety, and one group may not be combined with another. In other words, elements of guidelines may not be mixed and matched to create the exemption the educator seeks. For example, a teacher wishing to record a PBS *Frontline* documentary to show to his or her American Government class must stay strictly within the confines of the Broadcast Guidelines described above. While the instructor may show this taped program to a face-to-face class, he or she may not send it to a regional campus, because these guidelines specifically limit transmissions to "classrooms or similar places devoted to instruction within a single building, cluster or campus."

To circumvent this restriction, the same teacher may *not* also rely on Section 110(2) of the Copyright Act, which allows transmissions to any location because that exemption requires the use of a copy "lawfully made and acquired." In our example, the videotape of the PBS documentary was "lawfully acquired" only pursuant to the Broadcast Guidelines and must be exclusively used in accordance therewith. Lawfully obtaining a copyrighted work under one exemption does not carry with it the right to use it under another. In this case, if our instructor wanted to broadcast the documentary to a regional campus, he or she would have to either purchase or rent a version from the neighborhood video store or obtain permission or a license from the local PBS station.

Similarly, an instructor may not videotape a movie, such as *Gladiator*, off a pay-per-view or cable channel (e.g., Showtime or HBO) and show it to his History of the Roman Empire class under the theory that the TEACH Act now permits the use of any work, including audiovisual ones, in a nonprofit, educational broadcast. The educator has once again combined portions of two different guidelines (or a guideline and a statute in this case) to arrive at his desired result. He cannot do so because the Broadcast Guidelines apply only to programming being provided to the general public without charge. As such, an HBO or Showtime program is not covered thereunder. Instead, the teacher may purchase or rent the DVD version to show to his class. However, while he can play the entire movie for his live lecture class,[305] only a "reasonable and limited" portion thereof may be transmitted to any distance learning class setting.[306]

---

305. 17 U.S.C. § 110(1).
306. 17 U.S.C. § 110(2).

Lastly, the portion limitations set forth in the Multimedia Guidelines apply only to specific uses thereunder. They have no direct relevance to what percentage of a work may be placed on a library or electronic reserve system to comply with fair use, nor can they be used as a substitute for portion limits contained in the Photocopying or Music Guidelines. The percentage or volume limits of the Multimedia Guidelines may, however, provide a useful measuring stick when attempting a general fair use analysis (outside of any set guidelines) in an educational context, or in trying to ascertain a "reasonable and limited" portion of a work for purposes of complying with the TEACH Act.

Agreement on Guidelines for Classroom Photocopying

I. *Single Copying for Teachers*

A single copy may be made of any of the following by or for a teacher at his or her individual request for his or her scholarly research or use in teaching or preparation to teach a class:

A. A chapter from a book;

B. An article from a periodical or newspaper;

C. A short story, short essay or short poem, whether or not from a collective work;

D. A chart, graph, diagram, drawing, cartoon or picture from a book, periodical, or newspaper;

II. *Multiple Copies for Classroom Use*

Multiple copies (not to exceed in any event more than one copy per pupil in a course) may be made by or for the teacher giving the course for classroom use or discussion; *provided that:*

A. The copying meets the tests of brevity and spontaneity as defined below; *and,*

B. Meets the cumulative effect test as defined below; *and,*

C. Each copy includes a notice of copyright.

Definitions

Brevity

(i) Poetry:

(a) A complete poem if less than 250 words and if printed on not more than two pages or,

(b) from a longer poem, an excerpt of not more than 250 words.

(*ii*) Prose:
  (a) Either a complete article, story or essay of less than 2,500 words, or
  (b) an excerpt from any prose work of not more than 1,000 words or 10% of the work, whichever is less, but in any event a minimum of 500 words.

  [Each of the numerical limits stated in "i" and "ii" above may be expanded to permit the completion of an unfinished line of a poem or of an unfinished prose paragraph.]

(*iii*) Illustration: One chart, graph, diagram, drawing, cartoon or picture per book or per periodical issue.

(*iv*) "Special" works: Certain works in poetry, prose or in "poetic prose" which often combine language with illustrations and which are intended sometimes for children and at other times for a more general audience fall short of 2,500 words in their entirety.

  Paragraph "ii" above notwithstanding such "special works" may not be reproduced in their entirety; however, an excerpt comprising not more than two of the published pages of such special work and containing not more than 10% of the words found in the text thereof, may be reproduced.

Spontaneity
  (*i*) The copying is at the instance and inspiration of the individual teacher, and
  (*ii*) The inspiration and decision to use the work and the moment of its use for maximum teaching effectiveness are so close in time that it would be unreasonable to expect a timely reply to a request for permission.

Cumulative Effect
  (*i*) The copying of the material is for only one course in the school in which the copies are made.
  (*ii*) Not more than one short poem, article, story, essay or two excerpts may be copied from the same author, nor more than three from the same collective work or periodical volume during one class term.
  (*iii*) There shall not be more than nine instances of such multiple copying for one course during one class term.

[The limitations stated in "ii" and "iii" above shall not apply to current news periodicals and newspapers and current news sections of other periodicals.]

III. *Prohibitions as to I and II Above*

Notwithstanding any of the above, the following shall be prohibited:

(A) Copying shall not be used to create or to replace or substitute for anthologies, compilations or collective works. Such replacement or substitution may occur whether copies of various works or excerpts therefrom are accumulated or reproduced and used separately.

(B) There shall be no copying of or from works intended to be "consumable" in the course of study or of teaching. These include workbooks, exercises, standardized tests and test booklets and answer sheets and like consumable material.

(C) Copying shall not:

(a) substitute for the purchase of books, publishers' reprints or periodicals;

(b) be directed by higher authority;

(c) be repeated with respect to the same item by the same teacher from term to term.

(D) No charge shall be made to the student beyond the actual cost of the photocopying.

Agreed MARCH 19, 1976.

Ad Hoc Committee on Copyright Law Revision:
BY SHELDON ELLIOTT STEINBACH.

Author-Publisher Group:

Authors League of America:
BY IRWIN KARP, *Counsel.*

Association of American Publishers, Inc.:
BY ALEXANDER C. HOFFMAN,
Chairman, Copyright Committee.

Photocopying by Libraries for Patrons and Preservation

Section 108 of the Copyright Act specifies those conditions pursuant to which libraries and archives may duplicate copyrighted works to meet the needs of patrons and preserve items within their collections. Pertinent provisions of Section 108 are excerpted below:

1. GENERAL CONDITIONS.

In general, it is not an infringement of copyright for a library or archives, or any of their employees acting within the scope of their employment, to reproduce and distribute no more than one copy of a work (except as provided in Section 2 below), under the following conditions:

- the reproduction or distribution is made without any purpose of direct or indirect commercial advantage;
- the collections of the library or archives are open to the public or available to researchers affiliated with the institution and other persons doing research in a specialized field; and
- the reproduction of the work includes a notice of copyright appearing on the copy being reproduced or a legend stating the work may be protected by copyright if no notice can be found on the original work (*e.g.*, "Notice: This material may be protected by Copyright Law (Title 17 U.S.C.)").

2. COPYING FOR PRESERVATION PURPOSES.

- *Unpublished Works.* A library or archive may reproduce and distribute no more than three copies of any unpublished work solely for purposes of preservation and security, or for deposit for research use in another library, if the copy reproduced is currently in the library's collection.
- *Published Works.* A library or archive may reproduce and distribute no more than three copies of any published work solely for the purpose of replacement of a copy that is damaged, deteriorating, lost or stolen, or if the existing format in which the work is stored has become obsolete, if the library, after reasonable effort, has determined that an unused replacement cannot be obtained at a fair price (e.g., the work is out-of-print).
- *Digital Formats.* Any copy of a published or unpublished work made for the above purposes in digital format may not be made available to the public in such format outside the premises of the library.

3. COPYING FOR PATRONS.

A library or archive may copy and distribute from its own collection to a patron or another library or archive:

- one article or other contribution to a collection or periodical issue;
- a small part of any work; or
- an entire work, or a substantial part of a work

if all the following conditions are met:

a. in the case of an entire work, or substantial part thereof, the library has first determined, on the basis of a reasonable investigation, that a copy cannot be obtained at a fair price.
b. the copy becomes the property of the user.
c. the library had no notice that the copy would be used for any purpose other than private study, scholarship or research.
d. the library permanently displays, at the place where orders are accepted, and includes on its order form the notice described below:

NOTICE WARNING CONCERNING COPYRIGHT RESTRICTIONS

The copyright law of the United States (Title 17, United States Code) governs the making of photocopies or other reproductions of copyrighted material.

Under certain conditions specified in the law, libraries and archives are authorized to furnish a photocopy or other reproduction. One of these specific conditions is that the photocopy or reproduction is not to be "used for any purpose other than private study, scholarship, or research." If a user makes a request for, or later uses, a photocopy or reproduction for purposes in excess of "fair use," that user may be liable for copyright infringement.

This institution reserves the right to refuse to accept a copying order if, in its judgment, fulfillment of the order would involve violation of copyright law.

   (i) *A Display Warning of Copyright* must be printed on heavy paper or other durable material in type at least 18 points in size, and displayed prominently, in such manner and location as to be clearly visible, legible, and comprehensible to a casual observer within the immediate vicinity of the place where orders are accepted.

   (ii) *An Order Warning of Copyright* must be printed within a box located prominently on the order form itself, either on the front side of the form or immediately adjacent to the space calling for the name or signature of the person using the form. The notice must be printed in type size no smaller than that used predominantly throughout the form, but in no case smaller than 8 points, and be clearly legible, comprehensible, and readily apparent to a casual reader of the form.

  e. the copied item is not a musical work, a pictorial, graphic or sculptural work (unless part of a larger work), or a motion picture or other audiovisual work (other than an audiovisual work dealing with news).

4. MULTIPLE COPIES AND SYSTEMATIC REPRODUCTION.

The rights of reproduction and distribution under Section 108 of the Copyright Act extend to the isolated and unrelated reproduction or distribution of a single copy of the same material on separate occasions, but do not extend to cases where the library or archives, or any employee thereof:

- is aware or has substantial reason to believe that it is engaging in the related or concerted reproduction of multiple copies of the same material, whether made on one occasion or over a period of time, and whether intended for aggregate use by one or more individuals or for separate use by the individual members of a group; or

- engages in the systematic reproduction or distribution of single or multiple copies of single articles or small parts of works.

5. EDUCATIONAL USES.

During the last twenty years of any copyright term of a published work, a library or archives, including a non-profit educational institution that functions as such, may reproduce, distribute, display, or perform in facsimile or digital form a copy of such work, or portions thereof, for purposes of preservation, scholarship, or research, if such library or archives has first determined, on the basis of a reasonable investigation, that:

- the work is not subject to normal commercial exploitation;
- a copy of the work cannot be obtained at a reasonable price; and
- the copyright owner or its agent has not provided notice pursuant to regulations promulgated by the Register of Copyrights that either of the conditions set forth above applies.

Fair Use Guidelines for Electronic Reserve Systems

Revised: March 5, 1996

These guidelines were developed by the Conference on Fair Use (CONFU). The guidelines did not gain consensus support at the end of the CONFU process and were not approved as CONFU guidelines. However, libraries are using them as guidelines for developing electronic reserves systems.

A. Introduction
B. Scope of Material
C. Notices and Attributions
D. Access and Use
E. Storage and Reuse

A. INTRODUCTION

Many college, university, and school libraries have established reserve operations for readings and other materials that support the instructional requirements of specific courses. Some educational institutions are now providing electronic reserve systems that allow storage of electronic versions of materials that students may retrieve on a computer screen, and from which they may print a copy for their personal study. When materials are included as a matter of fair use, electronic reserve systems should constitute an ad hoc or supplemental source of information for students, beyond a textbook or other materials. If included with permission from the copyright owner, however, the scope and range of materials is potentially unlimited, depending upon the permission granted. Although fair use is determined on a case-by-case basis, the following guidelines identify an understanding of fair use for the reproduction, distribution, display, and performance of materials in the context of creating and using an electronic reserve system.

Making materials accessible through electronic reserve systems raises significant copyright issues. Electronic reserve operations include the making of a digital version of text, the distribution and display of that version at workstations, and downloading and printing of copies. The complexities of the electronic environment, and the growing potential for implicating copyright infringements, raise the need for a fresh understanding of fair use. These guidelines are not intended to burden the facilitation of reserves unduly, but instead offer a workable path that educators and librarians may follow in order to exercise a meaningful application of fair use, while also acknowledging and respecting the interests of copyright owners.

These guidelines focus generally on the traditional domain of reserve rooms, particularly copies of journal articles and book chapters, and their accompanying graphics. Nevertheless, they are not meant to apply exclusively to textual materials and may be instructive for the fair use of other media. The guidelines also focus on the use of the complete article or the entire book chapter. Using only brief excerpts from such works would most likely also be fair use, possibly without all of the restrictions or conditions set forth in these guidelines. Operators of reserve systems should also provide safeguards for the integrity of the text and the author's reputation, including verification that the text is correctly scanned.

The guidelines address only those materials protected by copyright and for which the institution has not obtained permission before including them in an electronic reserve system. The limitations and conditions set forth in these guidelines need not apply to materials in the public domain—such as works of the U.S. government or works on which copyright has expired—or to works for which the institution has obtained permission for inclusion in the electronic reserve system. License agreements may govern the uses of some materials. Persons responsible for electronic reserve systems should refer to applicable license terms for guidance. If an instructor arranges for students to acquire a work by some means that includes permission from the copyright owner, the instructor should not include that same work on an electronic reserve system as a matter of fair use.

These guidelines are the outgrowth of negotiations among diverse parties attending the Conference on Fair Use ("CONFU") meetings sponsored by the Information Infrastructure Task Force's Working Group on Intellectual Property Rights. While endorsements of any guidelines by all conference participants is unlikely, these guidelines have been endorsed by the organizations whose names appear at the end. These guidelines are in furtherance of the Working Group's objective of encouraging negotiated guidelines of fair use.

This introduction is an integral part of these guidelines and should be included with the guidelines wherever they may be reprinted or adopted by a library, academic institution, or other organization or association. No copyright protection of these guidelines is claimed by any person or entity, and anyone is free to reproduce and distribute this document without permission.

B. SCOPE OF MATERIAL

1. In accordance with fair use (Section 107 of the U.S. Copyright Act), electronic reserve systems may include copyrighted materials at the request of a course instructor.
2. Electronic reserve systems may include short items (such as an article from a journal, a chapter from a book or conference proceedings, or a poem from a collected work) or excerpts from longer items. "Longer items" may include articles, chapters, poems, and other works that are of such length as to constitute a substantial portion of a book, journal, or other work of which they may be a part. "Short items" may include articles, chapters, poems, and other works of a customary length and structure as to be a small part of a book, journal, or other work, even if that work may be marketed individually.
3. Electronic reserve systems should not include any material unless the instructor, the library, or another unit of the educational institution possesses a lawfully obtained copy.
4. The total amount of material included in electronic reserve systems for a specific course as a matter of fair use should be a small proportion of the total assigned reading for a particular course.

C. NOTICES AND ATTRIBUTIONS

1. On a preliminary or introductory screen, electronic reserve systems should display a notice, consistent with the notice described in Section 108(f)(1) of the Copyright Act. The notice should include additional language cautioning against further electronic distribution of the digital work.

2. If a notice of copyright appears on the copy of a work that is included in an electronic reserve system, the following statement shall appear at some place where users will likely see it in connection with access to the particular work:

    "The work from which this copy is made includes this notice: [restate the elements of the statutory copyright notice: e.g., Copyright 1996, XXX Corp.]"

3. Materials included in electronic reserve systems should include appropriate citations or attributions to their sources.

D. ACCESS AND USE

1. Electronic reserve systems should be structured to limit access to students registered in the course for which the items have been placed on reserve, and to instructors and staff responsible for the course or the electronic system.
2. The appropriate methods for limiting access will depend on available technology. Solely to suggest and not to prescribe options for implementation, possible methods for limiting access may include one or more of the following or other appropriate methods:
    a. individual password controls or verification of a student's registration status; or
    b. password system for each class; or
    c. retrieval of works by course number or instructor name, but not by author or title of the work; or
    d. access limited to workstations that are ordinarily used by, or are accessible to, only enrolled students or appropriate staff or faculty.
3. Students should not be charged specifically or directly for access to electronic reserve systems.

E. STORAGE AND REUSE

1. Permission from the copyright holder is required if the item is to be reused in a subsequent academic term for the same course offered by the same instructor, or if the item is a standard assigned or optional reading for an individual course taught in multiple sections by many instructors.
2. Material may be retained in electronic form while permission is being sought or until the next academic term in which the material

might be used, but in no event for more than three calendar years, including the year in which the materials are last used.

3. Short-term access to materials included on electronic reserve systems in previous academic terms may be provided to students who have not completed the course.

CONTU Guidelines on Photocopying under Interlibrary Loan Arrangements

Coalition for Networked Information

Information Policies: A Compilation of Position Statements, Principles, Statutes, and Other Pertinent Statements

CONTU
(National Commission on New Technological Uses of Copyright Works)

The CONTU guidelines were developed to assist librarians and copyright proprietors in understanding the amount of photocopying for use in interlibrary loan arrangements permitted under the copyright law. In the spring of 1976 there was realistic expectation that a new copyright law, under consideration for nearly twenty years, would be enacted during that session of Congress. It had become apparent that the House subcommittee was giving serious consideration to modifying the language concerning "systematic reproduction" by libraries in Section 108(g)(2) of the Senate-passed

Source: Final Report of the National Commission on New Technological Uses of Copyrighted Works, July 31, 1978, Library of Congress, Washington, DC, 1979, pages 54–55.

bill to permit photocopying under interlibrary arrangements, unless such arrangements resulted in the borrowing libraries obtaining "such aggregate quantities as to substitute for a subscription to or purchase of" copyrighted works.

The Commission discussed this proposed amendment to the Senate bill at its meeting on April 2, 1976. Pursuant to a request made at that meeting by the Register of Copyrights, serving in her ex officio role, the Commission agreed that it might aid the House and Senate subcommittees by offering its good offices in bringing the principal parties together to see whether agreement could be reached on a definition of "such aggregate quantities." This offer was accepted by the House and Senate subcommittees and the interested parties, and much of the summer of 1976 was spent by the Commission in working with the parties to secure agreement on "guidelines" interpreting what was to become the proviso in Section 108(g)(2) relating to "systematic reproduction" by libraries. The pertinent parts of that section, with the proviso added by the House emphasized, follow:

> (g) The rights of reproduction and distribution under this section extend to the isolated and unrelated reproduction or distribution of a single copy or phonorecord of the same material on separate occasions, but do not extend to cases where the library or archives, or its employee . . . .

> (2) engages in the systematic reproduction or distribution of single or multiple copies or phonorecords of material described in subsection (d): Provided, That nothing in this clause prevents a library or archives from participating in interlibrary arrangements that do not have, as their purpose of effect, that the library or archives receiving such copies or phonorecords for distribution does so in such aggregate quantities as to substitute for a subscription to or purchase of such work.

Before enactment of the new copyright law, the principal library, publisher, and author organizations agreed to the following detailed guidelines defining what "aggregate quantities" would constitute the "systematic reproduction" that would exceed the statutory limitations on a library's photocopying activities.

PHOTOCOPYING—INTERLIBRARY ARRANGEMENTS

Introduction

Subsection 108(g)(2) of the bill deals, among other things, with limits on interlibrary arrangements for photocopying. It prohibits systematic photocopying of copyrighted materials but permits interlibrary arrangements "that do not have, as their purpose or effect, that the library or archives receiving such copies or phonorecords for distribution does so in such aggregate quantities as to substitute for a subscription to or purchase of such work."

The National Commission on New Technological Uses of Copyrighted Works offered its good offices to the House and Senate subcommittees in bringing the interested parties together to see if agreement could be reached on what a realistic definition would be of "such aggregate quantities." The Commission consulted with the parties and suggested the interpretation which follows, on which there has been substantial agreement by the principal library, publisher, and author organizations. The Commission considers the guidelines which follow to be a workable and fair interpretation of the intent of the proviso portion of subsection 108(g)(2).

These guidelines are intended to provide guidance in the application of section 108 to the most frequently encountered interlibrary case: a library's obtaining from another library, in lieu of interlibrary loan, copies of articles from relatively recent issues of periodicals—those published within five years prior to the date of the request. The guidelines do not specify what aggregate quantity of copies of an article or articles published in a periodical, the issue date of which is more than five years prior to the date when the request for the copy thereof is made, constitutes a substitute for a subscription to such periodical. The meaning of the proviso to subsection 108(g)(2) in such case is left to future interpretation.

The point has been made that the present practice on interlibrary loans and use of photocopies in lieu of loans may be supplemented or even largely replaced by a system in which one or more agencies or institutions, public or private, exist for the specific purpose of providing a central source for photocopies. Of course, these guidelines would not apply to such a situation.

Guidelines for the Proviso of Subsection 108(g)(2)

1. As used in the proviso of subsection 108(g)(2), the words ". . . such aggregate quantities as to substitute for a subscription to or purchase of such work" shall mean:
   (a) with respect to any given periodical (as opposed to any given issue of a periodical), filled requests of a library or archives (a "requesting entity") within any calendar year for a total of six or more copies of an article or articles published in such periodical within five years prior to the date of the request. These guidelines specifically shall not apply, directly or indirectly, to any request of a requesting entity for a copy or copies of an article

or articles published in any issue of a periodical, the publication date of which is more than five years prior to the date when the request is made. These guidelines do not define the meaning, with respect to such a request, of ". . . such aggregate quantities as to substitute for a subscription to [such periodical]."

(b) With respect to any other material described in subsection 108(d) (including fiction and poetry), filled requests of a requesting entity within any calendar year for a total of six or more copies or phonorecords of or from any given work (including a collective work) during the entire period when such material shall be protected by copyright.

2. In the event that a requesting entity:

(a) shall have in force or shall have entered an order for a subscription to a periodical, or

(b) has within its collection, or shall have entered an order for, a copy or phonorecord of any other copyrighted work, materials from either category of which it desires to obtain by copy from another library or archives (the "supplying entity"), because the material to be copied is not reasonably available for use by the requesting entity itself, then the fulfillment of such request shall be treated as though the requesting entity made such copy from its own collection. A library or archives may request a copy or phonorecord from a supplying entity only under those circumstances where the requesting entity would have been able, under the other provisos of section 108, to supply such copy from materials in its own collection.

3. No request for a copy or phonorecord of any materials to which these guidelines apply may be fulfilled by the supplying entity unless such request is accompanied by a representation by the requesting entity that the request was made in conformity with these guidelines.

4. The requesting entity shall maintain records of all requests made by it for copies or phonorecords of any materials to which these guidelines apply and shall maintain records of the fulfillment of such requests, which records shall be retained until the end of the third complete calendar year after the end of the calendar year in which the respective request shall have been made.

5. As part of the review provided for in subsection 108(i), these guidelines shall be reviewed not later than five years from the effective date of this bill.

These guidelines were accepted by the Conference Committee and were incorporated into its report on the new act. During the ensuing twenty months, both library and publisher organizations have reported considerable progress toward adapting their practices to conform with the CONTU guidelines.

The guidelines specifically leave the status of periodical articles more than five years old to future determination. Moreover, institutions set up for the specific purpose of supplying photocopies of copyrighted material are excluded from coverage of the guidelines.

Guidelines for Educational Uses of Music

The purpose of the following guidelines is to state the minimum and not the maximum standards of educational fair use under Section 107 of HR 2223. The parties agree that the conditions determining the extent of permissible copying for educational purposes may change in the future; that certain types of copying permitted under these guidelines may not be permissible in the future, and conversely that in the future other types of copying not permitted under these guidelines may be permissible under revised guidelines.

Moreover, the following statement of guidelines is not intended to limit the types of copying permitted under the standards of fair use under judicial decision and which are stated in Section 107 of the Copyright Revision Bill. There may be instances in which copying which does not fall within the guidelines stated below may nonetheless be permitted under the criteria of fair use.

A. PERMISSIBLE USES

1. Emergency copying to replace purchased copies which for any reason are not available for an imminent performance provided purchased replacement copies shall be substituted in due course.
2. For academic purposes other than performance, single or multiple copies of excerpts of works may be made, provided that the excerpts do not comprise a part of the whole which would constitute a performable unit such as a section, movement or aria, but in no case more than 10 percent of the whole work. The number of copies shall not exceed one copy per pupil.

3. Printed copies which have been purchased may be edited or simplified provided that the fundamental character of the work is not distorted or the lyrics, if any, altered or lyrics added if none exist.
4. A single copy of recordings of performances by students may be made for evaluation or rehearsal purposes and may be retained by the educational institution or individual teacher.
5. A single copy of a sound recording (such as a tape, disc or cassette) of copyrighted music may be made from sound recordings owned by an educational institution or an individual teacher for the purpose of constructing aural exercises or examinations and may be retained by the educational institution or individual teacher. (This pertains only to the copyright of the music itself and not to any copyright which may exist in the sound recording.)

B. PROHIBITIONS

1. Copying to create or replace or substitute for anthologies, compilations or collective works.
2. Copying of or from works intended to he "consumable" in the course of study or of teaching such as workbooks, exercises, standardized tests and answer sheets and like material.
3. Copying for the purpose of performance, except as in A(1) above.
4. Copying for the purpose of substituting for the purchase of music, except as in A(1) and A(2) above.
5. Copying without inclusion of the copyright notice which appears on the printed copy.

Guidelines for Off-Air Recording of Broadcast Programming for Educational Purposes

In March 1979, Congressman Robert Kastenmeier, Chairman of the House Subcommittee on Courts, Civil Liberties and Administration of Justice, appointed a Negotiating Committee consisting of representatives of educational organizations, copyright proprietors, and creative guilds and unions. The following guidelines reflect the Negotiating Committee's consensus as to the application of "fair use" to the recording, retention, and use of television broadcast programs for educational purposes. They specify periods of retention and use of such off-air recordings in classrooms and similar places devoted to instruction and for homebound instruction. The purpose of establishing these guidelines is to provide standards for both owners and users of copyrighted television programs.

(1) The guidelines were developed to apply only to off-air recording by non-profit educational institutions.

(2) A broadcast program may be recorded off-air simultaneously with broadcast transmission (including simultaneous cable transmission) and retained by a non-profit educational institution for a period not to exceed the first forty-five (45) consecutive calendar days after date of recording. Upon conclusion of such retention period, all off-air recordings must be erased or destroyed immediately. "Broadcast programs" are television programs transmitted by television stations for reception by the general public without charge.

(3) Off-air recordings may be used once by individual teachers in the course of relevant teaching activities, and repeated once only when instructional reinforcement is necessary, in classrooms and similar places devoted to instruction within a single building, cluster, or campus, as well as in the homes of students receiving formalized home instruction, during the first ten (10) consecutive school days in the forty-five (45) day calendar day retention period. "School days" are school session days—not counting weekends, holidays, vacations, examination periods, or other scheduled interruptions— within the forty-five (45) calendar day retention period.

(4) Off-air recordings may be made only at the request of, and used by, individual teachers, and may not be regularly recorded in antici- pation of requests. No broadcast program may be recorded off-air more than once at the request of the same teacher, regardless of the number of times the program may be broadcast.

(5) A limited number of copies may be reproduced from each off-air recording to meet the legitimate needs of teachers under these guidelines. Each such additional copy shall be subject to all provi- sions governing the original recording.

(6) After the first ten (10) consecutive school days, off-air recording may be used up to the end of the forty-five (45) calendar day reten- tion period only for teacher evaluation purposes, i.e., to determine whether or not to include the broadcast program in the teaching curriculum, and may not be used in the recording institution for student exhibition or any other non-evaluation purpose without authorization.

(7) Off-air recordings need not be used in their entirety, but the recorded programs may not be altered from their original content. Off-air recordings may not be physically or electronically combined or merged to constitute teaching anthologies or compilations.

(8) All copies of off-air recordings must include the copyright notice on the broadcast program as recorded.

(9) Educational institutions are expected to establish appropriate con- trol procedures to maintain the integrity of these guidelines.

Educational Fair Use Guidelines: Distance Learning

These guidelines were developed
during the CONFU process.

Performance & Display of Audiovisual
and Other Copyrighted Works

November 18, 1996

1. INTRODUCTION

1.1 PREAMBLE

Fair use is a legal principle that provides certain limitations on the exclusive rights of copyright holders. The purpose of these guidelines is to provide guidance on the application of fair use principles by educational institutions, educators, scholars and students who wish to use copyrighted works for distance education under fair use rather than by seeking authorization from the copyright owners for non-commercial purposes. The guidelines apply to fair use only in the context of copyright.

There is no simple test to determine what is fair use. Section 107 of the Copyright Act sets forth the four fair use factors which should be considered in each instance, based on the particular facts of a given case, to determine whether a use is a fair use: (1) the purpose and character of the use, including whether use is of a commercial nature or is for non-profit educational purposes, (2) the nature of the copyrighted work, (3) the amount and substantiality of the portion used in relation to the copyrighted work as a whole, and (4) the effect of the use upon the potential market for or value of the copyrighted work.

While only the courts can authoritatively determine whether a particular use is a fair use, these guidelines represent the participants' consensus of conditions under which fair use should generally apply and examples of when permission is required. Uses that exceed these guidelines may or may not be fair use. The participants also agree that the more one exceeds these guidelines, the greater the risk that fair use does not apply. The limitations and conditions set forth in these guidelines do not apply to works in the public domain—such as U.S. government works or works on which the copyright has expired for which there are no copyright restrictions—or to works for which the individual or institution has obtained permission for the particular use. Also, license agreements may govern the uses of some works and users should refer to the applicable license terms for guidance.

The participants who developed these guidelines met for an extended period of time and the result represents their collective understanding in this complex area. Because digital technology is in a dynamic phase, there may come a time when it is necessary to revise these guidelines. Nothing in these guidelines should be construed to apply to the fair use privilege in any context, outside of educational and scholarly uses of distance education. The guidelines do not cover non-educational or commercial digitization or use at any time, even by nonprofit educational institutions. The guidelines are not intended to cover fair use of copyrighted works in other educational contexts such as educational multimedia projects, electronic reserves or digital images which may be addressed in other fair use guidelines.

This Preamble is an integral part of these guidelines and should be included whenever the guidelines are reprinted or adopted by organizations and educational institutions. Users are encouraged to reproduce and distribute these guidelines freely without permission; no copyright protection of these guidelines is claimed by any person or entity.

1.2 BACKGROUND

Section 106 of the Copyright Act defines the right to perform or display a work as an exclusive right of the copyright holder. The Act also provides, however, some exceptions under which it is not necessary to ask the copyright holder's permission to perform or display a work. One is the fair use exception contained in Section 107, which is summarized in the preamble. Another set of exceptions, contained in Sections 110(1)–(2), permit instructors and students to perform or display copyrighted materials without permission from the copyright holder under certain carefully defined conditions.

Section 110(1) permits teachers and students in a nonprofit educational institution to perform or display any copyrighted work in the course of face-to-face teaching activities. In face-to-face instruction, such teachers and students may act out a play, read aloud a poem, display a cartoon or a slide, or play a videotape so long as the copy of the videotape was lawfully obtained. In essence, Section 110(1) permits performance and display of any kind of copyrighted work, and even a complete work, as a part of face-to-face instruction.

Section 110(2) permits performance of a nondramatic literary or musical work or display of any work as a part of a transmission in some distance learning contexts, under the specific conditions set out in that Section. Section 110(2) does not permit performance of dramatic or audiovisual works as a part of a transmission. The statute further requires that the transmission be directly related and of material assistance to the teaching content of the transmission and that the transmission be received in a classroom or other place normally devoted to instruction or by persons whose disabilities or special circumstances prevent attendance at a classroom or other place normally devoted to instruction.

The purpose of these guidelines is to provide guidance for the performance and display of copyrighted works in some of the distance learning environments that have developed since the enactment of Section 110 and that may not meet the specific conditions of Section 110(2). They permit instructors who meet the conditions of these guidelines to perform and display copyrighted works as if they were engaged in face-to-face instruction. They may, for example, perform an audiovisual work, even a complete one, in a one-time transmission to students so long as they meet the other conditions of these guidelines. They may not, however, allow such transmissions to result in copies for students unless they have permission to do so, any more than face-to-face instructors may make copies of audiovisual works for their students without permission.

The developers of these guidelines agree that these guidelines reflect the principles of fair use in combination with the specific provisions of Sections 110(1)–(2). In most respects, they expand the provisions of Section 110(2).

In some cases students and teachers in distance learning situations may want to perform and display only small portions of copyrighted works that may be permissible under the fair use doctrine even in the absence of these guidelines. Given the specific limitations set out in Section 110(2), however, the participants believe that there may be a higher burden of demonstrating that fair use under Section 107 permits performance or display of more than a small portion of a copyrighted work under circumstances not specifically authorized by Section 110(2).

1.3 DISTANCE LEARNING IN GENERAL

Broadly viewed, distance learning is an educational process that occurs when instruction is delivered to students physically remote from the location or campus of program origin, the main campus, or the primary resources that support instruction. In this process, the requirements for a course or program may be completed through remote communications with instructional and support staff including either one-way or two-way written, electronic or other media forms.

Distance education involves teaching through the use of telecommunications technologies to transmit and receive various materials through voice, video and data. These avenues of teaching often constitute instruction on a closed system limited to students who are pursuing educational opportunities as part of a systematic teaching activity or curriculum and are officially enrolled in the course. Examples of such analog and digital technologies include telecourses, audio and video teleconferences, closed broadcast and cable television systems, microwave and ITFS, compressed and full-motion video, fiber optic networks, audiographic systems, interactive videodisk, satellite-based and computer networks.

2. APPLICABILITY AND ELIGIBILITY

2.1 APPLICABILITY OF THE GUIDELINES

These guidelines apply to the performance of lawfully acquired copyrighted works not included under section 110(2) (such as a dramatic work or an audiovisual work) as well as to uses not covered for works that are included in Section 110(2). The covered uses are (1) live interactive distance learning classes (i.e., a teacher in a live class with all or some of the students at remote locations) and (2) faculty instruction recorded without students present for later transmission. They apply to delivery via satellite, closed circuit television or a secure computer network. They do not permit circumventing anti-copying mechanisms embedded in copyrighted works.

These guidelines do not cover asynchronous delivery of distance learning over a computer network, even one that is secure and capable of limiting access to students enrolled in the course through PIN or other identification system. Although the participants believe fair use of copyrighted works applies in some aspects of such instruction, they did not develop fair use guidelines to cover these situations because the area is so unsettled. The technology is rapidly developing, educational institutions are just beginning to experiment with these courses, and publishers and other creators of copyrighted works are in the early stages of developing materials and experimenting with marketing strategies for computer network delivery of distance learning materials. Thus, consideration of whether fair use guidelines are needed for asynchronous computer network delivery of distance learning courses perhaps should be revisited in three to five years.

In some cases, the guidelines do not apply to specific materials because no permission is required, either because the material to be performed or displayed is in the public domain, or because the instructor or the institution controls all relevant copyrights. In other cases, the guidelines do not apply because the copyrighted material is already subject to a specific agreement. For example, if the material was obtained pursuant to a license, the terms of the license apply. If the institution has received permission to use copyrighted material specifically for distance learning, the terms of that permission apply.

2.2 ELIGIBILITY

2.2.1 ELIGIBLE EDUCATIONAL INSTITUTION

These guidelines apply to nonprofit educational institutions at all levels of instruction whose primary focus is supporting research and instructional activities of educators and students but only to their nonprofit activities. They also apply to government agencies that offer instruction to their employees.

2.2.2 ELIGIBLE STUDENTS

Only students officially enrolled for the course at an eligible institution may view the transmission that contains works covered by these guidelines. This may include students enrolled in the course who are currently matriculating at another eligible institution. These guidelines are also applicable to government agency employees who take the course or program offered by the agency as a part of their official duties.

3. WORKS PERFORMED FOR INSTRUCTION

3.1 RELATION TO INSTRUCTION

Works performed must be integrated into the course, must be part of systematic instruction and must be directly related and of material assistance to the teaching content of the transmission. The performance may not be for entertainment purposes.

4. TRANSMISSION AND RECEPTION

4.1 TRANSMISSION (DELIVERY)

Transmission must be over a secure system with technological limitations on access to the class or program such as a PIN number, password, smart-card or other means of identification of the eligible student.

4.2 RECEPTION

Reception must be in a classroom or other similar place normally devoted to instruction or any other site where the reception can be controlled by the eligible institution. In all such locations, the institution must utilize technological means to prevent copying of the portion of the class session that contains performance of the copyrighted work.

5. LIMITATIONS

5.1 ONE TIME USE

Performance of an entire copyrighted work or a large portion thereof may be transmitted only once for a distance learning course. For subsequent performances, displays or access, permission must be obtained.

5.2 REPRODUCTION AND ACCESS TO COPIES

5.2.1 RECEIVING INSTITUTION

The institution receiving the transmission may record or copy classes that include the performance of an entire copyrighted work, or a large portion thereof, and retain the recording or copy for up to 15 consecutive class days (i.e., days in which the institution is open for regular instruction) for viewing by students enrolled in the course. Access to the recording or copy for such viewing must be in a controlled environment such as a class-room, library or media center, and the institution must prevent copying by students of the portion of the class session that contains the performance of the copyrighted work. If the institution wants to retain the recording or copy of the transmission for a longer period of time, it must obtain permission from the rightsholder or delete the portion which contains the performance of the copyrighted work.

5.2.2 TRANSMITTING INSTITUTION

The transmitting institution may, under the same terms, reproduce and provide access to copies of the transmission containing the performance of a copyrighted work; in addition, it can exercise reproduction rights provided in Section 112(b).

6. MULTIMEDIA

6.1 COMMERCIALLY PRODUCED MULTIMEDIA

If the copyrighted multimedia work was obtained pursuant to a license agreement, the terms of the license apply. If, however, there is no license, the performance of the copyrighted elements of the multimedia works may be transmitted in accordance with the provisions of these guidelines.

7. EXAMPLES OF WHEN PERMISSION IS REQUIRED

7.1 COMMERCIAL USES

Any commercial use including the situation where a nonprofit educational institution is conducting courses for a for-profit corporation for a fee such as supervisory training courses or safety training for the corporation's employees.

7.2 DISSEMINATION OF RECORDED COURSES

An institution offering instruction via distance learning under these guidelines wants to further disseminate the recordings of the course or portions that contain performance of a copyrighted work.

7.3 UNCONTROLLED ACCESS TO CLASSES

An institution (agency) wants to offer a course or program that contains the performance of copyrighted works to non-employees.

7.4 USE BEYOND THE 15-DAY LIMITATION

An institution wishes to retain the recorded or copied class session that contains the performance of a copyrighted work not covered in Section

110(2). (It also could delete the portion of the recorded class session that contains the performance.)

ENDORSING ORGANIZATIONS:

Organizations Participating in Developing but Not Necessarily Endorsing or Supporting These Guidelines:

American Association of Community Colleges
American Association of Law Libraries
American Council of Learned Societies
Association of American Publishers
Association of American Universities
Association of College and Research Libraries
Association of Research Libraries
Broadcast Music, Inc.
City University of New York
Coalition of College and University Media Centers
Creative Incentive Coalition
Houghton-Mifflin
Indiana Partnership
John Wiley & Sons, Inc.
Kent State University
National Association of State Universities and Land Grant Colleges
National Geographic
National School Board Association
Special Libraries Association
State University of New York
U.S. Copyright Office
University of Texas System
Viacom

Fair Use Guidelines for Educational Multimedia

These guidelines were developed during the CONFU process.*

TABLE OF CONTENTS

---

*These Guidelines shall not be read to supersede other preexisting education fair use guidelines that deal with the Copyright Act of 1976.

1. INTRODUCTION

1.1 Preamble

Fair use is a legal principle that defines the limitations on the exclusive rights** of copyright holders. The purpose of these guidelines is to provide guidance on the application of fair use principles by educators, scholars and students who develop multimedia projects using portions of copyrighted works under fair use rather than by seeking authorization for noncommercial educational uses. These guidelines apply only to fair use in the context of copyright and to no other rights.

There is no simple test to determine what is fair use. Section 107 of the Copyright Act*** sets forth the four fair use factors which should be considered in each instance, based on particular facts of a given case, to determine whether a use is a "fair use": (1) the purpose and character of use, including whether such use is of a commercial nature or is for nonprofit educational purposes, (2) the nature of the copyrighted work, (3) the amount and substantiality of the portion used in relation to the copyrighted work as a whole, and (4) the effect of the use upon the potential market for or value of the copyrighted work.

While only the courts can authoritatively determine whether a particular use is fair use, these guidelines represent the participants'**** consensus of conditions under which fair use should generally apply and examples of when permission is required. Uses that exceed these guidelines may nor may not be fair use. The participants also agree that the more one exceeds these guidelines, the greater the risk that fair use does not apply.

The limitations and conditions set forth in these guidelines do not apply to works in the public domain—such as U.S. Government works or works on which copyright has expired for which there are no copyright restrictions—or to works for which the individual or institution has obtained permission for the particular use. Also, license agreements may govern the uses of some works and users should refer to the applicable license terms for guidance.

The participants who developed these guidelines met for an extended period of time and the result represents their collective understanding in this complex area. Because digital technology is in a dynamic phase, there may come a time when it is necessary to review the guidelines. Nothing in these

---

** See Section 106 of the Copyright Act.

*** The Copyright Act of 1976, as amended, is codified at 17 U.S.C. Sec.101 et seq.

**** The names of the various organizations participating in this dialog appear at the end of these guidelines and clearly indicate the variety of interest groups involved, both from the standpoint of the users of copyrighted material and also from the standpoint of the copyright owners.

guidelines shall be construed to apply to the fair use privilege in any context outside of educational and scholarly uses of educational multimedia projects.

This Preamble is an integral part of these guidelines and should be included whenever the guidelines are reprinted or adopted by organizations and educational institutions. Users are encouraged to reproduce and distribute these guidelines freely without permission; no copyright protection of these guidelines is claimed by any person or entity.

1.2 Background

These guidelines clarify the application of fair use of copyrighted works as teaching methods are adapted to new learning environments. Educators have traditionally brought copyrighted books, videos, slides, sound recordings and other media into the classroom, along with accompanying projection and playback equipment. Multimedia creators integrated these individual instructional resources with their own original works in a meaningful way, providing compact educational tools that allow great flexibility in teaching and learning. Material is stored so that it may be retrieved in a nonlinear fashion, depending on the needs or interests of learners. Educators can use multimedia projects to respond spontaneously to students' questions by referring quickly to relevant portions. In addition, students can use multimedia projects to pursue independent study according to their needs or at a pace appropriate to their capabilities. Educators and students want guidance about the application of fair use principles when creating their own multimedia projects to meet specific instructional objectives.

1.3 Applicability of These Guidelines

Certain basic terms used throughout these guidelines are identified in bold and defined in this section. These guidelines apply to the use, without permission, of portions of lawfully acquired copyrighted works in educational multimedia projects which are created by educators or students as part of a systematic learning activity by nonprofit educational institutions.

Educational multimedia projects created under these guidelines incorporate students' or educators' original material, such as course notes or commentary, together with various copyrighted media formats including but not limited to, motion media, music, text material, graphics, illustrations, photographs and digital software which are combined into an integrated presentation. **Educational institutions** are defined as nonprofit organizations whose primary focus is supporting research and instructional activities of educators and students for noncommercial purposes.

For the purposes of the guidelines, **educators** include faculty, teachers, instructors, and others who engage in scholarly, research and instructional activities for educational institutions. The copyrighted works used under these guidelines are **lawfully acquired** if obtained by the institution or individual through lawful means such as purchase, gift or license agreement but not pirated copies. Educational multimedia projects which incorporate portions of copyrighted works under these guidelines may be used only for **educational purposes** in systematic learning activities including use in connection with non-commercial curriculum-based learning and teaching activities by educators to students enrolled in courses at non-profit educational institutions or otherwise permitted under Section 3. While these guidelines refer to the creation and use of educational multimedia projects, readers are advised that in some instances other fair use guidelines such as those for off-air taping may be relevant.

2. PREPARATION OF EDUCATIONAL MULTIMEDIA PROJECTS USING PORTIONS OF COPYRIGHTED WORKS

These uses are subject to the Portion Limitations listed in Section 4. They should include proper attribution and citation as defined in Sections 6.2.

2.1 By students:

Students may incorporate portions of lawfully acquired copyrighted works when producing their own educational multimedia projects for a specific course.

2.2 By Educators for Curriculum-Based Instruction:

Educators may incorporate portions of lawfully acquired copyrighted works when producing their own educational multimedia programs for their own teaching tools in support of curriculum-based instructional activities at educational institutions.

3. PERMITTED USES OF EDUCATIONAL MULTIMEDIA PROGRAMS CREATED UNDER THESE GUIDELINES

Uses of educational multimedia projects created under these guidelines are subject to the Time, Portion, Copying and Distribution Limitations listed in Section 4.

3.1 Student Use:

Students may perform and display their own educational multimedia projects created under Section 2 of these guidelines for educational uses in the course for which they were created and may use them in their own portfolios as examples of their academic work for later personal uses such as job and graduate school interviews.

3.2 Educator Use for Curriculum-Based Instruction:

Educators may perform and display their own educational multimedia projects created under Section 2 for curriculum-based instruction to students in the following situations:

3.2.1 for face-to-face instruction,

3.2.2 assigned to students for directed self-study,

3.2.3 for remote instruction to students enrolled in curriculum-based courses and located at remote sites, provided over the educational institution's secure electronic network in real-time, or for after class review or directed self-study, provided there are technological limitations on access to the network and educational multimedia project (such as a password or PIN) and provided further that the technology prevents the making of copies of copyrighted material.

If the educational institution's network or technology used to access the educational multimedia project created under Section 2 of these guidelines cannot prevent duplication of copyrighted material, students or educators may use the multimedia educational projects over an otherwise secure network for a period of only 15 days after its initial real-time remote use in the course of instruction or 15 days after its assignment for directed self-study. After that period, one of the two use copies of the educational multimedia project may be placed on reserve in a learning resource center, library or similar facility for on-site use by students enrolled in the course. Students shall be advised that they are not permitted to make their own copies of the multimedia project.

3.3 Educator Use for Peer Conferences:

Educators may perform or display their own multimedia projects created under Section 2 of these guidelines in presentations to their peers, for example, at workshops and conferences.

3.4 Educator Use for Professional Portfolio:

Educators may retain educational multimedia projects created under Section 2 of these guidelines in their personal portfolios for later personal uses such as tenure review or job interviews.

4. LIMITATIONS—TIME, PORTION, COPYING AND DISTRIBUTION

The preparation of educational multimedia projects incorporating copyrighted works under Section 2, and the use of such projects under Section 3, are subject to the limitations noted below.

4.1 Time Limitations

Educators may use their educational multimedia projects created for educational purposes under Section 2 of these guidelines for teaching courses, for a period of up to two years after the first instructional use with a class. Use beyond that time period, even for educational purposes, requires permission for each copyrighted portion incorporated in the production. Students may use their educational multimedia projects as noted in Section 3.1.

4.2 Portion Limitations

Portion limitations mean the amount of a copyrighted work that can reasonably be used in educational multimedia projects under these guidelines regardless of the original medium from which the copyrighted works are taken. **In the aggregate** means the total amount of copyrighted material from a single copyrighted work that is permitted to be used in an educational multimedia project without permission under these guidelines. These limits apply cumulatively to each educator's or student's multimedia project(s) for the same academic semester, cycle or term. All students should be instructed about the reasons for copyright protection and the need to follow these guidelines. It is understood, however, that students in kindergarten through grade six may not be able to adhere rigidly to the portion limitations in this section in their independent development of educational multimedia projects. In any event, each such project retained under Sections 3.1 and 4.3 should comply with the portion limitations in this section.

4.2.1 Motion Media

Up to 10% or 3 minutes, whichever is less, in the aggregate of a copyrighted motion media work may be reproduced or otherwise incorporated as part of a multimedia project created under Section 2 of these guidelines.

4.2.2 Text Material

Up to 10% or 1000 words, whichever is less, in the aggregate of a copyrighted work consisting of text material may be reproduced or otherwise incorporated as part of a multimedia project created under Section 2 of these guidelines. An entire poem of less than 250 words may be used, but no more than three poems by one poet, or five poems by different poets from any anthology may be used. For poems of greater length, 250 words may be used but no more than three excerpts by a poet, or five excerpts by different poets from a single anthology may be used.

4.2.3 Music, Lyrics, and Music Video

Up to 10%, but in no event more than 30 seconds, of the music and lyrics from an individual musical work (or in the aggregate of extracts from an individual work), whether the musical work is embodied in copies, or audio or audiovisual works, may be reproduced or otherwise incorporated as a part of a multimedia project created under Section 2. Any alterations to a musical work shall not change the basic melody or the fundamental character of the work.

4.2.4 Illustrations and Photographs

The reproduction or incorporation of photographs and illustrations is more difficult to define with regard to fair use because fair use usually precludes the use of an entire work. Under these guidelines a photograph or illustration may be used in its entirety but no more than 5 images by an artist or photographer may be reproduced or otherwise incorporated as part of an educational multimedia project created under Section 2. When using photographs and illustrations from a published collective work, not more than 10% or 15 images, whichever is less, may be reproduced or otherwise incorporated as part of an educational multimedia project created under Section 2.

4.2.5 Numerical Data Sets

Up to 10% or 2500 fields or cell entries, whichever is less, from a copyrighted database or data table may be reproduced or otherwise incorporated as part of an educational multimedia project created under Section 2 of these guidelines. A field entry is defined as a specific item of information, such as a name or Social Security number, in a record of a database file. A cell entry is defined as the intersection where a row and a column meet on a spreadsheet.

4.3 Copying and Distribution Limitations

Only a limited number of copies, including the original, may be made of an educator's educational multimedia project. For all of the uses permitted by Section 3, there may be no more than two use copies only one of which may be placed on reserve as described in Section 3.2.3.

An additional copy may be made for preservation purposes but may only be used or copied to replace a use copy that has been lost, stolen, or damaged. In the case of a jointly created educational multimedia project, each principal creator may retain one copy but only for the purposes described in Sections 3.3 and 3.4 for educators and Section 3.1 for students.

5. EXAMPLES OF WHEN PERMISSION IS REQUIRED

5.1 Using Multimedia Projects for Non-Educational or Commercial Purposes

Educators and students must seek individual permissions (licenses) before using copyrighted works in educational multimedia projects for commercial reproduction and distribution.

5.2 Duplication of Multimedia Projects Beyond Limitations Listed in These Guidelines

Even for educational uses, educators and students must seek individual permissions for all copyrighted works incorporated in their personally created educational multimedia projects before replicating or distributing beyond the limitations listed in Section 4.3.

5.3 Distribution of Multimedia Projects Beyond Limitations Listed in These Guidelines

Educators and students may not use their personally created educational multimedia projects over electronic networks, except for uses as described in Section 3.2.3, without obtaining permissions for all copyrighted works incorporated in the program.

6. IMPORTANT REMINDERS

6.1 Caution in Downloading Material from the Internet

Educators and students are advised to exercise caution in using digital material downloaded from the Internet in producing their own educational multimedia projects, because there is a mix of works protected by copyright and works in the public domain on the network. Access to works on the Internet does not automatically mean that these can be reproduced and reused without permission or royalty payment and, furthermore, some copyrighted works may have been posted to the Internet without authorization of the copyright holder.

6.2 Attribution and Acknowledgment

Educators and students are reminded to credit the sources and display the copyright notice © and copyright ownership information if this is shown in the original source, for all works incorporated as part of the educational multimedia projects prepared by educators and students, including those prepared under fair use. Crediting the source must adequately identify the source of the work, giving a full bibliographic description where available (including author, title, publisher, and place and date of publication). The copyright ownership information includes the copyright notice (©, year of first publication and name of the copyright holder).

The credit and copyright notice information may be combined and shown in a separate section of the educational multimedia project (e.g., credit section) except for images incorporated into the project for the uses described in Section 3.2.3. In such cases, the copyright notice and the name of the creator of the image must be incorporated into the image when, and to the extent, such information is reasonably available; credit and copyright notice information is considered "incorporated" if it is attached to the image file and appears on the screen when the image is viewed. In those cases when displaying source credits and copyright ownership information on the screen with the image would be mutually exclusive with an instructional objective (e.g., during examinations in which the source credits and/or copyright information would be relevant to the examination questions), those images may be displayed without such information being simultaneously displayed on the screen. In such cases, this information should be linked to the image in a manner compatible with such instructional objectives.

6.3 Notice of Use Restrictions

Educators and students are advised that they must include on the opening screen of their multimedia program and any accompanying print material a notice that certain materials are included under the fair use exemption of the U.S. Copyright Law and have been prepared according to the multimedia fair use guidelines and are restricted from further use.

6.4 Future Uses Beyond Fair Use

Educators and students are advised to note that if there is a possibility that their own educational multimedia project incorporating copyrighted works under fair use could later result in broader dissemination, whether or not as commercial product, it is strongly recommended that they take steps to obtain permissions during the development process for all copyrighted portions rather than waiting until after completion of the project.

6.5 Integrity of Copyrighted Works: Alterations

Educators and students may make alterations in the portions of the copyrighted works they incorporate as part of an educational multimedia project only if the alterations support specific instructional objectives. Educators and students are advised to note that alterations have been made.

6.6 Reproduction or Decompilation of Copyrighted Computer Programs

Educators and students should be aware that reproduction or decompilation of copyrighted computer programs and portions thereof, for example the transfer of underlying code or control mechanisms, even for educational uses, are outside the scope of these guidelines.

6.7 Licenses and Contracts

Educators and students should determine whether specific copyrighted works, or other data or information are subject to a license or contract. Fair use and these guidelines shall not preempt or supersede licenses and contractual obligations.

APPENDIX A: (AS OF DECEMBER 12, 1996)

1. ORGANIZATIONS ENDORSING THESE GUIDELINES:

Agency for Instructional Technology (AIT)
American Association of Community Colleges (AACC)
American Society of Journalists and Authors (ASJA)
American Society of Media Photographers, Inc. (ASMP)
American Society of Composers, Authors and Publishers (ASCAP)
Association for Educational Communications and Technology (AECT)
Association for Information Media and Equipment (AIME)
Association of American Publishers (AAP)*
Association of American Colleges and Universities (AAC&U)
Association of American University Presses, Inc. (AAUP)
Broadcast Music, Inc. (BMI)
Consortium of College and University Media Centers (CCUMC)

---

* ADDITIONAL INFORMATION ON SOME OF THE ORGANIZATIONS WHO HAVE ENDORSED THESE GUIDELINES:

The Association of American Publishers (AAP) membership includes over 200 publishers.

The Information Industry Association (IIA) membership includes 550 companies involved in the creation, distribution and use of information products, services and technologies.

The Software Publishers Association (SPA) membership includes 1200 software publishers.

Creative Incentive Coalition (CIC)**
Iowa Association for Communications Technology (IACT)
Information Industry Association (IIA)
Instructional Telecommunications Council (ITC)
Maricopa Community Colleges/Phoenix
Motion Picture Association of America (MPAA)
Music Publishers' Association of the United States (MPA)
National Association of Regional Media Centers (NARMC)
Recording Industry Association of America (RIAA)
Software Publishers Association (SPA)

2. U.S. GOVERNMENT AGENCIES SUPPORTING THESE GUIDELINES:

U.S. National Endowment for the Arts (NEA)
U.S. Copyright Office
U.S. Patent and Trademark Office

3. INDIVIDUAL COMPANIES AND INSTITUTIONS ENDORSING THESE GUIDELINES:

Houghton-Mifflin
John Wiley & Sons, Inc.
McGraw-Hill
Time Warner, Inc.

** The Creative Incentive Coalition membership includes the following organizations:
Association of American Publishers
Association of Independent Television Stations
Association of Test Publishers
Business Software Alliance
General Instrument Corporation
Information Industry Association
Information Technology Industry Council
Interactive Digital Software Association
Magazine Publishers of America
The McGraw-Hill Companies
Microsoft Corporation
Motion Picture Association of America, Inc.
National Cable Television Association
National Music Publisher's Association
Newspaper Association of America
Recording Industry Association of America
Seagram/MCA, Inc.
Software Publishers Association
Time Warner, Inc.
Turner Broadcasting System, Inc.
West Publishing Company
Viacom, Inc.

APPENDIX B: ORGANIZATIONS PARTICIPATING IN GUIDELINE DEVELOPMENT:

Being a participant does not necessarily mean that the organization has or will endorse these guidelines.

Agency for Instructional Technology (AIT)
American Association of Community Colleges (AACC)
American Association of Higher Education (AAHE)
American Library Association (ALA)
American Society of Journal Authors, Inc. (ASJA)
American Society of Media Photographers (ASMP)
Artists Rights Foundation
Association of American Colleges and Universities (AAC&U)
Association of American Publishers (AAP)
   —Harvard University Press
   —Houghton Mifflin
   —McGraw-Hill
   —Simon and Schuster
   —Worth Publishers
Association of College Research Libraries (ACRL)
Association for Educational Communications and Technology (AECT)
Association for Information Media and Equipment (AIME)
Association of Research Libraries (ARL)
Authors Guild, Inc.
Broadcast Music, Inc. (BMI)
Consortium of College and University Media Centers (CCUMC)
Copyright Clearance Center (CCC)
Creative Incentive Coalition (CIC)
Directors Guild of America (DGA)
European American Music Distributors Corp.
Educational institutions represented
   —American University
   —Carnegie Mellon University
   —City College/City University of New York
   —Kent State University
   —Maricopa Community Colleges/Phoenix
   —Penn State University
   —University of Delaware
Information Industry Association (IIA)
Instructional Telecommunications Council (ITC)
International Association of Scientific, Technical and Medical Publishers

Motion Picture Association of America (MPAA)
Music Publishers Association (MPA)
National Association of State Universities and Land-Grant Colleges (NASULGC)
National Council of Teachers of Mathematics (NCTM)
National Educational Association (NEA)
National Music Publishers Association (NMPA)
National School Boards Association (NSBA)
National Science Teachers Association (NSTA)
National Video Resources (NVR)
Public Broadcasting System (PBS)
Recording Industry Association of America (RIAA)
Software Publishers Association (SPA)
Time-Warner, Inc.
U.S. Copyright Office
U.S. National Endowment for the Arts (NEA)
Viacom, Inc.

Prepared by the Educational Multimedia Fair Use Guidelines Development Committee, July 17, 1996

CHAPTER 4

Locating and Negotiating with Creators

Any educator seeking to use another person's copyrighted work has, in essence, the following four options to choose from if he or she wishes to avoid copyright infringement liability.

1. Rely on exemptions contained in the Copyright Act, such as fair use and the classroom privilege;
2. Use only works whose term of protection has expired or that were never covered by copyright, more commonly known as works in the public domain;
3. Obtain the permission of the copyright owner to use the work without payment of any fee or other restriction; or
4. Negotiate a license agreement with the owner or his representative that usually requires the payment of a royalty and includes other use constraints.

While Chapters Two and Three dealt extensively with the first two areas, this chapter covers options 3 and 4. Section 4.1 discusses conducting copyright searches. This may also have relevance for option 2 because these searches are often undertaken to determine whether a copyrighted work's term of protection has expired. Section 4.2 looks at seeking permission from owners after they have been located. If a proposed use affects the market for the copyrighted work, the party seeking permission will likely be asked to enter into a license with the copyright holder. Sections 4.3 and 4.4 herein deal with such licensing arrangements in greater detail. Section 4.5 covers the protection (or lack thereof) of databases often contained in licensed works and recent legislative efforts to address this issue.

4.1 INVESTIGATING THE COPYRIGHT STATUS OF A WORK

[1] Methods of Approaching a Copyright Investigation

Several methods are available to investigate whether a work is protected by copyright and, if so, the elements thereof. These include

- Examining the work for items such as a copyright notice, place and date of publication, author and publisher—or, if the work is a sound recording, examining the CD, tape cartridge, or cassette in which the sound is fixed, or the album cover, sleeve, or container in which the recording is sold;
- Making a search of the Copyright Office catalogs and other records;
- Having the Copyright Office conduct the search; or
- Using private information resources.

Copyright investigations often involve more than one of these methods. Even if the inquirer conducts all four, the results are not necessarily conclusive. Moreover, as explained below, changes brought about by the Copyright Act of 1976, the Berne Convention Implementation Act of 1988,[1] the Copyright Renewal Act of 1992,[2] and the Sonny Bono Copyright Term Extension Act of 1998[3] (hereinafter CTEA) must also be considered when investigating the copyright status of a work.

The best place to begin is obviously the work itself. A physical examination thereof should reveal its creator and date of publication. Often the publisher of the work holds its copyright. If this fails because the information is either missing or incomplete, a more comprehensive investigation must be undertaken. Subsections [2] through [6] offer some practical guidance on what to look at in conducting such a search. It is important to realize, however, that these subsections contain only general information and that several exceptions apply to the principles outlined therein. In many cases, it is still prudent to consult with an attorney before reaching any final conclusions regarding a work's status.

[2] Searching Copyright Office Catalogs and Records

[a] Catalog of Copyright Entries

The United States Copyright Office published the *Catalog of Copyright Entries* ("Catalog") in printed format from 1891 through 1978 and in

---

1. Pub. L. No. 100–568, 102 Stat. 2853 (1988) (Berne Convention Act).
2. Pub. L. No. 102–307, 106 Stat. 264 (1992) (CRA).
3. Pub. L. No. 105–298, 112 Stat. 2827 (1998) (CTEA).

microfiche from 1979 through 1982. The Catalog was divided into classes of works registered, with each segment covering all registrations made during a particular period of time. Many libraries throughout the United States maintain copies of the Catalog, which still provides a good starting point for any search. There are many cases, however, in which a Catalog search alone will prove insufficient to obtain the needed information. For example, the Catalog does not include entries for assignments or other recorded instruments. Thus, it cannot be used to search for the transfer or assignment of ownership rights. Any Catalog entry will contain essential facts concerning a registration, but not a transcript of the registration record. As such, it will not usually contain the copyright claimant's address.

The Catalog was discontinued in 1982. Most researchers today use the Internet to access the Automated Catalog, which contains entries from 1978 to the present. The following files are now available at the Copyright Office website (http://www.copyright.gov): COHM, which includes registration of most works and renewals thereof; COHD, which references copyright ownership documents, such as name changes and transfers; and COHS, which involves serials. "Serials" are generally periodicals, magazines, journals, and newspapers. Currently, the Office is conducting a business analysis to determine the feasibility of digitizing millions of Copyright Office paper records filed from 1790 to 1977. It is estimated that such an effort could achieve basic online access within six years at a cost of $6 million to $11 million.[4]

[b] Individual Searches of Copyright Records

If the Catalog and Internet prove insufficient, one may physically conduct a search at the Copyright Office, which is located in the Library of Congress, James Madison Memorial Building, 101 Independence Avenue, S.E., Washington, D.C., 20559-6000. Most Copyright Office records are open for public inspection from 8:30 a.m. to 5:00 p.m., Eastern Time, Monday through Friday, except federal holidays. The various public records include an extensive card catalog, the Automated Catalog, record books, and microfilm of assignments and related documents. Some materials, including correspondence files and deposit copies, are not available to the public for searching. However, they may be inspected upon request and by paying a fee. Anyone conducting an individual examination of Copyright

---

4. *Annual Report of the Copyright Office for Fiscal Year 2006* (hereinafter 2006 *Annual Report*), at 45.

Office files may request assistance in locating records or learning search procedures.[5]

[3] Searching by the Copyright Office

[a] In General

If traveling to Washington, D.C., is not in your plans, you may request the Copyright Office staff to search its records at the statutory rate of $75 per hour or the fraction thereof consumed. The Office can provide a fee estimate first, based on information furnished by the inquiring person. This fee does not include the cost of additional certificates or photocopies of deposits or other Copyright Office records, however. Anyone asking for a Copyright Office search should send the estimated fee along with the request. The Copyright Office will then commence the search and provide the inquirer a written report or, if the person prefers, an oral report by telephone.[6]

Search reports may be certified for an additional fee of $80 per hour. Certified searches are most frequently requested to meet the evidentiary requirements of litigation. Any search request or other correspondence should be addressed or communicated to:

Library of Congress
Copyright Office
Reference and Bibliography Section, LM-451
101 Independence Avenue, S.E.
Washington, D.C. 20559-6000
Tel: (202) 707-6850
Fax: (202) 252-3485
TTY: (202) 707-6737

[b] Information Needed

Supplying detailed information will normally reduce the cost of any search. Therefore, it is advisable to provide the Copyright Office with as many of the following facts as known:

- Title of the work, with any possible variations;
- Name of the author, including possible pseudonyms;

---

5. In fiscal 2006, the Reference and Bibliography Section of the Office assisted close to 9,000 such users. In addition, the Clerical Support Unit responded to 12,906 letter requests, 40,471 telephone calls, and 12,643 e-mail inquiries from the public for forms and other publications. See 2006 Annual Report at 46.

6. The Office prepared 832 such search reports in fiscal 2006. See 2006 Annual Report at 45.

- Name of the likely copyright owner, usually the publisher or creator;
- Approximate year when the work was published or registered;
- Type of work involved (book, play, musical composition, sound recording, photograph, etc.);
- For a work originally published as part of a periodical or collection, the title of that publication and any other information, such as the volume or issue number, to help identify it; and
- Registration number or any other available copyright data.

A specific request must be made for information on an underlying work, such as music from a movie. In such cases, it is best to first identify the underlying work and furnish the specific titles, authors, and approximate dates thereof, if known.

For the standard hourly fee, the Copyright Office will also search the records of assignments and other documents concerning copyright ownership. The final report will outline the facts derived from the Office's indexes but offer no interpretation or legal opinion thereof. As such, a copyright lawyer may still need to be retained to interpret the results. In determining whether to request a search, the following facts should also be considered:

- The Copyright Office does not maintain listings of works by subject or that are in the public domain.
- Individual works such as stories, poems, articles, or musical compositions published as contributions to a copyrighted periodical or collection are usually not listed separately by title.
- The Copyright Office does not compare works to determine possible infringement.
- Copyright law does not protect names and titles, so the Copyright Office records will list many different works identified by the same or similar titles.

[4] Private Information Services

Apart from the Copyright Office, third-party or private compilations play an important role in the gathering and maintenance of copyright ownership information. Therefore, they serve as additional resources for copyright searchers. Typically, these materials are accumulated where industry groups have an incentive to centralize this information, such as for collective rights administration and licensing purposes.[7] In other cases, interested

---

7. Collective licensing organizations such as ASCAP, BMI, and the Harry Fox Agency all have databases containing extensive contact information for owners of copyrights; they also have staff available to assist with inquiries.

users and researchers have developed their own databases.[8] Generally these third-party services tend to provide reliable, if not exhaustive, information about copyright ownership.

[5] Search Limitations

[a] Searches Not Always Conclusive

While searches of Copyright Office and private industry records are useful in ascertaining the copyright status of a work, they are not always definitive. For instance, the absence of information about a work does not necessarily mean it is unprotected. Consider that:

- Before 1978, unpublished works were entitled to protection under common law without the need of registration.
- Works published with notice prior to 1978 may be registered at any time within the first twenty-eight-year term.
- Works copyrighted between January 1, 1964, and December 31, 1977, are affected by the Copyright Renewal Act of 1992,[9] which automatically extends the copyright term and makes renewal registrations optional.
- For works under copyright protection on or after January 1, 1978, registration may be made at any time during the term of protection.
- A search report may not cover recent registrations for which records are not yet available.
- The information in the search request may not always be complete or specific enough to identify the work.
- The work may have been registered under a different title or as part of a larger work.
- Works created after March 1, 1989, are no longer required to contain a copyright notice to be protected.

[b] Protection in Foreign Countries

A work considered to be in the public domain in the United States may not necessarily have the same status in other countries. Every nation has its own laws governing the length and scope of copyright protection, and these laws typically apply to all works used within that country.[10] Thus, the

---

8. *See, e.g.,* The Online Books Page: *Information About the Catalog of Copyright Entries,* http://onlinebooks.library.upenn.edu/cce/; U.S. Catalog of Copyright Entries (Renewals), http://www.kingkong.demon.co.uk/ccer/ccer.htm.

9. CRA, *supra* note 2.

10. For a more detailed discussion of the international implications of copyright law, *see* Section 2.2 of Chapter Two.

expiration or loss of copyright protection in the United States is not always determinative of permitted use abroad.

[6] Impact of Copyright Act Amendments

On October 19, 1976, President Gerald R. Ford signed into law a comprehensive revision of the Copyright Act. Most provisions of the new statute came into force on January 1, 1978, superseding the Copyright Act of 1909.[11] Further important changes arose from the Berne Convention Implementation Act of 1988,[12] which took effect March 1, 1989; the Copyright Renewal Act of 1992,[13] which amended the renewal provisions of the law; and CTEA,[14] which extended the term of copyrights for an additional twenty years. For copyright investigations, these four statutes have had the following impact.

[a] Copyright Registration

The Copyright Act of 1976[15] (the "1976 Act") altered the procedural requirements for securing and maintaining full copyright protection. The former system was more rigid and involved copyright notice, deposit, and registration, along with the recording of transfers of ownership and licenses. In general, while retaining some formalities, the 1976 Act reduced the chances of mistakes, softened the consequences of omissions, and allowed for the correction of errors. For instance, under current law, copyright extends immediately to original works of authorship created and fixed in any tangible medium of expression from which they can be perceived, reproduced, or otherwise communicated with the aid of a machine or device.[16] In other words, copyright is an incident of creative authorship no longer dependent on statutory formalities. Thus, registration with the Copyright Office is no longer required, but certain advantages still arise therefrom.[17]

[b] Copyright Notice

As enacted, the 1976 Act prescribed that all visually perceptible published copies of a work had to bear a copyright notice. Such was the state of the

---

11. Copyright Act of March 4, 1909, 35 Stat. 1045 (1909).

12. Berne Convention Act, *supra* note 1.

13. CRA, *supra* note 2.

14. CTEA, *supra* note 3.

15. Copyright Revision Act of 1976, Pub. L. No. 94–553, 90 Stat. 2541 (1976) (the "1976 Act").

16. 17 U.S.C. § 102(a).

17. *See* Chapter Two, Section 2.1[5], for further information on the advantages of copyright registration.

law until the United States joined the Berne Convention. Beginning on March 1, 1989, notice of copyright on all works became optional.[18] Before that date, the notice requirement applied equally whether the work was published in the United States or elsewhere. However, for works published from January 1, 1978, through February 28, 1989, omission of the required notice, or use of a defective one, did not necessarily result in forfeiture of copyright protection. Protection was lost, however, if certain corrective steps were not taken in time. Adding the notice is still recommended because certain advantages arise therefrom when defending a copyright in court.[19] Acceptable positions for the notice of copyright are set forth in regulations promulgated by the Copyright Office.[20]

[c] Works Already in the Public Domain

Neither the 1976 Act, the Berne Convention Implementation Act of 1988, the Copyright Renewal Act of 1992, nor the CTEA restored protection to works that had already fallen into the public domain. However, the North American Free Trade Agreement Implementation Act[21] and the Uruguay Round Agreements Act (URAA)[22] may restore copyright in certain foreign works that had previously fallen into the public domain in the United States.[23]

4.2 OBTAINING PERMISSION AND "ORPHAN" WORKS

[1] Contacting the Owner

An educator wishing to incorporate a copyrighted work into her classroom materials must either rely on an exemption contained in the Copyright Act or obtain permission from the content owner before such use. Authors, publishers, and other copyright holders are often amenable to allowing legitimate educational uses of their works. In fact, many publishers have personnel or offices specifically designated to review and approve such requests for permission.

---

18. Berne Convention Act, *supra* note 1.

19. *See* Chapter Two, Section 2.1[8][f], note 357.

20. 37 C.F.R. § 201.20 (1990).

21. Pub. L. No. 103–182, 107 Stat. 2057 (1993).

22. Pub. L. No. 103–465, 108 Stat. 4809 (1994).

23. This "restoration" of works from the public domain is currently being challenged in the federal courts, however. *See, e.g., Golan v. Gonzalez,* No. 05-1259, slip. op. at 27 (10th Cir. Sept. 4, 2007) ("the URAA . . . contravened a bedrock principle of copyright law that works in the public domain remain in the public domain").

A permission seeker should always submit his or her request in writing. Appendix 4-A hereto contains a sample letter that may be used to obtain approval from a publisher for repeated photocopying of copyrighted content for classroom use. Appendix 4-B contains a sample letter seeking permission for republication of material as part of another work. No formal legal language needs to be included in these requests. The writer should take care, however, to be precise—but not verbose—regarding his intended use of the work.

Generally, it simplifies matters if the copyright owner can grant permission by merely countersigning the letter and returning it. Some publishers prefer to use their own consent letters and may send back a different form. These should be reviewed carefully to ensure any additional provisions do not interfere with the educator's intended use. While the teacher's request usually anticipates using the work for no charge, publishers sometimes seek payment in exchange for permission. These fees are often nominal, however. If the compensation is for more than a token amount, the educator may wish to propose a more formal licensing arrangement to protect his university or school's investment.[24]

Additional points to consider when seeking permission are as follows. First, make sure copies of the publisher's consent are retained by the school in case an issue arises later regarding the existence or scope of permission. Second, when using another's work, even with the owner's authority, it is still advisable (if not required) to place the original copyright notice on all copies. Third, an educator should submit her request far enough in advance to give the copyright holder sufficient time to review it, ask questions, and/or negotiate additional terms, if necessary. It is not unusual for such a process to consume two to three months, even for simple matters. Finally, never assume the failure to receive a response from a copyright holder or his publisher means the work is in the public domain or constitutes implied consent. Nothing could be further from the truth. In those cases, it is best to renew the request or obtain alternative materials.

[2] Issues with Orphan Works

When contemplating using the work of another, obviously the first and wisest course of action is to obtain the owner's permission. Situations often arise, however, where the copyright owner cannot be identified and/or located by the would-be user, and such user is otherwise unable to rely

---

24. For more information on license agreements and their contents, *see* Section 4.4. Most often, the content owner will submit a licensing agreement he or she wants the educational institution or school system to sign.

on an exemption (such as fair use) in the law. In these cases, that person faces a dilemma. He could use the work but then face the prospect, however remote, that an owner would appear later and sue for infringement. Alternatively, he could refrain from employing the work, thus possibly forestalling a productive and beneficial use thereof—not because the copyright holder objected or even failed to acquiesce to licensing terms, but merely because the parties never had the opportunity to meet and discuss the situation.

Copyrighted items in this category are often referred to as "orphan" works, and numerous concerns have been raised about them over the years. When the 1976 Act extended the copyright term of a work and protected it automatically upon fixation (without formal requirements such as registration or notice),[25] the rules of the game changed dramatically. Educators, in particular, expressed concern that these amendments would inhibit (if not foreclose) scholarly uses of those works no longer being commercially marketed.[26]

When examining CTEA in 1998[27] (which extended copyright protection again by twenty years), the Copyright Office observed that a term extension could exacerbate problems with orphan works.[28] The Office noted similar problems one year later, during its study on Copyright and Digital Distance Education, when it reported that attempting to locate copyright owners "can be time-consuming, difficult or even impossible."[29] It is difficult to quantify

---

25. 17 U.S.C. § 102(a).

26. Congress summarized these concerns as follows:

A point that has concerned some educational groups arose from the possibility that, since a large majority (now about 85 percent) of all copyrighted works are not renewed, a life-plus-fifty-year term would tie up a substantial body of material that is probably of no commercial interest, but that would be more readily available for scholarly use if free of copyright restrictions. H.R. Rep. No. 94-1476, at 1365 (1976) (hereinafter *House Report*).

27. *See* CTEA, *supra* note 3.

28. As Register of Copyrights, Marybeth Peters testified:

[F]inding the current owner can be almost impossible. Where the copyright registration records show that the author is the owner finding a current address or the appropriate heir can be extremely difficult. Where the original owner was a corporation, the task is somewhat easier but here too there are many assignments and occasionally bankruptcies with no clear title to works.

Copyright Term Extension: Hearing on S. 483 Before the Senate Committee on the Judiciary, 104th Cong. 18–19 (1995) (statement of Marybeth Peters, Register of Copyrights); *see also* Letter from Larry Urbanski, Chairman, American Film Heritage Association, to Senator Strom Thurmond Opposing S. 505 (Mar. 31, 1997), http://homepages.law.asu .edu/~dkarjala/OpposingCopyrightExtension/letters/AFH.html (stating that 75% of motion pictures from the 1920s are no longer clearly owned by anyone).

29. *See* U.S. Copyright Office, *Report on Copyright and Digital Distance Education* 41–43 (1999).

the actual scope of the "orphan works" problem. All works published before January 1, 1923, have now fallen into the public domain and can be used without permission of the author.[30] Conversely, most works published over the last thirty years contain an ISBN number permitting their authors to be located fairly easily.[31] It is those works created in the intervening fifty years or so, estimated in the millions, for which problems most generally arise.

[a] Obstacles to Identifying and Locating Copyright Owners

A copyright owner search typically begins with information available from the work itself. However, many copyrighted items bear no information at all about their author or creator. Because placing a copyright notice on a work became optional when the United States acceded to the Berne Convention,[32] a searcher may encounter serious difficulties from the outset. Without even a name to start with, potential users must rely on circumstantial or contextual information, to the extent available, to determine whether to exploit the work.

Even if the author is named, events subsequent to the work's creation may affect one's ability to identify or locate her. Copyright is, after all, a form of property. As with other property, a work's chain of title is often difficult to trace. Even where "title" to a work has not changed, the owner's circumstances may have. For instance, she could have moved, died, become bankrupt, or otherwise ceased doing business.

Transfer of copyright ownership to descendants by will, or otherwise, creates a separate set of issues. Rights may be fractionally distributed among several heirs, some or all of whom may be remote from each other or the potential user. Occasionally, descendants are completely unaware of their rights or may have elected to dispose of them, further complicating the trail.

In light of these difficulties, the Copyright Office remains the primary source of information regarding copyright ownership. The Office maintains extensive records related to registrations, renewals, assignments, and transfers of copyrights and any security interests held therein.[33] However, conducting such research is often costly and time-consuming. Potential users can incur substantial expense without any guarantee their efforts will yield the needed information. Sometimes the mere prospect of a long

---

30. *See* "Flowchart for Determining When U.S. Copyrights in Fixed Works Expire," http://www.bromson.com/practice/copyright-portfolio-development/flowchart.htm.

31. Christopher T. Heun, *Courts Unlikely to Stop Google Book Copying*, Internetweek .com (Sept. 2, 2005), at 2.

32. The United States formally acceded to the Berne Convention in 1988. *See* Berne Convention Act, *supra* note 1. The Convention itself went into effect in the United States on March 1, 1989.

33. 17 U.S.C. § 205.

and arduous search dissuades interested parties. For instance, in academic circles, even minimal investigation costs will outweigh the expected monetary (if not educational) return of any classroom use.

[b] Legal Background

In general, the orphan works issue is driven by factual circumstances and considerations; that is, the user is not as concerned about what law applies as she is about how to locate the copyright owner. The legal background, however, remains relevant to the situation in several ways. An analysis of the Copyright Act reveals some provisions that compound the orphan works problem, and others that solve it, but only for limited sets of works, users, or uses.

[i] Historical Factors Affecting Orphan Works

As mentioned above, the orphan works issue is, in many respects, a result of several major revisions to federal copyright law that began in 1976.[34] Consequently, copyright now subsists in original works of authorship upon fixation in any tangible medium of expression. Works need not be filed or registered with the Copyright Office to obtain protection, as was the case earlier.[35]

The 1976 Act also made it easier to *maintain* protection into the future. Prior to the amendment, copyright duration was split into two periods—an initial 28-year term followed by an additional 28-year renewal. Protection for the second term could be accomplished only by registration with the Copyright Office during the final year of the first term. Failure to renew resulted in a complete loss of copyright.

The 1976 Act changed the basic measure of a copyright's existence, however, by establishing a unified term composed of the actual life of the author, *plus* 50 years, which was extended to 70 years in 1998.[36] This single term applies to works created on or after January 1, 1978.[37] Works created before that date and in their first term under the old law were still subject to the renewal requirement until 1992, when such renewal was made automatic by statute.[38]

The aforementioned changes were key steps toward the United States assuming a more prominent role in the international copyright commu-

---

34. 1976 Act, *supra* note 15.
35. 17 U.S.C. § 102(a).
36. 17 U.S.C. § 302(a).
37. *Id.*
38. CRA, *supra* note 2 (amending 17 U.S.C. § 304 to add an automatic renewal term).

nity. Specifically, these amendments harmonized American copyright law with prevailing international norms, moving the United States closer to membership in the Berne Convention.[39] Berne, the oldest and most widely accepted international treaty on the protection of literary and artistic works, forbids "formalities" such as notice, registration, and renewal as conditions to copyright protection.[40] This prohibition on technical requirements has remained a fundamental principle of international copyright law for nearly a century. Moreover, substantial evidence was presented to Congress during consideration of the 1976 Act that such formalities, along with drastic forfeiture penalties, had served as a "trap for the unwary" and caused the loss of many valuable copyrights.[41]

Notwithstanding the benefits, these amendments exacerbated the orphan works problem in several ways. Starting in 1989, the Berne Convention Implementation Act no longer made the placement of a copyright notice on a work mandatory. Since such notices typically contained the name of the owner and year of creation, their omission led to immediate difficulties in locating authors and/or calculating whether a work had fallen into the public domain. By extending the term of protection, the 1976, 1992, and 1998 amendments also elongated the time during which a

---

39. Berne Convention for the Protection of Literary and Artistic Works (Paris Act 1971) (hereinafter "Berne Convention" or "Berne"). *See* Chapter Two, Section 2.2, for a more detailed discussion of international copyright treaties.

40. "The enjoyment and exercise of these rights shall not be subject to any formality; . . ." *See* Berne Convention art. 5(2).

41. *See, e.g., House Report* at 134 ("One of the worst features of the present copyright law is the provision for renewal of copyright. A substantial burden and expense, this unclear and highly technical requirement results in incalculable amounts of unproductive work. In a number of cases it is the cause of inadvertent and unjust loss of copyright. Under a life-plus-50 system the renewal device would be inappropriate and unnecessary."); *Copyright Law Revision: Hearings on S. 1006 before the Subcommittee on Patents, Trademarks, and Copyrights of the Committee on the Judiciary, United States Senate,* 89th Cong. 68 (1965) (statement of Abraham Kaminstein, Register of Copyrights) ("It is important for the revised term provisions to do away with the present system of copyright renewal, which is a nightmare of complexity and which frequently results in the inadvertent loss of protection."); *Copyright Law Revisions: Hearings on S. 597 Before the Subcommittee on Patents, Trademarks, and Copyrights of the Committee of the Judiciary, United States Senate,* 90th Cong. 27 (1967) (statement of John Dos Passos, Authors League of America) ("The present system by which copyright has to be renewed every 28 years has worked a great deal of hardship. It is very easy for an author to let the time of renewal slip by. A number of American and foreign authors or their heirs have lost their copyrights through ignorance or inadvertence. A man who makes his living by writing finds it hard to keep track of a great number of different items. In some cases, the renewal fees can become a real burden. If you do not renew the copyright at the specified time, there is no remedy whatsoever.").

work could "lose" its author or fall out of commercial use, but still be protected by copyright. Congress was indeed cognizant of such consequences when it passed these bills, but considered them outweighed by the advantages of the new system.[42]

[ii] Provisions in U.S. Copyright Law Relating to Orphan Works

While federal copyright law contains no universal provision addressing orphan works, it permits *selected* persons to utilize *some* of those works in *certain* circumstances. Relevant provisions include Sections 108(h), 115(b), 504(c)(2), and the so-called termination provisions (Sections 203, 304(c), and 304(d)).[43] Each provision is discussed below.

1) Section 108(h)   Section 108(h) was enacted as part of CTEA in 1998[44] and is often referred to as an "orphan works remedy."[45] Intended to permit

---

42. *See, e.g., House Report* at 136 ("It is true that today's ephemera represent tomorrow's social history, and that works of scholarly value, which are now falling into the public domain after 29 years, would be protected much longer under the bill. Balanced against this are the burdens and expenses of renewals, the near impossibility of distinguishing between types of works in fixing a statutory term, and the extremely strong case for a life-plus-50 system. Moreover, it is important to realize that the bill would not restrain scholars from using any work as source material or from making 'fair use' of it; the restrictions would extend only to the unauthorized reproduction or distribution of copies of the work, its public performance, or some other use that would actually infringe the copyright owner's exclusive rights. The advantages of a basic term of copyright enduring for the life of the author and for 50 years after the author's death outweigh any possible disadvantages.").

43. Other provisions in the Copyright Act such as statutory licenses available under Sections 112, 114, and 118 can also permit use of an orphan work. *See* 37 C.F.R. §§ 253.9, 260.7, 261.8, 262.8.

44. CTEA, *supra* note 3.

45. The Preservation of Orphan Works Act (POWA) was Title IV of the Family Entertainment and Copyright Act of 2005, Pub. L. No. 109–9, 119 Stat. 218, 226 (April 27, 2005). POWA contained a single provision, which amended Section 108(i). Section 108(i) had provided that the rights of reproduction and distribution granted by Section 108 do not apply to certain classes of works: musical, pictorial, graphic or sculptural works, or motion pictures or other audiovisual works other than audiovisual works dealing with news. However, Section 108(i) also excluded from this rule the reproduction and distribution rights granted under Section 108(b) (allowing certain reproductions and distributions for purposes of preservation and security or for deposit for research use in another library or archives) and 108(c) (allowing certain reproductions solely for the purpose of replacement of a copy or phonogram that is damaged, deteriorating, lost or stolen, or if the existing format in which the work was stored has become obsolete). POWA extended the exemption to the rights granted under Section 108(h): therefore, library reproductions allowed under Section 108(h) are no longer limited by Section 108(i). This provision promotes the preservation of orphan works because it enables libraries and archives to take advantage of Section 108(h) for previously excluded classes of works.

libraries and archives to use older works in their collections without incurring infringement liability, the provision allows such institutions—for purposes of preservation, scholarship, or research—to reproduce, distribute, display, or perform works in the last twenty years of their term if, after a reasonable investigation, it is determined that

- The work is not subject to normal commercial exploitation;
- A copy of the work cannot be obtained at a reasonable price; and
- The copyright owner or its agent has not provided notice pursuant to regulations promulgated by the Register of Copyrights that either of the above conditions applies.

Section 108(h), in other words, allows libraries and archives to use works still subject to copyright protection, but not readily available or obtainable at a fair price. The provision encompasses both orphan and non-orphan works, but it does not require the owner to be unlocatable nor the library to conduct a reasonable search for him (although such a search may determine whether the library conducted a reasonable investigation of the market for and availability of the work).

While the terms "reasonable investigation" and "reasonable price" are central to the law's operation, neither concept, nor the phrase "normal commercial exploitation," is defined by the statute.[46] Interestingly, while 108(h)(2)(C) allows the copyright owner to "opt out" of the exception, the registry established to enable this option has never been used in the years[47] since the provision became law.[48]

2) Section 115(b)   The Copyright Act provides owners of works certain exclusive rights that, of course, can be waived or negotiated away in the form of a license.[49] However, the Act also permits users to obtain so-called statutory (or compulsory) licenses instead of negotiated ones under certain

---

46. In his dissent in *Eldred v. Ashcroft*, 537 U.S. 186 (2003), Justice Breyer called Section 108(h) a "limited" exception, and expressed his view that the term "reasonable investigation" is "open-ended." *Id.* at 252.

47. CTEA, *supra* note 3, became effective on October 27, 1998.

48. The law provides no incentive for a copyright owner to file a notice before discovering that one of his works is being used. By its terms, a notice can be filed at any time, even after a library or archive begins utilizing a work determined to have met the criteria. Once the notice is filed, the library or archives must stop the impermissible activity. It would thus seem more efficient for a copyright owner to "wait and see" whether a work is being used under Section 108(h) rather than to file such notices proactively.

49. 17 U.S.C. § 106. *See infra* Section 4.3 for a more detailed discussion about licensing.

circumstances. Pursuant to these arrangements, the owner is paid a royalty previously established by law or regulation.

The Section 115 statutory license permits a person to distribute phonorecords of a nondramatic musical work when copies thereof have previously been distributed to the American public with the owner's permission, provided the primary purpose is dissemination for private use.[50] To obtain this "license," the would-be user must give notice of her intention to the copyright holder.[51] The statute provides, however, that "[i]f the registration or other public records of the Copyright Office do not identify the copyright owner and include an address at which notice can be served, it shall be sufficient to file the notice of intention in the Copyright Office."[52]

Further, such owner must be identified in those records in order for her to receive royalties under the license.[53] Thus, a potential user unable to locate the owner may make and distribute phonorecords of the orphan work provided the conditions of Section 115(b)(1) are satisfied. He may even continue to do so royalty-free until the owner files the requisite registration with the Copyright Office.[54]

Interestingly, actual knowledge of the owner's identity is not relevant. The key issue, instead, is whether such identity is reflected in the Copyright Office records. If not, no royalty payments are due her. As such, the user may still file the required notice with the Copyright Office even if he knows who holds the copyright[55] or could have obtained such information

---

50. There are still more limitations on eligibility, see 17 U.S.C. § 115(a)(1)(i)–(ii), as well as on various procedural requirements, see 17 U.S.C. § 115(b).

51. The Copyright Office recently adopted regulations that allow, among other things: service on an agent; the listing of multiple works on a single notice; the filing of a notice to cover all possible configurations, including those not specifically listed on the notice, and use of an address other than the one listed in the Copyright Office records. See 69 Fed. Reg. 34,578 (June 22, 2004).

52. 17 U.S.C. § 115(b)(1); accord 27 C.F.R. § 201.18(f)(3). If the Copyright Office's records do identify an owner and an address, but the would-be user sends the notice to that address and the notice is returned or refused, the user may file the rejected notice with the Copyright Office, along with a statement that the notice was sent to the last address listed in the records, but was returned. 37 C.F.R. § 201.18(f)(2).

53. 17 U.S.C. § 115(c)(1).

54. The legislative history states that the requirement of filing an official document with the Copyright Office helps to ensure accurate payment should the owner appear. See House Report at 109–10 (the owner does not receive the royalties until identified in the records of the Copyright Office, because "proper identification is an important precondition of recovery").

55. See 37 C.F.R. § 201.18(f)(4) (providing that, "alternatively," if the user knows the name and address of the owner, the user "may" serve the notice on the owner).

after a reasonable search. In either case, while the work in question is not truly an orphan work, it remains eligible for royalty-free treatment.

Does this mean a search by the potential user is never necessary? Is the filing of the requisite notice with the Copyright Office sufficient to escape royalty payments? No, because while Sections 115(b)(1) and (c)(1) do not expressly require a search, the federal regulations promulgated thereunder do.[56]

3) Section 504(c)(2) Limitation on Damages   Under Sections 504(a) and (b) of the Copyright Act, an owner is entitled to elect, in an action for infringement, between (1) actual damages plus any additional profits of the infringer (minus any overlap between these) or (2) "statutory" damages. While Section 504(c)(1) establishes the range for statutory damages between $750 and $30,000, Section 504(c)(2) provides for adjustments thereto under certain circumstances. For instance, where the infringement is deemed "willful," the upper limit increases to $150,000. Conversely, the bottom limit is remitted completely where "an infringer believed . . . that his or her use of the copyrighted work was a fair use under section 107, if the infringer was an employee or agent of a nonprofit educational institution, library, or archives acting within the scope of his or her employment."

Thus, some remedies are based on the user's actual knowledge and state of mind. For example, a library employee who legitimately believes he is making "fair use" of a work can proceed without fear of incurring liability. Section 504(c)(2)'s provisions can also benefit the library in its planning, especially when multiple uses of several works are involved. Note the statute does not distinguish between orphan and non-orphan works or require that a search for the owner be conducted by the would-be user.

4) Sections 203, 304(c), and 304(d)   While the so-called termination provisions of existing copyright law do not permit use of an orphan work, they do address situations where an owner or his descendants cannot be located. For instance, under Section 203, a work's creator, or certain of his survivors, have an inalienable right to terminate a transfer or license of the copyright therein where such transfer was executed on or after January 1, 1978. Section 304(c) provides a similar right for copyright renewal transfers, while

---

56. *See* 37 C.F.R. § 201.18(d)(1)(vi) (the user must include in the notice "an affirmative statement that with respect to the non-dramatic musical work named in the Notice of Intention, the registration records of the Copyright Office have been searched and found not to identify the name and address of the copyright owner of such work").

304(d) extends the privilege to the additional twenty years of protection afforded by CTEA.

To effect such action, the terminating party must give notice to the grantee or his successor. Since those persons may have become unlocatable between the time of the original grant and the deadline for notice,[57] an author (or other terminating party) may not be able to timely serve them. In this situation, the federal regulations provide:

> The service provision of section 203, section 304(c) or section 304(d) of title 17, U.S.C., whichever applies, will be satisfied if, before the notice of termination is served, a reasonable investigation is made by the person or persons executing the notice as to the current ownership of the rights being terminated, and based on such investigation:
>
> (i)   If there is no reason to believe that such rights have been transferred by the grantee to a successor in title, the notice is served on the grantee; or
>
> (ii) If there is reason to believe that such rights have been transferred by such grantee to a particular successor in title, the notice is served on such successor in title.[58]

The regulation also specifies that "reasonable investigation"

> [i]ncludes, but is not limited to, a search of the records in the Copyright Office; in the case of a musical composition with respect to which performing rights are licensed by a performing rights society, a "reasonable investigation" also includes a report from that performing rights society identifying the person or persons claiming current ownership of the rights being terminated.[59]

Finally, the terminating party may serve the grantee or his successor at an address "which, after a reasonable investigation, is found to be the last known address of the grantee or successor in title."[60] Note the similarity of these regulations to Sections 108(h) and 115—all require a reasonable

---

57. The time span between a grant and notice of termination will always be significant. These periods vary from 25 years after the execution of the grant in the case of Section 203, to 46 years after the copyright was originally secured in the case of Section 304(c), to 65 years after the copyright was originally secured in the case of Section 304(d).

58. 37 C.F.R. § 201.10(d)(2).

59. 37 C.F.R. § 201.10(d)(3).

60. 37 C.F.R. § 201.10(d)(1).

investigation—a concept embedded in copyright law and the genesis for proposed amendments to the Copyright Act discussed below.

5) Other Exemptions An orphan work may be affected by other exemptions in the Copyright Act as part of a larger class of works encompassed by such provision. For instance, the preservation, replacement, and patron use exceptions contained in Section 108 cover all works described therein, in addition to those in the last twenty years of their term.[61] Other permitted uses of orphan works might fall within the fair use provisions of Section 107 or one of the educational[62] or religious and/or charitable[63] exemptions contained in Section 110. Lastly, Section 117 permits owners of a computer program copy to duplicate and adapt such program in certain situations involving so-called abandonware.[64] No searches for the actual owner are a prerequisite for reliance on these exemptions.

[c] Recent Proposals

The Copyright Office recently completed a study[65] on orphan works and concluded that (1) the orphan works problem was real, but difficult to quantify and describe comprehensively; (2) while some orphan works situations are addressed by existing copyright law, many are not; and (3) new legislation is needed to provide a meaningful solution to the problem.[66]

Specifically, the Office recommended that any would-be user of an orphan work first be required to perform a reasonably diligent search for the copyright owner. In doing so, the user would have to demonstrate that the search was conducted and completed before the potentially infringing use began. Additionally, each user would have to perform her own search, although one could rely on the efforts of others under certain circumstances.[67] The Copyright Office further recommended that all such works be attributed to their creator, if possible, to avoid confusion regarding

---

61. 17 U.S.C. § 108. In 2005, the Section 108 Study Group was formed to examine whether and how that section needs to be amended to account for changes wrought by digital technology. Sponsored by the Library of Congress and the Copyright Office, the Study Group hopes to have its recommendations published sometime in 2008. *See* http://www.loc .gov/section108 to follow the workings of this group.

62. *See* Chapter Six for a detailed discussion of the educational use exemptions contained in Sections 110(1) and 110(2).

63. 17 U.S.C. §§ 110(3) and (4).

64. 17 U.S.C. § 117(a)(1).

65. *See* U.S. Copyright Office, *Report on Orphan Works* (Jan. 2006).

66. *Id.* at 7.

67. *Id.* at 9.

actual origin.[68] If a user met those two conditions, the remedies available to a rights holder appearing later to sue for infringement would be limited in two ways.

First, monetary damages would be restricted to only reasonable compensation for the use (e.g., damages would approximate a suitable licensing fee for the transaction). Such damages would be eliminated completely where the use was noncommercial and terminated expeditiously upon notice. The latter provision would be important to and primarily benefit nonprofit institutions such as universities, libraries, and museums, since their uses are almost always noncommercial.[69] Second, injunctive relief could not be granted in cases where the orphan work had been transformed into a derivative piece, such as a motion picture or book, thus permitting continued use thereof. Only money damages equivalent to a fair licensing arrangement would be permitted in such cases.[70]

On May 22, 2006, Representative Lamar Smith of Texas introduced a bill[71] on the floor of the House of Representatives essentially tracking the Copyright Office's recommendations for orphan works. The legislation was promptly forwarded to the Judiciary Subcommittee on Courts, the Internet, and Intellectual Property, where it was approved by voice vote and returned to the full House Judiciary Committee for consideration.[72] The 109th Congress ended, however, before the bill could be addressed by the full body.

4.3 LICENSING OF COPYRIGHTED WORKS

[1] Elements of Traditional Licensing

Licensing traditionally plays a role in education when preexisting copyrighted works are incorporated into the school's curricula. Normally, a copyright holder is reluctant to permit his work to be used without restriction or payment. Therefore, he often requires the educational institution or school system to enter into some type of licensing agreement governing the use thereof. To understand current licensing practices, it is helpful to know how works are used, who the participants in the process are, and what types of licenses are commonly sought by educators.

---

68. *Id.* at 16.

69. *Id.* at 13.

70. *Id.* at 11–12.

71. H.R. 5439, 109th Cong., 2d Sess., 152 Cong. Rec. H3015 (2006).

72. *See* http://thomas.loc.gov/cgi-bin/bdquery/z?d109:HR05439:@@@x.

[a] Use of Preexisting Copyrighted Works

Teachers and schools use preexisting copyrighted works in a variety of ways. The most common is making and distributing copies of textual material. The purchase and use of textbooks by students continues to be standard practice in education; however, instructors often provide students with supplemental written content. Sometimes these materials are distributed to students in hard copies or electronically as "coursepacks." They may also be set aside for the student's use in traditional or electronic reserve (e-reserve) format, generally accessed through the institution's library.[73]

Copyrighted works may also be incorporated into the lesson plan itself as an integral part of instruction.[74] Integrating preexisting content is different from supplementing texts for which the instructor intends the student to experience the material independently. Incorporating a copyrighted work into a lesson is usually accomplished by performing or displaying that work in the physical or electronic classroom. Examples include projecting slides of paintings, putting on a play, listening to music, reciting portions of a novel, or reading a poem. Class discussion either accompanies or follows such activities.

[b] Participants in the Licensing Process

Educational institutions, copyright owners, and collective licensing organizations are the three main participants in the scholastic licensing process.[75] For purposes of this text, the term "educational institutions" includes administrators, librarians, and faculty who make decisions about the use and licensing of copyrighted material. "Copyright owners" are individuals or entities who own the rights in a copyrighted work. In this context, the term also includes publishers who manage permissions for works they distribute but do not necessarily own.

While educational institutions have traditionally been viewed as users or licensees, and copyright owners as licensors, a growing overlap in these roles has recently developed. Educators also create works, and copyright owners often use preexisting content. This blurring is especially pronounced in the field of digital distance education. Educational institutions that create online courses sometimes license those classes to other schools.

---

73. *See* I. Hinds, *Marketplace for Licensing in Digital Distance Education* 8–12 (1998) (hereinafter *Hinds Report*).

74. *Id.* at 12–13.

75. Intermediaries, such as commercial establishments known as "copy shops," may also be relied upon by these parties to engage in licensing transactions.

Likewise, with greater emphasis on multimedia works, publishers often need to incorporate more and varied preexisting works into their products, thus increasing their need to license content from other sources.

Collective licensing organizations (CLOs) are entities that administer copyrights and facilitate transactions between users and owners. These organizations do not own the content but are authorized by copyright holders to index and license certain uses thereof. In the United States, each licensing organization primarily manages one type of work (such as text or music), sometimes in competition with other CLOs. These companies facilitate licensing in a number of ways. Primarily, they provide a central "warehouse" for prospective users to contact. Due to their infrastructure and experience, they can process licensing requests relatively quickly and easily. In some cases, they offer "blanket licenses" typically involving payment of a flat fee for all requested uses during a set period of time.

Several established CLOs do business in the United States today. For example, ASCAP, BMI, and SESAC administer licenses for the performance of nondramatic musical works. The Harry Fox Agency primarily handles the reproduction and distribution of musical works in phonorecords, as well as synchronization rights. The Copyright Clearance Center (CCC) is well recognized in the corporate and academic world as a central source for licensing reproductions of text.[76] On June 28, 2004, CCC announced it was forming a strategic partnership with Online Computer Library Center, Inc. (OCLC), a nonprofit organization, to provide access to copyright licensing directly from two of OCLC's leading reference services. OCLC provides computer-based cataloging and resource-sharing services to 50,000 libraries in 84 counties. Pursuant to the partnership, member libraries will be provided with convenient and efficient ways of determining copyright fees and obtaining permission.[77]

[c] Types of Licenses

Transactional licenses for analog and digital uses and site licenses are the three types of instruments used primarily in conjunction with educational courses.[78] The fee structure thereof typically depends on the user's identity

---

76. The term "text" is used here to refer to all types of printed material, including graphs, pictures, and diagrams as well as traditional literary works. *See* 17 U.S.C. § 101 (definition of "literary works").

77. "Copyright Clearance Center and OCLC Deliver Integrated Copyright Permission Service," Businesswire.com (June 28, 2004), http://findarticles.com/p/articles/mi_mOEIN/is_2004_June_28/ai_n6088022.

78. *See Hinds Report* at 6–7.

and its purpose. Educators are often charged lower fees than commercial users are.

Transactional licenses for analog uses are employed to authorize coursepacks or other supplementary printed materials. This text is then distributed in class or sometimes mailed to distance education students. If a license fee is required, it is typically paid by the institution for each student. (Often these charges are passed on to the student as an extra class fee of some sort, however.) Transactional licenses for digital uses typically authorize specific uses of electronic works. Besides creating e-reserves or coursepacks, such licenses often permit an educator to digitize analog materials or to reproduce, distribute, perform, or display a work in digital form. In most cases, the fee is directly calibrated to such use.

In contrast to fee-per-use transactional licenses, site licenses authorize all uses of a copyrighted work or works, by a particular user or group, for specified periods of time.[79] These licenses are often obtained in the academic community to permit university-wide use of software or of databases of scholarly material, such as journal or periodical collections.[80] The site license is negotiated to cover multiple projected uses, based on the size and nature of the community served. Typically, the authorized group is limited to one physical site, such as a college campus, although these licenses can also apply to a defined group of users, regardless of their location. The latter type is customarily used for distance education environments.

[2] Licensing for Digital Distance Education

As digital distance education has expanded, so have issues concerning the use of copyrighted works in electronic reserves, the amount of content being licensed, the types of works being used, and the practices or doctrines relied upon by institutions as alternatives to licensing. These issues are considered in more detail below.

[a] Amount and Types of Material Licensed

Substantial licensing activity on campus currently involves providing content to distance education students.[81] The bulk of contemporary licensing

---

79. When the works included in a site license belong to a number of copyright owners and the use is priced on an established annual fee, the license is often referred to as a "blanket license."

80. *See Hinds Report* at 7.

81. K–12 levels tend to incorporate less preexisting content into their distance education activities since they engage in less remote delivery of mediated instruction and use primarily prepackaged software for self-paced learning activities.

for distance education still relates to supplementary materials in analog form, such as coursepacks that are photocopied and sent to students.[82] Licensing for digital uses remains relatively limited but is growing. Here too, most of the activity involves the use of supplemental materials such as electronic coursepacks or other resources. Frequently, the use of digital materials is authorized through site licenses, often library based, applicable to the entire university. To avoid the need for separate arrangements, professors tend to limit their supplemental requests to electronic resources already licensed by their institutions.

Digital use of copyrighted works incorporated into the class session itself still remains the least common form of licensing, though.[83] Such instructional activity typically involves performances or displays of copyrighted works as examples or for conceptual reinforcement. The overwhelming majority of licensing for digital works still involves textual materials, primarily because text was the first type of content to be digitized.[84] Even so, the overall proportion of licensing for digital uses, compared to paper copies, remains relatively small.[85] Photographs and slides are also licensed for instructional purposes, but much less frequently than text. However, several projects are currently under way to license high-quality digital archives of museum collections for pedagogical purposes.[86] Producers of audiovisual works, including both educational videos and commercial motion pictures, also report relatively low licensing requests for digital activity.[87]

Licensing of musical works for education is also sporadic.[88] ASCAP and BMI, the two largest CLOs in the field, have traditionally offered low-cost blanket licenses to educational institutions for analog performances,[89] and licenses permitting digital performances are increasing.[90] ASCAP and BMI also license websites; but, as yet, this practice has met with little interest in the academic community.[91] As for digital sound recordings, licensing for performance first became a possibility in 1996, following enactment

---

82. *See Hinds Report* at 9–10.
83. *See Hinds Report* at 37.
84. *Id.* at 15.
85. *Id.* at 44–45.
86. *Id.* at 60–61.
87. *Id.* at 51.
88. *Id.* at 59–60.
89. *Id.* at 59.
90. *Id.* at 60.
91. *Id.*

of the Digital Performance Rights in Sound Recordings Act.[92] Recording companies report having received few licensing requests from educational institutions, however.[93]

Computer software is licensed rarely, if at all, for use as the subject of study in class. In contrast, software licenses for ordinary functional purposes are common. Institutions also often obtain licenses for software packages to use in creating or delivering distance education courses.[94]

[b] Alternatives to Licensing

Educational institutions have several alternatives to obtaining licenses for digital or analog material. One method is to completely avoid incorporating copyrighted content into a course. Many college classes use few, if any, preexisting works (other than the textbooks purchased by students). In the years since online classes became popular, faculty members have tended to create their own content without using third-party material.[95] Initially, this occurred because the technology used to create these courses was still in its infancy. That situation changed dramatically as faculty became more technologically sophisticated and new software packages were developed to help incorporate the works of others.[96] Notwithstanding these new capabilities, many instructors still prefer to use only their own creations in their lesson plans.

A second major alternative to licensing involves relying on exemptions contained in the Copyright Act such as "fair use." While fair use is the most commonly relied on exemption in deciding not to seek a license,[97] schools often evince uncertainty about how far the doctrine extends into the digital environment.[98] Other exemptions in the Copyright Act include Sections 110(1) and (2),[99] which deal with performances and displays of works in the physical classroom and via electronic transmission. These

---

92. Pub. L. No. 104–39 (1995).

93. *See Hinds Report* at 57.

94. *Id.*

95. *Id.* at 12–13.

96. *See* J. Band, *Educational Fair Use Today*, Paper Prepared for the Association of Research Libraries, at 14, http://www.arl.org ("Tools like Blackboard permit an instructor to create an online anthology for a class, including copyrighted works, commentary, lecture notes, and student reactions.").

97. *See* Chapter Three for a more detailed discussion of this issue.

98. Some institutions factor in their good faith attempt to obtain a license, resolving doubts in favor of fair use if a response is not received from the copyright owner. *See Hinds Report* at 29–30. This approach is not encouraged by the author.

99. *See* Chapter Six for a more detailed discussion of these two provisions of the Copyright Act.

exemptions are not always easy for educators without formal legal training to comprehend, however. A third alternative is to use only those materials already in the public domain. Again, though, effort is often required to ascertain whether the term of protection for a work has expired or never existed in the first place. These difficulties make relying on such alternatives a risky and uncertain proposition as well.

[3] Licensing Procedures

Licensing is handled in several ways between educational institutions and copyright owners. In both communities, licensing responsibilities are often decentralized, and those entrusted with such tasks sometimes possess little or no training in the field. In general, the process becomes more efficient with greater centralization and as more resources are devoted to it.

[a] Educational Institutions

Educational institutions tend to delegate licensing responsibility to a variety of persons or offices. Sometimes a single staff member is designated to handle all such requests. Librarians are usually asked to obtain licenses as a natural extension of their copyright management duties. At some schools, the legal counsel's office, academic department heads, or campus bookstore managers are involved.[100] Licensing responsibility is often allocated according to the type of work used. For example, the multimedia center may license audiovisual materials, while the library staff is responsible for e-reserves, and the campus bookstore for coursepacks.[101] Sometimes individual teachers bear the sole responsibility to obtain licenses for their own courses.

Educational institutions seek licenses from both copyright holders and licensing organizations. Many educators have experience and are acquainted with CLO procedures. An educational institution may also contact the copyright owner directly, especially when that person is well known and easy to locate. Before making such contacts, however, the school must first determine whether a license is even necessary. Such an analysis is not always a simple one. Given the vagaries of the fair use doctrine and the complexity of the other educational use exemptions, even intellectual property scholars might disagree on when a license is required.[102] Further

---

100. *See Hinds Report* at 19–23.

101. *Id.* at 20–21.

102. W. Fisher & W. McGeveran, *Obstacles to Educational Uses of Copyrighted Material*, 77 (Aug. 10, 2006), Berkman Center Research Publication No. 2006–09, http://ssrn.com/abstract=923465 (hereinafter *Fisher Report*).

complicating matters is the need to ascertain whether existing "blanket" or individual licenses may already cover the intended use.[103]

[b] Copyright Owners

Copyright owners also face challenges in managing licensing procedures. Evaluating and responding to such requests is not always centralized or efficient.[104] For instance, staff handling such requests are often unfamiliar with new and rapidly changing technology, or they lack established policies to generate a response.

License management can also differ substantially according to the size and sophistication of the copyright owner, her degree of interest in the educational market, and the types of works she creates. Larger copyright holders, or those with substantial experience in licensing, have more established and consistent practices, particularly if they serve academic clients. For example, major educational publishers typically establish a "permissions" department to respond to school requests quickly and predictably.[105] In contrast, individual authors or smaller organizations may lack standard licensing mechanisms and therefore process requests slower or more erratically.[106]

[4] Problems in Licensing

Educational institutions have often expressed dissatisfaction with the licensing process in both the traditional and digital environment. In light of the perceived threat of piracy and lack of a substantial revenue stream from the educational market, many rights owners simply refuse to license their works to universities or school systems.[107] Other problems commonly faced include (1) difficulty locating the copyright owner; (2) inability to obtain a timely response; and (3) encountering unreasonable prices and/or contract terms. As one prominent educator has summarized it: "Although in theory there are many ways to identify and pay licenses for the use of [copyrighted] materials, in practice, it is demanding, tedious, and oftentimes ignored by the copyright owner."[108]

---

103. *Id.* at 78.

104. *Hinds Report* at 40–41.

105. *Id.* at 48.

106. *Id.* at 49.

107. *Fisher Report* at 69.

108. *See* comments of Dr. Kimberly B. Kelley, *Public Comment on Library and Archive Exemption, Section 108 Study Group,* 5 (2006).

Finding owners of older, out-of-print, or unpublished works, or those not marked with copyright notices, can be particularly burdensome. This problem is exacerbated in the digital environment, where individual authors can disseminate works without using an established publisher.[109] Even after a copyright owner or publisher is located, he or she may not be able to license all components of the work.[110] At times, educators experience lengthy delays in getting owners to reply. Copyright holders may take months to answer a request or not respond at all. Such delays obviously jeopardize an educator's ability to prepare his course materials in a timely fashion.

Licensing costs also present a significant hurdle for many educators.[111] Digital use charges are normally higher than comparable analog licenses and may prove unaffordable. Problems often arise with journal articles and audiovisual works due to the perception (if not the accurate realization) of copyright holders that the prospect of unauthorized duplication and dissemination is much greater for these works.[112] To compensate for this increased risk, content owners tend to charge higher prices or impose more restrictive conditions for these arrangements.[113] For example, university site licenses sometimes attempt to limit use to only on-campus students. As such, these licenses prevent remote students or distance learners from accessing the material or necessitate additional fees to include them.

A more recent phenomenon involves copyright holders or their agents obligating users to employ digital rights management (DRM) systems to "lock up" their works to further ensure against the risk of unlawful dissemination.[114] Such restrictions further increase the licensee's costs and may lead to unlicensed content being rendered inaccessible as well. For instance, an instructor attempting to "protect" a copyrighted article placed on his website may need to prohibit access to the entire website to all but a few.[115] More problematic is that smaller colleges and local school systems

---

109. *See, e.g., Hinds Report* at 17–18. *See also* Section 4.2[2] *supra* for a more detailed discussion of the "orphan works" problem.

110. Where the contract between the author and publisher of a work predated the development of today's technologies, it is often uncertain whether the publisher has authority to grant permission for digital uses. In other situations, the chain of title to a work may be unclear. *See Hinds Report* at 42.

111. *Fisher Report* at 83.

112. *Fisher Report* at 67 ("copying of digital works is substantially easier than the copying of traditional analog works").

113. *See Hinds Report* at 38.

114. *See Fisher Report* at 70.

115. *Id.* at 71.

often lack the technological resources or funds to employ DRM systems and thus are rendered unable to acquire such works.[116]

[5] Trends and Future Developments

Several current technological and organizational trends should foster more effective digital licensing in the future as well as positively influence copyright owners' attitudes toward digital distance education.

[a] Technological Protections and Online Licensing Systems

Continuing advances in technology will likely facilitate increased digital licensing for educational uses. For example, improved protective measures should provide copyright owners with greater comfort. In addition, technology enabling copyright management information and licensing terms to be imbedded into a digital work has become more prevalent. This allows prospective users to more easily locate sources or even link to a website authorized to license the work. Numerous projects are under way to facilitate and standardize online licensing of digital works.[117] Online permission systems, licensing databases, and digital archives are proliferating.[118] Some educational publishers have established online mechanisms to quickly and easily license their products,[119] while other companies are creating digital archives to make these works available faster to consumers.[120]

[b] Collective Management

New collective initiatives are also making the process simpler. For example, CCC's Electronic Course Content Service was launched in 1997 to license digital material for electronic coursepacks and e-reserves. In 1998, it managed about forty transactions per week, but it does far in excess of that number today.[121] Certain limitations preclude collective management from serving as an across-the-board solution, though. Because CLOs in the United States are specialized and normally license only one type of work, the prospect of "one-stop" shopping appears unlikely.[122] For a growing

---

116. *Id.*

117. For a more detailed discussion of these developments, *see* Gervais, *Electronic Rights Management and Digital Identifier Systems*, 4 Elec. Pub. 27 (1999).

118. *See Hinds Report* at 61–64.

119. *Id.* at 62–63 (discussing ITP and CopyrightDirect projects).

120. *Id.* at 61–64 (discussion of online licensing sites, CCC's electronic licensing, iCopyright project, and digital archiving of audiovisual and graphic works).

121. *See generally Hinds Report* at 59.

122. *See Hinds Report* at 42–43.

number of uses, however, collective licensing will be an increasingly valuable and important mechanism.[123]

[c] Evolving Approaches to Digital Licensing

Experience with digital licensing remains in a nascent stage as both licensing mechanisms and copyright holders struggle to keep pace with technology.[124] Once technological protective measures become more available and accessible, however, content owners should be more amenable to participate in the process.[125] Predicting precisely when this will happen is difficult, however. As long as the perception remains that digitizing works merely expands the risks and exposure for copyright owners, prices and other terms will remain more burdensome than for analog uses. In addition, for certain categories of works, distance education may never be perceived as a profitable market.

4.4 NEGOTIATING EFFECTIVE LICENSE AGREEMENTS

Regardless of the type of work one seeks to license, or its medium (analog or digital), ultimately the owner and educator must reach agreement, almost always in writing, governing the terms and conditions of their arrangement. While licenses may take several forms, some elements are, or at least should be, common to all. The most important points are discussed below. The importance of any particular provision will depend greatly on the role one plays in the process, for example, whether that person is the copyright owner or *licensor*, or the requesting educator or *licensee*. Of course, these roles may be reversed when the educational institution is being asked to license its intellectual property to someone else.

[1] Fundamental Requirements

However broad or narrow its coverage, any effective licensing agreement should satisfy four basic requirements. First, the party granting the license

---

123. For example, CCC currently manages rights relating to over 1.75 million works and represents more than 9,600 publishers and hundreds of thousands of authors and creators, directly or through their representatives. CCC-licensed customers in the U.S. number over 10,000 corporations and subsidiaries, as well as thousands of government agencies, law firms, document suppliers, libraries, academic institutions, copy shops, and bookstores. *See Fisher Report* at 80 to place such numbers in context, however. ("Relative to the 29 million books and other printed materials in the . . . Library of Congress, however, CCC's portfolio is a mere drop in the bucket.").

124. *See Hinds Report* at 42–43.

125. *Id.* at 45.

must either own the copyright in the work or be delegated by the owner to do so. A person may not convey rights he or she does not possess without triggering a fraud charge or other liability.[126] A licensee negotiating with a third-party representative, such as a CLO, should seek verification from such entity that it has obtained the proper authorization from the copyright owner to enter into and fulfill the terms of the contract.

Second, the license should accurately identify the parties. Contracts may be signed only by natural persons or business entities that can be legally bound. Normally these include individuals over a certain age or other "persons" recognized under state law.[127] For instance, a division of a publishing house is usually not deemed a separate corporation with the right to contract, but a wholly owned subsidiary thereof is. Conversely, a college library or media center should never enter into a license; the university itself should fulfill that role. Also, the person signing the contract on behalf of either party should have the proper authority to do so. While an individual professor may not be able to bind her university contractually, a department head or academic dean might. Much depends on the school's charter and bylaws or internal decision-making structure.

Third, the contract should precisely identify the rights being licensed. Unlike a property deed or bill of sale that transfers unfettered ownership, a license conveys only certain rights in the copyrighted work. The agreement should, therefore, delineate what uses are being granted to the licensee and which are reserved to the licensor. For instance, the contract will usually permit the licensee to duplicate and distribute the work to students in class or over an electronic network, but not to change its fundamental character and thereby create a derivative work.

Fourth and finally, a licensing agreement should set forth the price being charged. Most often, this amount is based on the number of persons who may access the material over the license term. In other instances, a flat fee payable upon signing or periodically is assessed. Sometimes, the parties negotiate a standard agreement for all works and attach a separate fee schedule each time a new work is requested. Obviously, the longer the work is licensed for, the higher the fee.

---

126. *See* J. Dratler, *Licensing of Intellectual Property* §1.01[2] (1998), for an excellent and thorough discussion of the critical elements involved in negotiating any intellectual property license.

127. For example, under the General Corporation Law of the State of Ohio, a "person" includes a "natural person, a corporation, whether nonprofit or for-profit, a partnership, a limited liability company, an unincorporated society or association, and two or more persons having a joint or common interest." *See* O.R.C. § 1701(G) (2003). Schools are usually organized as nonprofit corporations or associations.

[2] Key Definitions

Every copyright license should contain definitions of important terms so as to avoid confusion about the scope of the owner's grant. Four key terms are discussed below.

[a] Authorized Users

Establishing who may access the copyrighted work at the school is an important consideration for both parties. This factor often determines the amount of the licensee fee as well. The definition is particularly critical if the licensed work is to be placed on an electronic network. The licensee will seek a broad scope so as to include members of its faculty (whether on a permanent, temporary, contract, or visiting basis), all students (whether part-time or full-time), and other persons eligible to use the school's library or information services. The licensor may prefer more limited access and a smaller defined group.

[b] Fee

As noted above, the parties may wish to establish a fee in a separate schedule to the license. As such, they do not have to "hammer out" a new license each time a work is used. In other words, they may develop a contract with terms and conditions both are comfortable with and negotiate price only when the need arises.

[c] Licensed Materials

The parties should specify what material is subject to the license. For ease of reference, a separate attachment may also be the simplest method to handle this issue. In that way, if the parties wish to add or delete certain works to or from the contract, they may simply amend the schedule without the need to enter into a new license agreement.

[d] Secure Network

The definition of a "secure network" is particularly important to the licensor if the school plans to place the licensed materials on any electronic network, such as the educational institution's intranet or library electronic reserve. More attention needs to be paid to digitized works because of how easily they can be duplicated and redistributed. A licensor should request the institution's network be accessible only to authorized users who are approved by the licensee and subject to its regulation and discipline. The licensee should also be required to issue a password or other authentication device ensuring each user can be individually identified both before and after any access.

[3] Usage Rights

The contract should also delineate what the school or any authorized user can do with the licensed work.

[a] Licensee Rights

In general, the licensee (usually the educational institution) should be permitted to:

- Load the licensed materials onto its server on the secure network.
- Make such archival copies of the licensed materials as are reasonably necessary.
- Make such temporary local electronic copies of the licensed materials as necessary to ensure efficient use by authorized users.
- Allow authorized users to access the licensed materials via the secure network.
- Provide authorized users with an integrated author, article, title, and keyword index to the licensed materials.
- Display, download, or print the licensed materials for the purpose of training authorized users.
- Use the licensed materials to create an online course available only to authorized users via the secure network.

[b] Authorized User Rights

The educational institution should negotiate with the licensor to, at a minimum, permit each of its authorized users to:

- Search, view, retrieve, and display the licensed materials.
- Electronically save portions of the licensed materials for educational use.
- Print off portions of the licensed materials for the sole purpose of research, teaching, or private study.
- Distribute portions of the licensed materials in print or electronic form to other authorized users for the sole purpose of research, teaching, or private study.

Some licensors may, of course, object to any right to make and distribute copies; but this seems to place an undue burden on the school's mission, particularly if it is observing the other restrictions of the agreement. Students often need to copy and highlight portions of traditional textbooks to aid in their study of the material, not to mention discussing it with classmates. The fact that the material is now in electronic rather than physical form should not subject it to disparate treatment.

[c] Fair Use Exemption

Very often, a school may request a clause be added to the license that no portion thereof be interpreted to modify or affect its rights under the Copyright Act. While seemingly straightforward, this provision can prove troublesome for the unwary. This language potentially permits the licensee to extract a portion of the licensed materials and use it in a way different from that envisioned by the licensor. A school generally seeks such a clause so it can continue to avail itself of the fair use privilege, a cornerstone of education. The copyright owner, on the other hand, is concerned that her work may be diluted even further and used in ways she is not being compensated for. Alternatively, she may request to have the educational institution waive its fair use privilege in the contract.

This issue often delays the negotiation process and sometimes results in failure to reach agreement.[128] In truth, such language is best omitted for the following reasons. First, whether the provision is included or not, the licensee (or any other person) is probably still able to avail himself of the fair use privilege. Fair use is an inherent part of federal copyright law and cannot be waived by contract. [129] In essence, this is because the interpretation and enforceability of written agreements is a matter of state law. As a general Constitutional principle, federal law prevails over state law when

---

128. The author speaks from personal experience here as he has often had this issue arise in negotiations between educational institutions and copyright owners.

129. *Vault Corp. v. Quaid Software Ltd.*, 847 F.2d 255 (5th Cir. 1988) (state law authorizing contracts prohibiting reverse engineering of computer programs was preempted by federal law); *Wrench LLC v. Taco Bell Corp.*, 256 F.3d 446, 457 (6th Cir. 2001) ("If the promise amounts only to a promise to refrain from reproducing, performing, distributing or displaying the work, then the contract claim is preempted."); *Endemol Entertainment B.V. v. Twentieth Television, Inc.*, No. CV 98-0608 ABC (BQRX), 1998 WL 785300, 48 U.S.P.Q. 2d 1524, 1528 (C.D. Cal. Sept. 29, 1988) (plaintiff's implied contract claim was preempted because it fell "squarely into the category of contract claims that allege no additional rights other than promising not to benefit from the copyrighted work").

the two are in conflict.[130] In other words, the party seeking to enforce the "fair use waiver" would need to rely on state contract law, which by nature is subordinate to a federally created right.[131] As such, an educational institution may typically make fair use of a copyrighted work, whether such work is licensed to it or not.[132]

Even though the licensee can potentially make fair use of the licensed work without the owner's consent, from a business perspective, it makes little sense to do so. First, a license typically permits use of an entire work, while fair use normally allows only a small portion to be utilized. Most license agreements should therefore grant larger rights in a work than what could be obtained under the fair use doctrine. Second, and more importantly, it behooves the educational institution, like any other party entering into a contract, to meet its obligations and "live within the four corners of its agreement," as lawyers like to say. The licensor and licensee may wish to continue doing business in the future. Such a relationship is immediately placed in jeopardy when one party starts to conduct itself in a manner not foreseen or anticipated by the other. The fact that a licensee may ultimately prevail in court on the issue is of little long-term benefit if it garners the reputation among copyright owners and CLOs that it cannot be trusted to adhere strictly to the contract it makes.

---

130. *McCullogh v. Maryland*, 4 Wheat 316, 4 L. Ed. 579 (1819); *Martin v. Hunter's Lessee*, 1 Wheat 304 (1816); *Sperry v. Florida*, 373 U.S. 379 (1963); *Sola Elec. Co. v. Jefferson Elec. Co.*, 317 U.S. 173, 176 (1942) (when state law touches upon the area of federal statutes, it is "familiar doctrine" that the federal policy "may not be set at naught, or its benefits denied" by state law); *Bonito Boats, Inc. v. Thunder Craft Boats, Inc.*, 489 U.S. 141, 152 (1989) ("Thus our past decisions have made clear that state regulation of intellectual property must yield to the extent that it clashes with the balance struck by Congress in our patent laws."); *Gonzales v. Raich*, 545 U.S. 1 (2005) (federal antidrug laws trump state laws that permitted the use of marijuana for medical purposes).

131. This principle has also been established for other provisions of the Copyright Act. *See, e.g.*, Laura G. Lape, *Ownership of Copyrightable Works of University Professors: The Interplay Between the Copyright Act and University Copyright Policies*, 37 VILL. L. REV. 223, 239 (1992) (". . . an agreement between employer and employee [cannot] determine whether a work is a 'work made for hire' within the terms of the [Copyright Act]").

132. *Wrench LLC, supra* note 129. *But see Bowers v. Bay State Technologies, Inc.*, 320 F.3d 1317 (Fed. Cir. 2003) (holding that the Copyright Act did not preempt the prohibition of reverse engineering embodied in a patent holder's shrink-wrap licensing agreements). This also assumes the institution can gain access to the work to copy it without circumventing technological protective measures as proscribed by 17 U.S.C. § 1201(a). *See* Chapter Five, Section 5.4, for a more in-depth discussion of this restriction.

[4] Prohibited Uses

While, under most circumstances, rights not specifically granted to the licensee are reserved and retained by the licensor, it is still prudent to list in the contract those uses of the copyrighted work that are strictly prohibited.

[a] Explicit Prohibitions

The copyright license should specify those acts that are disallowed by obtaining the licensee's agreement *never* to

- Remove or alter the author's name, publisher's copyright notices, or other means of identification from the licensed materials;
- Make print or electronic copies of the licensed materials for any purpose, other than those permitted under the license;
- Place or distribute the licensed materials on any unauthorized electronic network, including, without limitation, the Internet or World Wide Web;
- Use the licensed materials for commercial or private business purposes;
- Distribute the whole or any part of the licensed materials to anyone other than authorized users;
- Create works based on the licensed materials or combine them with any other products; or
- Alter, abridge, adapt, or modify the licensed materials, except as otherwise permitted under the license.

As an alternative, the licensor may grant the licensee permission to engage in the aforementioned conduct, but only if it receives prior notice thereof and consents thereto. Uses for which such consent is required should be listed separately in the agreement with appropriate caveats.

[b] Issues Regarding "Policing" Students

Copyright owners and educational institutions negotiating a license should anticipate and discuss potential violations of the agreement by students, as opposed to administrators or faculty members. If the term "authorized user" includes students, as it most often does, then any improper act by a pupil may violate the license, thereby subjecting the school to contractual penalties and possible cancellation of the agreement. This presents a host of potential problems for educational institutions.

Should a school be held accountable for its students' actions in the same way it is responsible for the deeds or misdeeds of its employees? Several points should be considered in answering this question. First, the educational institution has, theoretically at least, more control over its staff than it has over its students. Faculty may be readily sanctioned or even dismissed for their conduct under employment arrangements. Students, however, are not subject to contracts or collective bargaining agreements like traditional school employees. As such, their dismissal or discipline may carry with it time-consuming procedural processes or legal ramifications the university wishes to avoid.

Second, the nature of the employer–employee relationship grants educational institutions enhanced ability to monitor faculty rather than student conduct. Courts have upheld employers' rights to read employees' e-mail and review what websites they visit.[133] Faculty members and teachers are not exempt from these rulings. These oversight abilities, however, have not been applied to students. An employer is also permitted, under certain circumstances, to search the offices and "tools" of its employees if located on company property.[134] This would include university-owned computers and hardware. Such searches have not been extended to students' dormitory rooms or homes, however.[135] In short, one's "expectation of privacy" is significantly lower within the scope of an employment relationship than outside it. Third, and perhaps most importantly, faculty members are normally older and more mature than the students they teach. Thus, they are more likely to adhere to the rules of the institution and comprehend the ramifications of not doing so.

So what is the university or school system to do? How does it protect itself from the actions of those over whom it can exercise only limited oversight? The answer, as with most potential pitfalls in contracts, is artful negotiation and drafting. One suggestion is to structure the license to hold the educational institution strictly liable for the misdeeds of its faculty, staff members, and administrators, but only accountable for its failure to use "reasonable efforts" to ensure students fulfill the same standards. Copyright owners may object to such language because of its amorphousness, but the school should be able to overcome this objection.

---

133. *Smyth v. Pillsbury Co.*, 914 F. Supp. 97 (E.D. Pa. 1996); *Bohach v. City of Reno*, 932 F. Supp. 1232 (D. Nev. 1996).

134. *O'Connor v. Ortega*, 480 U.S. 709, 718–20 (1987) (Even an employee's expectation of privacy must be "balanced against the employer's need for supervision, control, and efficient operation of the workplace").

135. *See People v. Superior Court (Walker)*, 143 Cal. App. 4th 1183 (2006) ("[W]e conclude the defendant enjoyed the same Fourth Amendment protection from unreasonable searches and seizures in his dormitory room as would any other citizen in a private home.").

The educational organization should point out that despite its subjective nature, a "reasonable efforts" standard still imposes significant burdens upon it. The institution must, under any test of reasonableness, implement and maintain a method of notifying and educating students about their obligations under the license and the implications of violating it. Such objectives are, in reality, no less burdensome than the school's current responsibility to promote compliance with copyright law among its faculty, staff, and students under the TEACH Act.[136]

Therefore, the clause in question could be worded as follows: "Licensee and any Authorized User who is an employee of Licensee may not, and Licensee shall use all reasonable efforts to ensure that an Authorized User who is a student does not, engage in any of the following activities." The license should then list the specific prohibitions. This simple change provides a fair compromise in dealing with this controversial issue.

[5] Representations and Warranties

The representations and warranties in a copyright license sometimes become the most important provisions in the contract. They are essentially statements about the parties' status and property that each legally affirms to the other. While the use and fee provisions are of initial concern to the licensee, the representations and warranties of the licensor, among other things, serve to guarantee that the copyright owner can perform its obligations under the agreement.

Representations and warranties customarily come in two forms. The first are so-called institutional warranties; these are normally routine and usually not subject to much negotiation. They typically concern the background of the signatories and their procedures in approving the agreement. These warranties attest to the due formation of the parties and verify each has the power and authority to enter into the contract. Normally, each party represents that the agreement has been properly executed; that it constitutes a valid, legal, and binding obligation of the signatory; and that it does not contradict its charter or bylaws or any other previously signed contract. The second type of warranty relates directly to the licensed materials and is discussed in more detail below.

[a] Representations and Warranties of the Licensor

The licensee should seek a broad range of representations from the licensor and attempt to obtain at least the following ownership warranties therefrom:

---

136. Pub. L. No. 107–273, 116 Stat. 1758 (2002). *See* Chapter Six for further information on the TEACH Act and its requirements.

- Licensor is the owner of all right, title, and interest in and to the licensed materials, having good title thereto, free and clear of all mortgages, liens, security interests, and charges;
- No other person has any claim of ownership with respect to the licensed materials;
- The licensed materials do not infringe the copyright or any other proprietary interests of any person;
- Licensor is not a party to any legal action or administrative proceeding that involves a claim by any person that the licensed materials infringe on the intellectual property rights of such person; and
- Licensor has no direct or indirect knowledge of any infringement by others of its licensed materials.

The licensor, of course, will take a different approach by attempting to limit or even eliminate the representations and warranties described above.[137] A copyright holder will often resist warranting that it is the sole owner of the licensed materials, or that no third-party rights are infringed upon. Nevertheless, the licensee should aggressively seek these representations. This warranty is particularly important to obtain since a licensee may be held liable for infringement of another's work even if it had no direct knowledge thereof.[138]

If a legitimate question about ownership arises, the licensee should seek to obtain more information before entering into the agreement. Short of fraud, a licensor may hesitate to give a noninfringement warranty for several strategic business reasons. First, claims of plagiarism may be common in a particular field of scholarship. The licensor may therefore wish to avoid litigation each time a disgruntled academic or researcher feels he has accumulated all rights in an area. Without a warranty, the licensee is left to fend for itself if this "aggrieved" person surfaces looking for someone with resources to sue, whether legitimately or for nuisance value.

Second, authors often cite short excerpts from other works to supplement or buttress their theories. Most often, they have relied on the doctrine of fair use to justify incorporating these citations into their writings. Since, as discussed in Chapters Two and Three, the concept of fair use remains amorphous, the author may wish to avoid, in essence, rendering a guarantee on the doctrine's applicability to her personal "borrowings." Seasoned authors who properly attribute and footnote their sources generally do not raise this objection, however.

---

137. *Hart Engineering Co. v. FMC Corp.*, 593 F. Supp. 1471, 1480 (D.R.I. 1984) ("the dimensions and scope of warranties are fair game for negotiation").

138. *See* discussion of vicarious liability in Chapter Two, Section 2.1[8][c], *supra*.

Third, creators occasionally incorporate another's materials into their works by obtaining express permission to do so. Sometimes, the author's acquired rights do not extend to other parties or the specific uses contemplated by the licensee. In such cases, the licensor should disclose this fact and provide the licensee a description of any "unauthorized" materials. The licensee must then determine whether it needs to independently obtain and pay for such privileges.

Sometimes a licensor may wish to reserve the ability to extract from the licensed materials any items that it has lost the right to use because its agreement with a third party creator has expired. In such cases, the licensor should inform the licensee of such withdrawal sufficiently in advance to enable it to make alternate arrangements. However, the licensee should retain the right to terminate the agreement and receive a refund (either in whole or in part) of its license fee if the content withdrawn materially interferes with its expected use of the licensed materials.

A licensee should also be careful that the representations and warranties it obtains are not limited or weakened by other sections of the contract. For instance, the copyright holder may attempt to confine "ownership" warranties "to the best of its knowledge." This places a burden on the licensee to show the licensor actually knew about an infringement in advance. Another strategy is to indemnify a licensee only for losses exceeding a set amount, also known as a "basket" provision. Hence, in the event of an infringement, the licensee essentially self-insures for the "deductible" and seeks coverage only when its damages exceed a certain total. Conversely, the licensor may agree to cover damages only up to a maximum figure, a so-called ceiling provision. All such concessions may prove risky and ultimately costly for a licensee, depending upon the number of works infringed.[139]

A licensor often requests not to be held responsible for consequential or "special" damages, that is, damages or costs incurred as an *indirect* result of the licensor's failure to meet its contractual obligations. Obviously, what events flow "directly" or "indirectly" out of a breach of contract has been the subject of countless court cases.[140] Ideally, a licensor wants to be accountable only for damages directly related to its failure to perform. For example, if the licensor does not deliver its product by the start of the semester as promised, it would strongly prefer only to be required

---

139. For instance, copyright law permits statutory damages to be awarded in an amount from $750 to $30,000 per work infringed. *See* 17 U.S.C. § 504(c)(1). For a more detailed discussion of indemnification, *see* Section 4.4[6], *infra*.

140. Calamari & Perillo, *The Law of Contracts* § 14-5 (1981).

to refund the licensee's money. In addition, it may have to reimburse the licensee for its extra costs incurred in contracting with another publisher to obtain substitute materials. These are *direct* damages. Conversely, the licensor will want to avoid responsibility for revenue lost by the school after canceling the class, or so-called *indirect* damages. An example of such a limiting clause is as follows:

> Under no circumstances shall Publisher be liable to Licensee for any special, exemplary, incidental, or consequential damages of any character arising out of the inability to use, or the use of, the Licensed Materials. Irrespective of the cause or form of action, Publisher's aggregate liability to Licensee for any claims, losses, or damages arising out of any breach of this License shall in no circumstances exceed the Fee paid by Licensee to Publisher hereunder.

In addition to any *explicit* representations and warranties contained in a contract, certain *implied* warranties are granted by operation of law if the transaction involves goods.[141] While the licensing of copyrighted material does not typically constitute a sale of goods, the licensing of software generally does.[142] Depending on the circumstances, courts tend to classify software licensing as the sale of a product rather than a service. Under the Uniform Commercial Code, contracts for sales of goods trigger the implied warranties of merchantability and fitness for a particular purpose.[143]

U.C.C. § 2-314(2) sets forth the six elements of merchantability with respect to goods, which include that the products (1) "pass without objection in the trade"; (2) "are of fair average quality within the description"; (3) "are fit for the ordinary purpose for which such goods are used"; (4) "run, within the variations permitted by the agreement"; (5) "are adequately contained, packaged, and labeled as the agreement may require"; and (6) "conform to the promise or affirmations of fact made on the container or label." These warranties may be disclaimed or nullified in writing, however. While not always relevant, licensors of intellectual property tend to include these disclaimers in their contracts as a precautionary measure. Any such disclaimer must be conspicuous,[144] usually meaning it is included in boldface capital letters in the contract as follows:

---

141. *Id.* at § 11-24.
142. *See* Section 4.4[10] *infra* for a more detailed discussion of this issue and the U.C.C. in general.
143. U.C.C. §§ 2-314, 2-315.
144. U.C.C. § 2-316(2).

EXCEPT AS EXPRESSLY PROVIDED IN THIS LICENSE, THE PUBLISHER MAKES NO REPRESENTATIONS OR WARRANTIES OF ANY KIND, EXPRESS OR IMPLIED, INCLUDING, BUT NOT LIMITED TO, WARRANTIES OF DESIGN, ACCURACY OF THE INFORMATION CONTAINED IN THE LICENSED MATERIALS, MERCHANTABILITY, OR FITNESS OF USE FOR A PARTICULAR PURPOSE.

[b] Representations and Warranties of the Licensee

A licensor will also seek to obtain certain representations and warranties from the licensee, particularly if the licensed materials are to be digitized and/or placed on an educational institution's electronic network. In such instances, the school will usually be requested to represent that it will:

- Notify all authorized users of the importance of respecting the copyright in the licensed materials and the sanctions imposed for failing to do so;
- Ensure the authorized users are made aware of and undertake to abide by the terms and conditions of the license;
- Monitor compliance and take all reasonable and appropriate steps, including disciplinary action, to ensure any infringing activity ceases and does not reoccur;
- Issue passwords only to authorized users and ensure such persons do not divulge their access information to any third party;
- Keep full and complete records of all authorized users and their access details; and
- Take reasonable measures to ensure only authorized users can access the licensed materials.

Ultimately, what the licensee agrees to is a direct consequence of its bargaining power in the negotiations. It can attempt to limit or even eliminate these representations if it is a particularly valued customer of the publisher. While some larger universities may wield such clout, in most instances the licensor can demand and obtain almost any representation it seeks.[145]

One major disadvantage educational institutions face in negotiations with copyright holders is that, unlike other goods and services a school bargains for, there is only one "supplier" to deal with—the licensed work's owner or his agent. In essence, the licensor wields "monopoly" power in the process. While seemingly unfair, this is naturally a result of the exclu-

---

145. *Fisher Report* at 71.

sive rights granted a copyright owner. In most circumstances, the licensee is not faced with a choice between competing contractual language but rather with the decision to accept the terms imposed upon it by the licensor or do without the material.

[6] Indemnification Provisions

In the event of a dispute, "indemnification" clauses in a license take on paramount significance. The indemnification section is sometimes triggered when a breach of the agreement occurs. More likely, it comes into play when a third party files suit against either or both the licensor and licensee for copyright infringement. Indemnification provisions are intended to protect the "innocent" party being sued for acts or omissions of the "culpable" party. In other words, indemnification is intended to force the "wrongdoer," or *indemnitor*, to step into the shoes of the party being indemnified, or *indemnitee*, and defend it from the claims being brought. For example, if the licensor conveys rights it does not possess, it must defend the licensee in the event it is sued for infringement by the legitimate owner.

The indemnification section usually obligates the indemnitor to (1) hire legal counsel to defend any claims brought against the indemnitee and (2) if necessary, pay any damages awarded by a court. The indemnitee is generally not required to do anything more than promptly advise the indemnitor of any claim raised against it, and perhaps provide reasonable assistance to the defense. The indemnitor should cover any costs the indemnitee incurs in providing such assistance, however.

Indemnification provisions are customarily mutual, with each party promising to indemnify the other if it breaches the contract or is found to have violated one of its warranties. For example, the licensee will seek indemnification in the event the licensed property infringes on the rights of a third party, assuming the licensor gave an ownership representation. Conversely, the licensor will want to be indemnified for the educational institution's unauthorized use of the copyrighted material. Indemnification clauses need to be carefully negotiated and drafted so that one party is not taking on more responsibility (and ultimately legal fees) than it had intended.

As noted earlier, a licensor often seeks to place a monetary limit on its indemnification coverage. An owner or publisher may attempt to "cap" this amount at the level of the license fee. In other words, it offers a "money-back guarantee" in the event the licensee is sued for some act or omission of the licensor. A school should aggressively resist such a provision. The legal bills and penalties associated with copyright infringement may easily exceed the original license fee and expose the educational institution to costs and expenses far beyond those anticipated.[146]

[7] Termination Events

Termination clauses in a license may also prove critically important to the parties.[147] Such provisions accomplish two objectives. First, they establish what conditions prematurely terminate the agreement, that is, cause the contract to end before it is set to expire. Committing a material breach, such as the licensee's failure to pay its fee on time or institute appropriate technological protective measures, typically triggers a termination of the license. In such events the publisher "withdraws" the license, forcing the licensee to stop using the work immediately. In fact, a licensor should always specify that its license is granted upon or subject to the terms and conditions set forth in the contract. This makes clear that if the school violates the agreement, its rights to the licensed materials may be canceled.

Second, termination provisions usually set forth the obligations of the parties after the contract has ended. As such, portions of a license may stay in force even after its term has expired. While this may seem incongruous to laypersons, lawyers are well acquainted with this "life after death" notion of contract law. It seems illogical that parties would continue to have to honor obligations toward each other following the termination of their business deal, but this is normally the case. In fact, unless deemed against public policy, post-termination provisions can be quite onerous.[148]

Indemnification should always survive a license's term or termination because a third party may not always raise an infringement claim prior to the contract's expiration. A copyright owner has three years to bring a civil action for infringement. In addition, the statute of limitations runs from the occurrence of the last, not the first, infringing activity.[149] Therefore, the time to bring a suit can, in reality, run much longer than three years. These claims may thus surface well after the copyright holder and school have ceased doing business. As such, a licensee with expired indemnity

---

146. Current studies estimate the costs of defending a major copyright infringement action at close to $1 million. *See Fisher Report* at 57.

147. *See* M. Epstein & F. Politano, "Drafting License Agreements," in *Drafting License Agreements* § 1.02[3], at 1–5 (M. Epstein & F. Politano eds. 1999).

148. *Id.* at 1–6, *citing Murphy Door Bed Co., Inc. v. Interior Sleep Systems, Inc.*, 874 F.2d 95, 102–03 (2d Cir. 1989) (court held former trademark licensee was precluded from using a generic term otherwise available to everyone else).

149. 17 U.S.C. § 507.

protection could be forced to defend a lawsuit with its own resources, even though it may not have known about the infringement.

By the same token, a violation by the licensee may not be discovered until years after the agreement expires. For example, a school employee illegally duplicating and distributing a portion of licensed materials containing third-party content may not immediately be detected. In such a case, the aggrieved third party would eventually likely sue both the copyright holder and educational institution for infringement. Since the licensor was not at fault, it would turn to the licensee for indemnification. If the indemnity has already expired, the licensor would have to find other means to recoup its defense costs.

How long should this indemnity protection last? One or two years? Longer? Perhaps forever? While perpetual indemnities are rare, those ranging from 5 to 10 years are not. Again, much will depend on the bargaining power of the contracting parties and the school's need for the copyrighted material. Since the prospect that licensed material could infringe upon third-party rights is probably higher than the school engaging in illegal activity, educational institutions tend to seek longer indemnity periods. Licensors generally attempt to negotiate shorter terms for the same reason.

[8] Assignments and Sublicensing

One key advantage of licensing is that it permits the copyright owner to "sell" its product, yet still maintain dominion over it. The licensor controls who is entitled to use its property and how. Most copyright licenses are "nonexclusive" in nature, meaning the owner may grant exactly the same license, or some derivative thereof, to many persons simultaneously, hence maximizing his income. In rare instances, the license may be granted only to one person (an "exclusive" license). The licensor is compensated for this exclusivity by demanding (and usually obtaining) a higher price therefor.

While a content owner may permit a licensee to transfer or "sublease" its rights to others, this provision is typically resisted. Under the common law, a licensee is permitted to assign or sublicense its rights unless the contract specifically precludes her from doing so.[150] Therefore, it is prudent for a licensor to prohibit this conduct in writing. To protect the licensor's interest, any rights granted to a licensee should be described as "non-transferable,

---

150. "Drafting License Agreements," *supra* note 147, at 1–5, *citing Hapgood v. Hewitt*, 119 U.S. 226 (1986); *PPG Industries, Inc. v. Guardian Industries Corp.*, 597 F.2d 1090 (6th Cir.), *cert. denied*, 444 U.S. 930 (1979).

non-assignable, and without the right to sub-license."[151] If the licensor is amenable to certain assignments, an alternative clause may be:

> The Licensee may not assign this License to any other person or organization without the prior written consent of the Publisher, which consent shall not be unreasonably withheld.

[9] Miscellaneous Provisions

Most copyright licenses contain a string of "boilerplate" provisions at the end of the contract. These usually cover an array of issues governing potential legal disputes between the parties. Normally, they do not affect the terms of the actual transaction (e.g., price, content, and length of contract). Such clauses are often referred to as "miscellaneous" or "general" terms and conditions. These labels should not mitigate their significance, however. In the event of litigation, these provisions often influence which party prevails. As such, they should be carefully reviewed, discussed, negotiated, and drafted. Below are examples and a brief discussion of the most common boilerplate clauses appearing in license agreements.

[a] Acceptance

Since it typically prepares the contract, a licensor will also want to control the final steps of the negotiating process. An acceptance clause, similar to the provision below, gives the licensor the final authority to approve the transaction. In most cases, the content owner grants a few select individuals in its organization the right to sign (and thus accept) the license.[152]

> This agreement shall be binding on the Licensor only after acceptance at Licensor's principal office, and execution hereof by a duly designated officer thereof.

[b] Amendment and Waiver

Because business relationships are dynamic and subject to change, parties often need to amend their contractual arrangements. At times, these modifications are effectuated by correspondence and other extraneous writings. Oral statements made after the license is signed may also be intended to amend the written contract. While sometimes clarifying matters, these writings or statements may undermine and confuse the original

---

151. *Id.*

152. Turner, "Contracts," in *Start-up Companies, Planning, Financing and Operating the Successful Business* § 18.02[7][a], at 18–27 (R. Harroch ed. 1987).

intent of the parties. To avoid such issues, licenses often contain "formal amendment" provisions.[153] For instance, the Uniform Commercial Code, or U.C.C., expressly requires that any modification be accomplished by a signed writing.[154] Below is an example of such a provision in a non-U.C.C.-governed transaction. This clause also restricts a waiver's effectiveness to a specific situation.

> Alterations, modifications, or amendments to this License are valid only if reduced to writing and signed by both parties. Either party's waiver, or failure to require performance by the other, of any provision of this License will not affect its full right to require such performance at any subsequent time, or be taken or held to be a waiver of the provision itself.

Under the U.C.C., a party may retract a waiver by reasonable notice unless such retraction would be unjust in light of the other party's reliance thereon in materially changing its position.[155]

[c] Integration

Licensors typically include an integration clause in their agreements. Such provisions prevent the introduction into evidence of terms or conditions the parties may have discussed but did not incorporate into their final contract.[156] Under the U.C.C., written terms intended by the parties as a final expression of their agreement may not be contradicted by other prior or contemporaneous oral statements. A written contract may be supplemented, however, by *consistent* additional terms, unless the court finds the writing to have been a complete and exclusive statement of the parties' relationship.[157] An integration clause (sometimes also referred to as a "merger provision") serves to ensure a court makes such a finding.

A merger provision is therefore designed to motivate the parties to include all their agreements within the actual written license.[158] Sometimes, though, the parties may wish to include other documents to supplement the main contract. The licensee, for example, may insist on incorporating specific descriptions of the product being offered,[159] such as those included

---

153. *Id.* at 18–28.
154. U.C.C. § 2-209(2). *See* subsection [10] *infra* for more information regarding the applicability of the U.C.C. to licensing transactions.
155. U.C.C. § 2-209(5).
156. *See* "Contracts," *supra* note 152, at § 18.02[7][b].
157. U.C.C. § 2-202(b).
158. *See* "Contracts," *supra* note 152, at § 18.03[7][b].
159. *Id.*

in brochures or advertising literature previously received. Conversely, the copyright owner typically prefers the contract address the entire transaction, including all the representations and warranties the licensee intends to rely upon.[160] As such, the licensor will tend to reject the incorporation of other documents or materials into the contract. Regardless, claimants may still introduce evidence of contemporaneous *oral* agreements regarding issues referenced but not specifically addressed in their agreement.[161]

Typical integration or merger clauses include the following.

Option 1:

This License constitutes the entire agreement of the parties and supersedes all prior communications, understandings, and agreements relating to the subject matter thereof, whether oral or written.

Option 2:

This License shall be the complete and exclusive statement of the terms of the agreement between Licensor and Licensee, including all representations and warranties of the parties, and shall not be modified, supplemented, or qualified by any previous discussions, related documentation, course of dealing, or usage of trade.

[d] Severability

Courts in almost all states are permitted to strike or reform a provision in a contract found objectionable for public policy reasons, while still preserving the remaining terms of the agreement between the parties.[162] The clauses below adopt this concept by documenting the parties' intent

---

160. *Id.* The licensor may be particularly concerned about oral representations or statements regarding the product made by overzealous salesmen who simply wish to collect their commission; therefore, the licensor often insists that all warranties being relied upon by the licensee be in writing.

161. *Id.* at 18–29.

162. For instance, Ohio employs this "blue pencil" doctrine, thus permitting an overly broad noncompete covenant to be "tailored" to comply with Ohio law. *Economou v. Physicians Weight Loss Ctrs.*, 756 F. Supp. 1024, 1031 (N.D. Ohio 1991), *citing Raimonde v. Van Vlerah*, 325 N.E. 2d 544 (Ohio 1975). Conversely, under Georgia law, such blue-penciling is not permitted, thereby rendering the entire contract unenforceable. *See Advance Tech. Consultants, Inc. v. RoadTrac L.L.C.*, 551 S.E.2d 735, 738–39 (Ga. App. 2001) (invaliding entire noncompete agreement containing an overbroad restriction), and *Morgan Stanley DW, Inc. v. Frisby*, 163 F. Supp. 2d 1371, 1377–78 (N.D. Ga. 2001) (applying Georgia law and refusing to blue-pencil a restrictive convenant).

to retain all other contract provisions while the invalid or unenforceable language is eliminated or reformed.

Option 1:

The invalidity or unenforceability of any provision of this License shall not affect the continuation or enforceability of the remainder thereof.

Option 2:

If any provision of this License is deemed invalid, ruled illegal, or held unenforceable by a court of competent jurisdiction, the remainder of this License shall not be affected thereby. In lieu of each provision which is invalid, illegal, or unenforceable, there shall be added as part of this License a provision that shall be as similar as possible but be valid, legal, and enforceable.

[e] Force Majeure

Sometimes parties are unable to perform their obligations under a contract due to unforeseen circumstances such as natural disasters or work stoppages. To avoid being deemed in breach of their agreement, force majeure clauses will be placed into the contract. These provisions typically absolve a party from liability for a delay or failure to perform its obligations caused by events beyond its control.[163] The U.C.C. excuses failed performance arising from unexpected events. A breach of contract under the Code is not deemed to occur because of a delay in delivery or nondelivery in whole or part by a seller if "performance as agreed has been made impracticable by the occurrence of a contingency the non-occurrence of which was a basic assumption on which the contract was made."[164]

If such events affect only a portion of the seller's capacity to perform, it must allocate production and deliveries among its customers, or "in any manner which is fair and reasonable."[165] Generally, under common law, in order for its performance to be excused, a seller must demonstrate that the "precluding" event must not have been (1) reasonably foreseeable when the contract was entered into; (2) caused by the seller's negligence; and (3) an immaterial event.[166]

---

163. *See* "Contracts," *supra* note 152, at § 18.02[7][d].

164. U.C.C. § 2-615(a).

165. U.C.C. § 2-615(b).

166. *See* W. H. Henning & G. F. Wallach, *The Law of Sales Under the Uniform Commercial Code* ¶ 5.11, at 5–29 (rev. ed. 1992).

Force majeure clauses in license agreements attempt to serve these same purposes. Unlike the rule at common law, however, a specifically described circumstance will excuse performance whether or not it was foreseeable,[167] so long as the event is "due to causes beyond licensor's control and not occasioned by its fault or negligence."[168] Whether a force majeure provision is mutual or unilateral is sometimes the subject of discussion. Obviously, a licensor will always want to be excused for not performing due to unforeseen events beyond its control. Since a licensee's obligation is usually just to pay money, it is in less need of such protection. In fact, the failure to meet payment obligations is often "carved out" from a list of force majeure events. A sample mutual provision would read:

> Neither party's delay or failure to perform any provision of this License, as result of circumstances beyond its reasonable control (including, without limitation, war, strikes, floods, governmental restrictions, power or telecommunications failures, or damage to or destruction of any network facilities) shall be deemed to be, or to give rise to, a breach of this License.

[f] Governing Law and Forum

As noted above, most contracts are governed by state (not federal) law, and the laws of all states are not identical. It therefore benefits both parties to establish in advance what jurisdiction's law will govern their agreement. Most often, the law of the state where the licensor does business is the one selected. Some licensors prefer the law of a state where neither party does business, but which is deemed favorable to vendors or commercial entities.[169] A typical governing law provision would read: "This License shall be governed by and construed in accordance with the laws of the State of [to be determined by the parties], without regard to its conflicts of law provisions."

Sometimes a license may go beyond selecting what law will govern any dispute and impose an obligation on the parties to bring suit in a specific court. Here is an example of such a provision: "Each party hereto submits to the exclusive jurisdiction of any state or federal court sitting in [identify

---

167. See "Contracts," *supra* note 152, § 18.02[7][d], at 18–30.

168. Wallach, *supra* note 166, ¶ 5.12, at 5–40.

169. These choice-of-law provisions are not always honored by the courts, however. *See Allstate v. Hague*, 449 U.S. 302 (1981) ("[t]he law of the jurisdiction chosen by parties to a contract to govern their contractual rights will not be applied by . . . courts where application of the chosen law would contravene the policy of, or would be prejudicial to the interests of, this state.").

jurisdiction, e.g., the Northern District of California, the State of Illinois] in any action or proceeding relating to or arising out of any offer or sale of seller's products or services hereunder."

Parties to a license agreement may also choose to forgo litigation in the event of a dispute and submit all claims to binding arbitration. Unfortunately, neither word in the phrase "binding arbitration" bears a settled legal meaning. "Arbitration" can be a very different exercise in various contexts and cases since no universally applicable rules of practice, procedure, or evidence govern the conduct thereof. In addition, the parties usually decide whether their arbitration is to be heard by a single person or panel and how to choose those individuals. Typically, the selection method is set forth in the contract.

"Binding" arbitration traditionally means that judicial review of the arbitral decision is narrowly limited, as opposed to nonbinding arbitration in which each party remains free to disregard any ruling. The limitation on judicial review can take several forms—from no review, to review only under a very limited standard, such as fraud by the arbitrator(s) or arbitrary and capricious decision making, to appealable on procedural or evidentiary matters. In any event, the parties should take great care in negotiating and drafting this section.

[g] Notice

Parties to a license agreement will often need to communicate after entering into their business arrangement. While technical information may be solicited and exchanged over the telephone or by e-mail, problems regarding performance of the contract should be relayed more formally. Notice provisions in the license prescribe the means for the parties to do so. While these clauses take many forms, it is best to select those methods that prove convenient but also leave a written record. Two standard examples follow.

Option 1:

Any notices to be served on one party by the other shall be sent by prepaid, recorded delivery or registered post to the address of the addressee set out in this License or to such other address as given by either party to the other as its address for service of notices. All such notices shall be deemed to have been received within five (5) days of posting.

Option 2:

All notices, requests, demands, directions, and other communications ("notices") provided for hereunder shall be in writing, and mailed, telegraphed, or hand-delivered to the applicable party at the address thereof provided herein; or, as to each party, at such other address as shall be designated thereby in a written notice to each other party complying as to delivery with the terms hereof. Each such notice shall be effective on the date of actual hand delivery, or when mailed or telegraphed, be effective on the third business day after it has been deposited in the mails or delivered to the telegraph company, respectively, addressed as aforesaid; and, when mailed shall be sent by first class certified mail, return receipt requested, enclosed in a postage-prepaid envelope.

While telegrams and regular mail may seem outdated in today's electronic environment, using e-mails for legal notice is strongly discouraged due to the inability to confirm acceptance and the easy deletion of such messages from computer systems.

[10] Licensing, the U.C.C., and UCITA

One cannot depart from a discussion of negotiating license agreements without referring to the application of the Uniform Commercial Code to such instruments. While the preceding sections contained several references to the U.C.C., these citations were included to demonstrate how the Code treats similar issues arising from the sale of goods. In most instances today, the U.C.C. does not apply to intellectual property licenses.

[a] History and Construction of the Uniform Commercial Code

Prior to the creation and enactment of the Uniform Commercial Code, commercial law in the United States was "largely non-statutory and developing piecemeal from state to state."[170] Various states had enacted statutes, based on the Uniform Sales Act, the Uniform Negotiable Instruments Law, the Uniform Warehouse Receipts Act, the Uniform Bills of Lading Act, the Uniform Trusts Receipt Act, the Uniform Conditional Sales Act, the Uniform Stock Transfer Act, and similar legislation dealing with banking and secured transactions. Unfortunately, "[t]his arrangement proved deeply problematic for business enterprises because it created a patchwork quilt of unstable law."[171]

"Uniform Acts" in the United States, such as those mentioned above, are customarily sponsored and promulgated by the National Conference of Commissioners on Uniform State Laws (NCCUSL). The NCCUSL nor-

---

170. D. Litowitz, "Introduction to Law Students," in Perspectives on the Uniform Commercial Code XV (D. Litowitz ed. 2001).

171. *Id.*

mally develops a model statute, which it then recommends as a uniform state law.[172] State legislatures then determine whether to enact the model as their state's law, and, if so, to adopt it either in its entirety or with modifications. Obviously, major changes are discouraged by the conference as they endanger the model act's "uniformity" and undermine the process.[173]

In an effort to replace the confusing myriad of commercial statutes and bring cohesion to the field, the NCCUSL, joined by the American Law Institute (ALI), undertook an ambitious effort in the 1940s to develop a uniform body of commercial law.[174] The U.C.C's drafters wanted to resolve two major problems. "First, the law of commercial transactions was an uncertain mixture of case decisions and occasional statutes, and second, commercial law was not uniform from state to state."[175] Meetings and drafting seminars were completed by 1950, and the first official draft of the new U.C.C. was enacted into law by Pennsylvania in 1953. From 1953 through 1962, various changes were made to the U.C.C. to correct deficiencies and incorporate other recommendations (the "1962 Code").[176]

The 1962 Code was eventually adopted by every state (except Louisiana, which has not enacted the sales and leasing provisions), the District of Columbia, and the territories of Guam and the Virgin Islands.[177] The U.C.C. has been called "the most spectacular success story in the history of American law."[178] It is composed of the following nine articles:

Article 1—General Principles
Article 2—Sales
Article 3—Commercial Paper
Article 4—Bank Deposits and Collections
Article 5—Letters of Credit
Article 6—Bulk Transfers
Article 7—Documents of Title
Article 8—Investment Securities
Article 9—Secured Transactions

Each article is divided into various sections and subsections addressing multiple issues. The U.C.C. has been an evolving piece of legislation.

---

172. *See* Uniform Law Commissioners website, http://www.nccusl.org/update/.

173. Litowitz, *supra* note 170, at xiii.

174. *Id.* at xv.

175. *Id.*

176. R. Braucher, "Legislative History of the Uniform Commercial Code," in *Perspectives of the Uniform Commercial Code* 24 (D. Litowitz ed. 2001).

177. *Id.*

178. J. White & R. Summers, *Uniform Commercial Code* (1988).

From its beginnings through today, it has been amended and revised periodically to address changes in commercial practices and correct certain "gaps" discovered since its implementation.

[b] Intellectual Property Licenses

Section 2-102 of the U.C.C. provides:

> Unless the context otherwise requires, this Article applies to transactions in goods; it does not apply to any transaction which although in the form of an unconditional contract to sell or present sale is intended to operate only as a security transaction nor does this Article impair or repeal any statute regulating sales to consumers, farmers or other specified classes of buyers.

In short, the U.C.C. governs only "sales" and "contracts to sell" *goods.* Goods are defined therein as "all things . . . which are moveable at the time of identification to the contract for sale other than the money in which the price is to be paid, investment securities and things in action."[179] Consequently, Article 2 does not apply to contracts for *services,* except where application is appropriate (i.e., a sale involving both goods and services in which the sale of goods predominates). This broad language also makes the article sometimes applicable to non-sale transactions such as leases, bailments, and gifts. Courts tend to apply Article 2 to non-sales matters only if the policies underlying the section are applicable to such transactions.[180]

Where, then, does a copyright license fit into this equation? Is it deemed to be more a contract for goods or for services? Since a circumscribed set of rights to use someone else's intellectual property is not a "tangible moveable," courts tend to view these transactions as services.[181] In considering a patent license, one federal court viewed it as "in essence nothing more than a promise by the licensor not to sue the licensee . . . ."[182] The U.C.C. would similarly not apply to a copyright license, since the same factors are at work.

---

179. U.C.C. § 2-105.

180. *See W.E. Johnson Equipment v. United Airlines,* 238 So. 2d 98 (Fla. 1970) (warranty of fitness for a particular purpose (§ 2-315) held to apply to a lease of goods because similar factors and considerations arose as in a sale thereof).

181. *Data Processing Services, Inc. v. L.H. Smith Oil Corp.,* 492 N.E.2d 1329, 1 UCC Rep. Serv.2d 29 (Ind. Ct. App. 1986); *Micro-Managers, Inc. v. Gregory,* 147 Wisc.2d 500, 434 N.W.2d 97 (Wisc. Ct. App. 1988).

182. *Spindelfabrik Suessen-Schurr v. Schubert & Salzer,* 829 F.2d 1075, 1081 (Fed. Cir. 1987), *cert. denied,* 484 U.S. 1063 (1988). *See also Cohen v. Paramount Pictures Corp.,* 845 F.2d 851 (9th Cir. 1988).

One growing exception to this principle of non-applicability arises in the area of mass-marketed software. Software companies usually include agreements, commonly known as "shrink-wrap licenses," with their products. The term "shrink wrap" refers to the transparent plastic in which the software box is often encased.[183] These licenses are intended to replace customary business contracts between software producers and users. The typical mass-market transaction does not involve a negotiated agreement, however. Instead, the purchase is customarily made by a consumer at a retail store, through the mail, or on the Internet, with little discussion or bargaining between the parties. In encasing its product with a shrink-wrap license, the software producer usually seeks, among other things, to (1) prohibit unauthorized copies; (2) preclude software rental; (3) forbid reverse engineering and any modifications thereto; (4) restrict the use thereof to one central processing unit; (5) disclaim warranties; and (6) limit its liability.[184]

The widespread use of shrink-wrap licenses has generated intense debate in the academic and legal community, but not much case law.[185] In addressing the issue, courts must deal with how to properly classify a sale of software. Should it be viewed as a sale of goods or merely as providing services? Unlike patent and copyright licenses, most courts have opted for the first approach and applied the U.C.C. to mass-market software transactions.[186] Legal commentators also generally conclude the U.C.C. should govern computer software sales.[187] The major reasons cited are that (1) buyers of mass-market software usually pay a single purchase price instead of making periodic payments; (2) the software company does not retain title for the purpose of obtaining a security interest; and (3) no expiration date

---

183. Lemley, *Intellectual Property and Shrinkwrap Licenses*, 68 S. Cal. L. Rev. 1239, 1241 (1995).

184. Rich, *Mass Market Software and the Shrinkwrap License*, 23 Colo. Law. 1321 (1994).

185. *See Step-Saver Data Sys., Inc. v. Wyse Technology*, 939 F.2d 91 (3d Cir. 1991); *Vault Corp. v. Quaid Software Ltd.*, 847 F.2d 255 (5th Cir. 1988); *Arizona Retail Sys., Inc. v. Software Link, Inc.*, 831 F. Supp. 759 (D. Ariz. 1993). The enforceability of shrink-wrap licenses in general seems to have been accepted by the courts. *See, e.g., Pro CD, Inc. v. Zeidenberg*, 86 F.3d 1447 (7th Cir. 1996).

186. Lemley, *supra* note 183, at 1244 n.23 (citing numerous federal and state law cases); also *see Microsoft Corp. v. Harmony Computers & Electronics, Inc.*, 846 F. Supp. 208 (E.D.N.Y. 1994).

187. *See* Horovitz, *Note, Computer Software as a Good Under the Uniform Commercial Code: Taking a Byte out of the Intangibility Myth*, 65 B.U.L. Rev. 129 (1985); Lemley, *supra* note 183, at 1244 n.23.

exists for the "licensed" right.[188] As such, these factors correlate more with transfers of goods rather than typical licensing schemes.

Expanding the Uniform Commercial Code to cover licensing arrangements has been seriously considered over the last ten years. In the 1990s, the NCCUSL formed a committee to propose legislation regulating licenses.[189] To date, however, the manifestation of this effort, U.C.C. Article 2B, has not gained the consensus needed to proceed.[190] Thus, with the exceptions noted above, intellectual property issues remain outside the scope and coverage of U.C.C. Therefore, as with other business contracts, licenses are governed by the "common law" of the state where the parties are located (unless they choose another forum). However, some cases continue to challenge the validity of forum selection clauses in licenses and other contracts.[191]

[c] UCITA

A separate body of law potentially applicable to the licensing of intellectual property is the Uniform Computer Information Transactions Act (UCITA). UCITA is a *proposed* uniform state statute designed to provide default rules for licensing software and other forms of digital information. To date, UCITA has been enacted only in Maryland and Virginia.[192] UCITA was modeled on the U.C.C. and originally proposed as an amendment thereto. The act was initially developed by the NCCUSL and ALI.[193]

---

188. *See* Hamilton & Hood, *The Shrink-Wrap License—Is It Really Necessary?* 10 Computer Law 16 (1993).

189. The full text of proposed Article 2B along with comments is available at http://www.law.upenn.edu/library/ulc/ucc2/ucc2b997.htm.

190. A.L.I./NCCUSL Press Release (April 7, 1999), http://www.law.upenn.edu/bll/archives/ulc/ucita/2brel.htm ("it has become apparent that this area does not presently allow the sort of codification that is represented by the Uniform Commercial Code"); *See also* Memorandum from Todd J. Paglia to the American Law Institute regarding "Uniform Commercial Code Article 2B" (Mar. 10, 1998), http://www.cptech.org/ucc/ali3-10.htm.

191. *See* Karayanni, *The Public Policy Exception to the Enforcement of Forum Selection Clauses*, 34 Duq. L. Rev. 1009 (1996); *see also* Montana ex rel. Polaris Industries v. District Court, 695 P.2d 471 (Mont. 1985); Davenport v. Adolph Coors, 314 N.W.2d 432 (Iowa 1982); Cerami-Kote, Inc. v. Energywave Corp., 116 Idaho 56, 773 P.2d 1143 (1989); Disctronics Ltd. v. Disc Mfg. Inc., 686 So. 2d 1154 (Ala. 1996) ("[C]ontractual forum selection clauses are not enforceable in Alabama's courts."). However, Alabama has since validated a forum selection clause in a commercial transaction; *see Professional Ins. Corp. v. Sutherland*, 700 So. 2d 347 (Ala. 1997); *see also* North Carolina's statute, which overrules forum selection clauses (N.C. Gen. Stat. § 22B-3 (1994)).

192. Va. Code § 59.1-501.1 *et. seq.*; 1999 Md. Laws § 21-102.

193. Press Release of National Conference of Commissioners on Uniform State Laws Institute (April 7, 1999), http://www.law.upenn.edu/bll/ulc/ucita/2brel.htm.

ALI withdrew its support of the legislation in 1999, however, after it could not reach agreement with the NCCUSL on certain key provisions.[194] The NCCUSL also abandoned the measure in 2003, citing widespread political opposition to the proposed law.[195] As a result, the act's future remains in limbo.

UCITA applies to information obtained electronically and encompasses computer software, online databases, electronic journals, e-books, computer games, and multimedia products as well as "shrink-wrap" and "click-wrap" licenses.[196] As noted earlier, these latter agreements are seldom, if ever, negotiable. UCITA contains a choice of law provision enabling the parties to select which state's law governs the contract, regardless of their physical location.[197] The act also provides a forum selection clause, allowing parties to choose a UCITA state in which to have all of their disputes heard.[198] In response to this clause, three states (Iowa, West Virginia, and North Carolina) have enacted "bomb shelter" legislation designed to protect their citizens from such far-reaching clauses.[199] These statutes essentially void both the choice of law and choice of forum provisions in a contract, resulting in the application of the law of the consumer's domicile.[200]

[i] UCITA's Objectives

UCITA's drafters wanted it to provide a clearer, more predictable set of rules governing electronic transactions and information.[201] The legislation promotes freedom of contract by making its default rules applicable only in those instances where specific issues are not covered in the parties' agreement. UCITA was intended not to conflict with federal statutes, but

---

194. J.W. Fiscus, "American Law Institute Withdraws Sponsorship," SFWA Bulletin (Summer 1999), http://www.sfwa.org/News/2b.htm.

195. Thibodeau, "Sponsor Pulls Support For Controversial UCITA Law," Computerworld (Aug. 1, 2003), http://www.computerworld.com/governmenttopics/government/legalissues/story/0,10801,83676,00.html.

196. *NCCUSL Report to the American Bar Association, Recommendation*, American Bar Association website, http://www.abanet.org/leadership/recommendations03/113G.pdf. The act covers "information in electronic form that is obtained from or through the use of a computer, or that is in digital or equivalent form capable of being processed by a computer." Uniform Computer Information Transactions Act § 102 (11) (2002). The act is hereinafter referred to as UCITA and is available in its entirety at http://www.law.upenn.edu/bll/archives/ulc/ucita/2002final.htm.

197. UCITA § 109.

198. UCITA § 110.

199. *See* Iowa Code § 554D.104; N.C. Gen. Stat. § 66-329; and W. Va. Code § 55-8-15.

200. *Id.*

201. UCITA, Prefatory Note.

at the same time to address inconsistencies in state cases.[202] For example, some courts currently enforce "browse-wrap" agreements if a visitor merely uses a website, while others require an affirmative act to manifest assent.[203] UCITA adopts the latter approach and provides that users should have a reasonable opportunity to review the terms of a contract beforehand.[204]

Similarly, UCITA seeks to reconcile state common law with Article 2 of the U.C.C. and balance the competing interests between licensees and licensors[205] by permitting courts to strike "unconscionable" terms[206] and prohibiting clauses that conflict with public policy.[207] UCITA retains the common law defenses of fraud and duress in addition to consumer protection law.[208]

[ii] UCITA's Proponents

Advocates of UCITA contend that licensing electronic information requires different default rules than does the sale of goods.[209] They suggest that pre-written shrink-wrap contracts enhance trade by allowing customization of agreements and pricing depending on customers' needs, thereby reducing costs to consumers.[210] Proponents argue that UCITA also benefits those states where major software industry companies and distributors are located by increasing protection for such entities.[211] In addition, they suggest that UCITA encourages competition, development, and innovation by limiting liability for small start-up companies.[212] UCITA promoters claim its primary benefits include clarity of law, enhancing developing technology, and providing consumer protection.

---

202. Rosenfeld, *Spiders and Crawlers and Bots, Oh My: The Economic Efficiency and Public Policy of Online Contracting that Restrict Data Collection*, 2002 Stan. Tech. L. Rev. 3, 9 (2002).

203. Robertson, *Is Assent Still a Prerequisite for Contract Formation in Today's E-Conomy?* 78 Wash. L. Rev. 265, 280–81 (2003) (discussing four federal district court opinions).

204. UCITA § 112.

205. Report to American Bar Association, *supra* note 196.

206. UCITA § 111(a).

207. UCITA § 105(b).

208. Prefatory Note, *supra* note 201. UCITA § 105(c).

209. Nimmer, *Licensing in the Contemporary Information Economy*, 8 Wash. U.J.L. & Pol'y 99, 121 (2002).

210. Dreyfuss & Ginsberg, *Draft Convention on Jurisdiction and Recognition of Judgements in Intellectual Property Matters*, 77 Chi.-Kent. L. Rev. 1065, 1102–03 (2002).

211. Tichy, *Computer Software Transactions in Washington State—What Commercial Laws Can the State Provide for this Industry? Is UCITA the Answer?* 37 Gonz. L. Rev. 377, 378–79 (2001).

212. *Id.* at 394.

UCITA's choice of law provision admittedly allows greater predictability for online vendors,[213] while still permitting parties the option of choosing default provisions or negotiating their own terms.[214] Advocates further contend that UCITA demonstrates a national ability to provide uniformity and deal effectively and efficiently with changing legal and regulatory needs.[215] UCITA supporters suggest it provides greater protection for consumers by recognizing the creation of express warranties through advertising[216] and extending the implied warranty of merchantability to computer programs.[217] The "merchantability" warranties may be waived, however, by mentioning such terms or using "words of similar impact" that are "conspicuous."[218]

As noted above, UCITA provides consumers with a reasonable opportunity to review a contract before manifesting assent and limits a software developer's right to add later terms absent the consumer's knowledge.[219] UCITA also prohibits many forms of "electronic self-help" or repossession whereby the manufacturer can interrupt the use of an electronic product if the consumer allegedly breaches his agreement.[220] Lastly, unlike current practice, licensing rights are presumed to be transferable under UCITA unless the transfer would lead to material harm or be precluded by law or the language of the contract.[221]

[iii] UCITA's Opponents

UCITA has been criticized by consumer advocates, software user interest groups, insurance companies, library organizations, and state attorneys general, as well as the American Bar Association (ABA) and ALI.[222] These groups have expressed concern that UCITA more closely reflects

---

213. *Id.* at 387.

214. UCITA § 113(a).

215. Razook, *The Politics and Promise of UCITA*, 36 Creighton L. Rev. 643, 665 (2003).

216. UCITA § 402(a)(1). However, the advertisement must be known by the licensee and become part of the basis of the bargain under which he acquired the computer information. UCITA § 402, comment 3.

217. The act provides, however, that the "presence of certain defects may be consistent with merchantability." UCITA § 403, comment 3(a).

218. UCITA § 406 (b)(1)(A).

219. UCITA § 303(d).

220. UCITA § 816.

221. Report to American Bar Association, *supra* note 196; UCITA § 503(1).

222. *See* list of UCITA opponents compiled by James Huggins, http://www.jameshuggins.com/h/tek1/ucita.htm.

a regulatory system than a freedom of contract model.[223] UCITA's critics believe it unfairly favors software companies by permitting them to contract out of warranties, obtain signed agreements before disclosing all conditions,[224] and alter terms unilaterally by posting changes on a website.[225]

UCITA's critics further suggest it inhibits the free flow of information.[226] As an example, they note UCITA may impede operation of the "fair use" doctrine because "[b]y implicitly making shrinkwrap licenses enforceable without limitation, anyone clicking on an 'I Agree' icon [would] be 'agreeing' to waive copyright privileges."[227] By conceptually separating transfer of title from ownership of software products,[228] UCITA also conceivably negates the "first sale" doctrine by preventing the donation of software to libraries and other institutions.[229]

The act's opponents further point out that UCITA decreases protections for consumers who are usually less sophisticated than large companies and cannot examine software like a tangible product.[230] Opponents also note consumers may be left without warranty protection for software content because UCITA permits post-payment disclosure of contract terms.[231] Lastly, critics observe that "one of the major problems with UCITA is its categorization of [all] software as licenses"[232] and not goods. This may in turn nullify rights afforded to consumers under the Magnuson-Moss Warranty

---

223. Mann, *Balancing Issues and Overlapping Jurisdictions in the Global Electronic Marketplace: The UCITA Example*, 8 Wash. U.J.L. & Pol'y 215, 241–45 (2002). Letter from Attorney Generals of 14 states to Gene Lebrum, NCCUSL President, "Proposed Uniform Computer Information Transactions Act" (July 23, 1999), http://www.2Bguide.com/docs/71399ags.html.

224. D. Tuomey, *Weathering the Commercial Storm: Why Everyone Should Steer Clear of the Uniform Computer Information Transactions Act*, J. Inform. & Tech. (Mar. 22, 2002), http://www2.warwick.ac.uk/fac/soc/law/elj/jilt/2002_1/tuomey.

225. *Id.* at 4.1 ("UCITA validates post-payment disclosures of contract terms by software producers and software sellers."); UCITA § 112(e)(3).

226. Thibodeau, *supra* note 195.

227. Paglia Memorandum, *supra* note 190, at 3 ("The broad validation of these licenses will disturb the balance achieved in copyright law and erode the rights traditionally granted to information users . . . [such as] quoting a portion of the text.").

228. Alford, *Negotiating and Analyzing Electronic License Agreements*, 94 Law Libr. J. 621, 642 (2002).

229. *See* Chapter Two, Section 2.1[7][c], for a more detailed discussion of the first sale doctrine.

230. Razook, *supra* note 215, at 650–55.

231. Tuomey, *supra* note 224, at 6 ("All terms, even important ones such as warranties, can be hidden from the consumer until after the deal has been closed.").

232. *Id.* at 4.

Act[233] because "[such] warranty protections do not apply to licenses and apply only to consumer products or goods."[234]

Regardless of whether additional states enact its provisions, UCITA should have minimal impact on copyright licensing for digital distance learning lessons. By its own terms, UCITA does not apply to "an agreement to create, perform or perform in . . . use, modify, reproduce . . . transmit, license or display . . . a motion picture, sound recording, musical work or phonorecord" as defined in the Copyright Act.[235] More likely its influence would be felt on licensing textual databases and e-journals for academic use.

4.5 DATABASE LEGISLATION

Often programs and other materials licensed to schools and universities contain large amounts of data, statistics, or other types of factual information that the licensor has gone to great length to accumulate and incorporate into its product. Under current law, such accumulations of facts are ineligible for copyright protection. Therefore, the owner faces the depressing prospect that the licensee or some other person could extract such data from his or her program and use it for other purposes, including entering into direct competition with the licensor.

As an example, consider the case of *Pro CD Inc. v. Matthew Zeidenberg.*[236] The plaintiff therein, a Massachusetts corporation, invested several million dollars to create a comprehensive, national directory of over 95,000,000 residential and business listings containing full names, street addresses, telephone numbers, zip codes, and industry or "SIC" codes where appropriate. The company marketed and sold this information on CD-ROM discs under the trade name "Select Phone TM."

Mr. Zeidenberg, a graduate student at the University of Wisconsin, purchased a copy of Select Phone TM and subsequently downloaded certain data from the program onto his own computer. Zeidenberg then incorporated a new business in order to make such information available over

---

233. 15 U.S.C. § 2302(c).

234. Tuomey, *supra* note 224, at 14.

235. UCITA § 103(2)(B).

236. 908 F. Supp. 640 (W.D. Wis. 1996), *rev'd and remanded in part*, 86 F.3d 1447 (7th Cir. 1996). On appeal, the Seventh Circuit upheld the plaintiff's contention that its database could not be appropriated by the defendant because of the existence of a shrink-wrap license that prohibited any commercial use by a purchaser of the product. *Id.* at 1448. The lower court's conclusion that collections of facts are not eligible for copyright protection was not in dispute, however.

the Internet for commercial purposes. Defendant wrote his own computer program, however, to allow users to search the new database. No one who accessed Zeidenberg's website, therefore, ever used or copied Pro CD's proprietary software, only the raw data included therein. Upon learning of Defendant's business, Plaintiff promptly filed suit seeking to enjoin his activity. Defendant countered by claiming Pro CD was not entitled to copyright protection for the factual information contained in its products.

The *Zeidenberg* case and others like it concern the seemingly contradictory propositions that while facts are not copyrightable, compilations thereof generally are. Each of these principles is rooted in case law and federal statutes. A fundamental axiom of copyright law is that "no author may copyright his ideas or the facts he narrates."[237] At the same time, however, it is acknowledged that collections of facts are within the subject matter of copyright. "Compilations" were expressly mentioned in both the Copyright Act of 1909 and the 1976 Act.

An undeniable tension therefore exists between these two objectives. Many compilations consist of nothing but raw data—that is, wholly factual information not accompanied by any original written expression, such as a book on baseball statistics. On what basis may one claim copyright in such a work? Common sense dictates that 100 uncopyrightable batting averages of famous players do not magically change status when gathered together in one place. Yet copyright law contemplates that compilations consisting exclusively of facts are potentially within its scope.[238]

The key to comprehending the issue lies in understanding why facts are not copyrightable. Recall that to qualify for copyright protection, a work must be *original* to the author.[239] "Originality," as used in copyright law, means only that the work was independently created (as opposed to copied from others), and that it possesses at least some minimal degree of creativity.[240] The requisite level of creativity is extremely low; even a slight amount will suffice. Most works therefore make the grade quite easily, as they possess some creative spark, "no matter how crude, humble or obvious"[241] they may be. Unlike patent law, in copyright law "originality" does

---

237. *Harper & Row, Publishers, Inc. v. Nation Enterprises*, 471 U.S. 539, 556 (1985).

238. Mark F. Radcliffe & Diane Brinson, *Copyright Law*, findlaw.com (1999) ("A compilation of facts is protected by copyright only to the extent of the author's originality in the selection, coordination, and arrangement [thereof].").

239. *Harper & Row*, supra note 237, at 547–49.

240. 1 M. Nimmer & D. Nimmer, *Copyright* §§ 2.01[A], [B] (1994) (hereinafter *Nimmer on Copyright*).

241. *Id.* at § 1.08[C][1].

not signify "novelty"—meaning a work may be original even though it closely resembles other works, so long as the similarity is fortuitous.[242]

The requirement of originality arises directly from the U.S. Constitution, although the term is not specifically mentioned therein. The source of legislative power to enact copyright laws is Article I, § 8, cl. 8, which authorizes Congress to "secure for limited Times to Authors . . . the exclusive Right to their respective Writings." In two decisions from the late 1800s—*The Trade-Mark Cases*[243] and *Burrow-Giles Lithographic Co. v. Sarony*,[244] the Supreme Court defined both "authors" and "writings." In so doing, the Court made clear these terms presuppose a degree of originality.[245] In *The Trade-Mark Cases*, the Court determined "originality is required" for a particular work to be classified "under the head of writings of authors."[246]

In *Burrow-Giles*, the Supreme Court distilled the same requirement from the Constitution's use of the word "authors" by defining the term to mean "he to whom anything owes its origin; originator; maker."[247] As in *The Trade-Mark Cases*, the Court emphasized creativity by describing copyright as limited to "original intellectual conceptions of the author,"[248] and stressed "the existence of . . . originality, of intellectual production, of thought, and conception."[249] The originality requirement established in those early cases remains sacrosanct[250] and the very "premise of copyright law."[251] It is, therefore, "constitutionally mandated for all works."[252]

This principle in turn mandates the law's seemingly disparate treatment of facts and collections thereof. "No one may claim originality as to facts,"[253] because they do not owe their existence to an act of authorship.[254] For instance, the first person to find and report a particular fact did not

---

242. *Sheldon v. Metro-Goldwyn Pictures Corp.*, 81 F.2d 49, 54 (2d Cir. 1936).

243. 100 U.S. 82 (1879).

244. 111 U.S. 53 (1884).

245. *See supra* note 243, at 94.

246. *Id.*

247. *See supra* note 244, at 58 (internal quotation marks omitted).

248. *Id.*

249. *Id.* at 59–60.

250. *See Goldstein v. California*, 412 U.S. 546, 561–62 (1973).

251. *Miller v. Universal City Studios, Inc.*, 650 F. 2d 1365, 1368 (5th Cir. 1981).

252. Patterson & Joyce, *Monopolizing the Law: The Scope of Copyright Protection for Law Reports and Statutory Compilations,* 36 UCLA L. Rev. 719, 763, n. 155 (1989); *Nimmer on Copyright* § 1.06[A] ("Originality is a statutory as well as a constitutional requirement."); *id. at* § 1.08[C][1] ("[A] modicum of intellectual labor . . . clearly constitutes an essential constitutional element.").

253. *Nimmer on Copyright* § 2.11[A].

254. *See supra* note 244, at 58.

create it; he or she merely discovered it.[255] Census takers, for example, do not "create" the population figures emerging from their efforts; they simply accumulate those statistics from the world around them.[256] Population numbers are therefore not copyrightable, because they are not "original" in any Constitutional sense.[257] The same is true of all facts, whether scientific, historical, biographical, or just news of the day. "They may not be copyrighted and are part of the public domain available to every person."[258]

Factual compilations, on the other hand, may at times possess the requisites to garner copyright protection. The accumulating author typically chooses which facts to include and how to arrange them. These selection and arrangement choices may be sufficiently creative to trigger eligibility for copyright.[259] This protection is limited by the fact that to copyright a work does not mean every element thereof is included.[260] Copyright protection may extend only to those portions of the work original to the author.[261] For instance, in *Harper & Row, Publishers, Inc. v. Nation Enterprises*, the Supreme Court held that President Gerald R. Ford could not prohibit others from using bare historical facts from his autobiography,[262] but could prevent copying of his "subjective descriptions and portraits of public figures."[263]

In short, copyright in a factual compilation remains thin,[264] typically permitting others to use the facts contained in the original publication, so long as the new work does not feature the same selection and arrangement.[265] For example, someone may cite a player's statistics from a baseball encyclopedia, but not duplicate specific listings therefrom. "No matter how much original authorship the work displays, the facts and ideas it exposes are free for the taking. . . . The very same facts and ideas may be divorced from the context imposed by the author, and restated or reshuf-

---

255. *Nimmer on Copyright* § 2.03[E].

256. Denicola, *Copyright in Collections of Facts: A Theory for the Protection of Nonfiction Literary Works*, 81 Colum. L. Rev. 516, 525 (1981).

257. *Nimmer on Copyright* § 2.03[E].

258. *Miller, supra* note 251, at 1369.

259. *Nimmer on Copyright* §§ 2.11[D], 3.03; Denicola, *supra* note 256, at 523, n.38.

260. *See Harper & Row, supra* note 237, at 547; *see also Nimmer on Copyright* § 3.03.

261. Patterson & Joyce, *supra note* 252, at 80002; Ginsburg, *Creation and Commercial Value: Copyright Protection of Works of Information*, 90 Colum. L. Rev. 1865, 1868, n.12 (1990).

262. *Harper & Row, supra* note 237, at 556–57.

263. *Id.* at 563.

264. See Patry, *Copyright in Compilations of Facts (or Why the "White Pages" Are Not Copyrightable)*, 12 Com. & Law 37, 64 (1990).

265. *See* Patterson & Joyce, *supra note* 252, at 776.

fled by second comers, even if the author was the first to discover the facts or to propose the ideas."[266]

While using the fruits of another's labor without compensation may strike one as unfair, this was not "some unforeseen byproduct of a statutory scheme,"[267] but rather "the essence of copyright,"[268] the primary objective of which was not to reward the labor of authors, but "to promote the Progress of Science and useful Arts."[269] Thus, copyright assures creators the right to their original expression, but encourages others to build freely upon the ideas and information conveyed by them.[270] "The very object of publishing a book on science or the useful arts is to communicate to the world the useful knowledge which it contains. [This goal] would be frustrated if the knowledge could not be used without incurring the guilt of piracy of the book."[271]

Early versions of the Copyright Act may have obscured some of its objectives, however.[272] For instance, the subject matter of copyright was described in Sections 3 and 4 of the Copyright Act of 1909. Section 4 provided that copyright was available to "all the writings of an author."[273] By using the terms "writings" and "author"—the same words used in the Constitution and subsequently defined by the Supreme Court—the statute necessarily incorporated the originality requirement, but only implicitly, thereby leaving room for error. Section 3 was similarly ambiguous in that it protected only "the copyrightable component parts of the work," without specifically mentioning originality.

Most lower courts construed the 1909 Act correctly, notwithstanding its less than perfect language, by underscoring there could be no copyright without originality.[274] "[T]he 1909 Act neither defined originality, nor even expressly required that a work be 'original' in order to command protection. However, the courts uniformly inferred the requirement from the fact that copyright protection [could] only be claimed by 'authors' . . .

---

266. Ginsburg, *supra* note 261, at 1868.

267. *Harper & Row, supra* note 237, at 589 (dissenting opinion).

268. *Id.*

269. Art. I, § 8, cl. 8. *See also Twentieth Century Music Corp. v. Aiken,* 422 U.S. 151, 156 (1975).

270. *Harper & Row, supra* note 237, at 556–57.

271. *Baker v. Selden,* 101 U.S. 99, 103 (1880).

272. *Nimmer on Copyright* § 2.01.

273. 35 Stat. 1076 (1909).

274. *See* Patterson & Joyce, *supra note* 252, at 760–61.

reason[ing] that since an author is 'the . . . creator, originator' it follows that a work is not [his] product . . . unless . . . original."[275]

Unfortunately, some courts misinterpreted the 1909 Act by ignoring Sections 3 and 4 and instead focusing on Section 5, which provided that anyone registering a new work had to specify its category.[276] One such category was "books, including composite and cyclopedic works, directories, gazetteers, and other compilations."[277] Section 5 did *not* mean all compilations were eligible for copyright; and, in fact, it expressly referenced "the subject-matter of copyright [to be] defined in section four." Nevertheless, because "compilations" were specifically mentioned, some courts mistakenly concluded that directories and the like were copyrightable "without any further or precise showing of original . . . authorship."[278]

Making matters worse, other courts invented a new theory of law to justify the protection of factual compilations. Known alternatively as "sweat of the brow" or "industrious collection," the concept was that copyright could legitimately serve as a reward for the labor associated with compiling facts. The theory's premise was as follows:

> [T]he right to copyright a book upon which one has expended labor in its preparation does not depend upon whether the materials which he has collected consist or not of matters which are *publici juris*, or whether such materials show literary skill or originality, either in thought or in language, or anything more than industrious collection. The man who goes through the streets of a town and puts down the names of each of the inhabitants, with their occupations and their street number, acquires material of which he is the author.[279]

The "sweat of the brow" doctrine had numerous flaws; the most glaring was that it extended copyright protection in a compilation beyond the selection and arrangement of facts to the facts themselves. Under "industrious collection," a subsequent compiler had to prove independent creation or face infringement liability. A researcher was "not entitled to take one word of information previously published," but rather had to "independently work out the matter for himself, so as to arrive at the same result

---

275. *Nimmer on Copyright* § 2.01 (footnotes omitted) (citing cases).

276. *See, e.g., Leon v. Pacific Telephone & Telegraph Co.*, 91 F.2d 484 (9th Cir. 1937); *Jeweler's Circular Publishing Co. v. Keystone Publishing Co.*, 281 F. 83 (2d Cir. 1922).

277. Copyright Act of 1909, § 5(a).

278. Ginsburg, *supra* note 261, at 1895.

279. *Jeweler's Circular Publishing Co., supra* note 276, at 88.

from the same common sources of information."[280] "Sweat of the brow" holdings therefore ignored a fundamental axiom of copyright law—that facts alone are simply not copyrightable.[281]

Supreme Court decisions applying the 1909 Act firmly rejected this new doctrine, however. For example, in *International News Service v. Associated Press*,[282] the Court held the Act conferred protection only on those elements of a work original to the author. Recognizing Section 5 specifically mentioned "periodicals, including newspapers," the Court acknowledged news articles were copyrightable,[283] but flatly rejected that protection also extended to the factual information contained therein by holding that "[t]he news element—the information respecting current events contained in the literary production—is not the creation of the writer, but is a report of matters that ordinarily are *publici juris*."[284]

The "sweat of the brow" doctrine indisputably flouted basic copyright principles. Throughout history, copyright law has "recognized a greater need to disseminate factual works than works of fiction or fantasy."[285] But the "industrious collection" cases took a contrary view by deciding authors were precluded from saving time and effort by using material contained in prior works. In truth, "it is just such wasted effort that the proscription against the copyright of ideas and facts [was] designed to prevent."[286] "Protection for the fruits of such research . . . may in certain circumstances be available under a theory of unfair competition. But to accord copyright protection on this basis alone distorts [the law] in that it creates a monopoly in public domain materials without the necessary justification of protecting and encouraging the creation of 'writings' by 'authors.'"[287]

After taking into account the aforementioned precedents and analysis, the federal district court in *Zeidenberg* found for the Defendant and ruled that the names, addresses, and other information downloaded from the Pro CD product were not eligible for copyright protection. Specifically,

---

280. *Id.* at 88–89 (internal quotations omitted).

281. *Miller, supra* note 251, at 1372 (criticizing "sweat of the brow" courts because "ensuring that later writers obtain the facts independently . . . is precisely the scope of protection given . . . copyrighted matter, and the law is clear that facts are not entitled to such protection").

282. 248 U.S. 215 (1918).

283. *Id.* at 234.

284. *Id.*

285. *Harper & Row, supra* note 237, at 563; *See also* Gorman, *Fact or Fancy: The Implications for Copyright*, 29 J. Copyright Soc. 560, 563 (1982).

286. *Rosemont Enterprises, Inc. v. Random House, Inc.*, 366 F.2d 303, 310 (2d Cir. 1966), *cert. denied*, 385 U.S. 1009 (1967).

287. *Nimmer on Copyright* § 3.04.

the court held such a "collection of facts arranged in a commonplace, non-original fashion"[288] lacked both the necessary elements of originality and creativity. The district court further dispensed with the "sweat of the brow" doctrine by writing: "Without originality, time and effort do not factor into the copyright equation."[289]

In light of rulings such as *Zeidenberg* and in response to pressure from commercial vendors, legislation was introduced in Congress to deter the reproduction of factual information from subscription or purchased databases. One such bill, known as the Database and Collections of Information Misappropriation Act (DCIMA),[290] would target anyone who copies large portions of factual databases, "such as those containing on-line legal records, stock quotes, school data, sports scores, among other widely circulated nuggets of information."[291] While proponents argue the bill affects only those causing financial harm to corporations, its critics contend the law would place "news and other public knowledge under corporate lock and key."[292]

Supporting the bill's passage were groups and companies such as the Software Information Industry of America, Reed Elsevier, owner of LEXIS-NEXIS, and a myriad of small and large domestic database compilers. On the other side, the legislation was criticized by both educational and library organizations, including the Association of American Universities, the National Association of State Universities and Land Grant Colleges, the American Council of Education, the National Academies, and the American Association for the Advancement of Science.[293]

If enacted, the DCIMA would impose liability on anyone who, without authorization, made available in commerce a quantitatively substantial part of the information contained in another person's qualifying database. Qualifying databases must be "generated, gathered, or maintained through a substantial expenditure of financial resources or time." Thus, the bill would protect collections of facts merely because they arose from the "sweat of the brow" of their creator, a principle clearly rejected by the U.S. Supreme Court.

---

288. *Zeidenberg, supra* note 236, at 647.

289. *Id.*

290. H.R. 3261, 108th Cong., 1st Sess. (2002).

291. C. Murray, *Database-Protection Bill Raises Copyright Concerns*, eSchool News Online (Apr. 1, 2004), http://www.eschoolnews.com/news/top-news/index.cfm?i=35699&CFID=3832484&CFTOKEN=93671806.

292. *Id.*

293. *Id.* at 2.

The DCIMA would provide exceptions for (1) independently generated or gathered information; (2) certain reasonable use by nonprofit educational, scientific, or research institutions ("exempted institutions"); (3) hyperlinking one online location to another; and (4) making information available for the primary purpose of news reporting. The proposed legislation further absolves from liability any employees of exempted institutions acting within the scope of their employment or any students enrolled thereat. The bill provides for civil remedies, including temporary and permanent injunctions, monetary relief for damages, and impoundment of infringing copies. Any action to be brought thereunder would have to be commenced within two years after it arises.

Critics of the proposed measure contend it is critically vague on several points. First, it imposes civil liability upon anyone who copies a "quantitatively substantial" portion of a database without ever defining that term. Second, while it creates a "news reporting" exception, liability is still assessed if "the information is time sensitive and has been gathered by a news reporting entity . . . for the purpose of direct competition." Unfortunately, the bill fails to define such key terms as "time-sensitive," "news reporting entity," or "direct competition." One wonders, when is news is no longer time-sensitive? Isn't timeliness always the essence of "news"? What qualifies as a "news reporting entity"? Traditional sources of information, certainly, but what about political talk-show hosts or Internet bloggers? And who is really in "direct competition" with *The New York Times*? The *Washington Post*, probably, but what about the *Des Moines Register* or the local, small-town paper?[294] These questions are all left unanswered by the DCIMA.

Representatives of educational institutions and libraries have expressed their own set of concerns. Some believe database producers have not suffered any significant commercial harm from occasional data extraction.[295] Critics further point out the exception for exempted institutions applies only if a court "determines that the making available in commerce of the information in the database [was] reasonable under the circumstances, taking into consideration the customary practices associated with such uses." As such, any decision regarding what constitutes permissible conduct is made "*post facto* and only when such schools have already been

---

294. B. Karl, *How the Current Congressional Database Protection Bill Would Go Beyond Current Law*, Findlaw.com (Feb. 11, 2004), http://writ.news.findlaw.com/student/20040211_Karl.html.

295. Letter from Susan E. Fox, Executive Director, American Association of Law Libraries, to James Sensenbrenner, Jr., Chair, House Committee on the Judiciary, Washington Affairs Online (Sept. 4, 2003), http://www.arl.org/bm~doc/sensentauzin0903.pdf.

forced into a court under an allegation of misappropriation and a threat of quadruple damages."[296]

Finally, critics contend the bill does not ensure federally assembled information will remain in the public domain. For example, a publisher incorporating statistics compiled by the U.S. Government into his database could theoretically prevent others from subsequently using the data.[297] Such a result would directly contravene the congressional objective of making works of the federal government ineligible for copyright protection.[298]

---

296. *Id.* at 2.
297. *Id.*
298. 17 U.S.C. § 105 provides in pertinent part that "Copyright protection . . . is not available for works of the United States Government."

Request for Permission for Classroom Use

[INSTITUTION'S OR PERSON'S LETTERHEAD]

[Date]

[Name and address of copyright
owner or publisher]

Dear [Ms.] [Mr.]:

I am a [professor][teacher][instructor] of [course subject] at [name of
school] in   [city]   ,   [state]   . I would like to copy
and distribute the following material to students in my course(s)
entitled   [name of course(s)]   .

Title of Work: _____

Edition or Date:_____

Author:_____

Publisher:_____

Portion(s) of work to be used:_____

_____

_____

_____

[Describe by pages, sections, chapters, etc.]

This class is taught _____ times per academic year and I anticipate the material will be distributed to approximately _____ students.

Your work will contain your copyright notice and the statement: "Reprinted by permission of [name of copyright holder] from [title, edition, publisher, and date of work used]." If you would prefer some other type of credit, please write it in the space provided on the next page.

You may indicate your consent by signing the enclosed copy of this letter and returning it in the pre-addressed envelope. Also, please inform me of the name and address of any other person whose consent is required to use this material by completing the appropriate section on the next page.

Sincerely,

[name of person seeking permission]
[title]

I hereby grant my consent to use the material described on the first page of this letter in the manner set forth herein.

_____

[Legal name of copyright holder, if not a person]

By: _____
               [Signature]

Name: _____
                      [Please print]

Title: _____

Date: _____

Alternative form of credit requested:

_____

_____

_____

Other person to contact for consent:

Name: _____

Address: _____

Telephone No.: _____

Fax No.: _____

E-mail address: _____

Request for Permission to Publish

[INSTITUTION'S OR PERSON'S LETTERHEAD]

[Date]

[Name and address of copyright
owner or publisher]

Dear [Ms.] [Mr.]:

I am a [professor][teacher][instructor] of __[course subject]__ at ___[name of
school]__ in __[city]__ , ___[state]__ . I am preparing an [article][book][paper]
on the topic of _____ for publication [in or by]
_____. In doing so, I would like to use an
excerpt from your copyrighted work more fully described below. I would
greatly appreciate your consent in doing so.

Title of Work: _____

Edition or Date:_____

Author:_____

Publisher:_____

Portion(s) of work to be used:_____

_____

_____

[Describe by pages, sections, chapters, etc.]

Your work will contain your copyright notice and the statement "Reprinted by permission of [name of copyright holder] from [title, edition, publisher and date of work used]." If you would prefer some other type of credit, please write it in the space provided on the next page.

You may indicate your consent by signing the enclosed copy of this letter and returning it in the pre-addressed envelope. Also, please inform me of the name and address of any other person whose consent is required to use this material by completing the appropriate section on the next page.

Sincerely,

[name of person seeking permission]
[title]

I hereby grant my consent to use the material described on the first page of this letter in the manner set forth herein.

_____

[Legal name of copyright holder, if not a person]

By: _____

               [Signature]

Name: _____

                   [Please print]

Title: _____

Date: _____

Alternative form of credit requested:

_____

_____

_____

Other person to contact for consent:

Name: _____

Address: _____

Telephone No.: _____

Fax No.: _____

E-mail address: _____

CHAPTER 5

Distance Learning and the Internet

As more and more colleges and local school systems incorporate the Internet into their curriculums, using it both to offer online courses and supplement traditional classes, a growing interrelationship between the World Wide Web (the "WWW" or "Web") and educational distance learning has developed. The first three parts of this chapter address questions instructors at all levels must now face, such as:

- May I copy items from other Internet sites?
- May I freely link to the websites of others?
- Does the First Amendment protect linking as "speech"?
- Who owns a joint work posted by only one author?
- Does the institution or the instructor own the electronic course?

Section 5.4 of the chapter covers the Digital Millennium Copyright Act and the potential liability of educational institutions as Internet service providers thereunder. Section 5.5 discusses recent efforts to protect students from harmful influences found on the Internet.

5.1 COPYING AND LINKING ON THE WORLD WIDE WEB

[1] Principles of Law and the WWW

Thomas Jefferson once wrote:

> I am not an advocate for frequent changes in laws and constitutions. But laws and institutions must go hand and hand with the progress of the human mind. As that becomes more developed, more enlightened, as new discoveries are made, new truths discovered and manners and opinions change, with the change of

circumstances, institutions must advance also to keep pace with the times. We might as well require a man to wear the coat which fitted him when a boy.[1]

The lament that the law often struggles to keep stride with societal changes is a common one.[2] Nowhere has this gap been more pronounced than in the inability of legislative efforts to maintain pace with technological advances. While technology often moves at lightning speed, the law generally follows behind at a snail's pace.[3] One of the most problematic areas has been attempting to apply traditional legal concepts to the quickly evolving world of the Internet.[4]

The United States Supreme Court has described the WWW as "a vast library including millions of readily available and indexed publications" as well as "a sprawling mall offering goods and services."[5] Legal doctrines such as defamation, privacy, and contract law typically involved with other modes of publication do not translate well into Internet-related issues.[6] The Internet has also been called a "new frontier," where traditional legal principles "no longer seem to apply."[7] Recognizing that existing law was not created with the Internet in mind, one federal judge recently analogized the situation to "trying to board a moving bus."[8]

Copyright law and its application to the Internet suffers from the same fate and carries with it a host of misperceptions. Therefore, the remainder of Section 5.1 of this chapter is devoted to clarifying issues particularly relevant to educators regarding copying and linking to materials on the WWW.

---

1. Inscription at Jefferson Memorial in Washington, D.C.

2. *See* Tucker, *Information Superhighway Robbery: The Tortious Misuses of Links, Frames, Metatags and Domain Names*, 4 Va. J.L. & Tech. 8 (1999) (hereinafter "Tucker"), at *1 (Westlaw edition), citing *Klingenberg v. City of Raleigh*, 194 S.E. 297, 301 (N.C. 1937).

3. Tucker at *1, *citing* Howe, *Legal Tangles in the Web; Tips for Meeting Professionals on Setting Up Web Sites*, 33 Meetings & Conventions 36 (1998).

4. Tucker at *3. For a detailed discussion of the history and development of the Internet, *see* Beal, *The Potential Liability of Linking on the Internet: An Examination of Possible Legal Solutions*, 1998 BYU L. Rev. 703 (1998); *Reno v. ACLU*, 521 U.S. 844, 117 S. Ct. 2329, 2334 (1997).

5. Tucker at *9, *citing Reno, supra* note 4, at 2334.

6. Raysman & Brown, *Dangerous Liaisons: The Legal Risks of Linking Web Sites*, N.Y.L.J., April 8, 1997, at 3.

7. Tucker at *18, *citing* Davidson and Engisch, *Trademark Misuse in Domain Name Disputes*, 13 Computer Law 13 (1996).

8. Judge Ellsworth Van Graafeiland, *writing in Bensusan Restaurant Corp. v. King*, 937 F. Supp. 295 (S.D.N.Y. 1996), *aff'd,*126 F.3d 25, 27 (2d Cir. 1997).

[2] Using Materials from the Internet

One prevalent misperception is that material posted on the Internet is not subject to copyright protection and may, therefore, be freely copied and distributed by anyone accessing it. Several reasons account for this erroneous point of view. First, as mentioned above, recent court cases and legal commentators have noted traditional legal concepts do not always apply to the Internet. This does not mean, however, that *no* laws attach to the Web. Second, many laypersons simply misinterpret the term "public domain." They assume anything made available to the "public" without cost is placed in a "domain" where it can be used for any purpose. As discussed in Chapter Two, however, *public domain* is a legal term of art and means that copyright protection for a work has either expired or never existed in the first place.

Third, the ease of copying items on the Web leads many to conclude that the rules have changed. The WWW was not the first product to make reproduction and redistribution easier, however. Copy machines facilitated photocopying text, the VCR made it possible to tape movies, and floppy disks made it simpler to replicate computer programs.[9] No one would suggest these works are now subject to less protection just because the technology used to reproduce them has become more advanced and available.

Fourth, the absence of a copyright notice on many Internet sites causes some to assume the works located there are unprotected. As explained in Chapter Two, though, since American entry into the Berne Convention (the major international copyright treaty), affixing notice to a work is no longer needed to secure copyright protection for it. Other than originality and creativity, the only requirement is fixation of the work "in any tangible medium of expression . . . from which it can be perceived, reproduced or otherwise communicated, either directly or with the aid of a machine or device."[10] As such, once something is written on a piece of paper, spoken into a dictating machine, recorded on an audiocassette, or placed on film, it enjoys copyright protection. Similarly, loading items onto a disk or server, scanning pictures into a computer, or posting articles on a website all constitute sufficient fixation to qualify the work for copyright protection.[11]

Hence, the same principles used to protect works such as books, magazines, records, and film apply to the Internet as well. For instance, something seemingly as innocent as placing a picture of yourself or a colleague on your website can result in problems. The copyright of your picture may, for

---

9. *See* Oppedahl & Larson, *Web Law FAQ*, http://www.patents.com/weblaw.htm (hereinafter "Oppedahl & Larson").

10. 17 U.S.C. § 102(a).

11. *See* Chapter Two, Section 2.1[2][a].

instance, belong to the professional photographer who took it. Your colleague may need to sign a "model" release before his or her picture can be used.[12] Again, the safest course of action in such cases is to use only items already in the public domain or to obtain permission from the work's creator.

By the same token, the fair use doctrine,[13] which allows others to use portions of works without obtaining the author's permission, also applies to items placed on the WWW. To determine if the use is appropriate, the same four factors: *(1) the purpose for which the work will be used, (2) the amount of the work taken, (3) the nature of the original work, and (4) the impact of the use on the work's potential market or value,* must be taken into account, just as for published and recorded works. De minimis use would also be permitted,[14] as would the performance and display of certain legally obtained works in the course of nonprofit educational teaching pursuant to Sections 110(1) and 110(2) of the Copyright Act.[15]

Can applying traditional copyright principles to the Internet create a trap for the unwary user? Perhaps. For instance, since the law deems a typical website viewer to be "copying" the visited page in his computer's RAM, does that subject him to an infringement action? What if he "saves" material from the site on his hard drive or prints out a portion for later reference? Is that also potentially copyright infringement? The answer to the above questions, with some qualifiers, is no. While courts generally afford web page creators the same protections as book publishers, recording artists and filmmakers, they also understand the unique nature of the WWW and do not intend it as a legal minefield for the everyday Internet user.

Common sense dictates that if someone places material on his or her website, that person wishes others to see it. It would certainly be disingenuous for that person to create a web page and then turn around and institute copyright infringement actions against those visiting her site. To avoid these absurd consequences, courts have developed the notion of an "implied license,"[16] which permits someone engaging in normal Internet

---

12. Oppedahl & Larson at 3.

13. *See* Chapter Three for a detailed discussion the doctrine of fair use.

14. *See* discussion of copyright infringement defenses in Chapter Two, Section 2.1[8][f].

15. *See* Chapter Six, Section 6.3[2][a], for a detailed discussion of these educational use exemptions.

16. *Field v. Google, Inc.,* No. CV-S-04-0413-RCJ-LRL, slip op. at 10 (D. Nev. Jan. 12, 2006) ("An implied license can be found where the copyright holder engages in conduct from which the other party may properly infer that the owner consents to his use.") (internal citations omitted).

activity—viewing web pages,[17] bookmarking sites, and printing out text for personal use—to do so without triggering infringement liability.[18] This implied license has its limits, however. Just as with books and records, the Internet visitor cannot use this "license" to engage in wholesale copying and distribution of the protected work.[19]

As a general rule, unless it is for purely noncommercial and personal use, it is best not to copy large amounts of material from the Internet. If one wishes to share Web material with others, the best course of action is simply to provide a link to the site. Usually, one may link to the websites of others without triggering legal liability. However, as with all rules, exceptions exist. The next two subsections of this chapter deal with the legal implications of linking to websites and focus primarily on copyright issues associated therewith.

[3] The Use and Misuse of Links on the Internet

Three methods are customarily used to reach a site on the Web: (1) typing in its URL,[20] (2) using a search engine, or (3) linking directly to it. Linking is a major underpinning of the WWW.[21] Typically, a website can be viewed or linked to without the need to obtain prior consent.[22] Unlimited accessibility is part of the Web's culture.[23] Linking is even considered an advantage to the linked-to site.[24] As noted above, creating a website generally carries with it an implied license for others to link to it.[25] Therefore, absent trademark or copyright infringement, or breach of contract, establishing a link to another site is almost always permissible.[26] The possible exceptions thereto are discussed in the next three subsections.

[a] Copyright Infringement Claims

Unfortunately, due to the dearth of case law in the area, it is difficult to set forth clear guidelines involving copyright and linking. A few simple rules

---

17. Typical web browsing has also been held to constitute fair use. *See Perfect 10, Inc. v. Google, Inc.*, 416 F. Supp. 828, 852 n.17 (C.D. Cal. 2006); *Religious Technology Center v. Netcom On-Line Communications Services*, 907 F. Supp. 1361, 1378 n.25 (N.D. Cal. 1995).

18. Oppedahl & Larson at 2.

19. *Id.*

20. "URL" is an acronym for "uniform resource locator," the Internet address that identifies the location of a file in the Internet's infrastructure. *See In re DoubleClick Inc. Privacy Litig.*, 154 F. Supp. 2d 497, 501 (S.D.N.Y. 2001).

21. Tucker at *25.

22. *Id.*

23. Tucker at *25; *Potential Liability of Linking, supra* note 4, at 705.

24. Tucker at *26.

25. Madoff, *Freedom to Link Under Attack*, N.Y.L.J., June 23, 1997, at 51.

26. Tucker at *26.

should be followed, however. To begin with, citing a URL as a link does not constitute copyright infringement, because a URL is not copyrightable.[27] This locator functions more as a street address, merely directing someone to where information on the WWW can be found. As such, it contains no creative or original content protected by copyright.[28] However, arrangements of URLs found at a site may be subject to copyright protection because such organized selections may be deemed expression.[29]

It is now generally accepted, though, that merely linking to a website does not involve copyright infringement.[30] The main reason is that no copying of the website is involved. This notion was recently called into question, however, by a Federal circuit court. In *Kelly v. Arriba Soft Corporation*,[31] the Ninth Circuit affirmed in part and reversed in part a decision of the U.S. District Court for the Central District of California.[32] *Kelly* involved the application of copyright law to the world of Internet search engines.

The plaintiff, Leslie Kelly, was a professional photographer who had copyrighted many of his pictures of the American West. Some of these images were located on Kelly's website, while others were on sites personally licensed by him. The defendant, Arriba Soft Corp., operated an Internet search engine that displayed its results in the form of small pictures, called "thumbnails," rather than text. Arriba obtained its database of pictures by copying images from other websites. By clicking on one of these thumbnails, the user could then view a larger version of that same picture on the Arriba web page.

When Kelly discovered his photographs were part of Arriba's search engine database, he sued for copyright infringement. The District Court found Arriba's reproduction and display to constitute a noninfringing "fair use" under Section 107 of the Copyright Act. The Ninth Circuit upheld the District Court's ruling of fair use. The second part of the lower court's decision, however, concerned Arriba's inline linking to and framing of Kelly's full-sized images. This use did not entail copying but, rather, "import-

---

27. *Dangerous Liaisons, supra* note 6, at 3.
28. *Id.*
29. *Id.*
30. *See, e.g.,* Tucker at *36 ("The prevailing view is that a hypertext (HREF) link cannot constitute a basis for copyright infringement. . . ."); Gomez, *Washington Post v. Total News,* 13 Berkeley Tech. L.J. 21 (1998) ("Currently, there is an absence of case law addressing whether linking constitutes the creation of a 'copy' of another work. A technical understanding of linking suggests that it does not.").
31. 2002 U.S. App. LEXIS 1786 (9th Cir. 2002).
32. *Kelly v. Arriba Soft Corp.,* 77 F. Supp. 2d 116 (C.D. Cal. 1999).

ing" the images directly from Kelly's website. Therefore, the court could not find copyright infringement based on the *reproduction* of those works. Instead, this use of Kelly's images potentially infringed upon his exclusive right to "display the copyrighted work publicly."[33]

The Court reasoned that for plaintiff to prevail, Arriba must have displayed Kelly's works without his permission and made those displays available to the public. The Copyright Act defines "display" as showing a *copy* of a work.[34] Since Arriba made no copies, this would seem to have negated Kelly's argument. However, the act defines a copy as a material object in which a work is fixed, including the material object in which the work is *first* fixed.[35] The legislative history of the Copyright Act clarifies that "since 'copies' are defined as including the material object 'in which the work is first fixed,' the right of public display applies to original works of art as well as to reproductions of them."[36] By inline linking and framing Kelly's images,[37] the court found Arriba was showing Kelly's original works without his permission.

The legislative history of the Copyright Act also states that "'display' . . . include[s] the projection of an image on a screen or other surface by any method, the transmission of an image by electronic or other means, and the showing of an image on a cathode ray tube, or similar viewing apparatus connected with any sort of information storage and retrieval system."[38] This language supported the notion that showing Kelly's images on a computer screen constituted a display thereof.

The Copyright Act's definition of "publicly" encompasses a transmission of a display to the public "by means of any device or process, whether the members of the public capable of receiving the performance or display receive it in the same place or in separate places and at the same time or at different times."[39] A display is public even if none of its potential recipients were operating their receiving apparatus at the time of the transmission.[40] By making Kelly's images available on its website, the court found Arriba

---

33. 17 U.S.C. § 106(5).

34. 17 U.S.C. § 101.

35. *Id.*

36. H.R. Rep. No. 1476, 94th Cong., 2d Sess. 64 (1976) (hereinafter *House Report*).

37. While traditional "blue-underlined" linking, inline linking and framing may show up differently on a user's browser, "they are all fundamentally just 'links'—addresses where content may be found." Brief of Amicus Curiae, Electronic Frontier Foundation, at 7, *Perfect 10, Inc. v. Google, Inc.*, Case No. 06-55405, slip. op. (9th Cir. May 16, 2007).

38. *House Report* at 64.

39. 17 U.S.C. § 101.

40. *House Report* at 64–65.

was allowing public access to them. The ability to view those images was thus unrestricted to anyone with a computer and Internet access.

The court further noted the legislative history of the Copyright Act emphasized the broad nature of the display right, citing that "each and every method by which the images or sounds comprising a performance or display are picked up and conveyed is a 'transmission,' and if the transmission reaches the public in [any] form, the case comes within the scope of [the public performance and display rights] of section 106."[41] Looking strictly at the act's language and legislative history, the court concluded that when Arriba imported Kelly's images through its own web page, it had infringed upon Kelly's public display right.

As such, this panel of the Ninth Circuit (the "Panel") announced an unprecedented rule that would have imposed strict liability for "in-line" linking. If this ruling had been permitted to stand, many links on the Web would have given rise to a prima facie case of direct copyright infringement, and thus imposed strict liability on the link provider absent an affirmative defense or statutory exception.[42]

As discussed above, one of the Web's great strengths as a communications medium stems from its pervasive use of "hyperlinking"—the ability to embed in one document pointers to others. As one federal district court recently wrote:

> Links are what unify the [World Wide] Web into a single body of knowledge, and what makes the Web unique. . . . They often are used in ways that do a great deal to promote the free exchange of ideas and information that is a central value of our nation. Anything that would impose strict liability on a Web site operator for the entire contents of any Web site to which the operator linked therefore would raise grave constitutional concerns, as Web site operators would be inhibited from linking for fear of exposure to liability.[43]

Fortunately, the Ninth Circuit apparently realized the maelstrom its opinion would create and eventually withdrew it, ruling instead that a search engine's use of copyrighted photographs was a transformative fair use used to "improve access to information on the Internet."[44] The origi-

---

41. *Id.* at 64.

42. *See Religious Technology Center, supra* note 17, at 1367 n.10 (direct copyright infringement is a strict liability offense).

43. *Universal City Studios v. Reimerdes,* 111 F. Supp. 2d 294, 340 (S.D.N.Y. 2000) (hereinafter *Universal I*); *aff'd,* 273 F.3d 429 (2d Cir. 2001).

44. *Kelly v. Arriba Soft Corp.,* 336 F.3d 811, 819 (9th Cir. 2003).

nal Panel apparently went astray by failing to recognize "what [was] being transmitted and by whom."[45] While it correctly recognized infringement required a transmission of a display to the public, the only thing being "transmitted" by Arriba in this case was a URL, a bit of text instructing a viewer's web browser to retrieve an image directly from another server. As even the Panel recognized, Arriba did not itself reproduce or transmit the copyrighted images.[46]

Current case law also "provide[d] no support for the Panel's radical expansion of the public display right. No court has ever held a defendant directly liable for infringement under the transmit . . . to the public aspect of the public display right where he did not transmit the work, but rather caused a transmission by a third party."[47] Even in the cases cited by the Panel, the defendant directly transmitted the work.[48] Both in *Playboy Enters., Inc. v. Webbworld, Inc.,*[49] and *Playboy Enters., Inc. v. Russ Hardenburgh, Inc.,*[50] the defendants were chiefly involved in uploading and downloading images and transmitting them to other sites.[51] Thus, both cases "[stood] for the well-established proposition that a re-transmitter [could] be held directly liable for violating a copyright owner's public display or performance right,"[52] but not someone who merely causes a third party (in this case, the original website) to do the same.[53]

In another important case involving the confluence of linking and copyright, a California federal district court considered a dispute between two online ticket vendors.[54] In that case, the website of plaintiffs Ticketmaster Corporation and Ticketmaster Online-City Search, Inc. (hereinafter, collectively, "Ticketmaster") allowed consumers to purchase tickets to various events through an Internet connection. The site's home page contained instructions and a directory to subsequent event pages. These pages provided basic information (e.g., event, date, time, place, and price) and explained how to order tickets. Each event page was identifiable with an

---

45. *See* Brief of Amicus Curiae, Electronic Frontier Foundation (hereinafter "EFF Brief"), at 3, *Kelly v. Arriba Soft Corp.,* Case No. CV 99-560 (C.D. Calf. 2002).

46. *Kelly v. Arriba Soft Corp.,* 2002 WL 181351 (9th Cir. Feb. 6, 2002), at *8–9.

47. EFF Brief, *supra* note 45, at 4.

48. *Id.*

49. 991 F. Supp. 543 (N.D. Tex. 1997).

50. 982 F. Supp. 503 (N.D. Ohio 1997).

51. *See id.* at 505.

52. EFF Brief, *supra* note 45, at 5.

53. While search engines may indirectly promote transmissions by infringing websites, "[m]erely encouraging or facilitating those activities is not prescribed by the statute." *Hardenburgh, supra* note 50, at 512.

54. *Ticketmaster Corp. v. Tickets.com, Inc.,* 2000 U.S. Dist. LEXIS 4553 (C.D. Cal. 2002).

electronic address. Ticketmaster often had exclusive agreements with the events it carried so that tickets were not usually available elsewhere.

The defendant, Tickets.com, Inc. (hereinafter, "Tickets"), also operated a website that offered a somewhat different service. While Tickets sold admission to certain events on its own, it also provided information as to where and how the tickets it did not sell could be obtained. In such cases, its customers were provided with a link to another ticket broker or online seller. In many instances, the customer was immediately transferred to an interior web page of Ticketmaster (bypassing the home page) for the particular event, where he or she could then buy tickets.

To obtain information on Ticketmaster events, Tickets was alleged to have copied the interior web pages of Ticketmaster and extracted the basic raw data (event, place, time, date, and price) from them. Such information was then placed in a slightly different format on Tickets' own web pages. Tickets never copied the actual Ticketmaster event page; but, by the use of hyperlinking, simply "transferred" the customer there. In its suit, Ticketmaster claimed that posting the factual information derived from the Ticketmaster interior web pages on Tickets' site constituted infringement. The court promptly rejected that argument by acknowledging copyright could not be used to protect factual data.[55] While the expression, organization, and placement of facts could be protected, Tickets was not alleged to have copied the method of presentation. Rather, it had extracted the data and presented it in its own format. The court analogized this to taking historical facts from a reference work and reciting them in a different medium.

Most importantly, the court ruled that hyperlinking to the interior pages of the Ticketmaster site did not violate the Copyright Act, since no actual copying was involved. The court saw linking for what it truly was—the customer being automatically transferred to the particular web page of the original author. The court found no deception or confusion in what was happening. It simply compared the activity to using a library's card index to obtain references to particular items, albeit faster and more efficiently.

[b] Trademark Infringement Claims

The act of linking to sites has also occasionally resulted in trademark infringement or dilution claims being brought against the linker. In *Playboy Enterprises, Inc. v. Universal Tel-A-Talk*,[56] for instance, the defendant

---

55. *See, e.g., Feist Publications, Inc. v. Rural Telephone Service Company*, 499 U.S. 340 (1991).

56. 1998 U.S. Dist. LEXIS 17282 (E.D. Pa. 1998).

created and maintained several websites containing pornographic pictures. Playboy Enterprises, Inc. (hereinafter, "PEI") subsequently learned that Universal-Tel-A-Talk, Inc. was using PEI's registered trademarks PLAYBOY and BUNNY to advertise their photographs online. The defendant had also used the term "Bunny" on its navigational bar and "linked" its adult-sex website to PEI's site at "Playboy.com."

PEI sued defendant for infringement of the PLAYBOY trademark under Sections 32 and 43(a) of the Lanham Act and for trademark dilution. The test for infringement is typically whether the alleged action created a likelihood of confusion.[57] To succeed on the merits, a plaintiff must establish that its marks (1) are valid and legally protectable; (2) are owned by him or it; and (3) if used by the defendant, will likely create confusion concerning the origin thereof.[58]

In determining whether a likelihood of confusion exists, courts take into account: (1) the degree of similarity between the owner's mark and the alleged infringing one; (2) the strength of the owner's mark; (3) the price of the goods and other factors indicative of the care and attention expected of consumers when making a purchase; (4) the length of time the defendant has used the mark without evidence of actual confusion arising; (5) the intent of the defendant in adopting the mark; (6) any evidence of actual confusion; (7) whether the goods, though not competing, are marketed through the same channels of trade and advertised through the same media; (8) the extent to which the targets of the parties' sales efforts are similar; (9) the relationship of the goods in the minds of the public because of the proximity of function; and (10) other facts suggesting the consuming public might expect the prior owner to manufacture a product in the defendant's market.[59]

In *Universal Tel-A-Talk*, Defendant's use of the words "Playboy" and "Bunny" on its website and the identifying directories were identical to PEI's duly registered trademarks. PEI's registered trademarks had previously been adjudicated as very strong.[60] Suggestive marks are normally entitled to protection without proof of secondary meaning.[61] The court

---

57. *See Scott Paper Co. v. Scott's Liquid Gold*, 589 F.2d 1225 (3d Cir. 1978).

58. *Opticians Ass'n v. Independent Opticians*, 920 F.2d 187, 192 (3d Cir. 1990).

59. *Scott Paper Co., supra* note 57, at 1229.

60. *See Playboy Enterprises, Inc. v. Chuckleberry Pub, Inc.*, 687 F.2d 563 (2d Cir. 1982).

61. *See, e.g., Dominion Bankshares Corp. v. Devon Holding Co., Inc.*, 690 F. Supp. 338, 345 (E.D. Pa. 1988); *American Diabetes Assn. v. National Diabetes Ass'n*, 533 F. Supp. 16, 214 U.S.P.Q. 231, 233 (E.D. Pa. 1981).

found the PLAYBOY trademark was already famous, and had acquired significant secondary meaning, such that the public had come to always associate it with PEI. Thus, the court ruled that the defendant had intentionally adopted the PLAYBOY and BUNNY trademarks in an effort to capitalize on PEI's established reputation. Significantly, the court found such intent was further evidenced by Defendant's establishment of a link between its website and that of PEI.[62]

The court next took up the dilution claim. "Dilution" refers to the lessening of a mark's distinctiveness. Factors considered in determining its existence are (1) similarity of the marks; (2) similarity of the products covered; (3) sophistication of customers; (4) predatory intent; (5) renown of the senior mark; (6) renown of the junior mark; (7) duration and extent of advertising of the mark; (8) geographical extent of the trading area in which the mark is used; and (9) the nature and extent of the mark's use by third parties.[63] Applying the foregoing factors, the court concluded PEI has established its dilution claims with respect to the PLAYBOY trademark.

The court's holding was thus "consistent with the generally accepted rule that using someone else's trade name, trademark, or protected logo as the *icon* for the *hyperlink* can constitute trademark infringement."[64] The use of a trademarked name (e.g., "Goodyear.com") as the URL of a hyperlink, standing alone, however, usually constitutes "a fair and descriptive use of the mark."[65] Thus, while including the URL of a site is unlikely to constitute a trademark violation, the use of another's distinctive logo to serve as the hypertext link could amount to infringement. Infringement is even more likely to be found if there is an express or implied suggestion the person using the "logo-link" is somehow affiliated with the linked-to site, when, in fact, no business connection exists.[66]

---

62. The Court also found that evidence of actual confusion was not required. *See, e.g., Coach Leatherware Co. v. Ann Taylor, Inc.*, 933 F.2d 162 (2d Cir. 1991); *Lois Sportswear U.S.A., Inc. v. Levi Strauss & Co.*, 631 F. Supp. 735, 743 (S.D.N.Y.), *aff'd*, 799 F.2d 867 (2d Cir. 1986); *Brockum Co. v. Blaylock*, 729 F. Supp. 438, 445 (E.D. Pa. 1990) (lack of evidence of actual confusion is not a bar to injunctive relief).

63. 15 U.S.C. § 1125(c)(1); *Wawa, Inc. v. Haaf*, 1996 U.S. Dist. LEXIS 11494 (E.D. Pa. 1996) (citing *Mead Data, Inc. v. Toyota Motor Sales*, 875 F.2d 1026, 1035 (2d Cir. 1989) (Sweet, J. concurring)).

64. Tucker at *42.

65. *Id.*

66. Levi, *Web-site Hypertext Links Raise Issues of Control*, Nat'l L.J., Aug. 12, 1996, at B12.

[c] Breach of Contract Claims

At common law, a contract is formed when parties manifest mutual, voluntary assent to be bound by a set of terms—typically through an offer and acceptance.[67] In the world of Internet contracting, one key question is whether an electronic offer and the simple use of the "accept" or "return" key in response thereto constitutes assent.[68] A second issue is whether such assent meets the mirror image rule—that is, whether there was a "meeting of the minds."[69] If the seller provides an online contract form with terms that are essentially nonnegotiable, then, like the "shrink-wrap" licenses used by software publishers,[70] the purchaser can only accept or reject the terms. If the purchaser accepts, the mirror image rule is met. However, when a consumer assents to such a "standard form" contract, and there is no alternative source for a similar service, the result may be a contract of adhesion.[71]

Assent in contracts of adhesion has been considered in the context of online services.[72] While there is no clear "rule," a traditional analysis looks to the reasonableness of terms and the applicability of the agreement's conditions to similarly situated parties.[73] The status of shrink-wrap licenses for software provides some guidance; however, these contracts have not been treated consistently by those courts looking at them.[74] In some cases, the U.C.C. has been applied, thus avoiding the question of adhesion by

---

67. *See* J. Calamari & J. Perillo, *The Law of Contracts* 25 (3d ed. 1987).

68. In *Corinthian Pharmaceutical v. Lederle Laboratories*, the court found that the "automated, ministerial act" of a seller issuing an electronic order tracking number to a purchaser's online purchase order did *not* constitute assent or acceptance by the seller. *See* 724 F. Supp. 605, 610 (S.D. Ind. 1989); *see also* B. Wright, *The Law of Electronic Commerce* 235, 236 (1991); Electronic Messaging Task Force, *The Commercial Use of Electronic Data Interchange—A Report and Model Trading Partner Agreement*, A.B.A. Sec. Bus. Law, *reprinted from* 45 Bus. Law 1647 (1990).

69. *See Step-Saver Data Systems, Inc. v. Wyse Technology*, 939 F.2d 91 (3d Cir. 1991).

70. *See id.* at 96 n.7.

71. *See Standard Oil Co. v. Perkins*, 347 F.2d 379, 385 n.5 (9th Cir. 1965).

72. *Compare* Johnson & Marks, *Mapping Electronic Data Communications onto Existing Legal Metaphors: Should We Let Our Conscience (and Our Contracts) be Our Guide?*, 38 Vill. L. Rev. 487, 488–89 (1993) *with* Note, *Offers Users Can't Refuse: Shrink-Wrap License Agreements as Enforceable Adhesion Contracts*, 10 Cardozo L. Rev. 2105, 2120 (1989).

73. See *Restatement (Second) of Contracts* § 211 (1981).

74. *Compare Step-Saver, supra* note 69, at 99 *with Arizona Retail Systems v. Software Link*, 831 F. Supp. 759 (D. Ariz. 1993).

inferring formation.[75] In addition, some states have attempted to statutorily "validate" such shrink-wrap licenses.[76]

A third issue involves writing and signature requirements.[77] On the
Internet, where transactions are entirely paperless, it may be unclear whether
electronic messages are "written" and what is considered an adequate signature.[78] However, many of these issues were resolved by the Uniform Electronic Transactions Act (UETA), a uniform act enacted by 46 states and
designed to facilitate electronic contracting for most types of commercial
transactions by, among other things, specifically recognizing the validity
of electronic signatures.[79]

Assuming a valid and binding electronic contract is formed, may its
terms govern linking arrangements? What if the site owner explicitly
announces that he or she does not want to be linked to? A simple statement such as this is probably not enforceable, since no consideration is
granted the mere visitor to a site. Hence, no binding contract is formed.
However, if any agreement between the visitor and site operator is formally
entered into, the situation changes. This contract aspect usually derives
from a notice stating that anyone using the site can do so only under certain conditions. Before continuing, the visitor must agree to these terms.

To establish evidence of acquiescence to such conditions, a website
operator may attempt to obtain assent by requiring the visitor to click on
an icon that says "I agree" or some equivalent thereof. The current law in
some states may require even less, however, to recognize a contract. Buy-
ing the product or service may be sufficient. For instance, the purchase of
a cruise ship ticket with a venue provision printed on the back has been
held enforceable, while several "shrink-wrap" cases have found the printed

---

75. *See Step-Saver, supra* note 69, at 99; *see also* Peys, Comment, *Commercial Law—The
Enforceability of Computer "Box-Top" License Agreements Under the U.C.C.*, 7 Whittier L.
Rev. 881, 885–92 (1985).

76. *See* Ill. Rev. Stat. ch. 29, para. 801–08 (1986); La. Rev. Stat. §§ 51:1961–66 (1987).
The Louisiana statute was declared partially invalid in a controversial decision in *Vault
Corp. v. Quaid Software, Ltd.* because the court found that it impinged on "rights" under the
U.S. copyright laws and was therefore preempted. *See* 847 F.2d 255, 270 (5th Cir. 1988).

77. *See* Contracts Restatement, *supra* note 73, § 131. Signed writings are also required
for exclusive licenses and assignments under the Copyright Act. *See* 17 U.S.C. § 204.

78. *See Wright, supra* note 68, at 274.

79. National Conference of Commissioners on Uniform State Laws, Unif. Electronic
Trans. Act, http://www.law.upenn.edu/bll/ulc/fnact99/1990s/ueta99.htm. Only Georgia, Illinois, New York, and Washington have not enacted UETA. For a list of the states where
UETA has been enacted and the corresponding statutory citation, *see* http://www.ncsl.org/
programs/lis/CIP/ueta-statutes.htm.

conditions plainly wrapped around the software or CD to be binding as well.[80]

No particular form of words is necessary to indicate assent, either. The offeror may simply specify that a certain action ripens into a contract when taken.[81] Thus, a contract can be formed by knowledge (or, in some cases, presumptive knowledge) of the conditions accepted when using a website. For instance, in *Specht v. Netscape Communs. Corp.*,[82] a court found no mutual assent only because license terms governing the use of software were not visible to Internet users. In other cases, plaintiff's terms were enforceable if shown to be plainly visible or known to the defendants.[83]

In short, users need to be extremely aware of what they are being asked to agree to when visiting and using any Internet site. An agreement or promise not to link to that site in the future may well be enforceable if a valid contract is formed between the website operator and any visitor to her site.

[4] Posting and Linking on the WWW and the First Amendment

One of the more interesting legal debates over the last few years concerns whether posting material on the Internet and/or providing links to it may be protected by the First Amendment. Most of these cases involve the use and potential misuse of decryption devices designed to circumvent technology intended to protect copyrighted works. Not surprisingly, the major movie and television studios are usually the plaintiffs in these actions, while the defendants are typically individuals with various motives for engaging in such conduct.

For decades, the film industry made movies available for viewing at home in "analog" format. These movies are normally placed on video-tapes, which are then played on a videocassette recorder (VCR). In the early 1990s, the studios began to consider distributing motion pictures in digital form as well. Such movies are placed on disks, known as DVDs, that are played on a DVD player (either a stand-alone device or a component of a computer). DVDs offer significant advantages over analog tapes—improved visual and audio quality, larger data capacity, and greater durability. However, creation of the digital movie brought with it the risk

---

80. *Carnival Cruise Lines v. Shute*, 499 U.S. 585 (1999), *Register.com, Inc. v. Verio, Inc.*, 126 F. Supp. 2d 238 (S.D.N.Y. 2000); *Pollstar v. Gigmania Ltd*, 170 F. Supp. 2d 974 (E.D. Ca. 2000).

81. *Binder v. Aetna Life Ins. Co.*, 75 Cal. App. 4th 832 (1999); *Penn Sec. Life Ins. Co. v. Rising*, 62 Cal. App. 3d 302 (1976).

82. 306 F.3d 17 (2d Cir. 2002).

83. *Id.* at 31.

that a virtually perfect copy could be readily made at the click of a mouse and then instantly distributed to countless recipients over the Internet.

For this reason, the studios were reluctant to release digital motion pictures until they were confident adequate safeguards against piracy existed. The industry took several steps to minimize this threat. First, it settled on the DVD as the standard medium for home distribution. Second, it sought an encryption scheme to protect DVDs by enlisting the help of the consumer electronics and computer industries, which in mid-1996 developed the Content Scramble System (CSS).

CSS essentially employs an algorithm configured by a set of "keys" to encrypt a DVD's contents. The algorithm is a mathematical formula that transforms the contents of the movie file into gibberish; the keys are actually strings of 0s and 1s that serve as values for the mathematical formula. Decryption in turn requires a set of "player keys," contained in compliant DVD players, as well as an understanding of the CSS encryption algorithm. Without the player keys and algorithm, a DVD player cannot access the contents of a digital movie. With these items, a DVD player can display the movie on a television or computer screen, but it denies the viewer the ability to copy or manipulate the movie.

In September 1999, a Norwegian teenager named Jon Johansen, collaborating with two other individuals he met on the Internet, reverse-engineered a DVD player and culled from it the player keys and other information necessary to decrypt CSS. Johansen was actually trying to develop a DVD player operable on Linux, rather than the Microsoft operating system. To accomplish this task, he developed a decryption program executable on Microsoft's operating system,[84] appropriately called, "DeCSS."

Shortly following Johansen's discovery, self-proclaimed "hackers" across the globe began placing copies of this decryption program on their websites and posting links to other Internet sites containing it. This so-called hacker community included serious scholars conducting research on protection techniques, computer buffs intrigued by the challenge of circumventing access-limiting devices, mischief makers interested in disrupting computer operations, and those who simply wanted to acquire copyrighted material without paying for it.[85]

---

84. An operating system works with the computer to perform the application's instructions. Generally, an executable application can be played only on the operating system for which it is designed, although interoperability has been improving.

85. Much of the above background material was derived from Judge Jon O. Newman's excellent discourse on these issues, contained in *Universal City Studios, Inc. v. Corley*, 2001 U.S. App. LEXIS 25330 (2d Cir. 2001).

To stave off widespread dissemination of DeCSS, the entertainment industry launched a massive effort to locate those individuals posting and linking to DeCSS software. To start with, the industry sought preliminary injunctions against those "trading" in this commodity.[86] Creatively, several defendants contended these injunctions violated their First Amendment rights because such judicial orders constituted a prior restraint on freedom of speech. While posting and linking to material on the Internet is normally a commercial activity, and thus subject to a lower level of scrutiny, First Amendment defenses are typically taken quite seriously by the courts and were so here.[87]

The first question in any such case is whether a program like DeCSS is, in fact, "speech" protected by the First Amendment. The First Amendment provides: "Congress shall make no law . . . abridging the freedom of speech . . . ."[88] "Speech" is an elusive term, and judges and legal scholars have debated its bounds for over two centuries. While some confine First Amendment protection to political speech,[89] others would expand it only to cover artistic expression.[90] Whatever the merits of these and other approaches, the law has not been so limited. Even dry information, devoid of advocacy, political relevance, or artistic expression, has been accorded First Amendment protection.[91] Thus, for example, courts have considered the dissemination of technical information,[92] scientific research,[93] and attempts to regulate the publication of instructions as potentially protected

---

86. *See, e.g., Universal I, supra* note 43.

87. *Virginia State Board of Pharmacy v. Virginia Citizens Consumer Council, Inc.*, 425 U.S. 748, 763 (1976).

88. U.S. Const. amend. I.

89. *E.g.*, Bork, *Neutral Principles and Some First Amendment Problems*, 47 Ind. L.J. 1 (1971).

90. *E.g.*, Hamilton, *Art Speech*, 49 Vand. L. R Rev. 73 (1996).

91. *See Miller v. California*, 413 U.S. 15, 34 (1973) ("The First Amendment protects works which, taken as a whole, have serious literary, artistic, political, or scientific value. . . ."); *Roth v. United States*, 354 U.S. 476 (1957) (First Amendment embraces "all ideas having even the slightest redeeming social importance," including the "'advancement of truth, science, morality, and arts in general.'" (quoting 1 Journals of the Continental Congress 108 (1774)); *Board of Trustees of Stanford University v. Sullivan*, 773 F. Supp. 472, 474 (D.D.C. 1991) ("It is . . . settled . . . that the First Amendment protects scientific expression and debate just as it protects political and artistic expression."); *cf. Virginia State Board of Pharmacy, supra* note 87, at 763 ("prescription drug price information" is "speech" because a consumer's interest in "the free flow of commercial information" may be "keener by far" than "his interest in the day's most urgent political debate").

92. *United States v. Progressive, Inc.*, 467 F. Supp. 990 (W.D. Wis. 1979).

93. *Stanford University, supra* note 91, at 473.

speech.[94] Computer programs may also potentially fall into the realm of First Amendment speech.[95]

The application of the First Amendment also does not depend on whether the publication occurred via electronic or more traditional means.[96] Likewise, it makes no difference that a defendant is a republisher rather than the original author. As one court opined: "It would be anomalous if the mere fact of publication and distribution were somehow deemed to constitute 'conduct' which in turn destroyed the right to freely publish."[97] Nor does it matter that the disclosure was made on a website rather than a newspaper or book. The right to freedom of speech "does not restrict itself 'depend[ing] upon the identity' or legal character of the speaker, 'whether corporation, association, union, or individual.'"[98]

Having established computer code conveying information to be "speech," courts must then consider the scope of protection to be afforded it. This test generally depends on whether the restriction is imposed due to the content of the speech.[99] Content-based restrictions are permissible only if they serve compelling state interests and do so by the least restrictive means available.[100] A content-neutral restriction is permissible if it serves a substantial governmental interest, the interest is unrelated to the suppression of free expression, and the regulation is narrowly tailored, which "in this context requires . . . that the means chosen do not 'burden substantially more speech than is necessary to further the government's legitimate interests.'"[101]

Based upon these tests, courts must then examine the individual facts and circumstances of each case to determine whether or not a particular web-based activity is protected by the First Amendment. To date, some

---

94. See, e.g., United States v. Raymond, 228 F.3d 804, 815 (7th Cir. 2000) (First Amendment does not protect instructions for violating the tax laws); United States v. Dahlstrom, 713 F.2d 1423, 1428 (9th Cir. 1983) (same); Herceg v. Hustler Magazine, Inc., 814 F.2d 1017, 1020–25 (5th Cir. 1987) (First Amendment protects instructions for engaging in a dangerous sex act); United States v. Featherston, 461 F.2d 1119, 1122–23 (5th Cir. 1972) (First Amendment does not protect instructions for building an explosive device); see also Bernstein v. United States Department of State, 922 F. Supp. 1426, 1435 (N.D. Cal. 1996) ("Instructions, do-it-yourself manuals, [and] recipes" are all "speech").

95. Junger v. Daley, 209 F.3d 481, 484, 485 (6th Cir. 2000).

96. Reno, supra note 4, at 870.

97. Wilson v. Superior Court, 13 Cal. 3d 652, 660 (1975).

98. Gerawan Farming, Inc. v. Lyons, 24 Cal. 4th 468, 485 (2000).

99. Universal I, supra note 43, at 327.

100. See Sable Communications of California, Inc. v. FCC, 492 U.S. 115, 126 (1989).

101. Turner Broadcasting System, Inc. v. FCC, 512 U.S. 622, 662 (1994) (quoting Ward v. Rock Against Racism, 491 U.S. 781, 799 (1989)).

courts have upheld preliminary injunctions barring DeCSS and similar programs from being posted and linked to on the WWW,[102] while others have declined to do so.[103] The reasons cited by the ruling judges in these decisions are beyond the scope of this discussion. Regardless, what is certain is that much more remains to be debated and written on this topic.

5.2 ISSUES CONCERNING JOINT WORKS

Professors and instructors often collaborate in teaching courses, devising curricula and writing textbooks. In the electronic age, many educators have teamed up to publish materials online and produce digital courses to be offered at their school. As long as relations remain cordial, these persons often work together for many years on a variety of projects. But what happens when relationships deteriorate and the parties decide to go their separate ways? Who owns the works they created together? What happens when one author subsequently modifies or updates a joint work without the consent or collaboration of the other? Section 5.2 of this chapter attempts to answer these inquiries.

We begin with the basic question of who owns a joint work. Section 201(a) of the Copyright Act provides: "Copyright in a work protected under [the Copyright Act] vests initially in the author or co-authors of the work." Section 101 of the act defines a "joint work" as one "prepared by two or more authors with the intention that their contributions be merged into inseparable or interdependent parts of a unitary whole." In a joint work, each author "automatically acquires an undivided ownership in the entire work" including any portion thereof.[104] Thus an action for infringement between joint owners cannot stand, because an individual may not infringe his own copyright. The only duty joint authors have with respect to their work is to account for profits from its use.[105]

But who owns a work modified by only one of its original joint authors? The person making the changes or both original creators? A review of Sections 101 and 103(b) of the Copyright Act and their legislative history reveals two basic criteria must be satisfied before one is deemed a joint author of a new "derivative" work. First, each putative author must have "contributed" to the "new" work. Second, each must have intended

---

102. *Corley, supra* note 85.

103. *DVD Copy Control Association v. Bunner*, 2001 Cal. App. LEXIS 1179 (Cal. Ct. App. 2001).

104. 1 M. Nimmer & D. Nimmer, *Nimmer on Copyright* § 6.03 (1994) (hereinafter *Nimmer on Copyright*).

105. *See Donna v. Dodd, Mead & Co.*, 374 F. Supp. 429, 430 (S.D.N.Y. 1974).

to contribute to a joint work at the time his or her alleged contribution was made. Because Section 103(b) extends independent protection to derivative works, an intent to contribute or an actual contribution to prior works does not establish ownership in the derivative work.[106] We consider these two tests in the following sections and then examine when the "new" work becomes a derivative work, thus making it eligible for independent protection.

[1] Contribution to the "New" Work

As noted above, the federal copyright statute envisions each author contributing to a joint work. "Under the Section 101 definition, a work would not be joint unless its authors collaborated among themselves or unless each of the authors knew, at the time the work was being written, that his contribution would be integrated as an 'inseparable' or 'interdependent' part of a 'unitary whole.'"[107]

In enacting this definition, Congress endeavored to "make plain that copyright in a derivative work is independent of, and does not enlarge the scope of rights in, any pre-existing material incorporated in it. There [was] thus no need to spell this conclusion out in the definition of 'joint work.'"[108] The legislative history clearly indicates one cannot be deemed a joint author without actually collaborating in the work's preparation. Critical therefore "is the intention, at the time the writing is done, that the parts be absorbed or combined into an integrated unit."[109] That intention must be associated with the work in which a copyright is claimed, not with respect to the prior works from which it is derived.[110] As such, one coauthor may revise a joint work in order to create an individual derivative work, with the other coauthor acquiring no property rights therein.[111]

---

106. *House Report* at 120.

107. *Supplementary Report of the Register of Copyrights on the General Revision of the U.S. Copyright Law: 1965 Revision Bill,* 89th Cong., 1st Sess., *Copyright Law Revision Part 6,* at 65 (House Comm. Print 1965), *reprinted in* 1 Copyright Law Revision (1964–1965).

108. *House Report* at 120.

109. *Id.*

110. *See MCA, Inc. v. Wilson,* 425 F. Supp. 443, 455 (S.D.N.Y. 1976) (owner of underlying work obtains no property rights in derivative work), *aff'd,* 677 F.2d 180 (2d Cir. 1981).

111. *See Dynamic Solutions, Inc. v. Planning and Control, Inc.,* 646 F. Supp. 1329, 1338–39 (S.D.N.Y. 1986) (even sole author/owner of preexisting material contained in derivative work has no property right in new matter created for the derivative work added without his participation); *see also Weinstein v. University of Illinois,* 811 F.2d 1091, 1095 (7th Cir. 1987); *House Report* at 120; *Nimmer on Copyright* § 6.06[B].

[2] Intent to Contribute to a Derivative Work

In addition to both contributing to a work, to create a joint work, the parties must evince "the intention that their contributions be merged at the time the writing is done,"[112] not at some later date.[113] In *Edward B. Marks Music Corp. v. Jerry Vogel Music Co.*,[114] it was held joint authorship requires each author intend his or her contribution, at the time it was created, become part of a unitary work. Or, as Judge Learned Hand stated it, "when both plan an undivided whole . . . their separate interests will be as inextricably involved, as are the threads out of which they have woven the seamless fabric of the work."[115]

Marks involved a situation in which one person had written the lyrics for a song while another had composed the music. Neither party knew the other, but both were aware that their individual efforts would not stand alone. In holding the resulting song was a joint work, the critical fact cited was that both parties were aware their authorship efforts would have to be combined to create the final integrated product—a commercially viable song.[116] From this, the rule has evolved that an author wishing to create a joint work must clearly demonstrate his or her intent to do so.[117] Although such an intent may, as in *Marks*, be inferred from the circumstances surrounding the work's creation, in the absence of this showing, the work is presumed to be the product and sole property of an individual author.[118]

To place this analysis in context, let us consider the example of two scholars (Professor Alvin and Professor Banes) who are faculty members of the History Department at the same university. The professors decide to collaborate on a research article exposing some newly found evidence

---

112. *House Report* at 120.

113. *See Nimmer on Copyright* § 6.03.

114. 140 F.2d 266 (2d Cir. 1944) (L. Hand, J.).

115. *Id.* at 267; *see also Shapiro, Bernstein & Co. v. Jerry Vogel Music Co. (Melancholy Baby)*, 161 F.2d 406, 409 (2d Cir. 1946), *cert. denied*, 331 U.S. 820 (1947).

116. *See Edward B. Marks, supra* note 114, at 267.

117. L. Lape, *A Narrow View of Creative Cooperation: The Current State of Joint Work Doctrine*, 61 Alb. L. Rev. 43, 58–59 (1997) ("The stricter intent standard imposed by these courts requires that the parties have the intent to be joint authors, rather than simply the intent that their contributions merge. . . . What the courts mean by the intent to be joint authors is the intent to share ownership in a work.").

118. *See, e.g., Gilliam v. American Broadcasting Cos., Inc.*, 538 F.2d 14, 22 (2d Cir. 1976) (Lumbard, J.) (reservation of rights by one party inconsistent with joint authorship and work not therefore joint); *Picture Music, Inc. v. Bourne, Inc.*, 314 F. Supp. 640, 645 (S.D.N.Y. 1970) (declining to find joint authorship where a "common design to create a single work" not shown to exist), *aff'd on other grounds*, 457 F.2d 1213 (2d Cir.), *cert. denied*, 409 U.S. 997; *cf. Community for Creative Non-Violence v. Reid*, 846 F.2d 1485, 1497 (D.C. Cir. 1988), *cert. granted*, 488 U.S. 940 (1988).

regarding the assassination of President Abraham Lincoln. The professors then post their work on the college's website with both their names affixed. Several years later, Professor Alvin decides to take a position at another school. Professor Banes subsequently, without the knowledge of Professor Alvin or his cooperation, updates and revises the Lincoln article to include some additional findings. Professor Banes then posts this revised piece on the university website with only his name attached. Professor Alvin, while surfing the Web one afternoon, discovers the "new" article by Professor Banes and contacts his former college employer to insist his name also appear as a coauthor. What should the university do?

Apart from considerations of professional courtesy, the answer is that the university need do nothing. Based on current law, it is clear that Professor Alvin and Professor Banes were joint owners of the original article and each had an undivided interest therein. However, since Professor Alvin neither contributed nor intended to contribute to the subsequent work, he is *not* deemed a joint author thereof. The updated work is deemed to belong solely to Professor Banes. Why can't Professor Alvin sue Professor Banes for copyright infringement? Because each author acquired an inseparable, undivided interest in their original joint work. As such, an action for infringement cannot be maintained, since an individual owner cannot infringe his own copyright.[119] In short, Alvin cannot sue Banes because he would, technically, be suing himself.

While all of this may seem counterintuitive, it is nonetheless the law. Professor Alvin may have one other argument, though—that the "new" work is so similar to the original collaborative effort, it is not entitled to protection since copyright law protects only "original" works.[120] Professor Banes will counter that the "new" piece constitutes a "derivative" work and is therefore eligible for protection as a separate creation. We now turn our attention to this issue.

[3] Qualification as a Derivative Work

Section 101 of the Copyright Act defines a "derivative work" as one based on "preexisting works." In addition, Section 103(b) provides that

---

119. *See* Lape, *supra* note 117, at 73 ("Since a joint author has the right to independently use or license the entire work, she cannot be liable to another joint author for copyright infringement of that work.").

120. *See* Chapter Two, Section 2.1[2], for a more detailed discussion of the "originality" requirement.

[t]he copyright in a compilation or derivative work extends only to the material contributed by the author of such work, as distinguished from the preexisting material employed in the work, and does not imply any exclusive right in the preexisting material. The copyright in such a work is independent of, and does not affect or enlarge the scope, duration, ownership, or subsistence of, any copyright protection in the preexisting material.

Section 101 of the statute further defines a derivative work as "[a] work consisting of editorial revisions, annotations, elaborations, or other modifications which, as a whole, represent an original work of authorship. . . ." Thus, it is clear that "the manner of expression, the author's analysis or interpretation of events, the way he structures his material and marshals facts, his choice of words, and the emphasis he gives to particular developments" are protected under the copyright laws.[121] The principle of derivative work protection is subject to two important limitations, however. To support a copyright, a derivative work must be more than trivial, and the protection afforded it must reflect the degree to which the derivative work relies on preexisting material.[122] This rule is premised on the notion that "'the one pervading element prerequisite to copyright protection regardless of the form of work' is the requirement of originality—that the work be the original product of the claimant."[123]

In the law of copyright, though, only a modicum of originality need be demonstrated. High standards of uniqueness and creativity are dispensed with.[124] In deciding whether the originality of the matter added to a writing is sufficient to qualify it for protection as a derivative work, "[a]ll that is needed to satisfy both the Constitution and the statute is that the 'author' contributed something more than a 'merely trivial' variation, something recognizably 'his own.'"[125] The originality requirement for a revised version remains a "minimal" or "modest" one.[126] Hence, even minor changes

---

121. *Wainwright Securities, Inc. v. Wall Street Transcript Corp.*, 558 F.2d 91, 95–96 (2d Cir. 1977), *cert. denied*, 434 U.S. 1014 (1978).

122. *Durham Indus., Inc. v. Tomy Corp.*, 630 F.2d 905, 909 (2d Cir. 1980).

123. *L. Batlin & Son v. Snyder*, 536 F.2d 486, 489–90 (2d Cir.) (*en banc*) (*quoting Nimmer on Copyright* § 10), *cert. denied*, 429 U.S. 857 (1976).

124. *Feist Publications, supra* note 55, at 345.

125. *Alfred Bell & Co. v. Catalda Fine Arts, Inc.*, 191 F.2d 99, 102–03 (2d Cir. 1951).

126. *See, e.g., Eden Toys, Inc. v. Florelee Undergarment Co.*, 697 F.2d 27, 35 (2nd Cir. 1982); *Durham Indus., supra* note 122, at 910; *Puddu v. Buonamici Statuary, Inc.*, 450 F.2d 401, 402 (2d Cir. 1971); *Millworth Converting Corp. v. Slifka*, 276 F.2d 443, 445 (2d Cir. 1960).

or modifications made by Professor Banes to the second article in our example would likely make it a separate, derivative work eligible for independent protection under the Copyright Act.

5.3 OWNERSHIP OF THE ELECTRONIC COURSE

If ownership of joint works has received some recent attention on college campuses, that discussion has paled in comparison to the issue over who owns the electronic course—the professor or the institution he or she works for? That controversy has become particularly heated and passionate over the last decade, for several reasons: first, the overall growth of distance learning and, second, the amount of human and technical resources needed to develop even a single distance course.[127] It is not unusual for a college or university to spend tens of thousands of dollars to produce just one online class.[128] In addition, the widespread use of multimedia course materials and Internet offerings has convinced some schools it is possible to "package" courses and make a profit by marketing them to other institutions.[129]

In light of these financial considerations, it is not surprising that conflicts have arisen between faculty and their schools over the ownership of such materials. Adding fuel to the fire is the seeming reversal of position by many educational institutions on this issue. Traditionally, teachers were permitted to retain ownership of works created in connection with their job or field of expertise. Since these works were primarily the products of individuals, faculty members maintained they should hold the copyright therein. Royalties generated therefrom were also seen as a way to supplement lower-paying teaching positions and encourage additional research and scholarship.[130]

The advent of distance learning changed these dynamics, however. Universities began to claim ownership if substantial institutional resources were used in creating the work. This was often the case where technical support, such as server time, licensed software, instructional designers, programmers, and graphics specialists, were needed to assemble a digital

---

127. *See* Olsen, *The Promise and Problems of a New Way of Teaching Math*, Chron. of Higher Educ., Oct. 8, 1999.

128. *See* Carr, *Is Anyone Making Money on Distance Education?*, Chron. of Higher Educ., Feb. 16, 2001.

129. *See* Guernsey and Young, *Who Owns Online Courses?* Chron. of Higher Educ., June 5, 1998.

130. *See* Gasaway, *Drafting a Faculty Copyright Ownership Policy*, The Tech. Source, Mar./April 2002, at 3.

course.[131] Schools also tended to justify ownership by granting release time to the instructor or offering supplemental compensation.[132] Often too, institutional ownership was deemed advantageous because the university, rather than an individual, was in the best position to market the work or evaluate its commercial potential.[133] These reasons more often clouded than resolved the issue.

Does copyright law help answer the question of who owns the electronic course? Yes, even though the final determination will largely depend on the facts and circumstances of each case. Ultimately, resolution of the query will turn on whether (1) the instructor is an employee or independent contractor of the institution, (2) the work in question was produced inside or outside the scope of a person's employment, and (3) any other type of writing, contract, institutional policy, or charter governs the relationship between the teacher and his school. We explore each of these factors below, but begin with an overview of the current law.

[1] Copyright Ownership and the Work for Hire Doctrine

The Copyright Act provides that copyright ownership "vests initially in the author or authors of the work."[134] Typically, the author is the party who actually creates the work, that is, the person who translates an idea into a fixed, tangible expression.[135] The act carves out an important exception, however, for "works made for hire."[136] If the work is for hire, "the employer or other person for whom the work was prepared is considered the author" under some circumstances, and owns such copyright, unless there is a written agreement to the contrary.[137]

---

131. One university has defined "substantial use of resources" as use of its "laboratory, studio, audio, audiovisual, video, television, broadcast, computer, computational or other facilities, resources and [s]taff or [s]tudents which: (i) falls outside of the scope of the faculty member's normal job responsibilities or (ii) entails a faculty member's use of such resources not ordinarily available to all faculty members." *See* "George Washington University Copyright Policy" (April 1, 2005), at 5.

132. A recent survey of college distance learning programs reveals that "nearly 70% of the colleges in the sample offer payments routinely to instructors who develop distance learning courses . . ." *See* Primary Research Group, Inc. ("PRG"), Press Release (Sept. 20, 2007), http://www.primaryresearch.com/release–200707233.html.

133. Gasaway, *supra* note 130, at 3.

134. 17 U.S.C. § 201(a).

135. 17 U.S.C. § 102.

136. The phrase "work for hire" is used interchangeably here with the more cumbersome statutory phrase "work made for hire."

137. 17 U.S.C. § 201(b).

Classifying a work as "made for hire" determines not only the initial ownership thereof but also the copyright's duration[138] as well as the owners' renewal rights,[139] termination rights,[140] and ability to import certain goods bearing the copyright.[141] The doctrine thus carries great significance for freelance creators—including artists, writers, photographers, designers, composers, adjunct professors, and website developers—and for the educational, publishing, advertising, music, and other industries that often commission their works.[142]

Section 101 of the Copyright Act provides a work is "for hire" under two sets of circumstances:

(1) a work prepared by an employee within the scope of his or her employment; or

(2) a work specially ordered or commissioned for use as a contribution to a collective work, as a part of a motion picture or other audiovisual work, as a translation, as a supplementary work, as a compilation, as an instructional text, as a test, as answer material for a test, or as an atlas, if the parties expressly agree in a written instrument signed by them that the work shall be considered a work made for hire.[143]

Note the key distinction here. In the employer/employee context of Section 101(1), the presumption is that the *employer* owns the work, absent an agreement to the contrary. For commissioned works where an independent contractor is used (the subject of Section 101(2)), the presumption is that the *contractor* owns the work unless it falls into a specified category *and* a written contract documenting the relationship is in place.

Thus, the initial inquiry in establishing ownership is to determine whether a project is "a work prepared by an employee within the scope of his or her employment." This really triggers two questions—first, whether the person is a true employee; and, second, if so, whether the work was created within

---

138. 17 U.S.C. § 302 (c).

139. 17 U.S.C. § 304 (a).

140. 17 U.S.C. § 203 (a).

141. 17 U.S.C. § 601(b)(1). *See Nimmer on Copyright* § 5.03[A].

142. As of 1955, approximately 40% of all copyright registrations were for works for hire, according to a Copyright Office study. *See* Varmer, *Works Made for Hire and on Commission, in Studies Prepared for the Subcommittee on Patents, Trademarks, and Copyrights of the Senate Committee on the Judiciary*, Study No. 13, 86th Cong., 2d Sess., 139, n.49 (Comm. Print 1960). The Copyright Office does not keep more recent statistics on the number of work-for-hire registrations.

143. Section 101 of the act defines each of the nine categories of "specially ordered or commissioned" works.

the scope of his or her employment. Unfortunately, the Copyright Act does not define the term "employee." In the absence thereof, four interpretations have emerged over time in the federal courts. The first held that a work was prepared by an employee whenever the hiring party[144] retained the right to control the product.[145]

A second, closely related view was that a work was prepared by an employee when the hiring party actually wielded control with respect to the product's creation. This approach was formulated by the Court of Appeals for the Second Circuit,[146] and subsequently adopted by the Fourth[147] and Seventh Circuits.[148] A third view endorsed by the Fifth Circuit was that the term "employee" carried its common law of agency meaning.[149] Finally, the Court of Appeals for the Ninth Circuit adopted the view that "employee" referred only to "formal, salaried" employees.[150]

Which of these interpretations is the most appropriate? What is the true meaning of "employee" under federal copyright law? The starting point for any interpretation of a statute is always its language.[151] It has been established that "[w]here Congress uses terms that have accumulated settled meaning under . . . the common-law, a court must infer, unless the statute otherwise dictates, that Congress means to incorporate the established meaning of these terms."[152] In the past, when Congress used the term "employee" without defining it, it typically intended to describe the conventional master–servant relationship as understood by common law agency doctrine.[153] Nothing appears in the text of the work-for-hire provisions to indicate Congress chose the words "employee" and "employment"

---

144. The term "hiring party," as used herein, refers to the party who claims ownership of the copyright by virtue of the work-for-hire doctrine.

145. *See Peregrine v. Lauren Corp.*, 601 F. Supp. 828, 829 (Colo. 1985); *Clarkstown v. Reeder*, 566 F. Supp. 137, 142 (S.D.N.Y. 1983).

146. *Aldon Accessories Ltd. v. Spiegel, Inc.*, 738 F.2d 548 (2d Cir. 1984), *cert. denied*, 469 U.S. 982 (1985).

147. *Brunswick Beacon, Inc. v. Schock-Hopchas Publishing Co.*, 810 F.2d 410 (4th Cir. 1987).

148. *Evans Newton, Inc. v. Chicago Systems Software*, 793 F.2d 889 (7th Cir. 1985), *cert. denied*, 479 U.S. 949 (1986).

149. *Easter Seal Society for Crippled Children & Adults of Louisiana, Inc. v. Playboy Enterprises*, 815 F.2d 323 (5th Cir. 1987).

150. *See Dumas v. Gommerman*, 865 F.2d 1093 (9th Cir. 1989).

151. *Consumer Products Safety Comm'n v. GTE Sylvania, Inc.*, 447 U.S. 102, 108 (1980).

152. *NLRB v. Amax Coal Co.*, 453 U.S. 322, 329 (1981); *see also Perrin v. United States*, 444 U.S. 37, 42 (1979).

153. *See, e.g., Kelley v. Southern Pacific Co.*, 419 U.S. 318, 322–23 (1974); *Baker v. Texas & Pacific R. Co.*, 359 U.S. 227, 228 (1959) (per curiam); *Robinson v. Baltimore & Ohio R. Co.*, 237 U.S. 84, 94 (1915).

to describe anything other than "the conventional relation of employer and employee."[154] On the contrary, congressional intent to incorporate the agency law definition is strongly suggested by Section 101(1) of the Copyright Act's use of the phrase "scope of employment," a common term of art in agency law.[155]

In other cases of statutory interpretation, courts have concluded Congress intended terms such as "employee," "employer," and "scope of employment" to be interpreted in light of agency law, rather than the law of any particular state.[156] This practice reflected the fact that "federal statutes are generally intended to have uniform nationwide application."[157] Establishment of a federal rule of agency was therefore particularly appropriate given the Copyright Act's express objective of creating national, uniform law by broadly preempting state statutory and common law copyright regulation.[158]

The United States Supreme Court ultimately resolved the split between the circuit courts and adopted the common law of agency view in *Community for Creative Non-Violence v. Reid*.[159] The *Reid* case involved the Community for Creative Non-Violence (CCNV), a Washington, D.C.–based organization dedicated to helping homeless people. CCNV had entered into an oral agreement with Mr. Reid, a sculptor, to produce a statue dramatizing the plight of the homeless for a Christmas display. While Reid worked on the project in his Baltimore studio, CCNV members visited him on several occasions to check on his progress and coordinate CCNV's construction of the sculpture's base. Reid accepted most of CCNV's suggestions and directions regarding the sculpture's configuration and appearance. After the work was completed, CCNV connected the sculpture to its base and displayed it. The parties, who had never discussed copyright, then filed competing registrations and fought for ownership of the statue.

CCNV was unable to claim ownership under the second prong of the "work for hire" definition because a "statue" was not a listed item therein,

---

154. *Kelley, supra* note 153, at 323, *quoting Robinson, supra* note 153, at 94; *cf. NLRB v. Hearst Publications, Inc.*, 322 U.S. 111, 124–32 (1944) (rejecting agency law conception of employee for purposes of the National Labor Relations Act where structure and context of statute indicated broader definition).

155. See *Restatement (Second) of Agency* § 228 (1958) (hereinafter *Restatement* 2d).

156. *See, e.g., Kelley, supra* note 153, at 323–24, n.5; *id.* at 332 (Stewart, J., concurring in judgment); *Ward v. Atlantic Coast Line R. Co.*, 362 U.S. 396, 400 (1960); *Baker, supra* note 153, at 228.

157. *Mississippi Band of Choctaw Indians v. Holyfield*, 490 U.S. 30, 43 (1989).

158. *See* 17 U.S.C. § 301(a).

159. 490 U.S. 730 (1989).

and no written agreement existed between the parties. Therefore, CCNV had to establish Mr. Reid was its employee in order to obtain copyright in the work. In determining whether Mr. Reid was an employee under agency law, the Supreme Court examined CCNV's right to control the manner and means by which the statue was produced.[160] Among the factors it considered were the skill required;[161] the source of instrumentalities and tools used;[162] the location of the work;[163] the duration of the relationship between the parties;[164] whether the hiring party had the right to assign additional projects to the hired party;[165] the extent of the hired party's discretion over when and how long to work;[166] the method of payment;[167] the hired party's role in hiring and paying assistants;[168] whether the work was part of the regular business of the hiring party;[169] whether the hiring party was in business;[170] the provision of employee benefits;[171] and the tax treatment of the hired party.[172] The *Reid* case held no one factor was determinative, and none was to be accorded any more weight than another.[173] The Supreme

---

160. *See, e.g., Hilton Int'l Co. v. NLRB*, 690 F. 2d 318, 320 (2d Cir. 1982); *NLRB v. Maine Caterers, Inc.*, 654 F. 2d 131, 133 (1st Cir. 1981), *cert. denied*, 455 U.S. 940 (1982); *Restatement 2d* § 220(1).

161. *See, e.g., Bartels v. Birmingham*, 332 U.S. 126, 132 (1947); *Hilton Int'l Co., supra* note 160, at 320; *NLRB v. A. Duie Pyle, Inc.*, 606 F. 2d 379, 382 (3d Cir. 1979); *Restatement 2d* § 220(2)(d).

162. *See, e.g., NLRB v. United Ins. Co. of America*, 390 U.S. 254, 258 (1968); *United States v. Silk*, 331 U.S. 704, 717, 718 (1947); *Restatement 2d* § 220(2)(e).

163. *See, e.g., United Ins. Co., supra* note 162, at 258; *Dumas, supra* note 150, at 1105; *Darden v. Nationwide Mutual Ins. Co.*, 796 F. 2d 701, 705 (4th Cir. 1986); *Restatement 2d* § 220(2)(e).

164. *See, e.g., United Ins. Co., supra* note 162, at 259; *Bartels, supra* note 161, at 132; *Restatement 2d* § 220(2)(f).

165. *See, e.g., Dumas, supra* note 150, at 1105.

166. *See, e.g., United Ins. Co., supra* note 162, at 258; *Short v. Central States, Southeast & Southwest Areas Pension Fund*, 729 F. 2d 567, 574 (8th Cir. 1984).

167. *See, e.g., Dumas, supra* note 150, at 1105; *Darden, supra* note 163, at 705; *Holt v. Winpisinger*, 811 F.2d 1532, 1540 (1987); *Restatement 2d* § 220(2)(g).

168. *See, e.g., Bartels, supra* note 161, at 132; *Silk, supra* note 162, at 719; *Darden, supra* note 163, at 705; *Short, supra* note 166, at 574.

169. *See, e.g., United Ins. Co., supra* note 162, at 259; *Silk, supra* note 162, at 718; *Dumas, supra* note 150, at 1105; *Hilton Int'l, supra* note 160, at 321; *Restatement 2d* § 220(2)(h).

170. *See, e.g., Restatement 2d* § 220(2)(j).

171. *See, e.g., United Ins. Co., supra* note 162, at 259; *Dumas, supra* note 150, at 1105; *Short, supra* note 166, at 574.

172. *See, e.g., Dumas, supra* note 150, at 1105.

173. *Reid, supra* note 159, at 753; *see also Ward v. Atlantic Coast Line R. Co.*, 362 U.S. 396, 400 (1960); *Hilton Int'l, supra* note 160, at 321.

Court also looked at the Restatement (Second) of Agency § 220(2), which sets forth a non-exhaustive list of similar tests.[174]

In analyzing these factors, the Supreme Court found Mr. Reid to be an independent contractor and *not* CCNV's employee. Hence, he was entitled to presumptive copyright ownership of the sculpture. The *Reid* case maintains its significance today because the factors enumerated therein often need to be weighed and analyzed by colleges and school systems in determining whether their instructors are traditional employees or independent contractors. This question typically arises at the university level in establishing whether part-time adjunct professors or graduate students working for the college are considered actual employees.[175] If they are, works prepared by them on behalf of the university belong to the institution. On the other hand, if they are considered independent contractors, they retain ownership of these works absent a written agreement to the contrary.

[2] Work for Hire and the "Teacher Exception"

One cannot leave the topic of "work for hire" without discussing and, unfortunately for most educators, dispensing with what has been termed the "teacher exception" thereto. In essence, this "exception" espoused the theory that teachers as a profession were exempt from a work-for-hire analysis when determining copyright ownership. Until 1976, the statutory term "work made for hire" was not defined in the Copyright Act and was interpreted under common law. Prior to that time, some courts had recognized a "teacher exception" whereby academic writing was always presumed to belong to the educator, regardless of his or her status as an employee or independent contractor.[176] The legal authority for this conclusion was quite thin, however.[177] Almost all law on the subject derived from a few old English cases.[178]

---

174. In determining whether a hired party is an employee under the general common law of agency, the Supreme Court has traditionally looked for guidance to the *Restatement of Agency. See, e.g., Kelley, supra* note 153, at 323–24, n.5; *id.* at 332 (Stewart, J., concurring in judgment); *Baker, supra* note 153, at 227, 228.

175. This is often a significant issue as a recent survey has revealed that "private colleges use adjunct faculty for 64.5% of the courses that they offer." *See* PRG Press Release, *supra* note 132, at 2.

176. *See* Dreyfuss, *The Creative Employee and the Copyright Act of 1976*, 54 U. Chi. L. Rev. 590, 597–98 (1987).

177. *See* Simon, *Faculty Writings: Are They "Works for Hire" Under the 1976 Copyright Act?*, 9 J. C. & Univ. L. 485, 495–99 (1982).

178. *Abernethy v. Hutchinson*, 3 L.J. (Ch.) 209 (1825), 1 H. & T. 28 (1825); *Caird v. Sime* [1887] 12 A.C. 326 (H.L.).

The most prominent United States case on the topic was *B. J. Williams v. J. Edwinweisser.*[179] In *Williams*, the defendant had paid a student to attend a class taught by Professor Williams at UCLA and take notes on the lectures. The student subsequently delivered the notes to the defendant, who reproduced and offered them for sale to other students. Professor Williams subsequently sued for copyright infringement. The court, relying primarily on case law from Great Britain, held defendant was prohibited from selling copies of the lecture notes because the instructor (and not the university) owned the copyright therein.

Ironically, virtually no one questioned, until the enactment of the Copyright Act of 1976, that academic authors were entitled to copyright in their creations. Even though instructors often produced works directly related to their academic responsibilities and normally used the school's resources in doing so, the universal practice was to permit the teacher to own the material.[180] There were good reasons for this arrangement as a university did not usually supervise its faculty in the preparation of books and articles, and was not always equipped to market their writings.[181]

Regardless, it is now widely accepted that the Copyright Act of 1976 abolished the teacher exception.[182] It may have done so accidentally, however, for there is no mention of the issue in the act's legislative history, nor any discussion of the reasons for doing so. Nevertheless, a literal reading of the statute makes clear academic writing prepared within the scope of employment constitutes work made for hire and, thus, belongs to the employer or institution.[183] Bolstering this interpretation is the fact that no case upholding the teacher exception has been reported in the United States subsequent to enactment of the 1976 Act.

---

179. 273 Cal. App. 2d 726 (1969).

180. *Hays v. Sony Corporation of America*, 847 F.2d 412, 416 (7th Cir. 1988).

181. *Id.*

182. *See* Dreyfuss, *supra* note 176, at 598–600; Simon, *supra* note 177, at 502–09; *Weinstein v. University of Illinois*, 811 F.2d 1091, 1093–94 (7th Cir. 1987). *But see contra*, L. Lape, *Ownership of Copyrightable Works of University Professors: The Interplay Between the Copyright Act and University Copyright Policies*, 37 Vill. L. Rev. 223, 237–38 (1992) ("[L]anguage of the work-made-for-hire provisions of the 1976 Act does not preclude the continued existence of an exception for professors").

183. The law provides a strong presumption that the plain meaning of any statute or contract should be afforded great weight without the need to examine extraneous materials or resources to further interpret it. For example, under Ohio law, if contract terms are clear and unambiguous, the court must presume the parties' intent resides in the words of the agreement. *See, e.g., Foster Wheeler Enviresponse, Inc., v. Franklin County Convention Facilities Authority*, 78 Ohio St. 3d 353, 678 N.E.2d 519 (1997); *Graham v. Drydak Coal Co.*, 76 Ohio St. 3d, 67 N.E.2d 949 (1996).

[3] The Scope of Employment

Having dispensed with the "teacher exception," establishing whether someone is an employee or independent contractor is only the first step in determining copyright ownership. Even if the creator is deemed an employee, the hiring party must still prove the work was created within the scope of the person's employment to obtain ownership.

For example, let us suppose a university asks one of its professors to develop a lab manual for use by students taking freshman chemistry. The professor then works on the manual at her on-campus office during normal business hours using the staff and resources of the college. In such case, there is no doubt the work was produced within the scope of the professor's employment and therefore belongs to the university. Conversely, let us say this same chemistry professor decides to write a spy novel. In doing so, she works on the book at her house, after hours, using only her home computer and the help of her spouse in conducting research and editing. In that case, all rights in the work clearly belong to the professor; the university would have no claim of ownership therein.

Unfortunately, real-world situations are rarely so clear-cut. Very often, a combination of home and office resources are used to create a work. The final product may also have applicability to both the university and commercial sector. Further complicating matters, an employee may create a work in order to enhance his job ranking or performance without, necessarily, being asked to do so. Sometimes a university will grant supplemental compensation for such a work, whether it requested it or not. All these factors muddy the waters and make it more difficult to determine ownership. Some recent cases have attempted to establish clearer parameters.

To begin with, a "scope of employment" determination is a highly factual inquiry. As noted above, terms such as "employee" and "scope of employment" are generally interpreted using common law agency definitions.[184] The test for falling within the scope of one's employment in agency, and thus copyright, law is tripartite: (1) the work must be of the type the employee was hired to perform; (2) the employee's creation of the work must occur substantially within the authorized time and space limits of his or her job; and (3) the work must be actuated at least in part by a purpose

---

184. *Reid, supra* note 159, at 740 (1989); *Cannon Group, Inc. v. Better Bags, Inc.*, 250 F. Supp. 2d 893, 900 (S.D. Ohio 2003) (citing to *Reid*).

to serve the employer's interest.[185] Generally, all three prongs of the test must be satisfied before a work is deemed to belong to the employer.[186]

We consider the first test. In ascertaining whether the work's creation was the type of task the employee was hired to do, courts will usually look to the employee's job description.[187] A court will also consider the kind of work performed by similar employees to decide if the preparation was at least incidental to the person's job responsibility.[188] If the employee's job description does not include preparation of such works, or he was never asked to work on a similar project, the work will customarily be viewed as an independent creation.[189] However, if the employee was even sporadically required to prepare such works or was responsible for a department doing so, it is more likely the work will be found to belong to the employer.[190]

The second prong of the analysis, whether preparation of the work occurred substantially within the authorized time and space limits of employment, is analyzed at the time of the work's creation.[191] Factors considered *outside* the time and space limits of employment include (1) preparation of the material on the employee's own time at home; (2) use of personal equipment purchased with the employee's own funds; (3) sporadic to no use of the facilities or equipment of the employer; and (4) no direction or authorization by the employer to create the work.[192] Criteria indicating a work was created *within* the time and space limits of employment are more easily established for a salaried employee.[193] For example, if the employee normally works off-site or from home as a telecommuter, or just on off hours, the work may still belong to the employer.[194]

---

185. *Cannon, supra* note 184, at 900; *Quinn v. City of Detroit*, 988 F. Supp. 1044, 1049 (E.D. Mich. 1997); *Avtec Systems, Inc. v. Peiffer*, 1995 U.S. App. LEXIS 25901, at *11 (4th Cir. 1995).

186. *Quinn, supra* note 185, at 1049. *See also Nimmer on Copyright* § 5.03[A][1][b][i].

187. *Moonstruck Design, LLC v. Metz*, 2002 U.S. Dist. LEXIS 14583, at *14 (S.D.N.Y. 2002).

188. *Quinn, supra* note 185, at 1050; *Vanderhurst v. Colorado Mounting College District*, 16 F. Supp. 2d 1297, 1307 (D. Colo. 1998).

189. *Quinn, supra* note 185, at 1051.

190. *Genzmer v. Public Health Trust of Miami-Dade County*, 219 F. Supp. 2d 1275, 1281 (S.D. Fla. 2002); *Miller v. CP Chemicals, Inc.*, 808 F. Supp. 1238, 1244 (D.S.C. 1992).

191. *Quinn, supra* note 185, at 1051; *Avtec, supra* note 185, at **13–14.

192. *Cannon, supra* note 184, at 901; *Quinn, supra* note 185, at 1051; *City of Newark v. Beasely*, 883 F. Supp. 3, 8 (D.N.J. 1995); *Avtec, supra* note 185, at **13–14.

193. *Cramer v. Crestar Finan. Corp.*, 1995 U.S. App. LEXIS 25906, at *14 (4th Cir. 1995).

194. *Id.*; *Genzmer, supra* note 190, at 1281–82.

The third prong of the test, a motivation to serve one's employer, is easier to satisfy. Creation of the work for the employer's interest does not have to be the employee's sole motivation, but simply a partial one.[195] If the work was created to make the employee's job easier or simplify his tasks, that also serves the employer.[196] An example of when an employer is not served occurs if the sole or partial motivation is to create new job opportunities for the employee.[197]

[4] Written Agreements Affecting Copyright Ownership

The prior three sections have discussed how copyright law serves to determine a work's ownership in an employment relationship. The relevant provisions of the Copyright Act are a "default" mechanism, however, and apply only if the parties have not already allocated ownership amongst themselves in a writing.[198] It is unlikely in today's educational environment (considering the costs and potential financial rewards associated with distance learning) that these "default" provisions will prove sufficient. Faculty members are likely to aggressively resist the notion that all works created within the scope of their employment belong to the university. Likewise, educational institutions will not be content to always permit the copyright for commissioned works they paid for to be owned by independent contractors.

The resolution of these issues rests in the "need for an institution to have a clear statement of its policy and a mechanism to ensure that the issue of [copyright] ownership is addressed as early as possible. . . ."[199] Since parties are able to alter the "default" positions regarding ownership by entering into a writing, they should, when appropriate, choose to do so.[200] These "writings" may take various forms, such as an employment agreement between a college and faculty member, a business contract between the institution and an independent contractor, a policy manual or handbook, or a labor union contract.

In the case of policy guidelines disseminated to faculty members, institutions should take appropriate measures to ensure the enforceability of such documents, for two reasons. First, under the law of most states, the distribution of a manual by an employer to an employee is not deemed

---

195. *Genzmer, supra* note 190, at 1282.

196. *Quinn, supra* note 185, at 1051–52; *Miller, supra* note 190, at 1244.

197. *Roeslin v. District of Columbia*, 921 F. Supp. 793, 798 (D.D.C. 1995).

198. 17 U.S.C. § 201(b); 17 U.S.C. § 101 (definition of "work made for hire").

199. *See* Twigg, "Who Owns Online Courses and Course Material?" *Intellectual Property Polices for a New Learning Environment* (2000), at 1.

200. Twigg, *supra* note 199, at 23.

sufficient to create an enforceable agreement between the parties. For instance, in a case where an employee sued his employer for breach of contract, relying on the employer's failure to give a verbal and written warning as specified in the company's employee handbook, the court ruled the handbook constituted no more than general guidelines, and not a contract expressing the sole means of terminating employment.[201]

Second, in determining ownership, the Copyright Act often requires a writing *signed* by the parties. For example, Section 201(b) of the act permits a variance from the principle that the employer owns those works created by his employees within the scope of their employment only when "the parties have expressly agreed otherwise in a written instrument *signed by them.*" Correspondingly, this same requirement of a signed writing must be fulfilled to alter the presumption that an independent contractor, rather than the customer, owns a commissioned work. Lastly, other than by operation of law, Section 204(a) recognizes a transfer of copyright ownership only when there exists "an instrument ... note or memorandum of the transfer ... in writing ... *signed* by the owner of the rights. ..." (emphasis added).

Since most "copyright guidelines" are seldom, if ever, negotiated individually between a faculty member and an institutional representative, their mere issuance as "policy" will likely not be legally sufficient to create a binding obligation between a teacher and his school. Therefore, even the parties' actual intent expressed in a manual that faculty retain copyright in their work or that the college own all electronic courses created by part-time instructors could easily be subverted or negated by operation of the Copyright Act. As such, the safest course of action is to have any such guidelines executed by all affected persons or "expressly incorporated by reference into a written employment contract signed by the professor and the university."[202]

At a minimum, such writings should designate copyright ownership for the following situations commonly encountered on campus:

- Works created by administration or staff
- Works created by independent contractors
- Works created by students who are not employees of the university
- Works created by students who are employed by the university
- Works created by faculty, such as:

---

201. *Reynolds Manufacturing Company v. Mendoza*, 644 S.W.2d 536 (Tex. App. 1982); *Williams v. Biscuitville, Inc.*, 253 S.E.2d 18 (N.C. App. 1979), *cert. denied*, 256 S.E.2d 810 (1979).

202. Lape, *supra* note 182, at 249.

- Traditional creative or nondirected work of faculty;
- Materials created by faculty for use in an electronic environment;
- Materials created by faculty for use in a traditional class offered by the university;
- Materials created by faculty with "substantial use of institutional resources";[203]
- Materials created by faculty at the specific direction of the university; and
- "Sponsored" work created pursuant funding under a grant, contract, or other arrangement

In establishing ownership, it is important to understand a copyright need not be transferred in its entirety.[204] As such, the rights of a copyright owner may be allocated between the institution and a faculty member. The arrangement may take the form of a license agreement, whereby one party retains ownership while the other obtains certain rights to use the material subject to payment obligations and geographic, time, or notice restrictions.[205] Such an "unbundling" or allocation of rights often results in a fair accord as opposed to the faculty or institution adhering to an all-or-nothing position.[206] For example, a college could enter into a contract that allocates ownership of a work to the professor who created it, but licenses back to the institution the right to:

- require an appropriate acknowledgment of institutional support for the creation of the work.
- borrow portions thereof for use in compilations or other composite works.
- be informed in advance of any uses, reproductions, distributions, or dispositions of the work by its author(s).
- duplicate the work solely for teaching, scholarship, and research at the university.
- require a return of royalties received by the faculty member until the institution's costs in developing the work are recouped.
- share in revenues if the work is marketed commercially.

---

203. *Id.* at 257 (This is the "most common standard employed by universities for claiming ownership of faculty works").

204. 17 U.S.C. § 201(d).

205. Twigg, *supra* note 199, at 23. *Also see* Chapter Four herein for a more detailed discussion of the licensing of copyrighted works.

206. *See* Consortium for Educational Technology for University Systems, *Ownership of New Works at the University: Unbundling of Rights and the Pursuit of Higher Learning* (1997), http://www.cetus.org/ownership.pdf (hereinafter *CETUS Report*).

- split royalties for products sold to students at the university or college.[207]

The permutations and combinations for such allocations of rights are, of course, endless. What is critical is that a written framework be in place as an avenue for discussion and ultimate resolution of these issues. Many institutions err in overcomplicating their copyright policies by trying to foresee all possible scenarios and then drafting for their eventuality.[208] Most often, faculty works never see the commercial market and such efforts are for naught. Other schools attempt to establish "trigger" mechanisms in an institutional policy that subject participants to a forum or arbitration for determining rights. For instance, an agreement may provide that the parties must allow an independent panel to allocate royalty rates if an electronic course is sold to another university.[209]

Regardless of the form these policies ultimately take, their genesis and development are often "political" and potentially sensitive to several university constituents. The preferred approach is first to obtain and solicit input from a variety of groups on campus. "A policy drafted solely by legal counsel with no faculty, staff, or student input will be much less palatable than one a broader group helps draft. It is critical that the process be viewed as fair and that the policy ultimately respects the rights and expectations of all parties, including the institution."[210] Ideally, components of the school's administration, faculty, staff, students, librarians, IS department, and legal counsel should be involved in the process.[211] Among faculty members, care should be taken to involve "various academic disciplines in order to reflect the broadest range of faculty-created works."[212]

This all-inclusive approach has its drawbacks, however. Often the benefit of obtaining a wide array of input is diminished or outweighed by two other factors. The first is time. Involving a cross section of the university in any decision-making endeavor is likely to be a slow and cumbersome procedure. The conflict of schedules and typical unavailability of personnel during breaks and over the summer abnormally prolongs the process. Even during the academic year, a disparity often exists between "corporate speed" and "college speed."[213] Private companies have shareholders

---

207. These recommendations are drawn directly from the *CETUS Report*.
208. Twigg, *supra* note 199, at 26.
209. *Id.*
210. *See* Gasaway, *supra* note 130, at 6.
211. *Id.*
212. *Id.*
213. Twigg, *supra* note 199, at 18.

and customers to answer to and therefore are more accustomed to setting and adhering to short-term deadlines. Colleges and universities, on the other hand, measure their success not by profits, but "by the quality of the educational experience they provide, the nature of the research they generate, and the credentials of the faculty they recruit and retain."[214] As such, their approach is often more deliberative, reflective, and ultimately time-consuming than that followed in the business world.

The second diminishing factor is the possibility (if not probability) of reaching a weak and unworkable compromise. Including a diverse sector of the school's community of minds in reviewing and drafting a copyright policy necessarily involves taking into account a wide range of viewpoints and backgrounds. Often, the objectives of those involved vary considerably. Both sides will crave some degree of ownership and control. The school may seek to maximize profit potential while faculty members wish instead to promote academic freedom. Sometimes professors, because of their long years of schooling and intellectual acumen, tend to take more didactic and intransigent positions on issues than do traditional businessmen.[215] This clash of intellectual power may result in a policy that lacks cohesion, is overly ambiguous, and ultimately proves of questionable value.[216]

5.4 THE DIGITAL MILLENNIUM COPYRIGHT ACT

We are in the infancy of a networked, digital society. The early benefits of this transformation are obvious to anyone who has replaced his or her VCR with a DVD player, downloaded or updated software products over the Internet, or sampled and purchased music without visiting a record store. New and exciting online markets for distributing legitimate content are becoming a reality every day, and with advances in technology there will be benefits we have not yet imagined. But with these opportunities come real risks. The Internet and the inexpensive-yet-powerful computers that people use to access it are technological marvels, but copyright pirates have employed the technology and the Internet to cause millions of dollars in harm to copyright owners.[217]

---

214. *Id.*

215. At least this has been the experience of the author based on many years of representing both private companies and nonprofit educational institutions.

216. The author has been asked to review many such policies over the years.

217. Brief of Amici Curiae at 1, *Recording Industry Association of America v. Verizon Internet Services*, Case Nos. 03-7015, 03-7053 (consolidated appeals) (D.C. Cir. 2003).

The Digital Millennium Copyright Act[218] (hereinafter, the DMCA) was enacted to address concerns such as these. In short, the act was intended to provide copyright owners with enhanced protection in an environment where their works could be copied and distributed more easily than ever.[219] At no cost, and with a few clicks of a mouse, virtually perfect copies of digital works can now be made and disseminated on a global scale. The DMCA was a national legislative response to this threat and the reality of digital piracy. In passing the law, Congress sought to advance the interests of both copyright owners and the public at large. By granting authors and creators more reliable procedural remedies to pursue copyright infringers, Congress hoped to create an incentive for such artists to continue producing and distributing works in digital formats.

The DMCA was signed into law by President Clinton on October 28, 1998. The legislation effectuated two 1996 World Intellectual Property Organization (WIPO) treaties—the WIPO Copyright Treaty and the WIPO Performances and Phonograms Treaty. The DMCA also addressed several other significant copyright-related issues. The act is divided into five titles. Title I, the "WIPO Copyright and Performances and Phonograms Treaties Implementation Act of 1998," implemented the WIPO treaties. Title II, the "Online Copyright Infringement Liability Limitation Act," placed limitations on the liability of online service providers for copyright infringement. Since colleges and universities may be deemed "online service providers," this title has particular significance for digital distance learning.

Title III, the "Computer Maintenance Competition Assurance Act," exempted copying a computer program when maintaining and repairing a computer. Title IV contained six miscellaneous provisions relating to the functions of the Copyright Office, distance education, exceptions in the Copyright Act for libraries and making ephemeral recordings, "webcasting" of sound recordings on the Internet, and applying collective bargaining agreement obligations when transferring rights in motion pictures. Finally, Title V, the "Vessel Hull Design Protection Act," created a new form of protection for the design of vessel hulls.

The next subsection summarizes the first two titles of the DMCA (which have the greatest applicability to educational institutions) and provides an overview of the act's provisions thereunder.

---

218. Pub. L. No. 105–304, 112 Stat. 2860 (1998).

219. Raysman and Brown, *Notice and Takedown Under the Digital Millennium Copyright Act*, N.Y.L.J., Feb. 11, 2002, at 3.

[1] WIPO Treaty Implementation

Title I of the DMCA implemented the WIPO treaties in two ways. First, it made certain technical amendments to federal copyright law in order to provide appropriate references to the treaties. Second, it created two new prohibitions in Title 17 of the U.S. Code—one on circumvention of technological measures used by copyright owners to protect their works and the other on tampering with copyright management information. It also added civil remedies and criminal penalties for violating these prohibitions. Lastly, Title I of the DMCA now requires the Copyright Office to perform two joint studies with the National Telecommunications and Information Administration of the Department of Commerce (NTIA).

[a] Technical Amendments

The WIPO Copyright Treaty (WCT) and the WIPO Performances and Phonograms Treaty (WPPT) each require member countries to protect certain works from other member countries or those works created by such countries' citizens. That protection must be no less favorable than that accorded domestic works. Section 104 of the Copyright Act establishes the eligibility requirments for U.S. law to protect foreign works. Section 102(b) of the DMCA amended the Copyright Act to add new definitions required to extend U.S. protection to those works now eligible for protection under the WCT and WPPT.

Both treaties require protection of preexisting works from other member countries that have not fallen into the public domain in the country of origin. A similar obligation is contained in both the Berne Convention and the TRIPS Agreement.[220] In 1995, this obligation was implemented in the Uruguay Round Agreements Act, creating a new Section 104A of the Copyright Act. That amendment restored protection to works from Berne or World Trade Organization (WTO) member countries still protected in the country of origin, but that had fallen into the public domain in the United States because of a failure to comply with then existing U.S. formalities, or due to a lack of treaty relations. Section 102(c) of the DMCA amended Section 104A of the Copyright Act to restore protection in these same circumstances to works from WCT and WPPT member countries.

The remaining technical amendments related to the prohibition in both treaties against conditioning the exercise or enjoyment of rights on legal formalities. Section 411(a) of the Copyright Act currently requires an owner to register her work with the Copyright Office before she can

---

220. *See* Chapter Two, Section 2.2, for a more detailed discussion of these international treaties.

initiate a lawsuit. However, many foreign works were exempted from this requirement in order to comply with existing treaty obligations under the Berne Convention. Section 102(d) of the DMCA amended Section 411(a) to broaden this exemption and cover all foreign works.

[b] Technological Protection Systems

Each WIPO treaty contains virtually identical language obligating member states to prevent circumvention of technological measures used to protect copyrighted works. These obligations serve as technological adjuncts to the exclusive rights granted by copyright law. They provide the legal protection which the international copyright community deemed critical to the safe and efficient exploitation of works on digital networks. Article 11 of the WCT states: "Contracting Parties shall provide adequate legal protection and effective legal remedies against the circumvention of effective technological measures that are used by authors in connection with the exercise of their rights under this Treaty or the Berne Convention and that restrict acts, in respect of their works, which are not authorized by the authors concerned or permitted by law." Article 18 of the WPPT contains similar language.

In furtherance of these objectives, Section 103 of the DMCA added a new Chapter 12 to the Copyright Act that implemented the anti-circumvention obligation. Section 1201 divided technological measures into the categories of those (1) preventing unauthorized *access* to a copyrighted work,[221] and (2) stopping unauthorized *copying*[222] thereof. Making or selling devices or services (otherwise known as "trafficking" in such

---

221. Section 1201 addresses only the prohibition on the conduct of circumventing measures that control "access" to copyrighted works, *e.g.*, prohibiting unauthorized decryption of an encrypted work or bypassing passwords used to restrict access to copyrighted works. The structure of Section 1201 is such that there exists no comparable prohibition on the conduct of circumventing technological measures that protect the traditional rights of the copyright owner, *e.g.*, the Section 106 rights to reproduce, adapt, distribute, publicly perform, or publicly display a work. Circumventing a technological measure that protects these rights is governed not by Section 1201, but rather by the traditional copyright rights and the applicable limitations in the Copyright Act. For example, if a person circumvents a measure that prohibits printing or saving an electronic copy of an article, there is no provision in Section 1201 that precludes this activity. Instead, it would be actionable as copyright infringement of the Section 106 right of reproduction unless an applicable limitation, such as fair use, applied.

222. "Copying" is used in this context as a shorthand for the exercise of any of the exclusive rights of an author under Section 106 of the Copyright Act. Consequently, a technological measure that prevents unauthorized distribution or public performance of a work would fall in this second category.

goods or services) used to circumvent either category is generally prohibited. Specifically, Section 1201 proscribes devices or services that:

- are primarily designed or produced to circumvent;
- have only limited commercially significant purpose or use other
  than to circumvent; or
- are marketed for use in circumventing.

As to the actual act of circumvention, the provision prohibits circumventing technological measures precluding access, but *not* those measures
preventing copying. For example, copyright law explicitly recognizes
copying a computer program for archival purposes as a limitation on the
exclusive rights of a copyright owner. Hence, if a manufacturer of computer programs applied a copy-control technology to prevent unauthorized
copying of its product, a lawful purchaser could legally circumvent that
technology to make an archival copy.

This distinction was also included to permit the continuing availability of
the doctrine of fair use, which permits copying under appropriate circumstances. By contrast, since fair use is not a defense to gaining unauthorized
access to a work, such an act is prohibited.[223] This raises the question of
how logical it is, however, to permit someone to *copy* portions of a work
that he or she is not legally allowed to gain *access* to in the first place (e.g.,
an encrypted DVD). The federal courts have apparently glossed over this
seemingly important distinction by finding that technological measures
qualify as access controls even though their primary purpose may be to
prevent copying. In considering the Conduct Scrambling System (CSS)
used to encrypt most commercial DVDs, the Second Circuit observed that
"[w]hile preventing unauthorized duplication may be the primary goal of
such a technological scheme, the courts have held that CSS is a technological measure that 'effectively controls access to a work.'"[224]

The foregoing illustrates an important principle in copyright law—
namely, that copyright owners have no affirmative obligation to facilitate
any activity that limits their exclusive rights or promotes fair use. While
the courts have embraced fair use, they have never elevated it to an absolute right. For instance, the U.S. Supreme Court has noted fair use "permits

---

223. Notice of Inquiry, Exemption to Prohibition on Circumvention of Copyright Protection Systems to Access Control Technologies, 70 Fed. Reg. 57526, 57529 (Oct. 3, 2005)
(to be codified at 30 C.F.R. § 201) ("traditional Copyright Act limitations are not defenses to
the act of circumventing a technological measure that controls access").

224. *See, e.g., Universal City Studios, Inc. v. Corley*, 273 F.3d 429 (2d Cir. 2001).

courts to avoid rigid application of the copyright statute."[225] However, this flexibility of interpretation is tempered because "fair use has never been held to be a guarantee of access to copyrighted material in order to copy it by the fair user's preferred techniques, or in the format of the original."[226] Fair use has always had its limitations.[227] Even before the DMCA, movie critics could not videotape motion pictures in theaters to aid their reviews, and art students were prohibited from photographing famous paintings in violation of museum policy.

In practice, there also is little current evidence the DMCA has impeded fair use. As one federal district court recently wrote: "[T]he impact of the anti-trafficking provisions of the DMCA on prospective fair users is scanty and fails adequately to address the issues."[228] In truth, educators, reviewers, and commentators still retain other means of using a work apart from making an exact duplicate thereof. For example, while someone may not digitally reproduce an encrypted DVD, he or she may still comment on its content, quote excerpts from the original screenplay, and even record portions thereof by pointing a video camera at the TV set. Regardless, the fact that the resulting copy is not as perfect or manipulable as a digital version provides no basis for a claim under existing copyright law.

While Section 1201 prohibits trafficking in circumvention devices, it does not require manufacturers of consumer electronics, telecommunications, or computing equipment to design their products affirmatively to respond to any particular technological measure.[229] Despite this general "no mandate" rule, Section 1201(k) requires all analog videocassette recorders to conform to certain defined technologies currently in use for preventing unauthorized copying of analog videocassettes and certain analog signals. The provision prohibits rights holders, however, from applying these specified technologies to free television and basic and extended basic tier cable broadcasts.

Section 1201 also contains two general "savings" clauses. First, Section 1201(c)(1) provides that nothing in the statute diminishes any rights,

---

225. *Stewart v. Abend*, 495 U.S. 207 (1990) (quoting *Iowa State University Research Foundation, Inc. v. American Broadcasting Cos.*, 621 F.2d 57, 60 (2d Cir. 1980)); *see also Harper & Row, Publishers, Inc. v. Nation Enterprises*, 471 U.S. 539, 560 (1985) (noting "the First Amendment protections already embodied in the Copyright Act's distinction between copyrightable expression and uncopyrightable facts and ideas, and the latitude for scholarship and comment traditionally afforded by fair use").

226. *Corley, supra* note 224, at 459.

227. *See generally* F. Patry, *The Fair Use Privilege in Copyright Law*, 573–82 (2d ed. 1995) (questioning First Amendment protection for fair use).

228. *Universal I, supra* note 43, at 338 n.246.

229. 17 U.S.C. § 1201(c)(3).

remedies, limitations, or defenses to copyright infringement, including fair use. Second, Section 1201(c)(2) provides the DMCA is neither intended to enlarge or diminish vicarious or contributory infringement liability. The prohibitions contained in Section 1201 are subject to several exceptions, however, including a blanket exemption for law enforcement, intelligence, and other governmental activities.[230] Other exemptions relate to Section 1201(a), which deals with certain technological measures that control access to works.

The broadest of these, Section 1201(a)(1)(B)–(E), establishes an ongoing administrative rule-making procedure to evaluate the impact of access-control measures and permit circumvention for users of works likely to be adversely affected thereby. The Librarian of Congress (the "Librarian") and Register of Copyrights (the "Register") are currently charged with conducting this periodic review to determine whether users of particular classes of copyrighted works are, or in the next three years are likely to be, adversely affected by the prohibition on circumvention in their ability to make noninfringing uses of such works. The primary responsibility of the Register and the Librarian in this rule-making proceeding is to assess whether the implementation of access control measures is diminishing the ability of individuals to use copyrighted works in ways that are otherwise lawful.[231]

Congress intended for the Register to solicit input that would enable consideration of a broad range of current or likely future adverse impacts as well. To that end, it delineated in Section 1201(a)(1)(c) of the Copyright Act that the following issues were to be examined in all such rule making:

1. The availability for use of copyrighted works;[232]
2. The availability for use of works for nonprofit archival, preservation, and educational purposes;

---

230. 17 U.S.C. § 1201(e).

231. House Committee on Commerce, *Report on the Digital Millennium Copyright Act of 1998*, H.R. Rep. No. 105-551, pt. 2, at 22 (1998). For example, a motion picture (or individual images from a motion picture) may be performed or displayed in the course of face-to-face teaching activities in a classroom of a not-for-profit academic institution. 17 U.S.C. §110 (1). In many cases, the reproduction of portions of motion pictures or other audiovisual works for classroom use by an instructor would constitute fair use. Making such resources unavailable to educators because of encryption technology thus frustrates otherwise lawful activity.

232. This inquiry demands that the Register consider whether "works" protected by technological measures of controlling access are also available in the marketplace in formats that are unprotected.

3. The impact that the prohibition on the circumvention of technological measures applied to copyrighted works has on criticism, comment, news reporting, teaching, scholarship, or research;
4. The effect of circumvention of technological measures on the market for or value of copyrighted works; and
5. Such other factors as the Librarian considers appropriate.

The factors to be considered in the rule-making process require the Register to carefully balance the availability of works for use, the effect of the
prohibition on particular uses, and the effect of circumvention on copyrighted works. The Register is required to take into account any evidence
that particular classes of works would not be produced by their authors if
it were not for the protection afforded by technological measures controlling access thereto.[233] Thus, the Register's inquiry must assess any benefits
to the public resulting from the prohibition as well as the adverse effects
created thereby.

Since the enactment of the DMCA, there have been three such rule
makings; the first set of exceptions were issued on October 20, 2000,[234]
and the second on October 31, 2003.[235] The most recent session concluded
on November 17, 2006,[236] with the announcement by the Librarian, on the
recommendation of the Register, that the prohibition against circumvention would not apply to persons who engage in noninfringing uses of the
following six classes of copyrighted works:

1. Audiovisual works included in the educational library of a college or
   university's film or media studies department, when circumvention
   is accomplished for the purpose of making compilations of portions
   of those works for educational use in the classroom by media studies or film professors.

---

233. Exemption to Prohibition on Circumvention of Copyright Protection Systems for
Access Control Technologies, *2000 Recommendation of the Register of Copyrights*, 65 Fed.
Reg. 64,556, 64,559 (Oct. 27, 2000) (hereinafter *2000 Recommendation of the Register of
Copyrights*).

234. *Id.* at 64,558.

235. Exemption to Prohibition on Circumvention of Copyright Protection Systems for
Access Control Technologies, 68 Fed. Reg. at 62,011 (Oct. 31, 2003). *Recommendation of the
Register of Copyrights in RM 2002-4; Rulemaking on Exemptions from Prohibition on Circumvention of Copyright Protection Systems for Access Control Technologies*, dated October
27, 2003 (hereinafter *2003 Recommendation of the Register of Copyrights*).

236. *Recommendation of the Register of Copyrights in RM 2005-11; Rulemaking on
Exemptions from Prohibition on Circumvention of Copyright Protection Systems for Access
Control Technologies*, dated November 17, 2006 (hereinafter *2006 Recommendation of the
Register of Copyrights*).

2. Computer programs and video games distributed in formats that have become obsolete and that require the original media or hardware as a condition of access, when circumvention is accomplished for the purpose of preservation or archival reproduction of published digital works by a library or archive. A format shall be considered obsolete if the machine or system necessary to render perceptible a work stored in that format is no longer manufactured or is no longer reasonably available in the commercial marketplace.

3. Computer programs protected by dongles that prevent access due to malfunction or damage and which are obsolete. A dongle shall be considered obsolete if it is no longer manufactured or if a replacement or repair is no longer reasonably available in the commercial marketplace.

4. Literary works distributed in e-book format when all existing e-book editions of the work (including digital text editions made available by authorized entities) contain access controls that prevent the enabling either of the book's read-aloud function or of screen readers that render the text into a specialized format.

5. Computer programs in the form of firmware that enable wireless telephone handsets to connect to a wireless telephone communication network, when circumvention is accomplished for the sole purpose of lawfully connecting to a wireless telephone communication network.

6. Sound recordings, and audiovisual works associated with those sound recordings, distributed in compact disc format and protected by technological protection measures that control access to lawfully purchased works and create or exploit security flaws or vulnerabilities that compromise the security of personal computers, when circumvention is accomplished solely for the purpose of good faith testing, investigating, or correcting such security flaws or vulnerabilities.

Exemptions to the prohibition on circumvention remain in force for three years following the date of issuance. In each rule-making proceeding, proposed exemptions are reviewed de novo. The existence of a previous exemption creates a presumption but no assurance of its continued viability. Instead, proponents of any exemption must make a prima facie case for each triennial period, with the opponents of each class also being given the opportunity to express their objections.[237] It is the proponents of any exemption who bear the burden of proof that such an exception is warranted for a particular class of works. To meet this burden, these proponents must provide evidence that actual harm exists or is likely to occur in the ensuing three-year period.[238]

Of the six current exemptions, the first has the most applicability to teaching situations. However, it is strictly limited to audiovisual works held in a college's film department library which are to be used in the classroom by media studies or film professors. The "classroom" proviso further restricts the exception to face-to-face teaching situations, thus nullifying any utilization in distance learning settings. This exemption was proposed by several cinema studies professors who asserted that, for purposes of effective instruction, they had to be able to compile portions of various DVD movies protected by CSS.

These educators expressed a desire to be able to circumvent CSS in order to produce higher-quality content and satisfy their teaching objectives in a reasonably efficient manner. As an example, they cited the considerable amount of time needed to prepare a disc for classroom use, particularly the minutes consumed to load the DVD and watch the obligatory copyright notice and warning screens. This delay was augmented in those instances when the professor wanted to show a clip from multiple DVDs because of the need to change discs and locate the relevant scenes. Advocates of the exemption further noted that certain features were available only in digital formats (e.g., wider aspect ratios, enhanced color, divergent cinema angles, director and actor interviews, and alternative or deleted scenes), all of which they deemed important to the study of film.[239] The Register and Librarian obviously concurred with this analysis in authorizing the exemption.

Ironically, none of the exemptions promulgated by the Register applies to the DMCA's prohibitions on trafficking in those devices or services that circumvent encryption. As such, while a film professor may now be able to decrypt a DVD, anyone who develops or gives him the means of doing so is still subject to the DMCA's restrictions thereon. Since many teachers, and others wishing to take advantage of these exemptions, are not technologically savvy, they will most always rely on others to assist them. Who

---

237. *2000 Recommendation of the Register of Copyrights* at 64,563.
238. Notice of Inquiry, *supra* note 223, at 6.
239. *2006 Recommendation of the Register of Copyrights* at 20–24.

would proffer such help when those very acts could expose him or her to both civil and criminal liability? Some have argued this loophole essentially "renders [the Register-promulgated] exemptions irrelevant."[240]

Future exemptions by the Register to assist educators also appear unlikely given the Copyright Office's position on the DMCA. For instance, the Register has written that "[u]nless one can show that a particular noninfringing use can only be accomplished by using the digital version, the existence of a public domain or other work in alternative, unprotected formats provides a safety valve for noninfringing uses."[241] The Copyright Office has used this rationale to deny exemptions involving DVDs based on the fact that copy-protected digital movies are also available on "unencrypted analog VHS cassettes."[242] The Office has further shown a disinclination to allow circumvention of "mere inconveniences"[243] such as "allowing consumers to [bypass] 'unskippable' promotional material included on DVDs."[244]

Apart from this triennial rule making, Section 1201 contains some other exceptions covering a variety of circumstances:

1. *Nonprofit libraries, archives, and educational institutions.* Nonprofit libraries, archives, and educational institutions may circumvent access-control measures solely for the purpose of making a good faith determination as to whether they wish to obtain authorized access to the work.[245]

2. *Reverse engineering.* Circumvention, and the development of technological means therefor, is permitted by a person who has lawfully obtained a right to use a copy of a computer program for the sole purpose of identifying and analyzing elements thereof necessary to achieve interoperability with other programs, to the extent that such acts are permitted under copyright law.[246]

3. *Encryption research.* Circumvention of access-control measures, and the development of the technological means to do so, is permitted in order to identify flaws and vulnerabilities within encryption technologies.[247]

---

240. Timothy B. Lee, *Circumventing Competition: The Perverse Consequences of the Digital Millennium Copyright Act,* 8 (March 21, 2006).

241. *2003 Recommendation of the Register of Copyrights* at 62,112.

242. Electronic Frontier Foundation, *DMCA Triennial Rulemaking: Failing the Digital Consumer,* 4 (Dec. 1, 2005).

243. *2003 Recommendation of the Register of Copyrights* at 62,124.

244. Electronic Frontier Foundation, *supra* note 242, at 5.

245. 17 U.S.C. § 1201(d).

246. 17 U.S.C. § 1201(f).

247. 17 U.S.C. § 1201(g).

4. *Protection of minors.* A court applying the circumvention prohibition to a component or part may consider the necessity for its incorporation in technology that prevents access by minors to material on the Internet.[248]
5. *Personal privacy.* Circumvention is permitted when the technological measure, or the work it protects, is capable of collecting or disseminating personally identifying information about the online activities of a natural person.[249]
6. *Security testing.* Circumvention of access-control measures, and the development of technological means therefor, is allowed for the purpose of testing the security of a computer, computer system, or computer network, with the authorization of its owner or operator.[250]

[c] Integrity of Copyright Management Information

Both WIPO treaties also mandate member states have laws preventing tampering with the integrity of so-called copyright management information (hereinafter, CMI). Article 12 of the WCT provides in relevant part:

> Contracting Parties shall provide adequate and effective legal remedies against any person knowingly performing any of the following acts knowing, or with respect to civil remedies having reasonable grounds to know, that it will induce, enable, facilitate or conceal an infringement of any right covered by this Treaty or the Berne Convention:
>
> > (i) to remove or alter any electronic rights management information without authority;
> >
> > (ii) to distribute, import for distribution, broadcast or communicate to the public, without authority, works or copies of works knowing that electronic rights management information has been removed or altered without authority.

Article 19 of the WPPT contains nearly identical language.

The United States implemented this obligation by adding a new Section 1202 to the Copyright Act. The scope of protection is set out in two separate provisions of the act. Section 1202(a) prohibits the knowing provision or distribution of false CMI, if done with the intent to induce, enable, facilitate, or conceal infringement. Section 1202(b) bars the intentional

---

248. 17 U.S.C. § 1201(h).
249. 17 U.S.C. § 1201(i).
250. 17 U.S.C. § 1201(j).

removal or alteration of CMI without authority, as well its dissemination on copies of works, knowing that the CMI has been removed or altered without authority. Liability under subsection (b) requires the act be done with knowledge or, with respect to civil remedies, with reasonable grounds to know that it would induce, enable, facilitate, or conceal an infringement.

Section 1202(c) defines CMI as identifying information about the work, the author, the copyright owner—and in certain cases, the performer, writer, or director thereof—as well as the terms and conditions for its use. Information concerning users of works is explicitly excluded. Like Section 1201, 1202 is subject to a general exemption for law enforcement, intelligence, and other governmental activities.[251] The provision also limits the liability of broadcast stations and cable systems for removal or alteration of CMI in those circumstances where there is no intent to induce, enable, facilitate, or conceal an infringement.[252]

[d] Remedies

Any person injured by a violation of Sections 1201 or 1202 may bring a civil action in federal court. Section 1203 confers upon courts the power to grant a range of equitable and monetary remedies, including statutory damages. A court also has discretion to reduce or remit damages in cases of innocent violations, if the violator can demonstrate he was not aware and had no reason to believe his acts constituted a violation.[253] Special protection is afforded nonprofit libraries, archives, and educational institutions, which are entitled to a complete remission of damages in these circumstances.[254] To qualify for such protection, however, the defendant institution bears the burden of proof.[255] Some commentators have questioned, though, how "any responsible educational institution [could] demonstrate such ignorance of a well-known legal restriction."[256] As a further limitation, the defense is not available to individuals.[257]

In addition, it is a criminal offense to violate Sections 1201 or 1202 wilfully and for purposes of commercial advantage or private financial gain.

---

251. 17 U.S.C. § 1202(d).

252. 17 U.S.C. § 1202(e).

253. 17 U.S.C. § 1203(c)(5)(A).

254. 17 U.S.C. § 1203(c)(5)(B).

255. Id.

256. W. Fisher & W. McGeveran, *Obstacles to Educational Uses of Copyrighted Material in the Digital Age*, 18 (Aug. 10, 2006), Berkman Center Research Publication No. 2006–09, http://ssrn.com/abstract=923465.

257. Id.

Under Section 1204, maximum penalties include a $500,000 fine and/or five years imprisonment for a first offense, and a $1,000,000 fine and/or 10 years imprisonment for subsequent violations. Similar to other provisions of the Copyright Act, Section 1204 entirely exempts nonprofit libraries, archives, and educational institutions from criminal liability.

[2] Online Copyright Infringement Liability Limitation

Enactment of Title II of the DMCA was significantly promoted by the Internet service provider (ISP) industry, which at that time—the mid-1990s—was increasingly concerned that continued growth of the WWW, coupled with existing theories of contributory and vicarious liability for copyright infringement, could subject ISPs to massive exposure for the illegal conduct of their customers.[258] The fears regarding the growth of Internet piracy, at least, have turned out to be well founded.

As one federal district judge recently wrote: "[t]he extent of copyright infringement and piracy of intellectual property over the Internet . . . is well-recognized and has reached epidemic proportions."[259] Advocates for copyright owners have expressed similar sentiments by noting: "[t]he . . . wave of digital theft has now crashed over the creative industries, facilitated by the provision of faster and faster Internet connections that, while providing enormous benefits for society, have also made it more practical for copyright pirates to copy and distribute large files, such as full-length motion pictures."[260] According to one report, over 30 million Americans now have home broadband connections.[261] Other studies estimate that 400,000 to 600,000 unauthorized downloads of copyrighted motion pictures occur each day.[262]

Since ISPs are often unaware of the material subscribers place on their networks, Congress sought to grant these providers protection from potential infringement liability. In exchange, however, ISPs had to adopt certain procedural requirements to facilitate the "taking down" of allegedly infringing material from their sites and help identify culpable parties. As discussed below, the definitions of "service provider" contained in the DMCA are sufficiently broad as to encompass most educational

---

258. *See* H.R. Rep. No. 105-551 (Amended), pt. 1, at 11 (1998).

259. *In re Verizon Internet Services, Inc.*, 257 F. Supp. 2d 244 (D.D.C. 2003) (hereinafter *Second Subpoena Decision*) (quoting *United States v. Elcom Ltd.*, 203 F. Supp. 2d 1111, 1132 (N.D. Cal 2002)).

260. Brief of Amici Curiae, *supra* note 217, at 7.

261. *See* Horrigan, *Broadband Adoption at Home: A Pew Internet Data Memo*, May 18, 2003, at 1, http://www.pewinternet.org/pdfs/PIP_Broadband_adoption.pdf.

262. Brief of Amici Curiae, *supra* note 217, at xi.

institutions providing electronic networking and other services to their students and faculty.

The DMCA added Section 512 to the Copyright Act to create new liability limitations for ISPs.[263] These protections involve the following four categories of conduct normally engaged in by a service provider:

- transitory communications;
- system caching;
- storage of information on systems or networks at the direction of users; and
- information location tools.

Section 512 also includes special rules regarding how these limitations apply to nonprofit educational institutions.[264]

Each limitation entails a complete bar to monetary damages and restricts the availability of injunctive relief.[265] Since each also relates to a separate and distinct ISP function, qualifying for one limitation does not necessarily entitle the ISP to eligibility for any of the other three.[266] An ISP's failure to qualify for the protection afforded by Section 512 does not automatically render it liable, however. The copyright owner must still demonstrate the subscriber and provider have infringed, and the ISP may raise any defenses, such as fair use, available to it.[267]

[a] Section 512(h) Subpoenas

In addition to limiting ISP liability, the DMCA established a procedure whereby copyright owners could obtain subpoenas from federal courts ordering service providers to disclose the identity of subscribers allegedly engaged in infringing activities.[268] To obtain such a subpoena, a copyright

---

263. Courts have held that the limitations on liability contained in Section 512 protect secondary infringers (*e.g.*, infringement based on contributory and vicarious liability) as well as direct infringers. *See A & M Records, Inc. v. Napster*, 239 F.3d 1004, 1025 (9th Cir. 2001).

264. *See infra* subsection [2][h].

265. 17 U.S.C. § 512(j).

266. 17 U.S.C. § 512(n).

267. 17 U.S.C. § 512(l). In enacting Section 512, Congress made it clear the DMCA was not intended to supplant existing judicial decisions governing contributory infringement. *See CoStar Group, Inc. v. LoopNet, Inc.*, 373 F.3d 544, 553 (4th Cir. 2004).

268. 17 U.S.C. § 512(h).

owner (or its agent) had to file three items: (1) a "notification of claimed infringement" identifying the copyrighted work(s) and the infringing material or activity, and providing information reasonably sufficient for the ISP to locate the material; (2) the proposed subpoena directed to the ISP; and (3) a sworn declaration that the purpose thereof was "to obtain the identity of an alleged infringer and that such information [would] only be used for the purpose of protecting" a lawful copyright.[269]

Upon receipt of these items, the clerk of a federal district court was required to "expeditiously issue and sign the proposed subpoena and return it to the requester for delivery to the [ISP]."[270] After that, the ISP was "authorize[d] and order[ed] to disclose to the copyright owner the identity of the alleged infringer."[271] These so-called Section 512(h) subpoenas promptly became the subject of dispute and subsequently litigation.

In *In re Verizon Internet Services, Inc.*,[272] the Recording Industry Association of America (RIAA, or the "Association") sued Verizon Internet Services ("Verizon") to compel compliance with a subpoena ordering Verizon to disclose the identity of several Verizon subscribers whom the RIAA suspected of copyright infringement. The principal issue before the court concerned whether an ISP acting as a "mere conduit" under Section 512(a) of the Copyright Act had to comply with such a subpoena, or whether the requirement applied only to providers of hosting and linking services under Sections 512(c) and (d). The federal district court ruled that Section 512(h) covered all ISP conduct.

When the RIAA then served a second subpoena on Verizon,[273] the defendant argued a federal clerk of court lacked the power under Article III of the U.S. Constitution to issue a subpoena unless a lawsuit had first been filed. Verizon further contended Section 512(h) violated its subscribers' First Amendment and privacy rights. Lastly, Verizon suggested a copyright owner could obtain a Section 512(h) subpoena only when the alleged infringer had stored her pirated catalogue on the ISP's server rather than her own computer. Admittedly, such a construction made it difficult to identify those persons using so-called peer-to-peer services that, as the district court had earlier noted, provided "the largest opportunity for copyright theft."[274]

---

269. 17 U.S.C. §§ 512(h)(2)(A)–(C).

270. 17 U.S.C. § 512(h)(4).

271. 17 U.S.C. §§ 512(h)(3), (5).

272. 240 F. Supp. 2d 34 (D.D.C. 2003) (hereinafter *First Subpoena Decision*).

273. *Second Subpoena Decision, supra* note 259.

274. *First Subpoena Decision, supra* note 272, at 35.

Again, the district court rejected Verizon's arguments and ordered disclosure of the subscribers' names. In doing so, it found no place in the DMCA or its legislative history where Congress had drawn a distinction between placing pirated works on an ISP server rather than a peer-to-peer (P2P) network.[275] In fact, the court reiterated that excluding peer-to-peer infringers "would create a huge loophole in Congress's effort to prevent copyright infringement on the Internet" and "allow infringement to flourish."[276]

Verizon promptly appealed the district court's ruling and presented three alternative arguments to support reversal: (1) Section 512(h) did not authorize the issuance of a subpoena to an ISP acting solely as a conduit for communications; (2) the statute was unconstitutional because the district court lacked Article III jurisdiction to issue a subpoena with no underlying "case or controversy" pending before it; and (3) Section 512(h) violated the First Amendment because it lacked sufficient safeguards to protect an Internet user's ability to speak and associate anonymously.

Specifically, Verizon argued that a legal request could never meet the requirement of Section 512(h)(2)(A) that any subpoena must contain "a copy of a notification [of claimed infringement, as] described in [§ 512](c)(3)(A)." In particular, Verizon maintained the two subpoenas obtained by the RIAA failed to meet the requirements of Section 512(c)(3)(A)(iii) in that they did not—because Verizon was not storing the infringing material on its server—and could not identify material "to be removed or access to which is to be disabled" by Verizon. Verizon further pointed out that Section 512(h)(4) made satisfaction of the notification requirement of Section 512(c)(3)(A) a condition precedent to the subpoena's issuance.

As the federal appeals court correctly observed, infringing material obtained or distributed via P2P file sharing is located in the computer (or in an off-line storage device, such as a compact disc) of an individual user. No matter what information the copyright owner may provide, the ISP could never "remove" nor "disable access to" the infringing material, because it was not stored on its servers. In other words, since Verizon did not control the content on its subscribers' computers, it could never comply with an order to disable access thereto—rendering the subpoenas superfluous.

---

275. Brief of Amici Curiae, *supra* note 217, at 11.
276. *First Subpoena Decision, supra* note 272, at 35–36.

As such, the appeals court found for Verizon and overturned the lower court ruling.[277] In doing so, it specifically held that Section 512(h) does not apply to Section 512(a) service providers, but rather was "structurally linked to the storage functions of an ISP and not to its transmission functions, such as those listed in § 512(a)."[278] Because of its interpretation of Section 512(h), the court deemed it unnecessary to rule on the two Constitutional arguments raised by the defendant. Realizing its ruling would create a major hindrance for the recording industry, however, the court wrote:

> We are not unsympathetic either to the RIAA's concern regarding the widespread infringement of its members' copyrights, or to the need for legal tools to protect those rights. It is not the province of the courts, however, to rewrite the DMCA in order to make it fit a new and unforeseen internet architecture, no matter how damaging that development has been to the music industry or threatens being to the motion picture and software industries. The plight of copyright holders must be addressed in the first instance by the Congress; only the "Congress has the constitutional authority and the institutional ability to accommodate fully the varied permutations of competing interests that are inevitably implicated by such new technology."[279]

On October 12, 2004, the U.S. Supreme Court refused to grant certiorari for the *Verizon* case, thereby permitting the federal appeals court decision to stand.[280] While this finding was a setback, the entertainment industry's efforts to combat piracy currently continue on several fronts. In addition to private citizens, colleges and universities across the country have been affected by Hollywood's tactics. For instance, in March 2003, Universal Studios lodged e-mail complaints with several educational institutions citing the Internet protocol (IP) addresses of machines on which it

---

277. *Recording Industry Association of America, Inc. v. Verizon Internet Services, Inc.*, 351 F.3d 1229 (D.C. Cir. 2003), *cert. denied*, ____U.S. ____, 125 S. Ct. 309 (2004). The Eighth Circuit has also followed the D.C. Circuit's reasoning on this matter. *See In re Charter Communications, Inc., Subpoena Enforcement Matter*, 393 F.3d 771 (8th Cir. 2005). The analysis employed by the court in *Verizon* has also been applied to universities holding they may be deemed Section 512(a) providers (or "mere conduits") and therefore not subject to Section 512(h) subpoenas. *See In Re Subpoena to University of North Carolina at Chapel Hill*, No. 1:03MC138, slip op. at 11 (M.D.N.C. April 14, 2005).

278. *Recording Industry Association, supra* note 277, at 1237.

279. *Id.* at 1238 (internal citations omitted) .

280. *U.S. Court Rejects Music Industry Appeal*, smh.com.au (Oct. 13, 2004), http://www.smh.com.au/articles/2004/10/13/1097607260002.html; Cong. Budget Office, *Copyright Issues in Digital Media*, at 19 n.34 (Aug. 2004) (hereinafter *CBO Report*).

says copyrighted films were shared illegally.[281] The University of Maryland was notified of 155 offending computers, while the University of Wisconsin at Madison was asked to investigate activity on 127 machines.[282]

Approximately one month later, the RIAA filed lawsuits against four college students who had offered access to copyrighted music files within their institutions' networks.[283] The complaints sought $150,000 in damages for each of the dozens of recordings the students had allegedly used illegally.[284] These cases were ultimately settled, and the defendants paid between $12,500 and $17,000 each.[285] In late April 2003, the RIAA announced it would be sending warning messages directly to millions of users of popular file-sharing programs—including college students.[286] On April 12, 2005, the RIAA filed 405 separate suits against students, at 18 different schools, who were allegedly trading copyrighted music using a faster version of the WWW called Internet 2, a separate network often used by colleges and universities for sharing research and other academic works.[287]

In response to its loss in *Verizon*, the RIAA also started to initiate "John Doe" lawsuits, which target groups of suspected copyright infringers. In these cases, plaintiffs are usually able to identify the ISP to which the defendants subscribed using a publicly available database to trace the IP address for that person. ISPs own or are assigned certain blocks or ranges of IP addresses. In turn, an ISP assigns an IP address to a subscriber. Thus, an ISP can identify the computer from which the alleged infringement occurred and obtain the name and address of the subscriber from its customer files.[288] In "John Doe" cases, the court may issue a collective subpoena to the ISP for identifying information on individuals within the

---

281. Read, *Film Studios Send Hundreds of Letters Alleging Illegal Downloading to Colleges*, Chron. of Higher Educ., Mar. 5, 2003.

282. *Id.*

283. Carlson, *Recording Industry Sues Four Students*, Chron. of Higher Educ., April 4, 2003.

284. *Id.*

285. *RIAA: We'll Spare the Small Fry*, Wired News, Aug. 19, 2003, http://www.wired.com/entertainment/music/news/2003/08/60092.

286. Carlson, *Record Industry Will Send Warnings to Millions of Users of P2P File Sharing Services*, Chron. of Higher Educ., April 30, 2003.

287. Ahrens, *Music Industry Sues Hundreds of File Sharers at Colleges*, Wash. Post, April 13, 2005, p. E01. It has been estimated that the music industry filed over 23,000 such suits between 2003 and 2006. *See Why the Music Industry's New Piracy Tactics Will Fail*, Times Online (July 19, 2006).

288. *Sony Music Entertainment, Inc. v. Does 1-40*, 326 F. Supp. 2d 556, 558 (S.D.N.Y. 2004).

group only after considering the merits of the case.[289] This contrasts sharply with Section 512(h)'s subpoena provisions, under which identifying information was obtained first and individual lawsuits filed thereafter.[290]

Apart from the DMCA and "John Doe" defenses, some universities have moved to quash information requests on the basis they conflict with the Family Education Rights and Privacy Act,[291] which requires educational institutions to notify students before releasing their personal information.[292] Conversely, many schools are now cooperating with the music industry and have dramatically increased efforts to discourage students from downloading copyrighted music and movie files via university networks.[293]

[b] Eligibility for ISP Limitations Generally

An Internet company or university seeking protection under the DMCA must initially qualify as a "service provider." For purposes of the first limitation, relating to transitory communications, "service provider" is defined in Section 512(k)(1)(A) of the Copyright Act as "an entity offering the transmission, routing, or providing of connections for digital online communications, between or among points specified by a user, of material of the user's choosing, without modification to the content of the material as sent or received." For purposes of the other three limitations, "service provider" is more broadly defined in Section 512(k)(1)(B) as "a provider of online services or network access, or the operator of facilities therefor." Thus, any educational institution providing or facilitating Internet or e-mail access for its students and/or faculty through its own network falls within this definition.

Two additional conditions must be met for an ISP to be eligible for the liability limitations. A service provider must (1) adopt and reasonably implement a policy of terminating in appropriate circumstances those subscribers who are repeat infringers; and (2) accommodate and not

---

289. *Id.* at 565 ("Plaintiffs have made a concrete showing of a prima facie claim of copyright infringement.").

290. One federal court requires that before an ISP is forced to disclose its subscribers, it must submit a notice to each "John Doe" explaining what has occurred and how to contest the charges. *See Elektra Entertainment Group, Inc. v. Does 1-6*, No. 04-1241, slip. op. at 2 (E.D. Pa. Oct. 13, 2004).

291. *CBO Report, supra* note 283, at 19.

292. 20 U.S.C. § 1232(g); 34 C.F.R. Part 99.

293. Graham, *Colleges Aggressively Cracking Down on Downloads of Music*, USA Today, April 27, 2003. *See* Chapter Three, Section 3.3[6][e], for a detailed discussion of the steps some universities are currently taking to discourage P2P file sharing among their students.

interfere with "standard technical measures."[294] "Standard technical measures" are defined as those that (1) copyright owners use to identify or protect copyrighted works; (2) have been developed pursuant to a broad consensus of copyright owners and service providers in an open, fair, and voluntary multi-industry process; (3) are available to anyone on reasonable nondiscriminatory terms; and (4) do not impose substantial costs or burdens on ISPs.

[c] Limitation for Transitory Communications

In general terms, Section 512(a) of the Copyright Act limits the liability of ISPs in those circumstances where they merely function as a data conduit, transmitting digital information from one point on a network to another at someone else's request. This limitation covers acts of transmission, routing, or providing connections for the information, as well as the intermediate and transient copies[295] automatically made during the network's operation. To qualify for this limitation, an ISP's activities must meet the following conditions:

- The transmission must be initiated by a person other than the provider.
- The transmission, routing, provision of connections, or copying must be carried out by an automatic technical process without the ISP selecting any material.
- The service provider must not determine the material's recipients.
- Any intermediate copies must not ordinarily be accessible to anyone other than anticipated recipients and must not be retained for longer than reasonably necessary.
- The material must be transmitted without modification of its content.

For these types of activities, the ISP is considered to be functioning only as a "mere conduit" of information, and is not required to remove or "take down" any content posted without the copyright owner's authorization.[296]

---

294. 17 U.S.C. § 512(i).

295. *See Ellison v. Robertson*, 357 F.2d 1072, 1081 (9th Cir. 2004) (storage by AOL of online postings for 14 days still considered "intermediate" and "transient" for purposes of Section 512(a)).

296. Jennifer M. Urban, *Efficient Process or 'Chilling Effects'? Takedown Notices Under Section 512 of the Digital Millennium Copyright Act*, 3 (Nov. 30, 2005), http://mylaw.usc .edu/documents/512Rep/.

[d] Limitation for System Caching

Section 512(b) limits ISP liability for retaining copies, for a specified time, of material made available online by a person other than the provider, which is then transmitted to a subscriber at his or her direction. The ISP retains the material so that subsequent requests therefor can be fulfilled by transmitting the retained copy, rather than retrieving it from the original source on the network. Thus, the limitation applies to acts of intermediate and temporary storage[297] carried out through an automatic technical process. It is subject to the following conditions:

- The content of the retained material may not be modified.
- The provider must comply with rules about "refreshing" material replacing retained copies thereof from the original location when specified in accordance with a generally accepted industry standard data communication protocol.
- The ISP may not interfere with technology meeting certain requirements that returns "hit" information to the person posting the material.
- The provider must limit users' access to the material in accordance with connection conditions (e.g., password protection) imposed by the person posting such material.
- Any content posted without the copyright owner's authorization must be removed or blocked promptly once the ISP has been notified that it has been removed, blocked, or ordered to be removed or blocked, at the originating site.

[e] Limitation for Information Residing on Systems or Networks at the Direction of Users

Section 512(c) of the Copyright Act limits a provider's liability for infringing material on websites (or other information repositories) hosted on its system. It applies to storage at the direction of a user. To be eligible, an ISP must meet the following conditions:

- The provider may not have actual knowledge of the infringing activity, or be aware of facts or circumstances from which the infringing acitivity is apparent.
- If the ISP has the right and ability to control the infringing activity, it must not receive a financial benefit directly attributable thereto.

---

297. *See Field, supra* note 16, at 24 (Google's cache of web pages for 14 to 20 days held to still be "intermediary and temporary storage" for purposes of Section 512(b)).

- Upon receiving proper notification of a claimed infringement, the provider must expeditiously take down or block access to the material.

In addition, the ISP has to file a designation of agent to receive infringement notices with the U.S. Copyright Office. This designation must contain the name, address, telephone number, and e-mail address of the agent. This notice must also be posted on the service provider's website. The Copyright Office has adopted certain rules for designated agent filings.[298]

[f] Limitation for Information Location Tools

Section 512(d) of the Copyright Act relates to hyperlinks, online directories, search engines, and the like. It limits liability for referring or linking users to sites that contain infringing material, if the following conditions are met:

- The service provider must not have the requisite level of knowledge that the material is infringing. The knowledge standard is the same as under the limitation for information residing on systems or networks.
- If the ISP has the right and ability to control the infringing activity, it must not receive a financial benefit directly attributable thereto.
- Upon receiving a notification of claimed infringement, the provider must expeditiously take down or block access to the material.

[g] Notice and Takedown Requirements

As noted above, three out of the four limitations make reference to the service provider having to take down allegedly infringing material upon receiving notice from an aggrieved copyright owner or his representative. A more detailed discussion of this requirement follows.

[i] General Provisions

The DMCA specifically established procedures for proper notification and rules regarding its effect.[299] Pursuant to this process, a copyright owner must submit a notification under penalty of perjury, including a list of specified elements, to the service provider's designated agent. If, upon receiving such notice, the service provider promptly removes or blocks access to the material identified therein, the provider becomes exempt from monetary liability. In addition, the ISP is shielded from any claims of

---

298. *See* 37 C.F.R. § 201.38. The Copyright Office provides a suggested form for the purpose of designating an agent (http://www.loc.gov/copyright/onlinesp/) and maintains a list of agents on its website, http://www.loc.gov/copyright/onlinesp/list/.

299. 17 U.S.C. § 512(c)(3).

the person originally posting the material on its server.[300] Once removed, the material must stay off the site for at least 10 to 14 days.

This provision is not intended as a substitute for copyright infringement claims, nor is it an exclusive remedy for a copyright owner.[301] The copyright holder may still elect to file an infringement action in a court of law without utilizing the DMCA. However, initially proceeding under the act has significant advantages. First, it provides a speedy and cost-effective resolution of the issue if the ISP complies and removes the infringing material.[302] Second, the burden shifts to the service provider, which loses its immunity if it fails to remove the questionable material.[303] Thus, the copyright owner has added another potential defendant to the mix. This may prove significant because often the actual copyright infringer has limited financial resources to pursue.

A "takedown" notice under the DMCA is not the same as a Section 512(h) subpoena, however, because it does *not* require the ISP to identify the alleged infringer. In addition, since the notice is not technically a court order, the provider may choose to ignore it. If the described material is not removed, however, the service provider loses its limited liability protection[304] but still retains all copyright defenses otherwise available to it.[305]

[ii] Requirements for "Notification of Claimed Infringement"

The DMCA requires an effective "notification of claimed infringement" to be a "written communication" provided to the ISP's "designated agent."[306] The notice must include "substantially"[307] the following six elements:

(i)   A physical or electronic signature of the copyright owner or his authorized agent (the "complaining party").

(ii) Identification of the work claimed to have been infringed, or, if multiple copyrighted works are involved, a representative list of such works.

---

300. 17 U.S.C. § 512(g)(1).

301. Raysman and Brown, *supra* note 219, at 4. *See also Ellison v. Robertson, supra* note 295, at 1077 ("the DMCA did not simply rewrite copyright law for the online world").

302. Some commentators have taken a different view, suggesting the DMCA "takedown" process is often used not to protect copyright but to intimidate competitors, inhibit fair use, and disguise other legal claims. *See* Urban, *supra* note 296, at 13.

303. *Id.*

304. *Id.*

305. 17 U.S.C. § 512(l).

306. 17 U.S.C. § 512(c)(3)(A).

307. *Id.*

(iii) Identification of the material to be removed or access to which is to be disabled, with information reasonably sufficient to permit the service provider to locate this content.

(iv) Information reasonably sufficient to permit the service provider to contact the complaining party, such as an address, telephone number, and, if available, an e-mail address.

(v) A statement that the complaining party has a good faith belief that display of the material in the manner used is not authorized by the copyright owner, its agent, or the law.

(vi) A statement that the information in the notice is accurate, and under penalty of perjury, that the complaining party is authorized to act to protect an exclusive right that has allegedly been infringed.[308]

The requisite level of knowledge resulting in potential liability for an ISP will not be attributed to it if a notice from the complaining party fails to comply with the above provisions. In a case where the notice substantially complies with only clauses (ii), (iii), and (iv) above, however (and not the others), the service provider must promptly attempt to contact the complaining party or take other reasonable steps to receive the information that substantially complies with all the provisions above.[309]

[iii] Recent Cases on the "Notice and Takedown" Provision

To date, only a few cases have interpreted the notice and takedown provisions of the DMCA, and none have done so for an educational setting. In *ALS Scan Inc. v. Remarq Communities Inc.*,[310] the Fourth Circuit held that providing information to the defendant ISP, which listed two news groups composed almost entirely of plaintiff's copyrighted works along with supplying hyperlinks to plaintiff's own versions of the material, "substantially complied" with the DMCA. In *Hendrickson v. eBay Inc.*,[311] a California federal district court held a copyright owner must supply a service provider with information sufficient to enable it to target the actual infringing material. In *Hendrickson*, the owner did not provide eBay enough detail

---

308. 17 U.S.C. §512 (c)(3)(A)(i)–(vi).

309. 17 U.S.C. §512(c)(3)(B)(i) and (ii).

310. 239 F.3d 619 (4th Cir. 2001).

311. 165 F. Supp. 2d 1082 (C.D. Cal. 2001).

to permit it to discern between the counterfeit and authorized copies of a video being auctioned on its site.[312]

A copyright owner's duty to conduct a preliminary investigation prior to sending a "takedown" notice was considered in the unreported case of *Rossi v. Motion Picture Association of America*.[313] In *Rossi*, plaintiff owned and operated an online movie news magazine. The defendant, Motion Picture Association of America (MPAA), was a trade association that, among other things, sought to limit unauthorized copying and distribution of its members' motion pictures.[314] MPAA representatives had previously visited plaintiff's website and reported it was offering full-length copyrighted movies to its subscribers.

MPAA subsequently sent a "takedown" notice to FlexNet, Inc. ("FlexNet"), the plaintiff's ISP, asking it to remove the website from its server because of the allegedly infringing content. In response thereto, Mr. Rossi filed suit against the Association, claiming (1) hindrance with contractual relations; (2) tortious interference with prospective economic advantage; (3) libel and defamation; and (4) intentional infliction of emotional distress. Mr. Rossi also claimed MPAA's notice was premature because it had failed to investigate whether the website *actually* infringed on any copyrights before sending the document.

In reviewing the matter, the court found the DMCA did not require a copyright holder to establish actual infringement prior to sending notice. Rather, the court ruled the law mandated only that a "good faith belief" of an alleged or "claimed" infringement be found before the notice could be sent.[315] This standard was deemed fulfilled in *Rossi* because plaintiff's website contained such statements as: "Join to download full length movies online now! New movies every month"; "Full Length Downloadable Movies"; and "NOW DOWNLOADABLE." Accordingly, the court ruled MPAA had more than a sufficient basis for asking FlexNet to disable the web page. The fact that movies could not be downloaded from the site (or that a further investigation may have revealed this) was not deemed relevant.

---

312. Raysman and Brown, *supra* note 219, at 6.

313. No. 02-00239BMK, slip op. (D. Haw. April 29, 2003).

314. MPAA's members include Columbia Pictures Industries, Inc., Disney Enterprises, Inc., Metro Goldwyn-Mayer Studios, Inc., Paramount Pictures Corporation, TriStar Pictures, Inc., Twentieth Century Fox Film Corporation, United Artists Pictures, Inc., United Artists Corporation, Universal City Studios, LLP, and Time Warner Entertainment Company, LP.

315. *See* 17 U.S.C. § 512(c)(3)(A)(v).

[iv] Counter-notices

To guard against erroneous or fraudulent notifications, Section 512 contains certain safeguards. Primarily, the service provider must promptly notify the allegedly infringing subscriber that it has removed or disabled access to what he or she had posted. The subscriber may then, under Section 512(g)(1), serve a counter-notification on the ISP.[316] This counter-notice must comply with certain statutory requirements, including a sworn statement that the material was removed or disabled through mistake or misidentification. If the provider receives such a notice, it must re-post the material. The ISP need not do so, however, if the copyright owner is in the process of obtaining a court order against the subscriber.

[v] Penalties

The DMCA imposes significant penalties for making material misrepresentations in either a notice or a counter-notice. Any person who knowingly misrepresents that certain content is infringing, or that it was removed or blocked through mistake or misidentification, is liable for any resulting damages (including costs and attorneys' fees) incurred by the alleged infringer, the copyright owner, its licensee, or the ISP, as the case may be.[317]

[h] *Special Rules Regarding Liability of Nonprofit Educational Institutions*

Section 512(e) of the Copyright Act, as added by the DMCA, determines when the actions or knowledge of a faculty member or graduate student employee[318] affect a nonprofit educational institution's eligibility to limit its liability. Traditionally, under the doctrine of respondeat superior, employers are responsible for the acts or omissions of their employees provided they occur within the scope of employment.[319] As such, a college or university would normally be held liable for acts of copyright infringement committed by its faculty or staff in the course of a person's job performance. The DMCA provides an exception to this doctrine for nonprofit

---

316. Search engine services are not subject to this requirement. As such, links to allegedly infringing material are "typically removed from the search engine's index, based only on the copyright holder's . . . letters, without any other notice or process." Urban, *supra* note 296, at 3.

317. 17 U.S.C. § 512(f).

318. The section does not apply to students who would normally be considered "subscribers" to the university's electronic network under the DMCA.

319. *See* Prosser, *Law of Torts* § 70 (4th ed. 1971).

educational institutions. The exception varies slightly among the four major categories of conduct carried on by an ISP.

For transitory communications or system caching, the faculty member or graduate student is considered a "person other than the provider," in essence circumventing the respondeat superior doctrine (which views the employer and its employee as a single person). As for the other two limitations, the knowledge or awareness of the faculty member or graduate student is not be attributed to the institution, thereby absolving it of liability. The following conditions must be met by the school in order for this immunity to take hold:

- The faculty member or graduate student employee must be performing a teaching or research function.
- The faculty member or graduate student's infringing activities may not involve providing online access to course materials required or recommended during the past three years.
- The institution has not received more than two notices over the past three years that the faculty member or graduate student was engaged in using infringing material.
- The institution must provide all of its faculty, staff and students with information describing and promoting compliance with copyright law.[320]

As such, Section 512(e) does not provide a blanket immunity to educational institutions. Schools are still potentially liable if their instructors or graduate student assistants use infringing material for online courses or have exhibited a pattern of questionable behavior over a period of time. In addition, since truly independent (i.e., non-course or research related) infringing conduct of a university employee already falls outside the scope of his or her employment (and is customarily not actionable against the employer), one questions how much added protection this provision actually affords the institution.

---

320. The legislative history of the DMCA suggests an educational institution will be in compliance with this test if it provides access to materials prepared by Register of Copyrights. As such, a college merely directing or linking its faculty to the U.S. Copyright Office website may fulfill this requirement. *See* K. Salomon, *Copyright Considerations in Distance Education and Technology-Mediated Instruction* (July 5, 2000), http://www.aacc.nche.edu/Content/ContentGroups/White_Papers1/copyright.pdf. The recently enacted TEACH Act contains a similar requirement but no guidance as to compliance standards. *See* Chapter Six for a more detailed discussion of the TEACH Act.

[3] Conclusion

The DMCA "safe harbor" provisions were enacted to bring copyright law into the Internet age and help balance the interests of copyright owners and ISPs by supplying both with "strong incentives ... to cooperate to detect and deal with copyright infringements" taking place online.[321] At the same time, the DMCA continues to demonstrate congressional support for nonprofit educational institutions by allowing them to circumvent certain technological protective measures, mitigate damages under specified circumstances, and be immunized from certain acts of their employees.

But can even the recently enacted DMCA keep pace with technology? Can any legislation in this area? Congress attempted to accommodate fair use and privacy concerns in crafting the anti-circumvention provisions of the DMCA. It also tried to give copyright owners enhanced protection for their works through the notice and takedown procedures. Technological advances are now outpacing both objectives. As consumers are able to enjoy creative works in constantly innovative ways (e.g., iPods, wireless receivers, P2P networks), additional obstacles arise in the efforts of copyright owners to identify and penalize copyright infringement.

Conversely, while new technology expands an owner's ability to control his work, it also strains the privileges of private citizens. For example, how can a teacher make fair use of even a small portion of a work when he or she is forever denied access to it as a whole? Technological advances therefore continue to place growing pressures on the already delicate balance existing between copyright owners and consumers. Whether a satisfactory equilibrium can ever be achieved remains the subject of much dispute and discussion.

5.5 THE CHILDREN'S INTERNET PROTECTION ACT

As referenced in Chapter One, most distance learning taking place at the postsecondary level occurs through mediated online instruction, both synchronously and asynchronously. Distance education instructors are generally separated from their students by either time, distance, or both. Most primary and secondary schools have not yet reached this plane of sophistication, however. Distance learning at the K–12 level primarily encompasses use of the Internet by students as a research and communications tool. As such, a chapter on "Distance Learning and the Internet"

---

321. H.R. Conf. Rep. No. 105-796, at 71 (1998), *reprinted at* 1998 U.S. Code Cong. & Admin. News, 649.

would be incomplete without a discussion of federal legislation regulating this interaction.

Current federal law requires local school systems to adopt Internet Acceptable Use Policies (often called "IAUPs" or "AUPs") for their students. Such policies are often integrated into or supplement copyright compliance manuals, which are used to meet the information requirements of the DMCA and TEACH Act.[322] The most relevant statute is the Children's Internet Protection Act (CIPA).[323] Its history, scope, and application are examined below.

[1] The Evolution of CIPA

Congress enacted CIPA in October 2000. Among other items, it requires schools and libraries receiving discounted telecommunications, Internet access, or internal connections services through federal funding to certify and adopt Internet safety policies. The law also forces local school systems to employ technological protections to block or filter out certain visual depictions deemed obscene, pornographic, or harmful to minors.

[a] Children and the Internet

The Internet's explosive growth in the United States has been fueled in part by the online activities of young people. Children and teenagers use computers and the Internet more than any other age group.[324] By the fall of 2001, 99% of public schools in the United States offered Internet access, and had expanded such access into 87% of instructional rooms.[325] Approximately 65% of American children between the ages 2 and 17 use the Internet from home, school, or other locations.[326] Access to the resources of the WWW has given these youngsters new research tools, information sources, avenues of expression, collaborative learning opportunities, and

---

322. Pub. L. No. 107–273, 116 Stat. 1758 (2002). *See* Chapter Six for a detailed discussion of the provisions and requirements of the TEACH Act.

323. Children's Internet Protection Act, Pub. L. No. 106–554 (2000) (codified at 20 U.S.C. §§ 6801, 6777, 9134; 47 U.S.C. § 254).

324. U.S. Department of Commerce, National Telecommunications and Information Administration, *A Nation Online: How Americans Are Expanding Their Use of the Internet*, at 1, 13 (Feb. 2002), http://www.ntia.doc.gov/ntiahome/dn/index.html.

325. National Center for Education Statistics, *Internet Access in U.S. Public Schools and Classrooms: 1994–2001*, at 3 (Sept. 2002), http://nces.ed.gov/pubs2002/2002018.pdf.

326. Corporation for Public Broadcasting, *Connected to the Future* (Mar. 2003), http://www.cpb.org/stations/reports/connected/connected_report.pdf.

connections to other communities.[327] However, it has also exposed them to the unseemly side of life—indecent material, pornography, hate sites, and online predators.[328]

In 2002, the National Academies released *Youth, Pornography, and the Internet*, a report that examined various tools and strategies for protecting children from online pornography. The study concluded no "foreseeable technological 'silver bullets' or single permanent solutions" existed to keep children safe from such material.[329] Rather, the report supported solutions balancing the Internet's potential benefits to children with the competing goals and values of local communities.[330] As online dangers to children have emerged, so have a variety of protective tools.[331] Some common technologies used to safeguard young people include:

- *Filtering with Yes or No lists.*
  - *Server-side filtering.* ISPs and online server software offer filtering techniques to customers that deny access to particular content sources preselected for blocking via automated processes, human review, and/or user options. The list of blocked URLs may or may not be disclosed and is regularly updated at the server level.[332]
  - *Client-side filtering.* This technology prohibits the browser from downloading material based on specified content sources identified by the user. Blocked sites may originate from both the software supplier and/or the user's decision. Users maintain control over these lists with a password and may periodically download updated lists from the supplier's website. Some software also filters out e-mail or instant messaging.[333]
  - *Filtering using text-based content analysis.* Combines PC-based and server software to conduct real-time analysis of a website's content to filter out illicit content. Some software analyzes e-mail and attach-

---

327. *See, e.g.,* U.S. Department of Commerce, *National Telecommunications and Information Administration, How Access Benefits Children: Connecting Our Kids to the World of Information* (Sept. 1999).

328. The Commission on Child Online Protection Act, *Final Report to Congress*, at 1 (Oct. 20, 2001).

329. National Research Council, *Youth, Pornography, and the Internet, Committee to Study Tools and Strategies for Protecting Kids from Pornography and Their Applicability to Other Inappropriate Internet Content*, at 387 (May 2002).

330. *Id.*

331. *Final Report to Congress, supra* note 328.

332. *Id.* at 19.

333. *Id.* at 21.

ments. The user may or may not gain access to how such content is excluded.[334]

- *Monitoring and time-limiting technologies.* Tracks a child's online activities and sets limits on the amount of time he or she may spend on the Internet. Monitoring software often covers the WWW, e-mail, and instant messaging activities.[335]
- *Age verification system.* Uses an independently issued ID and controls the flow of online content by making access to a web page conditioned upon use of a password issued by a third party.[336]

Even the most sophisticated technology tools are not 100 percent effective, though.[337] Public awareness campaigns and workshops have sought to supplement this approach.[338] In addition, Congress has passed several other bills to legislate a solution. These are examined below.

[b] Related Congressional Efforts to Protect Children from Inappropriate Online Content

In 1996, Congress first attempted to curb inappropriate online content by enacting the Communications Decency Act (CDA).[339] The CDA prohibited sending or posting obscene or indecent material via the Internet to persons under the age of eighteen. The United States Supreme Court declared the law unconstitutional, however, ruling it violated the First Amendment.[340] Specifically, the Court found the CDA's vague provisions chilled free speech unknown to the speaker generating the content and criminalized legitimate, protected speech, including some sexually explicit communications.

Congress responded by passing more narrowly tailored legislation in the form of the Child Online Protection Act of 1998 (COPA).[341] COPA, among other things, imposed a $50,000 fine and six months in prison for the knowing posting, for "commercial purposes," of Web content deemed "harmful to minors." It provided an affirmative defense, however, to commercial websites that restricted access to prohibited materials by "requiring use of a credit card" or "any other reasonable measures [found]

---

334. *Id.* at 22.

335. *Id.* at 34.

336. *Id.* at 25–26.

337. *Digital Chaperones for Kids: Which Internet Filters Protect the Best? Which Get in the Way?* Consumer Rep., Mar. 2001, at 2.

338. *See, e.g.,* http://www.GetNetWise.org and http://www.NetSmart.org.

339. Pub. L. No. 104–104, 110 Stat. 56 (codified at 47 U.S.C. § 223).

340. *Reno v. American Civil Liberties Union,* 521 U.S. 844 (1997).

341. Pub. L. No. 105–277, 112 Stat. 2681-2736 (codified at 47 U.S.C. § 231).

feasible under available technology." The United States District Court for the Eastern District of Pennsylvania subsequently ruled COPA's reference to "contemporary community standards" violated the First Amendment when applied to the WWW, and enjoined its enforcement.[342]

The Third Circuit affirmed, stating the reference to community standards in the definition of "material that is harmful to minors" resulted in an ambiguously broad statute.[343] In May 2002, the United States Supreme Court vacated the Third Circuit decision and remanded the case for further review.[344] The Supreme Court found that "contemporary community standards" by itself did not render the statute unconstitutional for First Amendment purposes.[345] On remand, the Third Circuit found COPA was not narrowly tailored enough to satisfy the First Amendment and affirmed the original District Court's ruling.[346]

The Third Circuit's decision was again appealed by the Justice Department to the United States Supreme Court. On June 29, 2004, the Supreme Court held the Third Circuit was correct to affirm the original District Court's ruling.[347] The Court noted the lower tribunal had relied heavily on the contention there were plausible, less restrictive alternatives to COPA.[348] The Court agreed that when a content-based speech restriction is challenged, the burden shifts to the defendants to show proposed alternatives would be less effective than the statute in question.[349] Thus, it became the government's obligation to prove speech would not be restricted any more than necessary to accomplish a congressional objective.[350] The Third Circuit had previously concluded COPA's proponents (i.e., Congress and the federal government) had failed to meet this critical burden.[351]

Those challenging the statute had already posited that blocking and filtering software constituted a less restrictive alternative.[352] As a result, the Supreme Court took judicial notice of the primary advantage of filters—

---

342. *The American Civil Liberties Union v. Reno*, 31 F. Supp. 2d. 473 (E.D. Pa. 1999).

343. *The American Civil Liberties Union v. Reno*, 217 F.3d 162 (3d Cir. 1999).

344. *Ashcroft v. The American Civil Liberties Union*, 535 U.S. 564 (2002).

345. *Id.* at 566.

346. *The American Civil Liberties Union v. Ashcroft*, 322 F.3d 240 (3d Cir. 2003) (hereinafter *ACLU v. Ashcroft*) (holding that the terms "material harmful to minors" and "for commercial purpose," as defined, were not sufficiently narrowly tailored).

347. *Ashcroft v. American Civil Liberties Union, et al.*, No. 03-218, slip. op. at 15 (U.S. S. Ct. June 29, 2004) (hereinafter *Ashcroft*).

348. *Reno, supra* note 342, at 495.

349. *Reno v. American Civil Liberties Union, supra* note 340, at 874.

350. *R.A.V. v. St. Paul*, 505 U.S. 377, 382 (1992).

351. *ACLU v. Ashcroft, supra* note 346, at 266–71.

352. *Ashcroft, supra* note 347, slip. op. at 8.

that while such devices placed selective restrictions on speech at the receiving end, they did not impose universal restrictions at the source.[353] Thus, under a filtering regime, childless adults could still access the speech they had a right to see without having to identify themselves or provide credit card information. Even adults with children could obtain access simply by turning off the filter on their home computers.[354] In addition, promoting filters did not condemn as criminal any category of speech, and so eliminated, or at least diminished, the potential chilling effect of COPA.[355]

The Supreme Court further recognized filters might prove a more effective tool than COPA, for several reasons. First, they could prevent minors from seeing all pornography, not just illicit material posted on the WWW from the United States.[356] Second, COPA's effectiveness would likely diminish if upheld, because providers of illicit material would probably move their operations overseas.[357] Third, verification systems could be subject to evasion and circumvention (e.g., by minors with access to credit cards).[358] Finally, filters could be applied to all forms of Internet communication, including e-mail and search engines, and not just the WWW.[359]

As such, the Supreme Court permitted the preliminary injunction to stand and remanded the case again to the District Court for a full trial on the merits. The Court cited several reasons for doing so. First, it believed the potential harms from reversal, including self-censorship,[360] outweighed those of leaving the injunction in place by mistake.[361] Second, substantial factual disputes remained in the record.[362] By remanding for trial, the Court, in essence, instructed the government to meet its burden and prove filters would be less effective than implementing COPA. Third, the factual record failed to reflect current technological reality.[363] The Supreme Court found it reasonable to assume significant scientific advancements had occurred in the five years since the original District Court ruling. A

---

353. *Id.* at 9.
354. *Id.*
355. *Id.*
356. *Id.* As simply a United States statute, COPA had no applicability abroad.
357. *Id.*
358. *Id.*
359. *Id.*
360. *United States v. Playboy Entertainment Group, Inc.*, 529 U.S. 803, 817 (2000).
361. *Ashcroft, supra* note 347, slip. op. at 12.
362. *Id.* at 13.
363. *Id.*

remand thus permitted the lower court to take any recent and relevant technological advancements into account.[364]

[c] CIPA Today

As noted above, CIPA conditions the receipt of certain federal funding on the adoption by schools of technological protections and Internet safety policies.[365] Sections 1712 and 1721 of CIPA, involving the use of filtered Internet access on public computers in libraries, were challenged by various library associations.[366] In May 2002, a federal district court struck down these provisions as unconstitutional, holding a technology's tendency to overblock material prohibits the flow of protected speech to library patrons.[367] Under a CIPA provision providing for fast-track hearings, the Justice Department immediately appealed the lower court's decision to the U.S. Supreme Court.[368]

In a plurality decision, the Court reversed the lower tribunal by finding the filtering provisions did not violate the First Amendment.[369] Four justices held that (1) the Internet access provided by libraries was not a public forum, and therefore, decisions to block pornography were not subject to heightened scrutiny; (2) the disabling provision eased fears of "overblocking"; and (3) requiring filtering and blocking technology was an appropriate condition for federal funding because libraries already excluded pornographic material from their other collections. The Supreme Court also underscored "the ease with which patrons [could] have the filtering software disabled."[370]

[d] NTIA's Evaluation of Technology Protection Measures and Internet Safety Policies

Section 1703(a) of CIPA requested the NTIA[371] to initiate a notice and comment proceeding, within eighteen months of the legislation's enactment, to (1) determine whether currently available blocking and

---

364. *Id.* at 14.

365. *Supra* note 323.

366. *See American Library Association v. United States,* No. 01-CV-1303 (E.D. Pa. Mar. 20, 2001); *Multnomah County Public Library v. United States,* No. 01-CV-1332 (E.D. Pa. Mar. 20, 2001).

367. *American Library Association v. United States,* 201 F. Supp. 2d. 401 (E.D. Pa. 2002).

368. *United States v. American Library Association,* 537 U.S. 1017 (2002).

369. *United States v. American Library Association,* 123 S. Ct. 2297 (2003).

370. *Id.* at 2306.

371. "NTIA" is the National Telecommunications and Information Administration of the U.S. Department of Commerce. *See* Section 5.4[1].

filtering technologies adequately address the needs of educational institutions, (2) make recommendations on how to foster the development of such technologies, and (3) evaluate current Internet safety policies.

NTIA subsequently published a "Request for Comment" in the *Federal Register* eliciting information about such technologies and policies.[372] NTIA invited interested parties, such as academics, technology developers, and consumer groups, to submit written comments on any issue of fact, law, or policy germane to its evaluation. The agency also encouraged the submission of relevant studies, surveys, research, or other empirical data. Eventually, forty-two responses from various associations, technology vendors, governmental agencies, university professors, schools, and libraries were received.[373] Those who commented identified the need of K–12 school systems to:

(1) allow children to use the Internet while protecting them from inappropriate material;

(2) access online educational materials with a minimum level of disruption;

(3) decide on the local level how best to protect children from Internet dangers;

(4) understand how to fully utilize Internet protection technology measures;

(5) consider a variety of technical, educational and economic factors when selecting such measures; and

(6) adopt an Internet safety strategy combining technology, human monitoring and education.[374]

[2] Internet Safety Policies

In its study, NTIA found that educational institutions often engaged in discussions with their respective communities to help create acceptable Internet safety policies.[375] Local schools tended to incorporate the values and needs of their community into their policy and, as a result, experienced

---

372. Request for Comment on the Effectiveness of Internet Protection Measures and Safety Policies, 67 Fed. Reg. 37396 (May 24, 2002).

373. *See* http://www.ntia.doc.gov/ntiahome/ntiageneral/cipacomments/ for copies of all comments. Comments are also on file at the National Telecommunications and Information Administration. Page numbers below refer to the location of the comments on file at NTIA.

374. Report to Congress, *Children's Internet Protection Act, Study of Technological Measures in Section 1703, Dept. of Commerce,* at 12 (Aug. 2003).

375. Comment by Karen Gillespie, Grayson County Public Library, at 1 (Aug. 8, 2002); Comment by Janice Friesen, eMINTS, at 2 (Aug. 9, 2002).

positive feedback about protecting children online.[376] Many public libraries already post Internet safety policies that appear whenever a patron logs onto a public computer.[377] In these instances, Internet access requires patrons to click an "acceptance button" whereby they agree to abide by the policy's terms. Usually, patrons are then informed they may access any online material, but cannot use the Internet in a manner inappropriate for a public area. Such policies generally list specific, prohibited behaviors, such as viewing obscene material or engaging in offensive, intimidating, or hostile conduct.

NTIA also asked commenters to discuss their experience with successful Internet safety approaches. These responses were grouped into the following categories: (1) acceptable use policies, (2) child media literacy, (3) parental education and awareness, (4) staff education and development, (5) identification of appropriate content, and (6) child-safe areas. Recommendations for each category included:

- Acceptable Use Policies:
  - *Post guidelines and consequences for Internet use:* Ensure appropriate behavior through awareness of policy guidelines and consequences for failure to follow them. Consistently enforce the policy by authorizing staff to terminate Internet sessions for repeat offenders.
  - *On-screen Appropriate Use Policy:* Require computer users to agree to abide by these policies before gaining Internet access.
  - *Age/Education criteria:* Establish flexible policies to accommodate different ages and implement settings with varying degrees of supervision.
- Child Media Literacy:
  - *Internet safety courses:* Teach students how to (a) use the Internet safely, (b) report suspicious activity, harassment or threats, (c) protect their privacy and personal information, and (d) detect inappropriate content.
  - *Online safety videos:* Provide students, parents and teachers with a video teaching Internet safety and successful use skills.

---

376. Comment by National Education Association, at 4 (Aug. 27, 2002); International Society for Technology in Education, at 4 (Aug. 27, 2002).

377. *See, e.g.,* Comment by Jason Stone, East Brunswick Public Library, East Brunswick, N.J., at 1 (Aug. 14, 2002); Comment by Nancy Ledeboer, Las Vegas–Clark County Library District, at 1, 2 (Aug. 21, 2002).

- *Internet search skills*: Teach students how to conduct effective, safe Internet searches using keywords and search engines.
- *Learning to evaluate online material*: Train children to evaluate the veracity, appropriateness, and educational value of websites.
- *Internet Drivers' Licenses*: Develop tests students must pass in order to obtain the privilege of using the Internet at school.
- Parental Education and Awareness:
  - *Educate families about the Internet*: Encourage parents to pay attention to how and when their children use the WWW.
  - *Parental supervision*: Rely not only on filters, but also on parental supervision, intervention and discipline as means to protect children from harmful material.
- Staff Education and Development:
  - *Curriculum tailored sites*: Educate teachers about how to find, bookmark, and direct students to websites that complement safe teaching materials.
  - *Teacher Training*: Train teachers to effectively use new technology.
- Identification of Appropriate Content:
  - *Pre-approved hotlinks*: Administrators and educators should pre-select safe and appropriate sites and limit student access only to them.
  - *Teacher lessons*: Create lesson plans tailored to specific subject areas and curriculum.
- Child-Safe Areas:
  - *Filtered*: Designate a specific children's computer room which combines filtered access with Internet education and safety.
  - *Children's monitors in public view*: Discourage violations by positioning monitors so supervisors and teachers can always see them.
  - *Enclosed Internet stations for adults*: Separate adult workstations from child-safe areas.[378]

The National Research Council report cited earlier also discussed several issues relating to IAUPs. The Council recommended such policies should (1) distinguish between adult and child use; (2) set different standards for younger and older children; (3) determine how to measure compliance; (4) avoid overly broad wording; (5) strive to list specific inappropriate behavior and material; (6) protect against liability; and (7) define a

---

378. *See Report to Congress, supra* note 374, at 30–32.

user's rights.[379] These approaches are intended to provide the information communities and schools should consider as they develop and implement Internet safety policies.

Appendix 5-A hereto contains a sample Internet Acceptable Use Policy for utilization by a local school system. Obviously, these types of policies can take many forms and vary significantly in the areas they cover.

---

379. National Research Council, *supra* note 329, at 238–40.

Sample Computer Acceptable Use Policy

The computer network and Internet access provided by the Jefferson County Local Schools (JCLS) is available solely to gather educational information, support learning, and enhance instruction.

The JCLS computer and information network (the "Network") is operated for the benefit of all students. Therefore, students should never disrupt the Network's operation, interfere with the learning of others, or impede the work of JCLS employees. The Network is connected to the Internet and the World Wide Web, which often contain content inappropriate for student viewing. As such, strict adherence to this policy is a prerequisite for use of the Network.

All access to the Network must be preapproved by a student's teacher or the person in the school responsible for Network use. The school may restrict or terminate any student's access, with or without prior notice, if necessary to maintain computer availability or provide security for others. If a student violates any provision of this Policy, he or she shall be subject to any or all of the following: (1) termination of Network access; (2) probation; (3) suspension; or (4) expulsion from the school system.

All student-produced web pages are subject to approval and ongoing review by the responsible teacher or school official and must always reflect the mission and character of the school.

Students are also required to adhere to the following guidelines:

(1) *Respect for Others*
   Students should always respect the rights of others using the Network by:
   - Using only those workstations assigned by their teacher.
   - Being considerate of others when using scarce resources.
   - Always logging off workstations after completing their work.

- Not attempting to disrupt Network performance or interfere with another's work.
- Leaving equipment and rooms in good condition for the next user.

(2) *Ethical Conduct for Users*

Accounts on the Network are considered private, although absolute security cannot be guaranteed. It is the student's responsibility to:

- Use only his or her account.
- Never give account access or password information to another person.
- Not copy or distribute work belonging to others.
- Not read, modify, or remove files owned by others.
- Restrict use of the Network to the mission and function of the school.
- Never use the Network for commercial or private purposes.
- Maintain the integrity of the Network by not accessing, tampering with, or experimenting with outside systems.

(3) *Respect for Property*

Students are instructed to:

- Use only software already loaded on the Network.
- Not modify any software on the Network.
- Not rearrange keyboards, monitors, printers, or any other peripheral computer equipment.
- Report computer problems immediately to their teacher or Network supervisor.

(4) *Prohibited Uses*

Students should *never*:

- Use offensive, obscene, or harassing language on the Network.
- Post information on the Network if it:
    - (i)   violates the privacy of others
    - (ii)   jeopardizes the health or safety of others
    - (iii) is obscene or libelous
    - (iv)   causes disruption of school activities
    - (v)   plagiarizes the work of others
    - (vi)   is a commercial advertisement, or
    - (vii) is not approved by the teacher or Network supervisor.
- Change or delete files belonging to others.
- Use real-time messaging without the permission of their teacher.
- Reveal any personal information when communicating with unknown persons.
- Access World Wide Web pages that do not promote the instructional mission of the school system.

CHAPTER 6

The TEACH Act

On November 2, 2002, President George W. Bush signed into law the "Technology, Education, and Copyright Harmonization Act," more commonly known as the "TEACH Act."[1] This bill updated the distance education provisions of the Copyright Act and impacted all colleges, universities, and K–12 school systems utilizing distance learning technologies. The act essentially changed the terms and conditions under which educational institutions could incorporate copyrighted works into their electronic courses.

Specifically, the TEACH Act amended Sections 110(2) and 112 of the Copyright Act to facilitate the growth and development of digital distance education. In doing so, it enlarged the number of copyrighted works an instructor could use in an electronic course, without the need to obtain permission, pay licensing fees, or rely on items already in the public domain. Among its benefits, the act expanded the categories of works the "distance learning" exemption applied to, allowed content to be transmitted to students at any location rather than just classrooms (as used to be the law), and permitted institutions to digitize certain works.

To secure these benefits, however, the TEACH Act imposed a host of new legal and technological requirements on those schools seeking to take advantage of its provisions. Those requirements included preventing unauthorized access to and downstream copying of educational broadcasts and assuring all copyrighted materials are used in conjunction with "mediated instructional activities." Of legal significance, the TEACH Act mandated that educational institutions establish policies regarding copyright and

---

1. Pub. L. No. 107–273, 116 Stat. 1758 (2002). For a more detailed discussion of the history and requirements of the TEACH Act, *see infra* Section 6.4.

provide information to faculty, students, and relevant staff members accurately describing and promoting compliance with copyright law.

Specific requirements of the act will be explored later in this chapter. First, however, we start with an examination of prior efforts to address the appropriate role of copyright law in distance education. Only by reviewing such history can one truly understand the advancements brought forth by the TEACH Act, the legislation's current benefits and disadvantages, and the gaps remaining in the treatment of distance versus traditional students.

This chapter is divided into several sections. Section 6.1 describes recent federal initiatives, other than the TEACH Act, designed to promote distance education. Section 6.2 considers the general concept of applying copyright law to digital distance learning. Section 6.3 gives a brief history of prior (and mostly failed) legislative measures designed to govern the performance and display of copyrighted material in educational transmissions. Section 6.4 examines in detail the provisions of the TEACH Act and the interpretation of its key terms. Lastly, Section 6.5 gives an overview of technological protective measures and the terminology associated therewith.

6.1 FEDERAL LEGISLATION PROMOTING DISTANCE LEARNING

[1] Postsecondary Student Financial Aid

[a] General

Many pupils taking distance education courses participate in federal student aid programs.[2] About one-third of all undergraduate and graduate students receiving 100 percent of their courses through distance education accept Title IV assistance.[3] As distance education grows, major provisions of federal laws and regulations will need to be reexamined and rewritten. Certain rules must be modified if a small, but increasing, number of schools are to remain eligible for aid. Students attending these institutions may lose eligibility because their distance programs could eventually exceed statutory and regulatory limits on the amount of distance education a school may offer. Other issues involve accounting for student par-

---

2. Mendels, *Distance Learning to Receive Some Federal Aid*, N.Y. Times, Oct. 21, 1998.

3. *See Growth in Distance Education Programs and Implications for Federal Policy: Hearings Before the Senate Committee on Health, Education, Labor and Pensions*, 107th Cong., 2nd Sess. 4 (2002) (statement of Cornelia M. Ashby; Director, Education, Workforce, and Income Security Issues); *reprinted in* GAO-02-1125T.

ticipation in distance education and adjusting differences in aid between distance and classroom students.

As the largest provider of financial aid to postsecondary students (an estimated $52 billion in fiscal year 2002), the federal government has a major stake in the quality of distance education. Under Title IV of the Higher Education Act of 1965[4] and its subsequent amendments (HEA), the U.S. Government provides grants, work-study wages, and loans to millions of students each year. For the most part, distance students can qualify for this aid in the same way as traditional classroom pupils.

Differences in the way distance and traditional education courses are offered pose challenges for federal aid programs, however. For example, in 1992, Congress added several requirements to HEA addressing problems of fraud and abuse at correspondence schools—the primary providers of distance education in the early 1990s.[5] Limitations on aid were imposed at these institutions due to poor-quality programs and high default rates on loans.

Federal aid is an important consideration for many distance students, but to a somewhat lesser degree than for traditional classroom pupils. Students taking their entire program through distance education applied for aid at a lower rate than those with no distance courses (about 40% compared to 50%), and fewer actually received federal aid (about 31% compared to 39%).[6] Nonetheless, even these lower percentages for distance education represent a substantial federal commitment.[7]

[b] Federal Assistance Rules

A number of issues related to distance education and federal student aid have surfaced and should receive attention when Congress considers reauthorization of HEA or the Department of Education (DOE)

---

4. Pub. L. No. 105–244, 112 Stat. 1581 (1965).

5. Title IV of HEA distinguishes between students enrolled in correspondence and telecommunications courses. For example, students enrolled in correspondence courses cannot be considered more than half-time students for student financial aid purposes, even though they may be taking a full credit load.

6. This data comes from the National Postsecondary Student Aid Study (NPSAS), a Department of Education database covering more than 19 million postsecondary students. The most recent NPSAS covers students attending over 6,000 Title IV eligible institutions during the 1999–2000 school year.

7. Students taking their entire program through distance education courses received an estimated $763 million in federal student aid in the 1999–2000 school year. Students who took at least one distance education course may also have received federal student aid; however, the data sources used by the NPSAS do not distinguish between aid awarded for distance education and aid for traditional classroom courses.

reexamines regulations related to distance education. Among these are the following.

[i] "Fifty Percent" Rule Limits Aid to Correspondence and Telecommunication Students in Certain Circumstances

A school is not eligible to participate in federal student aid programs if it (1) offers over half of its courses through correspondence, (2) has over half of its students enrolled in correspondence courses,[8] or (3) offers correspondence and telecommunication courses[9] that amount to half or more of all courses. Collectively, these restrictions are known as the "50-percent rules."[10] In the early 1990s, concerns about widespread fraud and abuse at

---

8. 134 C.F.R. § 600.2 defines a correspondence course as (1) a home study course provided by an institution under which the institution provides instructional materials, including examinations on the materials, to students who are not physically attending classes at the institution. When students complete a portion of the instructional materials, the students take the examinations relating to that portion of the materials and return the examinations to the institution for grading; (2) a home study course that provides instruction in whole or in part through the use of videocassettes or video discs in an award year unless the institution also delivers the instruction on the cassette or disc to students physically attending classes at the institution during the same award year, and (3) a course at an institution that may otherwise satisfy the definition of a "telecommunications course" if the sum of telecommunications and other correspondence courses offered by that institution equals or exceeds 50 percent of the total courses offered at that institution. In addition, if a course is part correspondence and part residential training, the course is considered to be a correspondence course.

9. 234 C.F.R. § 600.2 provides that a telecommunications course is one offered principally through the use of television, audio, or computer transmission, including open broadcast, closed circuit, cable, microwave, satellite, audio conferencing, computer conferencing, videocassettes, or discs. The term "telecommunications" does not include a course delivered using videocassettes or disc recordings unless the institution also delivers comparable instruction offered on the cassettes or discs to students physically attending classes at the institution during the same award year. If the course offered in the manner described above does not qualify as a telecommunications course, it is considered to be a correspondence course.

10. The 50-percent rules involve three main statutory restrictions. First, under 20 U.S.C. § 1002(a)(3)(A), a school that would otherwise be eligible for the federal student aid programs becomes ineligible if more than 50 percent of its courses are offered by correspondence. Second, under 20 U.S.C. § 1002(a)(3)(B), an otherwise eligible school becomes ineligible if 50 percent or more of its students are enrolled in correspondence courses. Third, under 20 U.S.C. § 1091(l)(1)(A), a student enrolled in a course of instruction that is offered in whole or in part through telecommunications and leads to a certificate for a program of one year or longer, or a recognized associate, baccalaureate, or graduate degree conferred by such institution, shall not be considered to be enrolled in correspondence courses unless the total amount of telecommunications and correspondence courses at such institution equals or exceeds 50 percent of the total number of courses at the institution.

some correspondence schools led Congress to enact these limiting policies in order to protect federal student aid programs. The rapid growth of distance education at mainstream schools, however, has led many to question whether these restrictions are still appropriate. In 1998, Congress authorized DOE to administer a Distance Education Demonstration Program (Demonstration Program) to, among other things, evaluate these restrictions.[11] The Demonstration Program had authority to waive certain statutory or regulatory requirements, such as the 50-percent rule, and fund up to fifty schools over a five-year period.[12]

While federal restrictions on the size of distance education programs currently affect only a small number of schools offering financial aid, the growing popularity of distance learning could cause this number to increase significantly. In a recent study, the U.S. Government Accounting Office (GAO) found that fourteen schools were either currently or soon would be adversely affected by the restrictions.[13] Collectively, these institutions serve nearly 225,000 students. Eight of the fourteen are currently exempt from size restrictions, however, because they participate in the Demonstration Program.[14]

According to DOE, the Demonstration Program revealed no negative consequences to waiving the current restrictions. However, deciding whether to eliminate or modify these rules involves the following factors: (1) the extent to which any changes would improve access to postsecondary schools, (2) the impact changes would have on DOE's ability to prevent fraudulent or abusive practices at schools, and (3) the cost of implementation. GAO's analysis indicated eliminating the restrictions without implementing management accountability would increase the risk for fraud and abuse.[15] Other options include continuing to allow waivers (and monitoring schools that receive them) or using other thresholds, such as student loan default rates, to decide which institutions should receive exemptions.[16]

---

11. U.S. Dep't of Education, *Implementing the Higher Education Amendments of 1998: Update on Key Issues Briefing Document* (1999), http://www.ed.gov/about/bdscomm/list/acsfa/jan99brief/edlite-index.html.

12. Mendels, *supra* note 2.

13. U.S. Government Accounting Office, *Distance Education: Improved Data on Program Costs and Guidelines on Quality Assessments Needed to Inform Federal Policy*, 5, GAO-04-279 (Feb. 2004).

14. *Id.*

15. *Id.* at 6.

16. *Id.*

To further deal with this issue, the House of Representatives passed the Internet Equity in Education Act in October 2001.[17] The House bill permitted schools to obtain waivers for the 50 percent rule if they had (1) already participated in the federal student loan program, (2) a default rate of less than 10 percent for each of the last three years, (3) notified the Secretary of Education of their election to qualify for the exemption, and (4) not been informed by the Secretary that such election would pose a significant risk to federal funds and the integrity of Title IV programs. The Senate ultimately considered this proposal but failed to act on it.

[ii] Federal Student Aid Policies Treat Living Expenses Differently for Some Distance Education Students

Currently, traditional students living off-campus or those students enrolled in telecommunications classes at least one-half of the time can receive an annual living allowance of at least $1,500 or $2,500, respectively. Students enrolled in correspondence classes are not eligible for this same allowance. Whether to continue to treat distance students differently for purposes of federal student aid is an open policy question.

[iii] Regulations Relating to "Seat" Time

Institutions offering distance learning not tied to standard course lengths such as semesters or quarters have had difficulty in interpreting and applying DOE's "seat rules," which govern the actual instructional time needed to qualify for federal aid.[18] In particular, a regulation called the "12-hour rule" had proved quite troublesome. This rule was implemented to curb abuses by schools that were stretching the length of their educational programs without providing any additional instruction time. In essence, such institutions were seeking to maximize the federal aid students could receive and ultimately pass on to the school in the form of tuition and fees.

The 12-hour rule therefore defined each week of teaching in a nonstandard program as twelve hours of instruction, examination, or preparation for examinations. Some distance courses, particularly self-paced ones, did not neatly fit into this model. As such, the rule produced significant disparities in federal aid students received for the same credits, based simply on whether or not their schools used standard academic terms. In August

---

17. H.R. 1992, 107th Cong., 1st Sess. (2001).

18. Under HEA, a pupil must receive at least thirty weeks of instructional time to be considered a full-time student for financial aid purposes. For students operating under standard terms such as semesters, this is relatively easy to translate into semester hours. An undergraduate attending a school operating on the semester system, for example, would need to complete twenty-four semester hours to be considered a full-time student.

2002, DOE proposed replacing the 12-hour rule with a "one-day rule," requiring one day of instruction per week for any course, whether the program used standard or nonstandard terms.

DOE published its final regulations regarding this matter and effectively replaced the 12-hour rule with the one-day rule on November 1, 2002. Although never precisely defined, the one-day rule had long been the standard for college programs operating in a traditional calendar format. DOE's action simply extended such requirement to nonstandard terms, and in turn to many distance education programs. While most comments received by DOE supported abolishing the 12-hour rule, some educators expressed concern its elimination would again result in the fraud and abuse the original regulation was intended to prevent.[19]

[2] Star Schools Program Assistance Act

Although HEA deals, at least in part, with postsecondary distance education efforts, federal funding is also available for grades K–12. The Star Schools Program, operated through the Office of Educational Research and Improvement at DOE, was begun in 1988 as part of a federal effort to support local school reforms.[20] The program was originally intended to increase foreign language, mathematics, and science offerings for elementary and high school students, but it has expanded in scope over time.

The Star Schools Program now provides grants to eligible telecommunications partnerships "to encourage improved instruction in mathematics, science, foreign language, literacy skills, vocational education, and other subjects, and to serve underserved populations through the development, construction, and acquisition of telecommunications facilities, equipment, and instructional programming."[21] These grants are used "to obtain telecommunications facilities and equipment; develop and acquire instructional programming for students, staff development for teachers and administrators, and educational programming for parents and community members; and to obtain technical assistance for teachers, school personnel, and other educators in the use of the facilities and programming."[22] Since its inception, the program has awarded more than $125 million to telecommunications partnerships, provided services to over 6,000 schools, and reached approximately 1,600,000 learners.[23]

---

19. *See* Carnevale, *12-Hour Rule Expires Today; Distance Education Providers Had Long Sought its Demise,* Chron. of Higher Educ., Nov. 1, 2002.

20. 20 U.S.C. §§ 6891–6900 (Title III, Part B).

21. U.S. Dep't. of Education, *Star Schools Program, Basic Information.*

22. *Id.*

23. U.S. Dep't. of Education, *Star Schools—What Is the Star Schools Program?*

[3] Assistance for Disabled Students

The United States Census Bureau reported in 2003 that over 77 million Americans suffered from a disability.[24] Correspondingly, increasing numbers of students with disabilities are enrolling in two- and four-year colleges and universities. By 1996, more than 9 percent of college freshmen (or over 140,000 students) reported having a disability.[25] Between 1985 and 1994, among first-time, full-time freshmen who reported having any disability, the subset of those with learning disabilities doubled from 15 to 32 percent.[26] Interestingly, freshmen who reported disabilities were more likely than their nondisabled peers to enroll in special programs (such as distance education) offered at colleges.[27]

The Copyright Act itself contains an exemption to assist disabled persons.[28] Specifically, certain nonprofit organizations and governmental agencies are absolved of infringement liability when reproducing or distributing copies of previously published, nondramatic literary works if such copies are reproduced in "specialized formats," defined as Braille, audio, or digital text to be used exclusively by persons with disabilities.[29] Thus, electronic copies of textbooks may be posted on a campus computer for disabled students who have no access to a personal computer.

Other federal laws regarding disability are also beginning to impact college distance education programs. For example, distance learning administrators are now required to establish written accommodation plans to provide disabled students and faculty the same access to their programs as nondisabled persons have. This arises from a recent determination by DOE's Office of Civil Rights that providing accommodation on an ad hoc basis is impermissible, thereby imposing a duty to promulgate a comprehensive policy in advance.[30]

---

24. U.S. Census Bureau, American FactFinder, http://factfinder.census.gov/home/saff/main.html?_lang=en.

25. Heath Resource Center, *College Freshman with Disabilities* (Oct. 1, 2001), http://www.heath.gwv.edu/files/active/0/college_freshmen_w_disabilities.pdf.

26. V. Barr, R. Hartman, and S. Spillane, *Getting Ready for College: Advising High School Students with Learning Disabilities* (Spring 1995), http://www.heath.gwv.edu/files/active/0/getting_ready_for_college.pdf.

27. Heath Resource Center, *supra* note 25.

28. 17 U.S.C. § 121. The most significant federal legislation affecting students with disabilities is the Individuals with Disabilities Education Act (20 U.S.C. § 1400 *et seq.*, Pub. L. No. 108–446), which both authorizes federal funding for special education and related services (*e.g.*, physical therapy) and sets out principles under which special education and related services are to be provided. However, it has no specific provisions regarding distance learning.

29. 17 U.S.C. § 121(c)(3).

30. M. Hricko, "Guidelines for Implementing an Accessible Distance Education Program," Presentation at OCDE Conference, Columbus, Ohio (Mar. 6, 2005).

In addition, all content components of a distance course, including virtual interactions (e.g., e-mail, bbs discussions, PowerPoint slides), must be made accessible for disabled students enrolled therein.[31] This is a consequence of "Section 504" of the Rehabilitation Act of 1973, which prohibits institutions of higher learning from excluding students from any course of study.[32] This law has been applied to include web-based course tools, if such instruments impact essential course communications (e.g., notes, graded discussion, assignments, and collaborative learning activities).[33]

Virtual environments also now comprise areas of "public accommodation" subject to regulation under the Americans with Disabilities Act (ADA). Title III of the ADA, in Section 302(a), provides that "no individual shall be discriminated against on the basis of disability in the full and equal enjoyment of the goods, services, facilities, privileges, advantages, or accommodations of any place of public accommodation" by the owner, lessee, or operator thereof.[34] In essence, the owner or operator of a store, hotel, restaurant, dentist's office, travel agency, theater, website, or other facility (whether in physical or electronic space), that is open to the public cannot exclude disabled persons from entering and, once in, from using such facility in the same way as the nondisabled do.[35] For instance, a barber shop cannot bar the door to the disabled, nor can it let them in but then refuse to cut their hair on the same terms as other customers.[36]

Does this mean, however, that college web pages available to the general public (i.e., the university's general Internet site used to promote itself) must be made accessible to the disabled? Not necessarily. While it may be prudent to do so, particularly if the institution wishes to attract (or at least not discourage) disabled applicants, it need not take special measures to achieve this objective. Current interpretations of the ADA provide that the actual goods and services offered by places of public accommodation are not subject to regulation. For example, while a photography store may not refuse to sell its wares to a disabled person, it is not required to

---

31. *Id.*

32. 29 U.S.C. § 794(a) provides: "No otherwise qualified individual with a disability in the United States . . . shall, solely by reason of his or her disability, be excluded from the participation in . . . any program or activity receiving Federal financial assistance."

33. Hricko, *supra* note 30.

34. 42 U.S.C. § 12182(a).

35. *Carparts Distribution Center, Inc. v. Automotive Wholesaler's Ass'n of New England, Inc.*, 37 F.3d 12, 19 (1st Cir. 1994).

36. *E.g., Johnson v. Gambrinus Co./Spoetzl Brewery*, 116 F.3d 1052 (5th Cir. 1997); *Paralyzed Veterans of America v. D.C. Arena L.P.*, 117 F.3d 579 (D.C. Cir. 1997); Department of Justice, Civil Rights Division, *The Americans with Disabilities Act: Title III Technical Assistance Manual*, § III3.2000 (Nov. 1993); 28 C.F.R. § 36.202.

stock cameras specially designed for the blind.[37] Had Congress intended to impose such a burden on the retail sector of the economy, it would have made this clearer in the statute.

Websites designed and used as part of teaching a distance course are another matter, however. Unlike private businesses, most universities receive some type of federal funding that, as previously discussed, alters which laws are applicable and what accommodations must be made for the disabled.[38]

In an effort to further assist disabled persons, Congress amended the Rehabilitation Act of 1973[39] in 1998 to require federal agencies to make their electronic and information technology accessible to people with disabilities.[40] Inaccessible technology obviously interferes with an individual's ability to obtain and use information quickly and easily. This amendment, more commonly known as "Section 508," was enacted to eliminate barriers in information technology, give disabled persons new opportunities, and encourage development of those resources needed to achieve such objectives.[41] The law applies to all federal agencies that develop, procure, maintain, or use electronic and information technology. Under Section 508, agencies must give disabled employees and members of the public the same access to information that others have.

In addition, the Assistive Technology Act of 1998[42] made compliance with Section 508 a requirement for states and sub-recipients of grants related to this program. As such, higher education institutions receiving federal funds for technology-related initiatives, including distance learning projects, also need to adhere to Section 508's technical specifications and requirements.[43] For instance, a school asked to develop a distance learning

---

37. A few courts have already addressed the issue. For example, it has been held that a bookstore is not required to alter its inventory in order to stock Braille texts. *Lennox v. Healthwise of Kentucky, Ltd.,* 149 F.3d 453, 457 (6th Cir. 1998); *See also* 28 C.F.R. § 36.307.

38. For a more detailed discussion of making distance learning facilities accessible to disabled persons, *see* M. Hricko, *Design and Implementation of web-enabled Tracking Tools* (Information Service Publishing, 2004); K. Schenker, "The Design of Accessible Distance Education Environments That Use Collaborative Learning," http://www.rit.edu/~easi/itd/ itdvo8n1/scadden.htm.

39. Act of Sept. 26, 1973, Pub. L. No. 93–112, Title V, § 508, as added Oct. 21, 1986; Pub. L. No. 99–506, Title VI, § 603(a), 100 Stat. 1830 (1986).

40. Act of Aug. 7, 1998, Pub. L. No. 105–220, Title V, § 408(b), 112 Stat. 1203 (1998).

41. 29 U.S.C. § 794(d).

42. Act of Nov. 13, 1998, Pub. L. No. 105–394, 112 Stat. 3627 (1998).

43. M. Hricko, "Implementing Accessibility Standards in the Campus Technology Plan," Paper presented to the Ohio Learning Network Conference (Mar. 3, 2003), http://www .oln.org/conferences/OLN2003/papers/Implementing_Accessibility_Standards_in_the_ Campus_Technology_Plan.pdf.

class for federal employees would have to comply with Section 508 in the design and implementation of such course. On December 21, 2000, the Architectural and Transportation Barriers Compliance Board, also known as the "Access Board," issued the final accessibility standards for electronic and information technology under Section 508.[44] These rules are summarized below.

[a] General

The standards define the types of technology covered and set forth provisions establishing minimum levels of accessibility for each. The application section outlines the scope and coverage of these standards.[45] These rules cover the full range of electronic and information technologies used in the federal sector, including those for communication, duplication, computing, storage, presentation, control, transport, and production. This includes computers, software, networks, peripherals, and other types of electronic office equipment. The standards define *electronic and information technology*, in part, as "any equipment or interconnected system or subsystem of equipment, that is used in the creation, conversion, or duplication of data or information."

Subpart A explains what is exempt,[46] defines terms,[47] and generally recognizes alternatives providing equal or greater access.[48] Consistent with the law, the standards exempt systems used for military command, weaponry, intelligence, and cryptologic activities, but not routine business and administrative systems used for other defense-related purposes or by defense agencies or personnel. The standards also exempt "back office" equipment used only by service personnel for maintenance, repair, or similar purposes.

The rules also cover technology procured by federal agencies under contract with a private entity, but apply only to those products directly relevant to the contract and its deliverables. An exception clarifies that the standards do not apply to technology incidental to a federal contract. Thus, products not specified as part of a government contract do not need to be in compliance. For instance, a firm producing a report for a federal agency would not have to procure accessible computers and word processing software even if they were used exclusively for that contract.

---

44. *See* Press Release of Access Board (Dec. 21, 2000), http://www.access-board.gov/sec508/preamble.htm. The Access Board formed an advisory committee in 2006 to conduct a review and update of its access standards. *See* "Update of the 508 Standards and the Telecommunications Act Guidelines," http://www.access-board.gov/sec508/update-index.htm.
45. 36 C.F.R. § 1194.2.
46. 36 C.F.R. § 1194.3.
47. 36 C.F.R. § 1194.4.
48. 36 C.F.R. § 1194.5.

However, compliance would be required if such products became the property of the federal agency as contract deliverables or if the agency purchased them as part of the project. Also, for example, if a federal agency contracted with a private firm to develop its website, the standards would apply to the new agency website, but not to the private company's Internet site.

[b] Technical Standards

The standards provide criteria specific for various technologies, including

- software applications and operating systems;
- web-based information or applications;
- telecommunications products;
- video and multimedia products;
- self-contained, closed products (e.g., information kiosks, calculators, and fax machines); and
- desktop and portable computers.

The regulations issued by the Access Board provide technical specifications and performance-based requirements focusing on the functional capabilities of covered technologies. This dual approach recognizes the dynamic and continually evolving nature of the technology used plus the need for clear and specific standards to facilitate compliance. Certain provisions are designed to ensure compatibility with adaptive equipment disabled persons commonly use for information and communication access, such as screen readers, Braille displays, and TTYs (an acronym used to describe telecommunications devices that assist disabled persons to communicate over the telephone).

[i] Software Applications and Operating Systems[49]

Most of the specifications for software pertain to usability for the visually impaired. For example, one provision requires alternative keyboard navigation, which is essential for persons who cannot rely on pointing devices, such as a mouse. Other provisions address animated displays, color, contrast settings, flash rate, and electronic forms.

[ii] Web-Based Intranet and Internet Information Applications[50]

The criteria for web-based technology and information are based on access guidelines developed by the Web Accessibility Initiative of the World Wide

---

49. 36 C.F.R. § 1194.21.
50. 36 C.F.R. § 1194.22.

Web Consortium. Many of these provisions ensure access for people with vision impairments who rely on various assistive products, such as screen readers. Screen readers translate what is on a computer monitor into automated audible output and refreshable Braille displays. Certain conventions, such as verbal tags or identification of graphics and format devices, like frames, are necessary so that these devices can "read" for the user in a sensible way.

The standards do not prohibit the use of website graphics or animation. Instead, they aim to ensure such information is also available in an accessible format. Generally, this means use of text labels or descriptors for graphics and certain format elements. (HTML code already provides an "Alt Text" tag that serves as a verbal descriptor for graphics.) These regulations also address the usability of multimedia presentations, image maps, style sheets, scripting languages, applets and plug-ins, and electronic forms.

The regulations apply to federal websites but not private sector ones (unless a site is provided under contract to a federal agency, in which case only that website or portion covered by the contract would need to comply). Accessible sites offer significant advantages beyond easing tasks for disabled persons. For example, those with "text-only" options provide a faster downloading alternative and can facilitate transmission of web-based data to cell phones and personal digital assistants.

[iii] Telecommunications Products[51]

These standards are designed primarily to ensure access to the hearing impaired. This includes compatibility with hearing aids, cochlear implants, assistive listening devices, and TTYs. One requirement calls for a standard non-acoustic TTY connection point for telecommunications products allowing voice communication but not TTY functionality. Other specifications address adjustable volume controls for output, product interface with hearing technologies, and the usability of keys and controls by people with impaired vision or limited dexterity.

[iv] Video or Multimedia Products[52]

Multimedia products involve more than one medium and include, but are not limited to, video programs, narrated slide projection, and computer-generated presentations. These standards address caption decoder circuitry (for any system with a screen larger than thirteen inches) and secondary audio channels for television tuners, including tuner cards used in

---

51. 36 C.F.R. § 1194.23.
52. 36 C.F.R. § 1194.24.

computers. The rules require captioning and audio description for certain training and informational multimedia products developed or procured by federal agencies. The regulations also provide that viewers be able to turn captioning or video description features on or off.

[v] Self-Contained, Closed Products[53]

These regulations cover products with imbedded software that is often designed to preclude a user from attaching assistive technology. Examples include information kiosks, transaction machines, copiers, printers, calculators, and fax machines. The standards require access features to be built into the system so users do not have to attach an assistive device to it. Other specifications address mechanisms for private listening (handset or a standard headphone jack), touch screens, auditory output and adjustable volume, and the location of controls in accessible reach ranges.

[vi] Desktop and Portable Computers[54]

This section focuses on keyboards and other mechanically operated controls, touch screens, use of biometric forms of identification, and ports and connectors.

[c] Functional Performance Criteria

These requirements are intended for overall product evaluation and technologies or components for which there is no specific requirement under the technical standards in Subpart B of the regulations. The criteria are designed to ensure individual components work together to create an accessible product. They cover operation, including input and control features, functioning of mechanical items, and access to visual and audible information. These provisions are structured to allow people with sensory or physical disabilities to locate, identify, and operate input, control, and mechanical functions and to access the information provided—including text, static or dynamic images, icons, labels, sounds, or incidental operating cues. For example, one provision requires that at least one mode allow operation by people with low vision (visual acuity between 20/70 and 20/2000) without relying on audio input since many visually challenged people also have hearing loss.

[d] Information, Documentation, and Support

These rules address access to all information, documentation, and support provided to end users (e.g., federal employees) of covered technologies.

---

53. 36 C.F.R. § 1194.25.
54. 36 C.F.R. § 1194.26.

This includes user guides, installation manuals for end-user devices, and customer and technical support communications. Such information must be available in alternate formats upon request at no additional charge. Alternate formats or methods of communication can include Braille, cassette recordings, large print, electronic text, Internet postings, TTY access, and captioning and audio description for video materials.

6.2 THE GENERAL APPLICATION OF COPYRIGHT LAW TO DISTANCE EDUCATION

The interaction between copyright law and *digital* distance education is a relatively new field. No reported case has yet specifically applied copyright law principles to distance learning transmissions.[55] Therefore, the analysis here is based on statutory language, legislative history, and analogous situations. We begin with a description of the general principles of copyright law[56] and then examine those provisions most relevant to digital distance education.

[1] General Principles of Copyright Law

Copyright law protects original works of authorship, including literature, movies, plays, computer programs, music, works of art, and sound recordings.[57] Copyright confers on the owner[58] the exclusive rights to (1) reproduce the work in copies or phonorecords; (2) prepare derivative works (such as adaptations or translations); (3) distribute copies to the public; (4) perform the work publicly, limited in the case of sound recordings to

---

55. The few reported cases dealing with distance education do not involve copyright, but address issues such as the right of the disabled to gain access to educational opportunities, institutional accreditation, or funding for distance education programs. *See, e.g., Maczaczyj v. New York*, 956 F. Supp. 403 (W.D.N.Y. 1997) (disabled plaintiff denied admission into master's degree program could not require college to enable him to participate in the program from home).

56. *See* Chapter Two for a much more detailed examination of the principles of copyright law. The discussion here is limited to those elements necessary to give the reader some basic grounding in copyright law and distance education.

57. 17 U.S.C. § 102.

58. The initial owner of a copyright is the author, who, in the case of a "work made for hire," is defined as the hiring party. 17 U.S.C. §§ 201(a), (b). The question of who is considered the owner of instructional materials created by faculty members is a topic of some controversy in the educational community. Since it is not directly relevant to the question of what uses of copyrighted materials are permitted in distance learning transmissions, it is beyond the scope of this Chapter. For a more detailed discussion of ownership issues and the "work for hire" doctrine, *see* Chapter Two, Section 2.1[3]. Chapter Five, Section 5.3, covers ownership of the electronic course in more detail.

performances by means of digital audio transmissions; and (5) display the work publicly.[59] These rights are divisible and may be licensed or sold together or separately.[60] Exercising any exclusive rights in a copyrighted work without the owner's authorization constitutes an infringement, unless an exception applies.[61] The Copyright Act contains numerous exceptions, including several particularly relevant to educational uses.[62]

Different rights are implicated by various educational activities, depending in part on the technologies used. A teacher using a work in class will almost invariably exercise one or more of the copyright owner's exclusive rights when she reads from a work, displays it, or hands out copies thereof. This is true whether the instruction is face-to-face or takes place over a distance. A public performance or display of a work accomplished by means of a digital transmission, however, may implicate additional author's rights in a manner not foreseen by the instructor. Unlike face-to-face teaching, acts perceived by the teacher and student as merely a performance or display, when transmitted over a digital network, will also involve the reproduction and distribution right.

Transmissions may or may not involve the automatic creation of copies during the process. While a live open- or closed-circuit television broadcast does not involve copying, computer network communications normally do. When material is sent electronically, temporary RAM copies are made in the computers through which the transmission passes.[63] The version of the work arriving on the recipient's computer is the ultimate copy in the process, and it is an essential function of the way information is transported over a digital network.

In addition to the necessary transient copies generated in the computer network, the reproduction right may be implicated in other ways. For example, digitizing an analog version of a work entails copying. This occurs when a teacher scans a text into a computer or a student downloads or prints it out after receipt. The distribution right is involved when copies of the transmission are made widely available. In almost every digital

---

59. 17 U.S.C. § 106.

60. 17 U.S.C. § 201(d).

61. 17 U.S.C. § 501(a).

62. 17 U.S.C. §§ 107–121.

63. The courts have consistently held that RAM copies implicate the copyright owner's reproduction right. *See, e.g., MAI Sys. Corp. v. Peak Computer, Inc.,* 991 F.2d 511 (9th Cir. 1993), *cert. dismissed,* 114 S.Ct. 671 (1994); *Stenograph L.L.C. v. Bossard Assocs.,* 144 F.3d 96, 101–02 (D.C. Cir. 1998).

transmission, a temporary copy is deposited on the recipient's computer, as well as, possibly, more permanent copies.[64]

A second kind of digital transmission is exemplified by television or radio signals sent by satellite, microwave, or cable. These typically do not involve the automatic creation of intermediate copies. Therefore, from a copyright perspective, they are closer to analog broadcasts than to online transmissions. Unless specifically noted, this chapter will treat such digital broadcasts[65] as comparable to analog television or radio signals under copyright law, and will use the term "digital transmission" to refer only to transmissions involving reproduction over computer networks.

An educational use involving one or more of the copyright owner's exclusive rights does not necessarily mean an infringement has occurred. Only *unauthorized* uses can infringe, and permission to use the work may have been expressly granted or implied. The copyright owner, being either the original author or his transferee, may grant permission through an express license.[66] An educator may always attempt to contact the copyright owner, or a licensing organization acting on his behalf, to obtain the right to use a work.

Even without such permission, courts may interpret conduct to create an implied license to use the work in a certain way.[67] For instance, an owner who posts her work on a website without restriction impliedly licenses users to view it, including the making of temporary RAM copies

---

64. Even technologies designed to transmit in "real time," such as audio and video streaming, result in the same creation of temporary copies along the network, as the material is broken up into packets and carried from sender to recipient. Unlike other transmissions, however, no complete copy of the transmitted material is "reassembled" on the recipient's computer, although segments of the material are briefly copied into the computer's memory as a buffer to create a continuous display. Future technology, and broader bandwidth, may support streaming transmissions that do not create these buffer copies on the recipient's computer. The intermediate RAM copies will still be created, however.

65. The term "digital broadcasts" is used throughout this chapter to refer to those types of digital transmissions that function similarly to analog broadcasts and that do not create automatic reproductions by virtue of the technical process of transmission. It is not intended as the equivalent to the term "broadcast" as defined and used in the Copyright Act. *See* 17 U.S.C. § 114(j).

66. 17 U.S.C. § 101 (definition of "transfer of copyright ownership"); § 201(d); § 204 (rules for transfers of ownership); M. Nimmer & D. Nimmer, *Nimmer on Copyright* § 10.03[A] (1994) (hereinafter *Nimmer on Copyright*).

67. *Effects Assoc., Inc., v. Cohen*, 908 F.2d 555 (9th Cir. 1990), *cert. denied*, 498 U.S. 1103 (1991).

required to do so.[68] Such an implied license is of limited utility to distance educators, however, because it does not authorize the making of copies for distribution in class or as part of an electronic course.

If express or implied permission is not granted, a work's use may still be lawful if it falls within one of the various "instructional" exemptions contained in the Copyright Act. These are examined in more detail in the following section.

[2] Lawful Uses

The Copyright Act contains numerous exemptions to infringement liability, thereby permitting various uses without having to obtain permission or a license. Two exemptions found in Section 110 of the act are especially designed for educators and involve both face-to-face teaching and instructional broadcasting. The fair use doctrine also serves as a major exemption for some educational uses. This section analyzes these laws, which together largely define the scope of permitted uses for copyrighted works in education. Several other obscure provisions of the Copyright Act having limited applicability to distance learning are also discussed.

[a] The Instructional Exemptions

In the Copyright Act of 1976 (the "1976 Act"), Congress provided two specific exemptions from potential copyright infringement for educational performances and displays. To understand the genesis and purpose of these provisions, some background is useful. Prior law granted owners rights in their nondramatic literary and musical works only if performed "for profit."[69] The right to perform dramatic works belonged solely to copyright owners, whether the activity was for profit or not. There was no general equivalent to the display right, however, and therefore no distinction between for-profit or nonprofit displays.[70] As such, both types of displays belonged solely to the owner thereof.

In the years preceding the 1976 Act amendments, several groups, including the educational community, exerted pressure on Congress to expand the "blanket exemption" to permit all nonprofit performances and displays to be immune from liability. Instead, public performance and display rights were granted to owners in all works whether or not exercised

---

68. Oppedahl & Larson, *Web Law FAQ*, http://www.patents.com/weblaw.htm. *See also Field v. Google, Inc.*, No. CV-S-04-0413-RCJ-LRL, slip. op. at 10 (D. Nev. Jan. 12, 2006).

69. House Comm. on the Judiciary, 87th Cong., *Report of The Register of Copyrights on the General Revision of the U.S. Copyright Law* 27 (Comm. Print 1961) (hereinafter *Register's Report*).

70. *See* 1909 Copyright Act, § 1(c)–(e).

for profit, subject to exceptions "that by their nature justify being exempted from copyright control."[71] In explaining the shift away from a blanket non-profit exemption, the Register of Copyrights (hereinafter, the "Register") wrote that "the present blanket exemption has become too broad in its application to the new conditions of today, and . . . would involve serious dangers to the author's rights if continued into the future."[72]

Two new 1976 Act exemptions specifically addressed works used in nonprofit education and reflected a general consensus that instructional uses justified special treatment.[73] One exemption addressed face-to-face classroom teaching, while the other concerned instructional broadcasting.[74] In Section 110's legislative history, Congress concluded "[c]lauses (1) and (2) between them [were] intended to cover all of the various methods by which performances or displays in the course of systematic instruction take place."[75] Together with fair use, these provisions essentially governed the range of exempted instructional uses for nearly twenty-five years.[76]

[i] Section 110(1)

Section 110(1) of the Copyright Act, which was adopted in 1976 and remains the law today, exempts the performance or display of *any* work in the course of face-to-face teaching, but it does not apply to distance education. By its terms, it permits the:

> performance or display of a work by instructors or pupils in the course of face-to-face teaching activities of a nonprofit educational institution, in a classroom or similar place devoted to instruction, unless, in the case of a motion picture or other audiovisual work, the performance, or the display of individual images, is given by means of a copy that was not lawfully made under this title, and

---

71. *Supplementary Report of the Register of Copyrights on the General Revision of the U.S. Copyright Law: 1965 Revision Bill, Pt. 6, House Comm. on the Judiciary*, 89th Cong. 31 (Comm. Print 1965) (hereinafter *Supplementary Report*).

72. *Id.* With prescience, the Register noted, "it is becoming increasingly apparent that the transmission of works by nonprofit broadcasting, linked computers, and other new media of communication, may soon be among the most important means of disseminating them, and will be capable of reaching vast audiences. Even when these new media are not operated for profit, they may be expected to displace the demand for authors' works by other users from whom the copyright owners derive compensation." *Supplementary Report* at 14.

73. *Supplementary Report* at 21.

74. 17 U.S.C. §§ 110(1), (2) (1976).

75. H.R. Rep. No. 1476, 94th Cong., 2d Sess. 81 (1976) (hereinafter *House Report*).

76. Section 110(2) was significantly modified by enactment of the TEACH Act in November 2002. *See infra* Section 6.4 for a more detailed discussion of the TEACH Act.

that the person responsible for the performance knew or had reason to believe was not lawfully made.

According to the then Register of Copyrights, Section 110(1) reflected "general agreement that most ordinary instructional activities in classrooms should be exempt from copyright control."[77] The potentially broad coverage of this exemption caused some concern among copyright owners, leading the drafters to confine the permitted uses to purely instructional ones.[78]

One limitation is that the performance or display must be made in the course of "face-to-face teaching activities," which the legislative history makes clear *excludes* educational broadcasts or transmissions.[79] The performance or display must also be made in a "classroom or similar place devoted to instruction," but not auditoriums used for school plays, graduations, or school assemblies.[80] The exemption may extend, however, beyond the physical classroom to situations where the instructor and students are "in the same building or general area," and devices for amplifying or reproducing sound, or projecting visual images, are used.[81] This clarification was intended to permit a live lecture feed into an adjoining or nearby classroom to accommodate a student overflow situation, as might occur with a large introductory survey class.

In addition, Section 110(1) applies only to the teaching activities of "a nonprofit educational institution." This parallels the prior law's differentiation between for-profit and nonprofit performances, as discussed above, and excludes "performances or displays in profit-making institutions such as dance studios and language schools."[82] As such, any private school not having 501(c)(3) tax status would not be eligible to rely on the exemption. The most prominent example of such an "unqualified" entity might be the

---

77. *Supplementary Report* at 32. In fact, the provision has seldom, if ever, been litigated. *See* W. Fisher & W. McGeveran, *Obstacles to Educational Uses of Copyrighted Material in the Digital Age*, 43 (Aug. 10, 2006), Berkman Center Research Publication No. 2006–09, http://ssrn.com/abstract=923465 (hereinafter *Fisher Report*).

78. *Supplementary Report* at 33–35.

79. *House Report* at 81.

80. *Id.* at 82. Obviously, Congress did not want the exemption to be used to circumvent the need for a school to obtain permission or a license from the copyright owner to show a movie solely for entertainment purposes or perform the annual spring musical. Using school auditoriums or libraries to house larger classes is still acceptable, however.

81. *Id.* at 81. As such, most aspects of digital distance learning, even a class web page with limited access to teachers and students falls outside of the provision's purview. *See Fisher Report* at 44.

82. *House Report* at 82.

University of Phoenix, ironically one of the largest purveyors of distance education in the world.[83]

Finally, Section 110(1) is limited in the rights it covers. It exempts only the *performance* or *display* of a work—the major ways a teacher would use copyrighted works in a traditional classroom setting. It does *not* authorize the reproduction or distribution of works, or the creation of derivatives therefrom. Educators wishing to copy works for distribution to students must still rely on the concept of fair use and the various guidelines promulgated thereunder, as discussed in Chapter Three.

[ii] Old Section 110(2)[84]

1) General Old Section 110(2) was designed to cover the electronic forms of distance education existing in the mid-1970s and to exempt certain uses of works in the course of instructional broadcasting. In the 1960s and early 1970s, distance learning (outside of traditional correspondence courses) consisted primarily of open- or closed-circuit television and radio broadcasts. A proposal to confine old Section 110(2) to closed-circuit, on-campus transmissions was considered but rejected as too narrow.[85] Ultimately, the scope of the provision applied to both open and closed-circuit technologies, provided several other requirements were met. Old Section 110(2) authorized the:

> performance of a non-dramatic literary or musical work or display of a work, by or in the course of a transmission, if—
> (A) the performance or display [was] a regular part of the systematic instructional activities of a governmental body or a nonprofit educational institution; and
> (B) the performance or display [was] directly related and of material assistance to the teaching content of the transmission; and
> (C) the transmission [was] made primarily for—
> > (i) reception in classrooms or similar places normally devoted to instruction, or

---

83. "The University of Phoenix," Wikipedia, http://en.wikipedia.org/wiki/University_of_Phoenix ("The University of Phoenix is the United States' largest, private accredited university. . . .").

84. This portion of the chapter concerns the Section 110(2) that was part of the Copyright Act of 1976 and is sometimes hereinafter referred to as "old Section 110(2)." References to "new Section 110(2)" deal with the provision as modified by the TEACH Act.

85. *Supplementary Report* at 36–37.

      (ii) reception by persons to whom the transmission [was] directed because their disabilities or other special circumstances prevent[ed] their attendance in classrooms or similar places normally devoted to instruction, or

      (iii) reception by officers or employees of governmental bodies as a part of their official duties or employment.

Like Section 110(1), old Section 110(2) exempted only performances and displays. It did not authorize the reproduction or distribution of any copyrighted materials or the creation of derivative works therefrom.[86] The law was also narrower than Section 110(1) regarding the categories of works covered. While it permitted all displays, it allowed *only* performances of *nondramatic* literary or *nondramatic* musical works. Thus, under this provision, an instructor could never show a television program, play a sound recording, project a movie, put on a play, or perform an opera during a transmitted educational broadcast. All these items fell outside the definition of a "non-dramatic literary or musical work" and thus were not exempt from infringement liability.

During the 1976 revision process, education proponents pushed for the exemption to permit the performance of all works. However, the Register recommended maintaining the traditional distinction between dramatic and nondramatic works, and nonprofit versus for-profit performances.[87] As justification for this position, the Register noted copyright owners had held a general right of public performance in dramatic works since 1856,[88] with the right to perform nondramatic ones limited to for-profit productions.[89] The Register's Report listed several reasons for this disparate treatment, including the observation that while "public performance is usually the main source of revenue from a dramatic work; in the case of nondramatic works, revenue is also available from the sale of copies and sound recordings."[90]

The protection of nonprofit performances of dramatic works was incorporated into the 1976 Act because of concern instructional broadcasts

---

86. In a separate section of the 1976 Copyright Act, nonprofit educational institutions were granted a narrow exemption allowing them to make up to thirty "ephemeral" copies of a transmission program embodying a performance or display permitted under Section 110(2), upon compliance with certain conditions. 17 U.S.C. § 112(b).

87. *Supplementary Report* at 35.

88. *Register's Report* at 27–28.

89. *Id.*

90. *Id.* at 28. At the time this language was written, the term "sound recordings" was used to refer to the physical embodiments of sounds, defined in the 1976 Act as "phonorecords." 17 U.S.C. § 101.

could influence the intended market for plays. Audiovisual works were also protected and therefore left out of the exemption to safeguard against the pirating of motion pictures and television programs. The performance of sound recordings was also not authorized by old Section 110(2) because no exclusive right existed at that time for the creators of such recordings. Therefore, such a provision would have been superfluous.[91]

Old Section 110(2) further limited the nature and content of an educational transmission, as well as the identity and location of its recipients. First, the performance or display had to be a regular part of systematic instructional activity given by a nonprofit educational institution or governmental body. According to the provision's legislative history, the concept of "systematic instructional activity" was "intended as the general equivalent of 'curriculums,' but it could be broader in a case such as that of an institution using systematic teaching methods not related to specific course work."[92] As such, the exemption could have applied to noncredit courses, such as adult education offerings.

Similar to Section 110(1), the transmitting educational institution had to be nonprofit. However, Congress indicated "[t]he use of commercial facilities, such as those of a cable service, to transmit the performance or display, would not affect the exemption as long as the actual performance or display was for nonprofit purposes."[93] This provision thus permitted colleges to use the facilities of local commercial television stations to transmit their courses.

Second, the performance or display had to be directly related, and of material assistance, to the teaching content. This test of relevance and materiality connected the copyrighted work to the curriculum, thereby precluding using a work for entertainment purposes such as background music for a class.[94] Similarly, a disqualification occurred if a larger portion of a work than necessary was used to teach the subject in order to make the class more appealing to students.[95]

---

91. Current law provides an exclusive right to perform sound recordings publicly by means of a digital audio transmission, subject to a number of limitations. *See* Digital Performance Right in Sound Recordings Act of 1995, Pub. L. No. 104–39, 109 Stat. 336 (1995).

92. *House Report* at 83.

93. *Id.*

94. *Cf. House Report* at 81 ("The 'teaching activities' exempted by [old Section 110(2)] encompass systematic instruction of a very wide variety of subjects, but they do not include performances or displays, whatever their cultural value or intellectual appeal, that are given for the recreation or entertainment of any part of their audience.").

95. This aspect of old Section 110(2) was consistent with the fair use doctrine's examination of the purpose and nature of the use and the amount used. *See* Chapter Three for a more detailed discussion of the fair use doctrine as applied to educational settings.

Third, the exemption restricted both where the transmission could be sent and who could view it. Recipients had to be located in a classroom or similar place of instruction, or be persons "to whom the transmission [was] directed because their disabilities or other special circumstances prevented their attendance in classrooms."[96] Legislative history indicated such "special circumstances" included the inability of university students to take standard daytime classes because of work or other commitments:

> There has been some question as to whether or not the language in this section of the bill is intended to include instructional television college credit courses. These telecourses are aimed at undergraduate and graduate students in earnest pursuit of higher educational degrees who are unable to attend daytime classes because of daytime employment, distance from campus, or some other intervening reason. So long as these broadcasts are aimed at regularly enrolled students and conducted by recognized higher educational institutions, the committee believes that they are clearly within the language of Section 110(2)(C)(ii). Like night school and correspondence courses before them, these telecourses are fast becoming a valuable adjunct of the normal college curriculum.[97]

Fourth, transmissions had to be made *primarily*, but not *solely*, for reception by these persons. "[T]he transmission could still be exempt even though it [was] capable of reception by the public at large. . . . Factors to consider in determining the 'primary' purpose of a program would include its subject matter, content, and the time of its transmission."[98] This flexibility was necessary because, using the technologies available in the 1970s, particularly open-circuit broadcasting, no practical way existed to ensure educational broadcasts would reach only eligible students.

Taken together, these limitations, which greatly exceeded those contained in Section 110(1), represented a legislative attempt to balance the benefits and risks inherent in instructional broadcasting. In addressing the benefits, the Register of Copyrights wrote that "it . . . cannot be denied that educational broadcasting is in a special category. Its general aim is public and community service, and some of its instructional activities are essen-

---

96. 17 U.S.C. § 110(2) (1976). Recipients could also have been officers or employees of governmental bodies receiving the transmission as a part of their employment.
97. *House Report* at 84.
98. *Id.* at 83.

tially an extension, to a larger audience, of what schools have been doing for centuries."[99] In explaining the risks, however, the Register stressed the implications a wider audience would have for copyright owners:

> Fully acknowledging the unique public value of educational broad-casting and its need for financial support, we must also recognize the large public audiences it is now reaching, the vast potential audiences that are awaiting it, and the fact that, as a medium for entertainment, recreation, and communication of information, a good deal of educational programming is indistinguishable from a good deal of commercial programming. . . . In terms of good education, it is certainly true that the more people reached the better; but in terms of the author's rights it is equally true that the more people reached the more he should be compensated. It does not seem too much to ask that some of the money now going to support educational broadcasting activities be used to compen-sate authors and publishers whose works are essential to those activities.[100]

2) Application to Digital Distance Education   As enacted in 1976, old Section 110(2) had extremely limited application to digital course offerings. Taking the exemption out of its original context of analog broadcasting, and plac-ing it in the realm of digital distance education, raised a host of issues and problems. While in 1976, Sections 110(1) and 110(2) of the Copyright Act may have been sufficient to cover "all of the various methods by which per-formances or displays in the course of systematic instruction took place,"[101] this was certainly not the case by the time digital distance learning had established a foothold in the United States.

A threshold question was whether the term "transmission" as used in old Section 110(2) included digital broadcasts. The section itself did not specify any particular technology. To "transmit" a performance or display was, and still is, defined in Section 101 of the Copyright Act as "to com-municate it by any device or process whereby images or sounds are received beyond the place from which they are sent." Since this definition was

---

99. *Supplementary Report* at 35. The term "educational broadcasts" was used in this context by the Register to refer to transmissions of educational programs in the course of systematic instruction, within the scope of old Section 110(2), rather than to broadcast pro-grams of a general educational nature.

100. *Id.*

101. *House Report* at 81.

explicitly technology neutral ("any device or process"), digital transmissions were clearly covered. This alone failed to resolve the matter, however. The real problem arose from the fact that most digital distance education occurred via computer networks. As such, old Section 110(2) did not effectively exempt those transmissions because, by definition, they involved multiple acts of reproduction and distribution, and not just performances and displays of copyrighted works.

Even when the transmissions took the form of "live" analog broadcasts, thus avoiding the reproduction and distribution concerns, significant problems still arose. Recall the exemption permitted the performance of only a "non-dramatic literary or musical work." What constituted such a work? A chemistry or history text? Was that sufficiently nondramatic? What about a novel? Could *Moby Dick* constitute *too* dramatic a work to read in class? Probably not, but the answer was not clear. Nevertheless, educators were severely constrained in what they could perform for their students. Most often they were confined to reading from standard textbooks or novels in order to remain compliant.

An additional problem was created by the limitation placed on eligible recipients. Due to advances in technology, far more people became exposed to distance learning in the 1980s and 1990s. Consequently, many new distance students fell outside the bounds of the exemption. Those taking classes because of daytime employment, geographic remoteness, child care, or similar reasons, would likely have qualified as persons whose "special circumstances prevent[ed] their attendance in classrooms." Conversely, however, students taking courses for simple convenience, or as a supplement to regular classroom offerings, would most likely have fallen outside the statute's scope.

By the early 1990s, old Section 110(2) had truly become a dinosaur and a major hindrance to distance educators. Frustrated by its outdated provisions, more and more educators supported its repeal. Its painfully slow demise and ultimate amendment by the TEACH Act is the subject of Sections 6.3 and 6.4 of this chapter.

[b] Fair Use

Fair use is the broadest and most general limitation on the exclusive rights of copyright owners. The doctrine operates independently of other exemptions contained in the Copyright Act. As such, it can exempt teaching activity not covered by traditional educational exemptions. Codified in Section 107, fair use is a flexible, technology-neutral doctrine allowing reasonable and socially desirable uses of copyright works not necessarily authorized by their owner.[102] The legislative history of Section 107 explicitly noted its potential application to distance education:

> The fair use doctrine would be relevant to the use of excerpts from copyrighted works in educational broadcasting activities not exempted under Section 110(2) or 112 and not covered by the licensing provisions of Section 118. In these cases the factors to be weighed in applying the criteria of this section would include whether the performers, producers, directors, and others responsible for the broadcast were paid, the size and nature of the audience, the size and number of excerpts taken and, in the case of recordings made for broadcast, the number of copies reproduced and the extent of their reuse or exchange. The availability of the fair use doctrine to educational broadcasters would be narrowly circumscribed in the case of motion pictures and other audiovisual works, but under appropriate circumstances it could apply to the nonsequential showing of an individual still or slide, or to the performance of a short excerpt from a motion picture for criticism or comment.[103]

As such, fair use continues to play an important role in educational distance learning activities. Its interplay with the TEACH Act is further discussed in Section 6.4[2][j] of this chapter.

[c] Other Exemptions Applicable to Distance Learning

Other Copyright Act provisions may exempt certain distance education uses in limited circumstances. While these exemptions are important to fully understand the Copyright Act's application to distance education, they are unlikely to significantly expand the scope of permitted instructional uses in a digital environment.

[i] Section 112—Ephemeral Recordings

Section 112 of the act permits the making of ephemeral recordings of programs embodying the performance or display of copyrighted works used in making transmissions authorized under other provisions of the Copyright Act. This section was based upon "the traditional concept of ephemeral

---

102. *See, e.g., Nimmer on Copyright* § 13.05; *Stewart v. Abend*, 495 U.S. 207, 236 (1990); *Sony Corp. v. Universal City Studios, Inc.*, 464 U.S. 417, 449–50 (1984). For a more detailed discussion of the fair use doctrine and its applicability to education, *see* Chapter Three.

103. *House Report* at 72.

recordings as mere technical adjuncts of broadcasting that have no appreciable effect on the copyright owner's rights or market for the copies or phonorecords."[104] Subsection (a) thereof permits any transmitting organization to make a single copy of its authorized broadcasts under certain circumstances, thus facilitating the making of limited reproductions to assist in those broadcasts.[105]

Subsection (b) permits governmental or nonprofit organizations entitled to transmit displays or performances under Section 110(2) or 114(a) (discussed below) to make up to thirty copies of such transmissions and retain those copies for seven years (other than a single archival copy),[106] provided no further reproductions are made therefrom.[107] The exemption therefore operates as an adjunct to Sections 110(2) and 114(a), allowing a nonprofit educational institution to make certain reproductions to facilitate the permitted performance or display without seeking a separate license to do so.

The exemption is available only to the transmitting organization and does not permit copying by students. Since an educational institution often needs to repeat a class during a school day or over a term, this provision was deemed essential.[108] In describing Section 112, the House Judiciary Committee noted it was "aware of the practical problems facing educational broadcasters and other transmitters if they [were] required to seek separate clearances of performing and recording rights. . . ."[109]

Section 112(b) had only limited applicability to distance transmissions under old Section 110(2), however. It permitted the reproduction, and retention for seven years, of thirty copies of a digital broadcast; but it failed to authorize the necessary transient reproductions associated with the technical process of transmission in online courses, for two reasons. First, it would be impossible to limit to thirty the RAM copies generated during a transmission. Second, such copies inevitably generate other copies along the network, further disqualifying the transmitting organization. Enactment of the TEACH Act in November 2002, however, eliminated

---

104. *Second Supplementary Report of the Register of Copyrights on the General Revision of the U.S. Copyright Law: 1975 Revision Bill* (1975) (hereinafter 2d *Supplementary Report*).

105. *House Report* at 101. An example of such a use would be a radio broadcaster recording all the songs scheduled for a program on one tape, so that it could more easily play them in order.

106. 17 U.S.C. § 112(b).

107. *Id.*

108. *Supplementary Report* at 44.

109. H.R. Rep. No. 83, 90th Cong., 1st Sess. 60 (1967).

many of these problems by specifically authorizing the making of transient reproductions in the course of a digital educational transmission.[110]

[ii] Section 114—Scope of Exclusive Rights in Sound Recordings

Until 1996, no performance right existed for creators of sound recordings under U.S. copyright law. The Digital Performance Right in Sound Recordings Act of 1995 (DPRA)[111] amended Section 106 of the Copyright Act to give owners of these recordings the exclusive right "to perform the copyrighted work publicly by means of a digital audio transmission."[112] DPRA also amended Section 114, which limits the scope of exclusive rights in sound recordings. Further amendments were subsequently made in 1998 pursuant to the Digital Millennium Copyright Act (DMCA).[113]

In its current form, Section 114(d) divides transmissions carrying performances of sound recordings into three categories. Depending on the category, such performance could be subject to no right at all, a statutory license, or full exclusive rights. The three categories are (1) non-subscription broadcast transmissions (and certain retransmissions), which are completely exempted from the performance right (and thus unprotected); (2) subscription transmissions and certain "eligible non-subscription transmissions" such as webcasting, which are eligible for statutory licenses, subject to a list of criteria; and (3) interactive (on-demand) transmissions and other nonexempt transmissions, which are subject to the full exclusive performance right (and thus protected). All of these terms are defined at length in the statute.[114]

Applying this complex structure to digital distance education depends on the activity involved. Distance learning entailing digital "broadcast transmissions" of sound recordings would not be subject to the performance right. "Broadcast" transmissions, however, are defined for this purpose as those carried out by FCC-licensed radio or television stations.[115] As such, broadcasts emanating directly from educational institutions would not be covered. Some distance education activities could potentially be eligible for a statutory license under Section 114(d)(2). To qualify, a digital transmission would have to be either a subscription or an "eligible non-subscription" transmission. Subscription transmissions are

---

110. *See infra* Section 6.4[2][h].
111. *See supra* note 91.
112. 17 U.S.C. § 106(6).
113. Pub. L. No. 105–304, 112 Stat. 2860 (1998) (hereinafter, the DMCA). *See* Chapter Five, Section 5.4, for a more detailed discussion of the DMCA.
114. 17 U.S.C. § 114(j).
115. *Id.*

those controlled and limited to particular recipients who have paid for the transmission.[116]

Eligible non-subscription transmissions include those carried out synchronously by streaming audio. For either one to qualify for the statutory license, it must be non-interactive and meet other criteria set out in Section 114. These include not publishing the titles of the sound recordings in advance and not transmitting too many selections from the same phonorecord or by the same performer.[117] Digital transmissions of sound recordings outside these first two categories would be subject to the full exclusive right under Section 106(6). Because most distance education activities are asynchronous and interactive, they would likely fall into the third category and not be exempt.

Section 114(b) may also have some limited application to distance education. This provision limits the exclusive rights of reproduction, distribution, and preparation of derivative works, so as not to apply to sound recordings included in "educational television and radio programs" distributed or transmitted by or through "public broadcasting entities."[118] These copies also must not be commercially distributed to the general public.[119] In an analog world, this means a sound recording could be performed, and the performance transmitted, reproduced, and distributed, since there is no analog performance right for sound recordings.[120] In the digital world, however, the right to perform the work under Section 106(6), not exempted by Section 114(b), would still apply.

[iii] Section 111—Secondary Transmissions

Section 111(a) of the Copyright Act exempts certain "secondary transmissions" embodying the performance or display of a work.[121] A secondary transmission is defined as "the further transmitting of a primary transmission simultaneously with the primary transmission," or nonsimultaneously by a cable system outside the United States.[122] Paragraph (a)(2) exempts secondary transmissions "made solely for the purpose and under the conditions specified by clause (2) of Section 110." This provision does not materially expand the exemption for distance educators, but simply "make[s] clear that an instructional transmission within the scope of Sec-

---

116. *Id.*
117. 17 U.S.C. § 114(d)(2).
118. 47 U.S.C. § 397 and 17 U.S.C. § 118(g), respectively; 17 U.S.C. § 114(b).
119. 17 U.S.C. § 114(b).
120. 17 U.S.C. §§ 106(4) and (6).
121. 17 U.S.C. § 111(a).
122. 17 U.S.C. § 111(f).

tion 110(2) is exempt whether it is a 'primary transmission' or a 'secondary transmission.'"[123] For U.S. educational institutions, it authorizes only simultaneous transmissions of original broadcasts permitted under Section 110(2). Since, as discussed later in this chapter, the TEACH Act now permits both synchronous and asynchronous transmissions, this provision has become largely superfluous for distance educators.

[d] Compulsory Licenses

Distance educators may obtain authorization to use some works in limited ways through a compulsory license. A compulsory license is a contract established by statute that permits particular uses of works subject to compliance with prescribed procedures, rates, and terms. In addition to the Section 114(d) license discussed above, two other provisions may be relevant to educators.[124] Section 115 establishes a compulsory license to make and distribute phonorecords of nondramatic musical works. Section 118(d) does the same for published nondramatic musical works—or pictorial, graphic, and sculptural works—in the course of a transmission made by a noncommercial educational broadcast station. The entity must also comply with the terms of any voluntary, industry-wide license agreement[125] and a number of eligibility restrictions. Because of their limited applicability, such licenses are not likely to be used in most distance education settings.

6.3 PRIOR INITIATIVES ADDRESSING COPYRIGHT AND DIGITAL DISTANCE EDUCATION

[1] Fair Use Guidelines

The first in-depth public discussion of reforming copyright law to promote digital distance education occurred in the 1990s as an outgrowth of the Conference on Fair Use (CONFU), which was convened by the Clinton administration's Information Infrastructure Task Force.[126] CONFU

---

123. *House Report* at 92.

124. Other compulsory licenses in the Copyright Act relate to secondary transmissions by cable systems or satellite carriers. 17 U.S.C. §§ 111(b)–(f) and 119.

125. In practice, virtually all of the uses covered by Section 118 have been governed by voluntary agreements that preempt the terms of the compulsory license since enactment of the 1976 Copyright Act.

126. Notice of First Meeting of Conference on Fair Use and the National Information Infrastructure, 59 Fed. Reg. 46, 823 (1994).

established panels on several topics, including distance learning.[127] The CONFU Distance Learning Working Group (the "Working Group") was formed to draft "fair use guidelines" related to digital distance education. In preparing these guidelines, the Working Group wanted to avoid the pitfalls of old Section 110(2). It submitted its proposal to the full conference in November 1996, explaining:

> The purpose of these guidelines is to provide guidance for the performance and display of copyrighted works in some of the distance learning environments that have developed since the enactment of Section 110 and that may not meet the specific conditions of [old] Section 110(2). They permit instructors who meet the conditions of these guidelines to perform and display copyrighted works as if they were engaged in face-to-face instruction.[128]

The proposed guidelines (the "DL Guidelines") applied to the performance and display of all lawfully acquired copyrighted works, even dramatic and audiovisual ones, and addressed the following uses: (1) live interactive distance learning classes (i.e., a teacher in a live class with all or some of the students at remote locations) and (2) faculty instruction recorded without students present for later transmission.[129] The guidelines covered delivery via satellite, closed circuit television or secure computer network."[130]

Although the DL Guidelines were supposedly an extension of the fair use doctrine, they adopted a number of concepts contained in old Section 110(2) as well. For instance, the guidelines applied only to nonprofit educational institutions and limited any use to noncommercial settings.[131] Thus, the DL Guidelines could not be used for non-degree-granting programs. Likewise, only students officially enrolled in the course could view the transmission.[132] Unlike old Section 110(2), the DL Guidelines allowed

---

127. Other working groups also addressed topics relevant to education, including the application of fair use to electronic reserve systems that permit storage, access, display, and downloading of electronic materials intended to support the instructional requirements of a specific course within a nonprofit educational institution. While a subset of this working group circulated draft guidelines in March 1996, they did not receive widespread acceptance and were not disseminated as a formal work product of CONFU.

128. *Proposal for Educational Fair Use Guidelines for Distance Learning* § 1.2 (hereinafter *DL Guidelines*). A complete copy of the *DL Guidelines* is included in Appendix 3-G.

129. *Id.* at § 2.1.

130. *Id.*

131. *Id.* at § 2.2.1, § 7.1.

132. *Id.* at § 2.2.2.

the instructor to use *any* copyrighted work in his or her lesson. However, these uses were permitted only if certain additional restrictions were met.

First, the works performed had to be "integrated into the course," be part of systematic instruction, and be directly related to and of material assistance to the teaching content of the transmission. As such, the performance could not be used for entertainment purposes.[133] Second, technological measures had to be implemented to prevent unauthorized access or copying. Third, the course could only be transmitted to a classroom or other location controlled by the institution.[134] Finally, if an entire work or a large portion thereof was performed during the transmission, it could be viewed only once without obtaining permission from the author.[135]

While the Working Group discussed many aspects of distance learning, the DL Guidelines focused exclusively on synchronous or real-time teaching activity. This resulted from some participants believing the time was not ripe for consideration of delayed delivery. Those members supported their position at the time by explaining that "the relevant technology is rapidly developing, educational institutions are only now beginning to experiment with such distance learning courses, and publishers and other content creators are in the early stages of developing materials and marketing strategies for publisher-produced computer network delivery of distance learning materials."[136]

Other participants believed asynchronous delivery should have been covered and that the failure to do so would quickly render the guidelines antiquated. Given this lack of consensus and the limited time available, the Working Group opted "not [to] cover asynchronous delivery of distance learning over a computer network, even one . . . secure and capable of limiting access to students enrolled in the course through PIN or other identification system."[137]

The DL Guidelines did address certain limited, non-real-time uses, however. For instance, an eligible institution was permitted to "record or copy classes that include[d] the performance of an entire copyrighted work, or a large portion thereof, and retain the recorded copy for up to 15 consecutive class days (i.e., days in which the institution [was] open for regular instruction) for viewing by students enrolled in the course."[138]

---

133. *Id.* at § 3.1.

134. *Id.* at § 4, § 5.2.1.

135. *Id.* at § 5.1.

136. Conference on Fair Use, *Final Report to the Commissioner on the Conclusion of the Conference on Fair Use*, 31 (1998) (hereinafter *CONFU Final Report*).

137. *Id.*

138. *DL Guidelines* at § 5.2.1.

Permission from the copyright owner was required, however, for further dissemination of such classes.[139]

The DL Guidelines were included as an appendix to CONFU's Interim Report, published in December 1996. The publication of the Interim Report opened a six-month period during which parties could review the proposed guidelines and determine whether or not to support them formally.[140] While many organizations endorsed the proposal, a significant number were dissatisfied and failed to do so. A major reason cited was the failure to address asynchronous computer network delivery.[141] In May 1997, the Working Group was expanded to include additional representatives from the educational community with the ultimate objective of addressing delayed transmissions. The reconstituted group met twice in the fall of 1997, but its discussions terminated prior to satisfactory resolution of pending issues.

Four major factors contributed to the Working Group's failure to reach consensus. First, the various participants simply brought widely divergent views to the table. While educators and librarians wanted to significantly expand old Section 110(2) to give teachers the same latitude for electronic transmissions as for face-to-face instruction, copyright owners favored little to no change. The latter group feared a widened exemption would lead to significant revenue loss.

Second, the Working Group extended the concept of fair use beyond its traditional limits. Fair use essentially serves as a gloss over the Copyright Act, providing users of works guidance in areas where Congress has elected not to legislate. For instance, Congress chose not to delineate how much of a book or article could be copied and given to students in a class. Instead, it permitted educators to make their own judgment by employing the four fair use factors. Where Congress has opted to specifically legislate, as it did in Section 110 of the Copyright Act, fair use generally plays a lesser role.

Rather than applying fair use principles to distance learning, the Working Group chose instead to act as a kind of super-legislature. While referring to the four factors in their introduction, the DL Guidelines failed to actually analyze or employ them. Instead, the drafters attempted to essentially rewrite old Section 110(2) to further the goals of distance education.

---

139. *Id.* at § 7.2.

140. A preliminary list of endorsements was published in September 1997, along with a summary of the status of the Working Group discussions, in the Conference on Fair Use, *Report to the Commissioner on the Conclusion of the First Phase of the Conference on Fair Use*, 54 (1997).

141. *CONFU Final Report* at 13.

Unfortunately for the Working Group, it failed to realize that amending federal law falls exclusively within the domain of the U.S. Congress.

Third, participants in the CONFU process believed federal legislation addressing the field was imminent. Thus, their enthusiasm to develop a new (but soon to be moot) policy may have been dampened. As discussed below, several bills dealing with copyright and distance education were also introduced in Congress around the time the Working Group was meeting. Unfortunately, these legislative efforts would not reach fruition until many years later.

Fourth, the DL Guidelines as proposed were internally inconsistent. While their self-described purpose was to "provide guidance for the *performance* and *display* of copyrighted works in . . . distance learning environments,"[142] they also implicated the reproduction right in certain areas. For instance, the guidelines specifically covered "faculty instruction recorded without students present for later transmission,"[143] and permitted the institution receiving a transmission to "record or copy classes that include[d] the performance of an entire copyrighted work. . . ."[144]

The DL Guidelines also applied to delivery via a "secure computer network,"[145] thereby permitting reproduction through the transient or temporary storage of material carried out through the automated technical process of a digital transmission. Since old Section 110(2) dealt exclusively with the performance and display of copyrighted works (and not the reproduction thereof), the DL Guidelines tended to create "new law." The Working Group may have had better success by instead trying to "quantify" fair use as applied to digital distance education, as other CONFU panels had attempted.[146]

The final DL Guidelines were ultimately endorsed by several entities, including libraries, educational associations, and content owners.[147] Their applicability following enactment of the TEACH Act is open to question, however, since the topic of incorporating copyrighted works into instructional broadcasts is now specifically addressed in new Section 110(2). Since the TEACH Act still embraces the fair use doctrine, however, educators

---

142. *DL Guidelines* at §1.2.

143. *Id.* at § 2.1.

144. *Id.* at §§ 5.1 and 5.2.2.

145. *Id.* at § 2.1.

146. For instance, the Educational Multimedia Guidelines discussed in Chapter Three attempt to place precise quantitative limits on those portions of copyrighted works used in a qualified multimedia project so as to assist educators in interpreting "the amount and substantiality of the portion used" factor.

147. *DL Guidelines* at 7 (final list of endorsing organizations).

may continue to rely on portions of the DL Guidelines that go beyond the permitted uses outlined in new Section 110(2). The interaction between the doctrine of fair use and the TEACH Act is discussed in more detail later in Section 6.4[2][j] of this chapter.

[2] Congressional Consideration

[a] Early Legislative Efforts

Following the failure of the CONFU process to produce consensus for the field of fair use and distance learning, efforts moved to the legislative arena. In 1997, two separate bills were introduced in the 105th Congress to address the topic of instructional broadcasting in conjunction with other efforts, such as the DMCA, to update the Copyright Act.[148] After floor debate revealed the complexity of the subject, the bills were not passed as part of the DMCA.[149] Instead, Congress asked the Copyright Office to study the issue further and report back with recommendations within six months.[150]

[b] The Congressional Mandate

Section 403 of the DMCA required the Register of Copyrights, "after consultation with representatives of copyright owners, nonprofit educational institutions, and nonprofit libraries and archives," to submit to Congress "recommendations on how to promote distance education through digital technologies, including interactive digital networks, while maintaining an appropriate balance between the rights of copyright owners and the needs of users of copyrighted works." These recommendations were to include any new legislation considered appropriate to achieve these objectives.

In formulating suggestions, the Register was asked to consider the following questions:

1. Was there a need for a distance learning exemption for digital networks?
2. What categories of works should be exempt, if any?
3. Should quantitative limits be placed on those works used?
4. Who should benefit from the exemption?
5. Who should receive distance education materials?
6. Should technological measures be required to safeguard against unauthorized access to or use of copyrighted materials?

---

148. S. 1146, 105th Cong., 1st Sess. (1997); H.R. 3048, 105th Cong., 1st Sess. (1997).
149. *See supra* note 113.
150. DMCA at § 403.

7. To what extent should the availability of licenses be considered in assessing eligibility?

[c] The Copyright Office Process

To implement its congressional charge, the Copyright Office identified all stakeholders, gathered factual information, and provided a mechanism for full and open consultation. The process began on November 16, 1998, when a Notice of Request for Information was published in the Federal Register, seeking to identify interested parties and relevant issues.[151] The first notice generated more than 170 responses. The Copyright Office published a second notice on December 23, 1998, requesting comments and eliciting views and information on four topics: (1) the nature of distance learning; (2) the role of licensing therein; (3) the use of technology to prepare, disseminate, and protect copyrighted works; and (4) the application of copyright law to digital distance education.[152]

Through this process, the Copyright Office heard testimony and received comments from many interested parties, including colleges, universities, educational associations, professors, academic and research libraries, publishers, software and database vendors, motion picture and record producers, authors, photographers, collective licensing organizations, and technology companies. Not surprisingly, conflicting positions were taken by the various stakeholders as to the need for legislative action.

The academic community believed the law should be changed to optimize the quality and availability of distance education.[153] Members of this group expressed uncertainty and confusion regarding the application of fair use to the digital environment. They considered old Section 110(2) outmoded because it did not cover the full range of activities involved in digital distance learning. Academic administrators reported licensing for educational uses was cumbersome and expensive. Since educators already viewed distance education as capital intensive, many warned adding new licensing fees could make it cost prohibitive.[154] Others merely wished to avoid discrimination against remote-site students.[155]

---

151. 63 Fed. Reg. 63,749 (1998).
152. 63 Fed. Reg. 71,167 (1998).
153. *See* "Executive Summary," *The Copyright Office Report on Copyright and Digital Distance Education*, xi (1999) (hereinafter *Executive Summary*).
154. *Id.*
155. *Id.* at xii.

Copyright owners, on the other hand, were wary of new statutory amendments.[156] They viewed fair use as a strong and healthy concept and feared that broadening the instructional exemption would reduce opportunities to license works—a growing and potentially lucrative market for them. Copyright holders were also concerned about unauthorized downstream uses of their works, noting the ease with which students could duplicate and distribute digital copies around the world.[157] This group believed more efficient licensing systems would develop, eventually making it easier to obtain permission. Finally, copyright owners viewed licensing fees as a normal cost of distance education, comparable to the purchase of necessary hardware and software.[158]

On related topics, almost all participants agreed fair use was fully applicable to distance learning.[159] As for promulgating a new set of guidelines, the messages were mixed. Many copyright owners recommended pursuing fair use guidelines and suggested further discussion about the topic.[160] Educational and library groups were less enthusiastic. Some saw guidelines as valuable road maps to decision making, while others criticized the concept and expressed doubt about its efficacy.[161]

[d] The Copyright Office Report

In May 1999, the Copyright Office issued its "Report on Copyright and Digital Distance Education"[162] which summarized its findings (hereinafter, the DDE Report). The DDE Report concluded the Copyright Act should be amended to promote distance learning through digital technologies.[163] Specifically, it recommended allowing performances and displays permitted in face-to-face teaching to also be delivered by digital transmissions[164] and suggested that broadcast receptions not be limited only to physical classrooms.[165] As such, students in remote locations, at home, or in dormitory rooms using a computer could participate. In addition, the DDE Report endorsed allowing limited performances of those copyrighted works not originally covered under the 1976 Act.[166]

---

156. *Id.* at xi.
157. *Id.* at xii.
158. *Id.* at xi.
159. *Id.*
160. *Id* at xii.
161. *Id.*
162. The full name of this document is *The Copyright Office Report On Copyright And Digital Distance Education* (1999) (hereinafter *DDE Report*).
163. *Executive Summary* at xi.
164. *Id.* at xvi.
165. *Id.* at xvii.
166. *Id.* at xix.

At the same time, to protect copyright owners, the DDE Report suggested incorporating safeguards into educational broadcasts to control unauthorized dissemination and ensure the continued effectiveness of existing restrictions.[167] The report further proposed amending the ephemeral recordings exemption in Section 112 of the Copyright Act to facilitate asynchronous broadcasts.[168] Finally, the Copyright Office recommended clarifying various aspects of the fair use doctrine as applied to distance learning.[169] Despite support from both educational organizations and copyright owners, Congress failed to take action on the DDE Report for nearly two years following its issuance. Eventually, significant portions of the report were incorporated into the TEACH Act, which is the subject of the next section.

6.4 ENACTMENT OF THE TEACH ACT

[1] Legislative Background

On March 7, 2001, Senator Orrin Hatch of Utah and Senator Patrick Leahy of Vermont introduced Senate Bill 487 (or S. 487), the Technology, Education and Copyright Harmonization Act of 2001 (the TEACH Act),[170] to implement many of the recommendations contained in the DDE Report. On March 17, 2001, the Senate Judiciary Committee met in executive session to consider S. 487.[171] After extensive discussions with educators and copyright owners, and further assistance from the Copyright Office, an amended version of the bill was adopted and favorably reported to the full Senate.[172] On June 7, 2001, S. 487, as amended, passed the Senate by unanimous consent.

The bill was then sent to the House Judiciary Subcommittee on Courts, the Internet, and Intellectual Property. On July 11, 2001, this subcommittee met in open session and favorably reported out the bill.[173] For various

---

167. *Id.* at xviii.

168. *Id.* at xxi.

169. *Id.* at xxii.

170. S. 487, 107th Cong., 1st Sess. (2001). *See* 2000 Cong. Rec. S2008–2009 (daily ed. Mar. 7, 2001).

171. *See* H.R. Rep. No. 687, 107th Cong., 2d Sess. 4 (2002) (hereinafter *TEACH Act Report*).

172. *Id.* The original version of the bill was viewed by some as overly favorable to educators. The amended version added several provisions supported by copyright owners, including a requirement that technological protective measures be employed by educators to limit the risk of illegal downstream dissemination. *See* A. Aull, *The TEACH Act: The Impact of Copyright and Compromise on Digital Distance Education*, 4 (2006), http://cyber .law.harvard.edu/publications.

173. *TEACH Act Report* at 4.

reasons, however, the legislation was not submitted to the entire House Judiciary Committee until over a year later. One cause for the delay was the insistence of then-House Judiciary Committee Chairman James Sensenbrenner of Wisconsin that the legislation be coupled with copyright protection for certain factual databases and their vendors. Eventually, Congressman Sensenbrenner relented.[174] On July 17, 2002, the House Judiciary Committee met in open session and favorably reported the act.[175]

Senate Bill 487 was passed by the House of Representatives on September 25, 2002. On November 2, 2002, as part of the larger Justice Department Reauthorization Bill, S. 487 was signed into law by President Bush.[176] Unlike some other federal legislation, the TEACH Act contained no phase-in or grace period. Its provisions took effect immediately, leaving colleges and universities scrambling to comprehend its coverage and complex provisions. As discussed later, many schools and educators continue to struggle to comply with the act's requirements even years after its passage. A copy of the final legislation is included as Appendix 6-A hereto.

[2] Understanding the TEACH Act

[a] Works Subject to the Exemption

The TEACH Act expanded the scope of old Section 110(2) to apply to performances and displays of *all* copyrighted works, subject to specific exclusions for (1) works "produced or marketed primarily for . . . mediated instructional activities transmitted via digital networks" and (2) performances or displays "given by means of a copy . . . not lawfully made and acquired," which the transmitting body "knew or had reason to believe" fell into such category.[177] The *performance* of works, other than nondramatic literary or musical ones, is confined, however, to "reasonable and limited portions"[178] thereof. Nondramatic literary or musical works may still be performed in their entirety. In determining what constitutes a "reasonable and limited" portion, educators are required to take into account

---

174. Andrea Foster, *House Committee Votes to Ease Copyright Restrictions on Distance Education*, Chron. of Higher Educ., July 18, 2002, http://chronicle.com/free/2002/07/2002071801t.htm. For more detailed information on the nature and scope of such database legislation, *see* Chapter Four, Section 4.5.

175. *TEACH Act Report* at 5.

176. *See* EDUCAUSE and American Library Ass'n, *Technological Requirements of the TEACH Act*, 1 (Dec. 13, 2002), http://www.ala.org/ala/washoff/woissues/copyrightb/federallegislation/distanceed/teachdrm.pdf.

177. 17 U.S.C. § 110(2).

178. *Id.*

both the nature of the market for the work and the pedagogical purposes of the performance.[179]

The "reasonable and limited portion" qualification does not apply to the display right, because showing an entire work is often appropriate in a classroom setting (e.g., short poems or essays, or images of pictorial, graphic, or sculptural works). However, because the "display" of works, such as text using an "e-book" reader, could substitute for traditional purchases thereof, that exemption is also limited to "an amount comparable to [what] is typically displayed in the course of a live classroom setting."[180] This limitation thus incorporates the "mediated instructional activity" principle described below. In simpler terms, an instructor attempting to circumvent photocopying restrictions, by instead "displaying" an entire book to his class (such as by creating and posting an electronic version thereof on a website), would not be permitted to do so.

The exclusion for works "produced or marketed primarily for performance or display as part of mediated instructional activities transmitted via digital networks" is intended to protect the market for those materials expressly designed for academic use. The exclusion does not apply to *all* educational materials, but only those digital products to be performed or displayed as an integral part of the class experience, such as PBS or National Geographic videos. Traditional items used in the physical classroom would not be covered by this language.

The exclusion of performances or displays "given by means of a copy . . . not lawfully made and acquired" arises from similar language in Section 110(1) for audiovisual works used in the classroom. Unlike Section 110(1), the exclusion applies to *any* work, but liability attaches only when the transmitting institution knew or had reason to believe it was using an illegal copy. This language was intended to further discourage the proliferation and exploitation of pirated works.[181] Therefore, educators using the TEACH Act are still required to purchase, license, rent, borrow, or otherwise lawfully obtain the work being used. Thus, materials not yet commercially available in tangible form (e.g., unreleased music CDs or movies not yet on DVD) are not eligible for performance or display under the exemption.

[b] Eligible Transmitting Entities

As under old Section 110(2), the revised exemption is limited to governmental bodies and nonprofit educational institutions. However, because

---

179. *TEACH Act Report* at 8.
180. 17 U.S.C. § 110(2).
181. *DDE Report* at 159.

"nonprofit educational institutions" are no longer an easily identifiable group, and almost anyone can now transmit "educational" material over the Internet, the TEACH Act now requires these entities be "accredited."[182] "Accreditation" is defined as the qualification of the institution as a whole, and not particular classes or departments. Thus, an accredited institution may use the exemption for all its courses, whether or not they are part of a degree or certificate-granting program.

Most professional advancement or adult education classes would thus qualify under the exemption, as long as the institution offering them was accredited. This had not been the case under old Section 110(2). For postsecondary institutions, accreditation is "determined by a national or regional accrediting agency recognized by the Council on Higher Education Accreditation or the United States Department of Education." Elementary and secondary schools must be "recognized by the applicable state certification or licensing procedures" to qualify.[183]

[c] Qualifying Performances and Displays; Mediated Instructional Activities

Under the TEACH Act, a performance or display must be made "by, at the direction of, or under the actual supervision of an instructor as an integral part of a class session offered as a regular part of . . . systematic mediated instructional activit[y]."[184] This provision includes three major requirements. First, the performance or display must be made by or fall under an instructor's direction or supervision. As such, an eligible activity may be initiated by either a teacher or student, provided the pupil is supervised.

"Actual" supervision requires the instructor to control the class activities in reality, not just in theory. This provision also ensures students cannot independently "broadcast" works for their own entertainment under cover of educational objectives. The language is not intended, however, to require either constant, real-time supervision or preapproval for the performance or display. Since asynchronous learning, at the student's pace, is a significant and beneficial characteristic of distance education, "supervision" is not intended as a limiting factor.

Second, educational performances or displays must fall within the purview of "mediated instructional activities." This principle requires use of works analogous to what would take place in a live classroom. Thus,

---

182. *TEACH Act Report* at 9.

183. These definitions are contained in the defined terms section of 17 U.S.C. § 110 contained at the end of the statute.

184. 17 U.S.C. § 110(2)(A).

although one could display an entire textbook through an e-book reader or similar device, this is *not* what typically occurs in a classroom setting. Congress had no intent to encourage the displacing of textbooks, course-packs, or other material usually purchased or acquired by students. In other words, "the law attempt[s] to prevent an instructor from scanning and uploading chapters from a textbook in lieu of having the students purchase the material for their own use."[185]

Limiting use to "mediated instructional activities" operates in conjunction with the exclusion for works "produced or marketed primarily for performance or display . . . via digital networks." An example of the interaction between these provisions is seen in the case of traditional textbooks. As noted above, displaying extensive material from a book normally purchased by students is not permitted by the TEACH Act, because such activity does not usually take place in a traditional classroom. Correspondingly, because textbooks are not produced for digital networks, they are not excluded as eligible works. Thus an instructor remains free to highlight a chart, table, or other short excerpt from an unassigned work or to emphasize items from the assigned text.

Third, the performance or display must constitute an "integral part of a class session." This mirrors the requirement of old Section 110(2) that "the performance or display [be] directly related and of material assistance to the teaching content." This test of relevance and materiality directly connects the copyrighted work to "teaching" the class. In essence, it means the work may not be used simply as entertainment or unrelated background material.[186] It must be employed to fulfill some legitimate educational objective of the class.

[d] *Limitations on Receipt of Transmissions*

The TEACH Act removed the old Section 110(2) requirement that transmissions had to be received in "classrooms or similar places normally devoted to instruction." The only exception to such restriction was for persons prevented by disability or special circumstances from attending school. In making this change, Congress recognized and attempted to enhance the ability of distance education to transcend the physical classroom and reach students anywhere at any time.

---

185. K. Crews, *New Copyright Law for Distance Education: The Meaning and Importance of the TEACH Act*, 8, (Sept. 30, 2002), http://www.ala.org/ala/washoff/woissues/copyrightb/distanceed/teachsummary.pdf.

186. *DDE Report* at 80.

The TEACH Act does require, however, that a transmission be made solely for—and, to the extent technologically feasible, that its reception be limited to—students officially enrolled in the class.[187] This provision does not require impenetrable network security. Rather, its objective is to force schools to use standard measures, such as password protection, to ensure transmissions reach only authorized persons. In other words, the educational institution must employ reasonable mechanisms to deliver secure broadcasts, but it need not guarantee the inaccessibility of such transmissions to outsiders. The school may thus be absolved from liability if someone circumvents "imperfect technology."[188]

[e] Additional Safeguards to Counteract New Risks

Computer or satellite transmissions pose greater risks to copyright owners than traditional analog broadcasts because digital technologies facilitate the creation of multiple copies for rapid and widespread dissemination. Accordingly, the TEACH Act introduces several safeguards not contained in old Section 110(2).

[i] Legal Documentation

First, a transmitting body must institute "policies regarding copyright" and provide information to faculty, students, and staff accurately describing and promoting compliance with copyright law.[189] Further, the organization has to provide notice to recipients that materials used in a course may be subject to copyright protection.[190] One objective of the TEACH Act is therefore to inform students and faculty of their responsibilities under copyright law, promote compliance therewith, and decrease the likelihood of unintentional and uninformed acts of infringement.

The requirement to notify students that course materials may be protected by copyright is the most straightforward and least ambiguous of the statute's directives. The provision is obviously intended to alert students not to freely replicate and/or distribute works created by others. Compliance with this directive appears most easily met by placing warning language on textual materials given to students, or on the introductory screens, slides, or web pages of distance courses. The remaining informational requirements of the act are more difficult to interpret.

For instance, neither the statute nor its legislative history explains what "policies regarding copyright" are intended to entail. Also unclear is

---

187. 17 U.S.C. § 110(2)(C)(i).
188. *See* Crews, *supra* note 185, at 6.
189. 17 U.S.C. § 110(2)(D)(i).
190. *Id.*

whether these policies are synonymous with or different from the requirement to provide copyright compliance information to faculty and students. As such, the prudent course of action for educational institutions is to interpret these as distinct directives. Instituting copyright policies should involve concerted and deliberative action to promulgate written guidelines regarding how copyright ownership will be allocated between the school and its faculty for works created on-campus.[191] Conversely, providing information about copyright law involves an educational rather than a policy-making function.

Institutions subject to the TEACH Act should thus take reasonable measures to ensure their faculty, students, and staff understand the basics of copyright law and the implications of infringement. These educational efforts may take the form of in-house seminars, web-based training, or distribution of written materials. Typically, more detailed information is provided to faculty to explain concepts such as fair use and how Sections 110(1) and 110(2) of the Copyright Act operate in order to help them teach effectively and legally. Conversely, students need less instruction in appropriate classroom use of copyrighted materials. More importantly, they need to understand the propriety of their conduct outside of class when copying the materials of others. It is critical for school authorities to impress upon their students the importance of copyright as a property right and the serious penalties that may be assessed for infringement.

For both audiences, distribution of written materials, such as a copyright compliance manual, is recommended. Such documents are quicker and less expensive to produce than engaging speakers or organizing web-based training. They also provide the school with enhanced institutional protection. An educational organization can always distribute packets of information to faculty and students during the academic year, thus meeting its institutional obligation.[192] It is obviously more difficult to ensure that every teacher and student attends the required "copyright education lecture" or completes the applicable web-based training.

[ii] Technological Requirements

An additional safeguard imposed by the TEACH Act requires the transmitting body or institution, in the case of digital transmissions, to apply technological measures to prevent (1) students from retaining a copyrighted work being sent to them for longer than the class session; and

---

191. *See* Chapter Five, Section 5.3, for a more detailed discussion of this topic.

192. Whether the material in the packets is read is another matter, but at least the school has done what it can to distribute the information.

(2) any unauthorized further dissemination thereof.[193] These requirements have no legal effect other than as a precondition for eligibility, however. In other words, if a school chooses not to use copyrighted works in educational transmissions (or employs only works already in the public domain or those for which it currently has a license), such measures need not be implemented. In fact, schools do not have to comply with any provision of the TEACH Act if they avoid all use of copyrighted works in their distance courses. The act exists for those wishing to take advantage of its exemptions, provided its additional "safeguards" are implemented as well.

The TEACH Act also directs an institution not to "engage in conduct that could reasonably be expected to interfere with technological measures used by copyright owners to prevent such retention or unauthorized further dissemination."[194] This requirement potentially conflicts with another provision of the TEACH Act, however. Recall that only "reasonable and limited" portions of most works may now be used in educational transmissions. How does a teacher extract such a "reasonable and limited" portion from a "copyright-protected" digital product?

The obvious answer is that he or she cannot without running afoul of the law.[195] Currently, an instructor may still be able to digitize the needed portion from an analog work, as will be discussed below. But what happens when an analog copy is no longer available because everything is digitized and "copy-protected"?[196] Neither Congress nor the courts have yet to address this issue, and time may be running out to do so. As technological protection systems become more prevalent and widespread, the lesser the content available for educational use becomes.[197]

---

193. 17 U.S.C. §§ 110(2)(D)(ii)(I)(aa), (bb). Unfortunately, these requirements are quite vague and provide little to no guidance to information technology personnel employed by educational institutions. See Fisher Report at 97 (describing IT professionals as being "horrified by the vagueness and the impracticality" of the TEACH Act's terms).

194. 17 U.S.C. § 110(2)(D)(ii)(II). This requirement appears to apply to both digital and analog works.

195. There is increasing evidence, however, that many educators are doing just that. See Fisher Report at 26 ("Our research indicates that many film studies professors—probably most of them—respond to these difficulties by circumventing [DRM systems], despite the likely illegality of doing so.").

196. Anyone visiting a video store recently can notice the decreasing availability of videocassettes and increasing market dominance of DVDs. Macrovision recently announced the release of a new "Rip Guard DVD technology" that can prevent much of the copying of DVDs facilitated by software currently available online. See J. Borland, New Copy-Proof DVDs on the Way? CNETnews.com (Feb. 15, 2005), http://news.com.com/New+Copy+proof +DVDs+on+the+way/2100-1026_3-5576375.html.

197. Fisher Report at 48.

As noted above, technological measures must also be employed so that a copyrighted work may not be retained by a student for longer than the "class session." The length of a "class session" in distance education is generally the period a student is logged onto the server of the transmitting institution. However, this often varies with the pupil's needs and the design of a course. The term is not specifically defined in the TEACH Act, but the legislative history suggests it is not meant to encompass the entire duration of a course (e.g., a semester or term). Rather, it is intended to describe the equivalent of an actual single, face-to-face classroom session.[198]

Congress did take into account, however, that such a session may be asynchronous or that one student could remain online longer than another. Since many distance courses are self-paced, students could be accessing the same material at different points during a term. As such, the TEACH Act's sponsors recognized flexibility was necessary to accomplish the pedagogical goals of distance education. Therefore, Congress did not choose to legislate how long a "class" could be posted on a server. In return, though, it anticipated that a copy used in a "class session" would never serve as a substitute for acquiring the original work.[199]

As previously mentioned, the TEACH Act also requires a transmitting institution to implement technological measures to reasonably prevent "further dissemination" of a copyrighted work beyond the class. As with the "eligible recipient" requirement, a school does not have to guarantee such dissemination never takes place. Nor does the provision imply an obligation to monitor recipient conduct. Instead, it simply imposes an objectively reasonable standard on the institution to prevent such occurrences.[200] The TEACH Act does not list particular methods to comply with this requirement. Rather, Congress realized an institution's obligation would evolve with science. As the years passed, an effective measure could become obsolete or unreliable, forcing the school to update its technology from time to time.

[f] Interaction with the DMCA

The liability of Internet service providers remains governed by Section 512 of the Copyright Act (which was added by the DMCA). The DMCA

---

198. *TEACH Act Report* at 12.

199. *Id.*

200. Examples of technological protection measures that would reasonably prevent retention and further dissemination include measures used to prevent the copying of streamed material, such as the Real Player "Secret Handshake/Copy Switch" technology discussed in *Real Networks v. Streambox*, 2000 WL 127311 (Jan. 18, 2000) or digital rights management systems.

expressly granted nonprofit educational institutions an exemption from liability for certain acts of their employees. However, subject to these provisions, an educational transmitting body is not absolved of liability when it selects material to be used in teaching a course, determines how it will be used, and specifies to whom it will be transmitted.[201] As such, schools still need to exercise caution when placing copyrighted materials on their networks over extended periods of time. Because the TEACH Act covers the use of copyrighted works in "mediated instructional activity" and not long-term posting, it does not serve to minimize or mitigate those protections the DMCA affords to copyright owners.

On a related note, nothing in the TEACH Act is construed to affect the application or interpretation of Section 1201 of the DMCA, which governs circumvention of technological measures used by copyright owners to protect their works.[202] As such, educators must abide by the same standards as others in not "cracking" copyright-protection devices. In other words, teachers "who circumvent the DRM systems in DVDs to enable such uses thereby expose themselves to civil or even criminal penalties."[203] Similarly, nothing in Section 1201 is construed to affect the application or interpretation of the TEACH Act.[204]

[g] Transient and Temporary Copies

Like its predecessor, old Section 110(2), the TEACH Act was principally designed to cover *performances* and *displays* of copyrighted works, and not the remaining rights of copyright owners. However, Congress realized that, in the world of digital transmissions and electronic computer networks, reproduction and distribution rights would unavoidably be implicated.[205] To address this issue, the TEACH Act was drafted so as not to impose infringement liability on educational institutions when copies of

---

201. 17 U.S.C. § 512(e).

202. This provision of the DMCA is covered in more detail in Chapter Five, Section 5.4[1][b].

203. *Fisher Report* at 24.

204. *TEACH Act Report* at 13.

205. Material sent from servers often creates additional temporary or transient copies of such content (known as "caches") in other servers in order to facilitate the transmission. In addition, transient or temporary copies are produced in the transmission stream, or in the recipient's computer. Thus, by way of example, a recipient's browser may create a cache copy of a transmitted file on the recipient's hard drive, and another one in the random access memory when viewed on the screen.

works or distributions thereof are made through the "automatic technical process of a digital transmission."[206]

The TEACH Act also absolves an institution from responsibility for third-party copying beyond its reasonable control. However, to prevent a school from being used as an unwitting conduit,[207] the act imposes restrictions on transient or temporary material stored on the institution's computer network. For instance, it requires that such copies not be maintained "in a manner ordinarily accessible to anyone other than anticipated recipients" or "for a longer period than is reasonably necessary to facilitate the transmissions" for which they are made.[208]

[h] Ephemeral Recordings

Distance learning has greatly expanded America's educational capacity by the use of asynchronous courses. By these means, students can take a class at any time, not just when their teachers are available. Asynchronous education also permits the pupil to proceed at his or her own pace, freeing instructors from long-term classroom duty. For non-real-time learning to work, however, schools must be able to load material onto their servers for later transmission to students. The TEACH Act's amendment to Section 112 of the Copyright Act makes that possible. Under new Section 112(f)(1), institutions may now upload copies of those performances or displays authorized to be transmitted without triggering infringement liability. This provision further recognizes the need to make ephemeral recordings to aid in efficiently transmitting digital broadcasts.

Section 112(f) imposes three limitations on these recordings, though. First, they must be retained and used solely by the educational institution creating them.[209] Second, no further reproductions may be made, except for "transient and temporary" copies authorized by the TEACH Act.[210] Third, the recordings must be used solely for Section 110(2) transmissions.[211] In other words, copies of these classes may be made by the school for use in rebroadcasts permitted by the TEACH Act. In short, the TEACH

---

206. 17 U.S.C. § 110(2) (definitional section at end of statute).
207. *DDE Report* at 80.
208. 17 U.S.C. § 110(2) (definitional section at end of statute).
209. 17 U.S.C. § 112(f)(1)(A).
210. *Id.*
211. 17 U.S.C. § 112(f)(1)(B).

Act continues to envision distance learning as being offered in a series of discrete packets, the content of which may "thereafter be placed in storage and outside the reach of students."[212]

The TEACH Act also did not amend or alter Section 112(b) of the Copyright Act, which permits up to thirty copies of a transmission containing a copyrighted performance or display to be retained for seven years following its initial use. Some educators, who apparently read only the text of new Section 110(2) after enactment of the TEACH Act, criticized the legislation for not permitting copies of classes to be made for later use.[213] The addition of Section 112(f)(1) and the unaltered condition of Section 112(b) makes this an unwarranted concern, however.

[i] Digitizing Copies of Works

In essence, the TEACH Act now requires educators to use digital versions of works in their distance classes. This is the case for three reasons. First, as a practical matter, most works must be digitized in some fashion before they can be transmitted over a computer or satellite network. Second, since distance educators are now restricted to using only "reasonable and limited" portions of works to be broadcast, such extractions are typically easier to accomplish from digital rather than analog products. Third, the act only permits the use of analog works during digital transmissions when no digital version of a work is available. This provision was added to placate copyright owners who feared the widespread, unauthorized digitization of their analog works.

Congress correctly recognized, however, that some works would be unavailable for distance educators, either because no digital version was produced or because obtainable versions would be subject to technological protective measures.[214] In those two circumstances, Section 112(f)(2) authorizes conversion from an analog copy. However, only the amount authorized to be performed or displayed—that is, a "reasonable and limited" portion—may be so converted.

---

212. *See* Crews, *supra* note 185, at 7.

213. Trotter, *Bill Would Ease Copyright Limits for E-learning*, Educational Week, Oct. 30, 2002, at 3 (quoting Virginia Education Dept. official that TEACH Act's requirement that digital materials not be retained for an extended period "puts us in a little bit of a jam").

214. Most DVDs are protected by CSS or the "Content Scrambling System." *See* Chapter Five, Section 5.1[4], and *intra* Section 6.5[2][a] for a more detailed discussion regarding the operation of CSS. While unprotected for many years, companies are now developing technologies to "copy-protect" music CDs as well. *See* J. Borland, *New CD Copy-Lock Technology Nears Market*, ZDNet News (Dec. 16, 2004), http://news.zdnet.com/2100-9588_22-5492395.html.

For example, if a history professor teaching a digital distance course on the development of the American West wished to show the John Wayne movie *Stagecoach* to her class, she would face several issues. First, the professor could not legally digitize the VHS version to use unless, pursuant to the TEACH Act, "no digital version of the work was available to the institution."[215] What does this mean? To what lengths must the professor go to obtain the digital version? What if the local Blockbuster outlet does not have it? Must she visit every video store in town? If that fails, does she have to order it from a distributor or movie studio? Neither the courts nor Congress has thus far provided an answer.

What if *Stagecoach* had never been released on DVD, or the located DVD was CSS-protected? Our instructor could then use an analog copy (i.e., the videocassette version) and digitize it to show her class. However, she would be permitted to digitize only the reasonable and limited portion thereof she was allowed to transmit to her students.[216] More problematic for the professor is what happens when the analog version is also copyright-protected, such as by the use of "Macrovision?"[217] How can she make the necessary duplicate without violating the TEACH Act's prohibition on interfering with technological protective measures?[218]

Unfortunately, the TEACH Act fails to define what constitutes such "interference." The closest corollary is the DMCA's description that "to 'circumvent a technological measure' means to descramble a scrambled work, to decrypt an encrypted work, or otherwise to avoid, bypass, remove, deactivate, or impair a technological measure, without the authority of the copyright owner."[219] Does using a commercial analog-to-digital conversion device constitute such interference on the copyright-protected

---

215. 17 U.S.C. § 112(f)(2)(A).

216. 17 U.S.C. § 112(f)(2) (authorizes conversion only up to the amount permitted by Section 110(2)).

217. Macrovision is actually the name of a company that develops and sells licensing, access control, and secure distribution technologies for various media. The name is sometimes used to refer to the various copy-protection schemes developed by the company. *See* "Macrovision," Wikipedia, http://en.wikipedia.org/wiki/macrovision.

218. 17 U.S.C. § 110(2)(D)(ii)(II).

219. 17 U.S.C. § 1201(a)(3)(A). The technological measures that Congress intended to protect were described as "technologies, such as encryption, which will be used to protect copyrighted works in the digital environment and to secure on-line licensing systems." *See Section-by-Section Analysis of H.R. 2281 as Passed by the United States House of Representatives on August 4, 1998.* House Comm. on the Judiciary, 105th Cong., (Comm. Print 1998), at 10.

videocassette? The courts have yet to address this issue vis-à-vis the TEACH Act.[220]

It appears though that, short of "cracking" a code or rewriting software, this type of activity would be permissible. If our professor were strictly risk averse, however, her only alternative in this case would be to play portions of the DVD by selecting certain scenes manually during the class. However, the physical mechanics of that approach make it more suited to a live lecture setting, thereby defeating a major advantage of asynchronous distance learning. She might also try using a digital camera to tape portions of the movie off a television set playing a VHS tape. While such activity is likely permissible under the TEACH Act (or even fair use), it will likely result in a presentation of inferior quality and thus detract from the learning experience.

Ironically, the Register of Copyrights has recently taken notice of the advantages of using DVDs over VHS tapes for pedagogical purposes by observing that:

> the encrypted DVD versions of motion pictures often are of higher quality than copies in other available formats and contain attributes that are extremely important to teaching about film for a number of reasons. For example, for older works, the DVD version of a motion picture can preserve the color balance and aspect ratio to accurately reflect how the original work would have appeared when it was originally released in theaters. . . . For instance, VHS versions of the films altered the color balance and aspect ratio. Similarly, . . . screen shots with a digital video recorder reveal dramatic color distortions and greatly reduce picture quality. While these options may have satisfied the needs of many types of noninfringing users and even many noninfringing educational uses—e.g., those wanting to comment on the historical context of a film or create a parody, or to show a film clip in class unrelated to cinematographic significance—the reduced quality of alternative formats was wholly insufficient for the ped-

---

220. Courts, however, have addressed the issue of what constitutes "circumvention" of an access control measure under the DMCA. *See, e.g., I.M.S. Inquiry Management Systems Ltd. v. Berkshire Information Sys. Inc.*, 307 F. Supp. 2d 521, 532 (S.D.N.Y. 2004) (unauthorized use of a user name/password combination do not "evince circumvention as that term is used in the DMCA"); *Universal City Studios, Inc. v. Corley*, 273 F.3d 429, 435 (2d. Cir. 2001) (DMCA "targets the circumvention of digital walls guarding copyrighted material").

agogical purposes for which the clips were sought in film and media studies classes.[221]

Such observations were made in connection with certain provisions of the DMCA, and not the TEACH Act, however, and therefore have no legislative impact on the latter.

[j] Relationship to Fair Use

When it suggested amending old Section 110(2), the Copyright Office made clear that "critical to [its conclusion and recommendations was] the continued availability of the fair use doctrine."[222] Therefore, nothing in the TEACH Act limits or otherwise alters the scope of fair use. As the Copyright Office explained:

> Fair use is a critical part of the distance education landscape. Not only instructional performances and displays, but also other educational uses of works, such as the provision of supplementary materials or student downloading of course materials, will continue to be subject to the fair use doctrine. Fair use could apply as well to instructional transmissions not covered by the changes to Section 110(2) recommended above. Thus, for example, the performance of more than a limited portion of a dramatic work in a distance education program might qualify as fair use in appropriate circumstances.[223]

Specifically, therefore, Congress enacted the TEACH Act in recognition of the following two principles:

1. the fair use doctrine is technologically neutral and applies to activities in the digital environment; and
2. the lack of established guidelines for any particular use does not imply fair use is inapplicable to it.[224]

Such qualifiers are somewhat confusing and counterintuitive, however. As discussed earlier, one impetus for enacting the TEACH Act was the concern voiced by the educational community over the amorphousness of the fair use doctrine and the difficulty in relying on it. The TEACH

---

221. The Recommendation of the Register of Copyrights in RM 2005-11; Rulemaking on Exemptions from Prohibition on Circumvention of Copyright Protection Systems for Access Control Technologies, at 20 (Nov. 17, 2006) [footnotes omitted].

222. *Executive Summary* at xvi.

223. *DDE Report* at 161–62.

224. *Id.*

Act was therefore intended to give educators specific guidance as to what constituted permitted uses of copyrighted works in distance learning. To also incorporate the fair use doctrine into the new law simply clouds the matter. Fair use is a valuable tool in those instances where Congress has chosen not to set specific parameters for use of a copyrighted work. When Congress has elected to establish clear (or at least clearer) boundaries (as it did in the TEACH Act), the inclusion of fair use merely begets confusion and further uncertainty.[225]

Ironically, if Congress intended to "merge" the fair use doctrine into the TEACH Act, it failed to provide some key protection to educators in doing so. Under Section 504(c)(2) of the Copyright Act, if an employee or agent of a nonprofit educational institution can prove that he or she believed or had reasonable grounds for believing that his or her use of a copyrighted work constituted fair use, a judge could absolve such person of all damages. Such a "reasonable belief defense" is not part of the TEACH Act, however. As such, "educators with a good-faith belief that their activity [complies with the statute] are not necessarily protected from statutory damages in the event their judgment is incorrect."[226]

[k] Contractual Obligations

While the Copyright Office also examined a variety of licensing issues, it made no legislative recommendations about them. Therefore, nothing in the TEACH Act directly affects the relationship between express copyright exemptions and those restrictions private parties may agree to in a contract.[227] The impact of this policy position is not clear, however. The most plausible interpretation is that the TEACH Act may not be used to override the terms of a license agreement entered into between an educational institution and copyright owner. For instance, a school would not be able to use any portion of an author's work in a distance learning class if the

---

225. As a corollary, it is a seminal principle of jurisprudence that where the language of a statute or regulation is clear on its face, legislative history may not be used to supplant it. *See Pipefitters Local Union v. United States*, 407 U.S. 385, 446 (1972). *See also K and N Engineering, Inc. v. Bulat*, 2007 WL 4394416 at *1 (9th Cir. Dec. 18, 2007) ("[i]f the text of the statute is clear, [a] court looks no further in determining the statute's meaning.").

226. *Fisher Report* at 60. To specifically address this issue, Rep. Richard Boucher of Virginia introduced the Fair Use Act of 2007 (H.R. 1201), http://www.ala.org/ala/washoff/woissues/copyrightb/FairUseAct2007.pdf, on the floor of Congress on February 27, 2007. The Fair Use Act would, among other things, amend Section 504(c)(2) to completely remit damages "under circumstances in which no reasonable person could have believed such conduct to be illegal." The outlook for the legislation's enactment is uncertain.

227. *TEACH Act Report* at 16.

contract under which it is licensed permits performances only in live lecture settings.

On the other hand, the assertion by Congress that fair use remains a component of the TEACH Act may countermand such an assumption. A contract, for example, precluding a school from making "fair use" copies of a work it has licensed is arguably unenforceable as to that specific provision. As discussed in Chapter Two, the federal preemption doctrine permits U.S. copyright law to supersede private contracts if the plaintiff fails to show an "extra element" to the agreement.[228] Therefore, in our example above, a school could still use "reasonable and limited portions" of the "licensed only for live lecture" work in distance courses, in contravention of its contract, because new Section 110(2) applies to *all* works. To date, the courts have yet to address or rule specifically on this issue in terms of the TEACH Act.

The development of copyright law as applied to distance education has been a long and arduous process. An examination of the various statutes and guidelines can be quite confusing for anyone new to the field. To assist the reader in more clearly visualizing the issues, Appendix 6-B herein contains a schematic diagram summarizing Section 110(1), old Section 110(2), the DL Guidelines, and the TEACH Act. The chart shows the evolution of these provisions and highlights their similarities and differences.[229]

[l] The USPTO Report

The TEACH Act requires the U.S. Commerce Department to submit periodic reports to Congress on technological systems designed to protect digitized copyrighted works. The act specifically directed the United States Patent and Trademark Office (USPTO) to include information on those "systems that have been implemented, are available for implementation, or are proposed to be developed to protect digitized copyrighted works and prevent infringement."[230] The USPTO report is "not to be construed to affect in any way, either directly or by implication, any provision"[231] of the Copyright Act in general or the TEACH Act in particular.

Some lawmakers worried these reports would "only provide a snapshot in time," while others feared they would be "out of date by the time they

---

228. *See* Chapter Two, Section 2.1[3][c], for a more detailed discussion of this issue. The presumption is that federal law normally preempts or "trumps" state law (under which private contracts are governed) pursuant to Constitutional principles of federalism.

229. The author has used this chart in numerous lectures and seminars across the country and found it to be a valuable tool in explaining unfamiliar concepts to both educators and lawyers.

230. Pub. L. No. 107–273, § 1(d)(1) (2002).

231. *Id.*

were finished due to continual advances in technology."[232] However, Congress also noted these studies could be "useful in establishing a baseline of knowledge for the Committee and our constituents with regard to what technology is or could be made available and how it is or could be implemented."[233] Obviously, Congress believed it important to be kept abreast of technological developments that could aid in stemming the tide of illegal pirating and distribution of copyrighted works. With this information, Congress could more intelligently decide whether to further restrict or, instead, significantly expand the exemptions for educational uses of copyrighted works in the future.

Pursuant to this mandate, on December 4, 2002, the USPTO solicited written comments from interested parties and scheduled public hearings.[234] In particular, the agency solicited responses to the following two questions:

1. What technological protection systems have or could be developed to protect digitized copyrighted works?
2. What systems have or could be developed in the private sector through a broad-based consensus process?[235]

On February 4, 2003, the USPTO conducted a public hearing to assist in the preparation of its study.[236] The final USPTO report was released to the public in May 2003.[237] Some of its findings are considered in Section 6.5 below.

[m] Conclusion

Enactment of the TEACH Act in late 2002 heralded the most significant development in the field of copyright law and distance learning in over twenty-five years.[238] Many who applauded its coming saw it as an opportunity to finally place distance education, at least for copyright purposes, on equal footing with face-to-face teaching.[239] While the TEACH Act narrowed major differences between exempt uses of copyrighted works in a

---

232. Cong. Rec. S5991 (daily ed. June 7, 2001).

233. *Id.*

234. 67 Fed. Reg. 72,920 (2002).

235. Copies of the public comments received on these questions are available on the USPTO website, http://www.uspto.gov.

236. A transcript of the hearing is available on the USPTO website, http://www.uspto.gov.

237. United States Patent and Trademark Office, *Technological Protection Systems for Digitized Copyrighted Works: A Report to Congress* (May 2, 2003), http://uspto.gov/web/offices/dcom/olia/teachreport.pdf.

238. Hutchinson, *The TEACH Act: Copyright Law and Online Education,* 78 N.Y.U. L. Rev. 2204, 2207 (2003) ("the TEACH Act is likely the most educator-friendly legislation that Congress will produce in the near future").

239. *See* Crews, *supra* note 185, at 3.

live classroom versus a distance setting, it still left significant gaps between the two environments.

Distance students continue to be more constrained regarding the performances they may receive in their educational experiences. For example, a professor wishing to show the movie *Ben Hur* to his Roman History course may play the entire movie for his on-campus class without the need to obtain permission. Conversely, only "reasonable and limited" portions thereof may be shown to students taking the same course over the Internet. Even students viewing the class simultaneously at a regional campus of the same university must receive an "edited" broadcast. This disparate treatment hardly seems justified.

While the TEACH Act, by most accounts, substantially improves conditions for distance educators and their students, it does so at a price.[240] Expanding the types of works eligible for use and the locations to which they may be transmitted is contingent upon compliance with a host of new requirements. Some of these directives are administrative in nature, such as the need to distribute information on copyright and develop institutional policies. Others, like the requirement to install protective measures to prevent unauthorized access to and the reproduction of copyrighted works, are more technical in scope.

These new mandates are all an integral part of the exemption, however. An educational institution showing only "reasonable and limited" portions of audiovisual works to its distance students is still not compliant unless it is concurrently putting these new administrative and technological measures in place. There is no "piecemeal" implementation or substantial compliance component to the TEACH Act. To take advantage of its provisions, its directive is "all or nothing." The defenses of "our school can't afford that" or "we haven't been able to get around to all of it yet" are not recognized in the law.

The TEACH Act's requirements are also more institutionally oriented than other Copyright Act provisions. While other educational exemptions, such as fair use, focus on the actions of individual instructors, the TEACH Act places duties squarely on the shoulders of the educational organization. It is the school itself that "must impose restrictions on access, develop new policy, and disseminate copyright information."[241] Since the institution is also the party most likely to be held accountable for violations of the law, educational bodies have strong incentives to see their faculty members

---

240. Some commentators believe too high a price. *See Fisher Report* at 46 ("these [new] restrictions so limit the reach of the TEACH Act . . . most observers believe the exception from liability it offers has little or no value"). *See also* Nimmer, *Codifying Copyright Comprehensibly*, 51 U.C.L.A. L. Rev. 1233, 1312 (2004) (describing the TEACH Act as "lacking national significance").

241. Crews, *supra* note 185, at 3.

adhere to the act's provisions. This enhanced role creates its own set of issues and problems, however.

College and university administrators may attempt to become more involved in day-to-day course offerings. This "oversight" may include auditing classes to ensure instructors' "broadcasts" are TEACH Act compliant.[242] More curriculum decisions could potentially need to be made by administrators rather than faculty to ensure "all programs [are] transmitted solely on centralized systems that meet the prescribed standard."[243] These "supervised" instructors might in turn view these procedures as an invasion of their "academic freedom"[244] and resent the presence of the "TEACH Act police"[245] on campus.

Even more troublesome for some schools will be the financial costs of compliance.[246] Hiring attorneys to draft copyright manuals or conduct training along with acquiring the hardware and software necessary to implement copyright protective measures are expensive ventures. While major private and state universities may be able to absorb these costs, smaller community colleges and K–12 school systems, already struggling under tight budgets, may not.

Due to the lack of technology, money, or both, many institutions may be forced to choose between compliance or tabling implementation of the TEACH Act.[247] In the latter case, schools could continue to rely on fair use and/or employ only works in the public domain for their distance courses. Others may simply limit their distance programs or attempt to obtain licenses from copyright owners. Ironically, while the TEACH Act was intended to facilitate a school's educational mission, it may actually hinder some aspects thereof until sufficient funds are allocated to meet its requirements. In fact, according to one recent study, "less than 7.8% of the survey respondents indicated their institutions were seeking to comply with TEACH Act requirements."[248]

To date, other than a congressional report accompanying its enactment, no federal rules or regulations have been promulgated regarding the TEACH Act, and no cases have been published specifically interpreting

---

242. *Id.*

243. *Id.*

244. *Id.*

245. This term is solely the creation of the author.

246. *Fisher Report* at 47.

247. Hutchinson, *supra* note 238, at 2207.

248. Comments of Dr. Kimberly B. Kelley, *Public Comment on Library and Archive Exemption, Section 108 Study Group*, 2 (2006) (*citing* University of Maryland Center for Intellectual Property research study).

its provisions. In view of the act's significance and potentially conflicting clauses, such releases and/or judicial rulings cannot be far behind.

6.5 TECHNOLOGICAL PROTECTION SYSTEMS

[1] Introduction

The 1996 World Intellectual Property Organization (WIPO) Copyright Treaty and the WIPO Performances and Phonograms Treaty (collectively, the "WIPO Treaties") require signatories to provide "adequate legal protection and effective legal remedies against the circumvention of effective technological measures."[249] The U.S. legislation implementing the WIPO Treaties, the DMCA,[250] generally divides technological measures into those preventing unauthorized *access* to a copyrighted work and those preventing unauthorized *copying* thereof. As noted earlier, the TEACH Act specifically prohibits transmitting institutions from engaging in "conduct that could reasonably be expected to interfere with technological measures used by copyright owners"[251] to regulate the retention or unauthorized dissemination of their works.

Although the term "technological measures" is not defined in the TEACH Act,[252] it generally refers to a range of methods that control unauthorized access to and copying of works. Few educators or lawyers are well versed in the language of these systems, however. As such, the next section briefly discusses a variety of core technologies in use today and introduces some common terminology.[253]

---

249. WIPO Copyright Treaty (WCT), Article 11, adopted December 20, 1996, WIPO Doc. CRNR/DC/94; WIPO Performances and Phonograms Treaty (WPPT), Article 18, adopted December 20, 1996, WIPO Doc. CRNR/DC/95; Agreed Statements Concerning the WIPO Copyright Treaty, adopted December 20, 1996, WIPO Doc. CRNR/DC/96. The treaties also require adequate legal protection and effective legal remedies for the protection of the integrity of copyright management information. WCT, Art. 12; WPPT, Art. 19.

250. *Supra* note 113. *Also see* Chapter Five, Section 5.4, for a more detailed discussion of the DMCA.

251. 17 U.S.C. § 110(2)(D)(ii)(II).

252. While the DMCA also does not specifically define "technological measures," it does provide that "a technological measure 'effectively controls access to a work' if the measure, in the ordinary course of its operation, requires the application of information, or a process or a treatment, with the authority of the copyright owner, to gain access to the work." *See* 17 U.S.C. § 1201(a)(3)(B).

253. For a recent survey of these technologies, *see* Committee on Intellectual Property Rights and the Emerging Information Infrastructure, National Research Council, Computer Science and Technology Board, *Protecting Digital Intellectual Property*; in *The Digital Dilemma: Intellectual Property in the Information Age* (1999).

[2] Core Technologies

[a] Encryption

Encryption is a process that "scrambles" data using sophisticated mathematical equations. In simple terms, encryption algorithms convert discernible data, such as a word processing document, into scrambled data. The encrypted material becomes readable again by use of a corresponding decryption key. If the decryption key is given only to authorized parties, and the encryption algorithm is sufficiently strong, unauthorized access is prevented. Encryption's objective is to ensure works cannot easily be manipulated without permission. A secret key or pair of keys, as discussed below, is required for the decryption of a scrambled file. Encryption technology can also be used to protect material sent over computer networks (such as e-mail and database information), or other delivery systems, including telephone, satellite, and cable.

Broadly speaking, encryption algorithms are characterized either as "secret key" (sometimes called "symmetric key") or "public key" (sometimes called "asymmetric") encryption. Secret key encryption uses a single key to encrypt and decrypt content. A common example is pay-per-view television, where the program is encrypted using the secret key that only paying customers have access to. Of course, as its name suggests, successfully applying this technology depends on keeping the key secret. Wide distribution thereof may thus result in compromising such a system.

Public key encryption uses an algorithm requiring two keys—a "public" and a "private" one. The data is encrypted using the public key, which is then made widely available. The private key is kept secret by individuals. Basically, encrypted content may be decrypted only by using the corresponding private key. For example, a copyright owner could encrypt a work by using the public key of the intended recipient. Following transmission, the recipient uses the private key to decrypt the work. No private keys need be exchanged in this transaction. Without the recipient's private key, the work cannot be read, manipulated, or otherwise deciphered easily by others.

The Content Scrambling System (CSS) illustrates how encryption technology is integrated into a copyright protection system. First, using CSS, digital audiovisual content (including the keys that enable a DVD player to access a movie) is encrypted on a DVD. Second, only DVD players licensed by the DVD Copy Control Association (DVD CCA), a private industry-led, nonprofit organization, may decrypt the content. Third, under DVD CCA's contract requirements, licensed players must, among other things, protect against copying and disclosure of the decryption keys.

[b] Digital Watermarking

Although encryption is an important tool, it does not address all potential issues. After receipt, for example, decrypted content is still subject to unauthorized use, manipulation, and further distribution. One way to prevent this is to directly embed control information into the media itself, commonly known as "digital watermarking."[254] Originally, digital watermarking referred only to techniques that inserted copyright information into a digitized work. The term "fingerprinting" is now used for watermarking that reveals the identity of the person receiving the protected content. Digital watermarking today also refers to technology aimed at concealing data in media content.

In its basic form, a digital watermark contains information about the origin, status, or destination of the host data. It may be embedded in almost any kind of digitized visual or audio work, including broadcast data, without degrading or interfering with its quality.[255] The hidden information cannot be removed without also perceptibly distorting or significantly reducing data quality. Thus, digital watermarks can be an important mechanism for content owners to monitor, audit, and index their works. These watermarks may also be used to identify the source and destination of data, thereby allowing owners to authenticate content when copyright infringement is suspected. Finally, these marks can detect the unauthorized manipulation of data, thereby controlling its integrity.

[c] Authentication

Technologies used to recognize devices and authenticate a user's identity are important elements of modern protection systems. One way to control user access in a centralized network is by Internet protocol addresses, or IP authentication. To protect content from off-site locations, a resource provider may provide password accounts to users. User data may also be stored in a cookie—a text string or small file placed on an end user's hard drive. Digital certificates are also used to authenticate a user's identity. Under this approach, a certificate authority issues a personal digital cer-

---

254. For a comprehensive treatment of the subject, *see* Cox, Bloom, & Miller, *Digital Watermarking Principles & Practice* (2001). *See also* de Vleeschouwer, Delaigle, & Macq, *Invisibility and Application Functionalities in Perceptual Watermarking—An Overview*, 90 Proc. of the IEEE 17 (2002).

255. Digital watermarks may be either "perceptible" (to humans) or "imperceptible." A "fragile" watermark becomes undetectable even after minor modifications of the work in which it is embedded. A "robust" watermark is capable of surviving manipulations over its lifetime such as compression, image processing, printing, or scanning. A "semi-fragile" watermark is fragile against certain distortions and robust against others.

tificate containing the owner's name and public key, the certificate expiration date, the certificate serial number, and the name and digital signature of the certificate issuer.

Techniques to detect tampering with works have become critically important as more and more businesses transmit digital data. For example, a medical publisher may depend on content authentication techniques to ensure that textual data (such as dosage amounts) or visual information (such as medical illustrations) have not been altered. One common cryptographic solution is the use of digital signatures, a technique that authenticates both the message contents and person signing it. Digital signatures may be transmitted with the work as either "metadata" (encoded identifying information about the content) or embedded directly as watermarks. More broadly, such technology may be used to authenticate the integrity of license terms and conditions associated with a copyrighted work.

[3] Digital Rights Management Systems

Advances in hardware and software technology permit content owners to assert much greater control over digital media embodying their works. These advances help authenticate users, verify content integrity, and deter piracy. The term "digital rights management" (DRM) commonly refers to systems designed to achieve these objectives.[256] Although DRM has no generally accepted definition,[257] such protective systems typically incorporate access and use controls and tracking functions. For purposes of this discussion, "DRM" refers to a broad range of technical, legal, and business issues pertaining to copyright management and the control of digital works. Some key concepts and elements underlying DRM are discussed below.

[a] Trusted Computing

A trusted computer system combines hardware and software (meeting certain specifications approved by the content provider) to create a secure

---

256. For a very useful introduction to DRM technologies and systems, *see* Rosenblatt, Trippe, & Money, *Digital Rights Management: Business and Technology* (New York: M&T Books, 2002).

257. One commentator broadly defined DRM systems as "technology systems facilitating the trusted and dynamic management of rights in any kind of digital information, throughout its life cycle, irrespective of how and where the digital information is distributed." *See* N. Garnett, "Outline of Presentation of Nic Garnett, representing InterTrust Technologies," Presentation to ALAI Congress (2001).

platform for the exchange of digital information.[258] In the DRM context, a trusted system is a computer (or other device) relied on to follow and enforce rules governing the access and use of protected content. The server relies on "trusted" elements of the recipient's device to identify it, transmit accurate information, and limit unauthorized manipulation of content.

[b] Rights Models and Expression Languages

Rights models and expression languages are two mechanisms used to facilitate transactions involving digital works. In essence, a rights model specifies the types of rights and users, the extent thereof, and associated costs. The model permits specified users (e.g., subscribers, enrolled students, or site licensees) to perform only certain functions (e.g., print, view, or play). The extent of such rights may be set out in either time or number of functions (i.e., print 5 times, view for 10 days, or play for 48 hours). This model also expresses costs associated with exercise of these rights.

In practice, the rights model is implemented through "rights expression language" (REL),[259] which establishes a structure for expressing permissions in machine (and human readable) form and a "rights data dictionary." This dictionary precisely defines the meaning of the permissions and conditions expressed. Electronic rights transactions also require the unique identification of each item of digital content. Such encoded information (e.g., author, title, date of creation, and other identifying information) is commonly referred to as "metadata."

[c] DRM Architecture

Although DRM systems vary widely depending on purpose and function, their overall architecture consists of three major components.[260] First, the "content server" contains the actual digital material, along with product and/or service information the provider wants to distribute. The server typically includes a "content repository," a database holding the content, along with associated metadata and a "DRM packager." The packager prepares the content for secure distribution (e.g., by encrypting the content and/or inserting metadata), creates specifications of rights associated therewith, and produces encryption keys to authenticate users and decrypt content, before passing the information along to the license server.

---

258. *See generally* M. Stefik, "Letting Loose the Light: Igniting Commerce in Electronic Publication"; in *Internet Dreams: Archetypes, Myths, and Metaphors* (1996). *See also* Stefik, *Shifting the Possible: How Trusted Systems and Digital Property Rights Challenge Us to Rethink Digital Publishing,* 12 Berkeley Tech. L.J. 137 (1997).

259. An example of a modern REL is Extensible Rights Markup Language.

260. *See Digital Rights Management, supra* note 256.

Second, the "license server" identifies the digital content, specifies the rights associated therewith (e.g., "play" or "copy"), and establishes the terms and conditions for the exercise thereof (e.g., an expiration date), whether by a user or device.[261] Third, on the "client" side of a DRM, the "DRM controller" receives the user's request to exercise rights regarding specific content, gathers information about its identity, obtains a license, authenticates the application that performs the rights exercise, retrieves the encryption keys, and decrypts the content for the appropriate "rendering" application (e.g., playing a song or viewing a movie).

[d] Types of DRM Systems

A wide range of DRM options are currently available, evidencing that no single technology or solution can fulfill the diverse requirements of the marketplace. In general terms, DRM systems may be hardware- or software-based, or they may be hybrid systems combining both elements. Hardware-based DRM solutions embed the technological protection in the hardware itself. Examples are smartcards and many conditional access systems, including direct broadcast satellite and digital cable television.

Software-based DRM technologies have been developed to provide secure delivery of content over the Internet and adherence to copy control instructions in the PC and home network environments. Some of these products (such as the Microsoft Windows Media Rights Manager) include built-in renewability, enabling the content owner to respond quickly to security breaches by renewing the protections applying to all other copies of the content. Finally, the CSS system discussed above is an example of a hybrid DRM solution that uses CSS-enabled DVD players to inspect DVDs for embedded code.

---

261. Digital content protection technologies help support a variety of "copy control states," including "copy never" (used in pay-per-view, video-on-demand, and prerecorded media), "copy once" (used in pay TV and basic and extended cable), and copy control not asserted, but no redistribution (free-to-air TV).

107th Congress
1st Session

S. 487

IN THE HOUSE OF REPRESENTATIVES
June 8, 2001
Referred to the Committee on the Judiciary

AN ACT

To amend chapter 1 of title 17, United States Code, relating to the exemption of certain performances or displays for educational uses from copyright infringement provisions, to provide that the making of copies or phonorecords of such performances or displays is not an infringement under certain circumstances, and for other purposes.

Be it enacted by the Senate and House of Representatives of the United States of America in Congress assembled,

SECTION 1. EDUCATIONAL USE COPYRIGHT EXEMPTION

(a) SHORT TITLE—This Act may be cited as the "Technology, Education, and Copyright Harmonization Act of 2001."

(b) EXEMPTION OF CERTAIN PERFORMANCES AND DISPLAYS FOR EDUCATIONAL USES—Section 110 of title 17, United States Code, is amended—

(1) by striking paragraph (2) and inserting the following:

"(2) except with respect to a work produced or marketed primarily for performance or display as part of mediated instructional activities transmitted via digital networks, or a performance or display that is given by means of a copy or phonorecord that is not lawfully made and acquired under this title, and the transmitting government body or accredited nonprofit educational institution knew or had reason to believe was not lawfully made and acquired, the performance of a nondramatic literary or musical work or reasonable and limited portions of any other work, or display of a work in an amount comparable to that which is typically displayed in the course of a live classroom session, by or in course of a transmission, if—

"(A) the performance or display is made by, at the direction of, or under the actual supervision of an instructor as an integral part of a class session offered as a regular part of the systematic mediated instructional activities of a governmental body or an accredited nonprofit educational institution;

"(B) the performance or display is directly related and of material assistance to the teaching content of the transmission;

"(C) the transmission is made solely for, and, to the extent technologically feasible, the reception of such transmission is limited to—

"(i) students officially enrolled in the course for which the transmission is made; or

"(ii) officers or employees of governmental bodies as a part of their official duties or employment; and

"(D) the transmitting body or institution—

"(i) institutes policies regarding copyright, provides informational materials to faculty, students, and relevant staff members that accurately describe, and promote compliance with, the laws of the United States relating to copyright, and provides notice to students that materials used in connection with the course may be subject to copyright protection; and

"(ii) in the case of digital transmissions—

"(I) applies technological measures that reasonably prevent—

"(aa) retention of the work in accessible form by recipients of the transmission from the transmitting body or institution for longer than the class session; and

"(bb) unauthorized further dissemination of the work in accessible form by such recipients to others; and

"(II) does not engage in conduct that could reasonably be expected to interfere with technological measures used by copyright owners to prevent such retention or unauthorized further dissemination;"; and

(2) by adding at the end the following:

"In paragraph (2), the term 'mediated instructional activities' with respect to the performance or display of a work by digital transmission under this section refers to activities that use such work as an integral part of the class experience, controlled by or under the actual supervision of the instructor and analogous to the type of performance or display that would take place in a live classroom setting. The term does not refer to activities that use, in 1 or more class sessions of a single course, such works as textbooks, course packs, or other material in any media, copies or phonorecords of which are typically purchased or acquired by the students in higher education for their independent use and retention or are typically purchased or acquired for elementary and secondary students for their possession and independent use.

"For purposes of paragraph (2), accreditation—

"(A) with respect to an institution providing postsecondary education, shall be as determined by a regional or national accrediting agency recognized by the Council on Higher Education Accreditation or the United States Department of Education; and

"(B) with respect to an institution providing elementary or secondary education, shall be recognized by the applicable state certification or licensing procedures.

"For purposes of paragraph (2), no governmental body or accredited nonprofit educational institution shall be liable for infringement by reason of the transient or temporary storage of material carried out through the automatic technical process of a digital transmission of the performance or display of that material as authorized under paragraph (2). No such material stored on the system or network controlled or operated by the transmitting body or institution under this paragraph shall be maintained on such system or network in a manner ordinarily accessible to anyone other than anticipated recipients. No such copy shall be maintained on the system or network in a manner ordinarily accessible to such anticipated recipients for a longer period than is reasonably necessary to facilitate the transmissions for which it was made."

(c) EPHEMERAL RECORDINGS—

(1) IN GENERAL—Section 112 of title 17, United States Code, is amended—

(A) by redesignating subsection (f) as subsection (g); and

(B) by inserting after subsection (e) the following:

"(f)(1) Notwithstanding the provisions of section 106, and without limiting the application of subsection (b), it is not an infringement of copyright for a governmental body or other nonprofit educational institution entitled under section 110(2) to transmit a performance or display to make copies or phonorecords of a work that is in digital form and, solely to the extent permitted in paragraph (2), of a work that is in analog form, embodying the performance or display to be used for making transmissions authorized under section 110(2), if—

"(A) such copies or phonorecords are retained and used solely by the body or institution that made them, and no further copies or phonorecords are reproduced from them, except as authorized under section 110(2); and

"(B) such copies or phonorecords are used solely for transmissions authorized under section 110(2).

"(2) This subsection does not authorize the conversion of print or other analog versions of works into digital formats, except that such conversion is permitted hereunder, only with respect to the amount of such works authorized to be performed or displayed under section 110(2), if—

"(A) no digital version of the work is available to the institution; or

"(B) the digital version of the work that is available to the institution is subject to technological protection measures that prevent its use for section 110(2).".

(2) TECHNICAL AND CONFORMING AMENDMENT—Section 802(e) of title 17, United States Code, is amended in the third sentence by striking "section 112(f)" and inserting "section 112(g)".

(d) PATENT AND TRADEMARK OFFICE REPORT—

(1) IN GENERAL—Not later than 180 days after the date of enactment of this Act and after a period for public comment, the Undersecretary of Commerce for Intellectual Property, after consultation with the Register of Copyrights, shall submit to the Committees

on the Judiciary of the Senate and the House of Representatives a report describing technological protection systems that have been implemented, are available for implementation, or are proposed to be developed to protect digitized copyrighted works and prevent infringement, including upgradeable and self-repairing systems, and systems that have been developed, are being developed, or are proposed to be developed in private voluntary industry-led entities through an open broad based consensus process. The report submitted to the Committees shall not include any recommendations, comparisons, or comparative assessments of any commercially available products that may be mentioned in the report.

(2) LIMITATIONS—The report under this subsection—

(A) is intended solely to provide information to Congress; and

(B) shall not be construed to affect in any way, either directly or by implication, any provision of title 17, United States Code, including the requirements of clause (ii) of section 110(2)(D) of that title (as added by this Act), or the interpretation or application of any such provision, including evaluation of the compliance with that clause by any governmental body or nonprofit educational institution.

Flowchart Comparing and Contrasting Section 110(1), Old Section 110(2), the CONFU Distance Learning Guidlines and the TEACH Act

For ease of reference, page 462 represents the top left quarter of the chart; p. 463, the top right quarter; p. 464, the bottom left quarter; and page 465, the bottom right quarter.

The flowchart can best be viewed if the pages are copied and laid out as follows:

Page 462	Page 463
Page 464	Page 465

Copyright Act § 110 (1) (1976)

Designed to permit instructors to incorporate performance and display of all works into their face-to-face teaching courses

Part of United States Code

Permits the:

Performance or display

Excludes:
Reproduction
Distribution
Derivative Works

Copyright Act § 110 (2) (1976)

Designed to cover then-extant forms of distance education
(1) open/closed circuit TV
(2) radio broadcasting

Part of United States Code from January 1, 1978 to November 1, 2002

Performance or display

"Reproduction" includes:
Recording
Taping
Residence in computer RAM

Narrow exception in § 112(b)—30 copies may be kept for seven (7) years for archival purposes

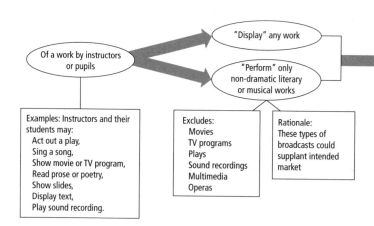

Of a work by instructors or pupils

"Display" any work

"Perform" only non-dramatic literary or musical works

Examples: Instructors and their students may:
Act out a play,
Sing a song,
Show movie or TV program,
Read prose or poetry,
Show slides,
Display text,
Play sound recording.

Excludes:
Movies
TV programs
Plays
Sound recordings
Multimedia
Operas

Rationale:
These types of broadcasts could supplant intended market

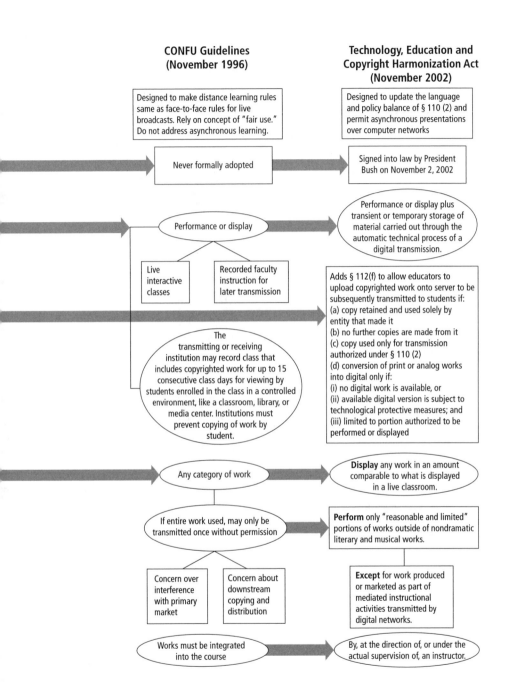

**CONFU Guidelines
(November 1996)**

**Technology, Education and
Copyright Harmonization Act
(November 2002)**

Designed to make distance learning rules same as face-to-face rules for live broadcasts. Rely on concept of "fair use." Do not address asynchronous learning.

Designed to update the language and policy balance of § 110 (2) and permit asynchronous presentations over computer networks

Never formally adopted

Signed into law by President Bush on November 2, 2002

Performance or display

Performance or display plus transient or temporary storage of material carried out through the automatic technical process of a digital transmission.

Live interactive classes

Recorded faculty instruction for later transmission

Adds § 112(f) to allow educators to upload copyrighted work onto server to be subsequently transmitted to students if:
(a) copy retained and used solely by entity that made it
(b) no further copies are made from it
(c) copy used only for transmission authorized under § 110 (2)
(d) conversion of print or analog works into digital only if:
(i) no digital work is available, or
(ii) available digital version is subject to technological protective measures; and
(iii) limited to portion authorized to be performed or displayed

The transmitting or receiving institution may record class that includes copyrighted work for up to 15 consecutive class days for viewing by students enrolled in the class in a controlled environment, like a classroom, library, or media center. Institutions must prevent copying of work by student.

Any category of work

Display any work in an amount comparable to what is displayed in a live classroom.

If entire work used, may only be transmitted once without permission

Perform only "reasonable and limited" portions of works outside of nondramatic literary and musical works.

Concern over interference with primary market

Concern about downstream copying and distribution

Except for work produced or marketed as part of mediated instructional activities transmitted by digital networks.

Works must be integrated into the course

By, at the direction of, or under the actual supervision of, an instructor.

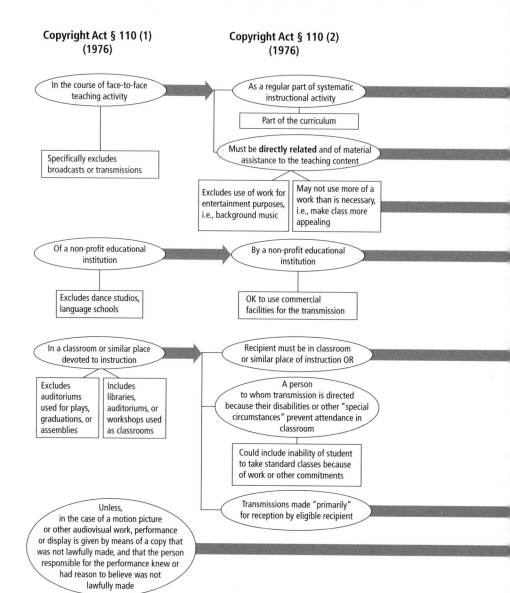

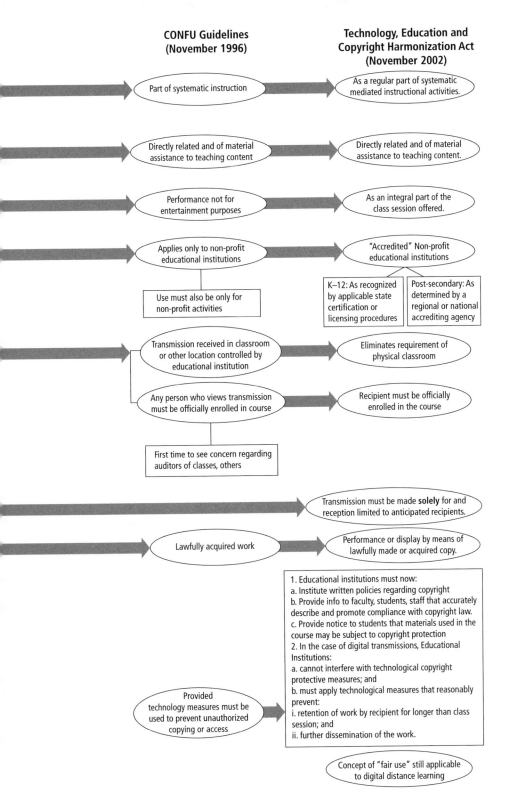

CONFU Guidelines (November 1996)

Part of systematic instruction

Directly related and of material assistance to teaching content

Performance not for entertainment purposes

Applies only to non-profit educational institutions

Use must also be only for non-profit activities

Transmission received in classroom or other location controlled by educational institution

Any person who views transmission must be officially enrolled in course

First time to see concern regarding auditors of classes, others

Lawfully acquired work

Provided technology measures must be used to prevent unauthorized copying or access

Technology, Education and Copyright Harmonization Act (November 2002)

As a regular part of systematic mediated instructional activities.

Directly related and of material assistance to teaching content.

As an integral part of the class session offered.

"Accredited" Non-profit educational institutions

K–12: As recognized by applicable state certification or licensing procedures

Post-secondary: As determined by a regional or national accrediting agency

Eliminates requirement of physical classroom

Recipient must be officially enrolled in the course

Transmission must be made **solely** for and reception limited to anticipated recipients.

Performance or display by means of lawfully made or acquired copy.

1. Educational institutions must now:
a. Institute written policies regarding copyright
b. Provide info to faculty, students, staff that accurately describe and promote compliance with copyright law.
c. Provide notice to students that materials used in the course may be subject to copyright protection
2. In the case of digital transmissions, Educational Institutions:
a. cannot interfere with technological copyright protective measures; and
b. must apply technological measures that reasonably prevent:
i. retention of work by recipient for longer than class session; and
ii. further dissemination of the work.

Concept of "fair use" still applicable to digital distance learning

465

Index

F